THE ESSENCE OF
BECKER

THE ESSENCE OF

B·E·C·K·E·R

Edited and with an Introduction by
Ramón Febrero
AND
Pedro S. Schwartz
Foreword by John Raisian

HOOVER INSTITUTION PRESS
Stanford University, Stanford, California

*The Hoover Institution on War, Revolution and Peace, founded
at Stanford University in 1919 by Herbert Hoover, who went on
to become the thirty-first president of the United States, is an
interdisciplinary research center for advanced study on domestic
and international affairs. The views expressed in its publications are
entirely those of the authors and do not necessarily reflect the views
of the staff, officers, or Board of Overseers of the Hoover Institution.*

www.hoover.org

Hoover Institution Press Publication No. 426

Hoover Institution at Leland Stanford Junior University,
Stanford, California 94305-6010

First printing, 1995
First paperback printing, 1995
21   20   19   18   17   16   15   14   11   10   9   8   7   6   5
Manufactured in the United States of America

The paper used in this publication meets the minimum requirements of the
American National Standard for Information Sciences—Permanence of Paper
for Printed Library Materials, ANSI/NISO Z39.48-1992. ∞

Library of Congress Cataloging-in-Publication Data
Becker, Gary Stanley, 1930–2014
[Selections. 1995]
The essence of Becker / edited and with an introduction by Ramón Febrero and
Pedro S. Schwartz : foreword by John Raisian
    p.   cm. — (Hoover Institution Press publication series ; 426)
Includes index.
ISBN 978-0-8179-9341-2 (cloth : alk. paper)
ISBN 978-0-8179-9342-9 (paperback : alk. paper)
ISBN 978-0-8179-9346-7 (epub)
ISBN 978-0-8179-9347-4 (mobi)
ISBN 978-0-8179-9348-1 (PDF)
    1. Human capital.   2. Time—Economic aspects.   3. Family—Economic aspects.
4. Economics.   5. Becker, Gary Stanley, 1930–2014.
I. Febrero, Ramón   II. Schwartz, Pedro, 1935–   .   III. Title.
HD4904.7.B43A25   1995
330—dc20   95-40219
                                                        CIP

WE DEDICATE THIS VOLUME
WITH ADMIRATION AND GRATITUDE TO
PROFESSOR GARY S. BECKER
—IN APPRECIATION OF HIS WISDOM AND INSIGHT—
ON THE OCCASION OF HIS 65TH BIRTHDAY.

CONTENTS

PART ONE: FOUNDATIONS OF HUMAN BEHAVIOR

PART TWO: FAMILY, MARRIAGE, AND FERTILITY

PART THREE: DISCRIMINATION

PART FOUR: LAW

PART FIVE: POLITICS

PART SIX: MONEY AND MACROBEHAVIOR

PART SEVEN: BECKER'S PERSONAL OVERVIEW

FOREWORD

This collection of essays is being published to honor one of the most innovative and influential economists of our time on the occasion of his sixty-fifth birthday. Gary Becker has long been recognized as a major force in the development of contemporary economic thinking, an achievement for which he was awarded the Nobel Prize in Economic Sciences in 1992. Having been affiliated with the Hoover Institution since 1973, when he was named to the Domestic Studies Advisory Board, Gary Becker was appointed as a senior fellow in 1990. Thus, his Hoover colleagues join me in offering this special tribute, *The Essence of Becker*.

A prolific scholar, Gary is perhaps best known for his work on labor economics, human capital, criminal behavior, and the economics of the family, in which he extended further than anyone previously the hypothesis of rational behavior as the explanation of many social phenomena. For example, in his book *A Treatise on the Family*, he applies economic theory to some of the most consequential personal decisions that individuals make in life, decisions such as choosing a spouse, having a family, or continuing in school. This has stimulated much additional study, not only among economists but by anthropologists, political scientists, sociologists, demographers, and biologists, constituting an important step in the unification of the social sciences. In the words of the late George J. Stigler, himself a Nobel laureate and Hoover fellow, "Gary Becker may well go down in history as the chief architect in the designing of a truly general science of society."

As important as Gary Becker's work is on the academic end of the spectrum, so too is his influence among wider audiences and on public opinion. As a teacher and mentor at the University of Chicago and earlier at Columbia University, he has for decades challenged and enlightened some of this country's brightest young minds. The same can be said of his regular column in *BusinessWeek*, which reaches and informs a reading audience nationwide. In it, he clearly, concisely, and consistently applies empirical economic analysis to address everyday social problems and public policy issues, ranging most recently from competition and deregulation in the telephone industry to changes in welfare policy.

Personally, I have been a great admirer of Gary Becker over many years, beginning with my days as a graduate student. Even in those early years, I had a tremendous respect for his intellectual breadth, his inexhaustible originality, and his unfailing persistence in forging ahead into interdisciplinary territory, even in the face of occasional skepticism. Since that time, thanks to our mutual affiliation with the Hoover Institution and the opportunities for interaction that it has afforded, my respect and admiration for him have continued to grow. Therefore, it is with special pleasure that I am participating in the production of this volume containing some of his most important and influential work. I hope it will intellectually enrich many and inspire further study of the work of Gary Becker.

The Essence of Becker is the fourth such collection in Hoover's salutes to its Nobel Prize winners in economics, the others being Milton Friedman, Friedrich Hayek, and George Stigler. For this volume, we are deeply indebted to Ramón Febrero and Pedro Schwartz, who worked with Gary to choose the essays contained herein, and to Patricia Baker and the entire staff of the Hoover Press, who worked tirelessly to bring this project to fruition.

On behalf of my colleagues here at Hoover, I extend warmest wishes to Gary on his birthday, along with continued good health, happiness, and intellectual vitality.

JOHN RAISIAN
Director, Hoover Institution

ACKNOWLEDGMENTS

I am honored to join Friedman, Hayek, and Stigler in the Hoover Essence series. Two excellent Spanish economists, Ramón Febrero and Pedro Schwartz, have collected my principal articles into categories that define the main subjects I have worked on, including discrimination, human capital, the allocation of time, the family, and political economy. They also provide an excellent overview of my approach to economics, political behavior, and social behavior. I am in debt to them for effectively capturing the "essence of Becker."

I also want to thank John Raisian and the Hoover Institution for the decision to include my work in this series.

GARY S. BECKER

THE ESSENCE OF BECKER: AN INTRODUCTION

Ramón Febrero
Pedro Schwartz

Give me a fulcrum and I will move the world.

Archimedes

It is often said or implied that the housewife . . . is actuated by a different set of motives in her economic transactions in the market and her noneconomic transactions at home; but this is obviously not so.

Philip Wicksteed

I. INTRODUCTION

A glance at any of his papers makes it apparent that Gary Becker's contributions to economics are anything but conventional. Becker is without a doubt the leading figure in nonconventional economics. This volume contains a selection of Becker's papers that represent his approach to economics.

The papers selected in this book are grouped under two broad headings: foundations of human behavior (Part One) and applications (Parts Two to six). Part One consists of nine papers through which the reader gains access to the basics of Becker's approach to human behavior: fundamental premises, the time allocation problem, the concept of human capital, social interactions, and preferences characterization. Parts Two, Three, Four, Five, and Six contain sixteen papers devoted to family, marriage and fertility, discrim-

We wish to thank Gary Becker for his comments and suggestions on an earlier version of this paper.

ination, law, politics, and macrobehavior (in that order). All but one of these papers are examples of Becker's unorthodox applications of economic theory. The exception is reading 23 (Part Six), one of the rare cases of Becker's orthodox use of economic tools (in the area of monetary economics). The volume ends with Part Seven, Becker's personal survey of his contributions.

The surfeit of economic publications during the last two decades by itself justifies the appearance of this volume. Let us just sketch two additional reasons. First, no single collection of Becker's papers is currently available, thus presenting a ready market for this book. Second, what better reason can there be than the awarding of a Nobel Prize to promote the diffusion of worthwhile ideas?

The organization of the introduction is as follows. Section II offers an abbreviated account of Becker's intellectual biography. Section III is a brief guide to the fundamental contributions Becker has made to economics, including the key concepts and their principal implications. After reviewing what we call Becker's first principles, we analyze three peculiar types of inputs: time, human assets, and children. Then we deal with two important examples of social interaction: marriage/divorce and discrimination. The last subsection concerns a singular kind of labor supply problem: criminal behavior. In Section IV, we discuss the meaning of economics in the light of Becker's work. Section V suggests some conclusions. An extensive bibliography, containing all Becker's books and main articles, is provided in the appendix.

Finally, we would remind readers that this paper is not intended to be an account of each and every contribution Gary Becker has made to economics. The following pages are thus an invitation to become acquainted with Becker's literature, beginning with the twenty-six papers in this volume.

II. Intellectual Biography

In presenting this selection of Professor Gary Becker's scientific papers, we wish to help the student of modern economics know, criticize, and extend the unconventional ideas developed in them. We also want to honor one of the most original economists of the twentieth century, who has contributed to widening the scope of economics to the point of being decried as an empire builder! His originality was one of the reasons the Swedish Academy awarded him the Nobel Prize for Economic Science in 1992.

His approach consists of questioning some assumptions taken for granted in most microeconomic modeling, such as given tastes, homogeneous labor, risk neutrality, households as one-person consumption units, and, with this

minimal deepening in the level of explanation, applying standard neoclassical cost and utility theory to throw new light on previously unconnected and
badly understood social phenomena. By using Occam's razor to cut away
ancillary assumptions, he reduces his axioms to one: that all actors in the
social game are *homines economici*—economic persons, rational agents who
maximize their advantages in different cost situations. Inductivists would not
believe it, but, by placing his models on this minimalist fulcrum, he shifts
huge problems that other social scientists found immovable.

For the normal science of economics, Becker's hunting ground is unconventional (or, rather, thanks to him, *was*). His minimal-assumption starting
point has allowed him to study persistent racial and sexual discrimination in
labor markets; investment in human capital; crime and punishment; marriage, divorce, and the quantity and quality of children; drug addiction; and
other apparently noneconomic dimensions of society. In recognition of the
breadth of his research, he is a professor at the University of Chicago in both
the Departments of Economics and Sociology.

Whatever opinion the reader may form of Becker's explanations, the test
by which Becker will allow himself to be judged is empirical refutation (see
Becker, Grossman, Kevin, and Murphy 1994). He is well within the tradition
of the older Chicago School, as represented by his friends and masters Milton
Friedman and George Stigler (both of whom he has written about), that
holds mere theorizing to be insufficient and that is ready to stand or fall by
the ability of its theories to solve empirical problems. Anybody disagreeing
with Becker should test his assumption shifts with economic laboratory
experiments and his conclusions with statistical observations. By questioning
the assumptions of standard microeconomic theory, Becker has gone a step
further than Friedman: for Becker the standard assumptions of neoclassical
economics can also be challenged empirically!

Gary Stanley Becker was born in Pottsville, Pennsylvania, in 1930. He
graduated from Princeton University in 1951 and obtained his master's and
Ph.D. degrees at the University of Chicago, the spirit and tradition of whose
Department of Economics left an indelible mark on him.

After holding an assistant professorship at Chicago, he moved to Columbia University in 1957, where he was made professor of economics in 1960.
He returned to Chicago as a one-year Ford Foundation Visiting Professor of
Economics, and George Stigler persuaded him to stay. This was a shrewd
move by a keen talent spotter: Becker became the fifth Chicago Nobel Prize
winner in economics.

Much of his mature thought can be found in his books, which, unchar-
acteristically for the profession, are as important as his articles. But the
articles themselves are sometimes indispensable and often illuminating,
which explains the need for the present collection.

After a few articles on macroeconomics and monetary theory, Becker published his reworked doctoral thesis, *The Economics of Discrimination* (Becker 1957). It went unnoticed for a time, perhaps because the problem he addressed was not yet in the news. In this work he tried to square the competitive model of labor markets with observed persistent color and sex differences in wages by introducing a "taste" for discrimination in the utility function of employers and employees. He thus started to dig below the assumption of identical preferences in market actors.

The second book, *Human Capital* (Becker 1964), again broke new ground, studying the formation of human capital by schooling, on-the-job learning, and labor training. This theory of differences in personal distribution of income had been adumbrated by Richard Cantillon and Adam Smith but was abandoned for nearly two centuries, with the exception of the labor market economist Jacob Mincer. Becker's idea was an immediate success that sparked off a spate of studies in the productivity of education, the causes of underdevelopment, wage differentials, and connected fields such as unemployment.

Becker was again innovative in considering time as a scarce resource constraining individual utility functions. In his article "A Theory of the Allocation of Time" (Becker 1965) and in a book he wrote with Gilbert Ghez entitled *The Allocation of Time and Goods over the Life Cycle* (Ghez and Becker 1974), he applied the view of time as a scarce input in production to modeling the family. Much later, he used the same view of time to model destructive and constructive addictions (such as addictions to classical music and sport or to drugs and alcohol).

His fourth fruitful idea was to treat delinquents as rational persons who calculate the utility of rewards and costs of their peculiar calling but who have a positive risk preference and discount the future. This "positivistic" view of crime had been explored initially by Jeremy Bentham in the late eighteenth and early nineteenth centuries but abandoned for a "normative" conception of crime and punishment. Becker published an article called "Crime and Punishment: An Economic Approach" (Becker 1968) and later edited *Essays in the Economics of Crime and Punishment* (Becker and Landes 1974). Many other authors have researched the sociology of crime following his suggestion that the criminal calculates the expected benefits and costs of crime.

Becker returned to parents and children in his *Treatise on the Family* (Becker 1981a), a topic he had previously approached in a number of articles. In his *Treatise*, after discarding the standard assumption that the family was a one-person consumption unit, he explained cooperative behavior within the family on the basis of the utility functions of its members. (He even accommodated altruistic behavior by selfish family members with his famous "rotten kid theorem.") He modeled the family as a multiperson production unit, as a "factory," he says, to shock sociologists. The family produces joint utility, the inputs being the time, skills, and knowledge of its different members. It is thus that he approaches one of the most intractable conundrums: "Altruism in the Family and Selfishness in the Marketplace," as he entitled a later article (Becker 1981b).

Becker uses the theory of the family to predict the choice of spouse, the increased frequency of divorce with female occupation in the market, and other phenomena such as monogamy and polygamy. He has even addressed the historical question of "Human Capital and the Rise and Fall of Families" (Becker and Tomes 1986).

His economic theory of the family also allowed Becker to rework and overturn the theory of population. For nearly two centuries economists had held that Malthus's theory of population (Malthus 1798) was a fruitful hypothesis but that it was contradicted by fact. The escape hatch had traditionally been normative preaching, telling people not to fall into the Malthusian trap and patting each other on the back for having been such successful neo-Malthusians. With his economics of the family, Becker was able to model parental choice in the matter of offspring: the choice between quantity and quality of children when wealth increases; the effect of one-parent families, of divorce, of female employment, on family size; the repercussions on children of the educational level of the mother.

Becker has also shown some interest, derived perhaps from his studies of the labor market and union restrictions on entry (Becker 1959), in public policy and pressure groups. But his latest unsettling move has been his attempt to model the formation of tastes. In an earlier article with George Stigler, "De Gustibus Non Est Disputandum" (Stigler and Becker 1977), he had unyieldingly held the neoclassical ground that questioning preferences and utility maximization was no way to solve social problems and that as much mileage as possible should be extracted from the structure of costs in each concrete case. In later years, however, and with the help of human capital theory and time scarcity, he has been able to model taste formation, constructive and destructive addiction, advertising as a good and a bad; he has even forayed into the direct relation between price and lines and demand.

Again he has modeled the addict as a rational being. A person may be rational *and* unhappy, pace Bentham, if her or his time and risk preference lead to acquiring an "addiction capital," which, like any capital, decays over time. He uses this capital, combined with a diminishing yield to increments in the consumption of the addictive "bad," to explain unwelcome continued addiction, as well as "binges" when the addiction has been suspended for a while (see Becker and Murphy 1988).

Conversely, constructive addictions, such as the enjoyment of classical music or art or jogging or tennis, are again explained by the contribution of current consumption to the accumulation or restoring of an "addiction capital." These are constructive because they have as a joint product the accumulation or restoration of other kinds of wanted human capital, such as pleasurable social intercourse or the maintenance of health.

Finally, we cannot conclude this section without mentioning his *Economic Approach to Human Behavior* (1976a). In the introductory chapter of that book, Becker emphasizes what he considers to be the fundamental premises of the economic approach to human behavior: maximizing behavior, stable preferences, and market equilibrium (see Section IV).

III. THE ECONOMICS OF GARY BECKER: A BRIEF GUIDE

First Principles

First impressions can be misleading where the explanation of human behavior is concerned. This, we may well say, is the advice implicitly given by Becker to economists (and noneconomists). Many activities performed by individuals or families are not what they seem to be; some economic activities traditionally interpreted as pure consumption actions are actually something else. A family outing to a restaurant or reading a good book are, for Becker, not simply consumption activities but are instead production of sustenance and investment in vocabulary activities, respectively. These activities cannot therefore be understood in the light of traditional consumption theory. A *reformulation of the economic theory of household behavior is needed that brings production and investment theories into consumption theory*. This is one of Becker's central contributions to economics (see Part One of the selected readings, in particular chapters 3 and 4).

Two ideas are fundamental to Becker's household economic theory. The first one refers to *time*, which now becomes a scarce factor input (also used in the production of nonmarket goods) and is the household's primary scarce resource. Time is also a new restriction for the behaviors of households; agents must now solve a more complex time allocation problem than the one involved in the textbook trade-off between leisure and work. The second idea is concerned with people seen as assets or durables; embodied in ourselves is our human capital.

In contrast, many activities thought to be noneconomic in nature (by both the general public and the profession itself) are actually economic problems. Economic theory can thus help explain phenomena traditionally located outside the scope of economics, in the areas of law, sociology, biology, political science, and anthropology. Exercising racial discrimination, choosing the number of children, entering the political arena, or behaving as a criminal is just a short list that economic theory can help comprehend.

There is no reason why the economist should not extend the frontiers of economics and apply the tools of economic theory to the long-neglected sphere of nonmarket activities. The development of this *economic imperialism* (see Parts Two through Five), especially in the areas of marriage and fertility, discrimination, and criminal behavior, is another significant contribution that Becker has made to modern economics.

The novelty of Becker's contributions does not reside in the tools employed but in the applications. By using standard (and mercifully nonsophisticated) economic tools, Becker has widened the range of applications of economics. In Becker's words, what is new is not the starting point but where one goes with the analysis.

Households as Small Factories

Ever since Adam Smith's *Wealth of Nations*, consumption has been regarded as the final stage of the economic process, with the ultimate goal of economic activity the maximization of utility by consumers. In conventional economic theory the arguments of utility functions are the quantities of nondurable market goods and services (including those provided by durable market goods) purchased by agents. No further transformation of these goods is needed for consumers to derive utility. In formal terms, households were traditionally assumed to maximize

$$U = U(x_1, \ldots x_m),$$

where U is a well-behaved utility function and x_i represents the ith market good purchased by the household.

In this respect, Becker's approach to consumption theory (Becker 1965; Michael and Becker 1973) represents an important departure from conventional theory. His *new* theory introduces a new category of goods, *basic goods*, as the arguments of the utility functions of consumers (i.e., as the only utility-yielding goods). Basic goods are goods not purchased or sold in the marketplace but are instead produced by consumers (for a given state of household technology), using both market-purchased goods and time as factor inputs. Now households derive utility from market goods only indirectly. Basic goods also exhibit another unconventional characteristic; that is, they have no explicit prices because there are no explicit markets for them. This, however, represents no impediment to the development of an operative theory of household behavior because *shadow prices* (i.e., prices based on home production costs) can always be assigned to basic goods. The new approach to the study of household behavior implies, then, the maximization of the utility function

$$U = U(Z_1, \ldots, Z_m),$$

where Z_i is the basic good i that the household produces via the well-behaved production function

$$Z_i = Z_i(x_i, t_i), \qquad i = 1, \ldots, m,$$

where x_i is a vector of market goods and t_i is a vector of time inputs used in producing the ith basic good.

An example of a basic good is sleeping, which can be seen as the output of a production process wherein a bed, a house, some amount of time, and, maybe, soft music, lullabies, or pills are used as inputs and combined via a production function. Households (individuals or families) are then regarded as production units or small factories. Now, not only firms (conventional theory) but also households produce goods and services. Although firms produce market goods, producing those goods that directly enter consumers' utility functions is under the control of households. Households, then, must make two kinds of decisions: how to produce at the minimum cost and how to consume at the maximum utility level. The *household production theory* points out that the relevant measure of an economy's global production is far from being the one estimated by national accounting standards.

Having said that, Why are market goods not *final goods*? What makes them *intermediate* goods from the point of view of households? Time is the answer. Consuming market goods takes time. Although obvious to economists and noneconomists alike, this simple fact has been ignored by traditional economic theory. Time is an input in both market (labor market) and nonmarket (home) activities. Washing up at home or going to the movies are two cases of common activities requiring time and market goods as factor inputs.

As economists often say, there is no such a thing as a free lunch. Time is no exception in that it is an input in fixed supply with the immediate implication that time has an explicit price in market activities and a shadow price (approximated by the market wage rate) in nonmarket activities. Another implication is that time, in itself, represents a restriction for consumers in addition to the conventional budget constraint. The new time restriction demonstrates that time not spent working in the labor market is not leisure, as traditional theory suggests, but time spent in nonmarket activities (i.e., time spent producing basic goods). The need to consider both restrictions led Becker to define a new scale variable in the utility maximization problem that households are supposed to solve. It is now *full income* (i.e., the maximum money income a household can achieve when devoting all the time and other resources to earning income) that is the relevant resource constraint that limits household choices.

The fact that *time is money* (i.e., has a positive price) is equivalent to saying that the relevant price of a good is not its market price. Several factors determine the *full* or *effective price* of a good. The full price depends on the price of time, the time and market goods intensities, the price of market goods, and the state of household technology. Differences in these factors will result in differences in the effective price of the same good, which brings us to a striking conclusion. Two different consumers do not (in general) pay the same price for the same good even if the market under consideration is perfectly competitive; rather than a price, there is a distribution of prices associated with each good.

The price of time is not equal for everyone; it changes, for example, through the week. Thus for working persons, the opportunity cost of time is normally lower at weekends than on working days. The price of time changes also with the level and composition of income. Thus time will be cheaper for a poor man than for a rich one, for a woman (generally) than for a man, for a worker than for a rentier, or for an unemployed person than for a person with a job. The importance of these conclusions for firms cannot be exaggerated. Firms can reduce the effective price of a given good without lowering its market price by offering more convenience to the consumer. They can either decrease the amount of time spent consuming that good (e.g., by offering free parking, quick service, etc.) or reduce the cost of time devoted to its purchase (e.g., by opening on weekends). These considerations allow us to define a new (full-income) budget constraint as

$$\sum_{i=1}^{m} \pi_i Z_i = S,$$

where π_i is the *full price* of a unit of Z_i and S is the household *full income*. The full price π_i is, in turn, defined as

$$\pi_i = a_i p_i + b_i w,$$

where p_i is the price of the market goods, w is the price of the time used per unit of Z_i, and the coefficients a_i and b_i measure the goods and time intensity, respectively, of Z_i.

A number of interesting conclusions can be derived from the comparative statics of Becker's model. One concerns the effects of a rise in wages. The first-order conditions of the household problem show that, for consumption to be optimal, the marginal rate of substitution between any two basic goods should equal their full price ratio and that optimal production requires that the marginal rate of technical substitution between time and market goods be equal to their relative prices. Thus, unlike conventional theory, an increase in the wage rate now leads to two types of substitution effects. The first one is the conventional substitution effect away from time spent on nonmarket activities (leisure, in the old-fashioned theory), which leads households to replace time by goods in the production of each basic good. The second type is the new substitution effect created by the changes in the relative full prices (or relative marginal costs) of nonmarket activities that the increase in the wage rate normally induces. A rise in the wage rate increases the relative full price of time-intensive goods, which leads to a substitution effect that moves households from high to low time-intensive activities. This new effect changes the optimal composition of household production. The two substitution effects reinforce each other, leading to a decline in the total time spent consuming and an increase in the time spent working in the labor market.

Another conclusion from the comparative statics of the model is that the effects of a rise in income differ according to the source of the rise. A rise in property income does not produce the same effect as that induced by a rise in wage income, for in the case of property income, no changes in full prices are involved. The model also enables us to evaluate the effects from shocks or differences in *environmental variables* (age, education, climate, and so on). In traditional theory, the effects of these variables were reflected in consumers' preferences; in Becker's theory, changes in these variables affect households' production functions that, in turn, cause changes in household behavior through income and substitution effects.

Becker's model has applications in areas such as labor supply, the sexual division of labor, income taxation, household technology, and the computation of income elasticities and explains a great number of everyday facts: for example, why rich people tend to prefer goods low in time intensity (say, having dinner at a restaurant instead of preparing a meal at home), why women, rather than men, tend to go to the supermarket, why consumers tend to buy labor-saving consumer durables or hire housekeeping services as they reach higher wages, or why husbands work fewer hours when their wives' wage rates are higher. Thanks to Becker's work, households and other ordinary aspects of household behavior, traditionally attributed to exogenous factors in conventional theory (usually differences in tastes or shifts in preferences), can now be endogenized and related to differences in prices and incomes.

Investing in Ourselves

Consumers not only carry out production activities as if they were small firms, they also engage in investment activities. We do not refer to investment in the conventional sense (i.e., investment in physical plant and equipment or financial capital) but to investment in a special kind of capital, the capital embodied in ourselves, our human capital. Apart from inherited talents and skills, people build up their human capital stock by investing in themselves. Schooling, on-the-job training, medical care, and acquiring information about the economic environment are the main forms of investment, but it is embodiment that distinguishes human from nonhuman capital. You cannot separate human assets from their owners (except under slavery), which is why you cannot buy or sell human capital units in modern societies (i.e., there are no human capital markets). Of course, this does not preclude the existence of a related market, the labor market, where you can offer the services rendered by your own human capital or hire someone else's.

The study of human capital is another field where Becker has become a leading figure. Traditionally, spending part of our income in, say, training or health has been considered to be a consumption activity. Becker's view (1964 [1st ed.], 1975 [2d ed.], 1993 [3d ed.]), which again signifies a departure from mainstream economics, is to treat your expenditure in education, training, health, and so on as what it is, additions to your human capital, in other words, applying to human capital the traditional framework used to analyze investment in other capital.

Investment in human capital, like any other type of investment, implies a transfer of resources from the present to the future. Behind any investment decision lies the problem of choosing between resources available today and resources that will be available tomorrow. The intertemporal nature of investment in human capital, however, does not fit in with the standard (static) theory of consumer behavior because you cannot compare costs of human capital today with benefits today to determine the optimal amount.

In Becker's model things are different. Households solve an intertemporal optimization problem when they maximize an intertemporal utility function subject to two production functions per period (one of consumption goods and the other of human capital), the law of motion of the stock of human capital, a new *time constraint* per period, and an intertemporal *goods budget constraint*. The new time constraint, which is a revised version of the one we encountered in the previous section, means that time has to be allocated among labor market activities, consumption activities, and investment in human capital (i.e., a third use added to the two considered in the previous section).

In this model a cost today need not be compensated by an equal benefit today. Instead, people must compare the present value of the marginal (*full*) costs of investing in human capital (i.e., including forgone earnings) with the present value of future returns. Investing in human capital is worthwhile only if the present value of benefits is as large as the present value of costs. As correctly emphasized by Rosen (1987), the compensatory nature of earnings on prior investments is the fundamental insight of human capital theory. This model of investment in human capital can explain, among other things, why the amount of time spent investing in human capital tends to decline with age (e.g., people are in school, attend college, participate in on-the-job training, change jobs and locations, or have children—see next section—at younger ages) and why *impatient* people (i.e., people with a low subjective discount factor) tend to invest less in human capital.

Viewing people as stocks resulting from both an initial inherited capital and a sequence of investments over time has important implications. One of them refers to the degree of heterogeneity of workers and the corresponding differences in their earnings. Differences in earnings tend to reflect differences in productivity that, in turn, reflect differences in the investment efforts made by people in the past. In this regard, a great deal of attention has been paid to education as a central factor in explaining earnings differences. Becker's empirical work (see his *Human Capital*) supports the proposition that a higher education level is correlated with higher earnings.

A second implication is obvious. Standard accounting procedures valuing exclusively physical and financial assets underestimate the true wealth of agents and nations. The same applies to the treatment given to family expenditures on education, health, and so on. Part of what national accounting regards as consumption activities is in fact an investment effort that will help expand future production.

Another implication concerns the interaction between financial markets and human capital. Embodiment necessarily limits efforts to finance human capital because it is not always possible to use human assets as collateral. Thus, people whose only asset is themselves will be liquidity constrained, an implication of great relevance for investment in education and one reason human capital theory has found a place in public policy discussions. Another reason is, of course, the externalities that education generates and the subsequent discrepancies between private and social returns.

Unlike the three previous implications, the fourth implication is related not to household behavior but to firm behavior. As Becker reminds us in his *Human Capital*, theories of firm behavior have traditionally ignored the effect of the productive process itself on worker productivity. When on-the-job training is explicitly taken into account, two interesting conclusions, among others, are obtained. The first, which refers to the profit-maximizing conditions for competitive firms, is that the equality between physical marginal product and real wage no longer holds, even if we assume a world with perfectly competitive labor and product markets. (Marginal productivity can be greater or less than the real wage rate.) The conventional profit-maximizing condition is replaced by the equality between the present value of receipts and the present value of expenditures (which would include training outlays in the periods when job training was given). The second conclusion, which is related to the first one and involves Becker's distinction between *general* and *firm-specific training*, implies that quit and layoff rates are inversely related to the amount of specific training. Therefore, the turnover of employees will be lower in firms that provide firm-specific training because that training cannot be used in other firms.

Becker's approach to human capital has given rise to a number of interesting predictions. Thus, it has important implications for the distribution of income (e.g., why the distribution of earnings is more skewed than the distribution of abilities), the shape of age-earnings profiles (e.g., age-earnings profiles tend to be steeper among more skilled and educated persons), and the effects of specialization on skill (e.g., the greater unemployment among unskilled than skilled workers may be because the latter have more specific human capital, and, as another example, profit-maximizing firms pay generally trained employees the same wage and specifically trained employees a higher wage than they could get elsewhere, although people tend to believe the contrary).

Another field where human capital theory has proven fruitful is growth theory. Although modern growth theorists have recognized the importance of human capital since *growth accounting* (see Denison 1962) showed in the 1960s how big was the "measure of their ignorance" (also called "Solow residual" or "total factor productivity"), it is only recently that human capital concepts have been given a proper role in growth models. Traditionally, growth models have overemphasized the role played by physical capital in explaining the rate of growth of per capita income. After Lucas (1988), the *endogenous growth* theory developed in the 1980s became a natural framework for the application of human capital theory.

Children as Consumer Durables

If people are assets or stocks of human capital, what would you expect children to be in Becker's view? The answer is that, for parents, children are consumer durable goods (although they may also become capital goods).

Becker's analysis of fertility is a natural extension of both his theory of allocation of time and his theory of human capital. Thus, children are seen as consumer durables, similar to cars or washing machines, who provide parents with a flow of valuable services (psychic and monetary in nature) over time. Of course, children also imply a flow of costs over time that include market-purchased goods (medical care, education, food, and so on) and parental time. All this makes having children (procreating or adopting them) an economic decision (to be more accurate, an investment decision).

Potential parents, then, must compare the present value of children's services with the present value of children's costs. Once again, Becker's way (Becker 1960; Becker 1981a [1st ed.], 1991 [2d ed.]; Becker and Lewis 1973; Becker and Tomes 1976) of addressing a nonconventional topic, in this case, fertility, has proven to be pathbreaking.

Becker's approach to fertility allows us to relate family size to economic variables so that optimal family size can be expressed as the outcome of a utility maximization program where parents choose between children and all other goods. As in standard economic theory, we can explain the demand for babies in terms of the price of children relative to other goods and the size of the parents' budget. The price of children will differ from one set of parents (or from one mother) to another (i.e., costs per child will vary with parental characteristics). Thus differences in the input mix (market goods versus time consumption) chosen by parents producing children (in the parents' price of time or in household technology) will be reflected in children's prices. Given that producing a child is a time-intensive activity, parents' price of time—particularly the mother's—has become a variable of especial relevance in Becker's analysis.

The aspect of child demand behavior that has attracted most attention from researchers concerns the role parents' income plays in the determination of family size. Children, like other durables, are expected to be normal goods. Empirical evidence, nevertheless, shows the opposite: wealthier families tend to have fewer children. Should we take this as a proof that babies are *inferior goods*? Becker rejects this interpretation. Two explanations can be given using Becker's framework: the *female time-cost hypothesis* and the *quantity-quality interaction hypothesis*, which is the one emphasized by Becker. In both explanations the *effective price* of children increases with income, which produces a substitution effect (away from children) strong enough to counteract the corresponding income effect.

Let us first consider the *female time-cost hypothesis*. How do exogenous changes in wage rates affect the demand for children? In principle, you cannot reach a conclusive answer because two effects of opposite signs are involved when the wage rate changes. On the one hand, a change (say a rise) in the wage rate makes children more expensive than other goods, which leads to a negative substitution effect away from children. But, on the other hand, this wage rise makes parents wealthier and induces a positive income effect (if we assume children are *normal* goods). The total effect on child demand will then be uncertain. A rise in the mother's wage rate, however, is likely to produce a strong substitution effect because the price of the mother's time is a major component of the price of children. Indeed, empirical evidence supports this prediction (i.e., married women's demand for children is negatively sloped). Given that women's wage rates have been rising over time as countries become more productive, families in modern societies tend to have fewer children. Also, given that richer men tend to have wives with higher prices of time, the female time-cost hypothesis would also explain why the desired number of children decreases with family income.

The *quantity-quality interaction hypothesis*, the explanation stressed by Becker, adds a new dimension to the demand for children: child quality. Most of the increased expenditure on children at higher income levels goes to increased child quality, not to increased numbers. In other words, richer parents prefer higher-quality children rather than higher numbers, which accounts for a negative relationship between income and family size, as we shall see in a moment.

Let us examine Becker's hypothesis in more detail. Parents care not only about the number but also about the quality of their children. These two arguments of parents' utility functions—quantity and quality of children—are not independent of each other. In fact, they interact in such a way that even a "pure" rise in income will increase the *effective price* of children, leading to a strong substitution effect away from the quantity of them. This is because the shadow price of children with respect to number is positively related to the level of quality and because the shadow price of quality, in turn, is positively related to income. This quantity-quality interaction works as follows. Higher-income families want children of higher quality, which raises the shadow price of numbers and induces an initial substitution effect away from numbers (fertility) and toward both quality and other goods. The induced reduction in numbers lowers the shadow price of quality, whereas the induced increase in quality further raises the shadow price of numbers. These two effects reinforce the initial substitution effect from numbers and toward quality, a process that will continue until an equilibrium position is reached. The final result will be a strong substitution effect away from numbers that will dominate the corresponding income effect even if the quantity and quality of children are not close substitutes. Thus, a decline in the demand for children (quantity) may occur, even though the "true" income elasticity of demand for children is positive and large.

In addition to the predictions already mentioned, Becker's theory of fertility can explain, for example, why rural fertility has traditionally exceeded urban fertility and why education per child tends to be lower in families having more children. Becker's approach can also improve our understanding of such topics as the relationship between parents' education and children's education and the relationship between child mortality and family size. Of interest are two recent extensions of the economic analysis of fertility that we shall just mention. The first one (Barro and Becker 1989), which refers to the relationship between fertility and economic growth, pioneers a discussion of the dynamics and comparative statics of a neoclassical growth model in which fertility choices are based on parental altruism. Barro and Becker (1989) show that fertility in open economies depends positively on the world's real rate of interest, the degree of altruism, and the growth of child-survival probabilities and negatively on the rate of technical progress and the growth rate of social security (see also the paper by Becker, Murphy, and Tamura 1990). The second extension concerns intergenerational mobility (Becker and Tomes 1979; Becker and Tomes 1986). A well-known and striking fiscal policy implication of Becker's analysis of intergenerational mobility is that a progressive tax and public expenditure system may widen the inequality in disposable income in the long run.

Marriage and the Importance of Gains from Trade

In modern economies there is a great diversity of markets through which agents can allocate their scarce resources. When the word *market* is used, people tend to think about explicit markets like the stock exchange or the market for bananas. Not all markets, however, are *explicit markets* where *explicit prices* are determined by the interaction of demand and supply. One of these nonexplicit markets is the *marriage market*, in which people compete for the best mate. In a marriage market equilibrium allocation, men and women are assigned to each other or remain single, awaiting better opportunities in the future. An important property of such an equilibrium allocation is that it implies a Pareto-optimal assignment (i.e., persons not assigned to each other could not be made better off by marrying each other).

As in any other aspect of human behavior, when deciding to marry, divorce, or remain single, people act as if they maximized their utility functions, subject to their budget and time constraints, both of which now depend on the marriage market equilibrium conditions (and, therefore, taking into account that no one could change mates and become better off). Accordingly, and given that participants in marriage markets act under uncertainty (owing to their imperfect information about the utility they can expect with potential mates), people will marry if they *expect* to be better off than if they remained single. (In the same way, people will divorce when the utility expected from marriage falls below the utility expected from divorcing and, if such is the case, remarrying.) Hence marrying is a decision related, ultimately, to the *expected net gains* (*benefits minus costs*) from marriage (compared with remaining single). Assuming risk neutrality, the necessary condition for marrying simplifies to the condition that the expected wealth or expected income (in a static framework) of potential mates should be higher when married than when remaining single. The above considerations constitute the unorthodox starting point of Becker's analysis of marriage (Becker

1973; Becker 1974b; Becker, Landes, and Michael 1977; two editions of his *Treatise*), making utility-maximizing behavior and marriage market equilibrium conditions the two fundamental premises of Becker's economic theory of marriage.

Again, Becker's approach deviates from conventional theory, in which marital status is seen as an exogenous aspect of human behavior, assumed to be determined by biological or institutional factors and, in any case, of no relevance to household behavior. Becker departs from this view by endogenizing marriage and divorce decisions in terms of preferences, prices, and incomes and by linking marital status to home production, fertility, labor market participation, and income distribution. For Becker, marriage is not simply a matter of physical attraction or cultural or institutional factors but an economic problem. When choosing the best mate, people behave as if trying to maximize the total income or wealth (in expected terms) produced by the marriage.

Becker's analysis has, among other things, important implications for the likelihood of marriage and divorce. The key factor for explaining the likelihood of marriage is, as we said before, the expected net gain from marriage; the greater this gain is, the greater the likelihood of marriage. The fundamental factor that influences the gain from marriage is the *complementarity* between men and women. The more complementary the time of spouses and market goods, the greater the gain because when substitution is imperfect, single persons cannot produce small-scale equivalents of the optimal combination of inputs achieved by married couples (Becker 1973). This complementarity between inputs is caused basically by the desire to produce or invest in *own children* (a desire that Becker considers to be the feature that best distinguishes married from other types of households) and explains why households with men and women are more efficient than households with only one sex. The importance of own children explains why the gain from marriage is lower for people desiring few or *low-quality* children. Not surprisingly, these people tend to marry later (or to divorce earlier).

The gain from marriage for any two persons is also positively related to their incomes, the relative difference between their wage rates, and the level of nonmarket, productivity-augmenting variables (such as beauty, intelligence, and education). Becker's analysis predicts that a rise in property income (necessarily) and a rise in wage rates (possibly) increase the incentive to marry. As Becker recognizes, this prediction (supported by empirical evidence) contrasts with the popular opinion that poor persons marry earlier (and divorce less) than rich persons.

Also of interest is the role played by the *husband-wife wage gap* in a number of aspects of household behavior (such as the household division of labor between husband and wife, the specialized investments in human capital made by married men and women, and the gain from marriage). Here we face a traditional problem of differences in *comparative advantage*, although now instead of countries, as in standard international economics, we are dealing with husbands and wives. Thus, other things being equal, the higher the husband's wage rate, relative to his wife's, the greater the opportunity for specialization within the household, the greater the gains from trade (marriage) to be shared by spouses, and, therefore, the greater the incentive to marry. Given the wage ratio (greater than one) between men and women in the labor market, husbands tend to have comparative advantage in market work and wives in home work. Acting rationally, each member of the household, then, tends to specialize in those activities in which she or he has comparative advantage (i.e., women in home activities and men in market activities) and invest in the type of human capital he or she uses (i.e., women in household capital and men in market capital). These specialized investments, in turn, reinforce the initially given difference in comparative advantage between husband and wife. Hence the husband-wife wage ratio and the corresponding *sexual division of labor* can be seen as due, at least in part, to the gain from specialized investments. Then, as Becker (1974b) concludes, married women spend less time in the labor force because their wage rates are lower because they spend less time there!

Specialized investments are not, however, the only explanation for the observed patterns of *sexual wage gap* and sexual division of labor. Suppose that men and women are equally productive in the sector market and earn the same wage rate. It can be argued that, even in this case, women will have comparative advantage in the home sector for biological reasons (especially in bearing and rearing children). As Becker admits, it is hard to disentangle biological from investment-induced causes of the division of labor between men and women. All we can say, in this regard, is that differences in the specialized investments made by men and women reinforce the effects of biological differences between them.

Having reached this point, it is worth nothing that Becker's conclusions about the household division of labor conflict with the claim that men and women should fully share household tasks. In this regard, one of Becker's predictions is that, if all members of an efficient household have different comparative advantages, all (except at most one of them) will tend to specialize in either the market or the household sector. This implies that fully sharing household tasks would lead to an inefficient allocation of resources.

Becker's analysis can be easily extended to an explanation of divorce. As the wife's wage rate rises, the difference in comparative advantage narrows and the gain from marriage reduces, making divorce more probable. This rise in the wife's wage will also increase her labor market participation. Both the change in her time allocation and the increased likelihood of divorce induce her to reduce her investment in home-specific capital (e.g., having children). (Note that the relation between divorce and fertility also works the other way around: a decline in fertility reduces the gain from marriage and raises the likelihood of divorce. The same can be said of the rise in women's labor force participation: it is a cause, as well as a result, of the rise in marital instability.)

Besides the expected gain from marriage (or, in this case, the gain from divorce), Becker also stresses that the imperfect information available before marriage in the marriage market is an important determinant of the likelihood of divorce. This factor makes deciding to marry risky (i.e., outcomes from marriage may be less favorable than expected). In the language of the *mean-variance approach* used in finance, the likelihood of divorce is higher, the lower the expected gain from marriage and the higher the variance of the probability distribution of gains from marriage. *Search theory* can also shed light on the determinants of divorce. Among others, one implication of the explicit consideration of searching in the marriage market is that, the longer the search, the more appropriate the mate chosen. This would explain why persons marrying younger than average are more likely to divorce.

Regarding Becker's conclusions about the likelihood of divorce, it should not go unnoticed that, contrary to popular opinion, the decision to divorce is largely independent of divorce laws. As Becker (1987a) points out, the legislation that affects the gains from divorce (aid to mothers with dependent children, negative income tax, and so on) is more important than the legislation that affects the conditions for divorce.

Another aspect of *marriage economics* discussed by Becker is the characterization of a marriage market equilibrium. Two kinds of properties are emphasized: assortative mating properties and efficiency properties. Becker's conclusion about efficiency properties is that a market equilibrium implies a Pareto-optimal assignment and involves the maximization of the aggregate output of household commodities (not the aggregate output conventionally defined in national accounting). Concerning assortative mating, Becker's theory predicts both positive and negative properties depending on the characteristic under consideration. Becker predicts a predominance of positive assortative mating with respect to personal characteristics that are complements in the production of commodity income (such as education, height, intelligence, age, property income, physical attractiveness, and so on) and negative assortative mating for substitutes (such as wages). This implies that marriage markets increase the inequality in traits, and thus in commodity income across families, but reduce the inequality in money income.

Finally, a few words on marital forms. Becker shows, under a number of simplifying assumptions (all men and all women identical, equal number of men and women, diminishing returns from additional spouses), that a monogamous sorting would be optimal and therefore would maximize the total output of commodities over all marriages. If the productivity of men differs, a polygynous sorting could be optimal. Becker's theory predicts that polygyny would be more frequent among more productive men, as shown by empirical evidence. In George Bernard Shaw's words, "The maternal instinct leads a woman to prefer a tenth share in a first-rate man to the exclusive possession of a third-rate one" (quoted by Becker 1981a, 90—91).

Discrimination, a Matter of Both Prejudice and Price

Discrimination was the first unconventional area to which Becker fruitfully applied price theory. The economic analysis of discrimination was the subject of his doctoral dissertation, which became *The Economics of Discrimination* (1957, 1st ed.; 1971, 2d ed.), wherein he used international trade theory to study the effects of discrimination in the marketplace. In this work Becker focused on racial discrimination by three different types of agents: employers, employees, and consumers.

The starting point of Becker's theory of discrimination is that people behave as if they derived utility or disutility from the personal characteristics of those with whom they have "contact" in the marketplace. These personal attributes or characteristics include race, gender, and religion. People are, then, not indifferent to the kind of group, defined in terms of these personal characteristics, they associate with. Becker's approach to discrimination implies a reformulation of the standard objective functions that economic agents are assumed to maximize (e.g., discriminatory employers do not maximize profits but rather their utility functions, which depend on both profits and the personal characteristics of those workers hired by the discriminator). The fact that person Y's characteristics enter the utility function of person X is, in Becker's view, the ultimate reason why X may practice discrimination (nepotism) against (toward) Y. Hence people can be said to have a *taste for discrimination* (or for nepotism). In sum, X discriminates against Y because the association with Y becomes in itself a source of disutility, a psychic cost, for X. Discrimination is, therefore, a matter of preferences or tastes.

Discrimination, however, is also a matter of prices. Because people have a taste for discrimination, they will be willing to pay something either directly, in the form of a higher price, or indirectly, in the form of a reduced income, to be associated with some groups instead of others. It is precisely this consideration that makes Becker's theory operative. Discrimination will have to be reflected in prices, which enables the analyst to move from unobservable preferences to observable market prices. To do so, Becker establishes the concept of a *discrimination coefficient* and distinguishes between individual and market discrimination coefficients.

The discrimination coefficient of an economic agent (employer, employee, or consumer) is a money measure of her or his "taste for discrimination" and thus allows Becker to differentiate between the *money* costs of a transaction and its *net* or *true* costs (i.e., net of psychic or nonpecuniary costs). Therefore, if an employer faces a money wage rate for w for workers, then $w(1 + d_i)$, defines the corresponding net wage rate where d_i is the discrimination coefficient against this factor. An employee, offered a wage rate of w_j for working with the factor discriminated against, acts as if the net wage rate were $w_j(1 - d_j)$, where d_j is his or her discrimination coefficient against this factor. A consumer, faced with a unit money price of p for the commodity produced by this factor, acts as if the net price were $p(1 + d_k)$, where d_k is the discrimination coefficient against this factor. These discrimination coefficients take on any value between zero and plus infinity, and the quantities wd_i, w_jd_j, and pd_k are the exact money equivalents of the above-mentioned psychic costs.

Market discrimination is said to occur against members of group N who are perfect substitutes in production for members of group W if their equilibrium wage rates differ. In the absence of discrimination and if the labor market were perfectly competitive, the equilibrium wage rate of W would equal that of N. Under discrimination, however, the equilibrium wages of W and N *could* differ. (Wage and price differentials are not the only possible outcomes of discrimination. Under certain conditions, discrimination is likely to produce segregation rather than differences in prices or wages.) The market discrimination coefficient (MDC) is defined as

$$MDC = \frac{w_W - w_N}{w_N},$$

where w_W and w_N are the equilibrium wage rates of W and N, respectively. The value of the MDC measures the extent of discrimination in the corresponding market.

The relation between individual discrimination coefficients and the market discrimination coefficient is more complex than is normally assumed. Individual discrimination coefficients interact with other factors to determine the degree of market discrimination. As Becker stresses, although the magnitude of the MDC depends in an important way on each individual discrimination coefficient, merely to use some measure of the average discrimination coefficient does not suffice. Becker shows that the MDC depends on the distribution of discrimination coefficients among individuals (i.e., not only the average taste for discrimination but also the dispersion around the average influence of the *MDC*), the degree of competition in the labor and product market (i.e., competitive industries tend to discriminate less than monopolistic industries), the degree of substitution between W and N workers (e.g., in the case of employee discrimination, if W workers and N workers are perfect substitutes in production, discrimination leads to market segregation, that is, separate establishments, but not to wage differentials between the two groups), and the relative size, in economic and quantitative terms (see below), of the group discriminated against (e.g., the larger the minority compared with the majority, the more harmed, in terms of their incomes, are the members of the majority; this could explain why South African apartheid eventually broke down).

Let us now turn our attention, for the remainder of this section, to Becker's international trade model of discrimination. To study the economic effects of discrimination, Becker develops a model in which N(egro) and W(hite) sectors are treated as if they were two different countries. The model assumes perfect competition, only one good in the world economy, two inputs (capital and labor), perfect substitutability between N and W factors, a higher capital-labor ratio in the W sector, and identical technology represented by a linear homogeneous production function (which implies trade only in the factors of production). In the absence of discrimination, W would export capital (or import labor) to the point where the marginal products of capital and labor are equal in both sectors. Now, if we assume that W members have a taste for discrimination against N members, exported capital must receive a higher equilibrium return (or marginal product) than at home to compensate for working with N labor. Discrimination, therefore, restricts trade between sectors W and N, that is, reduces capital exports and labor imports to a level below free trade and decreases output because of the induced inefficient allocation of resources. Discrimination is, consequently, equivalent to the imposition of a *tax on exported capital* in this model.

Two fundamental implications from this model are that the total net incomes of *both* N, $Y(N)$ and W, $Y(W)$ must decrease with discrimination and that all factors are not affected the same way. Thus, the return to W capital and N labor decreases, but the return to W labor and N capital increases. Hence, W capitalists and N workers lose with discrimination, and W workers gain. These conclusions question conventional wisdom about the effects of discrimination. As Becker (1971, 21–22) points out, "There is a remarkable agreement in the literature on the proposition that capitalists from the dominant group are the major beneficiaries of prejudice and discrimination in a competitive capitalistic economic system. If W is considered to represent whites or some other dominant group, the fallacious nature of this proposition becomes clear because discrimination harms W capitalists and benefits W workers. The most serious non sequitur in the mistaken analysis is the (explicit or implicit) conclusion that, if tastes for discrimination cause N laborers to receive a lower wage rate than W laborers, the difference between these wage rates must accrue as "profits" to W capitalists.

Another important set of implications stemming from Becker's model concerns what Becker calls *effective discrimination*. There is effective discrimination against N when the total MDC, defined as

$$MDC = \frac{Y(W)}{Y(N)} - \frac{Y_0(W)}{Y_0(N)},$$

is positive, $Y(W)$ and $Y(N)$ are the actual incomes of W and N, and $Y_0(W)$ and $Y_0(N)$ are their incomes without discrimination. Becker proves (1971, appendix to chapter 2) that a necessary and sufficient condition for effective discrimination to occur against N at all levels of discrimination by W is

$$\frac{Y_0(W)}{Y_0(N)} > \frac{l_N}{l_W},$$

where l_N and l_W are the amounts of labor supplied by N and W. That is, if in the absence of discrimination N's net total income relative to W's were less than W's supply of labor relative to N's, discrimination would reduce N's income by a greater percentage than it would W's. In this case, discrimination would cause a decrease in both absolute and relative income of N. Or, in Becker's words, "a necessary and sufficient condition for effective discrimination against N is that N be more of an economic minority than a numerical majority." In this model it is also shown that, if there is effective discrimination against N, N members cannot avoid the effects of discrimination by trying either to segregate themselves or to retaliate against members of W.

Becker's main predictions from his international trade and migration model of discrimination can, then, be summarized in the following simple terms. Discrimination decreases the total net incomes of both N and W. Minorities lose more than majorities when there is discrimination. Minorities lose still more if they try to segregate themselves or retaliate against majorities.

Crime as a Labor Supply Problem

Conventional wisdom about criminal behavior reflects the great influence of sociologists on this subject. From the sociological standpoint, criminals are either sick persons whose behavior is not far from being irrational or passive victims of the social environment. According to this view, people neither freely nor consciously nor rationally choose to be criminals. It is beyond their control to behave that way. Exogenous factors of a biological or social nature force people to behave as criminals. For sociologists, criminal behavior is a matter of mental illness or social oppression and, not surprisingly, a problem whose solution is rehabilitation. In this view, punishment is thought to be the wrong approach to public policy against crime.

Few fields show as clearly as criminal behavior does how incompatible the conclusions from sociologists and economists can be. Although the roots of the economics of crime can be traced back to Bentham, the seminal paper of the modern literature is Becker's "Crime and Punishment," published in 1968. Becker's analysis of criminal behavior rejects the sociological view subsumed in current conventional wisdom. For Becker, criminals are not different from other people as far as rationality, maximizing behavior, or preferences are concerned. The cost-benefit analysis employed in the study of households, firms, investment in human capital, marriage and fertility, and discrimination can also be fruitfully utilized in the area of criminal behavior.

Two closely related ideas are central to Becker's approach. The first one is that criminals are neither victims nor irrational agents. Criminals behave in the same manner as the average person. They act as if they maximized their (expected) utility subject to their full-income constraint in a world with uncertainty. Criminals are then *rational actors* faced with a standard time allocation problem. Choosing to become criminals is a decision problem not different from choosing any other occupation. "Crime is a part-time or full-time occupation like carpentry, engineering, or teaching" (Becker 1987b). People decide to become part-time or full-time criminals when the net return from this activity surpasses that of any other alternative occupation. It is therefore differences in return between legal and illegal activities, not differences in preferences, that lies behind criminal behavior. This explains, for example, why criminal activities like robbery and theft are committed mainly by poor persons: their insufficient education and training limit greatly the return they can obtain from legal activities. Thus, Becker relates criminal behavior to prior investment in human capital (training and education). Likewise unemployment increases the volume of crimes against property because it implies a reduction in the return from legal activities.

The second idea is that criminal behavior is, contrary to what is generally believed by sociologists, *price elastic*. Criminals (i.e., the suppliers in the market for illegitimate activities) react to changes in prices in the same way as consumers and workers do. Thus, all other things equal, the higher the net return from criminal activity, the higher the crime rate (i.e., the "production" of crimes). The most important "price" in the cost-benefit analysis that criminals apply when making a decision is punishment. A major public policy conclusion from the economic analysis of crime (and the most controversial) is that, the higher the punishment associated with an illegal activity, the lower will be the net return from this activity and the number of persons devoting their time to it. In Becker's words, "punishment works" (Becker 1987b), that is, punishment deters criminal activity. The equivalence between punishment and prices, and the consideration that criminals' preferences are not different from the preferences of other persons, invalidates the traditional distinction between crimes of passion and economic crimes regarding the deterrence effect of punishments. There is no reason why crimes of passion should be less price elastic than economic crimes. No less unconventional is the related conclusion that capital punishment is likely to have a strong deterrent effect on murder.

Unlike his other contributions, Becker's analysis of crime focuses on public policy issues. In developing a social welfare analysis applied to crime, Becker uses a particular form of a social loss function, in which the relevant criterion is social real income, to derive normative propositions concerning criminal activities (i.e., to determine "how to combat crime in an optimal fashion"). Of particular relevance for public authorities is the distinction between the two basic dimensions of punishment: severity, f, and likelihood, p (i.e., the probability of being caught). These are the two *policy variables* that authorities can use to minimize the social loss from crime, that is,

$$L = D(X) \cdot + C(p,X) + bpfX,$$

where L is the function measuring social loss, $D(X)$ is the net damage to society from X offenses, $C(p,X)$ is the total costs of apprehension and conviction, which depend on the probability p of apprehension and conviction and the number of offenses X, and $bpfX$ is the total social loss from punishments where b is a parameter greater than one if the punishments take the form of imprisonment.

From the first-order conditions of this social welfare problem, Becker deduces many interesting implications about the optimal magnitudes of severity and likelihood of punishments. One well-known conclusion is that "social welfare is increased if fines are used whenever possible" because probation and institutionalization use up resources and fines do not. Fines also provide compensation to victims.

The first-order conditions of the social welfare problem allow us to characterize *optimal fines*. An optimal fine can be seen as an *optimal tax* on a negative externality (in this case, crime). Optimal fines should be equal to the sum of the marginal harm and the marginal cost of apprehension and conviction. Criminals must compensate at the margin for the cost imposed on their victims and the cost of catching them.

Another important result is that, under certain conditions, authorities can exchange f for p without affecting the corresponding deterrent effect. Authorities could reduce the cost of crime by imposing large fines with a low probability, leading Becker to conclude that the *optimal probability of conviction* would be close to zero.

IV. Becker's Research Program

An Economic Approach to Human Behavior

As Becker said in his Nobel Prize acceptance speech, his is an "economic way of looking at behavior" (Becker 1993). For Becker, economics deals with more than the traditional economics of explicit markets and explicit prices, which he feels unnecessarily limits the scope of economics. What distinguishes economics from other sciences is not the area of human behavior under consideration (market activities, political behavior, criminal behavior, racial and other types of discrimination, and so on) but the *way of looking* at such diverse activities. In Becker's view the scope of economics is as wide as the range of aspects of human behavior in which two essential elements, *scarce means* and *competing ends*, are present. Becker, therefore, extends Robbins's (1935) definition of economics to *all* human behavior; "decisions about the allocation of a consumer's nonmarket time and decisions about his choice of religion, marriage mate, family size, divorce, political party, or 'lifestyle' all involve the allocation of scarce resources among competing ends" (Michael and Becker 1973).

Regarding those decisions, Becker emphasizes the importance of aggregate behavior as compared with the behavior of microunits like firms and households. Thus he claims (Becker 1971, 2) that "our main interest, as is that of most economists, is in the market behavior of aggregations of firms and households; although important inferences are drawn about individual firms and households, we try mainly to understand aggregate responses to changes in basic economic parameters like tax rates, tariff schedules, technology, or antitrust provisions."

But what can be said about the economic approach itself? What are the distinctive features of the economic approach? In Becker's introductory chaper to his *Economic Approach* (1976a, 5), we find the answer: "the combined assumptions of maximizing behavior, market equilibrium, and stable preferences, used relentlessly and unflinchingly, form the heart of the economic approach as I see it." In recent years, Becker has progressed to modeling preferences, and thus the above phrase could be amended to say "functionally stable preferences."

The assumption of *maximizing* or *rational behavior* implies that agents behave as if they maximized their own utility functions subject to their budget, time, and production constraints, which can all be combined into a single *full-income* (or full-wealth, in a dynamic model) *budget constraint*. The utility functions of households relate (in ordinal terms) their welfare to their consumption of *basic goods* (not market goods), that is, goods that are not purchased or sold but that are produced by households and whose prices (shadow prices) are determined by their production costs. Through the prices and incomes that enter their full-income budget constraints, household behavior is restricted by *market equilibria conditions*, even if there are no explicit markets and prices (e.g., marriage markets).

For Becker, rational behavior is a broader concept than *selfish behavior*, which means that *altruistic behavior* can also be interpreted as a form of rational behavior. Becker expresses the altruistic behavior of person X with respect to Y by considering Y's utility as an argument of the utility function of X. Proceeding this way, Y's welfare becomes a new basic good for X. This device enables Becker to solve the problem of aggregation of preferences in multiperson households and to define the decision-making problem of a household in terms of a single utility, the *household's* or *family's* utility function, the family's utility function being that of the "head" of the family. In his popular "rotten kid theorem," Becker (1974a) shows that, under certain conditions, if the head of a household is altruistic (and, therefore, incorporates in her or his utility function the utility functions of the other household members), all other household members, even if they are selfish (i.e., they are only interested in maximizing their own individual utility functions), will nevertheless behave as if they were altruistic toward the family head because that raises their own welfare. This implies that the household or family decision-making problem can be stated in terms of a single utility function, one representing the family head's preferences, and a single full-income (or wealth) budget constraint, one delimiting the possible uses of the joint income or wealth of the entire family.

Altruism is not the only kind of human behavior that is thought to threaten the validity of economic theory, for it is also argued that irrational behavior implies the rejection of standard economic predictions. Becker (1962) shows that economic theory is more compatible with irrational behavior than had been generally believed. By distinguishing between individual and market rationality, Becker proves that irrational consumers and firms would often be forced into rational *market* responses. Accordingly, the standard market demand (negatively sloped) and supply functions (positively sloped) can be derived even when households and firms behave irrationally. Becker comes to the astonishing conclusion that households and firms can be said to behave "as if" they were rational but also "as if" they were irrational. Becker's explanation relies on the role played by the *scarcity principle* in the allocation of resources, a principle general enough to include a wide class of irrational behavior as well as rational behavior.

The assumption of stable preferences serves as "a stable foundation for generating predictions about responses to various changes, and prevents the analyst from succumbing to the temptation of simply postulating the required shift in preferences to 'explain' all apparent contradictions to his predictions" (Becker 1976a, 5). To understand the assumption of stable preferences, we must remember that basic goods, not market goods, are the only utility-yielding goods. Accordingly, Becker's assumption about the stability of preferences refers to the stability of preferences with respect to basic goods such as health, prestige, sensual pleasure, and so on. This kind of stability need not imply the stability of preferences with respect to market goods, for, as Becker (1971) reminds us, basic goods do not always bear a stable relation to market goods and services. Stability should also be interpreted in both cross-section and intertemporal terms; in other words, "tastes neither change capriciously nor differ importantly between people" (Stigler and Becker 1977, 76).

The approach based on rational behavior and stable preferences differs greatly from the traditional economic approach. A comparative analysis of the two approaches is provided by Stigler and Becker (1977). "On the traditional view, an explanation of economic phenomena that reaches a difference in tastes between people or times is the terminus of the argument" (p. 76). In Becker's (and Stigler's) approach, however, "one never reaches this impasse, the economist continues to search for differences in prices or incomes to explain any differences or changes in behavior" (p. 76). The new approach has "partly translated 'unstable tastes' into variables in the household production functions for commodities. The great advantage, however, of relying only on changes in the arguments entering household production functions is that *all* changes in behavior are explained by changes in prices and incomes, precisely the variables that organize and give power to economic analysis" (p. 89). In conclusion, "when an apparently profitable opportunity to a firm, worker, or household is not exploited, the economic approach does not take refuge in assertions about irrationality, contentment with wealth already acquired, or convenient ad hoc shifts in values (i.e., preferences). Rather it postulates the existence of costs, monetary or psychic, of taking advantage of these opportunities that eliminates their profitability—costs that may not be easily seen by outside observers" (Becker 1976a, 7).

We end this section with a brief remark on the nature of the assumptions of maximizing behavior and stable preferences. For Becker (1976b), the postulates of maximizing behavior and stable preferences are not simply primitive assumptions. Behind them lies the principle of *natural selection*. These assumptions can be explained by the selection over time of traits having greater survival value. In Michael and Becker's (1973) words, "if genetical natural selection and rational behavior reinforce each other in producing speedier and more efficient responses to changes in environment, perhaps that common preference function has evolved over time by natural selection and rational choice as that preference function best adopted to human society."

Methodology and Becker's Approach

Methodological disputes are deemed singularly unproductive in economics. Ever since the *Methodenstreit* between Karl Menger and Gustav Schmoller, the prejudice of the profession has gone against wasting time on method. Becker has not made any overt pronouncements on these questions, but in practice he has profoundly transformed the way in which many economists look at how they should proceed in building their science. He can even be seen as innovative in relation to that luminary of the older Chicago School, Milton Friedman (Friedman 1953).

Freidman, Stigler, Becker, and other colleagues, such as Schultz and Fogel, all worked or are working within the general framework of Karl Popper's methodology (Popper 1959). For these economists, hypothesizing is free, to the point even of being "counterfactual" if necessary, but theory has to be tested by comparing its predictions with observations.

Some dross has accumulated around the views of Popper that has obscured their understanding. One sort of confusion arises from Imre Lakatos's belief that a school of thought is characterized by a common "research program." Another kind of confusion arises from another idea of Lakatos's—that a research program always has a hard core that none of the members ever question (Lakatos 1976).

Although Becker clearly conceives of economic research in the same Popperian spirit as Stigler or Friedman, it would be less than useful if all three were presented as having the same research program. All three can be seen as followers of Marshall in their wish to solve practical problems using partial equilibrium tools or, to speak more accurately, assuming away some systemic or general equilibrium feedbacks to focus on observable causes. But their research programs must be seen as differing in fruitful ways; Becker's is to apply little-used tools, such as human capital, time preference, risk aversion, to explain widely dispersed social phenomena.

Again Becker is the best refutation of the idea that the older Chicago School defended a crystallized citadel of first principles that they never questioned. One can observe Becker moving away from the principle that "tastes must not be caviled at" to endogenizing preferences and modeling them along the same lines that apply to individual consumption or savings or to a firm's production. As Popper maintained, each scientist, even though belonging to a school, can have her or his own research program or a number of them along the years; and no assumption or theoretical axiom need be immunized from criticism and revision.

Becker can be observed at present as receiving the influence of the new Chicago School, as he does not seem content with the comparative statics of his early years and is moving toward a more dynamic analysis, along the lines suggested by the new classical economics of Lucas, Sargent, and Barro.

V. CONCLUSIONS

Becker's implicit proposal for the profession seems to be that things are not necessarily what they appear to be and that the economist should go beyond surfaces to acquire a better knowledge of human behavior. Becker's share of this task has been fulfilled by bringing production and investment theory into consumer theory. Since Becker reformulated the theory of consumer behavior, households are seen not only as utility maximizers but as rational *producers* and *investors*. Households, then, are *producers* of basic goods, *investors* in themselves, in their human capital, and in their own children. They also have to make decisions about their *marital status* (remaining single, marrying, or divorcing), no longer taken as a given, and about the subsequent *home division of labor* among members. The additional structure Becker gives households means that aspects of household behavior traditionally attributed to exogenous factors in conventional theory (usually differences in tastes or shifts in preferences) can now be endogenized and related to differences in prices and incomes.

Becker's economics differs from traditional economics in two fundamental respects: scope and approach. Economic theory is a much more powerful tool than noneconomists and even professional economists tend to think, being not only the science of explicit markets and prices but a way of thinking. A whole world of nonmarket activities is waiting to be fruitfully analyzed by economic tools. The economic theories of marriage, fertility, and criminal and political behavior are outstanding examples of this *imperialistic* view of economics in which Becker has become a leading figure. Armed with the postulates of stable preferences, maximizing behavior, and market equilibrium, the economist can offer new insights into areas not traditionally viewed as the province of economics. More often than not, these insights are at variance with casual observation, conventional wisdom, or established propositions from other sciences. Thus, babies are not inferior goods, criminals are not passive victims of society, full sharing of household tasks between husbands and wives is not an efficient arrangement, capitalists do not gain by discriminating against black workers, marriage is not simply a matter of physical attraction or cultural or institutional factors, divorce is largely independent of divorce laws, and so on.

These considerations capture, we believe, the essence of Becker.

REFERENCES

Barro, R. J., and G. S. Becker. 1989. "Fertility Choice in a Model of Economic Growth." *Econometrica* 57, no. 2: 481–501.

Becker, G. S. 1957 (1st ed.), 1971 (2d ed.). *The Economics of Discrimination.* Chicago: University of Chicago Press.

Becker, G. S. 1959. "Union Restrictions on Entry." In P. D. Bradley, ed., *The Public Stake in Union Power.* Charlottesville: University of Virginia Press.

Becker, G. S. 1960. "An Economic Analysis of Fertility." In Becker, ed., *Demographic and Economic Change in Developed Countries.* Princeton, N.J.: Princeton University Press.

Becker, G. S. 1962. "Irrational Behavior and Economic Theory." *Journal of Political Economy* 70, no. 1: 1–13.

Becker, G. S. 1964 (1st ed.), 1975 (2d ed.), 1993 (3d ed.). *Human Capital.* Chicago: University of Chicago Press.

Becker, G. S. 1965. "A Theory of the Allocation of Time." *Economic Journal* 75 (September): 493–517.

Becker, G. S. 1968. "Crime and Punishment: An Economic Approach." *Journal of Political Economy* 76, no. 2: 169–217.

Becker, G. S. 1971. *Economic Theory.* New York: A. Knopf.

Becker, G. S. 1973. "A Theory of Marriage: Part I." *Journal of Political Economy* 81, no. 4: 813–46.

Becker, G. S. 1974a. "On the Relevance of the New Economics of the Family." *American Economic Review* 64, no. 2: 317–24.

Becker, G. S. 1974b. "A Theory of Marriage: Part II." *Journal of Political Economy* 82, no. 2: S11–S26.

Becker, G. S. 1974c. "A Theory of Social Interactions." *Journal of Political Economy* 82, no. 6: 1063–93.

Becker, G. S. 1976a. *The Economic Approach to Human Behavior.* Chicago: University of Chicago Press.

Becker, G. S. 1976b. "Altruism, Egoism, and Genetic Fitness: Economics and Sociobiology." *Journal of Economic Literature* 14, no. 3: 817–26.

Becker, G. S. 1981a (1st ed.), 1991 (2d ed.). *A Treatise on the Family.* Cambridge, Mass.: Harvard University Press.

Becker, G. S. 1981b. "Altruism in the Family and Selfishness in the Marketplace." Economica 48 (February): 1–15.

Becker, G. S. 1987a. "Family." In J. Eatwell, M. Milgate, and P. Newman, eds., The New Palgrave: A Dictionary of Economics. Vol. 2. New York: Macmillan.

Becker, G. S. 1987b. "Economic Analysis and Human Behavior." In L. Green and J. H. Kagel, eds., Advances in Behavioral Economics. Vol. 1. Norwood, N.J.: Ablex.

Becker, G. S. 1993. "Nobel Lecture: The Economic Way of Looking at Behavior." Journal of Political Economy 101, no. 3: 385–409.

Becker, G. S., and R. J. Barro. 1988. "A Reformulation of the Economic Theory of Fertility." Quarterly Journal of Economics 103, no. 1: 1–25.

Becker, G. S., M. Grossman, and K. M. Murphy. 1994. "An Empirical Analysis of Cigarette Addiction." American Economic Review 84, no. 3: 390–418.

Becker, G. S., E. M. Landes, and R. T. Michael. 1977. "An Economic Analysis of Marital Instability." Journal of Political Economy 85, no. 6: 1153–89.

Becker, G. S., and W. M. Landes, eds. 1974. Essays in the Economics of Crime and Punishment. New York: Columbia University Press for the National Bureau of Economic Research.

Becker, G. S., and H. G. Lewis. 1973. "On the Interaction between the Quantity and Quality of Children." Journal of Political Economy 81, no. 2: S279–S288.

Becker, G. S., and K. M. Murphy. 1988. "A Theory of Rational Addiction." Journal of Political Economy 96 (August): 675–700.

Becker, G. S., K. M. Murphy, and R. Tamura. 1990. "Human Capital, Fertility, and Economic Growth." Journal of Political Economy 98, no. 5, pt. 2: S12–S70.

Becker, G. S., and N. Tomes. 1976. "Child Endowments and the Quantity and Quality of Children." Journal of Political Economy 84, no. 4: S143–S162.

Becker, G. S., and N. Tomes. 1979. "An Equilibrium Theory of the Distribution of Income and Intergenerational Mobility." Journal of Political Economy 87, no. 6: 1153–89.

Becker, G. S., and N. Tomes. 1986. "Human Capital and the Rise and Fall of Families." Journal of Labor Economics 4, no. 3, pt. 2: S1–S39.

Denison, E. F. 1962. The Sources of Economic Growth in the United States and the Alternatives before Us. New York: Committee for Economic Development.

Friedman, M. 1953. "The Methodology of Positive Economics." In Friedman, ed., Essays in Positive Economics. Chicago: University of Chicago Press.

Ghez, G. R., and G. S. Becker. 1975. The Allocation of Time and Goods Over the Life Cycle. New York: Columbia University Press for the National Bureau of Economic Research.

Lakatos, I. 1970. "Falsification and the Methodology of Scientific Research Programmes." In I. Lakatos and A. Musgrave, eds., Criticism and the Growth of Knowledge. Cambridge, Eng.: Cambridge University Press.

Lucas, R. E. 1988. "On the Mechanics of Economic Development." Journal of Monetary Economics 22: 3–42.

Malthus, T. R. 1798. [*Anonymous First Essay on Population*] *An Essay on the Principle of Population as It Affects the Future Improvement of Society, with Remarks on the Speculations of Mr. Godwin and M. Condorcet, and Other Writers*. London: N.p.

Michael, R. T., and G. S Becker. 1973. "On the New Theory of Consumer Behavior." *Swedish Journal of Economics* 75, no. 4: 378–96.

Popper, K. 1959. *The Logic of Scientific Discovery*. Hutchinson.

Robbins, L. 1935. *The Nature and Significance of Economic Science*. London: Macmillan.

Rosen, S. 1987. "Human Capital." In J. Eatwell, M. Milgate, and P. Newman, eds., *The New Palgrave: A Dictionary of Economics*. Vol 2. New York: Macmillan.

Stigler, G. J., and G. S Becker. 1977. "De Gustibus Non Est Disputandum." *American Economic Review* 67, no. 2: 76–90.

APPENDIX:
BECKER'S BIBLIOGRAPHY

Monographs

A Treatise on the Family. 1981, expanded edition, 1991. Cambridge: Harvard University Press. Spanish translation, 1987; Chinese translation, 1988.

The Economic Approach to Human Behavior. 1976. Chicago: University of Chicago Press. German translation, 1982, Polish translation, 1990; Chinese translation, 1993.

Essays in Labor Economics in Honor of H. Gregg Lewis. 1976. Special Supplement to the *Journal of Political Economy* 84, no. 2, pt 2, August).

With Gilbert Ghez. *The Allocation of Time and Goods over the Life Cycle*. 1975. New York: Columbia University Press for the National Bureau of Economic Research.

With William M. Landes. 1974. *Essays in the Economics of Crime and Punishment*. New York: Columbia University Press for the National Bureau of Economic Research

Economic Theory. 1971. New York: A. Knopf. Japanese translation, 1976.

Human Capital and the Personal Distribution of Income: An Analytical Approach. 1967. Ann Arbor: University of Michigan.

Human Capital 1964: 2d edition, 1975; 3d edition, 1993. New York: Columbia University Press. Japanese translation, 1975; Spanish translation, 1984.

The Economics of Discrimination. 1957. Chicago: University of Chicago Press. 2d edition 1971.

Selected Articles

With Michael Grossman and Kevin M. Murphy. 1994. "An Empirical Analysis of Cigarette Addiction. *American Economic Review* 84, no. 3 (June) 390–418.

With Kevin M. Murphy. "A Simple Theory of Advertising as a Good or Bad." 1993. *Quarterly Journal of Economics* 108, no. 4 (November): 941–04.

"George Joseph Stigler: January 17, 1911–December 1, 1991." 1993. *Journal of Political Economy* 101, no. 5 (October): 701–67.

With Richard Posner. "Cross-Cultural Differences in Family and Sexual Life: An Economic Analysis." 1993. *Rationality and Society* 5, no. 4 (October): 421–31.

"Nobel Lecture: The Economic Way of Looking at Behavior." 1993. *Journal of Political Economy* 101, no. 3 (June): 385–409.

"Government, Human Capital, and Economic Growth." 1993. Presidential Address to the Mont Pelerin Society, Vancouver General Meeting, September 1992. *Industry of Free China* 79, no. 6 (June): 47–56.

With Michael Grossman and Kevin Murphy. "Rational Addiction and the Effect of Price on Consumption." 1992. In George Loewenstein and Jon Elster, eds. *Choice over Time.* Russell Sage Foundation.

"George Joseph Stigler." 1992. *Journal des Economistes et des Etudes Humaines* 3, no. 1 (March): 5–9.

With Kevin Murphy. "The Division of Labor, Coordination Costs, and Knowledge." 1992. *Quarterly Journal of Economics* 107, no. 4 (November): 1137–60.

"Fertility and the Economy." 1992. *Journal of Population Economics* 5, no. 3: 185–201.

"Habits, Addictions and Traditions." 1992. *Kyklos* 45, asc 3: 327–46.

"Human Capital and the Economy." 1992. *Proceedings of the American Philosophical Society* 136, no. 1 (March): 85–92.

"Education, Labor Force Quality and the Economy." 1992. *Business Economics* 27, no. 1 (January): 7–12.

"Milton Friedman." 1991. In Edward Shils, ed. *Remembering the University of Chicago: Teachers, Scientists, and Scholars.* Chicago: University of Chicago Press.

"A Note on Restaurant Pricing and Other Examples of Social Influences on Price." 1991. *Journal of Political Economy* 99, no. 1 (October): 1109–16.

With Michael Grossman and Kevin M. Murphy. 1991. "Rational Addiction and the Effect of Price on Consumption." *AEA Papers and Proceedings* 81, no. 2 (May): 237–41.

With Kevin M. Murphy and Robert Tamura. "Human Capital, Fertility, and Economic Growth." 1990. *Journal of Political Economy* 98, no. 5, Pt 2 (October): S12–S70.

With Robert Barro. "Fertility Choice in a Model of Economic Growth." 1989. *Econometrica* 57 (March): 481–501.

With Kevin M. Murphy. "A Theory of Rational Addiction." 1988. *Journal of Political Economy* 96 (August): 675–700.

With Kevin M. Murphy. "The Family and the State." 1988. *Journal of Law and Economics* 31 (April): 1–18.

"Family Economics and Macro Behavior." 1988. Presidential Address to the American Economic Association, December 29, 1988. *American Economic Review* 86, no. 1 (March).

With Robert J. Barro. "A Reformulation of the Economic Theory of Fertility." 1988. *Quarterly Journal of Economics* 103, no. 1 (February): 1–25.

With Nigel Tomes. 1986. "Human Capital and the Rise and Fall of Families." *Journal of Labor Economics* 4, no. 3, Pt. 2 (July): S1–S39.

"Special Interests and Public Policies." 1985. Acceptance Paper, the Frank E. Seidman Distinguished Award in Political Economy, Rhodes College, September 26.

"Public Policies, Pressure Groups, and Dead Weight Costs." 1985. *Journal of Public Economics* 28: 329–47.

"Pressure Groups and Political Behavior." 1985. In R. D. Coe and C. K. Wilbur, eds. *Capitalism and Democracy: Schumpeter Revisited*. Notre Dame, Ind.: University of Notre Dame Press.

"An Economic Analysis of the Family." 1985. Seventeenth Geary Lecture, the Economic and Social Research Institute, Dublin, Ireland.

"Human Capital, Effort, and the Sexual Division of Labor." 1985. *Journal of Labor Economics* 3, no. 1, Pt. 2 (January): S33–S58.

"A Theory of Competition among Pressure Groups for Political Influence." 1983. *Quarterly Journal of Economics* 97, no. 3 (August): 371–400.

"Altruism in the Family and Selfishness in the Market Place." 1981. *Economica* 48 (February): 1–15.

With Nigel Tomes. "An Equilibrium Theory of the Distribution of Income and Intergenerational Mobility." 1979. *Journal of Political Economy* 87, no. 6 (December): 1153–89.

"Economic Analysis and Human Behavior." 1979. In L. Levy-Garboua, ed. *Sociological Economics*. Beverly Hills, Calif.

With F. M. Landes and R. T. Michael. "An Economic Analysis of Marital Instability." 1977. *Journal of Political Economy* 85, no. 6 (December): 1153–89.

With G. J. Stigler. "De Gustibus Non Est Disputandum." 1977. *American Economic Review* 67, no. 2 (March): 76–90.

"Altruism, Egoism, and Genetic Fitness: Economics and Sociobiology." 1976. *Journal of Economic Literature* 14, no. 3 (September): 817–26.

With Nigel Tomes. "Child Endowments and the Quantity and Quality of Children." 1976. In G. S. Becker, ed. *Essays in Labor Economics in Honor of H. Gregg Lewis. Journal of Political Economy* 84, no. 4, pt. 2 (August): S143–62.

"A Theory of Social Interactions." 1974. *Journal of Political Economy* 82, no. 6 (November/December): 1063–93.

"A Theory of Marriage, Part II." 1974. *Journal of Political Economy* 82, no. 2 pt. 2) (March/April): S11–S20. Reprinted in T. W. Schultz, ed. *Economics of the Family*. Chicago: University of Chicago Press.

With G. J. Stigler. "Law Enforcement, Malfeasance, and Compensation of Enforcers." 1974. *Journal of Legal Studies* 3, no. 1 (January): 1–18.

With R. T. Michael. "On the New Theory of Consumer Behavior." 1973. *Swedish Journal of Economics* 75: 378–90.

"A Theory of Marriage: Part I." 1973. *Journal of Political Economy* 81, no. 4 (July/August): 813–46. Reprinted in T. W. Schutlz, ed. *Economics of the Family*. Chicago: University of Chicago Press.

With H. G. Lewis. "On the Interaction between the Quantity and Quality of Children." 1973. *Journal of Political Economy* 81, no. 2, pt. 2 (March/April): S279–S288.

With I. Ehrlich. "Market Insurance, Self-Insurance, and Self-Protection." 1972. *Journal of Political Economy* 80, no. 4 (July/August): 623–48.

"Crime and Punishment: An Economic Approach." 1968. *Journal of Political Economy* 76, no. 2 (March/April): 169–217.

With B. Chiswick. "Education and the Distribution of Earnings." 1966. *American Economic Review* LVI, no. 2 (May): 358–69.

"A Theory of the Allocation of Time." 1965. *Economic Journal* 75, no. 299 (September): 493–508.

"Underinvestment in College Education?" 1960. *American Economic Review* 50, no. 2: 346–54. Reprinted in E. Phelps, ed. *Problems of Economic Growth* New York: W. W. Norton, 1962.

"Investment in Human Capital: A Theoretical Analysis." 1962. *Journal of Political Economy* 70, no. 5, pt. 2 (October): 9–49.

"Irrational Behavior and Economic Theory." 1962. *Journal of Political Economy* 60, no. 1 (February): 1–13.

With W. J. Baumol. "The Classical Monetary Theory: The Outcome of the Discussion." 1960. In J. Spengler and W. Allen, eds. *Essays in Economic Thought*. Chicago: Rand McNally and Co.

"An Economic Analysis of Fertility." 1960. In *Demographic and Economic Change in Developed Countries, Conference of the Universities-National Bureau Committee for Economic Research, a Report of the National Bureau of Economic Research*. Princeton, N.J.: Princeton University Press.

"Union Restrictions on Entry." 1959. In *The Public Stake in Union Power*, ed. Philip D. Bradley. Charlottesville: University of Virginia Press.

"Competition and Democracy." 1958. *Journal of Law and Economics* 1: 105–9.

With M. Friedman. "A Statistical Illusion in Judging Keynesian Models." 1957. *Journal of Political Economy* 65, no. 1 (February): 64–75.

With W. J. Baumol. "The Classical Monetary Theory: The Outcome of the Discussion." 1952. *Economica* 19, 70 (November): 355–70.

"A Note on Multi-Country Trade." 1952. *American Economic Review*. 42, no. 4 (September): 558–68.

FOUNDATIONS OF
HUMAN BEHAVIOR

◆

• *PART* • *ONE* •

THE ECONOMIC APPROACH
TO HUMAN BEHAVIOR

· 1 ·

Economy is the art of making the most of life.

George Bernard Shaw

The following essays use an "economic" approach in seeking to understand human behavior in a variety of contexts and situations. Although few persons would dispute the distinctiveness of an economic approach, it is not easy to state exactly what distinguishes the economic approach from sociological, psychological, anthropological, political, or even genetical approaches. In this introductory essay I attempt to spell out the principal attributes of the economic approach.

Let us turn for guidance first to the definitions of different fields. At least three conflicting definitions of economics are still common. Economics is said to be the study of (1) the allocation of material goods to satisfy material wants,[1] (2) the market sector,[2] and (3) the allocation of scarce means to satisfy competing ends.[3]

The definition of economics in terms of material goods is the narrowest and the least satisfactory. It does not describe adequately either the market sector or what economists "do." For the production of tangible goods now provides less than half of all the market employment in the United States, and the intangible outputs of the service sector are now larger in value than

First published as chapter 1 in Gary S. Becker, *The Economic Approach to Human Behavior* (Chicago: University of Chicago Press, 1976) pp. 3–14. © 1976 by the University of Chicago. All rights reserved.

the outputs of the goods sector (see Fuchs 1968). Moreover, economists are as successful in understanding the production and demand for retail trade, films, or education as they are for autos or meat. The persistence of definitions which tie economics to material goods is perhaps due to a reluctance to submit certain kinds of human behavior to the "frigid" calculus of economics.

The definition of economics in terms of scarce means and competing ends is the most general of all. It defines economics by the nature of the problem to be solved, and encompasses far more than the market sector or "what economists do."[4] Scarcity and choice characterize all resources allocated by the political process (including which industries to tax, how fast to increase the money supply, and whether to go to war); by the family (including decisions about a marriage mate, family size, the frequency of church attendance, and the allocation of time between sleeping and waking hours); by scientists (including decisions about allocating their thinking time, and mental energy to different research problems); and so on in endless variety. This definition of economics is so broad that it often is a source of embarrassment rather than of pride to many economists, and usually is immediately qualified to exclude most nonmarket behavior.[5]

All of these definitions of economics simply define the scope, and none tells us one iota about what the "economic" approach is. It could stress tradition and duty, impulsive behavior, maximizing behavior, or any other behavior in analyzing the market sector or the allocation of scarce means to competing ends.

Similarly, definitions of sociology and other social sciences are of equally little help in distinguishing their approaches from others. For example, the statement that sociology "is the study of social aggregates and groups in their institutional organization, of institutions and their organization, and of causes and consequences of changes in institutions and social organization" (Reiss 1968) does not distinguish the subject matter, let alone the approach, of sociology from, say, economics. Or the statement that "comparative psychology is concerned with the behavior of different species of living organisms" (Waters and Brunnell 1968) is as general as the definitions of economics and sociology, and as uninformative.

Let us turn away from definitions, therefore, because I believe that what most distinguishes economics as a discipline from other disciplines in the social sciences is not its subject matter but its approach. Indeed, many kinds of behavior fall within the subject matter of several disciplines: for example, fertility behavior is considered part of sociology, anthropology, economics, history, and perhaps even politics. I contend that the economic approach is uniquely powerful because it can integrate a wide range of human behavior.

Everyone recognizes that the economic approach assumes maximizing behavior more explicitly and extensively than other approaches do, be it the utility or wealth function of the household, firm, union, or government bureau that is maximized. Moreover, the economic approach assumes the existence of markets that with varying degrees of efficiency coordinate the actions of different participants—individuals, firms, even nations—so that their behavior becomes mutually consistent. Since economists generally have had little to contribute, especially in recent times, to the understanding of how preferences are formed, preferences are assumed not to change substantially over time, nor to be very different between wealthy and poor persons, or even between persons in different societies and cultures.

Prices and other market instruments allocate the scarce resources within a society and thereby constrain the desires of participants and coordinate their actions. In the economic approach, these market instruments perform most, if not all, of the functions assigned to "structure" in sociological theories.[6]

The preferences that are assumed to be stable do not refer to market goods and services, like oranges, automobiles, or medical care, but to underlying objects of choice that are produced by each household using market goods and services, their own time, and other inputs. These underlying preferences are defined over fundamental aspects of life, such as health, prestige, sensual pleasure, benevolence, or envy, that do not always bear a stable relation to market goods and services (see Becker 1976, chap. 7). The assumption of stable preferences provides a stable foundation for generating predictions about responses to various changes, and prevents the analyst from succumbing to the temptation of simply postulating the required shift in preferences to "explain" all apparent contradictions to his predictions.

The combined assumptions of maximizing behavior, market equilibrium, and stable preferences, used relentlessly and unflinchingly, form the heart of the economic approach as I see it. They are responsible for the many theorems associated with this approach. For example, that (1) a rise in price reduces quantity demanded,[7] be it a rise in the market price of eggs reducing the demand for eggs, a rise in the "shadow" price of children reducing the demand for children, or a rise in the office waiting time for physicians, which is one component of the full price of physician services, reducing the demand for their services; (2) a rise in price increases the quantity supplied, be it a rise in the market price of beef increasing the number of cattle raised and slaughtered, a rise in the wage rate offered to married women increasing their labor force participation, or a reduction in "cruising" time raising the effective price received by taxicab drivers and thereby increasing the supply of taxicabs; (3) competitive markets satisfy consumer preferences more effectively than monopolistic markets, be it the market for aluminum or the market for ideas (see Director 1964; Coase 1974); or (4) a tax on the output of a market reduces that output, be it an excise tax on gasoline that reduces the use of gasoline, punishment of criminals (which is a "tax" on crime) that reduces the amount of crime, or a tax on wages that reduces the labor supplied to the market sector.

The economic approach is clearly not restricted to material goods and wants, or even to the market sector. Prices, be they the money prices of the market sector or the "shadow" imputed prices of the nonmarket sector, measure the opportunity cost of using scarce resources, and the economic approach predicts the same kind of response to shadow prices as to market prices. Consider, for example, a person whose only scarce resource is his limited amount of time. This time is used to produce various commodities that enter his preference function, the aim being to maximize utility. Even without a market sector, either directly or indirectly, each commodity has a relevant marginal "shadow" price, namely, the time required to produce a unit change in that commodity; in equilibrium, the ratio of these prices must equal the ratio of the marginal utilities.[8] Most important, an increase in the relative price of any commodity—i.e., an increase in the time required to produce a unit of that commodity—would tend to reduce the consumption of that commodity.

The economic approach does not assume that all participants in any market necessarily have complete information or engage in costless transactions. Incomplete information or costly transactions should not, however, be confused with irrational or volatile behavior.[9] The economic approach has developed a theory of the optimal or rational accumulation of costly information[10] that implies, for example, greater investment in information when undertaking major than minor decisions—the purchase of a house or entrance into marriage versus the purchase of a sofa or bread. The assumption that information is often seriously incomplete because it is costly to acquire is used in the economic approach to explain the same kind of behavior that is explained by irrational and volatile behavior, or traditional behavior, or "nonrational" behavior in other discussions.

When an apparently profitable opportunity to a firm, worker, or household is not exploited, the economic approach does not take refuge in assertions about irrationality, contentment with wealth already acquired, or convenient ad hoc shifts in values (i.e., preferences). Rather it postulates the existence of costs, monetary or psychic, of taking advantage of these opportunities that eliminate their profitability—costs that may not be easily "seen" by outside observers. Of course, postulating the existence of costs closes or "completes" the economic approach in the same, almost tautological, way that postulating the existence of (sometimes unobserved) uses of energy completes the energy system, and preserves the law of the conservation of energy. Systems of analysis in chemistry, genetics, and other fields are completed in a related manner. The critical question is whether a system is completed in a useful way; the important theorems derived from the economic approach indicate that it has been completed in a way that yields much more than a bundle of empty tautologies in good part because, as I indicated earlier, the assumption of stable preferences provides a foundation for predicting the responses to various changes.

Moreover, the economic approach does not assume that decision units are necessarily conscious of their efforts to maximize or can verbalize or otherwise describe in an informative way reasons for the systematic patterns in their behavior.[11] Thus it is consistent with the emphasis on the subconscious in modern psychology and with the distinction between manifest and latent functions in sociology (Merton 1968). In addition, the economic approach does not draw conceptual distinctions between major and minor decisions, such as those involving life and death[12] in contrast to the choice of a brand of coffee; or between decisions said to involve strong emotions and those with little emotional involvement,[13] such as in choosing a mate or the number of children in contrast to buying paint; or between decisions by persons with different incomes, education, or family backgrounds.

Indeed, I have come to the position that the economic approach is a comprehensive one that is applicable to all human behavior, be it behavior involving money prices or imputed shadow prices, repeated or infrequent decisions, large or minor decisions, emotional or mechanical ends, rich or poor persons, men or women, adults or children, brilliant or stupid persons, patients or therapists, businessmen or politicians, teachers or students. The applications of the economic approach so conceived are as extensive as the scope of economics in the definition given earlier that emphasizes scarce means and competing ends. It is an appropriate approach to go with such a broad and unqualified definition, and with the statement by Shaw that begins this essay.

For whatever its worth in evaluating this conclusion, let me indicate that I did not arrive at it quickly. In college I was attracted by the problems studied by sociologists and the analytical techniques used by economists. These interests began to merge in my doctoral study,[14] which used economic analysis to understand racial discrimination (see chapter 17, this volume, and Becker 1971). Subsequently, I applied the economic approach to fertility, education, the uses of time, crime, marriage, social interactions, and other "sociological," "legal," and "political" problems. Only after long reflection on this work and the rapidly growing body of related work by others did I conclude that the economic approach was applicable to all human behavior.

The economic approach to human behavior is not new, even outside the market sector. Adam Smith often (but not always!) used this approach to understand political behavior. Jeremy Bentham was explicit about his belief that the pleasure-pain calculus is applicable to all human behavior: "Nature has placed mankind under the governance of two sovereign masters, *pain and pleasure*. It is for them alone to point out what we ought to do, as well as to determine what we shall do. . . . They govern us in all we do, in all we say, in all we think" (1963). The pleasure-pain calculus is said to be applicable to *all* we do, say, and think, without restriction to monetary decisions, repetitive choices, unimportant decisions, etc. Bentham did apply his calculus to an extremely wide range of human behavior, including criminal sanctions, prison reform, legislation, usury laws, and jurisprudence as well as the markets for goods and services. Although Bentham explicitly states that the pleasure-pain calculus is applicable to what we "shall" do as well as to what we "ought" to do, he was primarily interested in "ought"—he was first and foremost a reformer—and did not develop a theory of actual human behavior with many testable implications. He often became bogged down in tautologies because he did not maintain the assumption of stable preferences, and because he was more concerned about making his calculus consistent with all behavior than about deriving the restrictions it imposed on behavior.

Marx and his followers have applied what is usually called an "economic" approach to politics, marriage, and other nonmarket behavior as well as to market behavior. But to the Marxist, the economic approach means that the organization of production is decisive in determining social and political structure, and he places much emphasis upon material goods, processes, and ends, conflict between capitalists and workers, and general subjugation of one class by another. What I have called the "economic approach" has little in common with this view. Moreover, the Marxist, like the Benthamite, has concentrated on what ought to be, and has often emptied his approach of much predictive content in the effort to make it consistent with all events.

Needless to say, the economic approach has not provided equal insight into and understanding of all kinds of behavior: for example, the determinants of war and of many other political decisions have not yet been much illuminated by this approach (or by any other approach). I believe, however, that the limited success is mainly the result of limited effort and not lack of relevance. For, on the one hand, the economic approach has not been systematically applied to war, and its application to other kinds of political behavior is quite recent; on the other hand, much apparently equally intractable behavior—such as fertility, child-rearing, labor force participation, and other decisions of families—has been greatly illuminated in recent years by the systematic application of the economic approach.

The following essays, through the variety of subjects covered, and (I hope) the insights yielded, provide some support for the wide applicability of the economic approach. Greater support is provided by the extensive literature developed in the last twenty years that uses the economic approach to analyze an almost endlessly varied set of problems, including the evolution of language (Marschak 1965), church attendance (Azzi and Ehrenberg 1975), capital punishment (Ehrlich 1975), the legal system (Posner 1973; Becker and Landes 1974), the extinction of animals (Smith 1975), and the incidence of suicide (Hammermesh and Soss 1974). To convey dramatically the flavor of the economic approach, I discuss briefly three of the more unusual and controversial applications.

Good health and a long life are important aims of most persons, but surely no more than a moment's reflection is necessary to convince anyone that they are not the only aims: somewhat better health or a longer life may be sacrificed because they conflict with other aims. The economic approach implies that there is an "optimal" expected length of life, where the value in utility of an additional year is less than the utility forgone by using time and other resources to obtain that year. Therefore, a person may be a heavy smoker or so committed to work as to omit all exercise, not necessarily because he is ignorant of the consequences or "incapable" of using the information he possesses, but because the life span forfeited is not worth the cost to him of quitting smoking or working less intensively. These would be unwise decisions if a long life were the only aim, but as long as other aims exist, they could be informed and in this sense "wise."

According to the economic approach, therefore, *most* (if not all!) deaths are to some extent "suicides" in the sense that they could have been postponed if more resources had been invested in prolonging life. This not only has implications for the analysis of what are ordinarily called suicides,[15] but also calls into question the common distinction between suicides and "natural" deaths. Once again the economic approach and modern psychology come to similar conclusions since the latter emphasizes that a "death wish" lies behind many "accidental" deaths and others allegedly due to "natural" causes.

The economic approach does not merely restate in language familiar to economists different behavior with regard to health, removing all possibility of error by a series of tautologies. The approach implies, for example, that both health and medical care would rise as a person's wage rate rose, that aging would bring declining health although expenditures on medical care would rise, and that more education would induce an increase in health even though expenditures on medical care would fall. None of these or other implications are necessarily true, but all appear to be consistent with the available evidence.[16]

According to the economic approach, a person decides to marry when the utility expected from marriage exceeds that expected from remaining single or from additional search for a more suitable mate (see Becker 1976, chap. 11). Similarly, a married person terminates his (or her) marriage when the utility anticipated from becoming single or marrying someone else exceeds the loss in utility from separation, including losses due to physical separation from one's children, division of joint assets, legal fees, and so forth. Since many persons are looking for mates, a *market* in marriages can be said to exist: each person tries to do the best he can, given that everyone else in the market is trying to do the best they can. A sorting of persons into different marriages is said to be an equilibrium sorting if persons not married to each other in this sorting could not marry and make each better off.

Again, the economic approach has numerous implications about behavior that could be falsified. For example, it implies that "likes" tend to marry each other, when measured by intelligence, education, race, family background, height, and many other variables, and that "unlikes" marry when measured by wage rates and some other variables. The implication that men with relatively high wage rates marry women with relatively low wage rates (other variables being held constant) surprises many, but appears consistent with the available data when they are adjusted for the large fraction of married women who do not work (see Becker 1976, chap. 11). The economic approach also implies that higher-income persons marry younger and divorce less frequently than others, implications consistent with the available evidence (see Keeley 1974) but not with common beliefs. Still another implication is that an increase in the relative earnings of wives increases the likelihood of marital dissolution, which partly explains the greater dissolution rate among black than white families.

According to the Heisenberg indeterminacy principle, the phenomena analyzed by physical scientists cannot be observed in a "natural" state because their observations change these phenomena. An even stronger principle has been suggested for social scientists since they are participants as well as analysts and, therefore, are supposed to be incapable of objective observation. The economic approach makes a very different but distantly related point: namely, that persons only choose to follow scholarly or other intellectual or artistic pursuits if they expect the benefits, both monetary and psychic, to exceed those available in alternative occupations. Since the criterion is the same as in the choice of more commonplace occupations, there is no obvious reason why intellectuals would be less concerned with personal rewards, more concerned with social well-being, or more intrinsically honest than others.[17]

It then follows from the economic approach that an increased demand by different interest groups or constituencies for particular intellectual arguments and conclusions would stimulate an increased supply of these arguments, by the theorem cited earlier on the effect of a rise in "price" on quantity supplied. Similarly, a flow of foundation or government funds into particular research topics, even "ill-advised" topics, would have no difficulty generating proposals for research on those topics. What the economic approach calls normal responses of supply to changes in demand, others may call intellectual or artistic "prostitution" when applied to intellectual or artistic pursuits. Perhaps, but attempts to distinguish sharply the market for intellectual and artistic services from the market for "ordinary" goods have been the source of confusion and inconsistency (see Director 1964; Coase 1974).

I am not suggesting that the economic approach is used by all economists for all human behavior or even by most economists for most. Indeed, many economists are openly hostile to all but the traditional applications. Moreover, economists cannot resist the temptation to hide their own lack of understanding behind allegations of irrational behavior, unnecessary ignorance, folly, ad hoc shifts in values, and the like, which is simply acknowledging defeat in the guise of considered judgment. For example, if some Broadway theater owners charge prices that result in long delays before seats are available, the owners are alleged to be ignorant of the profit-maximizing price structure rather than the analyst ignorant of why actual prices do maximize profits. When only a portion of the variation in earnings among individuals is explained, the unexplained portion is attributed to luck or chance,[18] not to ignorance of or inability to measure additional systematic components. The coal industry is called inefficient because certain cost and output calculations point in that direction (see Henderson 1958), although an attractive alternative hypothesis is that the calculations are seriously in error.

War is said to be caused by madmen, and political behavior, more generally, dominated by folly and ignorance. Recall Keynes's remark about "madmen in authority, who hear voices in the air" (1962, 383), and although Adam Smith, the principal founder of the economic approach, interpreted some laws and legislation in the same way that he interpreted market behavior, even he, without much discussion, lamely dismissed others as a result of folly and ignorance.[19]

Examples abound in the economic literature of changes in preferences conveniently introduced ad hoc to explain puzzling behavior. Education is said to change preferences—about different goods and services, political candidates, or family size—rather than real income or the relative cost of different choices.[20] Businessmen talk about the social responsibilities of business because their attitudes are said to be influenced by public discussions of this question rather than because such talk is necessary to maximize their profits, given the climate of public intervention. Or advertisers are alleged to take advantage of the fragility of consumer preferences, with little explanation of why, for example, advertising is heavier in some industries than others, changes in importance in a given industry over time, and occurs in quite competitive industries as well as in monopolistic ones.[21]

Naturally, what is tempting to economists nominally committed to the economic approach becomes irresistible to others without this commitment, and without a commitment to the scientific study of sociology, psychology, or anthropology. With an ingenuity worthy of admiration if put to better use, almost any conceivable behavior is alleged to be dominated by ignorance and irrationality, values and their frequent unexplained shifts, custom and tradition, the compliance somehow induced by social norms, or the ego and the id.

I do not mean to suggest that concepts like the ego and the id, or social norms, are without any scientific content. Only that they are tempting materials, as are concepts in the economic literature, for ad hoc and useless explanations of behavior. There is no apparent embarrassment in arguing, for example, both that the sharp rise in fertility during the late 1940s and early 1950s resulted from a renewed desire for large families, and that the prolonged decline starting just a few years later resulted from a reluctance to be tied down with many children. Or developing countries are supposed simply to copy the American's "compulsiveness" about time, whereas the growing value of their own time is a more fruitful explanation of their increased effort to economize in their use of time (see chapter 4, this volume). More generally, custom and tradition are said to be abandoned in developing countries because their young people are seduced by Western ways; it is not recognized that while custom and tradition are quite useful in a relatively stationary environment, they are often a hindrance in a dynamic world, especially for young people (see Stigler and Becker 1974).

Even those believing that the economic approach is applicable to all human behavior recognize that many noneconomic variables also significantly affect human behavior. Obviously, the laws of mathematics, chemistry, physics, and biology have a tremendous influence on behavior through their influence on preferences and production possibilities. That the human body ages, that the rate of population growth equals the birth rate plus the migration rate minus the death rate, that children of more intelligent parents tend to be more intelligent than children of less intelligent parents, that people need to breathe to live, that a hybrid plant has a particular yield under one set of environmental conditions and a very different yield under another set, that gold and oil are located only in certain parts of the world and cannot be made from wood, or that an assembly line operates according to certain physical laws—all these and more influence choices, the production of people and goods, and the evolution of societies.

To say this, however, is not the same as saying that, for example, the rate of population growth is itself "noneconomic" in the sense that birth, migration, and death rates cannot be illuminated by the economic approach, or that the rate of adoption of new hybrids is "noneconomic" because it cannot be explained by the economic approach. Indeed, useful implications about the number of children in different families have been obtained by assuming that families maximize their utility from stable preferences subject to a constraint on their resources and prices, with resources and prices partly determined by the gestation period for pregnancies, the abilities of children, and other noneconomic variables (see Becker 1976, chaps. 9 and 10; see also Schultz 1975). Similarly, the rate of adoption of hybrid corn in different parts of the United States has been neatly explained by assuming that farmers maximize profits: new hybrids were more profitable, and thus adopted earlier, in some parts because weather, soil, and other physical conditions were more favorable (Griliches 1957).

Just as many noneconomic variables are necessary for understanding human behavior, so too are the contributions of sociologists, psychologists, sociobiologists, historians, anthropologists, political scientists, lawyers, and others. Although I am arguing that the economic approach provides a useful framework for understanding all human behavior, I am not trying to downgrade the contributions of other social scientists, or even to suggest that the economist's are more important. For example, the preferences that are given and stable in the economic approach, and that determine the predictions from this approach, are analyzed by the sociologist, psychologist, and probably most successfully by the sociobiologist (see Wilson 1975). How preferences have become what they are and their perhaps slow evolution over time are obviously relevant in predicting and understanding behavior. The value of other social sciences is not diminished even by an enthusiastic and complete acceptance of the economic approach.

At the same time, however, I do not want to soften the impact of what I am saying in the interest of increasing its acceptability in the short run. I am saying that the economic approach provides a valuable unified framework for understanding *all* human behavior, although I recognize, of course, that much behavior is not yet understood, and that noneconomic variables and the techniques and findings from other fields contribute significantly to the understanding of human behavior. That is, although a comprehensive *framework* is provided by the economic approach, many of the important concepts and techniques are provided and will continue to be provided by other disciplines.

The heart of my argument is that human behavior is not compartmentalized, sometimes based on maximizing, sometimes not, sometimes motivated by stable preferences, sometimes by volatile ones, sometimes resulting in an optimal accumulation of information, sometimes not. Rather, all human behavior can be viewed as involving participants who maximize their utility from a stable set of preferences and accumulate an optimal amount of information and other inputs in a variety of markets.

14 • FOUNDATIONS OF HUMAN BEHAVIOR

If this argument is correct, the economic approach provides a unified framework for understanding behavior that has long been sought by and eluded Bentham, Comte, Marx, and others. The reader of the following essays will judge for himself the power of the economic approach.

NOTES

For very helpful comments I am indebted to Joseph Ben-David, Milton Friedman, Victor Fuchs, Robert T. Michael, Jacob Mincer, Richard Posner, and T. W. Schultz. I am especially indebted to George J. Stigler for many discussions, comments, and much-needed encouragement, and to Robert K. Merton for a very helpful and lengthy response to an earlier draft that provided a sociologist's perspective on the issues covered in this essay. The usual disclaimer to the effect that none of these persons should be held responsible for the arguments made in this essay is especially appropriate since several disagreed with the central theme.

1. "[Economics] is the social science that deals with the ways in which men and societies seek to satisfy their material needs and desires." Albert Rees (1968); "[Economics . . . is the study of the supplying of man's physical needs and wants," art. "Economics," *The Columbia Encyclopedia*, 3d ed., p. 624; and see the many earlier references to Marshall, Cannan, and others in L. Robbins (1962).

2. A. C. Pigou said, "[Economic welfare is] that part of social welfare that can be brought directly or indirectly into relation with the measuring rod of money" (1962, p. 11).

3. "Economics is the science which studies human behavior as a relationship between ends and scarce means which have alternative uses," Robbins (1962, p. 16); "Economics . . . is the study of the allocation of scarce resources among unlimited and competing uses," Rees (1968) and many other references.

4. Boulding (1966) attributes this definition of economics to Jacob Viner.

5. Almost immediately after giving the broad definition of economics, Rees (1968) gives one in terms of material needs, without explaining why he so greatly reduced the scope of economics. Even Robbins, after an excellent discussion of what an economic problem is in the first chapter of his classic work on the nature and scope of economics (1962), basically restricts his analysis in later chapters to the market sector.

6. An excellent statement of structural analysis can be found in Merton (1975).

7. That maximizing behavior is not necessary to reach this conclusion is shown below in chapter 2.

8. He maximizes $U = U(Z_1, \ldots Z_m)$ subject to $Z_i = f_i(t_i)$, and $\sum t_i = t$, where Z_i is the ith commodity, f_i the production function for Z_i, and t_i is the time input into Z_i. The well-known first-order equilibrium conditions for the allocation of his scarce resource, time, are:

$$\frac{\partial U}{\partial Z_i} = \lambda \frac{\partial t_i}{\partial Z_i} = \frac{\lambda}{\partial Z_i/\partial t_i} = \frac{\lambda}{MP_{t_i}},$$

where λ is his marginal utility of time.

9. Schumpeter appears to confuse them, although with considerable modification (1950, chap. 21, section "Human Nature in Politics").

10. The pioneering paper is Stigler's "The Economics of Information" (1961).

11. This point is stressed in Milton Friedman's seminal article, "The Methodology of Positive Economics" (1953).

12. The length of life itself is a decision variable in the important study by Grossman (1972).

13. Jeremy Bentham said, "As to the proposition that passion does not calculate, this, like most of these very general and oracular propositions is not true. . . . I would not say that even a madman does not calculate. Passion calculates, more or less, in every man" (1963). He does add, however, that "of all passions, the most given to calculation . . . [is] the motive of pecuniary interest."

14. Actually, a little earlier in an essay that applied economic analysis to political behavior.

15. Some of these implications are developed in Hammermesh and Soss (1974).

16. These implications are derived, and the evidence is examined, in Grossman (1971).

17. This example is taken from Stigler (1976). Also see the discussion of the reward system in science and of related issues in Merton (1973, esp. part 4).

18. An extreme example is Jencks (1972). Jencks even grossly understates the portion that can be explained because he neglects the important work by Mincer and others (see especially Mincer [1974]).

19. See Stigler (1971). Smith does not indicate why ignorance is dominant in the passage of certain laws and not others.

20. For an interpretation of the effects of education on consumption entirely in terms of income and price effects, Michael (1972).

21. For an analysis of advertising that is consistent with stable preferences, and implies that advertising might even be more important in competitive than monopolistic industries, see Stigler and Becker (1974). For a good discussion of advertising that also does not rely on shifts in preferences, see Nelson (1975).

References

Azzi, C., and R. Ehrenberg. 1975. "Household Allocation of Time and Church Attendance." *Journal of Political Economy* 83 (February).

Becker, G. S. 1957 (1st ed.), 1971 (2d ed.). *The Economics of Discrimination.* University of Chicago Press.

————. 1971. *See* Becker 1957.

————. 1976. *The Economic Approach to Human Behavior.* Chicago: University of Chicago Press.

Becker, G. S., and W. M. Landes, eds. 1974. *Essays in the Economics of Crime and Punishment.* New York: Columbia University Press for the National Bureau of Economic Research.

Bentham, J. 1963. *An Introduction to the Principles of Morals and Legislation.* New York: Hafner.

Boulding, K. 1966. *Economic Analysis.* New York: Harper and Row.

Coase, R. H. 1974. "The Market for Goods and the Market for Ideas." *American Economic Review* 64 (May).

Director, A. 1964. "The Parity of the Market Place." *Journal of Law and Economics* (October).

Ehrlich, I. 1975. "Capital Punishment: A Case of Life or Death." *American Economic Review* (June).

Friedman, M. 1953. "The Methodology of Positive Economics." In *Essays in Positive Economics.* Chicago: University of Chicago Press.

Fuchs, Victor. 1968. *The Service Economy.* New York: Columbia University Press for the National Bureau of Economic Research.

Griliches, Z. 1957. "Hybrid Corn: An Exploration in the Economics of 'Technical Change.'" *Econometrica* 25 (October).

Grossman, M. 1971. "The Economics of Joint Production in the Household." Report 7145, Center for Mathematical Studies in Business and Economics, University of Chicago.

————. 1972. *The Demand for Health: A Theoretical and Empirical Investigation.* New York: Columbia University Press for the National Bureau of Economic Research.

Hammermesh, D., and N. M. Soss. 1974. "An Economic Theory of Suicide." *Journal of Political Economy* 82 (January/February).

Henderson, J. M. 1958. *The Efficiency of the Coal Industry: An Application of Linear Programming.* Cambridge: Harvard University Press.

Jencks, C. 1972. *Inequality.* New York: Basic Books.

Keeley, M. C. 1974. "A Model of Marital Formation: The Determinants of the Optimal Age of First Marriage and Differences in Age of Marriage." Ph.D. dissertation, University of Chicago.

Keynes, J. M. 1962. *The General Theory of Employment, Interest, and Money.* Harcourt, Brace and World.

Marschak, J. 1965. "Economics of Language." *Behavioral Science* 10 (April).

Merton, R. K. 1958. *Social Theory and Social Structure.* New York: Free Press.

————. 1973. *The Sociology of Science.* University of Chicago Press.

————. 1975. "Structural Analysis in Sociology." In *Approaches to the Study of Social Structure,* ed. P. M. Blau. New York: Free Press.

Michael, R. T. 1972. *The Effect of Education on Efficiency in Consumption.* National Bureau of Economic Research.

Mincer, J. 1974. *Schooling, Experience, and Earnings*. New York: Columbia University Press for the National Bureau of Economic Research.

Nelson, P. J. 1975. "The Economic Consequence of Advertising." *Journal of Business* 48 (April).

Pigou, A. 1962. *The Economics of Welfare*, 4th ed. London: Macmillan.

Posner, R. 1973. *Economic Analysis of Law*. Boston: Little, Brown.

Rees, Albert. 1968. "Economics." In *International Encyclopedia of the Social Sciences*, ed. D. E. Sills. New York: Macmillan and Free Press.

Reiss, A. J. 1968. "Sociology." In *International Encyclopedia of the Social Sciences*, ed. D. E. Sills. New York: Macmillan and Free Press.

Robbins, L. 1962. *The Nature and Significance of Economic Science*. London: Macmillan.

Schultz, T. W., ed. 1975. *Economics of the Family: Marriage, Children, and Human Capital*. University of Chicago Press for the National Bureau of Economic Research.

Schumpeter, J. 1942. *Capitalism, Socialism, and Democracy*. Reprinted New York: Harper, 1950.

Smith, V. 1975. "The Primitive Hunter Culture, Pleistocene Extinction, and the Rise of Agriculture." *Journal of Political Economy* 83 (August).

Stigler, G. J. 1961. "The Economics of Information." *Journal of Political Economy* 69 (June).

———. 1971. "Smith's Travels on the Ship of State." *History of Political Economy* (fall).

———. 1974. "Do Economists Matter?" Mimeographed. University of Chicago. Published in 1976 in the *Southern Economic Journal* 42 (January).

Stigler, G. J., and G. S. Becker. 1974. "De Gustibus Non Est Disputandum." Mimeographed. University of Chicago.

Waters, R. H., and B. N. Brunnell. 1968. "Comparative Psychology." In *International Encyclopedia of the Social Sciences*, ed. D. E. Sills. New York: Macmillan and Free Press.

Wilson, E. O. 1975. *Sociobiology*. Cambridge: Harvard University Press.

IRRATIONAL BEHAVIOR AND
ECONOMIC THEORY

· 2 ·

I. INTRODUCTION

Although it has long been agreed that traditional economic theory "assumes" rational behavior, at one time there was considerable disagreement over the meaning of the word "rational." To many, the word suggested an outdated psychology, lightning-fast calculation, hedonistic motivation, and other presumably unrealistic behavior. As economic theory became more clearly and precisely formulated, controversy over the meaning of the assumptions diminished greatly, and now everyone more or less agrees that rational behavior simply implies consistent maximization of a well-ordered function, such as a utility or profit function.[1]

Strong and even violent differences developed, however, at a different level. Critics claim that households and firms do not maximize, at least not consistently, that preferences are not well ordered, and that the theory is not useful in explaining behavior. Some theorists have replied that economic theory is valid only as a broad tendency, not in each specific instance; some noted that the "proof of the pudding is in the eating," and argued that this theory gives useful predictions even though decisions do not "seem" to be

First published in the *Journal of Political Economy* 70, no. 1 (February 1962): 1–13. © 1962 by The University of Chicago. All rights reserved.

rational; still others claimed that only rational behavior has much chance of surviving a very harsh competitive world.

The purpose of this paper is not to contribute still another defense of economic rationality. Rather it is to show how the important theorems of modern economics result from a general principle which not only includes rational behavior and survivor arguments as special cases, but also much irrational behavior. No matter what the intent, some readers might believe that the effect of this demonstration is to provide another and more powerful defense of economic rationality. I believe it does provide an important defense of the *theorems* of modern economics, although, of course, the only ultimate defense is an empirical one, and no new empirical materials are introduced. Since, however, these theorems are shown to be consistent also with an extremely wide class of irrational behavior, a defense of them is not necessarily a defense of individual rational behavior. Indeed, perhaps the main conclusion of this study is that economic theory is much more compatible with irrational behavior than had been previously suspected.

Although economists have typically been interested in the reactions of large markets to changes in different variables, economic theory has been developed for the individual firm and household with market responses obtained simply by blowing up, so to speak, the response of a typical unit. Confusion resulted because comment and analysis were directed away from the market and toward the individual, or away from the economist's main interests. Those arguing that rationality is only a broad tendency, or that only a few units need behave rationally in order for markets to do so, were well aware of the difference between market and individual levels of analysis. Unfortunately, however, one can equally well argue that irrationality is only a broad tendency, or that only a few units need behave irrationally in order for markets to do so. An argument supporting rationality at the market level must imply that rational unit responses would tend to outweigh irrational ones. This paper clearly distinguishes between the market and individual levels and produces such an argument implying rationality at the market level. Perhaps it will help shift the analytical interests of economists toward the same level as their substantive interests.

Section II first presents the traditional theory of household choices and then shows why its main implication—that market demand curves are negatively inclined—can also be derived from a wide variety of irrational behavior. Section III develops similar arguments for firms, and Section IV summarizes the discussion and adds a few additional implications.

II. Households

Traditional Theory

Traditional theory assumes that households choose the best collection of commodities consistent with the limited resources available to them. To determine which collection is "best," a preference or utility function is introduced with the properties that any collection A always gives more, less, or the same utility as any other collection B (the consistency assumption), and that if A is preferred to B, and B to C, A must be preferred to C (the transitivity assumption). The best collection produces more utility than any feasible alternative. This theory is usually illustrated geometrically by the diagram shown in figure 1: commodity X is plotted along the horizontal axis, the "other" commodity Y along the vertical axis, AB is the budget line and OAB defines the feasible collections, and preferences are represented by the set of equal utility or indifference curves. The best collection must be on AB at the point p where AB is tangent to an indifference curve.

A change in relative prices or real income would change the location of the best collection, and the fundamental theorem of this theory is that the demand curve for any commodity, real income held constant, must be negatively inclined. In figure 1 a change in the budget line from AB to CD increases the relative price of X and reduces that of Y, and attempts to hold real income constant by holding the ratio of money income to a Laspeyres price index constant.[2] This is the method most commonly used in empirical demand studies to separate relative price from real income effects. The best collection is changed from p to p', and the fundamental theorem states that p' is to the left and above p, or less X and more Y is chosen. Since the demand curve of a market with many households is usually obtained by horizontal summation of the individual demand curves, it would simply be a blown-up or macroscopic reproduction of the individual microcurves and, consequently, would also be negatively inclined.[3]

Market demand curves of many commodities have been extensively investigated empirically and almost invariably are found to be negatively inclined,[4] as predicted by traditional theory, while household demand curves, on the other hand, have seldom been investigated and little is known about them. Other implications of utility theory[5] have almost never been empirically investigated at either the market or the household level and are of little practical use.

FIGURE I

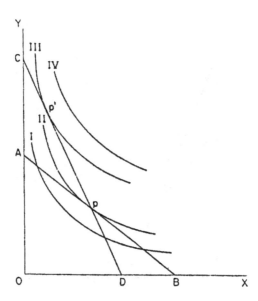

The utility approach to household decisions has been extensively criticized ever since its conception, although both formulation and criticism have changed drastically over time. Today, critics either deny that households maximize any function or that the function maximized is consistent and transitive. In effect, they deny that households act "rationally" since rational behavior is now taken to signify maximization of a consistent and transitive function.[6]

How can these extensive criticisms be reconciled with the fact that the main implication of utility theory—that market demand curves would be negatively inclined—has been consistently verified empirically and found extremely useful in practical problems? Perhaps one explanation is that the assumptions of a theory are often "tested" individually rather than as a whole, or what amounts to the same thing, rather than by their implications. Surely another is that many criticisms are really aimed only at the normative implications of utility theory. In this paper I suggest a reconciliation along very different lines: principally, by showing that negatively inclined market demand curves result not so much from rational behavior per se as from a general principle which includes a wide class of irrational behavior as well. Therefore, households can be said to behave not only "as if" they were rational but also "as if" they were irrational: the major piece of empirical evidence justifying the first statement can equally well justify the second.

FIGURE 2

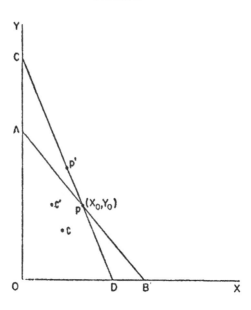

A General Approach

Economists have long been aware that some changes in the feasible or opportunity sets of households would lead to the same response *regardless of the decision rule used*. For example, a decrease in real income necessarily decreases the amount spent on at least one commodity, and the average percentage change in expenditures on all commodities must equal the percentage decrease in income. These theorems, although "obvious" and "arithmetic," have been extremely useful in practical problems. It has seldom been realized, however, that the change in opportunities resulting from a change in relative prices also tends to produce a systematic response, regardless of the decision rule. In particular, the fundamental theorem of traditional theory—that demand curves are negatively inclined—largely results from the change in opportunities alone and is largely independent of the decision rule.

Since the budget line CD in figure 2 has a higher relative price for commodity X and a lower price for Y than does AB, the set OCD enclosed by CD offers more opportunity to consume Y and less opportunity to consume X than does the set OAB. If point p represents the amounts of X and Y (X_0, Y_0) that would be chosen from OAB by a particular decision rule, OCD can be said to offer smaller opportunity to consume more than X_0 of X and greater opportunity to consume more than Y_0 of Y than OAB does. If the amount of any commodity chosen by a decision rule were positively related to its availability, less X than X_0 and more Y than Y_0 would necessarily be chosen from OCD. Demand would be negatively related to price for all such decision rules, no matter how they differed in other respects.

The traditional theory of rational behavior is easily shown to be a rule that depends on the effect of a change in relative prices on the distribution of opportunities. In equilibrium a rational household would gain the same utility from spending an additional dollar on any commodity. A change in relative prices would shift marginal as well as average consumption opportunities toward relatively cheaper and away from more expensive commodities because a dollar now buys more of the former and less of the latter. Consequently an additional dollar at the old equilibrium position would add more utility if it were spent on the former than the latter. Hence rational households would have an incentive to change their consumption, along with the opportunity set, toward relatively cheaper and away from more expensive commodities.

Not only utility maximization but also many other decision rules, incorporating a wide variety of irrational behavior,[7] lead to negatively inclined demand curves because of the effect of a change in prices on opportunities. This will be demonstrated with two models of irrational behavior that encompass both a wide and an allegedly "realistic" class of behavior. On the one hand, households are often said to be impulsive, erratic, and subject to never-ending whim and, on the other hand, inert, habitual, and sluggish. One view alleges that momentary impulses beget a confusing array of undirected change, the other that the past permits little current change or choice. Between these two extremes lies a wide spectrum of irrational behavior, partly determined by the past and partly by current impulses.

If the implications of such behavior are to be fully developed, the attributes of "impulsiveness" and "inertia" must be given a precise and quantitative formulation. To that end, impulsive behavior will be represented by a probabilistic model in which decisions are determined, so to speak, by the throw of a multisided die; inert behavior by a model in which decisions are determined by the past whenever possible (the meaning of this clause is fully developed shortly); and intermediate behavior by a weighted average of these extremes. I believe these models do effectively capture the spirit of the strongest and most frequent criticisms of utility theory, although this cannot be rigorously shown. In any case, they vividly illustrate how irrational choices can also be systematically affected by a change in the distribution of opportunities.

Impulsive households are assumed to act "as if" they only consulted a probability mechanism: no preference system or utility function is consulted. Indeed, to eliminate any vestige of utility maximization, it is assumed that every opportunity has an equal chance of being selected.[8] Although the consumption of a single household could not be determined in advance, the average consumption of a large number of independent households would almost certainly be at the middle of the opportunity set, which is also the (mathematically) expected consumption of a single household. If opportunities were initially restricted to the budget line AB in figure 2, the average consumption of many households would be close to p, the midpoint of AB, with different households uniformly distributed around p.

A change in relative prices which held a market-weighted Laspeyres price index constant would rotate the budget line through p, the point representing market consumption.[9] The line CD represents a compensated increase in the price of X, and points would now be chosen at random along CD instead of AB. Each household could be anywhere on CD, but again the average location of many independent households would almost certainly be at the middle, represented by p' in the figure. It should be clear geometrically and is easily shown algebraically that p' is not to the left and above p by accident: a compensated increase in the price of X always shifts the midpoint of the budget line upward and to the left, while a compensated decrease shifts it downward and to the right.[10]

The fundamental theorem of rational behavior, that market demand curves are negatively inclined, is, therefore, also implied by impulsive behavior, at least in markets with large numbers of households. The expected demand curve of each household must also be negatively inclined, although many actual individual curves would not be.[11] Both expected individual and actual market demand curves are negatively inclined because of the effect of a change in prices on the distribution of opportunities. An increase in the relative price of X shifts opportunities away from X, increases the fraction of those with less X than in the initial position, and thereby increases the probability that an impulsive household would reduce its consumption of X. And what is simply more probable for a particular household becomes a certainty for a large number of independent ones.

Consider now a model of inertia: wherever possible, households consume exactly what they did in the past. Point p can again represent the average consumption of a large group of households faced with the budget line AB, and CD the line resulting from a compensated increase in the price of X. Households initially in the region Ap could remain there indefinitely after the price change, the budget line. Some, however, would also have to be initially in the half-open region pB, unless all were at p, and they could not remain there indefinitely after prices changed, no matter how much they wanted to, because pB would be outside the new opportunity set OCD. Obviously, households forced to adjust are not by accident precisely those with an above average consumption of X, for an increase in X's price shifts opportunities away from X.

If the average household in pB had been consuming more than OD of X, the average amount of X consumed by all households would necessarily decline. Those in Ap would not change, and those in pB would have to reduce their X since OD is the maximum X permitted by the budget line CD. In general, the larger the change in relative prices and the larger the dispersion among households,[12] the more likely is it that the maximum X permitted by the new budget line would be smaller than the average in pB. Although the adjustments made by households in pB cannot be determined precisely until a decision rule is specified, their consumption of X would probably decline even when not arithmetically necessary: a wide variety of decision rules would do this because they were consuming relatively large amounts of X, and the opportunity set shifted away from X. The conclusion is warranted, therefore, that a group of inert consumers, along with rational and impulsive ones, would tend to have negatively inclined demand curves.

A broad class of irrational behavior, including inert and impulsive behavior as extreme cases, would be encompassed by a model in which current choices were partly determined by past ones and partly by a probability mechanism.[13] In other words, these choices are a weighted average of those made by impulsive and inert households. Since market demand curves at both these extremes would tend to be negatively inclined, the market curves of any weighted average would also tend to be. So all behavior in this class would reproduce the fundamental theorem of rational behavior.

A utility-maximizing household would necessarily have negatively inclined compensated demand curves and a consistent and transitive "revealed" preference system. A compensated change in prices to an irrational household, on the other hand, would have very different effects. For example, a compensated change to a single inert household, rather than to a group of them, would not cause any change in consumption; and although an impulsive household would tend to have negatively inclined demand curves and consistent and transitive revealed preferences, there would be many exceptions. The market demand curve in markets with many irrational households would, however, be negatively inclined, and the market's revealed preference system could be said to be rational (consistent and transitive) in the sense that a compensated change in prices would push the market outside its initial opportunity set.

Hence the market would act as if "it" were rational not only when households were rational, but also when they were inert, impulsive, or otherwise irrational. This analytical statement must be distinguished from the frequently encountered arithmetical statement that a market would behave rationally even if only a few households did, assuming always that the average consumption of other households did not move perversely. The same arithmetic demonstrates that a market would behave irrationally even if only a few households did, again assuming that the average consumption of others did not move "perversely." Our statement goes beyond arithmetic and stems from an analysis of the responses of rational and irrational households.

A "representative" household would act rationally even when actual ones did not if "representative" simply indicates a microscopic reproduction of market responses. Economists have gone further and constructed also a theory of an actual household that is simply a microscopic reproduction of the market. Observed market behavior is used to infer unobserved household behavior without any recognition that a theory of the household need not simply reproduce the market because market rationality is consistent with household irrationality. If we may join the trend toward borrowing analogies from the currently glamorous field of physics, the theory of molecular motion does not simply reproduce the motion of large bodies: the smooth, "rational" motion of a macrobody is assumed to result from the erratic, "irrational" motions of a very large number of microbodies.

Patterning the theory of households after market responses was not only unnecessary, but also responsible for much bitter and rather sterile controversy. Confidence in market rationality misled some into stout defenses of rationality at all levels, while confidence in household irrationality misled others into equally stout attacks on all rationality. What has apparently been overlooked is that both views may be partly right and partly wrong: households may be irrational and yet markets quite rational. If this were generally recognized, critics might be more receptive to models implying rational market responses, and economic theorists to models permitting erratic and other irrational household responses.

Utility analysis does not imply that market demand curves necessarily have sizable elasticities; nevertheless, rational behavior is popularly believed to produce sizable responses in at least some markets. Perhaps, therefore, it would be useful to show that irrational households can produce sizable as well as negative elasticities. The market response of inert households depends on the dispersion among them, the change in prices, and the response of those forced to adjust. If the price of X rose by 10 percent, if households were uniformly distributed along the initial budget line, and if those forced to adjust reduced their average consumption to the midpoint of the new budget line, market demand would decline by about 30 percent, giving a high elasticity of -3.[14] A smaller price change or a larger dispersion would yield a still higher elasticity. It is also significant that a large group of erratic households must have unitary elastic market demand curves.[15] So the broad class of irrational behavior explicitly discussed in this paper can generate sizable market elasticities, and thus can reproduce this attribute of "rational" behavior as well.

Inert households in the region *Ap* in figure 2 were forced off the boundary and into the interior of the opportunity set by a shift of the budget line from *AB* to *CD*. Although "commodities" can sometimes be usefully defined, and usually are defined, so that households must necessarily be on the boundary, I would usually prefer to treat this as an additional implication of rational behavior. Thus utility-maximizing households would be on the boundary not because of a definition, but because utility would be maximized (as long as the marginal utility of at least one commodity was nonnegative). Even if "expenditures" were defined so that the entire income had to be spent, irrational households might not "consume" it all because some "purchases" might be lost, spoil, or accumulate unused. These households would be located in the interior of their opportunity sets if the commodity space referred to "consumption" rather than to "expenditures."

Our assumption that opportunities are (at least initially) restricted to the budget line must go if the effect of "inefficient" consumption is to be investigated. Inefficient impulsive households might assign equal probabilities to all points in the opportunity set, not just to those on the boundary. The average consumption of a large number of these households would almost certainly be at the set's center of gravity, with households uniformly distributed around this point. Since a compensated change in prices would shift opportunity sets and thus centers of gravity away from commodities rising and toward those falling in price, these households would also have negatively inclined market demand curves. For example, point *c* in figure 2 would be the center of the set *OAB*, and *c'*, to the left and above *c*, would be the center of *OCD*.[16] Inefficient inert households would be initially distributed throughout the opportunity set. They too would tend to have negatively inclined market curves because a compensated change in prices would still force those consuming relatively large amounts of commodities rising in price to change, presumably toward a smaller consumption of these commodities. So an extension of irrational behavior to cover inefficient consumption does not alter the conclusion that irrational households would tend to have rational market responses to a change in prices.

III. Firms

The analysis can easily be extended to the demand for inputs by interpreting *X* and *Y* in figure 2 as inputs rather than commodities, and *AB* and *CD* as equal outlay rather than equal income lines. A fundamental theorem of rational behavior is that a compensated increase in the price of X would reduce the amount of X employed with a given outlay: less X would be employed with the outlay line CD than AB. The applicability of figure 2 is a hint that this theorem is derived not so much from rational behavior itself as from the general effect of a change in relative input prices on the distribution of employment opportunities. Even irrational firms would tend to respond "rationally" to a change in input prices; for example, a large number of impulsive firms would on the average be located at point p when faced with AB and at p', to the left and above p, when faced with CD.[17]

Figure 2 could not be directly applied to the demand for inputs if total outlays were permitted to vary because outlay lines could not then serve as budget lines. More generally, since the traditional analytical distinction between households and firms is that firms are not supposed to be subject to budget constraints,[18] our analysis of irrational households would seem to have little relevance to irrational firms. As long as the assumption of profit maximization is maintained, firm decisions can legitimately be analyzed without recourse to budgetary constraints, and the traditional distinction is valid. But as soon as other decision rules are permitted, the existence and importance of a budget constraint become patently clear, and the traditional distinction is blurred and perhaps even vanishes.

In my judgment the great achievement of the "survival" argument advanced by Alchian and others[19] is not a demonstration that surviving firms must act as if they were trying to maximize profits, for counterexamples can easily be developed, but rather a demonstration that the decisions of irrational firms are limited by a budgetary constraint. Indeed, the survival argument is really simply a special case of a general argument, developed for households in Section II, linking the behavior of all economic units to the distribution of their opportunities. Thus firms could not continually produce, could not "survive," outputs yielding negative profits, as eventually all the resources at their disposal would be used up.[20] For exactly the same reason households could not continually consume, in this sense could not "survive," outside the region covered by incomes. In both cases the word "survive" simply refers to a resource constraint on behavior and does not literally distinguish "life" from "death," although some households and firms may actually die from trying to "live" beyond their means. Had the meaning of survival in this context been understood, numerous pointless discussions of the application of biological survival theories in economics could have been avoided.

Since the region enclosed by the income constraint is called the consumption opportunity set of households, the region of nonnegative profits can appropriately and naturally be called the production opportunity set of firms. For example, households with the budget line AB in figure 2 have the

FIGURE 3

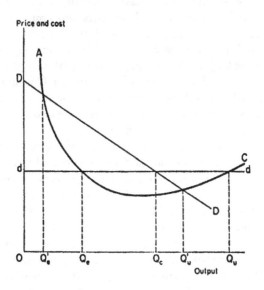

consumption opportunity set OAB, and firms with the average cost curve AC and demand curve *dd* shown in figure 3 have the production opportunity set Q_e, Q_u. Just as households choose their consumption subject to the limitation that they spend no more than the available income, so firms can be assumed to choose their output subject to the limitation that they spend no more than the maximum profit which could have been earned. The entire amount, so to speak, would be spent at outputs yielding zero profits; nothing would be spent if profits were maximized; and a positive but less than the entire amount would be spent at any other admissible output. The traditional conclusion that firms are not subject to a budget constraint is clearly valid when profits are maximized: nothing would be "spent" and so no constraint could be operative. With any other decision rule, however, a constraint on total expenditures might be operative because something would be spent.

A change in cost or demand conditions would change production opportunity sets and force even irrational firms to respond systematically. Many variables influence these sets, and I have not tried to determine the response of irrational firms to changes in all of them. It is instructive, however, to consider explicitly some differences between monopolistic and competitive outputs: a well-known theorem is closely associated with profit-maximizing behavior, and even skeptical readers might be impressed by a demonstration that a wide variety of irrational behavior would reproduce this theorem.

Industrial costs would be the same as a firm's, except for a difference in units, in industries having many independent, identical firms, but the industrial demand curve would be more elastic than the firm's. The AC curve in figure 3 can, therefore, measure both industry and firm average costs, DD industry and dd firm demand conditions. Line DD is drawn so that the competitive equilibrium of profit-maximizing firms occurs at a price of od and a per firm output of OQ_c where presumably marginal costs equal price. If the industry became a completely monopolistic cartel, DD would measure firm as well as industrial demand and dd would no longer be relevant. A famous and ancient theorem states that, if profits were always maximized, output per firm under the cartel would be less than OQ_c.

Completely impulsive firms would assign an equal probability to all available outputs and select one at random: no marginal cost function would be consulted and certainly no attempt would be made to equate marginal cost and marginal revenue. If the industry was "competitive," these firms would be uniformly distributed along the opportunity set Q_e, Q_u with an average output almost certainly at the midpoint. Let Od again be the equilibrium price and OQ_c average output, where OQ_c is now simply the midpoint of $Q'_e Q'_u$ and not necessarily a point equating marginal cost to price. Cartelization would shift the firm's demand curve to DD and shift the opportunity set to the left of $Q_e Q_u$ to $Q'_e Q'_u$. If outputs were again chosen randomly, firms would be uniformly distributed along $Q'_e Q'_u$ and average output would almost certainly be at its midpoint, which is to the left of Q_c.

In the same way inert and many other kinds of irrational firms can be shown to reproduce these famous theorems of neoclassical economics. The fundamental explanation is that a change from competition to monopoly shifts the production opportunity set toward lower outputs, which in turn encourages irrational firms to lower their outputs. At best only of indirect importance is the effect on the marginal revenue function, the explanation always given for profit-maximizing firms.

Our discussion of changes in input prices and the degree of competition indicates that irrational firms can give very rational market responses, and this seeming paradox offers a solution to the heated and protracted controversy between marginalists and antimarginalists. Confidence in the irrationality of firms induced the latter to conclude that market responses were also irrational, while confidence in the rationality of markets induced the former to conclude that firms were also rational. Apparently few realized that both kinds of "evidence" could be valid and yet both inferences invalid, so that each side might be partly right and partly wrong. Basically, what is missing in the controversy is a systematic analysis of the responses of irrational firms; in particular, of how opportunity sets and thus the decisions of irrational as well as rational firms are affected by changes in different variables. For such an analysis reveals that irrational firms would often be "forced" into rational market responses. Consequently, antimarginalists can believe that firms are irrational, marginalists that market responses are rational, and both can be talking about the same economic world.

IV. Summary and Conclusions

Economists have long recognized that consumption opportunities of households are limited to those costing no more than the income available, but not that production opportunities of firms are limited in *exactly the same way* to those yielding nonnegative profits—or to a somewhat larger set when income is also received from other sources. This neglect results from the almost exclusive concern with profit-maximizing firms, for they and they alone are not affected by the restraint on production opportunities. If firms maximized utility rather than profits[21] or behaved irrationally, the constraint on opportunities would be as real to firms as to households. The word "firm" in this context includes foundations and other private nonprofit organizations, governments, and persons choosing occupational and industrial employment as well as "commercial" organizations. Opportunity sets apply, then, to all decision units with limited resources.

Even irrational decision units must accept reality and could not, for example, maintain a choice that was no longer within their opportunity set. And these sets are not fixed or dominated by erratic variations, but are systematically changed by different economic variables: a compensated increase in the price of some commodities would shift consumption opportunities toward others; a compensated increase in the price of some inputs would shift production opportunities toward others; or a compensated decrease in the attractiveness of some occupations would shift employment opportunities toward others. Systematic responses might be expected, therefore, with a wide variety of decision rules, including much irrational behavior.

Indeed, the most important substantive result of this paper is that irrational units would often be "forced" by a change in opportunities to respond rationally. For example, impulsive households would tend to have negatively inclined demand curves because a rise in the price of one commodity would shift opportunities toward others, leaving less chance to purchase this one even impulsively. Other irrational households would likewise tend to have negatively inclined demand curves, irrational firms negatively inclined demand curves for inputs, and irrational workers positively inclined supply curves to occupations.

If irrational units, nevertheless, often respond rationally, what accounts for the deep and prolonged animosity between marginalists and antimargin-alists, Veblenites and neoclassicists, and other groups differing in the degree of rationality attributed to economic decision units? The major explanation undoubtedly is that formal models of irrational behavior have seldom been systematically explored—in particular, to determine how changes in oppor-tunities impinge on irrational behavior. A subsidiary explanation is that little attention has been paid to the distinction between group or market and individual responses. This distinction is unnecessary in traditional theories of rational behavior because a market's response is usually simply the mac-roversion of an individual's response. A group of irrational units would, however, respond more smoothly and rationally than a single unit would, and undue concentration at the individual level can easily lead to an over-estimate of the degree of irrationality at the market level.

When market responses of irrational units sometimes differ substantially from the responses of rational units, empirical evidence on actual responses would be crucially important in assessing the extent of individual rationality. The kind of evidence traditionally used, the negative slope of market demand curves or the positive slope of market demand curves or the positive slope of market supply curves, is equally consistent with individual irrationality and cannot discriminate between them. Inadequate attention has been paid to gathering relevant evidence apparently because opportunity sets and their effect on the market responses of irrational units have been inadequately appreciated.

I explicitly analyzed only simple models of irrational behavior in which current choices were partly determined by past ones and partly by probability considerations. Much additional work is required to formulate rigorously other models and to determine their implications. Although many of these would surely differ, an important area of agreement would result from com-mon responses to shifts in opportunities. Such is the main lesson to be learned from this paper.

NOTES

1. My greatest debt is to A. A. Alchian for the stimulation provided by his article of more than a decade ago ("Uncertainty, Evolution and Economic Theory," *Journal of Political Economy*, 63 [June 1950]), and for comments on various drafts beginning in the summer of 1957. I am also indebted to M. Friedman for insightful oral and written statements (see "The Methodology of Positive Economics," in *Essays in Positive Economics* [Chicago: University of Chicago Press, 1931]) on economic rationality, to seminar groups at Columbia, the National Bureau of Economic Research (NBER), North Carolina State College, UCLA, and Stanford, and to Z. Griliches, H. G.

Johnson, H. G. Lewis, J. Mincer, P. J. Nelson, and G. J. Stigler. I alone am responsible, however, for any remaining errors.

2. It is well known that real income would be approximately held constant in the sense that households would tend to remain on the same indifference curve.

3. Even if household demand curves were interdependent the market curve would tend to be negatively inclined, but more or less elastic than the average microcurve, depending on whether "bandwagon" or "snob" effects predominated.

4. Widespread confidence in the universality of negative market curves has, however, resulted in some "cheating." Other findings are often simply not published or altered until more "reasonable" findings emerge.

5. The whole set of implications can be summarized in the negative semi-definiteness of a certain quadratic form. See, e.g., P.A. Samuelson, *The Foundations of Economic Analysis* (Cambridge, Mass.: Harvard University Press, 1947), p. 114.

6. See, e.g., W. Edwards, "The Theory of Decision Making," *Psychological Bulletin*, 51 (July, 1954); reprinted in *Some Theories of Organization*, ed. A. H. Rubenstein and C. J. Haberetroh (Homewood, Ill.: Richard D. Irwin, Inc., 1960).

7. Any deviation from utility maximization is considered "irrational" in this paper: a more precise or philosophical definition is not required for our purposes and is not attempted.

8. Zvi Griliches pointed out to me that this model was also presented in a very brief appendix to the article by R. L. Marris, "Professor Hicks' Index Number Theorem," *Review of Economic Studies* 25 (October 1957): 25–39. The appendix is said to be based on a conversation with Harry Johnson.

9. Since utility maximization is not assumed, a compensated price change could no longer be said to hold the level of utility (approximately) constant. The important point for our purposes, however, is that empirical studies usually separate price from income effects in this way, and the negative slope of empirical demand curves is a valid and important regularity, regardless of whether utility "really" has been held constant.

10. Since the midpoint of any budget line is given by $(I/2P_x, I/2P_y)$, where I is money income and P_x and P_y are unit prices, a compensated change in the price of X must change the midpoint of X in the opposite and that of Y in the same direction.

11. An individual demand curve is more likely to be negatively inclined the greater the number of price observations and the longer the time period covered by each one. Averaging over prices or time is as effective in canceling out erratic behavior here as averaging over households is in a market.

12. Average consumption in pB is positively related to the dispersion around the overall average represented by p.

13. Mathematically this model is a first-order Markov process.

14. Initially, average consumption of X would be $X_0 = I/2 P_x$; subsequently, it would decline to

$$X_1 = 1/2\left(\frac{I}{4P_x}\right) + 1/2\left(\frac{I}{2.2P_x}\right) = \frac{31}{88}\frac{I}{P_x},$$

so

$$\frac{X_1 - X_0}{X_0} = \frac{\frac{31}{88} - \frac{44}{88}}{\frac{44}{88}} = -.3.$$

15. The amount of X consumed would be given by the function

$$X = k\frac{I}{P_x},$$

where X is market demand and I market income. A compensated change in the price of X would hold constant the ratio of market income to a Laspeyres price index. That is,

$$\frac{I}{P} = c,$$

hence

$$X = k' \cdot \frac{P}{P_x},$$

or

$$X \cdot \frac{P_x}{P} = k'.$$

16. The set OCD differs from OAB only because ApC differs from BpD ($OApD$ is common to both). Since ApC is to the left and above BpD, the center of OCD must be to the left and above that of OAB.

17. Just as a group of impulsive households would produce compensated commodity demand curves having unitary elasticity, so impulsive firms would produce compensated input demand curves having unitary elasticity, or exactly the same as that produced by firms maximizing profits subject to Cobb-Douglas production functions. It is rather amazing that these implications of Cobb-Douglas functions, which have been extensively acclaimed, should also result from the simplest model of impulsive behavior.

18. See, e.g., H. Hotelling, "Demand Functions with Limited Budgets," *Econometrica*, January 1935, pp. 66–78, and P. Samuelson, op. cit., p. 218.

19. See references in n. 1.

20. More generally, firms could not survive if the sum of profits and net income from other sources was less than zero.

21. See A. A. Alchian and R. A. Kessel, "Competition, Monopoly, and the Pursuit of Pecuniary Gains," paper given at the Universities–National Bureau Conference on Labor Economics, April 22–23, 1960, and my *The Economics of Discrimination* (Chicago: University of Chicago Press, 1951), chap. 3.

INVESTMENT IN
HUMAN CAPITAL:
A THEORETICAL ANALYSIS

· 3 ·

I. INTRODUCTION

Some activities primarily affect future well-being, while others have their main impact in the present. Dining is an example of the latter, while purchase of a car exemplifies the former. Both earnings and consumption can be affected: on-the-job training primarily affects earnings, a new sail boat primarily affects consumption, and a college education is said to affect both. The effects may operate either through physical resources, such as a sail boat, or through human resources, such as a college education. This paper is concerned with activities that influence future real income through the imbedding of resources in people. This is called investing in human capital.[1]

The many ways to invest include schooling, on-the-job training, medical care, vitamin consumption, and acquiring information about the economic system. They differ in the relative effects on earnings and consumption, in the amount of resources typically invested, in the size of returns, and in the extent to which the connection between investment and return is perceived. But all improve the physical and mental abilities of people and thereby raise real income prospects.

People differ substantially in their economic well-being, both among

First published in the *Journal of Political Economy* 70, no. 5 (October 1962): 9–49. © 1962 by The University of Chicago. All rights reserved.

countries and among families within a given country. For a while economists were relating these differences primarily to differences in the amount of physical capital since richer people had more physical capital than others. It has become increasingly evident, however, from studies of income growth[2] that factors other than physical resources play a larger role than formerly believed, thus focusing attention on less tangible resources like the knowledge possessed. A concern with investment in human capital, therefore, ties in closely with the new emphasis on intangible resources and may be useful in attempts to understand the inequality in income among people.

The original aim of my study was to estimate the money rate of return to college and high school education in the United States. In order to set these estimates in proper context I undertook a brief formulation of the theory of investment in human capital. It soon became clear to me, however, that more than a restatement was called for: while important and pioneering work had been done on the economic return to various occupations and education classes,[3] there have been few, if any, attempts to treat the process of investing in people from a general viewpoint or to work out a broad set of empirical implications. I began then to prepare a general analysis of investment in human capital.

As the work progressed, it became clearer and clearer that much more than a gap in formal economic analysis would be filled, for the analysis of human investment offered a unified explanation of a wide range of empirical phenomena which had either been given ad hoc interpretations or had baffled investigators. Among these are the following: (1) Earnings typically increase with age at a decreasing rate. Both the rate of increase and the rate of retardation tend to be positively related to the level of skill. (2) Unemployment rates tend to be negatively related to the level of skill. (3) Firms in underdeveloped countries appear to be more "paternalistic" toward employees than those in developed countries. (4) Younger persons change jobs more frequently and receive more schooling and on-the-job training than older persons do. (5) The distribution of earnings is positively skewed, especially among professional and other skilled workers. (6) Abler persons receive more education and other kinds of training than others. (7) The division of labor is limited by the extent of the market. (8) The typical investor in human capital is more impetuous and thus more likely to err than is the typical investor in tangible capital. What a diverse and possibly even confusing array! Yet all these as well as many other important empirical implications can be derived from very simple theoretical arguments. The purpose of this paper is to set out these arguments in some generality, with the emphasis placed on empirical implications, although little empirical material is presented. My own empirical work will appear in a later study.

First, a lengthy discussion of on-the-job training is presented and then, much more briefly, discussions of investment in schooling, information, and health. On-the-job training is dealt with so elaborately not because it is more important than other kinds of investment in human capital—although its importance is often underrated—but because it clearly illustrates the effect of human capital on earnings, employment, and other economic variables. For example, the close connection between forgone and direct costs or the effect of human capital on earnings at different ages is vividly brought out. The extended discussion of on-the-job training paves the way for much briefer discussions of other kinds of investment in human beings.

II. Different Kinds of Investment

On the Job

Theories of firm behavior, no matter how they differ in other respects, almost invariably ignore the effect of the productive process itself on worker productivity. This is not to say that no one recognizes that productivity is affected by the job itself; but the recognition has not been formalized, incorporated into economic analysis, and its implications worked out. We now intend to do just that, placing special emphasis on the broader economic implications.

Many workers increase their productivity by learning new skills and perfecting old ones while on the job. For example, the apprentice usually learns a completely new skill while the intern develops skills acquired in medical school, and both are more productive afterward. On-the-job training, therefore, is a process that raises future productivity and differs from school training in that an investment is made on the job rather than in an institution that specializes in teaching. Presumably, future productivity can be improved only at a cost, for otherwise there would be an unlimited demand for training. Included in cost are a value placed on the time and effort of trainees, the "teaching" provided by others, and the equipment and materials used. These are costs in the sense that they could have been used in producing current output if they were not used in raising future output. The amount spent and the duration of the training period depends partly on the type of training—more is spent for a longer time on an intern than on an operative—partly on production possibilities, and partly on the demand for different skills.

Each employee is assumed to be hired for a specified time period (in the limiting case this period approaches zero), and for the moment both labor and product markets are assumed to be perfectly competitive. If there were no on-the-job training, wage rates would be given to the firm and would be independent of its actions. A profit-maximizing firm would be in equilibrium when marginal products equaled wages, that is, when marginal receipts equaled marginal expenditures. In symbols

$$MP = W, \tag{1}$$

where W equals wages or expenditures and MP equals the marginal product or receipts. Firms would not worry too much about the relation between labor conditions in the present and future partly because workers were only hired for one period, and partly because wages and marginal products in future periods would be independent of a firm's current behavior. It can therefore legitimately be assumed that workers have unique marginal products (for given amounts of other inputs) and wages in each period, which are, respectively, the maximum productivity in all possible uses and the market wage rate. A more complete set of equilibrium conditions would be the set

$$MP_t = W_t, \tag{2}$$

where t refers to the tth period. The equilibrium position for each period would depend only on the flows during that period.

These conditions are altered when account is taken of on-the-job training and the connection thereby created between present and future receipts and expenditures. Training might lower current receipts and raise current expenditures, yet firms could profitably provide this training if future receipts were sufficiently raised or future expenditures sufficiently lowered. Expenditures during each period need not equal wages, receipts need not equal the maximum possible productivity, and expenditures and receipts during all periods would be interrelated. The set of equilibrium conditions summarized in equation (2) would be replaced by an equality between the *present values* of receipts and expenditures. If E_t and R_t represent expenditures and receipts during period t, and i the market discount rate, then the equilibrium condition can be written as

$$\sum_{t=0}^{n-1}\frac{R_t}{(1+i)^{t+1}}=\sum_{t=0}^{n-1}\frac{E_t}{(1+i)^{t+1}}, \tag{3}$$

where n represents the number of periods, and R_t and E_t depend on all other receipts and expenditures. The equilibrium condition of equation (2) has been generalized, for if marginal product equals wages in each period, the present value of the marginal product stream would have to equal the present value of the wage stream. Obviously, however, the converse need not hold.

If training were given only during the initial period, expenditures during the initial period would equal wages plus the outlay on training, expenditures during other periods would equal wages alone, and receipts during all periods would equal marginal products. Equation (3) becomes

$$MP_0 + \sum_{t=1}^{n-1} \frac{MP_t}{(1+i)^t} = W_0 + k + \sum_{t=1}^{n-1} \frac{W_t}{(1+i)^t},$$ (4)

where k measures the outlay on training.

If a new term is defined,

$$G = \sum_{t=1}^{n-1} \frac{MP_t - W_t}{(1+i)^t},$$ (5)

equation (4) can be written as

$$MP_0 + G = W_0 + k.$$ (6)

Since the term k only measures the actual outlay on training it does not entirely measure training costs, for excluded is the time that a person spends on this training, time that could have been used to produce current output. The difference between what could have been produced, call this MP_0', and what is produced, MP_0, is the opportunity cost of the time spent in training. If C is defined as the sum of opportunity costs and outlays on training, (6) becomes

$$MP_0' + G = W_0 + C.$$ (7)

The term G, the excess of future receipts over future outlays, is a measure of the return to the firm from providing training; and, therefore, the difference between G and C measures the difference between the return from, and the cost of, training. Equation (7) shows that marginal product would equal wages in the initial period only when the return equals costs, or $G = C$; it would be greater or less than wages as the return was smaller or greater than costs. Those familiar with capital theory might argue that this generalization of the simple equality between marginal product and wages is spurious because a full equilibrium would require equality between the return from an investment—in this case, made on the job—and costs. If this implied that $G = C$, marginal product would equal wages in the initial period. There is much to be said for the relevance of a condition equating the return from an investment with costs, but such a condition does not imply that $G = C$ or that marginal product equals wages. The following discussion demonstrates that great care is required in the application of this condition to on-the-job investment.

General. Our treatment of on-the-job training produced some general results—summarized in equations (3) and (7)—of wide applicability, but more concrete results require more specific assumptions. In this and the following section two types of on-the-job training are discussed in turn: general and specific. General training is useful in many firms in addition to the firm providing it, as a machinist trained in the army finds his skills of value in steel and aircraft firms, or a doctor trained (interned) at one hospital finds his skills useful at other hospitals. Most on-the-job training presumably increases the future marginal product of workers in the firm providing it, but general training would also increase their marginal product in many other firms as well. Since in a competitive labor market the wage rates paid by any firm are determined by marginal productivities in other firms, future wage rates as well as marginal products would increase to firms providing general training. These firms could capture some of the return from training only if their marginal product rose by more than their wages. "Perfectly general" training would be equally useful in many firms and marginal products would rise by the same extent in all of them. Consequently, wage rates would rise by exactly the same amount as the marginal product and the firms providing such training could not capture any of the return.

Why, then, do rational firms in competitive labor markets provide general training, for why provide training that brings no return? The answer is that firms would provide general training only if they did not have to pay any of the costs. Persons receiving general training would be willing to pay these costs since training raises their future wages. Hence the cost as well as the return from general training would be borne by trainees, not by firms.

These and other implications of general training can be more formally demonstrated with equation (7). Since wages and marginal products are raised by the same amount, MP_t must equal W_t for all $t = 1, \ldots n - 1$; and therefore

$$G = \sum_{t=1}^{n-1} \frac{MP_t - W_t}{(1+i)^t} = 0. \tag{8}$$

Equation (7) is reduced to

$$MP_0' = W_0 + C, \tag{9}$$

or

$$W_0 = MP_0' - C. \tag{10}$$

In terms of actual marginal product

$$MP_0 = W_0 + k, \tag{9'}$$

or

$$W_0 = MP_0 - k. \qquad (10')$$

The wage of trainees would not equal their opportunity marginal product but would be less by the total cost of training. In other words, employees would pay for general training by receiving wages below their current (opportunity) productivity. Equation (10) has many other implications, and the rest of this section is devoted to developing the more important ones.

Some might argue that a really "net" definition of marginal product obtained by subtracting training costs from "gross" marginal product must equal wages even for trainees. Such an interpretation of net productivity could formally save the equality between marginal product and wages here, but later I show (pp. 44–52) that it cannot always be saved. Moreover, regardless of which interpretation is used, training costs would have to be included in any study of the relation between wages and productivity.

Employees pay for general on-the-job training by receiving wages below what could be received elsewhere. "Earnings" during the training period would be the difference between an income or flow term, potential marginal product, and a capital or stock term, training costs, so that the capital and income accounts would be closely intermixed, with changes in either affecting wages. In other words, earnings of persons receiving on-the-job training would be net of investment costs and would correspond to the definition of *net* earnings used throughout this paper, which subtracts all investment costs from "gross" earnings. Therefore, our departure with this definition of earnings from the accounting conventions used for transactions in material goods—which separate income from capital accounts to prevent a transaction in capital from ipso facto[4] affecting the income side—is not capricious but is grounded in a fundamental difference between the way investment in material and human capital are "written off." The underlying cause of this difference undoubtedly is the widespread reluctance to treat people as capital and the accompanying tendency to treat all wage receipts as earnings.

Intermixing the capital and income accounts could make the reported "incomes" of trainees unusually low and perhaps negative, even though their long-run or lifetime incomes were well above average. Since a considerable fraction of young persons receive some training, and since trainees would tend to have lower current and higher subsequent earnings than other youth, the correlation between current consumption and current earnings of young people[5] would not only be much weaker than the correlation with long-run earnings, but the signs of these correlations might even differ.[6]

Doubt has been cast on the frequent assertion that no allowance is made in the income accounts for depreciation on human capital.[7] A depreciation-type item is deducted, at least from the earnings due to on-the-job training, for the cost would be deducted during the training period. Depreciation on

FIGURE I

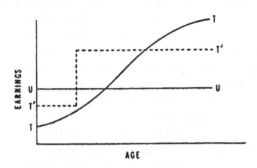

tangible capital does not bulk so large in any one period because it is usually "written off" or depreciated during a period of time designed to approximate its economic life. Hence human and tangible capital appear to differ more in the time pattern of depreciation than in its existence,[8] and the effect on wage income of a rapid "write-off" of human capital is what should often be emphasized and studied.

Our point can be put differently and more rigorously. The ideal depreciation on a capital asset during any period would equal its change in value during the period. In particular, if value rose, a negative depreciation term would have to be subtracted or a positive appreciation term added to the income from the asset. Since training costs would be deducted from earnings during the training period, the economic "value" of a trainee would at first increase rather than decrease with age, and only later would it begin to decrease.[9]

Training has an important effect on the relation between earnings and age. Suppose that untrained persons received the same earnings regardless of age, as shown by the horizontal line *UU* in figure 1. Trained persons would receive lower earnings during the training period because training is paid for then, and higher earnings at later ages because the return is collected then. The combined effect of paying for and collecting the return from training in this way would be to make the age earnings curve of trained persons, shown by *TT* in figure 1, steeper than that of untrained persons, the difference being greater the greater the cost of, and return from, the investment.

Not only does training make the curve steeper but, as indicated by figure 1, also more concave; that is, the rate of increase in earnings is affected more at younger than at older ages. Suppose, to take an extreme case, that training raised the level of marginal productivity but had no effect on the slope, so that the marginal productivity of trained persons was also independent of age. If earnings equaled marginal product, *TT* would merely be parallel to and higher than UU, showing neither slope nor concavity. Since, however, earnings of trained persons would be below marginal productivity during the training period and equal afterward, they would rise sharply at the end of the training period and then level off (as shown by the dashed line $T'T'$ in fig. 1), imparting a concave appearance to the curve as a whole. In this extreme case an extreme concavity appears; in less extreme cases the principle would be the same and the concavity more continuous.

Forgone earnings are an important, although neglected, cost of much human capital and should be treated on the same footing as direct outlays. Indeed, all costs appear as forgone earnings to workers receiving on-the-job training; that is, all costs appear as lower earnings than could be received elsewhere, although direct outlays, C, may really be an important part of costs. The arbitrariness of the division between forgone and direct costs and the resulting advantage of treating total costs as a whole[10] can be further demonstrated by contrasting training in a wide variety of skills and school and on-the-job training. Usually only the direct cost of school training is emphasized, even though the forgone cost is sometimes (as with college education) an important part of the total. A shift of training from schools to on the job would, however, reverse the emphasis and make all costs appear as forgone earnings, even when direct outlays were important.

Income-maximizing firms in competitive labor markets would not pay the cost of general training and would pay trained persons the market wage. If, however, training costs were paid, many persons would seek training, few would quit during the training period, and labor costs would be relatively high. Firms that did not pay trained persons the market wage would have difficulty satisfying their skill requirements and would also tend to be less profitable than other firms. Firms that both paid for training and less than the market wage for trained persons would have the worst of both worlds, for they would attract too many trainees and too few trained persons.

These principles have been clearly demonstrated during the last few years in discussions of problems in recruiting military personnel. The military offers training in a wide variety of skills, and many—such as piloting and machine repair—are very useful in the civilian sector. Training is provided during part or all of the first enlistment period and, it is hoped, during subsequent periods. This hope, however, is thwarted by the fact that reenlistment rates tend to be inversely related to the amount of civilian-type skills provided by the military.[11] Persons with these skills leave the military more readily because they can receive much higher wages in the civilian sector. Net military wages for those receiving training are higher relative to civilian wages during the first than during subsequent enlistment periods because training costs are largely paid by the military. Not surprisingly, therefore, first-term enlistments for skilled jobs are obtained much more easily than are reenlistments.

The military is a conspicuous example of an organization that both pays at least part of training costs and does not pay market wages to skilled personnel. It has had, in consequence, relatively easy access to "students" and heavy losses of "graduates." Indeed, its graduates make up the predominant part of the supply in several civilian occupations. For example, well over 90 percent of United States commercial airline pilots received much of their training in the armed forces. The military, of course, is not a commercial organization judged by profits and losses and has had no difficulty surviving and even thriving.

What about the old argument that firms in competitive labor markets have no incentive to provide on-the-job training because trained workers would be bid away by other firms? Firms that train workers are supposed to impart external economies to other firms because the latter can use these workers free of any training charge. An analogy with research and development is often drawn since a firm developing a process that cannot be patented or kept secret would impart external economies to competitors.[12] This argument and analogy would apply if firms were to pay training costs, for they would suffer a "capital loss" whenever trained workers were bid away by other firms. Firms can, however, shift training costs to trainees and have an incentive to do so when faced with competition for their services.

The difference between investment in training and in research and development can be put very simply. Without patents or secrecy, firms in competitive industries cannot establish property rights in innovations, and these innovations become fair game for all comers. Patent systems try to establish these rights so that incentives can be provided to invest in research. Property rights in skills, on the other hand, are automatically vested, for a skill cannot be used without permission of the person possessing it. This property right in skills is the source of the incentive to invest in training and explains why an analogy with unowned innovations is misleading.

Specific. Completely general training increases the marginal productivity of trainees by exactly the same amount in firms providing the training as in other firms. Clearly some kinds of training increase productivity by a different amount in firms providing the training than in other firms. Training that increases productivity more in firms providing it will be called specific training. Completely specific training can be defined as training that has no effect on the productivity of trainees that would be useful in other firms. Much on-the-job training is neither completely specific not completely general but increases productivity more in firms providing it and falls within the definition of specific training. The rest increases productivity by at least as much in other firms and falls within a definition of general training. The previous section discussed general training and this one will cover specific training. A few illustrations of the scope of specific training are presented before a formal analysis is developed.

The military offers some forms of training that are extremely useful in the civilian sector, as already noted. Training is also offered that is only of minor use to civilians: astronauts, fighter pilots, and missile men all illustrate this to a greater or lesser extent. Such training falls within the scope of specific training because productivity is raised in the military but not (much) elsewhere. Resources are usually spent by firms in familiarizing new employees with their organization,[13] and the knowledge so acquired is a form of specific training because productivity is raised more in the firms acquiring the knowledge than in other firms. Other kinds of hiring costs, such as employment agency fees, the expenses incurred by new employees in finding jobs (what Stigler calls the "costs of search"), or the time employed in interviewing, testing, checking references, and bookkeeping do not so obviously raise the knowledge of new employees, but they too are a form of specific investment in human capital, although not training. They are an investment because outlays over a short period create distributed effects on productivity; they are specific because productivity is raised primarily in the firms making the outlays; they are in human capital because they lose their value whenever employees leave. In the rest of this section I usually refer only to on-the-job specific training even though the analysis applies to all on-the-job specific investment.

Even after hiring costs are incurred, firms usually know only a limited amount about the ability and potential of new employees. They try to increase their knowledge in various ways—testing, rotation among departments, trial and error, etc.—for greater knowledge permits a more efficient utilization of manpower. Expenditures on acquiring knowledge of employee talents would be a specific investment if the knowledge could be kept from other firms, for then productivity would be raised more in the firms making the expenditures than elsewhere.

The effect of investment in employees on their productivity elsewhere depends on market conditions as well as on the nature of the investment. Very strong monopsonists might be completely insulated from competition by other firms, and practically all investments in their labor force would be specific. On the other hand, firms in extremely competitive labor markets would face a constant threat of raiding and would have fewer specific investments available.

These examples convey some of the surprisingly large variety of situations that come under the rubric of specific investment. This set is now treated abstractly in order that a general formal analysis can be developed. Empirical situations are brought in again after several major implications of the formal analysis have been developed.

If all training were completely specific, the wage that an employee could get elsewhere would be independent of the amount of training he had received. One might plausibly argue, then, that the wage paid by firms would also be independent of training. If so, firms would have to pay training costs, for no rational employee would pay for training that did not benefit him. Firms would collect the return from such training in the form of larger profits resulting from higher productivity, and training would be provided whenever the return—discounted at an appropriate rate—was at least as large as the cost. Long-run competitive equilibrium requires that the present value of the return exactly equals costs.

These propositions can be stated more formally with the equations developed earlier. According to equations (5) and (7) the equilibrium of a firm providing training in competitive markets can be written as

$$MP_0' + G\left[\sum_{t=1}^{n-1} \frac{MP_t - W_t}{(1+i)^t}\right] = W_0 + C, \qquad (11)$$

where C is the cost of training given only in the initial period, MP_0' is the opportunity marginal product of trainees, W_0 is the wage paid to trainees, and W_t and MP_t are the wage and marginal product in period t. If the analysis of completely specific training given in the preceding paragraph was correct, W would always equal the wage that could be received elsewhere, $MP_t - W_t$ would be the full return in t from training given in 0, and G would be the present value of these returns. Since MP_0' measures the marginal product elsewhere and W_0 would measure the wage elsewhere of trainees, $MP_0' = W_0$. As a consequence $G = C$, or, in full equilibrium, the return from training equals costs.

Before claiming that the usual equality between marginal product and wages holds when completely specific training is considered, the reader should bear in mind two points. The first is that the equality between wages and marginal product in the initial period involves opportunity, not actual marginal product. Wages would be greater than actual marginal product if some productivity was forgone as part of the training program. The second is that, even if wages equaled marginal product initially, they would be less in the future because the differences between future marginal products and wages constitute the return to training and are collected by the firm.

All of this follows from the assumption that firms pay all costs and collect all returns. But could not one equally well argue that workers pay all specific training costs by receiving appropriately lower wages initially and collect all returns by receiving wages equal to marginal product later? In terms of equation (11), W_t would equal MP_t, G would equal zero, and $W_0 = MP_0'$ – C, just as with general training. Is it more plausible that firms rather than workers pay for and collect the return from training?

An answer can be found by reasoning along the following lines. If a firm had paid for the specific training of a worker who quit to take another job, its capital expenditure would be partly wasted, for no further return could be collected. Likewise, a worker fired after he had paid for specific training would be unable to collect any further return and would also suffer a capital loss. The willingness of workers or firms to pay for specific training should, therefore, closely depend on the likelihood of labor turnover.

To bring in turnover at this point may seem like a deus ex machina since it is almost always ignored in traditional theory. In the usual analysis of competitive firms, wages equal marginal product, and since wages and marginal product are assumed to be the same in many firms, no one suffers from turnover. It would not matter whether a firm's labor force always contained the same persons or a rapidly changing group. Any person leaving one firm could do equally well in other firms, and his employer could replace him without any change in profits. In other words, turnover is ignored in traditional theory because it plays no important role within the framework of the theory.

Turnover becomes important when costs are imposed on workers or firms, which are precisely the effects of specific training. Suppose a firm paid all the specific training costs of a worker who quit after completing it. According to our earlier analysis he would have been receiving the market wage and a new employee could be hired at the same wage. If the new employee were not given training, his marginal product would be less than that of the one who quit since presumably training raised the latter's productivity. Training could raise the new employee's productivity but would require additional expenditures by the firm. In other words, a firm is hurt by the departure of a trained employee because an equally profitable new employee could not be obtained. In the same way an employee who pays for specific training would suffer a loss from being laid off because he could not find an equally good job elsewhere. To bring turnover into the analysis of specific training is not, therefore, a deus ex machina but is made necessary by the important link between them.

Firms paying for specific training might take account of turnover merely by obtaining a sufficiently large return from those remaining to counterbalance the loss from those leaving. (The return on "successes"—those remaining—would, of course, overestimate the average return on all training expenditures.) Firms could do even better, however, by recognizing that the likelihood of a quit is not fixed but depends on wages. Instead of merely recouping on successes what is lost on failures, they might reduce the likelihood of failure itself by offering higher wages after training than could be received elsewhere. In effect, they would offer employees some of the return from training. Matters would be improved in some respects but worsened in others, for the higher wage would make the supply of trainees greater than the demand, and rationing would be required. The final step would be to shift some training costs as well as returns to employees, thereby bringing supply more in line with demand. When the final step is completed firms no longer pay all training costs nor do they collect all the return but they share both with employees.[14] The shares of each depend on the relation between quit rates and wages, layoff rates and profits, and on other factors not discussed here, such as the cost of funds, attitudes toward risk, and desires for liquidity.[15]

If training were not completely specific, productivity would increase in other firms as well, and the wage that could be received elsewhere would also increase. Such training can be looked upon as the sum of two components, one completely general, the other completely specific, with the former being relatively larger the greater the effect on wages in other firms relative to the firms providing the training. Since firms do not pay any of completely general costs and only part of completely specific costs, the fraction of costs paid by firms would be negatively related to the importance of the general component, or positively related to the specificity of the training. Our conclusions can be stated formally in terms of the equations developed earlier. If G is the present value of the return from training collected by firms, the fundamental equation is

$$MP' + G = W + C. \qquad (12)$$

If G' measures the return collected by employees, the total return, G'', would be the sum of G and G'. In full equilibrium the total return would equal total costs, or G'' = C. Let a represent the fraction of the total return collected by firms. Since G = aG'' and G'' = C, equation (12) can be written as

$$MP' + aC = W + C, \qquad (13)$$

or

$$W = MP' - (1 - a)C.[16] \qquad (14)$$

Employees pay the same fraction of costs, $1 - a$, as they collect in returns, which generalizes the results obtained earlier. For if training were completely general, $a = 0$, and equation (14) reduces to equation (10); if firms collected all the return from training, $a = 1$, and (14) reduces to $MP'_0 = W_0$; if $0 < a < 1$, none of the earlier equations are satisfactory.

A few major implications of this analysis of specific training are now developed.

Rational firms pay generally trained employees the same wage and specifically trained employees a higher wage than they could get elsewhere. A reader might easily believe the contrary, namely, that general training would command a higher wage relative to alternatives than specific training does, since, after all, competition for persons with the latter is apt to be weaker than for those with the former. This view, however, overlooks the fact that general training raises the wages that could be received elsewhere while (completely) specific training does not, so a comparison with alternative wages gives a misleading impression of the absolute effect on wages of different types of training. Moreover, firms are not too concerned about the turnover of employees with general training and have no incentive to offer them a premium above wages elsewhere because the cost of such training is borne entirely by employees. Firms are concerned about the turnover of employees with specific training, and a premium is offered to reduce their turnover because firms pay part of their training costs.

The part of specific training paid by employees has effects similar to those discussed earlier for general training: it is also paid by a reduction in wages during the training period, tends to make age-earnings profiles steeper and more concave, etc. The part paid by firms has none of these implications, since current or future wages would not be affected.

Specific, unlike general, training would produce certain "external" effects, for quits would prevent firms from capturing the full return on costs paid by them, and layoffs would do the same to employees. Note, however, that these are external *diseconomies* imposed on the employees or employers of firms providing the training, not external economies accruing to other firms.

Employees with specific training have less incentive to quit, and firms have less incentive to fire them, than employees with no or general training, which implies that quit and layoff rates would be inversely related to the amount of specific training. Turnover would be least for employees with extremely specific training and most for those receiving such general training that productivity was raised less in firms providing the training than elsewhere. These propositions are as applicable to the large amount of irregular quits and layoffs that continually occur as to the more regular cyclical and secular movements in turnover; in this section, however, only the more regular movements are discussed.

Consider a firm that experiences an unexpected decline in demand for its output, the rest of the economy being unaffected. The marginal product of employees without specific training—such as untrained or generally trained employees—presumably initially equaled wages, and their employment would be reduced to prevent their marginal productivity from falling below wages. The marginal product of specifically trained employees initially would have been greater than wages. A decline in demand would reduce these marginal products too, but as long as they were reduced by less than the initial difference with wages, firms have no incentive to lay off such employees. For sunk costs are sunk, and there is no incentive to lay off employees whose marginal product is greater than wages, no matter how unwise it was, in retrospect, to invest in their training. Thus workers with specific training seem less likely to be laid off as a consequence of a decline in demand than are untrained or even generally trained workers.[17]

If the decline in demand were sufficiently great so that even the marginal product of specifically trained workers was pushed below wages, would the firm just proceed to lay them off until the marginal product was brought into equality with wages? To show the danger here, assume that all the cost and return from specific training was paid and collected by the firm. Any worker laid off would try to find a new job, since nothing would bind him to the old one.[18] The firm might be hurt if a new job was found, for the firm's investment in his training might be lost forever. If specifically trained workers were not laid off, the firm would lose now because marginal product would be less than wages but would gain in the future if the decline in demand proved temporary. There is an incentive, therefore, not to lay off workers with specific training when their marginal product is only temporarily below wages, and the larger a firm's investment the greater the incentive not to lay off such workers.

A worker collecting some of the return from specific training would have less incentive to find a new job when temporarily laid off than others would: he does not want to lose his investment. His behavior while laid off in turn affects his chances of being laid off, for if it were known that he would not readily take another job, the firm could lay him off without much fear of losing its investment.

The conclusion here can be briefly summarized. When one firm alone experiences an unexpected decline in demand, relatively few workers with specific training would be laid off, if only because their marginal product was initially greater than their wage. If the decline were permanent, all workers would be laid off when their marginal product became less than their wage and all those laid off would have to find jobs elsewhere. If the decline were temporary, specifically trained workers might not be laid off even though their marginal product was less than their wage because the firm would suffer if they took other jobs. The likelihood of their taking other jobs would be inversely related, and therefore the likelihood of their being laid off would be positively related, to the extent of their own investment in training.

The analysis can easily be extended to cover general declines in demand; suppose, for example, a general cyclical decline occurred. Let me assume that wages are sticky and remain at the initial level. If the decline in business activity were not sufficient to reduce the marginal product below the wage, workers with specific training would not be laid off even though others would be, just as before. If the decline reduced marginal product below wages, only one modification in the previous analysis is required. A firm would have a greater incentive to lay off specifically trained workers than when it alone experiences a decline because laid-off workers would be less likely to find other jobs when unemployment was widespread. In other respects the implications of a general decline with wage rigidity are the same as those of a decline in one firm alone.

The discussion has concentrated on layoff rates, but the same kind of reasoning shows that a rise in wages elsewhere would cause fewer quits among specifically trained workers than among others. For specifically trained workers initially receive higher wages than are available elsewhere and the wage rise elsewhere would have to be greater than the initial difference before they would consider quitting. Thus both the quit and layoff rate of specifically trained workers would be relatively low and fluctuate relatively less during business cycles. These are important implications that can be tested with the data available.

Although quits and layoffs are influenced by considerations other than investment costs, some of these, such as the presence of pension plans, are more strongly related to investments than may appear at first blush. A pension plan with incomplete vesting privileges[19] penalizes employees quitting before retirement and thus provides an incentive—often an extremely powerful one—not to quit. At the same time pension plans "insure" firms against quits for they are given a lump sum—the nonvested portion of payments—whenever a worker quits. Insurance is needed for specifically trained employees because their turnover would impose capital losses on firms. Firms can discourage such quits by sharing training costs and the return with employees, but they have less need to discourage them and would be more willing to pay for training costs if insurance was provided. The effects on the incentive to invest in one's employees may have been a major stimulus to the development of pension plans.[20]

An effective long-term contract would insure firms against quits, just as pensions do, and also insure employees against layoffs. Firms would be more willing to pay for all kinds of training—assuming future wages were set at an appropriate level—since a contract, in effect, converts all training into completely specific training. A casual reading of history suggests that long-term contracts have, indeed, primarily been a means of inducing firms to undertake large investments in employees. These contracts are seldom used today in the United States,[21] and while they have declined in importance over time, they were probably always the exception here largely because courts have considered them a form of involuntary servitude. Moreover, any enforceable contract could at best specify the hours required on a job, not the quality of performance. Since performance can vary widely, unhappy workers could usually "sabotage" operations to induce employers to release them from contracts.

Some training may be useful neither in most nor only in a single firm but in a set of firms defined by product, type of work, or geographical location. For example, carpentry training would raise productivity primarily in the construction industry, and French legal training would be ineffective in the United States, with its different language and legal institutions. Such training would tend to be paid by trainees, since a single firm could not readily collect the return,[22] and in this respect would be the same as general training. In one respect, however, it is similar to specific training. Workers with training "specific" to an industry, occupation, or country are less likely to leave that industry, occupation, or country (via migration) than other workers, so their industrial, occupational, or country "turnover" would be less than average. The same result is obtained for specific training, except that a firm rather than an industry, occupation, or country is used as the unit of observation in measuring turnover. An analysis of specific training, therefore, is helpful also in understanding the effects of certain types of "general" training.

Although a discrepancy between marginal product and wages is frequently taken as evidence of imperfections in the competitive system, it would occur even in a perfectly competitive environment where there is investment in specific training. The investment approach provides a very different interpretation of some common phenomena, as can be seen from the following examples.

A positive difference between marginal product and wages is usually said to be evidence of monopsony power, and just as the ratio of product price to marginal cost has been suggested as a measure of monopoly power, so has the ratio of marginal product to wages been suggested as a measure of monopsony power. But specific training would also make this ratio greater than one. Does the difference between the marginal product and the earnings of major-league baseball players, for example, measure monopsony power or the return on a team's investment? Since teams do spend a great deal on developing players, some and perhaps most of the difference must be considered a return on investment even were there no uncertainty about the abilities of different players.[23]

Earnings might differ greatly among firms, industries, and countries and yet there may be relatively little worker mobility. The usual explanation would be that workers were either irrational or faced with formidable obstacles in moving. However, if specific[24] training were important, differences in earnings would be a misleading estimate of what "migrants" could receive, and it might be perfectly rational not to move. For example, although French lawyers earn less than American lawyers, the average French lawyer could not earn the average American legal income simply by migrating to the United States, for he would have to invest in learning English and American law and procedures.[25]

In extreme types of monopsony, exemplified by an isolated company town, job alternatives for both trained and untrained workers are nil, and all training, no matter what the nature, would be specific to the firm. Monopsony combined with control of a product or an occupation (due, say, to anti-pirating agreements) converts training specific to that product or occupation into firm-specific training. These kinds of monopsony increase the importance of specific training and thus the incentive to invest in employees.[26] The effect on training of less extreme monopsony positions is more difficult to assess. Consider the monopsonist who pays his workers the best wage available elsewhere. I see no reason why training should have a systematically different effect on the forgone earnings of his employees than of those in competitive firms and, therefore, no reason why specific training should be more (or less) important to him. But monopsony power as a whole, including the more extreme manifestations, would appear to increase the importance of specific training and the incentive for firms to invest in human capital.

Schooling

A school can be defined as an institution specializing in the production of training, as distinct from a firm that offers training in conjunction with the production of goods. Some schools, like those for barbers, specialize in one skill while others, like universities, offer a large and diverse set. Schools and firms are often substitute sources of particular skills. The shift that has occurred over time in both law and engineering is a measure of this substitution. In acquiring legal skills the shift has been from apprenticeships in law firms to law schools, and in engineering skills from on-the-job experience to engineering schools.[27]

Some types of knowledge can be mastered better if simultaneously related to a practical problem; others require prolonged specialization. That is, there are complementarities between learning and work and between learning and time. Most training in the construction industry is apparently still best given on the job, while the training of physicists requires a long period of specialized effort. The development of certain skills requires both specialization and experience and can be had partly from firms and partly from schools. Physicians receive apprenticeship training as interns and residents after several years of concentrated instruction in medical schools. Or to take an example closer to home, a research economist not only spends many years in school but also a rather extensive apprenticeship in mastering the "art" of empirical and theoretical research. The complementarity with firms and school depends in part on the amount of formalized knowledge available: price theory can be formally presented in a course, while a formal statement of the principle used in gathering and handling empirical materials is lacking.

Training in a new industrial skill is usually first given on the job, since firms tend to be the first to be aware of its value, but as demand develops, some of the training shifts to schools. For example, engineering skills were initially acquired on the job, and over time engineering schools have been developed.

A student does not work for pay while in school but may do so "after" or "before" school, or during "vacations." His earnings are usually less than if he were not in school since he cannot work as much or as regularly. The difference between what could have been and is earned is an important and indirect cost of schooling. Tuition, fees, books and supplies, unusual transportation and lodging expenses are other, more direct, costs. Net earnings can be defined as the difference between actual earnings and direct school costs. In symbols,

$$W = MP - k, \tag{15}$$

where MP is actual marginal product (assumed equal to earnings) and k is direct costs. If MP_0 is the marginal product that could have been received, equation (15) can be written as

$$W = MP_0 - (MP_0 - MP + k) = MP_0 - C, \tag{16}$$

where C is the sum of direct and forgone costs and where net earnings are the difference between potential earnings and total costs. These relations should be familiar since they are the same as those derived for general on-the-job training, which suggests that a sharp distinction between schools and firms is not always necessary: for some purposes schools can be treated as a special kind of firm and students as a special kind of trainee. Perhaps this is most apparent when a student works in an enterprise controlled by his school, which frequently occurs at many colleges.

Our definition of student net earnings may seem strange since tuition and other direct costs are not usually subtracted from "gross" earnings. Note, however, that indirect school costs are implicitly subtracted, for otherwise earnings would have to be defined as the sum of observed and forgone earnings, and forgone earnings are a major cost of high school, college, and adult schooling. Moreover, earnings of on-the-job trainees would be net of *all* their costs, including direct "tuition" costs. Consistent accounting, which is particularly important when comparing earnings of persons trained in school and on the job, would require that earnings of students be defined in the same way.[28]

Regardless of whether all costs or merely indirect costs are subtracted from potential earnings, schooling would have the same kind of implications as general on-the-job training. Thus schooling would steepen the age-earnings profile, mix together the income and capital accounts, introduce a negative relative between the permanent and current earnings of young persons, and allow for depreciation on human capital. This supports our earlier assertion that an analysis of on-the-job training leads to general results that apply to other kinds of investment in human capital as well.

Other Knowledge

On-the-job and school training are not the only activities that raise real income primarily by increasing the knowledge at a person's command. Information about the prices charged by different sellers would enable a person to buy from the cheapest, thereby raising his command over resources, or information about the wages offered by different firms would enable him to work for the firm paying the highest (see G. J. Stigler, *Journal of Political Economy*, October 1962, pp. 594–605). In both examples information about the economic system, of consumption and production possibilities, is increased as distinct from knowledge of a particular skill. Information about the political or social system—the effect of different parties or social arrangements—could also significantly raise real incomes.[29]

Let us consider in more detail investment in information about employment opportunities. A better job might be found by spending money on employment agencies and situation-wanted ads, using one's time to examine want ads, talking to friends and visiting firms, or in Stigler's language by "search." When the new job requires geographical movement, additional time and resources would be spent in moving.[30] These expenditures constitute an investment in information about job opportunities that would yield a return in the form of higher earnings than would otherwise have been received. If workers paid costs and collected the return, an investment in search would have the same implications about age-earnings profiles, depreciation, and the like as general on-the-job training and schooling, although it must be noted that the direct costs of search, like the direct costs of schooling, are usually added to consumption rather than deducted from earnings. If firms paid costs and collected the return, search would have the same implications as on-the-job specific training.

Whether workers or firms pay for search depends on the effect of a job change on alternatives: the larger the number of alternatives made available by a change, the larger, not the smaller, the fraction of costs that have to be paid by workers. Consider a few examples. Immigrants to the United States usually found many firms that could use their talents, and these firms should have been reluctant to pay the large cost of transporting workers to the United States. In fact, immigrants almost always had to pay their own way. Even the system of contract labor, which we have seen is a means of protecting firms against turnover, was singularly unsuccessful in the United States and has been infrequently used.[31] Firms that are relatively insulated from competition in the labor market have an incentive to pay the costs of workers coming from elsewhere since they have little to worry about in the way of competing neighboring firms. In addition, firms would be willing partly to pay for search within a geographical area because some costs—such as an employment agency's fee—would be specific to the firm doing the hiring since they must be repeated at each job change.

Productive Wage Increases

One way to invest in human capital is to improve emotional and physical health. In Western countries today earnings are much more closely geared to knowledge than to strength, but in an earlier day, and elsewhere still, strength had a significant influence on earnings. Moreover, emotional health increasingly is considered an important determinant of earnings in all parts of the world. Health, like knowledge, can be improved in many ways. A decline in the death rate at working ages may improve earning prospects by extending the period during which earnings are received; a better diet adds strength and stamina, and thus earning capacity; or an improvement in working conditions—higher wages, coffee breaks, and so on—might affect morale and productivity.

Firms can invest in the health of employees through medical examinations, luncheons, or steering them away from activities with high accident and death rates. An investment in health that increased productivity to the same extent in many firms would be a general investment and would have the same effect as general training, while an investment in health that increased productivity more in the firms making them would be a specific investment and would have the same effect as specific training. Of course, most investments in health in the United States are made outside firms, in households, hospitals, and medical offices. A full analysis of the effect on earnings of such "outside" investment in health is beyond the scope of this paper, but I would like to discuss a relation between on-the-job and "outside" human investments that has received much attention in recent years.

When on-the-job investments are paid by reducing earnings during the investment period, less is available for investments outside the job in health, better diet, schooling, and other factors. If these "outside" investments were more productive, some on-the-job investments would not be undertaken even though they were very productive by "absolute" standards.

Before I proceed further, one point needs to be made. The amount invested outside the job would be related to current earnings only if the capital market was very imperfect, for otherwise any amount of "outside" investment could be financed with borrowed funds. The analysis assumes, therefore, that the capital market is extremely imperfect, earnings and other income being a major source of funds.[32]

A firm would be willing to pay for investment in human capital made by employees outside the firm if it could benefit from the resulting increase in productivity. The only way to pay, however, would be to offer higher wages during the investment period than would have been offered since direct loans to employees are prohibited by assumption. When a firm gives a productive wage increase—that is, an increase that raises productivity—"outside" investments are, as it were, converted into on-the-job investments. Indeed, such a conversion is a natural way to circumvent imperfections in the capital market and the resultant dependence of the amount invested in human capital on the level of wages.

The discussion can be stated more formally. Let W represent wages in the absence of any investment, and let a productive wage increase costing an amount C be the only on-the-job investment. Total costs to the firm would be $\pi = W + C$, and since the investment cost is received by employees as higher wages, π would also measure total wages. The cost of on-the-job training is not received as higher wages, so this formally distinguishes a productive wage increase from other on-the-job investments. The term MP can represent the marginal product of employees when wages equal W, and G the gain to firms from the investment in higher wages. In full equilibrium,

$$MP + G = W + C = \pi. \tag{17}$$

Investment would not occur if the firm's gain was nil ($G = 0$), for then total wages (π) would equal the marginal product (MP) when there is no investment.

We have shown that firms would benefit more from on-the-job investment the more specific the productivity effect, the greater their monopsony power, and the longer the labor contract; conversely, the benefit would be less the more general the productivity effect, the less their monopsony power, and the shorter the labor contract. For example, a wage increase spent on a better diet with an immediate impact on productivity might well be granted,[33] but not one spent on general education with a very delayed impact.[34]

The effect of a wage increase on productivity depends on the way it is spent, which in turn depends on tastes, knowledge, and opportunities. Firms might exert an influence on spending by exhorting employees to consume good food, housing, and medical care, or even by requiring purchases of specified items in company stores. Indeed, the company store or truck system in nineteenth-century Great Britain has been interpreted as partly designed to prevent an excessive consumption of liquor and other debilitating commodities.[35] The prevalence of employer paternalism in underdeveloped countries has been frequently accepted as evidence of a difference in temperament between East and West. An alternative interpretation suggested by our study is that an increase in consumption has a greater effect on productivity in underdeveloped countries, and that a productivity advance raises profits more there either because firms have more monopsony power or because the advance is less delayed. In other words "paternalism" may simply be a way of investing in the health and welfare of employees in underdeveloped countries.

An investment in human capital would usually steepen age-earnings profiles, lowering reported earnings during the investment period and raising them later on. But an investment in an increase in earnings may have precisely the opposite effect, raising reported earnings more during the investment period than later and thus flattening age-earnings profiles. The cause of this difference is simply that reported earnings during the investment period tend to be net of the cost of general investments and gross of the cost of a productive earnings increase.[36]

The productivity of employees depends not only on their ability and the amount invested in them both on and off the job but also on their motivation, or the intensity of their work. Economists have long recognized that motivation in turn partly depends on earnings because of the effect of an increase in earnings on morale and aspirations. Equation (17), which was developed to show the effect of investments outside the firm financed by an increase in earnings, can also show the effect of an increase in the intensity of work "financed" by an increase in earnings. Thus W and MP would show initial earnings and productivity, C the increase in earnings, and G the gain to firms from the increase in productivity caused by the "morale" effect of the increase in earnings. The incentive to grant a morale-boosting increase in earnings, therefore, would depend on the same factors as does the incentive to grant an increase used for outside investments. Many recent discussions of wages in underdeveloped countries have stressed the latter;[37] while earlier discussions often stressed the former.[38]

III. Relation between Earnings, Costs, and Rates of Return

Thus far little attention has been paid to the factors determining the amount invested in human capital. The most important single determinant is the profitability or rate of return, but the effect on earnings of a change in the rate of return has been difficult to distinguish empirically from a change in the amount invested. For investment in human capital usually extends over a long and variable period, so the amount invested cannot be determined from a known "investment period." Moreover, the discussion of on-the-job training clearly indicated that the amount invested is often merged with gross earnings into a single net earnings concept (which is gross earnings minus the cost or plus the return on investment).

In the following, some rather general relations between earnings, investment costs, and rates of return are derived. They permit one to distinguish, among other things, a change in the return from a change in the amount invested. The discussion proceeds in stages from simple to complicated situations. First, investment is restricted to a single period and returns to all remaining periods; then investment is permitted to be distributed over a known group of periods called the investment period. Finally, we show how the rate of return, amount invested, and the investment period can all be derived from information on net earnings alone.

Let Y be an activity providing a person entering at a particular age, called age zero, with a real net earnings stream of Y_0 during the first period, Y_1 the next period, and so on until Y_n is provided during the last period. The general term "activity" rather than occupation or another more concrete term is used to indicate that any kind of investment in human capital is permitted, not just on-the-job training but also schooling, information, health, and morale. By "net" earnings I continue to mean that tuition costs during any period have been subtracted and returns added to "gross" earnings during the same period (see discussion in Section II). "Real" earnings are the sum of monetary earnings and the monetary equivalent of psychic earnings. Since many persons appear to believe that the term "investment in human capital" must be restricted to monetary costs and returns, let me emphasize that essentially all my analysis applies independently of the division of real earnings into monetary and psychic components. Thus the analysis applies to health, an activity with a large psychic component, as well as to on-the-job training, an activity with a large monetary component. When psychic components dominate, the language associated with consumer durable goods might be considered more appropriate than that associated with investment goods, but to simplify the presentation, I use investment language throughout.

The present value of the net earnings stream in Y would be

$$V(Y) = \sum_{j=0}^{n} \frac{Y_j}{(1+i)^{j+1}},^{39} \tag{18}$$

where i is the market discount rate, assumed for simplicity to be the same in each period. If X were another activity providing a net earning stream of X_0, $X_1, \ldots X_n$, with a present value of $V(X)$, the present value of the gain from choosing Y would be given by

$$d = V(Y) - V(X) = \sum_{j=0}^{n} \frac{Y_j - X_j}{(1+i)^{j+1}}. \tag{19}$$

Equation (19) can be reformulated to bring out explicitly the relation between costs and returns. The cost of investing in human capital equals the net earnings forgone by choosing to invest rather than choosing an activity requiring no investment. If activity Y requires an investment only in the initial period and if X does not require any, the cost of choosing Y rather than X is simply the difference between their net earnings in the initial period, and the total return would be the present value of the differences between net earnings in later periods. If $C = X_0 - Y_0$, $k_j = Y_j - X_j$, $j = 1, \ldots$ n, and if R measures the total return, the gain from Y could be written as

$$d = \sum_{j=1}^{n} \frac{k_j}{(1+i)^j} - C = R - C. \tag{20}$$

The relation between costs and returns can be derived in a different and, for our purposes, preferable way by defining the internal rate of return,[40] which is simply a rate of discount equating the present value of returns to the present value or costs. In other words, the internal rate, r, is defined implicitly by the equation

$$C = \sum_{1}^{n} \frac{k_j}{(1+r)^j}, \tag{21}$$

which clearly implies

$$\sum_{j=0}^{n} \frac{Y_j}{(1+r)^{j+1}} - \sum_{0}^{n} \frac{X_j}{(1+r)^{j+1}} = d = 0, \tag{22}$$

since $C = X_0 - Y_0$ and $k_j = Y_j - X_j$. So the internal rate is also a rate of discount equating the present values of net earnings. These equations would be considerably simplified if the return were the same in each period, or $Y_j = X_j + k$, $j = 1, \ldots n$. Thus equation (21) would become

$$C = \frac{k}{r}[1 - (1 + r)^{-n}], \tag{23}$$

where $(1 + r)^{-n}$ is a correction for the finiteness of life that tends toward zero as people live longer.

If investment is restricted to a single known period, cost and rate of return are easily determined from information on net earnings alone. Since, however, investment in human capital is distributed over many periods—formal schooling is usually more than ten years in the United States, and long periods of on-the-job training are also common—the analysis must be generalized to cover distributed investment. The definition of an internal rate in terms of the present value of net earnings in different activities obviously applies regardless of the amount and duration of investment, but the definition in terms of costs and returns is not generalized so readily. If investment were known to occur in Y during each of the first m periods, a simple and superficially appealing approach would be to define the investment cost in each of these periods as the difference between net earnings in X and Y, total investment costs as the present value of these differences, and the internal rate would equate total costs and returns. In symbols,

$$C_j^1 = X_j - Y_j, \quad j = 0, \ldots m - 1,$$
$$C^1 = \sum_0^{m-1} C_j^1 (1 + r)^{-j},$$

and

$$C^1 = \frac{k}{r}\left[\frac{1 - (1 + r)^{m-1-n}}{(1 + r)^{m-1}} \right]. \tag{24}$$

If $m = 1$, this reduces to equation (23).

Two serious drawbacks mar this appealing, straightforward approach. The estimate of total costs requires a priori knowledge and specification of the investment period. While the period covered by formal schooling is easily determined, the period covered by much on-the-job training and other investment is not, and a serious error might result from an incorrect specification: to take an extreme example, total costs would approach zero as the investment period is assumed to be longer and longer.[41]

A second difficulty is that the differences between net earnings in X and Y do not correctly measure the cost of investing in Y since they do not correctly measure earnings forgone. A person who invested in the initial period could receive more than X_1 in period 1 as long as the initial investment yielded a positive return.[42] The true cost of an investment in period 1 would be the total earnings forgone, or the difference between what could have been received and what is received. The difference between X_1 and Y_1 could greatly underestimate true costs; indeed, Y might be greater than X_1 even though a large investment was made in period 1.[43] In general, therefore, the amount invested in any period would be determined not only from net earnings in the same period but also from net earnings in earlier periods.

If the cost of an investment is consistently defined as the earnings forgone, quite different estimates of total costs emerge. Although superficially a less natural and straightforward approach, the generalization from a single period to distributed investment is actually greatly simplified. So let C_j be the forgone earnings in the jth period, r_j the rate of return on C_j, and let the return per period on C_j be a constant k_j, with $k = \sum k_j$ being the total return on the whole investment. If the number of periods was indefinitely large, and if investment occurred only in the first m periods, the education relating costs, returns, and internal rates has the strikingly simple form of[44]

$$C = \sum_{0}^{m-1} C_j = \frac{k}{\bar{r}}, \tag{25}$$

where

$$\bar{r} = \sum_{0}^{m-1} w_j r_j, \qquad w_j = \frac{C_j}{C},$$

and

$$\sum_{0}^{m-1} w_j = 1. \tag{26}$$

Total cost, defined simply as the sum of costs during each period, would equal the capitalized value of returns, the rate of capitalization being a weighted average of the rates of return on the individual investments. Any sequence of internal rates or investment costs is permitted, no matter what the pattern of rises and declines, or what form the investments take, be they a college education, an apprenticeship, ballet lessons, or a medical examination. Different investment programs would have the same ultimate effect on earning whenever the average rate of return and the sum of investment costs were the same.[45]

Equation (25) can be given an interesting interpretation if all rates of return were the same. The term k/r would then be the value at the beginning of the mth period of all succeeding net earning differentials between Y and X discounted at the internal rate, r.[46] Total costs would equal the value also at the beginning of the mth period—which is the end of the investment period—of the first m differentials between X and Y.[47] The value of the first m differentials between X and Y must equal the value of all succeeding differentials between Y and X, since r would be the rate of return equating the present values in X and Y.

The internal rate of return and the amount invested in each of the first m periods could be estimated from the net earnings streams in X and Y alone if the rate of return was the same on all investments. For the internal rate r could be determined from the condition that the present value of net earnings must be the same in X and Y, and the amount invested in each period seriatim from the relations[48]

$$C_0 = X_0 - Y_0, \qquad C_1 = X_1 - Y_1 + rC_0$$
$$C_j = X_j - Y_j + r \sum_{k=0}^{j-1} C_k, \qquad 0 \le j \le m-1 . \tag{27}$$

So costs and the rate of return can be estimated from information on net earnings. This is fortunate since the return on human capital is never empirically separated from other earnings and the cost of such capital is only sometimes and incompletely separated.

The investment period of education can be measured by years of schooling, but the period of on-the-job training, the search for information, and other investments is not readily available. Happily, one need not know the investment period to estimate costs and returns, since all three can be simultaneously estimated from information on net earnings. If activity X were known to have no investment (a zero investment period) the amount invested in Y during any period would be defined by

$$C_j = X_j - Y_j + r \sum_0^{j-1} C_k, \quad \text{all } j , \tag{28}$$

and total costs by

$$C = \sum_0^{\infty} C_j . \tag{29}$$

The internal rate could be determined in the usual way from the equality between present values in X and Y, costs in each period from equation (28), and total costs from equation (29).

The definition of costs presented here simply extends to all periods the definition advanced earlier for the investment period.[49] The rationale for the general definition is the same: investment occurs in Y whenever earnings there are below the sum of those in X and the income accruing on prior investments. If costs were found to be greater than zero before some period m and equal to zero thereafter, the first m periods would be the empirically derived investment period. But costs and returns can be estimated from equation (28) even when there is no simple investment period.

A common objection to an earlier draft of this paper is that the general and rather formal definition of costs advanced here is all right when applied to on-the-job training, schooling, and other recognized investments, but goes too far by also including as investment cost many effects that should be treated otherwise. For example, the protest runs, suppose that learning was essentially unavoidable in an activity Z, so that earnings "automatically" grow rapidly with experience. Since earnings in Z would tend to be lower than those in X at younger ages and higher later on, my approach would say that investment occurs in Z. Critics have argued that there really is no investment in Z since the rise in earnings results from *unavoidable* learning rather than from an attempt to improve skills, knowledge, or health. Although the argument is superficially plausible I am convinced it is as reasonable to say that investment in human capital occurs in Z as in activities requiring training or schooling. Indeed, an important virtue rather than defect in my concept of human capital is that learning—both on and off the job—is included along with training and schooling.

If Z were preferred to X the higher earnings at later ages presumably outweigh the earnings forgone initially. Similarly, a person entering an activity requiring much education is said to value the stream of future higher earnings more than the net earnings forgone initially. If the lower earnings due to education are called investment costs, the higher earnings investment returns, and if costs are related to returns by an internal rate of return, logical consistency and economic sense would require that similar concepts apply to learning. Thus the lower initial earnings of high school graduates who enter occupations "with a future" have as much right to be considered investment, both from the social and private viewpoints, as do the lower net earnings of those enrolled in college. In general, since the private and social ranking of different economic activities depend only on their net earning streams, if one activity was said to require a given investment and to yield a given return, another activity with the same net earning stream must be said to require the same investment and yield the same return, no matter how they differ in other respects.

So much in defense of our approach. To estimate costs empirically still has required a priori knowledge that nothing is invested in activity X. Without such knowledge, only the difference between the amounts invested in any two activities with known net earning streams could be estimated from the definitions in equation (28). Were this done for all available streams the investment in any activity beyond that in the activity with the smallest investment could be determined.[50] The observed minimum investment would not be zero, however, if the rate of return on some initial investment was sufficiently high to attract everyone. A relevant question is, therefore: can the shape of the stream in an activity having zero investment be specified a priori so that the total investment in any activity can be determined?

The statement "nothing is invested in an activity" means only nothing would be invested after the age when information on earnings first became available; investment can have occurred before that age. If, for example, the data begin at age eighteen, some investment in schooling, health, or information surely must have occurred at younger ages. The earning stream of persons who do not invest after age eighteen would have to be considered, at least in part, as a return on the investment before eighteen Indeed, in the developmental approach to child-rearing most if not all of these earnings would be so considered.

The earning stream in an activity with no investment beyond the initial age (activity X) would be flat if the developmental approach was followed and earnings were said to result entirely from earlier investment.[51] The minimum investment could then be determined if an assumption was made about its rate of return. My discussion of the shape of the earning stream in X is, however, highly conjectural,[52] and further investigation may well indicate that another approach is preferable.

Our assumption that lifetimes are infinite, although descriptively unrealistic, is often a very close approximation. For example, I have shown elsewhere that the average rate of return on college education in the United States could only be slightly raised if people remained in the labor force indefinitely. A finite earning period has, however, a greater effect on the rate of return of investments occurring at later ages, say after age forty; indeed, it helps explain why schooling and other investments are primarily made at younger ages.

An analysis of finite earning streams can be approached in two ways. One simply applies the concepts developed for infinite streams and says there is disinvestment in human capital when net earnings are above the amount that could be maintained indefinitely. Investment at younger ages would give way to disinvestment at older ages until no human capital remained at death (or retirement). This approach has several important applications and is used in parts of my study. An alternative that is more useful for some purposes lets the earning period itself influence the definitions of accrued income and cost. The income resulting from an investment during period j would be defined as

$$k_j = \frac{r_j C_j}{1 - (1 + r_j)^{j-n}}, \tag{30}$$

where $n + 1$ is the earning period, and the amount invested during j would be defined by

$$C_j = X_j - Y_j + \sum_{k=0}^{k=j-1} \frac{r_k C_k}{1 - (1 + r_k)^{k-n}}. \tag{31}$$

IV. THE INCENTIVE TO INVEST

Number of Periods

The discussion summarized in equations (28) and (31) shows how total costs, rates of return, and the investment period can be estimated from information on net earnings alone, and thus how the effect on earnings of a change in the amount invested can be distinguished empirically from the effect of a change in rates of return. Our attention now turns to the factors influencing the amount invested in different activities and by different persons. Economists have long believed that the incentive to expand and improve physical resources depends on the rate of return expected. They have been very reluctant, however, to interpret improvements in the effectiveness and amount of human resources in the same way, namely, as systematic responses or "investments" resulting in good part from the returns expected. In this section I try to show that an investment approach to human resources is a powerful and simple tool capable of explaining a wide range of phenomena, including much that has either been ignored or given ad hoc interpretations.

An increase in the life span of an activity would, other things the same, increase the rate of return on the investment made in any period. The influence of life span on the rate of return and thus on the incentive to invest is important and takes many forms. A few of these forms will now be discussed.

The number of periods is obviously affected by mortality and morbidity rates, for the lower they are, the longer the expected life span, and the larger the fraction of a lifetime that can be spent at any activity. The major secular decline of these rates in the United States and elsewhere may have increased the rates of return on investment in human capital,[53] thereby encouraging such investment. This conclusion is independent of whether the secular improvement in health itself resulted from investment; if so, the secular increase in rates of return would be part of the return to investment in health.

A relatively large fraction of younger persons are in school, enter on-the-job training, change jobs and locations, and add to their knowledge of economic, political, and social opportunities. The entire explanation of these differences between young and old persons may not be that the young are more interested in learning, more able to absorb new ideas, less tied down by family responsibilities, more easily supported by parents, or more flexible about changing their routine and place of living. One need not rely only on life-cycle effects on capabilities, responsibilities, or attitudes as soon as one recognizes, as we have throughout, that schooling, training, mobility, and the like are ways to invest in human capital and that younger people have a greater incentive to invest because they can collect the return over more years.[54] Indeed, a greater incentive would be present even if age had no effect on capabilities, responsibilities, and attitudes.

Although the unification of these different kinds of behavior by the investment approach is important evidence in its favor, other evidence is needed. A powerful test can be developed along the following lines.[55] Suppose that investment in human capital raised earnings for p periods only, where p varied between 0 and n. The size of p would be affected by many factors, including the rate of obsolescence since the more rapidly an investment became obsolete the smaller p would be. The advantage in being young would be less the smaller p was, since the effect of age on the rate of return would be positively related to p. For example, if p equaled two years, the rate would be the same at all ages except the two nearest the "retirement" age. If the investment approach was correct, the difference between the amount invested at different ages would be positively correlated with p, which is not surprising since an expenditure with a small p would be less of an "investment" than one with a large p, and arguments based on an investment framework would be less applicable. None of the life-cycle arguments seem to imply any correlation with p, so this provides a powerful test of the importance of the investment approach.

The time spent in any one activity is determined not only by age, mortality, and morbidity but also by the amount of switching between activities. Women spend less time in the labor force than men and, therefore, have less incentive to invest in market skills; tourists spend little time in any one area and have less incentive than residents of the area to invest in knowledge of specific consumption opportunities;[56] temporary migrants to urban areas have less incentive to invest in urban skills than permanent residents; and, as a final example, draftees have less incentive than professional soldiers to invest in purely military skills.

Women, tourists, and the like have to find investments that increase productivity in several activities. A woman wants her investment to be useful both as a housewife and as a participant in the labor force, or a frequent traveler wants to be knowledgeable in many environments. Such investments would be less readily available than more specialized ones—after all, an investment increasing productivity in two activities also increases it in either one alone, extreme complementarity aside, while the converse does not hold; specialists, therefore, have greater incentive to invest in themselves than others do.

Specialization in an activity would be discouraged if the market were very limited; thus the incentive to specialize and to invest in oneself would increase as the extent of the market increased. Workers would be more skilled the larger the market, not only because "practice makes perfect," so often stressed in discussions of the division of labor,[57] but also because a larger market would *induce* a greater investment in skills.[58] Put differently, the usual analysis of the division of labor stresses that efficiency, and thus wage rates, would be greater the larger the market, and ignores the potential earnings period in any activity, while ours stresses that this period, and thus the incentive to become more efficient, would be directly related to market size. Surprisingly little attention has been paid to the influence of market size on the incentive to invest in skills.

Wage Differentials and Secular Changes

According to equation (30) the internal rate of return depends on the ratio of the return per unit time to investment costs. A change in the return and costs by the same percentage would not change the internal rate, while a greater percentage change in the return would change the internal rate in the same direction. The return is measured by the absolute income gain, or by the absolute income difference between persons differing only in the amount of their investment. Note that absolute, not relative, income differences determine the return and the internal rate.

Occupational and educational wage differentials are sometimes measured by relative, sometimes by absolute, wage differences,[59] although no one has adequately discussed their relative merits. Marginal productivity analysis relates the derived demand for any class of workers to the ratio of their wages to those of other inputs,[60] so wage ratios are more appropriate in understanding forces determining demand. They are not, however, the best measure of forces determining supply, for the return on investment in skills and other knowledge is determined by absolute wage differences. Therefore neither wage ratios nor wage differences are uniformly the best measure, ratios being more appropriate in demand studies and differences in supply studies.

The importance of distinguishing between wage ratios and differences, and the confusion resulting from the practice of using ratios to measure supply as well as demand forces, can be illustrated by considering the effects of technological progress. If progress were uniform in all industries and neutral with respect to all factors, and if there were constant costs, initially all wages would rise by the same proportion and the prices of all goods, including the output of industries supplying the investment in human capital,[61] would be unchanged. Since wage ratios would be unchanged, firms would have no incentive initially to alter their factor proportions. Wage differences, on the other hand, would rise at the same rate as wages, and since investment costs would be unchanged, there would be an incentive to invest more in human capital, and thus to increase the relative supply of skilled persons. The increased supply would in turn reduce the rate of increase of wage differences and produce an absolute narrowing of wage ratios.

In the United States during much of the last eighty years, a narrowing of wage ratios has gone hand in hand with an increasing relative supply of skill, an association that is usually said to result from the effect of an *autonomous* increase in the supply of skills—brought about by the spread of free education or the rise in incomes—on the return to skill, as measured by wage ratios. An alternative interpretation suggested by our analysis is that the spread of education and the increased investment in other kinds of human capital were in large part induced by technological progress (and perhaps other changes) through the effect on the rate of return, as measured by wage differences and costs. Clearly a secular decline in wage ratios is not inconsistent with a secular increase in real wage differences if average wages were rising, and, indeed, one important body of data on wages shows a decline in ratios and an even stronger rise in differences.[62]

The interpretation based on autonomous supply shifts has been favored partly because a decline in wage ratios has erroneously been taken as evidence of a decline in the return to skill. While a decision ultimately can be based only on a detailed reexamination of the evidence,[63] the induced approach can be made more plausible by considering trends in physical capital. Economists have been aware that the rate of return on capital could be rising or at least not falling while the ratio of the "rental" price of capital to wages was falling. Consequently, although the rental price of capital declined relative to wages over time, the large secular increase in the amount of physical capital per man-hour is not usually considered autonomous, but rather induced by technological and other developments that, at least temporarily, raised the return. A common explanation based on the effects of economic progress may, then, account for the increase in both human and physical capital.

Risk and Liquidity

An informed, rational person would invest only if the expected rate of return was greater than the sum of the interest rate on riskless assets and the liquidity and risk premiums associated with the investment. Not much need be said about the "pure" interest rate, but a few words are in order on risk and liquidity. Since human capital is a very illiquid asset—it cannot be sold and is rather poor collateral on loans—a positive liquidity premium, perhaps a sizable one, would be associated with such capital.

The actual return on human capital varies around the expected return because of uncertainty about several factors. There always has been considerable uncertainty about the length of life, one important determinant of the return. People are also uncertain about their ability, especially younger persons who do most of the investing. In addition, there is uncertainty about the return to a person of given age and ability because of numerous events that are not predictable. The long time required to collect the return on an investment in human capital reduces the knowledge available, for required is knowledge about the environment when the return is to be received, and the longer the average period between investment and return the less such knowledge is available.

Informed observation as well as calculations I have made suggest that there is much uncertainty about the return to human capital.[64] The response to uncertainty is determined by its amount and nature and by tastes or attitudes. Many have argued that attitudes of investors in human capital are very different from those of investors in physical capital because the former tend to be younger,[65] and young persons are supposed to be especially prone to overestimate their ability and chance of good fortune.[66] Were this view correct, a human investment which promised a large return to exceptionally able or lucky persons would be more attractive than a similar physical investment. However, a "life-cycle" explanation of attitudes toward risk may be no more valid or necessary than life-cycle explanations of why investors in human capital are relatively young (discussed on pp. 65–66). Indeed, an alternative explanation of reactions to large gains has already appeared.[67]

Capital Markets and Knowledge

If investment decisions respond only to earning prospects, adjusted for risk and liquidity, the adjusted marginal rate of return would be the same on all investments. The rate of return on education, training, migration, health, and other human capital is supposed to be higher than elsewhere, however, because of financing difficulties and inadequate knowledge of opportunities. These will now be discussed briefly.

Economists have long emphasized that it is difficult to borrow funds to invest in human capital because such capital cannot be offered as collateral and courts have frowned on contracts which even indirectly suggest involuntary servitude. This argument has been explicitly used to explain the "apparent" underinvestment in education and training and also, although somewhat less explicitly, underinvestment in health, migration, and other human capital. The importance attached to capital market difficulties can be determined not only from the discussions of investment but also from the discussions of consumption. Young persons would consume relatively little, productivity and wages might be related, and some other consumption patterns would follow only if it were difficult to capitalize future earning power. Indeed, unless capital limitations applied to consumption as well as investment, the latter could be indirectly financed with "consumption" loans.[68]

Some other implications of capital market difficulties can also be mentioned:

1. Since large expenditures would be more difficult to finance, investment in (say) a college education would be more affected than in (say) short-term migration.

2. Internal financing would be common, and consequently wealthier families would tend to invest more than poorer ones.

3. Since employees' specific skills are part of the intangible assets or goodwill of firms and can be offered as collateral along with tangible assets, capital would be more readily available for specific than for general investments.

4. Some persons have argued that opportunity costs (forgone earnings) are more readily financed than direct costs because they require only to do "without," while the latter require outlays. Although superficially plausible, this view can easily be shown to be wrong: opportunity and direct costs can be financed equally readily, given the state of the capital market. If total investment costs were $800, potential earnings $1,000, and if all costs were forgone earnings, investors would have $200 of earnings to spend; if all were direct costs, they would initially have $1,000 to spend, but just $200 would remain after paying "tuition," so their *net* position would be exactly the same as before. The example can be readily generalized and the obvious inference is that indirect and direct investment costs are equivalent in imperfect as well as perfect capital markets.

While it is undeniably difficult to use the capital market to finance investments in human capital, there is some reason to doubt whether otherwise equivalent investments in physical capital can be financed much more easily. Consider an eighteen-year-old who wants to invest a given amount in equipment for a firm he is starting rather than in a college education. What is his chance of borrowing the whole amount at a "moderate" interest rate? Very slight, I believe, since he would be untried and have a high debt-equity ratio; moreover, the collateral provided by his equipment would probably be very imperfect. He, too, would either have to borrow at high interest rates or self-finance. Although the difficulties of financing investments in human capital have usually been related to special properties of human capital, in large measure they seem also to beset comparable investments in physical capital.

A recurring theme is that young persons are especially prone to be ignorant of their abilities and of the investment opportunities available. If so, investors in human capital, being younger, would be less aware of opportunities and thus more likely to err than investors in tangible capital. I suggested earlier (pp. 65–66) that investors in human capital are younger partly because of the cost in postponing their investment to older ages. The desire to acquire additional knowledge about the return and about alternatives provides an incentive to postpone any risky investment, but since an investment in human capital is more costly to postpone, it would be made earlier and presumably with less knowledge than comparable nonhuman investments. Therefore, investors in human capital may not have less knowledge because of their age; rather both might be a *joint* product of the incentive not to delay investing.[69]

The eighteen-year-old in our example who could not finance a purchase of machinery might, without too much cost, postpone the investment for a number years until his reputation and equity were sufficient to provide the "personal" collateral required to borrow funds. Financing may prove a more formidable obstacle to investors in human capital because they cannot postpone their investment so readily. Perhaps this accounts for the tendency of economists to stress capital market imperfections when discussing investments in human capital.

V. Some Effects of Human Capital

Examples

Differences in earnings among persons, areas, or time periods are usually said to result from differences in physical capital, technological knowledge, ability, or institutions (such as unionization or socialized production). Our analysis indicates, however, that investment in human capital also has an important effect on observed earnings because earnings tend to be net of investment costs and gross of investment returns. Indeed, an appreciation of the direct and indirect importance of human capital appears to resolve many otherwise puzzling empirical findings about earnings. Consider the following examples:

1. Almost all studies show that age-earnings profiles tend to be steeper among more skilled and educated persons. I argued earlier (pp. 40–42) that on-the-job training would steepen age-earnings profiles and the analysis in Section III generalizes the argument to all human capital. Since observed earnings are gross of returns and net of costs, investment in human capital at younger ages would reduce observed earnings then and raise them at older ages, thus steepening the age-earnings profile.[70]

2. In recent years students of international trade theory have been somewhat shaken by findings that the United States, said to have relative scarcity of labor and abundance of capital, apparently exports relatively labor-intensive commodities and imports relatively capital-intensive commodities. For example, one study found that export industries pay higher wages than import competing ones.[71]

An interpretation consistent with the Ohlin-Heckscher emphasis on the relative abundance of different factors argues that the United States has an even more (relatively) abundant supply of human than of physical capital. An increase in human capital would, however, show up as an apparent increase in labor intensity since earnings are gross of the return on such capital. Thus export industries might pay higher wages than import competing ones primarily because they employ more skilled or healthier workers.[72]

3. Several recent studies have tried to estimate empirically the elasticity of substitution between capital and labor. Usually a ratio of the input of physical capital to the input of labor is regressed on the wage rate in different areas or time periods, the regression coefficient being an estimate of the elasticity of substitution.[73] Countries, states, or time periods that have relatively high wages and inputs of physical capital also tend to have much human capital. Just as a correlation between wages, physical capital, and human capital seems to obscure the relationship between relative factor supplies and commodity prices, so it obscures the relationship between relative factor supplies and factor prices. For if wages were high primarily because of human capital, a regression of the relative amount of physical capital on wages could give a seriously biased picture of the effect of factor proportions on wages.[74]

4. A secular increase in average earnings has usually been said to result from increases in technological knowledge and physical capital per earner. The average earner, in effect, is supposed to benefit indirectly from activities by entrepreneurs, investors, and others. Another explanation put forward in recent years argues that earnings can rise because of direct investment in earners.[75] Instead of only benefiting

from activities by others, the average earner is made a prime mover of development through the investment in himself.[76]

Ability and the Distribution of Earnings

An emphasis on human capital not only helps explain differences in earnings over time and among areas but also among persons or families within an area. This application will be discussed in greater detail than the others because a link is provided among earnings, ability, and the incentive to invest in human capital.

Economists have long been aware that conventional measures of ability—intelligence tests or aptitude scores, school grades, and personality tests—while undoubtedly relevant at times, do not reliably measure the talents required to succeed in the economic sphere. The latter requires a particular kind of personality, persistence, and intelligence. Accordingly, some writers have gone to the opposite extreme and argued that the only relevant way to measure economic talent is by results, or by earnings themselves.[77] Persons with higher earnings would simply have more ability than others, and a skewed distribution of earnings would imply a skewed distribution of abilities. This approach goes too far, however, in the opposite direction. The main reason for an interest in relating ability to earning is to distinguish its effects from differences in education, training, health, and other such factors and a definition equating ability and earnings ipso facto precludes such a distinction. Nevertheless, results are very relevant and should not be ignored.

A compromise might be reached through defining ability by earnings only when several variables had been held constant. Since the public is very concerned about separating ability from education, on-the-job training, health, and other human capital, the amount invested in such capital would have to be held constant. Although a full analysis would also hold discrimination, nepotism, and several other factors constant, a reasonable first approximation would say that if two persons have the same investment in human capital, the one who earns more is demonstrating greater economic talent.

Since observed earnings are gross of the return on human capital they are affected by changes in the amount and rate of return. Indeed, after the investment period earnings (Y) can be simply approximated by

$$Y = X + rC, \qquad (32)$$

where C measures total investment costs, r the average rate of return, and X earnings when there is no investment in human capital. If the distribution of X is ignored for now, Y would depend only on r when C was held constant, so "ability" would be measured by the average rate of return on human capital.[78]

The amount invested is not the same for everyone, or even in a very imperfect capital market rigidly fixed for any given person, but depends in part on the rate of return. Persons receiving a high marginal rate of return would have an incentive to invest more than others.[79] Since marginal and average rates are presumably positively correlated[80] and since ability is measured by the average rate, one can say that abler persons would invest more than others. The end result would be a positive correlation between ability and the investment in human capital,[81] a correlation with several important implications.

One is that the tendency for abler persons to migrate, continue their education,[82] and generally invest more in themselves can be explained without recourse to an assumption that noneconomic forces or demand conditions favor them at higher investment levels. A second implication is that the separation of "nature from nurture" or ability from education and other environmental factors is apt to be difficult, for high earnings would tend to signify both more ability and a better environment. Thus the earnings differential between college and high school graduates does not measure the effect of college alone since college graduates are abler and would earn more even without the additional education. Or reliable estimates of the income elasticity of demand for children have been difficult to obtain because higher-income families also invest more in contraceptive knowledge.[83]

The main implication, however, is in the field of personal income distribution. At least ever since the time of Pigou economists have tried to reconcile the strong skewness in the distribution of earnings and other income with a presumed symmetrical distribution of abilities.[84] Pigou's own solution, that property income is not symmetrically distributed, does not directly help explain the skewness in earnings. Subsequent attempts have largely concentrated on developing ad hoc random and other probabilistic mechanisms that have little relation to the mainstream of economic thought.[85] The approach presented here, however, offers an explanation that is not only consistent with economic analysis but actually relies on one of its fundamental tenets; namely, that the amount invested is a function of the rate of return expected. In conjunction with the effect of human capital on earnings this tenet can explain several well-known properties of earnings distributions.

By definition, the distribution of earnings would be exactly the same as the distribution of ability if everyone invested the same amount in human capital; in particular, if ability were symmetrically distributed, earnings would also be. Equation (32) shows that the distribution of earnings would be exactly the same as the distribution of investment if all persons were equally able; again, if investment were symmetrically distributed, earnings would also be.[86] If ability and investment both varied, earnings would tend to be skewed even when ability and investment were not, but the skewness would be small as long as the amount invested was statistically independent of ability.[87]

Our analysis has shown, however, that abler persons would tend to invest more than others, so ability and investment would be positively correlated, perhaps quite strongly. Now the product of two symmetrical distributions is more positively skewed the higher the positive correlation between them, and might be quite skewed.[88] The economic incentive given abler persons to invest relatively large amounts in themselves does seem capable, therefore, of reconciling a strong positive skewness in earnings with a presumed symmetrical distribution of abilities.

Variations in X help explain an important difference among skill categories in the degree of skewness. The smaller the fraction of total earnings resulting from investment in human capital—the smaller rC relative to X— the more would the distribution of earnings be dominated by the distribution of X. Higher skill categories have a greater average investment in human capital and thus presumably a large rC relative to X. The distribution of "unskilled ability," X, would, therefore, tend to dominate the distribution of earnings in relatively unskilled categories while the distribution of a product of ability and the amount invested, rC, would dominate in skilled categories. Hence if abilities were symmetrically distributed, earnings would tend to be more symmetrically distributed among the unskilled than among the skilled.[89]

Equation (32) holds only when investment costs are small, which tends to be true at later ages, say after age thirty-five. Net earnings at earlier ages would be given by

$$Y_j = X_j + \sum_0^{j-1} r_i C_i + (-C_j),$$

where j refers to the current year and i to previous years, C_i measures the investment cost of age i, C_j current costs, and r_i the rate of return on C_i. The distribution of $-C_j$ would be an important determinant of the distribution of Y_j since investment is large at these ages. Hence our analysis would predict a smaller (positive) skewness at younger than at older ages because the presumed negative correlation between $-C_j$ and $\sum_0^{j-1} r_i C_i$ would counteract the positive correlation between ability and investment.

A simple analysis of the incentive to invest in human capital seems capable of explaining, therefore, not only why the overall distribution of earnings is more skewed than the distribution of abilities, but also why earnings are more skewed among older and skilled persons than among younger and less skilled ones. The renewed interest in investment in human capital may provide the means of bringing the theory of personal income distribution back into economics.

VI. Summary and Conclusions

Most investments in human capital both raise observed earnings at older ages, because returns are added to earnings then, and lower them at younger ages, because costs are deducted from earnings then. Since these common effects are produced by very different kinds of human capital, a basis is provided for a unified and powerful theory. The analysis proceeded from a discussion of specific kinds of human capital, with greatest attention paid to on-the-job training because it clearly illustrates and emphasizes the common effects, to a general theory applying to any kind.

The general theory has a wide variety of important implications, ranging from interpersonal and interarea differences in earnings, to the shape of age-earnings profiles, to the effect of specialization on skill. For example, since earnings are gross of the return on human capital, some persons may earn more than others simply because they invest more in themselves. And since "abler" persons tend to invest more than others, the distribution of earnings could be very unequal and even skewed, even though "ability" were symmetrically and not too unequally distributed. To take another example, learning, both on and off the job, and other activities appear to have exactly the same effects on observed earnings as do education, training, and other traditional investments in human capital. We argue that a relevant concept should cover all activities with identical effects and show that the total amount invested in a generalized concept of human capital and its rate of return can be estimated from information on earnings alone.

Some investments in human capital do not affect earnings because costs are paid and returns are collected by the firms, industries, or countries using the capital. These "specific" investments range from hiring costs to executive training and are more important than is commonly believed. To take a couple of examples, we showed that the well-known greater unemployment among unskilled than skilled workers may result from the latter having more specific capital; or incompletely vested pension plans may be a means of insuring firms against a loss on their specific investments.

This paper has concentrated on developing a theory of investment in human capital, with an emphasis on empirical implications rather than on formal generalization. Of course, empirical usefulness is the only justification for any theory, and although I did not try to bring in even the quite limited evidence on the role of human capital, my own work and that of many others support the view that investment in human capital is a pervasive phenomenon and a valuable concept. The next few years should provide much stronger evidence on whether the recent emphasis placed on this concept is just another fad or a development of great and lasting importance.

NOTES

1. I am greatly indebted to the Carnegie Corporation of New York for the support given to the National Bureau of Economic Research to study investment in education and other kinds of human capital. I benefited greatly from many discussions with my colleague Jacob Mincer, and also with other participants in the Labor Workshop of Columbia University. Although many persons offered valuable comments on the draft prepared for the conference, I am especially indebted to the detailed comments of Theodore Schultz, George Stigler, and Shirley Johnson.

2. The evidence for the United States appears to show that the growth in capital per capita explains only a small part of the growth in per capita income and that the growth in "technology" explains most of it. On this see S. Fabricant, *Economic Progress and Economic Change: 34th Annual Report of the National Bureau of Economic Research* (New York: National Bureau of Economic Research, 1954).

3. In addition to the earlier works of Smith, Mill, and Marshall, see H. Clark, *Life Earnings in Selected Occupations in the U.S.* (New York: Harper & Bros., 1937); J. R. Walsh, "Capital Concept Applied to Man," *Quarterly Journal of Economics*, February 1935; M. Friedman and S. Kuznets, *Income from Independent Professional Practice* (New York: National Bureau of Economic Research, 1945); G. Stigler and D. Bland, *The Demand and Supply of Scientific Personnel* (New York: National Bureau of Economic Research, 1957); and T. W. Schultz, "Investment in Man: An Economist's View," *Social Service Review*, June 1959.

4. Of course, a shift between assets having different productivities would affect the income account on material goods even with current accounting practices.

5. I say "young people" rather than "young families" because, as J. Mincer has shown (in a paper to be published in a National Bureau of Economic Research conference volume on labor economics), the labor force participation of wives is positively correlated with the difference between husbands' long-run and current income. Participation of wives, therefore, makes the correlation between a family's current and a husband's long-run income greater than that between a husband's current and long-run income.

6. A difference in signs is impossible in Friedman's analysis of consumer behavior because he assumes that transitory and long-run (that is, permanent) incomes are uncorrelated (see his *A Theory of the Consumption Function* [Princeton, N.J.: Prince-

ton University Press, 1959]); we are suggesting that they may be *negatively* correlated for young persons.

7. See, for example, A. Marshall, *Principles of Economics*, 8th ed. (New York: Macmillan Co., 1949); C. Christ, "Patinkin on Money, Interest, and Prices," *Journal of Political Economy*, August 1957, p. 352; and W. Hamburger, "The Relation of Consumption to Wealth and the Wage Rate," *Econometrica*, January 1955.

8. In a recent paper, R. Goode has argued (see "Educational Expenditures and the Income Tax," in Selma J. Mushkin, ed., *Economics of Higher Education* [Washington, D.C.: United States Department of Health, Education, and Welfare (1962)]) that educated persons should be permitted to subtract from income a depreciation allowance on tuition payments. Such an allowance is apparently not required for on-the-job training costs; indeed, one might argue, on the contrary, that too much or too rapid depreciation is permitted on such investment.

9. In my study for the National Bureau of Economic Research I try to measure the relation between depreciation and age for several education classes.

10. The equivalence between forgone and direct costs applies to consumption as well as to investment decisions. A household can be assumed to maximize a utility function

$$U(X_1, X_2, \ldots X_r),$$

$X_1, \ldots X_r$ being consumption goods, subject to the constraint

$$\sum_{i=1}^{r} p_i X_i = W\left(h - \sum_{j=1}^{r} h_j X_j\right) + y,$$

where p_i is the market price of the ith good, W the average wage rate, y nonwage income, h the total number of hours available for either consumption or work, and h_j the number of hours required to consume a unit of the jth good. By transposing terms the constraint can be written as

$$\sum (p_i + W h_i) X_i = W h + y.$$

The total cost or price of consuming a unit of the ith good is the sum of two components: the market price or direct outlay per unit, p_i, and the forgone earnings per unit, Wh_i. I expect to show in another paper that this formulation of household decisions gives extremely useful insights into a number of important economic problems, such as the choice between labor and "leisure," the effect of price control on prices, the role of queues, and the cause of differences among income classes in price elasticities of demand.

11. See *Manpower Management and Compensation*. Vol. I. (Washington, D.C.: Government Printing Office, 1957), chart 3, and the accompanying discussion. The military not only wants to eliminate the inverse relation but apparently would like to create a strong positive relation because they have such a large investment in heavily trained personnel (see ibid.).

12. These arguments can be found in Marshall, op. cit., pp. 565–66, although he compares training to land-tenure systems.

13. To judge by a sample of firms recently analyzed, formal orientation courses are quite common, at least in large firms (see H. F. Clark and H. S. Sloan, *Classrooms in the Factories* [New York: New York University Press, 1955], chap. iv).

14. Marshall was clearly aware of specific talents and their effect on wages and productivity: "Thus the head clerk in a business has an acquaintance with men and things, the use of which he could in some cases sell at a high price to rival firms. But in other cases it is of a kind to be of no value save to the business in which he already is; and *then his department could perhaps injure it by several times the value of his salary*, while probably he could not get half that *salary elsewhere*" (op. cit., p. 626; my italics). However, he overstressed the element of indeterminacy in these wages ("their earnings are determined . . . by a bargain between them and their employers, the terms of which are theoretically arbitrary" [ibid., fn.]) because he ignored the effect of wages on turnover.

15. The rate used to discount costs and returns is the sum of a (positive) rate measuring the cost of funds, a (positive or negative) risk premium, and a liquidity premium that is presumably positive since capital invested in specific training is very illiquid (see the discussion in Section IV.

16. If G'' did not equal C, these equations would be slightly more complicated. Suppose, for example, $G'' = G + G' = C + n$, $n \geq 0$, so that the present value of the total return would be greater than total costs. Then $G = aG'' = aC + an$, and

$$MP' + aC + an = W + C,$$

or

$$W = MP' - [(1 - a)C - an].$$

17. A very similar argument is developed by Walter Oi in "Labor as a Quasi-fixed Factor of Production" (Ph.D. dissertation, University of Chicago).

18. Actually one need only assume that the quit rate of laid-off workers tends to be significantly greater than that of employed workers, if only because the cost of searching for another job is less for laid-off workers.

19. According to the National Bureau of Economic Research study of pensions, most plans still have incomplete vesting (see D. Holland's report in *A Respect for Facts: National Bureau of Economic Research Annual Report* [New York: National Bureau of Economic Research, 1960], pp. 44–46).

20. In recent years pensions have also been an important tax-saving device, which certainly has been a crucial factor in their mushrooming growth.

21. The military and entertainment industry are the major exceptions.

22. Sometimes firms cooperate in paying training costs, especially when training apprentices (see *A Look at Industrial Training in Mercer County, N.J.* [Washington, D.C.: Bureau of Apprenticeship and Training, 1951], p. 3).

23. S. Rottenberg ("The Baseball Players' Labor Market," *Journal of Political Econ-*

omy, June 1956, p. 254) argues that the strong restrictions on entry of teams into the major leagues is prima facie evidence that monopsony power is important, but the entry or threat of new leagues, such as have occurred in professional basketball and football, is a real possibility.

24. Specific, that is, to the firms, industries, or countries in question.

25. Of course, persons who have not yet invested in themselves would have an incentive to migrate, and this partly explains why young persons migrate more than older ones. For a further explanation see my discussion on p. 66.

26. A relatively large difference between marginal product and wages in monopsonies might measure, therefore, the combined effort of economic power and a relatively large investment in employees.

27. State occupational licensing requirements often permit on-the-job training to be substituted for school training (see S. Rottenberg, "The Economics of Occupational Licensing" [paper given at the National Bureau of Economic Research Conference on Labor Economics, April 1960]).

28. Students often have negative net earnings and in this respect differ from most on-the-job trainees, although at one time many apprentices also had negative earnings.

29. The role of political knowledge is systematically discussed in A. Downs, *An Economic Theory of Democracy* (New York: Harper & Bros., 1957), and more briefly in my "Competition and Democracy," *Journal of Law and Economics* 1 (fall 1958).

30. Studies of large geographical moves—those requiring both a change in employment and consumption—have tended to emphasize the job change more than the consumption change. Presumably money wages are considered to be more dispersed geographically than prices.

31. For a careful discussion of the contract labor system see C. Erickson, *American Industry and the European Immigrant, 1886–1885* (Cambridge, Mass.: Harvard University Press, 1957).

32. Imperfections in the capital market with respect to investment in human capital are discussed in Section IV.

33. The more rapid the impact the more likely that it comes within the (formal or de facto) contract period. Leibenstein apparently initially assumed a rapid impact when discussing wage increases in underdeveloped countries (see his "Theory of Underemployment in Backward Economies," *Journal of Political Economy* 65 [April 1957]). In a later comment he argued that the impact might be delayed ("Underemployment in Backward Economies: Some Additional Notes," *Journal of Political Economy* 66 [June 1958]).

34. Marshall discusses delays of a generation or more and notes that profit-maximizing firms in competitive industries have no incentive to grant such wage increases.

> Again, in paying his workpeople high wages and in caring for their happiness and culture, the liberal employer confers benefits which do not end with his own

generation. For the children of his workpeople share in them, and grow up stronger in body and in character than otherwise they would have done. The price which he has paid for labour will have borne the expenses of production of an increased supply of high industrial facilities in the next generation: but these facilities will be the property of others, who will have the right to hire them out for the best price they will fetch: neither he nor even his heirs can reckon on reaping much material reward for this part of the good that he has done (op. cit., p. 566).

35. See G. W. Hilton, "The British Truck System in the Nineteenth Century," *Journal of Political Economy* 65 (April 1957): 246–47.

36. If E represents reported earnings during the investment period and MP the marginal product when there is no investment, $E = MP - C$ with a general investment, $E = MP$ with a specific investment paid by the firm, and $E = MP + C$ with a productive earnings increase.

37. See the papers by Leibenstein, op. cit., and H. Oshima, "Underdevelopment in Backward Economies: An Empirical Comment," *Journal of Political Economy* 66 (June 1958).

38. For example, Marshall stressed the effect of an increase in earnings on the character and habits of working people (op. cit., pp. 529–32, 566–69).

39. Our discussion assumes discrete income flows and compounding, even though a mathematically more elegant formulation would have continuous variables, with sums replaced by integrals and discount rates by continuous compounding. The discrete approach is, however, easier to follow and yet yields the same kind of results as the continuous approach. Extensions to the continuous case are straightforward.

40. A substantial literature has developed on the difference between the income gain and internal return approaches. See, for example, Friedrich and Vera Lutz, *The Theory of Investment of the Firm* (Princeton, N.J.: Princeton University Press, 1951), chap. ii, and the articles in *The Management of Corporate Capital*, ed. Ezra Solomon (Glencoe, Ill.: Free Press, 1959).

41. Since

$$C^1 = \sum_0^{m-1} (X_j - Y_j)(1+r)^{-j},$$

$$\lim_{m \to n} C^1 = \sum_0^{n-1} (X_j - Y_j)(1+r)^{-j} = 0,$$

by definition of the internal rate.

42. If C_0 was the initial investment, r_0 its internal rate, and if the return were the same in all years, the amount

$$X_1^1 = X_1 + \frac{r_0 C_0}{1 - (1 + r_0)^{-n}}$$

could be received in period 1.

43. Y_1 is greater than X_1 if

$$X_1 + \frac{r_0 C_0}{1-(1+r_0)^{-n}} - C_1 > X_1,$$

or if

$$\frac{r_0 C_0}{1-(1+r_0)^{-n}} > C_1,$$

where C_1 is the investment in period 1.

44. A proof is straightforward. An investment in period j would yield a return of the amount $k_j = r_j C_j$ in each succeeding period if the number of periods was infinite and the return was the same in each. Since the total return is the sum of individual returns,

$$k = \sum_0^{m-1} k_j = \sum_0^{m-1} r_j C_j = C \sum_0^{m-1} \frac{r_j C_j}{C} = \bar{r} C.$$

I am indebted to Helen Raffel for important suggestions which led to this simple proof.

45. Note that the rate of return equating the present values of net earnings in X and Y is not necessarily equal to $\bar{r}$, for it would weigh more heavily than $\bar{r}$ does the rates of return on earlier investments. For example, if rates were higher on investments in earlier than later periods, the over-all rate would be greater than $\bar{r}$, and vice versa if rates were higher in later periods. The difference between the over-all internal rate for X and Y and $\bar{r}$ would be small, however, as long as the investment period was not very long and the systematic difference between internal rates not very great.

46. That is

$$\sum_{j=m}^{\infty} (Y_j - X_j)(1+r)^{m-1-j} = k \sum_m^{\infty} (1+r)^{m-1-j} = \frac{k}{r}.$$

47. Since, by definition,

$$X_0 - Y_0 = C_0, \qquad X_1 - Y_1 = C_1 - rC_0,$$

and more generally

$$X_j - Y_j = C_j - r \sum_{k=0}^{j-1} C_k, \qquad 0 \le j < m,$$

then

$$\sum_{j=0}^{m-1} (X_j - Y_j)(1+r)^{m-1-j} = \sum_{j=0}^{m-1} \left(C_j - r \sum_0^{j-1} C_k \right)(1+r)^{m-1-j}$$

$$= \sum_0^{m-1} C_j \{(1+r)^{m-1-j} - r[1+(1+r)+\cdots+(1+r)^{m-2-j}]\} = \sum_0^{m-1} C_j = C.$$

The analytical difference between the naive definition of costs advanced earlier and one in terms of forgone earnings is that the former measures total costs by the value of earning differentials at the beginning of the investment period and the latter by the value at the end of the period. Therefore, $C^1 = C(1+r)^{1-m}$, which follows from eq. (24) when $n = \infty$.

48. If the rate of return was not the same on all investments there would be $2m$ unknowns—$C_0, \ldots C_m - 1$, and $r_0, \ldots r_{m-1}$—and only $m+1$ equations—the m cost definitions and the equation

$$k = \sum_0^{m-1} r_i C_i .$$

An additional $m - 1$ relation would be required to determine the $2m$ unknowns. The condition $r_0 = r_1 = \cdots = r_{m-1}$ is one form these $m - 1$ relations can take.

49. Therefore, since the value of the first m earning differentials has been shown to equal

$$\sum_0^{m-1} C_j$$

at period m (see n. 47), total costs could be estimated from the value of all differentials at the end of the earning period. That is,

$$C = \sum_0^{\infty} C_j = \sum_0^{\infty} (X_j - Y_j)^{\infty - 1 - j} .$$

Thus the value of all differentials would equal zero at the beginning of the earning period—by definition of the internal rate—and C at the end. The apparent paradox results from the infinite horizon, as can be seen from the following equation relating the value of the first f differentials at the beginning of the gth period to costs:

$$V(f, g) = \sum_{j=0}^{f-1} (X_j - Y_j) (1 + r)^{g-1-j} = \sum_{j=0}^{f-1} C_j (1 + r)^{g-f} .$$

When $f = \infty$ and $g = 0$, $V = 0$, but whenever $f = g$,

$$V = \sum_0^{f-1} C_j .$$

In particular, if $f = g = \infty$, $V = C$.

50. The technique is applied and further developed by Mincer.

51. If C measured the cost of investment before the initial age and r its rate of return, $k = rC$ would measure the return per period. If earnings were attributed entirely to this investment, $X_i = k = rC$, where X_i represents earnings at the ith period past the initial age.

52. But note that empirical evidence indicates that age-earnings profiles in unskilled occupations are very flat.

53. I say *may* because rates of return are adversely affected by the increase in labor

force that would result from a decline in death and sickness. If the adverse effect was sufficiently great, a decline in death and sickness would reduce rates of return on human capital. I am indebted to my wife for emphasizing this point.

54. Younger persons would also have a greater incentive to invest if the cost of any investment rose with age, say, because potential and thus forgone earnings rose with age.

55. This test was suggested by George Stigler's discussion of the effect of different autocorrelation patterns on the incentive to invest in information (see "The Economics of Information," *Journal of Political Economy* 69 [June 1961]).

56. This example is from Stigler, "The Economics of Information," op. cit.

57. See, for example, Marshall, op. cit., Bk. IV, chap. ix.

58. If "practice makes perfect" means that age-earnings profiles slope upward, then according to my approach it must be treated along with other kinds of learning as a way of investing in human capital. The distinction above between the effect of an increase in the market on practice and on the incentive to invest would simply be that the incentive to invest in human capital is increased even aside from the effect of practice on earnings.

59. See A. M. Ross and W. Goldner, "Forces Affecting the Interindustry Wage Structure," *Quarterly Journal of Economics* 64 (May 1950); P. H. Bell, "Cyclical Variation and Trend in Occupational Wage Differentials in American Industry Since 1914," *Review of Economics and Statistics* 23 (November 1951); F. Meyers and R. L. Bowlby, "The Interindustry Wage Structure and Productivity," *Industrial and Labor Relations Review* 7 (October 1953); Stigler and Blank, op. cit., table 11; P. Keat, "Long-Term Trends in Occupational Wage Differentials," *Journal of Political Economy* 68 (December 1960).

60. Thus the elasticity of a substitution is usually defined as the percentage change in the ratio of quantities employed per 1 percent change in the ratio of wages.

61. Some persons have argued that only direct investment costs would be unchanged, indirect costs or forgone earnings rising along with wages. Neutral progress implies, however, the same increase in the productivity of a student's time as in his teacher's time or in the use of raw materials, so even forgone earnings would not change.

62. Keat's data for 1906–53 in the United States show both an average annual decline of 0.8 percent in the coefficient of variation of wages and an average annual rise of 1.2 percent in the real standard deviation. The decline in the coefficient of variation was shown in his study (op. cit.); I computed the change in the real standard deviation from data made available to me by Keat.

63. For those believing that the evidence overwhelmingly indicates a secular decline in rates of return on human capital, I reproduce Adam Smith's statement on earnings in some professions. "The lottery of the law, therefore, is very far from being a perfectly fair lottery; and that, as well as many other liberal and honorable professions, is, in point of pecuniary gain, evidently under-recompensed" (*The Wealth of Nations* [New York: Modern Library 1937], p. 106). Since economists tend to believe that law and most other liberal professions are now overcompensated relative to non-

professional work "in point of pecuniary gain," the return to professional work could not have declined continuously if Smith's observations were accurate.

64. For example, Marshall said: "Not much less than a generation elapses between the choice by parents of a skilled trade for one of their children, and his reaping the full results of their choice. And meanwhile the character of the trade may have been almost revolutionized by changes, on which some probably threw long shadows before them, but others were such as could not have been foreseen even by the shrewdest persons and those best acquainted with the circumstances of the trade" (op. cit., p. 571), and "the circumstances by which the earnings are determined are less capable of being foreseen [than those for machinery]" (ibid.).

65. Note that our argument on p. 66 implied that investors in human capital would be younger.

66. Smith said: "The contempt of risk and the presumptuous hope of success, are in no period of life more active than at the age at which young people choose their professions" (op. cit., p. 109). Marshall said that "young men of an adventurous disposition are more attracted by the prospects of a great success than they are deterred by the fear of failure" (op. cit., p. 554).

67. See M. Friedman and L. J. Savage, "The Utility Analysis of Choices Involving Risk," reprinted in *Readings in Price Theory*, ed. C. J. Stigler and K. Boulding (Chicago: Richard D. Irwin, Inc., 1952).

68. A person with an income of X and investment costs of Y ($y < X$) could either use X for consumption and receive an *investment loan* of Y, or use $X - Y$ for consumption, Y for investment, and receive a *consumption loan* of Y. He ends up with the same consumption and investment in both cases, the only difference being in the names attached to loans.

69. Marshall (op. cit., pp. 571–73) appears to argue that it is also intrinsically more difficult to acquire knowledge about the return from an investment in human capital.

70. According to eq. (28) earnings at age j can be approximated by

$$Y_j = X_j + \sum_{k=0}^{k=j-1} r_k C_k - C_j,$$

where X_j are earnings at j of persons who have not invested in themselves, C_k is the investment at age k, and r_k is its rate of return. The rate of increase in earnings would be at least as steep in Y as in X at each age and not only from "younger" to "older" ages if and only if

$$\frac{\Delta Y_j}{\Delta j} \geq \frac{\Delta X_j}{\Delta j},$$

or

$$r_j C_j \geq \frac{\Delta C_j}{\Delta j}.$$

This condition is usually satisfied since $r_jC_j \geq 0$ and the amount invested tends to decline with age.

71. See I. Kravis, "Wages and Foreign Trade," *Review of Economics and Statistics* 33 (February 1956).

72. This kind of interpretation has been put forward by many writers; see, for example, the discussion in W. Leontief, "Factor Proportions and the Structure of American Trade: Further Theoretical and Empirical Analysis," *Review of Economics and Statistics* 33 (November 1956).

73. Interstate estimates for several industries can be found in J. Minasian, "Elasticities of Substitution and Constant-Output Demand Curves for Labor," *Journal of Political Economy* 69 (June 1961): 261–70; intercountry estimates in Kenneth Arrow, Hollis B. Chenery, Bagicha Minhas, and Robert M. Solow, "Capital-Labor Substitution and Economic Efficiency," *Review of Economics and Statistics*, August 1961; unpublished papers by Philip Nelson and Robert Solow contain both interstate and time-series estimates.

74. Minasian's argument (op. cit., p. 264) that interstate variations in skill level necessarily bias his estimates toward unity is actually correct only if skill is a perfect substitute for "labor." (In correspondence Minasian states that he intended to make this condition explicit.) If, on the other hand, human and physical capital were perfect substitutes the estimates would always have a downward bias, regardless of the true substitution between labor and capital. Perhaps the most reasonable assumption would be that physical capital is more complementary with human capital than with labor; I have not, however, been able to determine the direction of bias in this case.

75. The major figure here undoubtedly is T. W. Schultz. Of his many articles see esp. "Education and Economic Growth" in *Social Forces Influencing American Education* (Sixtieth Yearbook of the National Society for the Study of Education, Part II [Chicago: University of Chicago Press, 1961]).

76. One caveat is called for, however. Since observed earnings are not only gross of the return from investments in human capital but also are net of some costs, an increased investment in human capital would both raise and reduce earnings. Although average earnings would tend to increase as long as the rate of return was positive, the increase is less than it would be if the cost of human capital, like that of physical capital, was not deducted from national income.

77. Let me state again that whenever the word "earnings" appears I mean real earnings, or the sum of monetary earnings and the monetary equivalent of psychic earnings.

78. Since r is a function of C, Y would indirectly as well as directly depend on C, and therefore the distribution of ability would depend on the amount of human capital. Some persons might rank high in earnings and thus high in ability if everyone were unskilled, and quite low if education and other training were widespread.

79. In addition, they would find it easier to invest if the marginal return and the resources of parents and other relatives were positively correlated.

80. According to a well-known formula

$$r_m = r_a \left(1 + \frac{1}{e_a}\right),$$

where r_m is the marginal rate of return, r_a, the average rate, and e_a the elasticity of the average rate with respect to the amount invested. The rates r_m and r_a would be positively correlated unless r_a and $1/e_a$ were sufficiently negatively correlated.

81. This kind of argument is not new. Marshall argued that business ability and the ownership of physical capital would be positively correlated: "[economic] forces . . . bring about the result that there is a far more close correspondence between the ability of business men and the size of the businesses which they own than at first sight would appear probable" (op. cit., p. 312).

82. The first is frequently alleged (see, for example, Marshall, op. cit., pp. 199, 684). Evidence on the second is discussed in my forthcoming study for the National Bureau of Economic Research.

83. See my "An Economic Analysis of Fertility" in *Demographic and Economic Change in Developed Countries* (Princeton, N.J.: Princeton University Press, 1960).

84. See A. C. Pigou, *The Economics of Welfare*, 4th ed. (London: Macmillan & Co., 1950), Part IV, Chap. ii.

85. A sophisticated example can be found in B. Mandelbrot, "The Pareto-Levy Law and the Distribution of Income," *International Economic Review* 1 (May 1960). In a recent paper, however, Mandelbrot has brought in maximizing behavior (see "Paretian Distributions and Income Maximization," *Quarterly Journal of Economics* 76 [February 1962]).

86. Jacob Mincer ("Investment in Human Capital and Personal Income Distribution," *Journal of Political Economy* 66 [August 1958]) concluded that a symmetrical distribution of investment in education implies a skewed distribution of earnings because he defines educational investment by school years rather than costs. If we follow Mincer in assuming that everyone was equally able, that schooling was the only investment, and that the cost of the nth year of schooling equaled the earnings of persons with $n - 1$ years of schooling, then, say, a normal distribution of schooling can be shown to imply a log-normal distribution of school costs, and thus a log-normal distribution of earnings.

The difference between the earnings of persons with $n - 1$ and n years of schooling would be $k_n = Y_n - Y_{n-1} = r_n C_n$. Since r_n is assumed to equal r for all n, and $C_n = Y_{n-1}$, this equation becomes $Y_n = (1 + r) Y_{n-1}$, and therefore

$$C_1 = Y_0$$
$$C_2 = Y_1 = Y_0 (1 + r)$$
$$C_3 = Y_2 = Y_1 (1 + r) = Y_0 (1 + r)^2$$
$$C_n = Y_{n-1} = \cdots = Y_0 (1 + r)^{n-1},$$

or the cost of each additional year of schooling increases at a constant rate. Since total costs have the same distribution as $(1 + r)^n$, a symmetrical, say a normal, distribution of school years, n, implies a log-normal distribution of costs and hence by eq. (32) a log-normal distribution of earnings. I am indebted to Mincer for a helpful discussion of the comparison and especially for the stimulation provided by

90 ◆ FOUNDATIONS OF HUMAN BEHAVIOR

his pioneering work. Incidentally, his article and the dissertation on which it is based cover a much broader area than has been indicated here.

87. For example, C. C. Craig has shown that the product of two independent normal distributions is only slightly skewed (see his "On the Frequency Function of XY," *Annals of Mathematical Statistics* 7 [March 1936]: 3).

88. Craig (op. cit., pp. 9–10) showed that the product of two normal distributions would be more positively skewed the higher the positive correlation between them, and that the skewness would be considerable with high correlations.

89. As noted earlier, X does not really represent earnings when there is no investment in human capital, but only earnings when there is no investment after the initial age (be it fourteen, twenty-five, or six). Indeed, the developmental approach to child-rearing argues that earnings would be close to zero if there was no investment at all in human capital. The distribution of X, therefore, would be at least partly determined by the distribution of investment before the initial age, and if it and ability were positively correlated, X might be positively skewed, even though ability was not.

A THEORY OF THE
ALLOCATION OF TIME

· 4 ·

I. INTRODUCTION

Throughout history the amount of time spent at work has never consistently been much greater than that spent at other activities. Even a workweek of fourteen hours a day for six days still leaves half the total time for sleeping, eating, and other activities. Economic development has led to a large secular decline in the workweek, so that whatever may have been true of the past, today it is below fifty hours in most countries, less than a third of the total time available. Consequently the allocation and efficiency of nonworking time may now be more important to economic welfare than that of working time; yet the attention paid by economists to the latter dwarfs any paid to the former.

Fortunately, there is a movement under way to redress the balance. The time spent at work declined secularly, partly because young persons increasingly delayed entering the labor market by lengthening their period of schooling. In recent years many economists have stressed that the time of students is one of the inputs into the educational process, that this time could be used to participate more fully in the labor market, and therefore that one of the costs of education is the forgone earnings of students. Indeed, various esti-

First published in the *Economic Journal* 75, no. 299 (September 1965): 493–508. Reprinted by permission of Blackwell Publishers, Oxford, England.

mates clearly indicate that forgone earnings is the dominant private and an important social cost of both high school and college education in the United States.[1] The increased awareness of the importance of forgone earnings has resulted in several attempts to economize on students' time, as manifested, say, by the spread of the quarterly and trimester systems.[2]

Most economists have now fully grasped the importance of forgone earnings in the educational process and, more generally, in all investments in human capital, and criticize educationalists and others for neglecting them. In the light of this it is perhaps surprising that economists have not been equally sophisticated about other nonworking uses of time. For example, the cost of a service like the theater or a good like meat is generally simply said to equal their market prices, yet everyone would agree that the theater and even dining take time, just as schooling does, time that often could have been used productively. If so, the full costs of these activities would equal the sum of market prices and the forgone value of the time used up. In other words, indirect costs should be treated on the same footing when discussing all nonwork uses of time, as they are now in discussions of schooling.

In the last few years a group of us at Columbia University have been occupied, perhaps initially independently but then increasingly less so, with introducing the cost of time systematically into decisions about nonwork activities. J. Mincer has shown with several empirical examples how estimates of the income elasticity of demand for different commodities are biased when the cost of time is ignored;[3] J. Owen has analyzed how the demand for leisure can be affected;[4] E. Dean has considered the allocation of time between subsistence work and market participation in some African economies;[5] while, as already mentioned, I have been concerned with the use of time in education, training, and other kinds of human capital. Here I attempt to develop a general treatment of the allocation of time in all other nonwork activities. Although under my name alone, much of any credit it merits belongs to the stimulus received from Mincer, Owen, Dean and other past and present participants in the Labor Workshop at Columbia.[6]

The plan of the discussion is as follows. The first section sets out a basic theoretical analysis of choice that includes the cost of time on the same footing as the cost of market goods, while the remaining sections treat various empirical implications of the theory. These include a new approach to changes in hours of work and "leisure," the full integration of so-called productive consumption into economic analysis, a new analysis of the effect of income on the quantity and "quality" of commodities consumed, some suggestions on the measurement of productivity, an economic analysis of queues, and a few others as well. Although I refer to relevant empirical work that has come to my attention, little systematic testing of the theory has been attempted.

II. A Revised Theory of Choice

According to traditional theory, households maximize utility functions of the form

$$U = U(y_1, y_2, \ldots, y_n) \tag{1}$$

subject to the resource constraint

$$\sum p_i' y_i = I = W + V \tag{2}$$

where y_i are goods purchased on the market, p_i' are their prices, I is money income, W is earnings, and V is other income. As the introduction suggests, the point of departure here is the systematic incorporation of nonworking time. Households will be assumed to combine time and market goods to produce more basic commodities that directly enter their utility functions. One such commodity is the seeing of a play, which depends on the input of actors, script, theater, and the playgoer's time; another is sleeping, which depends on the input of a bed, house (pills?), and time. These commodities will be called Z_i and written as

$$Z_i = f_i(x_i, T_i) \tag{3}$$

where x_i is a vector of market goods and T_i a vector of time inputs used in producing the ith commodity.[7] Note that, when capital goods such as refrigerators or automobiles are used, x refers to the services yielded by the goods. Also note that T_i is a vector because, e.g., the hours used during the day or on weekdays may be distinguished from those used at night or on weekends. Each dimension of T_i refers to a different aspect of time. Generally, the partial derivatives of Z_i with respect to both x_i and T_i are nonnegative.[8]

In this formulation households are both producing units and utility maximizers. They combine time and market goods via the "production functions" f_i to produce the basic commodities Z_i, and they choose the best combination of these commodities in the conventional way by maximizing a utility function

$$U = U(Z_i, \ldots Z_m) \equiv U(f_1, \ldots f_m) \equiv U(x_1, \ldots x_m; T_1, \ldots T_m) \tag{4}$$

subject to a budget constraint

$$g(Z_i \ldots Z_m) = Z \tag{5}$$

where g is an expenditure function of Z_i and Z is the bound on resources. The integration of production and consumption is at odds with the tendency for economists to separate them sharply, production occurring in firms and consumption in households. It should be pointed out, however, that in recent years economists increasingly recognize that a household is truly a "small factory":[9] it combines capital goods, raw materials, and labor to clean, feed, procreate, and otherwise produce useful commodities. Undoubtedly the fundamental reason for the traditional separation is that firms are usually given control over working time in exchange for market goods, while "discretionary" control over market goods and consumption time is retained by households as they create their own utility. If (presumably different) firms were also given control over market goods and consumption time in exchange for providing utility the separation would quickly fade away in analysis as well as in fact.

The basic goal of the analysis is to find measures of g and Z which facilitate the development of empirical implications. The most direct approach is to assume that the utility function in equation (4) is maximized subject to separate constraints on the expenditure of market goods and time, and to the production functions in equation (3). The goods constraint can be written as

$$\sum_1^m p_i x_i = I = V + T_w \overline{w} \qquad (6)$$

where p_i is a vector giving the unit prices of x_i, T_w is a vector giving the hours spent at work, and $\overline{w}$ is a vector giving the earnings per unit of T_w. The time constraints can be written as

$$\sum_1^m T_i = T_c = T - T_w \qquad (7)$$

where T_c is a vector giving the total time spent at consumption and T is a vector giving the total time available. The production functions (3) can be written in the equivalent form

$$\left. \begin{array}{l} T_i \equiv t_i Z_i \\ x_i \equiv b_i Z_i \end{array} \right\} \qquad (8)$$

where t_i is a vector giving the input of time per unit of Z_i and b_i is a similar vector for market goods.

The problem would appear to be to maximize the utility function (4) subject to the multiple constraints (6) and (7) and to the production relations (8). There is, however, really only one basic constraint: (6) is not independent of (7) because time can be converted into goods by using less time at consumption and more at work. Thus, substituting for T_w in (6) its equivalent in (7) gives the single constraint[10]

$$\sum p_i x_i + \sum T_i \bar{w} = V + T\bar{w} \tag{9}$$

By using (8), (9) can be written as

$$\sum (p_i b_i + t_i \bar{w}) Z_i = V + T\bar{w} \tag{10}$$

with

$$\left. \begin{array}{l} \pi_i \equiv p_i b_i + t_i \bar{w} \\ S' \equiv V + T\bar{w} \end{array} \right\} \tag{11}$$

The full price of a unit of Z_i (π_i) is the sum of the prices of the goods and of the time used per unit of Z_i. That is, the full price of consumption is the sum of direct and indirect prices in the same way that the full cost of investing in human capital is the sum of direct and indirect costs.[11] These direct and indirect prices are symmetrical determinants of total price, and there is no analytical reason to stress one rather than the other.

The resource constraint on the right side of equation (10), S', is easy to interpret if $\bar{w}$ were a constant, independent of the Z_i. For then S' gives the money income achieved if all the time available were devoted to work. This achievable income is "spent" on the commodities Z_i either directly through expenditures on goods, $\Sigma p_i b_i Z_i$, or indirectly through the forgoing of income, $\Sigma t_i \bar{w} Z_i$, i.e., by using time at consumption rather than at work. As long as $\bar{w}$ were constant, and if there were constant returns in producing Z_i so that b_i and t_i were fixed for given p_i and $\bar{w}$, the equilibrium condition resulting from maximizing (4) subject to (10) takes a very simple form:

$$U_i = \frac{\partial U}{\partial Z_i} = \lambda \pi_i \qquad i = 1, \ldots m \tag{12}$$

where λ is the marginal utility of money income. If $\bar{w}$ were not constant the resource constraint in equation (10) would not have any particularly useful interpretation: $S' = V + T\bar{w}$ would overstate the money income achievable as long as marginal wage rates were below average ones. Moreover, the equilibrium conditions would become more complicated than (12) because marginal would have to replace average prices.

The total resource constraint could be given the sensible interpretation of the maximum money income achievable only in the special and unlikely case when average earnings were constant. This suggests dropping the approach based on explicitly considering separate goods and time constraints and substituting one in which the total resource constraint necessarily equaled the maximum money income achievable, which will be simply called "full income."[12] This income could in general be obtained by devoting all the time and other resources of a household to earning income, with no regard for consumption. Of course, all the time would not usually be spent "at" a job: sleep, food, even leisure are required for efficiency, and some time (and other resources) would have to be spent on these activities in order to maximize money income. The amount spent would, however, be determined solely by the effect on income and not by any effect on utility. Slaves, for example, might be permitted time "off" from work only insofar as that maximized their output, or free persons in poor environments might have to maximize money income simply to survive.[13]

Households in richer countries do, however, forfeit money income in order to obtain additional utility, i.e., they exchange money income for a greater amount of psychic income. For example, they might increase their leisure time, take a pleasant job in preference to a better-paying unpleasant one, employ unproductive nephews, or eat more than is warranted by considerations of productivity. In these and other situations the amount of money income forfeited measures the cost of obtaining additional utility.

Thus the full income approach provides a meaningful resource constraint and one firmly based on the fact that goods and time can be combined into a single overall constraint because time can be converted into goods through money income. It also incorporates a unified treatment of all substitutions of nonpecuniary for pecuniary income, regardless of their nature or whether they occur on the job or in the household. The advantages of this will become clear as the analysis proceeds.

If full income is denoted by S, and if the total earnings forgone or "lost" by the interest in utility is denoted by L, the identity relating L to S and I is simply

$$L(Z_1, \ldots, Z_m) \equiv S - I(Z_1, \ldots, Z_m) \qquad (13)$$

I and L are functions of the Z_i because how much is earned or forgone depends on the consumption set chosen; for example, up to a point, the less leisure chosen the larger the money income and the smaller the amount forgone.[14] Using equations (6) and (8), equation (13) can be written as

$$\sum p_i b_i Z_i + L(Z_1, \ldots, Z_m) \equiv S \qquad (14)$$

This basic resource constraint states that full income is spent either directly on market goods or indirectly through the forgoing of money income. Unfortunately, there is no simple expression for the average price of Z_i as there is in equation (10). However, marginal, not average, prices are relevant for behavior, and these would be identical for the constraint in (10) only when average earnings, $\overline{w}$, was constant. But, if so, the expression for the loss function simplifies to

$$L = \overline{w}T_c = \overline{w}\sum t_i Z_i \qquad (15)$$

and (14) reduces to (10). Moreover, even in the general case the total marginal prices resulting from (14) can always be divided into direct and indirect components: the equilibrium conditions resulting from maximizing the utility function subject to (14)[15] are

$$U_i = T(p_i b_i + L_i), \quad i = 1, \ldots, m \qquad (16)$$

where $p_i b_i$ is the direct and L the indirect component of the total marginal price $p_i b_i + L_i$.[16]

Behind the division into direct and indirect costs is the allocation of time and goods between work-oriented and consumption-oriented activities. This suggests an alternative division of costs; namely, into those resulting from the allocation of goods and those resulting from the allocation of time. Write $L_i = \partial L/\partial Z_i$ as

$$L_i = \frac{\partial L}{\partial T_i}\frac{\partial T_i}{\partial Z_i} + \frac{\partial L}{\partial x_i}\frac{\partial x_i}{\partial Z_i} \qquad (17)$$

$$= l_i t_i + c_i b_i \qquad (18)$$

where $l_i = \dfrac{\partial L}{\partial T_i}$ and $c_i = \dfrac{\partial L}{\partial x_i}$ are the marginal forgone earnings of using more time and goods respectively on Z_i. Equation (16) can then be written as

$$U_i = T[b_i(p_i + c_i) + t_i l_i] \qquad (19)$$

The total marginal cost of Z_i is the sum of $b_i(p_i + c_i)$, the marginal cost of using goods in producing Z_i and $t_i l_i$, the marginal cost of using time. This division would be equivalent to that between direct and indirect costs only if $c_i = 0$ or if there were no indirect costs of using goods.

The figure on page 98 shows the equilibrium given by equation (16) for a two-commodity world. In equilibrium the slope of the full income opportunity curve, which equals the ratio of marginal prices, would equal the slope of an indifference curve, which equals the ratio of marginal utilities. Equilibrium occurs at p and p' for the opportunity curves S and S' respectively.

The rest of the paper is concerned with developing numerous empirical implications of this theory, starting with determinants of hours worked and concluding with an economic interpretation of various queuing systems. To simplify the presentation, it is assumed that the distinction between direct and indirect costs is equivalent to that between goods and time costs; in

FIGURE I

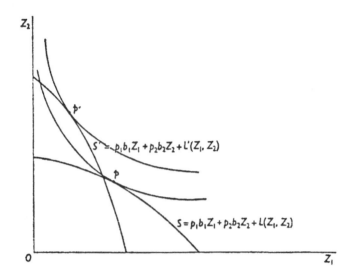

other words, the marginal forgone cost of the use of goods, c_i, is set equal to
zero. The discussion would not be much changed, but would be more cum-
bersome were this not assumed.[17] Finally, until Section IV goods and time
are assumed to be used in fixed proportions in producing commodities; that
is, the coefficients b_i and t_i in equation (8) are treated as constants.

III. Applications

Hours of Work

If the effects of various changes on the time used on consumption, T_c,
could be determined their effects on hours worked, T_w, could be found
residually from equation (7). This section considers, among other things,
the effects of changes in income, earnings, and market prices on T_c, and thus
on T_w, using as the major tool of analysis differences among commodities in
the importance of forgone earnings.

The relative marginal importance of forgone earnings is defined as

$$\alpha_i = \frac{l_i t_i}{p_i b_i + l_i t_i} \tag{20}$$

The importance of forgone earnings would be greater the larger l_i and t_i, the forgone earnings per hour of time and the number of hours used per unit of Z_i respectively, while it would be smaller the larger p_i and b_i, the market price of goods and the number of goods used per unit of Z_i respectively. Similarly, the relative marginal importance of time is defined as

$$\gamma_i = \frac{t_i}{p_i b_i + l_i t_i} \tag{21}$$

If full income increased solely because of an increase in V (other money income) there would simply be a parallel shift of the opportunity curve to the right with no change in relative commodity prices. The consumption of most commodities would have to increase; if all did, hours worked would decrease, for the total time spent on consumption must increase if the output of all commodities did, and by equation (7) the time spent at work is inversely related to that spent on consumption. Hours worked could increase only if relatively time-intensive commodities, those with large γ, were sufficiently inferior.[18]

A uniform percentage increase in earnings for all allocations of time would increase the cost per hour used in consumption by the same percentage for all commodities.[19] The relative prices of different commodities would, however, change as long as forgone earnings were not equally important for all; in particular, the prices of commodities having relatively important forgone earnings would rise more. Now the fundamental theorem of demand theory states that a compensated change in relative prices would induce households to consume less of commodities rising in price. The figure shows the effect of a rise in earnings fully compensated by a decline in other income: the opportunity curve would be rotated clockwise through the initial position p if Z_1 were the more earnings-intensive commodity. In the figure the new equilibrium p' must be to the left and above p, or less Z_1 and more Z_2 would be consumed.

Therefore a compensated uniform rise in earnings would lead to a shift away from earnings-intensive commodities and toward goods-intensive ones. Since earnings and time intensiveness tend to be positively correlated,[20] consumption would be shifted from time-intensive commodities. A shift away from such commodities would, however, result in a reduction in the total time spent in consumption, and thus an increase in the time spent at work.[21]

The effect of an uncompensated increase in earnings on hours worked would depend on the relative strength of the substitution and income effects. The former would increase hours, the latter reduce them; which dominates cannot be determined a priori.

The conclusion that a pure rise in earnings increases and a pure rise in

income reduces hours of work must sound very familiar, for they are traditional results of that well-known labor-leisure analysis. What, then, is the
relation between our analysis, which treats all commodities symmetrically
and stresses only their differences in relative time and earning intensities,
and the usual analysis, which distinguishes a commodity having special
properties called "leisure" from other more commonplace commodities? It is
easily shown that the usual labor-leisure analysis can be looked upon as a
special case of ours in which the cost of that commodity called leisure consists
entirely of forgone earnings and the cost of other commodities entirely of
goods.[22]

As a description of reality such an approach, of course, is not tenable,
since virtually all activities use both time and goods. Perhaps it would be
defended either as an analytically necessary or extremely insightful approximation to reality. Yet the usual substitution and income effects of a change
in resources on hours worked have easily been derived from a more general
analysis which stresses only that the relative importance of time varies among
commodities. The rest of the paper tries to go further and demonstrate that
the traditional approach, with its stress on the demand for "leisure," apparently has seriously impeded the development of insights about the economy,
since the more direct and general approach presented here naturally leads to
a variety of implications never yet obtained.

The two determinants of the importance of forgone earnings are the
amount of time used per dollar of goods and the cost per unit of time. Reading
a book, taking a haircut, or commuting use more time per dollar of goods
than eating dinner, frequenting a nightclub, or sending children to private
summer camps. Other things the same, forgone earnings would be more
important for that former set of commodities than the latter.

The importance of forgone earnings would be determined solely by time
intensity only if the cost of time was the same for all commodities. Presumably, however, it varies considerably among commodities and at different
periods. For example, the cost of time is often less on weekends and in the
evenings because many firms are closed then,[23] which explains why a famous
liner intentionally includes a weekend in each voyage between the United
States and Europe.[24] The cost of time would also tend to be less for commodities that contribute to productive effort, traditionally called "productive
consumption." A considerable amount of sleep, food, and even "play" fall
under this heading. The opportunity cost of the time is less because these
commodities indirectly contribute to earnings. Productive consumption has
had a long but banditlike existence in economic thought; our analysis does
systematically incorporate it into household decision making.

Although the formal specification of leisure in economic models has
ignored expenditures on goods, cannot one argue that a more correct speci-

fication would simply associate leisure with relatively important forgone earnings? Most conceptions of leisure do imply that it is time intensive and does not indirectly contribute to earnings,[25] two of the important characteristics of earnings-intensive commodities. On the other hand, not all of what are usually considered leisure activities do have relatively important forgone earnings: nightclubbing is generally considered leisure, and yet, at least in its more expensive forms, has a large expenditure component. Conversely, some activities have relatively large forgone earnings and are not considered leisure: haircuts or child care are examples. Consequently, the distinction between earnings-intensive and other commodities corresponds only partly to the usual distinction between leisure and other commodities. Since it has been shown that the relative importance of forgone earnings rather than any concept of leisure is more relevant for economic analysis, less attention should be paid to the latter. Indeed, although the social philosopher might have to define precisely the concept of leisure,[26] the economist can reach all his traditional results as well as many more without introducing it at all!

Not only is it difficult to distinguish leisure from other nonwork[27] but also even work from nonwork. Is commuting work, nonwork, or both? How about a business lunch, a good diet, or relaxation? Indeed, the notion of productive consumption was introduced precisely to cover those commodities that contribute to work as well as to consumption. Cannot pure work then be considered simply as a limiting commodity of such joint commodities in which the contribution to consumption was nil? Similarly, pure consumption would be a limiting commodity in the opposite direction in which the contribution to work was nil, and intermediate commodities would contribute to both consumption and work. The more important the contribution to work relative to consumption, the smaller would tend to be the relative importance of forgone earnings. Consequently, the effects of changes in earnings, other income, etc., on hours worked then become assimilated to and essentially a special case of their effects on the consumption of less earnings-intensive commodities. For example, a pure rise in earnings would reduce the relative price, and thus increase the time spent on these commodities, *including the time spent at work*; similarly, for changes in income and other variables. The generalization wrought by our approach is even greater than may have appeared at first.

Before concluding this section a few other relevant implications of our theory might be briefly mentioned. Just as a (compensated) rise in earnings would increase the prices of commodities with relatively large forgone earnings, induce a substitution away from them, and increase the hours worked, so a (compensated) fall in market prices would also induce a substitution away from them and increase the hours worked: the effects of changes in direct and indirect costs are symmetrical. Indeed, Owen presents some evidence indicating that hours of work in the United States fell somewhat more in the first thirty years of this century than in the second thirty years, not because wages rose more during the first period, but because the market prices of recreation commodities fell more then.[28]

A well-known result of the traditional labor-leisure approach is that a rise in the income tax induces at least a substitution effect away from work and toward "leisure." Our approach reaches the same result only via a substitution toward time-intensive consumption rather than leisure. A simple additional implication of our approach, however, is that if a rise in the income tax were combined with an appropriate excise on the goods used in time-intensive commodities or subsidy to the goods used in other commodities there need be no change in full relative prices, and thus no substitution away from work. The traditional approach has recently reached the same conclusion, although in a much more involved way.[29]

There is no exception in the traditional approach to the rule that a pure rise in earnings would not induce a decrease in hours worked. An exception does occur in ours, for if the time and earnings intensities (i.e., $l_{i}t_{i}$ and t_{i}) were negatively correlated a pure rise in earnings would induce substitution toward time-intensive commodities, and thus away from work.[30] Although this exception does illustrate the greater power of our approach, there is no reason to believe that it is any more important empirically than the exception to the rule on income effects.

The Productivity of Time

Most of the large secular increase in earnings, which stimulated the development of the labor-leisure analysis, resulted from an increase in the productivity of working time due to the growth in human and physical capital, technological progress, and other factors. Since a rise in earnings resulting from an increase in productivity has both income and substitution effects, the secular decline in hours worked appeared to be evidence that the income effect was sufficiently strong to swamp the substitution effect.

The secular growth in capital and technology also improved the productivity of consumption time: supermarkets, automobiles, sleeping pills, safety and electric razors, and telephones are a few familiar and important examples of such developments. An improvement in the productivity of consumption time would change relative commodity prices and increase full income, which in turn would produce substitution and income effects. The interesting point is that a very different interpretation of the observed decline in hours of work is suggested because these effects are precisely the opposite of those produced by improvements in the productivity of working time.

Assume a uniform increase only in the productivity of consumption time, which is taken to mean a decline in all t_i, time required to produce a unit of Z_i, by a common percentage. The relative prices of commodities with large forgone earnings would fall, and substitution would be induced toward these and away from other commodities, causing hours of work also to fall. Since the increase in productivity would also produce an income effect,[31] the demand for commodities would increase, which, in turn, would induce an increased demand for goods. But since the productivity of working time is assumed not to change, more goods could be obtained only by an increase in work. That is, the higher real income resulting from an advance in the productivity of consumption time would cause hours of work to *increase*.

Consequently, an emphasis on the secular increase in the productivity of consumption time would lead to a very different interpretation of the secular decline in hours worked. Instead of claiming that a powerful income effect swamped a weaker substitution effect, the claim would have to be that a powerful substitution effect swamped a weaker income effect.

Of course, the productivity of both working and consumption time increased secularly, and the true interpretation is somewhere between these extremes. If both increased at the same rate there would be no change in relative prices, and thus no substitution effect, because the rise in l_i induced by one would exactly offset the decline in t_i induced by the other, marginal forgone earnings ($i_i t_i$) remaining unchanged. Although the income effects would tend to offset each other too, they would do so completely only if the income elasticity of demand for time-intensive commodities was equal to unity. Hours worked would decline if it was above and increase if it was below unity.[32] Since these commodities have probably on the whole been luxuries, such an increase in income would tend to reduce hours worked.

The productivity of working time has probably advanced more than that of consumption time, if only because of familiar reasons associated with the division of labor and economies of scale.[33] Consequently, there probably has been the traditional substitution effect toward and income effect away from work, as well as an income effect away from work because time-intensive commodities were luxuries. The secular decline in hours worked would only imply therefore that the combined income effects swamped the substitution effect, not that the income effect of an advance in the productivity of working time alone swamped its substitution effect.

Cross-sectionally, the hours worked of males have generally declined less as incomes increased than they have over time. Some of the difference between these relations is explained by the distinction between relevant and reported incomes, or by interdependencies among the hours worked by different employees;[34] some is probably also explained by the distinction between working and consumption productivity. There is a presumption that persons distinguished cross-sectionally by money incomes or earnings differ more in working than consumption productivity because they are essentially distinguished by the former. This argument does not apply to time series because persons are distinguished there by calendar time, which in principle is neutral between these productivities. Consequently, the traditional substitution effect toward work is apt to be greater cross-sectionally, which would help to explain why the relation between the income and hours worked of men is less negatively sloped there, and be additional evidence that the substitution effect for men is not weak.[35]

Productivity in the service sector in the United States appears to have advanced more slowly, at least since 1929, than productivity in the goods sector.[36] Service industries like retailing, transportation, education, and health use a good deal of the time of households that never enters into input, output, and price series, or therefore into measures of productivity. Incorporation of such time into the series and consideration of changes in its productivity would contribute, I believe, to an understanding of the apparent differences in productivity advance between these sectors.

An excellent example can be found in a recent study of productivity trends in the barbering industry in the United States.[37] Conventional productivity measures show relatively little advance in barbers' shops since 1929, yet a revolution has occurred in the activities performed by these shops. In the 1920s shaves still accounted for an important part of their sales, but declined to a negligible part by the 1950s because of the spread of home safety and electric razors. Instead of traveling to a shop, waiting in line, receiving a shave, and continuing to another destination, men now shave themselves at home, saving traveling, waiting, and even some shaving time. This considerable advance in the productivity of shaving nowhere enters measures for barbers' shops. If, however, a productivity measure for general barbering activities, including shaving, was constructed, I suspect that it would show an advance since 1929 comparable to most goods.[38]

Income Elasticities

Income elasticities of demand are often estimated cross-sectionally from the behavior of families or other units with different incomes. When these units buy in the same marketplace it is natural to assume that they face the same prices of goods. If, however, incomes differ because earnings do, and cross-section income differences are usually dominated by earnings differences, commodities prices would differ systematically. All commodities prices would be higher to higher-income units because their forgone earnings would be higher (which means, incidentally, that differences in real income would be less than those in money income), and the prices of earnings-intensive commodities would be unusually so.

Cross-sectional relations between consumption and income would not therefore measure the effect of income alone, because they would be affected by differences in relative prices as well as in incomes.[39] The effect of income would be underestimated for earnings-intensive and overestimated for other commodities, because the higher relative prices of the former would cause a substitution away from them and toward the latter. Accordingly, the income elasticities of demand for "leisure," unproductive and time-intensive commodities would be understated, and for "work," productive and other goods-intensive commodities overstated by cross-sectional estimates. Low apparent income elasticities of earnings-intensive commodities and high apparent elasticities of other commodities may simply be illusions resulting from substitution effects.[40]

Moreover, according to our theory demand depends also on the importance of earnings as a source of income. For if total income were held constant an increase in earnings would create only substitution effects: away from earnings-intensive and toward goods-intensive commodities. So one unusual implication of the analysis that can and should be tested with available budget data is that the source of income may have a significant effect on consumption patterns. An important special case is found in comparisons of the consumption of employed and unemployed workers. Unemployed workers not only have lower incomes but also lower forgone costs, and thus lower relative prices of time and other earnings-intensive commodities. The propensity of unemployed workers to go fishing, watch television, attend school, and so on are simply vivid illustrations of the incentives they have to substitute such commodities for others.

One interesting application of the analysis is to the relation between family size and income.[41] The traditional view, based usually on simple correlations, has been that an increase in income leads to a reduction in the number of children per family. If, however, birth control knowledge and other variables were held constant economic theory suggests a positive relation between family size and income, and therefore that the traditional negative correlation resulted from positive correlations between income, knowledge, and some other variables. The data I put together supported this interpretation, as did those found in several subsequent studies.[42]

Although positive, the elasticity of family size with respect to income is apparently quite low, even when birth control knowledge is held constant. Some persons have interpreted this (and other evidence) to indicate that family-size formation cannot usefully be fitted into traditional economic analysis.[43] It was pointed out, however, that the small elasticity found for children is not so inconsistent with what is found for goods as soon as quantity and quality income elasticities are distinguished.[44] Increased expenditures on many goods largely take the form of increased quality—expenditure per pound, per car, etc.—and the increase in quantity is modest. Similarly, increased expenditures on children largely take the form of increased expenditures per child, while the increase in number of children is very modest. Nevertheless, the elasticity of demand for number of children does seem somewhat smaller than the quantity elasticities found for many goods. Perhaps the explanation is simply the shape of indifference curves; one other factor that may be more important, however, is the increase in forgone costs with income.[45] Child care would seem to be a time-intensive activity that is not "productive" (in terms of earnings) and uses many hours that could be used at work. Consequently, it would be an earnings-intensive activity, and our analysis predicts that its relative price would be higher to higher-income families.[46] There is already some evidence suggesting that the positive relation between forgone costs and income explains why the apparent quantity income elasticity of demand for children is relatively small. Mincer found that cross-sectional differences in the forgone price of children have an important effect on the number of children.[47]

Transportation

Transportation is one of the few activities where the cost of time has been explicitly incorporated into economic discussions. In most benefit-cost evaluations of new transportation networks the value of the savings in transportation time has tended to overshadow other benefits.[48] The importance of the value placed on time has encouraged experiment with different methods of determination: from the simple view that the value of an hour equals average hourly earnings to sophisticated considerations of the distinction between standard and overtime hours, the internal and external margins, etc.

The transport field offers considerable opportunity to estimate the marginal productivity or value of time from actual behavior. One could, for example, relate the ratio of the number of persons traveling by airplane to those traveling by slower mediums to the distance traveled (and, of course, also to market prices and incomes). Since relatively more people use faster mediums for longer distances, presumably largely because of the greater importance of the saving in time, one should be able to estimate a marginal value of time from the relation between medium and distance traveled.[49]

Another transportation problem extensively studied is the length and mode of commuting to work.[50] It is usually assumed that direct commuting costs, such as train fare, vary positively and that living costs, such as space, vary negatively with the distance commuted. These assumptions alone would imply that a rise in incomes would result in longer commutes as long as space ("housing") were a superior good.[51]

A rise in income resulting at least in part from a rise in earnings would, however, increase the cost of commuting a given distance because the forgone value of the time involved would increase. This increase in commuting costs would discourage commuting in the same way that the increased demand for space would encourage it. The outcome depends on the relative strengths of these conflicting forces: one can show with a few assumptions that the distance commuted would increase as income increased if, and only if, space had an income elasticity greater than unity.

For let Z_1 refer to the commuting commodity, Z_2 to other commodities, and let

$$Z_1 = f_1(x, t) \qquad (22)$$

where t is the time spent commuting and x is the quantity of space used. Commuting costs are assumed to have the simple form $a + l_1t$, where a is a constant and l_1 is the marginal forgone cost per hour spent commuting. In other words, the cost of time is the only variable commuting cost. The cost per unit of space is $p(t)$, where by assumption $p' < 0$. The problem is to maximize the utility function

$$U = U(x, t, Z_2) \qquad (23)$$

subject to the resource constraint

$$a + l_1t + px + h(Z_2) = S \qquad (24)$$

If it were assumed that $U_t = 0$—commuting was neither enjoyable nor irksome—the main equilibrium condition would reduce to

$$l_1 + p'x = 0\,^{52} \qquad (25)$$

which would be the equilibrium condition if households simply attempt to maximize the sum of transportation and space costs.[53] If $l_1 = kS$, where k is a constant, the effect of a change in full income on the time spent commuting can be found by differentiating equation (25) to be

$$\frac{\partial t}{\partial S} = \frac{k(\epsilon_x - 1)}{p''x} \qquad (26)$$

where ϵ_x is the income elasticity of demand for space. Since stability requires that $p'' > 0$, an increase in income increases the time spent commuting if, and only if, $\epsilon_x > 1$.

In metropolitan areas of the United States higher-income families tend to live further from the central city,[54] which contradicts our analysis if one accepts the traditional view that the income elasticity of demand for housing is less than unity. In a definitive study of the demand for housing in the

United States, however, Margaret Reid found income elasticities greater than unity.[55] Moreover, the analysis of distance commuted incorporates only a few dimensions of the demand for housing; principally the demand for outdoor space. The evidence on distances commuted would then only imply that outdoor space is a "luxury," which is rather plausible[56] and not even inconsistent with the traditional view about the total elasticity of demand for housing.

The Division of Labor within Families

Space is too limited to do more than summarize the main implications of the theory concerning the division of labor among members of the same household. Instead of simply allocating time efficiently among commodities, multiperson households also allocate the time of different members. Members who are relatively more efficient at market activities would use less of their time at consumption activities than would other members. Moreover, an increase in the relative market efficiency of any member would effect a reallocation of the time of all other members toward consumption activities in order to permit the former to spend more time at market activities. In short, the allocation of the time of any member is greatly influenced by the opportunities open to other members.

IV. SUBSTITUTION BETWEEN TIME AND GOODS

Although time and goods have been assumed to be used in fixed proportions in producing commodities, substitution could take place because different commodities used them in different proportions. The assumption of fixed proportions is now dropped in order to include many additional implications of the theory.

It is well known from the theory of variable proportions that households would minimize costs by setting the ratio of the marginal product of goods to that of time equal to the ratio of their marginal costs.[57] A rise in the cost of time relative to goods would induce a reduction in the amount of time and an increase in the amount of goods used per unit of each commodity. Thus, not only would a rise in earnings induce a substitution away from earnings-intensive commodities but also a substitution away from time and towards goods in the production of each commodity. Only the first is (implicitly) recognized in the labor-leisure analysis, although the second may well be of considerable importance. It increases one's confidence that the substitution effect of a rise in earnings is more important than is commonly believed.

The change in the input coefficients of time and goods resulting from a change in their relative costs is defined by the elasticity of substitution between them, which presumably varies from commodity to commodity. The only empirical study of this elasticity assumes that recreation goods and "leisure" time are used to produce a recreation commodity.[58] Definite evidence of substitution is found, since the ratio of leisure time to recreation goods is negatively related to the ratio of their prices. The elasticity of substitution appears to be less than unity, however, since the share of leisure in total factor costs is apparently positively related to its relative price.

The incentive to economize on time as its relative cost increases goes a long way toward explaining certain broad aspects of behavior that have puzzled and often disturbed observers of contemporary life. Since hours worked have declined secularly in most advanced countries, and so-called leisure has presumably increased, a natural expectation has been that "free" time would become more abundant, and be used more "leisurely" and "luxuriously." Yet, if anything, time is used more carefully today than a century ago.[59] If there was a secular increase in the productivity of working time relative to consumption time (see Section III) there would be an increasing incentive to economize on the latter because of its greater expense (our theory emphatically cautions against calling such time "free"). Not surprisingly, therefore, it is now kept track of and used more carefully than in the past.

Americans are supposed to be much more wasteful of food and other goods than persons in poorer countries, and much more conscious of time: they keep track of it continuously, make (and keep) appointments for specific minutes, rush about more, cook steaks and chops rather than time-consuming stews, and so forth.[60] They are simultaneously supposed to be wasteful—of material goods—and overly economical—of immaterial time. Yet both allegations may be correct and not simply indicative of a strange American temperament because the market value of time is higher relative to the price of goods there than elsewhere. That is, the tendency to be economical about time and lavish about goods may be no paradox, but in part simply a reaction to a difference in relative costs.

The substitution toward goods induced by an increase in the relative cost of time would often include a substitution toward more expensive goods. For example, an increase in the value of a mother's time may induce her to enter the labor force and spend less time cooking by using precooked foods and less time on child care by using nurseries, camps, or baby-sitters. Or barbers' shops in wealthier sections of town charge more and provide quicker service than those in poorer sections, because waiting by barbers is substituted for waiting by customers. These examples illustrate that a change in the quality of goods[61] resulting from a change in the relative cost of goods may simply reflect a change in the methods used to produce given commodities, and not any corresponding change in their quality.

Consequently, a rise in income due to a rise in earnings would increase the quality of goods purchased not only because of the effect of income on quality but also because of a substitution of goods for time; a rise in income due to a rise in property income would not cause any substitution, and should have less effect on the quality of goods. Put more dramatically, with total income held constant, a rise in earnings should increase while a rise in property income should decrease the quality chosen. Once again, the composition of income is important and provides testable implications of the theory.

One analytically interesting application of these conclusions is to the recent study by Margaret Reid of the substitution between store-bought and home-delivered milk.[62] According to our approach, the cost of inputs into the commodity "milk consumption at home" is either the sum of the price of milk in the store and the forgone value of the time used to carry it home or simply the price of delivered milk. A reduction in the price of store relative to delivered milk, the value of time remaining constant, would reduce the cost of the first method relatively to the second, and shift production toward the first. For the same reason a reduction in the value of time, market prices of milk remaining constant, would also shift production toward the first method.

Reid's finding of a very large negative relation between the ratio of store to delivered milk and the ratio of their prices, income and some other variables held constant, would be evidence both that milk costs are a large part of total production costs and that there is easy substitution between these alternative methods of production. The large, but not quite as large, negative relation with income simply confirms the easy substitution between methods, and indicates that the cost of time is less important than the cost of milk. In other words, instead of conveying separate information, her price and income elasticities both measure substitution between the two methods of producing the same commodity, and are consistent and plausible.

The importance of forgone earnings and the substitution between time and goods may be quite relevant in interpreting observed price elasticities. A given percentage increase in the price of goods would be less of an increase in commodity prices the more important forgone earnings are. Consequently, even if all commodities had the same true price elasticity, those having relatively important forgone earnings would show lower apparent elasticities in the typical analysis that relates quantities and prices of goods alone.

The importance of forgone earnings differs not only among commodities but also among households for a given commodity because of differences in income. Its importance would change in the same or opposite direction as income, depending on whether the elasticity of substitution between time and goods was less or greater than unity. Thus, even when the true price elasticity of a commodity did not vary with income, the observed price elasticity of goods would be negatively or positively related to income as the elasticity of substitution was less or greater than unity.

The importance of substitution between time and goods can be illustrated in a still different way. Suppose, for simplicity, that only good x and no time was initially required to produce commodity Z. A price ceiling is placed on x, it nominally becomes a free good, and the production of x is subsidized sufficiently to maintain the same output. The increased quantity of x and Z demanded due to the decline in the price of x has to be rationed because the output of x has not increased. Suppose that the system of rationing made the quantity obtained a positive function of the time and effort expended. For example, the quantity of price-controlled bread or medical attention obtained might depend on the time spent in a queue outside a bakery or in a physician's office. Or if an appointment system were used a literal queue would be replaced by a figurative one, in which the waiting was done at "home," as in the Broadway theater, admissions to hospitals, or air travel during peak seasons. Again, even in depressed times the likelihood of obtaining a job is positively related to the time put into job hunting.

Although x became nominally a free good, Z would not be free, because the time now required as an input into Z is not free. The demand for Z would be greater than the supply (fixed by assumption) if the cost of this time was less than the equilibrium price of Z before the price control. The scrambling by households for the limited supply would increase the time required to get a unit of Z, and thus its cost. Both would continue to increase until the average cost of time tended to the equilibrium price before price control. At that point equilibrium would be achieved because the supply and demand for Z would be equal.

Equilibrium would take different forms depending on the method of rationing. With a literal "first come first served" system the size of the queue (say outside the bakery or in the doctor's office) would grow until the expected cost of standing in line discouraged any excess demand;[63] with the figurative queues of appointment systems, the "waiting" time (say to see a play) would grow until demand was sufficiently curtailed. If the system of rationing was less formal, as in the labor market during recessions, the expected time required to ferret out a scarce job would grow until the demand for jobs was curtailed to the limited supply.

Therefore, price control of x combined with a subsidy that kept its amount constant would not change the average private equilibrium price of Z,[64] but would substitute indirect time costs for direct goods costs.[65] Since, however, indirect costs are positively related to income, the price of Z would be raised to higher-income persons and reduced to lower-income ones, thereby redistributing consumption from the former to the latter. That is, women, the poor, children, the unemployed, etc., would be more willing to spend their time in a queue or otherwise ferreting out rationed goods than would high-earning males.

V. SUMMARY AND CONCLUSIONS

This paper has presented a theory of the allocation of time between different activities. At the heart of the theory is an assumption that households are producers as well as consumers; they produce commodities by combining inputs of goods and time according to the cost-minimization rules of the traditional theory of the firm. Commodities are produced in quantities determined by maximizing a utility function of the commodity set subject to prices and a constraint on resources. Resources are measured by what is called full income, which is the sum of money income and that forgone or "lost" by the use of time and goods to obtain utility, while commodity prices are measured by the sum of the costs of their goods and time inputs.

The effect of changes in earnings, other income, goods prices, and the productivity of working and consumption time on the allocation of time and the commodity set produced has been analyzed. For example, a rise in earnings, compensated by a decline in other income so that full income would be unchanged, would induce a decline in the amount of time used at consumption activities, because time would become more expensive. Partly goods would be substituted for the more expensive time in the production of each commodity, and partly goods-intensive commodities would be substituted for the more expensive time-intensive ones. Both substitutions require less time to be used at consumption, and permit more to be used at work. Since the reallocation of time involves simultaneously a reallocation of goods and commodities, all three decisions become intimately related.

The theory has many interesting and even novel interpretations of, and implications about, empirical phenomena. A few will be summarized here.

A traditional "economic" interpretation of the secular decline in hours worked has stressed the growth in productivity of working time and the resulting income and substitution effects, with the former supposedly dominating. Ours stresses that the substitution effects of the growth in productivity of working and consumption time tended to offset each other, and that hours worked declined secularly primarily because time-intensive commodities have been luxuries. A contributing influence has been the secular decline in the relative prices of goods used in time-intensive commodities.

Since an increase in income partly due to an increase in earnings would raise the relative cost of time and of time-intensive commodities, traditional cross-sectional estimates of income elasticities do not hold either factor or commodity prices constant. Consequently, they would, among other things, be biased downward for time-intensive commodities, and give a misleading impression of the effect of income on the quality of commodities consumed. The composition of income also affects demand, for an increase in earnings, total income held constant, would shift demand away from time-intensive commodities and input combinations.

Rough estimates suggest that forgone earnings are quantitatively important and therefore that full income is substantially above money income. Since forgone earnings are primarily determined by the use of time, considerably more attention should be paid to its efficiency and allocation. In particular, agencies that collect information on the expenditure of money income might simultaneously collect information on the "expenditure" of time. The resulting time budgets, which have not been seriously investigated in most countries, including the United States and Great Britain, should be integrated with the money budgets in order to give a more accurate picture of the size and allocation of full income.

NOTES

1. See T. W. Schultz, "The Formation of Human Capital by Education," *Journal of Political Economy* (December 1960), and my *Human Capital* (Columbia University Press for the NBER, 1964), chapter IV. I argue there that the importance of forgone earnings can be directly seen, e.g., from the failure of free tuition to eliminate impediments to college attendance or the increased enrollments that sometimes occur in depressed areas or time periods.

2. On the cause of the secular trend toward an increased school year see my comments, ibid., p. 103.

3. See his "Market Prices, Opportunity Costs, and Income Effects," in *Measurement in Economics: Studies in Mathematical Economics and Econometrics in Memory of Yehuda Grunfeld* (Stanford University Press, 1963). In his well-known earlier study Mincer considered the allocation of married women between "housework" and labor force participation. (See his "Labor Force Participation of Married Women," in *Aspects of Labor Economics* [Princeton University Press, 1962].)

4. See his "The Supply of Labor and the Demand for Recreation" (Ph.D. dissertation, Columbia University, 1964)

5. See his "Economic Analysis and African Response to Price" (Ph.D. dissertation, Columbia University, 1963).

6. Let me emphasize, however, that I alone am responsible for any errors.

I would also like to express my appreciation for the comments received when presenting these ideas to seminars at the Universities of California (Los Angeles), Chicago, Pittsburgh, Rochester and Yale, and to a session at the 1963 Meetings of the Econometric Society. Extremely helpful comments on an earlier draft were provided by Milton Friedman and by Gregory C. Chow; the latter also assisted in the mathematical formulation. Linda Kee provided useful research assistance. My research was partially supported by the IBM Corporation.

7. There are several empirical as well as conceptual advantages in assuming that households combine goods and time to produce commodities instead of simply assuming that the amount of time used at an activity is a direct function of the amount of goods consumed. For example, a change in the cost of goods relative to time could cause a significant substitution away from the one rising in relative cost. This, as well as other applications, are treated in the following sections.

8. If a good or time period was used in producing several commodities I assume that these "joint costs" could be fully and uniquely allocated among the commodities. The problems here are no different from those usually arising in the analysis of multi-product firms.

9. See, e.g., A. K. Cairncross. "Economic Schizophrenia," *Scottish Journal of Political Economy* (February 1958).

10. The dependency among constraints distinguishes this problem from many other multiple-constraint situations in economic analysis, such as those arising in the usual theory of rationing (see J. Tobin, "A Survey of the Theory of Rationing," *Econometrica* [October 1952]). Rationing would reduce to a formally identical single-constraint situation if rations were salable and fully convertible into money income.

11. See my *Human Capital*, op. cit.

12. This term emerged from a conversation with Milton Friedman.

13. Any utility received would only be an incidental by-product of the pursuit of money income. Perhaps this explains why utility analysis was not clearly formulated and accepted until economic development had raised incomes well above the subsistence level.

14. Full income is achieved by maximizing the earnings function

$$W = W(Z_1, \ldots Z_m) \qquad (1')$$

subject to the expenditure constraint in equation (6), to the inequality

$$\sum_1^m T_1 \leq T \qquad (2')$$

and to the restrictions in (8). I assume for simplicity that the amount of each dimension of time used in producing commodities is less than the total available, so that (2') can be ignored; it is not difficult to incorporate this constraint. Maximizing (1') subject to (6) and (8) yields the following conditions

$$\frac{\partial W}{\partial Z_i} = \frac{p_i b_i \sigma}{1 + \sigma} \tag{3'}$$

where σ is the marginal productivity of money income. Since the loss function $L = (S - V) - W$, the equilibrium conditions to minimize the loss are the same as (3') except for a change in sign.

15. Households maximize their utility subject only to the single total resource constraint given by (14), for once the full income constraint is satisfied, there is no other restriction on the set of Z_i that can be chosen. By introducing the concept of full income the problem of maximizing utility subject to the time and goods constraints is solved in two stages: first, full income is determined from the goods and time constraints, and then utility is maximized subject only to the constraint imposed by full income.

16. It can easily be shown that the equilibrium conditions of (16) are in fact precisely the same as those following in general from equation (10).

17. Elsewhere I have discussed some effects of the allocation of goods on productivity (see my "Investment in Human Capital: A Theoretical Analysis," *Journal of Political Economy*, special supplement [October 1962], Section 2); essentially the same discussion can be found in *Human Capital*, op. cit., Chapter II.

18. The problem is: under what conditions would

$$\frac{-\partial T_w}{\partial V} = \frac{\partial T_e}{\partial V} = \sum t_i \frac{\partial Z_i}{\partial V} < 0 \tag{1'}$$

when

$$\sum (p_i b_i + l_i t_i) \frac{\partial Z_i}{\partial V} = 1 \tag{2'}$$

If the analysis were limited to a two-commodity world where Z_1 was more time-intensive, then it can be easily shown that (1') would hold if, and only if,

$$\frac{\partial Z_1}{\partial V} < \frac{-\gamma_2}{(\gamma_1 - \gamma_2)(p_1 b_1 + l_1 t_1)} < 0 \tag{3'}$$

19. By a uniform change of β is meant

$$W_1 = (1 + \beta) W_0 (Z_1, \ldots Z_n)$$

where W_0 represents the earnings function before the change and W_1 represents it afterward. Since the loss function is defined as

$$L = S - W - V$$
$$= W(\hat{Z}) - W(Z),$$

then

$$L_1 = W_1(\hat{Z}) - W_1(Z)$$
$$= (1 + \beta) [W_0(\hat{Z}) - W_0(Z)] = (1 + \beta) L_0$$

Consequently, all opportunity costs also change by β.

20. According to the definitions of earning and time intensity in equations (20) and (21), they would be positively correlated unless l_i and t_i were sufficiently negatively correlated. See the further discussion later on.

21. Let it be stressed that this conclusion usually holds, even when households are irrational; sophisticated calculations about the value of time at work or in consumption, or substantial knowledge about the amount of time used by different commodities is not required. Changes in the hours of work, even of nonmaximizing, impulsive, habitual, etc., households would tend to be positively related to compensated changes in earnings because demand curves tend to be negatively inclined even for such households (see G. S. Becker, "Irrational Behavior and Economic Theory," *Journal of Political Economy* [February 1962]).

22. Suppose there were two commodities Z_1 and Z_2, where the cost of Z_1 depended only on the cost of market goods, while the cost of Z_2 depended only on the cost of time. The goods-budget constraint would then simply be

$$p_1 b_1 Z_1 = I = V + T_w \bar{w}$$

and the constraint on time would be

$$t_2 Z_2 = T - T_w$$

This is essentially the algebra of the analysis presented by Henderson and Quandt, and their treatment is representative. They call Z_2 "leisure," and Z_1 an average of different commodities. Their equilibrium condition that the rate of substitution between goods and leisure equals the real wage rate is just a special case of our equation (19) (see *Microeconomic Theory* [New York: McGraw-Hill, 1958], p. 23).

23. For workers receiving premium pay on the weekends and in the evenings, however, the cost of time may be considerably greater then.

24. See the advertisement by the United States Lines in various issues of the *New Yorker* magazine: "The S.S. *United States* regularly includes a weekend in its 5 days to Europe, saving [economic] time for businessmen" (my insertion).

25. For example, *Webster's Collegiate Dictionary* defines leisurely as "characterized by leisure, taking *abundant time*" (my italics); or S. de Grazia, in his recent *Of Time, Work and Leisure*, says, "Leisure is a state of being in which activity is performed for its own sake or as its own end" (New York: The Twentieth Century Fund, 1962, p. 15).

26. S. de Grazia has recently entertainingly shown the many difficulties in even reaching a reliable definition and, a fortiori, in quantitatively estimating the amount of leisure. See ibid., chapters III and IV; also see W. Moore, *Man, Time and Society* (New York: Wiley, 1963), chapter II; J. N. Morgan, M. H. David, W. J. Cohen and H. E. Brazer, *Income and Welfare in the United States* (New York: McGraw-Hill, 1962), p. 322, and Owen, op. cit., chapter II.

27. Sometimes true leisure is defined as the amount of discretionary time available (see Moore, op. cit., p. 18). It is always difficult to attach a rigorous meaning to the word "discretionary" when referring to economic resources. One might say that in

the short run consumption time is and working time is not discretionary, because the latter is partially subject to the authoritarian control of employers. (Even this distinction would vanish if households gave certain firms authoritarian control over their consumption time; see the discussion in Section II.) In the long run this definition of discretionary time is suspect too because the availability of alternative sources of employment would make working time also discretionary.

28. See op. cit., chapter VIII. Recreation commodities presumably have relatively large forgone earnings.

29. See W. J. Corbett and D. C. Hague, "Complementarity and the Excess Burden of Taxation," *Review of Economic Studies* 21 (1953–54); also A. C. Harberger, "Taxation, Resource Allocation and Welfare," in the *Role of Direct and Indirect Taxes in the Federal Reserve System* (Princeton University Press, 1964).

30. The effect on earnings is more difficult to determine because, by assumption, time-intensive commodities have smaller costs per unit time than other commodities. A shift toward the former would, therefore, raise hourly earnings, which would partially and perhaps more than entirely offset the reduction in hours worked. Incidentally, this illustrates how the productivity of hours worked is influenced by the consumption set chosen.

31. Full money income would be unaffected if it were achieved by using all time at pure work activities. If other uses of time were also required it would tend to increase. Even if full money income were unaffected, however, full real income would increase because prices of the Z_i would fall.

32. So the "Knight" view that an increase in income would increase "leisure" is not necessarily true, even if leisure were a superior good and even aside from Robbins's emphasis on the substitution effect (see L. Robbins, "On the Elasticity of Demand for Income in Terms of Effort," *Economica* [June 1930]).

33. Wesley Mitchell's justly famous essay "The Backward Art of Spending Money" spells out some of these reasons (see the first essay in the collection, *The Backward Art of Spending Money and Other Essays* [New York: McGraw-Hill, 1932]).

34. A. Finnegan does find steeper cross-sectional relations when the average incomes and hours of different occupations are used (see his "A Cross-Sectional Analysis of Hours of Work," *Journal of Political Economy* [October 1962]).

35. Note that Mincer has found a very strong substitution effect for women (see his "Labor Force Participation of Married Women," op. cit.).

36. See the essay by Victor Fuchs, "Productivity Trends in the Goods and Service Sectors, 1929–61: A Preliminary Survey," NBER Occasional Paper, October 1964.

37. See J. Wilburn, "Productivity Trends in Barber and Beauty Shops," mimeographed report, NBER, September 1964.

38. The movement of shaving from barbers' shops to households illustrates how and why even in urban areas households have become "small factories." Under the impetus of the general growth in the value of time they have been encouraged to find

ways of saving on traveling and waiting time by performing more activities themselves.

39. More appropriate income elasticities for several commodities are estimated in Mincer, "Market Prices," op. cit.

40. In this connection note that cross-sectional data are often preferred to time-series data in estimating income elasticities precisely because they are supposed to be largely free of colinearity between prices and incomes (see, e.g., J. Tobin, "A Statistical Demand Function for Food in the U.S.A.," *Journal of Royal Statistical Society*, Series A [1950]).

41. Biases in cross-sectional estimates of the demand for work and leisure were considered in the last section.

42. See G. S. Becker, "An Economic Analysis of Fertility," *Demographic and Economic Change in Developed Countries* (NBER Conference Volume, 1960); R. A. Easterlin, "The American Baby Boom in Historical Perspective," *American Economic Review* (December 1961); I. Adelman, "An Econometric Analysis of Population Growth," *American Economic Review* (June 1963); R. Weintraub, "The Birth Rate and Economic Development: An Empirical Study," *Econometrica* (October 1962); Morris Silver, "Birth Rate, Marriages, and Business Cycles" (Ph.D. dissertation, Columbia University, 1964); and several other studies; for an apparent exception, see the note by D. Freedman, "The Relation of Economic Status to Fertility," *American Economic Review* (June 1963).

43. See for example, Duesenberry's comment on Becker, op. cit.

44. See Becker, op. cit.

45. In ibid., p. 214 fn. 8, the relations between forgone costs and income was mentioned but not elaborated.

46. Other arguments suggesting that higher-income families face a higher price of children have generally confused price with quality (see ibid., pp. 214–15).

47. See Mincer, "Market Prices," *op. cit.*. He measures the price of children by the wife's potential wage rate, and fits regressions to various cross-sectional data, where number of children is the dependent variable, and family income and the wife's potential wage rate are among the independent variables.

48. See, for example, H. Mohring, "Land Values and the Measurement of Highway Benefits," *Journal of Political Economy* (June 1961).

49. The only quantitative estimate of the marginal value of time that I am familiar with uses the relation between the value of land and its commuting distance from employment (see ibid.). With many assumptions I have estimated the marginal value of time of those commuting at about 40 percent of their average hourly earnings. It is not clear whether this value is so low because of errors in these assumptions or because of severe kinks in the supply and demand functions for hours of work.

50. See L. N. Moses and H. F. Williamson, "Value of Time, Choice of Mode, and the Subsidy Issue in Urban Transportation," *Journal of Political Economy* (June 1963), R. Muth, "Economic Change and Rural-Urban Conversion," *Econometrica* (January

1961), and J. F. Kain, *Commuting and the Residential Decisions of Chicago and Detroit Central Business District Workers* (April 1963).

51. See Muth, op. cit.

52. If $U_t \neq 0$, the main equilibrium condition would be

$$\frac{U_t}{U_x} = \frac{l_1 + p'x}{p}$$

Probably the most plausible assumption is that $U_t < 0$, which would imply that $l_1 + p'_x < 0$.

53. See Kain, op. cit., pp. 6–12.

54. For a discussion, including many qualifications, of this proposition see L. F. Schnore, "The Socio-Economic Status of Cities and Suburbs," *American Sociological Review* (February 1963).

55. See her *Housing and Income* (University of Chicago Press, 1962), p. 6 and passim.

56. According to Reid, the elasticity of demand for indoor space is less than unity (ibid., chapter 12). If her total elasticity is accepted this suggests that outdoor space has an elasticity exceeding unity.

57. The cost of producing a given amount of commodity Z_i would be minimized if

$$\frac{\partial f_i/\partial x_i}{\partial f_i/\partial T_i} = \frac{P_i}{\partial L/\partial T_i}$$

If utility were considered an indirect function of goods and time rather than simply a direct function of commodities the following conditions, among others, would be required to maximize utility:

$$\frac{\partial U/\partial x_i}{\partial U/\partial T_i} \equiv \frac{\partial Z_i/\partial x_i}{\partial Z_i/\partial T_i} = \frac{p_i}{\partial L/\partial T}$$

which are exactly the same conditions as above. The ratio of the marginal utility of x_i to that of T_i depends only on f_i, x_i, and T_i, and is thus independent of other production functions, goods, and time. In other words, the indirect utility function is what has been called "weakly separable" (see R. Muth, "Household Production and Consumer Demand Functions," unpublished manuscript).

58. See Owen, op. cit., chapter X.

59. See, for example, de Grazia, op. cit., chapter IV.

60. For a comparison of the American concept of time with others see Edward T. Hall, *The Silent Language* (New York: Doubleday, 1959), chapter 9.

61. Quality is usually defined empirically by the amount spent per physical unit, such as pound of food, car, or child. See especially S. J. Prais and H. Houthakker, *The Analysis of Family Budgets* (Cambridge, 1955); also my "An Economic Analysis of Fertility," op. cit.

62. See her "Consumer Response to the Relative Price of Store versus Delivered Milk," *Journal of Political Economy* (April 1963).

63. In queueing language the cost of waiting in line is a "discouragement" factor that stabilizes the queueing scheme (see, for example, D. R. Cox and W. L. Smith, *Queues* [New York: Wiley 1961]).

64. The social price, on the other hand, would be double, for it is the sum of private indirect costs and subsidized direct costs.

65. Time costs can be criticized from a Pareto optimality point of view because they often result in external diseconomies; e.g., a person joining a queue would impose costs on subsequent joiners. The diseconomies are real, not simply pecuniary, because time is a cost to demanders, but is not revenue to suppliers.

MARKET INSURANCE, SELF-INSURANCE, AND SELF-PROTECTION

Isaac Ehrlich
Gary S. Becker

· 5 ·

*The article develops a theory of demand for insurance that em-
phasizes the interaction between market insurance, "self-insurance," and "self-protection." The effects of changes in "prices,"
income, and other variables on the demand for these alternative
forms of insurance are analyzed using the "state preference"
approach to behavior under uncertainty. Market insurance and
self-insurance are shown to be substitutes, but market insurance
and self-protection can be complements. The analysis challenges
the notion that "moral hazard" is an inevitable consequence of
market insurance, by showing that under certain conditions the
latter may lead to a reduction in the probabilities of hazardous
events.*

The incentive to insure and its behavioral implications have usually been
analyzed by applying the expected utility approach without reference to the
indifference curve analysis ordinarily employed in consumption theory. In
this paper insurance is discussed by combining expected utility and an indifference curve analysis within the context of the "state preference" approach

First published in the *Journal of Political Economy* 80, no. 4 (July–August 1972): 623–48. ©
1972 by the University of Chicago. All rights reserved.

to behavior under uncertainty (the preferences in question relating to states of the world).[1] We use this framework to restate and reinterpret in a simpler and more intuitive way some familiar propositions concerning insurance behavior; more important, we derive a number of apparently new results, especially those concerned with self-insurance and self-protection. Our approach separates objective opportunities from "taste" and other environmental factors, which facilitates an independent investigation of each class of factors analytically as well as empirically. In addition, we consider not only the incentive to insure, but also how much insurance is purchased under varying "opportunities"[2] and in view of the existence of the alternatives of self-insurance and self-protection. We use the basic analytical tools employed throughout traditional consumption and production theory.

It has been argued that insurance is different from "ordinary" goods and services because it is not desired per se, but as a means of satisfying more basic needs.[3] Recent developments in consumption theory[4] suggest, however, that the distinction between goods and services purchased in the market and more basic needs they satisfy is not a unique characteristic of insurance, but applies to all goods and services. The demand for the latter is also derived from the needs they satisfy, just as the demand for factors of production in ordinary production theory is derived from their contribution to final products.

The basic needs underlying the purchase of insurance will be identified with consumption opportunities contingent upon the occurrence of various mutually exclusive and jointly exhaustive "states of the world."[5] Market insurance in this approach redistributes income and, consequently, consumption opportunities, toward the less well-endowed states. Self-insurance, however, redistributes income similarly, self-protection has a related effect, and either might be pursued when market insurance was not available. Moreover, optimal decisions about market insurance depend on the availability of these other activities and should be viewed within the context of a more comprehensive "insurance" decision.

The first part of this paper spells out a model of market insurance and discusses the effects of changes in terms of trade, "income," and other environmental factors on optimal insurance decisions. Self-insurance, self-protection, and a simultaneous determination of the full insurance decision are then discussed in the second and more original part.

FIGURE I

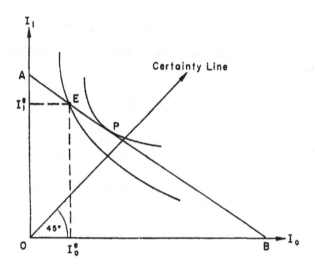

I. Market Insurance

We assume for simplicity that an individual is faced with only two states of the world (0, 1) with probabilities p and $1 - p$, respectively, and that his real income endowment in each state is given with certainty by I_0^ε and I_1^ε where $I_1^\varepsilon - I_0^\varepsilon$ is the prospective loss if state 0 occurs. If income in state 1 can be exchanged for income in state 0 at the fixed rate

$$- \frac{dI_1}{dI_0} = \pi \,, \tag{1}$$

π can be called the "price of insurance" measured in terms of income in state 1. The amount of insurance purchased in state 0 can be defined as the difference between the actual and endowed incomes:[6]

$$s = I_0 - I_0^\varepsilon \,. \tag{2}$$

The expenditure on insurance measured in terms of state 1's income is

$$b = I_1^\varepsilon - I_1 = s\pi \,. \tag{3}$$

Substituting (2) in (3) gives the opportunity boundary

$$I_1^\varepsilon - I_1 = \pi(I_0 - I_0^\varepsilon) \,, \tag{4}$$

or the line $\overline{AB}$ in figure 1.[7] It is assumed that the individual chooses the optimal income in states 1 and 0 by maximizing the expected utility of the income prospect,

$$U^* = (1 - p) U(I_1) + pU(I_0),[8] \qquad (5)$$

subject to the constraint given by the opportunity boundary. The first-order optimality condition is

$$\pi = \frac{pU_0'}{(1-p)U_1'}, \qquad (6)$$

where $(pU_0')/(1-p)U_1'$ is the slope of the indifference curve (defined along $dU^* = 0$), and π is the slope of the budget line. In equilibrium, they must be the same (see point P).

One can more completely separate tastes from environmental factors by dividing $p/(1 - p)$ through in (6) to obtain

$$\overline{\pi} = \frac{1-p}{p}\pi = \frac{U_0'}{U_1'}. \qquad (7)$$

Further, $\overline{\pi}$, the price of insurance deflated by the actuarially "fair"[9] price, $p/(1 - p)$, is a measure of the "real" price of insurance because a fair price is "costless" to the individual (see the second paragraph below). Equation (7) thus implies that, in equilibrium, the real price of insurance equals the ratio of the marginal utility of I_0 to that of I_1, the ordinary result in consumer demand theory.

The second-order condition requires that the indifference curve be convex to the origin at the equilibrium point, or

$$D = -pU_0'' - \pi^2(1-p) U_1'' > 0. \qquad (8)$$

A sufficient condition is that the marginal utility of income is strictly declining.[10]

An immediate implication of equation (7) is that insurance would be demanded—some I_1 would be traded for I_0—if the slope of the indifference curve exceeded the price of insurance at the endowment point, E:

$$\overline{\pi} < \frac{U'(I_0^e)}{U'(I_1^e)}. \qquad (9)$$

If the opposite were true, "gambling" would be demanded, provided similar terms of trade apply in redistributions of income toward state 1. Note that gambling can occur without increasing marginal utility of income if the opportunities available are sufficiently favorable. Therefore, inferences about attitudes toward risk cannot be made independently of existing market opportunities: a person may appear to be a "risk avoider" under one combination of prices and potential losses and a "risk taker" under another.[11]

If the price of insurance were actuarially fair, equation (7) would reduce to $1 = U_0'/U_1'$: incomes would be equalized in both states of the world if the marginal utility of income were always diminishing. This is "full insurance" in the sense that a person would be indifferent as to which state occurred.[12] In particular, for small changes around the equilibrium position, he would act as if he were indifferent toward risk and interested only in maximizing his expected income. Indeed, his income in each state would equal his expected income;[13] therefore, fair insurance can be regarded as costless to him.[14]

Substitution Effects

The effect of an exogenous increase in the price of insurance on the demand for I_0, with the probability of loss and the initial endowment being the same, can be found by partially differentiating the first-order optimality condition with respect to π:

$$\frac{\partial I_0}{\partial \pi} = \frac{1}{D} [-(1-p) U_1' + (I_0 - I_0^\varepsilon) \pi (1-p) U_{11}''] . \tag{10}$$

Since the denominator D has already been shown to be positive, the sign of equation (10) is the same as the sign of the numerator, or negative if $I_0 > I_0^\varepsilon$, since we are assuming $U_{11}'' < 0$. An increase in the relative cost of income in state 0 necessarily decreases the demand for income in this state. Moreover, it also reduces the amount of insurance purchased, since I_0^ε remains unchanged: $\partial s/\partial \pi = \partial I_0/\partial \pi - \partial I_0^\varepsilon/\partial \pi = \partial I_0/\partial \pi$.

Similarly, the effect of an increase in π on I_1, and thus on the amount spent on insurance, is

$$\frac{\partial I_1}{\partial \pi} = \frac{1}{D} [(1-p) U_1' \pi + (I_0 - I_0^\varepsilon) p U_0''] . \tag{11}$$

Here the result is ambiguous since U_1' is positive whereas

$$(I_0 - I_0^\varepsilon) p U_0'' = s p U_0''$$

is negative if $U_0'' < 0$ and $s > 0$. The result is ambiguous because, although an increase in π reduces the amount of insurance purchased, each unit purchased becomes more expensive. Consequently, the amount spent on insurance would decline only if the price elasticity of demand for insurance exceeded unity[15] (a proof is obvious).

Equations (10) and (11) do not isolate a "pure" substitution effect because an increase in π lowers the opportunities available (if $s > 0$). If both

FIGURE 2

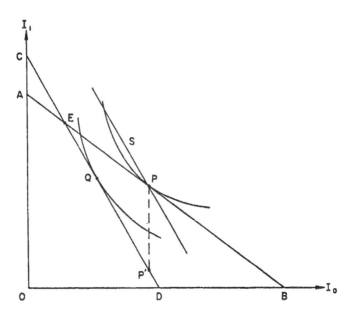

I_1 and I_0 are superior goods, the income and substitution effects both reduce the demand for I_0, whereas they have opposite effects on the demand for I_1. Diagrammatically, as the opportunity boundary changes from $\overline{AB}$ to $\overline{CD}$ (see fig. 2), the equilibrium point shifts from P to Q. If I_0 were a superior good, Q must be to the left of P'. Even if I_0 were an inferior good, however, a "pure" (that is, expenditure-compensated) increase in the terms of trade must always reduce the demand for I_0 and increase I_1: the equilibrium must shift from P to a point to its left, like S.

Income Effects

Equation (4) can be written as

$$I_1^\varepsilon + \pi I_0^\varepsilon = W = I_1 + \pi I_0, \qquad (12)$$

where W is a measure of the total opportunities available. (This is shown in fig. 1 by the intercept $\overline{OA}$ on the I_1 axis.) The effect of a change in the endowments on the income demanded in each state can be determined by differentiating the first-order condition:

$$\frac{\partial I_0}{\partial W} = \frac{\partial I_0}{\partial I_0^\varepsilon} = \frac{\partial I_0}{\partial I_1^\varepsilon}\frac{\partial I_0^\varepsilon}{\partial W} = -\frac{D_{31}}{D}$$

$$\frac{\partial I_1}{\partial W} = \frac{\partial I_1}{\partial I_0^\varepsilon} = \frac{\partial I_1}{\partial I_1^\varepsilon}\frac{\partial I_0^\varepsilon}{\partial W} = -\frac{D_{32}}{D}$$
(13)

where $D_{31} = \pi(1-p)U_1''$, and $D_{32} = pU_0''$. The income demanded in each state necessarily increases with opportunities if the marginal utility of income is falling. Hence, an increase in each state's endowment increases the demand for income in other states as well. The effects on the demand for insurance are more complicated, however, since they depend on how different endowments change. For example, if I_1^ε alone increased,

$$\frac{\partial s}{\partial I_1^\varepsilon} = \frac{\partial I_0}{\partial I_1^\varepsilon} > 0,$$
(14)

and the demand for insurance would increase. Similarly, if I_0^ε alone increased,

$$\frac{\partial s}{\partial I_0^\varepsilon} = \frac{\partial I_0}{\partial I_0^\varepsilon} - 1 < 0,[16]$$
(15)

and the demand for insurance would decrease. Equations (14) and (15) imply that if the difference in endowed income—the endowed loss from the hazard—increased either because I_0^ε decreased or I_1^ε increased, the demand for insurance would increase. Put differently, a person would be more likely to insure large rather than small losses (see Lees and Rice 1965).[17] The effects of a change in total opportunities on the demand for insurance cannot be derived without knowledge of the way opportunities change essentially because insurance is a "residual" that bridges the gap between endowed and desired levels of income in different states of the world.[18]

For example, if both endowments (and hence the size of the loss) are changed by the same percentage, then

$$(\epsilon_s W - 1) = \frac{I_0}{s}(\eta_0 - 1),$$
(16)

where $\epsilon_{sw} = \partial s/\partial W \cdot W/s$ and $\eta_0 = \partial I_0/\partial W \cdot W/I_0$ are the opportunity elasticities of demand for s and I_0, respectively.[19]

Equation (16) incorporates the rather obvious conclusion that the effect of a change in opportunities on the demand for insurance depends on the effects on the income demanded in each state. If the slopes of the indifference curves are constant along a given ray from the origin (the indifference curves are like EPF and GQ_1H in fig. 3)—there is constant relative risk aversion[20]—then all equilibrium positions lie on a given ray from the origin, as P and Q_1 do in figure 3, and $\eta_0 = \eta_1 = 1$. An equal proportional increase in all

FIGURE 3

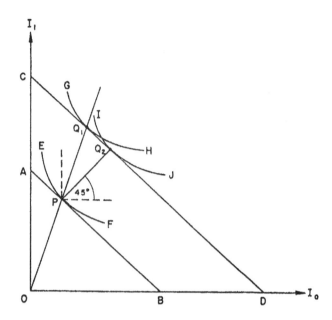

endowments would then increase the demand for insurance by the same proportion. If the slopes of the indifference curves increase along a given ray from the origin, as shown by EPF and IQ_2J in figure 3, there is increasing relative risk aversion, and η_0 and thus ϵ_{sW} would exceed unity. Increasing relative risk aversion implies that the elasticity of substitution between I_0 and I_1 tends to decline as opportunities increase.[21] Regardless of the shape of preferences elsewhere in the preference space, however, relative (and absolute) risk aversion remains constant along the certainty line. This constancy always characterizes choices when the price of insurance is actuarially fair (see fig. 4).

Rare Losses

An inspection of the necessary conditions for insurance given in equation (9) shows that changes in p, the probability of loss, do not affect the incentive to insure as long as the real price of insurance is independent of p. If insurance were actuarially fair, the real price would always equal unity, and thus would be independent of p.

The deviation from a fair price, or the "loading" in insurance terminology, can be defined from the identity

FIGURE 4

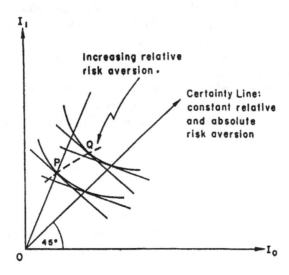

$$\pi \equiv \frac{(1+\lambda)p}{1-p}, \tag{17}$$

where λ is the "loading factor." If λ were independent of p, so also would be the real price of insurance and p would have no effect on the incentive to insure. In particular, there would *not* then be a greater incentive to insure "rare" losses of a given size.[22]

Since, apparently, rare losses are more frequently insured,[23] λ is presumably positively related to p, perhaps because processing and investigating costs increase as p increases.[24] (An alternative explanation is provided by the interaction between market and self-insurance analyzed in the next section.) Even if the *incentive* to insure were independent of p, the *amount* insured would decline and the expenditure on insurance would increase as p increased.[25]

II. Self-Insurance and Self-Protection

Two alternatives to market insurance that have not been systematically analyzed in the literature on insurance are self-insurance—a reduction in the size of a loss—and self-protection—a reduction in the probability of a loss.[26] For example, sprinkler systems reduce the loss from fires; burglar alarms reduce the probability of illegal entry; cash balances reduce fluctuations in consumption; medicines, certain foods, and medical checkups reduce vulnerability to illness; and good lawyers reduce both the probability of conviction and the punishment for crime. As these examples indicate, it is somewhat artificial to distinguish behavior that reduces the probability of a loss from behavior that reduces the size of a loss, since many actions do both. Nevertheless, we do so for expository convenience and because self-insurance clearly illustrates the insurance principle of redistributing income toward less favorable states.

Self-Insurance

Assume that market insurance is unavailable and write the loss to a person as $L = L(L^e, c)$, where $L^e = I_1^e - I_0^e$ is the endowed loss, c is the expenditure on self-insurance, and $\dfrac{\partial L}{\partial c} = L'(c) \leq 0$. The expected utility can be written as

$$U^* = (1 - p) U(I_1^e - c) + pU(I_1^e - L(L^e, c) - c).^{27} \qquad (18)$$

The value of c that maximizes equation (18), c^0, satisfies the first-order condition

$$-\frac{1}{L'(c^0) + 1} = \frac{pU_0'}{(1 - p) U_1'}. \qquad (19)$$

This maximizes expected utility if the marginal utility of income and the marginal productivity of self-insurance are decreasing, that is, if the indifference curves are convex and if the production transformation curve between income in states 1 and 0 (TN in fig. 5) is concave to the origin.[28] A necessary condition for a positive amount of self-insurance obviously is $-L'(c^0) > 1$, or that there be a net addition to income in state 0. A sufficient condition, if the transformation and indifference curves do not have kinks, is that

$$-\frac{1}{L'(L^e, 0) + 1} < \frac{pU'(I_0^e)}{(1 - p)U'(I_1^e)}.^{29} \qquad (20)$$

An increase in the unit cost of self-insurance, measured by the marginal productivity of self-insurance, would reduce the demand for self-insurance, measured by c^0:[30]

FIGURE 5

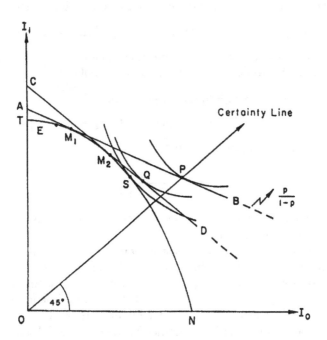

$$\frac{\partial c^0}{\partial \alpha} < 0,^{31} \qquad (21)$$

where α is a parameter that reduces the absolute value of L' for a given c. Similarly, a reduction in I_0^e would increase the demand for self-insurance:

$$-\frac{\partial c^0}{\partial I_0^e} > 0.^{32} \qquad (22)$$

Equation (20) shows clearly that the incentive to self-insure, unlike the incentive to use market insurance, is smaller for rare losses. The reason is that the loading factor of self-insurance is *larger* for rare losses because its price, unlike the price of market insurance, can be presumed to be independent of the probability of loss.[33]

An increase in endowed incomes that resulted from investment in human capital would probably be associated with an increase in the marginal productivity of self-insurance.[34] Therefore, the effect on self-insurance of a change in income has to be separated from the effect of the associated change in marginal productivity.

If market and self-insurance were both available, values of c and s would be chosen simultaneously to maximize the expected utility function,

$$U^* = (1-p)\, U\, (I_1^e - c - s\pi) + pU(I_1^e - L(L^e, c) - c + s). \quad (23)$$

If the price of market insurance were independent of the amount of self-insurance, the first-order optimality conditions would be

$$-(1-p)\, U_1'\, \pi + pU_0' = 0.$$
$$-(1-p)U_1' - pU_0'[L'(c) + 1] = 0. \quad (24)$$

By combining these equations we get

$$\pi = -\frac{1}{L'(c)+1}. \quad (25)$$

In equilibrium, therefore, the "shadow price" of self-insurance would equal the price of market insurance.

Clearly, market insurance and self-insurance are "substitutes" in the sense that an increase in π, the probability of loss being the same, would decrease the demand for market insurance and increase the demand for self-insurance.[35] For example, a change in the market insurance line from $\overline{AB}$ to $\overline{CD}$ in figure 5 would increase self-insurance by the horizontal distance between M_1 and M_2 and reduce market insurance by the horizontal distance between Q and P. In particular, the purchase of market insurance would reduce the demand for self-insurance—compare points S and, say, M_1.

When market insurance is available at a fair price, the equilibrium condition (25) becomes

$$-\frac{1}{L'(c)+1} = \frac{p}{1-p}, \quad (26)$$

or

$$-L'(c) = \frac{1}{p},$$

precisely the condition that maximizes expected income.[36] Even with diminishing marginal utility of income, a person would act as if he were risk neutral and choose the amount of self-insurance that maximized his expected income. Consequently, apparent attitudes toward risk are dependent on market opportunities, and real attitudes cannot easily be inferred from behavior.

More generally, even if the price of market insurance were not fair, the optimal amount of self-insurance would maximize the market value of income (given by W in equation [12]), and would not depend on the shape of the indifference curves or even on the probability distribution of states.[37] Geo-metrically, optimal self-insurance is determined by moving along the trans-formation curve in figure 5 to the point of tangency between this curve and a market insurance line; since the market value of income is the intercept on the y-axis, that intercept would be maximized at such point of tangency.

The effects of specific parameters on the demand for market and self-insurance when both are available often are quite different from their effect when market insurance or self-insurance alone is available. For example, although an increase in the endowed loss increases the demand for self- or market insurance when either alone is available since an increase in market insurance itself reduces self-insurance, and vice versa, the indirect effects can offset the direct effects when both market and self-insurance are positive (see Appendix A for an example of this). Similarly, because a decrease in the probability of loss with no change in the market loading factor reduces the demand for self-insurance, it increases the demand for market insurance. Therefore, people may be more likely to use the market to insure rare losses not necessarily because of a positive relation between the probability of loss and the loading factor (see the discussion on rare losses on pages 126–27), but because of a substitution between market and self-insurance.

Self-Protection, Subjective Probabilities, and "Moral Hazard"

Self-insurance and market insurance both redistribute income toward hazardous states, whereas self-protection reduces the probabilities of these states. Unlike insurance, self-protection does not redistribute income, be-cause the amount spent reducing the probability of a loss decreases income in all states equally, leaving unchanged the absolute size of the loss (its relative size actually increases).

Studies using the states-of-the-world approach to analyze decision mak-ing under uncertainty have assumed that the probability of a state is entirely determined by "nature" and is independent of human actions. With this approach there is no such thing as self-protection; the activities we call by this name would be subsumed under self-insurance. It has been claimed that states can always be defined to guarantee the independence of their proba-bilities from human actions,[38] but we deny that this can be done in a meaningful way. Consider, for example, the probability that a given house will be damaged by lightning.[39] Since this probability can be reduced by the installation of lightning rods, independent state probabilities could be ob-tained only by using a more fundamental state description: the probability of a stroke of lightning itself. If control of the weather is ruled out, the proba-bility of lightning can be assumed to be unaffected by human actions. We are concerned, however, about the probability of damage to the house—we do

FIGURE 6

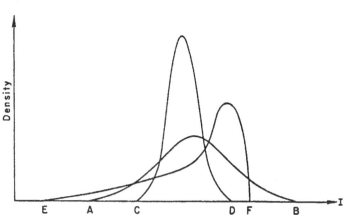

not care about the probability of lightning per se—and the probability of damage is affected by lightning rods.

In other words, although an appropriate definition of states would produce state probabilities that are independent of human actions, it would not produce a probability distribution of outcomes—the relevant probability distribution—that is independent of these actions. Since one of the main purposes of the state-of-the-world approach is to equate the probability distribution of outcomes with the probability distribution of states, a search for state probabilities that are independent of human actions would be self-defeating.

To look at the difference between self-protection and self-insurance from the viewpoint of outcomes, assume the probability distribution of endowed outcomes given by AB in figure 6. Self-insurance, by contracting the distribution to, say, CD, lowers the probability of both high and low outcomes, thereby unambiguously reducing the dispersion of outcomes. Self-protection, on the other hand, by shifting the whole distribution to the left to, say, EF, reduces the probability of low outcomes and raises the probability of high ones and does not have an unambiguous effect on the dispersion.[40]

Since the preceding discussion shows that self-insurance is to be distinguished from self-protection, we develop a formal analysis of the latter. Let us assume that the probability of a hazardous state can be reduced by appropriate expenditure: $p = p(p^e, r)$, where p^e is the endowed probability of hazard, r is the expenditure on self-protection, and $\partial p / \partial r = p'(r) \leq 0$. If no market or self-insurance were available, the optimal expenditure on self-protection would maximize

$$U^* = [1 - p(p^e,r)] \, U(I_1^e - r) + p(p^e,r) \, U(I_0^e - r); \qquad (27)$$

the optimality condition is

$$-p'(r^0) \, (U_1 - U_0) = (1 - p) \, U_1' + p U_0'. \qquad (28)$$

The term on the left is the marginal gain from the reduction in p; that on the right, the decline in utility due to the decline in both incomes, is the marginal cost. In equilibrium, of course, they must be equal.

The second-order optimality condition requires that

$$U_{r\,r}^* = -p''(r^0) \, (U_1 - U_0) + 2p'(r^0) \, (U_1' - U_0')$$
$$+ \, (1 - p) \, U_1'' + p U_0'' < 0. \qquad (29)$$

Decreasing marginal utility of income is neither a necessary nor a sufficient condition. If $p''(r^0) > 0$, equation (29) is always satisfied if the marginal utility of income is constant and may or may not be satisfied if the marginal utility is decreasing or increasing. This shows that the incentive to self-protect, unlike the incentive to insure, is not so dependent on attitudes toward risk, and could be as strong for risk preferrers as for risk avoiders.

As with market and self-insurance, the effect of a change in incomes on the demand for self-protection depends on the source of the change as well as on preferences.[41] A decline in I_0^e alone might not increase the demand for self-protection, even if the marginal utility of income were falling because a decline in I_0^e would increase the marginal cost of self-protection.[42]

A decline in the marginal productivity of self-protection—an increase in the shadow price of protection—always decreases the demand for self-protection regardless of attitudes toward risk.[43] Therefore, if the endowed probabilities and incomes were the same, more efficient providers of self-protection would have lower equilibrium probabilities of hazard. Consequently, different persons use different probabilities in their decision-making process not only because of differences in "temperament," or optimism, but also because of differences in productivity at self-protection. As suggested in the last section, differences in productivity, in turn, may be attributed to differences in education and other forms of "human capital."

If market insurance and self-protection were jointly available, the function

$$U^* = [1 - p(p^e,r)] \, U \, (I_1^e - r - s\pi(r)) + p(p^e,r) \, U \, (I_0^e - r + s) \qquad (30)$$

would be maximized with respect to r and s; the first-order optimality conditions are

$$-(1 - p) \, U_1' \pi + p U_0' = 0 \qquad (31)$$

$$-p'(r^*) \, (U_1 - U_0) - (1 - p) \, U_1' \, [1 + s^* \pi'(r^*)] - p U_0' = 0. \qquad (32)$$

The term $\pi'(r^*)$ measures the effect of a change in self-protection on the price of market insurance through its effects on p and the loading factor λ. From the definition of π in equation (17) we obtain:

$$\frac{\partial \pi}{\partial r} = \pi'(r) = \pi'(p)\,p'(r) + \pi'(\lambda)\lambda'(r). \tag{33}$$

The effect of market insurance on the demand for self-protection has generally been called "moral hazard." In particular, moral hazard refers to an alleged deterrent effect of market insurance on self-protection[44] that increases the actual probabilities of hazardous events (Arrow 1962). Consequently, moral hazard is said to be "a relevant cost of producing insurance that is imposed by the insured on the insurance company" (Demsetz 1969, 7) and to provide a "limit to the possibilities of insurance" (Arrow 1962, 612). We showed in the last section that market insurance does reduce self-insurance, but no one has shown rigorously why, or under what conditions, market insurance reduces self-protection.

Market insurance has two opposite effects on self-protection. On the one hand, self-protection is discouraged because its marginal gain is reduced by the reduction of the difference between the incomes and thus the utilities in different states (see equation [28]); on the other hand, it is encouraged if the price of market insurance is negatively related to the amount spent on protection through the effect of these expenditures on the probabilities. Consider the relative importance of these opposite effects in two extreme cases:

If market insurance were always available at an actuarially fair price regardless of the amount spent on self-protection, then $\pi = p/(1-p)$, and equation (31) implies that the optimal amount of market insurance (s^*) equalizes income in both states of the world. There is still an incentive to spend on self-protection, however, because π is negatively related to these expenditures (r):

$$\pi'(r) = \frac{p'(r)}{(1-p)^2}. \tag{33a}$$

Substituting $U_1 = U_0$ and $U_1' = U_0'$ into equation (32), and using equation (33a) and the fact that $s^* = (1-p)(I_1^e - I_0^e)$, we get

$$p'(r^*) = -\frac{1-p}{s^*} = -\frac{1}{I_1^e - I_0^e}, \tag{34}$$

precisely the condition to maximize expected income. As with self-insurance, a fair price of market insurance encourages an expenditure on self-protection that maximizes expected income. Consequently, moral hazard would not then increase the real cost of insurance, reduce an economy's technical efficiency, or limit the development of market insurance since an amount of market insurance equalizing income in all states would be chosen.

Even more important is that, contrary to the moral hazard argument, the optimal expenditure on self-protection, r^*, can be *larger* than the amount spent in the absence of market insurance, r^0. By equations (34) and (28), and the condition $p'(r) < 0$, r^* would be larger than r^0 if

$$\frac{U(I_1^e - r^0) - U(I_0^e - r^0)}{I_1^e - I_0^e} = \overline{U}'$$

$$< (1-p) U'(I_1^e - r^0) + pU'(I_0^e - r^0), \quad (35)$$

which is likely provided p is not very small and U is concave. Indeed, if utility were a quadratic function of income, r^* would be larger than r^0 if p were larger than one-half.[45] Not only are market insurance and self-protection complements in the sense that the availability of the former could increase the demand for the latter, but also in the sense that an increase in the productivity of self-protection or a decrease in the real cost of market insurance would increase the demand for both (see Appendix B).

Suppose, at the other extreme, that the price of market insurance was independent of expenditures on self-protection—the loading factor increased sufficiently to offset exactly the reduction in the probability of loss. Self-protection would then usually be discouraged by market insurance—moral hazard would exist—because the main effect of introducing market insurance would be to narrow the differences between incomes in different states.[46] Moreover, since the demand for market insurance is negatively related to the degree of loading, it would be negatively related to expenditures on self-protection. Consequently, for those kinds of market insurance with prices that are largely independent of expenditures on self-protection, one should observe either a large demand for insurance and a small demand for self-protection, or the converse. In our judgment, this is the major reason why certain kinds of hazards, like failure in business, are not considered insurable by the market.

Since the price of self-insurance is independent of the probability of hazard (see the discussion on pages 130–33) and thus of expenditures on self-protection, our analysis of market insurance implies that self-insurance is likely to create a moral hazard. That is to say, the availability of self-insurance would discourage self-protection and vice versa. Moreover, technological progress in the provision of one would tend to discourage the other.

This analysis of moral hazard applies not only to the relation between self-protection and insurance as ordinarily conceived, but also to the relation between protection and insurance for all uncertain events that can be influenced by human actions. For example, do unemployment compensation, relief, or negative income tax rates increase the probability that someone becomes unemployed? Does the presence of underground shelters increase the probability that a country goes to war, the use of seat belts the probability of an automobile accident, or generous parental support the probability that children become "irresponsible"?

Since each of these, in effect, relates a form of insurance to a form of protection, our answers are not necessarily "yes," and depend on how responsive the cost of insurance is to the amount spent on protection. Shelters and seat belts are ways to self-insure, and have costs that are essentially unrelated to the probability of the hazards; therefore they would tend to reduce (perhaps only slightly) the incentive to avoid a war or an automobile accident. On the other hand, if the cost—in time, embarrassment, etc.—of applying for relief, unemployment compensation, or parental support were sufficiently positively related to its frequency, the answers might well be "no": the availability of insurance might encourage the insured to make his own efforts.

APPENDIX A:
SELF-INSURANCE AND MARKET INSURANCE

If both self-insurance and market insurance are available, the expected utility is

$$U^* = (1-p) U (I_1^e - c - s\pi) + pU (I_1^e - L(L^e, c) - c + s) . \quad (A1)$$

The values of c and s that maximize this function must satisfy the first-order optimality conditions

$$U_s^* = -(1-p) U_1' \pi + pU_0' = 0 \quad (A2)$$

$$U_c^* = -(1-p) U_1' - pU_0' [L'(c^*) + 1] = 0 . \quad (A3)$$

Clearly, equation (A3) would be satisfied only if $\delta = [L'(c^*) + 1] < 0$: only if expenditures on self-insurance increased the net income in the hazardous state.

Second-order optimality conditions are

$$U_{ss}^* = (1-p) U_1'' \pi^2 + pU_0'' < 0 \quad (A4)$$

$$U_{cc}^* = (1-p) U_1'' + p U_0'' \delta^2 - pU_0' L'' < 0 \quad (A5)$$

$$\Delta = U_{ss}^* U_{cc}^* - (U_{sc}^*)^2 > 0 . \quad (A6)$$

Equations (A4) and (A5) are obviously satisfied if everywhere $U'' < 0$ and $L'' = \partial^2 L / \partial c^2 > 0$, that is, if the marginal utility of income and the marginal productivity of self-insurance are both decreasing. These assumptions are also sufficient to satisfy equation (A6) since

$$U_{sc}^* = (1-p)\, U_1'' \pi - p\, U_0'' \delta < 0 . \tag{A7}$$

Utilizing the first-order condition $\pi\delta = -1$, we can write

$$\Delta = -p(1-p)\, U_0'\, U_1''\, L''\, \pi^2 - p^2\, U_0'\, U_0''\, L'',$$

which is positive if $U'' < 0$ and $L'' > 0$.

Terms of Trade Effects

The effect of an increase in π on the optimal values of s and c—I_1^ε, L^ε, and p held constant—can be found by differentiating equations (A2) and (A3) with respect to π. By Cramer's rule,

$$\frac{ds^*}{d\pi} = \frac{A_1 U_{cc}^* - A_2 U_{sc}^*}{\Delta} = \frac{1}{\Delta}[(1-p)^2\, U_1'\, U_1'' + p(1-p)\, U_1'\, U_0'' \delta^2$$

$$- p(1-p)\, U_0'\, U_1'\, L'' + p(1-p)\, U_0'\, U_1''\, s^*\, \pi L''] = \frac{(-)}{(+)} < 0 \tag{A8}$$

where $-A_1 = -(1-p)U_1' + (1-p)U_1''s^*\pi$ and $-A_2 = (1-p)U_1''s^*$ are the partial derivatives of (A2) and (A3) with respect to π. Similarly,

$$\frac{dc^*}{d\pi} = \frac{A_2 U_{ss}^* - A_1 U_{sc}^*}{\Delta}$$

$$= \frac{1}{\Delta}[-(1-p)^2\, U_1'\, U_1''\pi + p(1-p)\, U_1'\, U_0'' \delta] = \frac{(+)}{(+)} > 0. \tag{A9}$$

Hence, market insurance and self-insurance can be considered substitutes.

By similar reasoning, the effect of an increase in p on the optimal values of s and c, given that λ in $\pi = [(1+\lambda)p]/(1-p)$, I_1^ε and L_1^ε are constant, is found to be

$$\frac{ds^*}{dp} = \frac{B_1 U_{cc}^* - B_2 U_{sc}^*}{\Delta} = \frac{1}{\Delta}[U_0'U_1''L''s^*\pi^2 + (1-p)U_1'U_1''\pi$$

$$+ (1-p)U_0'U_1'' - pU_1'U_0''\delta + pU_0'U_0''\delta^2] = \frac{(-)}{(+)} < 0; \tag{A10}$$

also

$$\frac{dc^{*}}{dp} = \frac{B_2 U_{cc}^{*} - B_1 U_{sc}^{*}}{\Delta} = \frac{1}{\Delta}[-(1-p)\,U_1'\,U_1''\,\pi^2$$

$$- (1-p)\,U_0'\,U_1''\,\pi - p U_1'\,U_0'' + p U_0'\,U_0''\,\delta] = \frac{(+)}{(+)} > 0 \quad \text{(A11)}$$

where $-B_1 = (1-p)U_1''s^{*}\pi'(p)\pi$, $-B_2 = U_1' - U_1'\delta + (1-p)U_1''s^{*}\pi'(p)$, and $\pi'(p) = \partial\pi/\partial p = \pi/[p(1-p)]$.

An Endowment Effect

The effect of a decrease in $I_0^{\varepsilon} = I_1^{\varepsilon} - L^{\varepsilon} - I_1^{\varepsilon}$, π, p, and L' held constant— can be shown to be

$$-\frac{ds^{*}}{dI_0^{\varepsilon}} = \frac{-p^2 U_0' U_0'' L''}{\Delta}\frac{\partial L}{\partial L^{\varepsilon}} = \frac{(+)}{(+)} > 0, \quad \text{(A12)}$$

where, by assumption, $\partial L/\partial L^{\varepsilon} > 0$; and

$$-\frac{dc^{*}}{dI_0^{\varepsilon}} = \frac{-p U_0''\delta U_{ss}^{*} - p U_0'' U_{sc}^{*}}{\Delta}\frac{\partial L}{\partial L^{\varepsilon}} = 0, \quad \text{(A13)}$$

since by equations (A7) and (A8) $U_{sc}^{*} = -\delta U_{ss}^{*}$. If the change in I_0^{ε} also changed L', the results would be different.

APPENDIX B:
SELF-PROTECTION AND MARKET INSURANCE

If both market insurance and self-protection are available, the expected utility is

$$U^{*} = [1 - p\,(p^{\varepsilon}, r)]\,U\,(I_1^{\varepsilon} - r - s\,\pi\,(r)) + p\,(p^{\varepsilon}, r)\,U\,(I_0^{\varepsilon} - r + s). \quad \text{(B1)}$$

The first-order optimality conditions are

$$U_s^{*} = -(1-p)\,U_1'\,\pi + p U_0' = 0 \quad \text{(B2)}$$

$$U_r^{*} = -p'\,(r^{*})\,(U_1 - U_0) - (1-p)\,U_1'$$
$$[1 + s^{*}\pi'(r)] - p U_0' = 0 \quad \text{(B3)}$$

where $p'(r^{*}) < 0$ and $\pi'(r^{*}) \le 0$.

Second-order conditions are that

$$U_{ss}^{*} = (1-p)\,U_1''\,\pi^2 + p U_0'' < 0 \quad \text{(B4)}$$

$$U_{rr}^{*} = -p''\,(r^{*})\,(U_1 - U_0) + (1-p)\,U_1''[1 + s^{*}\pi'\,(r^{*})]^2 + p U_0'' \quad \text{(B5)}$$

$$+ 2p'(r^*) \{U_1'[1 + s^*\pi'(r)] - U_0'\} - (1-p) U_1's^*\pi''(r^*) < 0. \quad (B6)$$

$$\sum = U_{ss}^* U_{rr}^* - (U_{s,r}^*)^2 > 0.$$

Equations (B4) and (B5) would be satisfied if $U'' < 0$, if both $p''(r^*)$ and $\pi''(r^*) > 0$, and if $D = 2p'(r^*)\{U_1'[1 + s^*\pi'(r^*)] - U_0'\}$ (which is positive if $U'' < 0$)[47] were small in absolute value relative to the other terms in equation (B5). These conditions are also sufficient to satisfy equation (B6) if, in particular, $D < (1-p)U_1's^*\pi''(r^*) + p''(r^*)(U_1 - U_0)$.

Since $\pi = [(1 + \lambda)p]/(1 - p)$, the effect of an increase in r on π would be

$$\pi'(r) = \frac{(1 + \lambda)p'(r)}{(1 - p)^2} + \frac{p\lambda'(r)}{(1 - p)}, \quad (B7)$$

where $\lambda'(r)$ gives the effect on the loading of an additional expenditure on self-protection and is generally assumed to be positive.[48]

If insurance were always available at an actuarially fair price, then $\lambda(p) = 0$ for all p; hence

$$\pi = \frac{p(r)}{1 - p(r)}, \quad \pi'(r) = \frac{p'(r)}{(1 - p)^2}, \text{ and}$$

$$\pi''(r) = \frac{p''(r)}{(1-p)^2} + \frac{2[p'(r)]^2}{(1 - p)^3} > 0.$$

Equation (B2) reduces to

$$U_1' = U_0', \quad (B8)$$

and equation (B3) to

$$p'(r^*) = -\frac{(1-p)}{s^*}. \quad (B9)$$

Therefore, $\pi'(r^*) = -1/[s^*(1-p)]$ and $1 + s^*\pi'(r^*) = -\pi$.

Terms of Trade Effects

If an initially fair price $\pi = [p(r^*)]/[1 - p(r^*)]$ were increased by an increase in the loading with no change in $\pi'(r)$,[49] the change in the optimal values of s and r would be given by

$$\frac{ds^*}{d\pi} = \frac{C_1 U^*_{rr} - C_2 U^*_{sr}}{\Sigma}$$

$$= \frac{C_1 \left[\dfrac{2U'_1}{s^*} - (1-p) U'_1 s^* \pi''(r) \right]}{\Sigma} = \frac{(-)}{(+)} < 0,^{50} \quad \text{(B10)}$$

$$\frac{dr^*}{d\pi} = \frac{C_2 U^*_{ss} - C_1 U^*_{sr}}{\Sigma} = \frac{-2(1-p) U'_1 U^*_{sr}}{\Sigma} = \frac{(-)}{(+)} < 0, \quad \text{(B11)}$$

where

$$-C_1 = U^*_{s\pi} \Big]_{\substack{s^*, r^*, p, \pi'(r^*) \\ \text{constant}}} = -(1-p) U'_1 + (1-p) U''_1 s^* \pi$$

and

$$-C_2 = U^*_{r\pi} \Big]_{\substack{s^*, r^*, p, \pi'(r^*) \\ \text{constant}}} = p'(r^*) U'_1 s^* + (1-p) U''_1 s^* [1 + s^* \pi'(r^*)]$$

$$= -(1-p) U'_1 - (1-p) U''_1 s^* \pi$$

(from equation [B9]). Hence, if the price of insurance increased from an initially fair level, the demand for both self-protection and market insurance would decrease.

If the price of insurance were always actuarially fair, the effect of an exogenous increase in the productivity of self-protection on s^* and r^* with no change in the endowed probabilities and in the endowed incomes would be given by

$$\frac{ds^*}{d\beta} = \frac{D_2 U^*_{sr}}{\Sigma} = \frac{(+)}{(+)} > 0 \quad \text{(B12)}$$

and

$$\frac{dc^*}{d\beta} = \frac{-D_2 U^*_{ss}}{\Sigma} = \frac{(+)}{(+)} > 0, \quad \text{(B13)}$$

where $D_2 = -U'_1 [s/(1-p)] \, \partial p'/\partial \beta$ and, by assumption, $\partial p'/\partial \beta < 0$. Technological improvements in self-protection are thus seen to increase the demand for both market insurance and self-protection.

The Effect of Exogenous Changes in p and L

If insurance were provided at an actuarially fair price, and if the endowed probability increased due to an exogenous factor γ with no change in $p'(r)$, then

$$\frac{ds^*}{d\gamma} = \frac{\left[-(1-p)\,U_1''s^*\,\pi\,\pi'(p)\right]\left[\dfrac{2U_1'}{s} - (1-p)\,U_1's^*\,\pi''(r)\right]}{\Sigma}$$

$$\cdot \frac{\partial p}{\partial \gamma} = \frac{(-)}{(+)} < 0 \quad (B14)$$

where, by assumption, $\partial p/\partial \gamma > 0$, and

$$\frac{dr^*}{d\gamma} = \frac{(1-p)U_1''s^*\,\pi\,\pi'(p)[U_{s,s}^* + U_{s,r}^*]}{\Sigma}\frac{\partial p}{\partial \gamma} = 0, \quad (B15)$$

since $U_{s,s}^* = -U_{s,r}^*$.[51] The last result is intuitively obvious since a fair price of insurance implies that $-p'(r^*) = 1/(I_1^e - I_0^e)$; therefore, r^* is independent of p provided that $p'(r)$ is unaffected by changes in γ. By the same reasoning one can show that an increase in the size of the prospective loss increases the optimal values of both s and r.

NOTES

Becker's contribution was primarily an unpublished paper that sets out the approach developed here. Ehrlich greatly extended and applied that approach and was primarily responsible for writing this paper. We have had many helpful comments from Harold Demsetz, Jacques Drèze, Jack Hirshleifer, and members of the Labor Workshop at Columbia University and the Industrial Organization Workshop at the University of Chicago.

1. An approach originally devised by Arrow (1963–64) and worked out in application to investment decisions under uncertainty by Hirshleifer (1970).

2. Theorems concerning optimal insurance decisions have been derived in two recent contributions by Smith (1968) and Mossin (1968). Our approach differs not only in form but also in substance; for example, in the analysis of the interaction between market insurance, self-insurance, and self-protection.

3. For example, Arrow (1965) says, "Insurance is not a material good . . . its value to the buyer is clearly different in kind from the satisfaction of consumer's desires for medical treatment or transportation. Indeed, unlike goods and services, transactions involving insurance are an exchange of money for money, not money for something which directly meets needs" (p. 45).

4. See, for example, Becker and Michael (1970).

5. By consumption opportunities in each state of the world is meant command over commodities, C_i, produced by combining market goods, X_i, time spent in consumption, t_i, and the "state environment," E_i, via household production functions (for the latter concept see Becker and Michael 1970): $C_{ij} = f_{ij}(X_{ij}, t_{ij}, E_i) \; j = 1, \ldots, m$ where j refers to different commodities. If the production functions fully incorporate the effects of environment, the utility function of commodities would not depend on which state occurred. In particular, for an aggregate commodity C, $U(C_0) = U(C_1)$ if $C_0 = C_1$ where 0, 1 denote different states.

6. Note that insurance is defined not in terms of the liability "coverage" of potential losses, as in Smith's (1968) and Mossin's (1968) papers, but in terms of "coverage minus premium," or the net addition to income in state 0.

7. In figure 1, the opportunity boundary $\overline{AB}$ is drawn as a straight line. This assumes that the same terms of trade apply to both insurance and "gambling," that is, to movements to the right and to the left of E, the endowment position. In practice, the opportunity boundary may be kinked about the endowment point.

8. For analytical simplicity we ignore the time and environment inputs and assume only a single aggregate commodity in each state. Then the output of commodities can be identified with the input of goods and services, or with income.

9. An actuarially fair exchange is an exchange of $p/(1-p)$ units of income in state 1 for an additional unit of income in state 0, where $p/(1-p)$ is the odds that state 0 would occur.

10. Hirshleifer (1970, 233) points out that although diminishing marginal utility of income is not a necessary condition for equilibrium at any given point, it is a necessary condition for the indifference curve to be convex at all points.

11. Indeed, when faced with several independent hazards, a person might "gamble" and "insure" at the same time, provided the different hazards were associated with different opportunities. For example, given a fair price of theft insurance, he may fully insure his household against theft and at the same time engage in a risky activity if his expected earnings there were greater than his earnings in alternative "safe" activities (see Ehrlich 1970).

12. Full insurance can be identified with full coverage of potential losses, since the equation $I_1 = I_0$ implies that $I_1^e - b = I_0^e + d - b$, where d is the gross coverage and b is the premium. Clearly, then, $d = I_1^e - I_0^e$. By the same reasoning, since an "unfair" price of insurance $\overline{\pi} > 1$ implies that $I_1 > I_0$, it also implies necessarily less than full coverage of potential losses.

13. If $I_0 = I_1 = I$, that is, $I_1 = I_1^e - s\pi = I_0 = I_0^e + s$, where $\pi = p/(1-p)$, then $I = pI_0^e + (1-p)I_1^e$.

14. Although the model has been developed for two states of the world, the analysis applies equally well to n states. We define the state with the highest income— say, state n—as the state without hazard and define all the states with hazard ($h = 1, \ldots, n - 1$) relative to that state. Denoting by p_h the probability of state h, by

$$p = 1 - \sum_{h=1}^{n-1} p_h$$

the probability of state n, and by π_h the implicit terms of trade between income in state n and income in state h, it can easily be shown that if the terms of trade were fair ($\overline{\pi}_h = [p/p_h] \, \pi_h = 1$), s_h would be chosen to equalize incomes in all states of the world and losses would be "fully covered." If the real terms of trade were unfair but constant ($\overline{\pi}_h = \pi = 1 + \lambda > 1$ for all h), s_h would be chosen to equalize incomes in states with hazard only, that is, we would achieve what has been called full insurance above a deductible (for a definition of this concept and an alternative proof see Arrow 1963).

15. This analysis, therefore, also shows that the effect of a change in π on the "fullness" of insurance (the difference $I_1 - I_0$) and thus on the degree of gross coverage is generally not unambiguous.

16. According to equation (13), $\partial I_0 / \partial I_0^\varepsilon = [-\pi^2 (1-p) \, U_1''] / [-p U_0'' - \pi^2 (1-p) \, U_1''] = \delta$, where clearly $0 < \delta < 1$ if U_1'' and $U_0'' < 0$. But since $s = I_0 - I_0^\varepsilon$, $\partial s / \partial I_0^\varepsilon = \delta - 1 < 0$.

17. Similarly, he would be less likely to take large gambles (see the discussion in Hirshleifer 1966). Of course, if insurance is fair he will fully insure all losses, large or small.

18. Note the analogy between insurance and savings: the latter bridges the gap between "endowed" and desired levels of consumption at different points in time.

19. Given $s = I_0 - I_0^\varepsilon$ and $I_1^\varepsilon = \gamma I_0^\varepsilon$, then $(\partial s / \partial W) \, (W/s) = (ds/dI_0^\varepsilon) \, (I_0^\varepsilon / s) = \eta_0 (I_0/s) - (I_0^\varepsilon / s)$; by collecting terms, we get equation (16). Since $I_0 \geq s$, $e_{sW} \geq 1$ if $\eta_0 \geq 1$.

If the loss is unaffected by an equal increase in endowments, that is, if $I_0^\varepsilon = I_1^\varepsilon - L$ where L is a constant, then $\epsilon_{se} = (ds/dI_1^\varepsilon) \, (I_1^\varepsilon / s) = (I_0/s) \eta_0 (d \log W)/(d \log I_1^\varepsilon) - (I_1^\varepsilon / s)$. This implies that

$$\epsilon_{se} \gtreqqless 0 \quad \text{as} \quad \eta_0 \gtreqqless \frac{W}{I_0(1+\pi)} \geq 1 \quad (\text{if} \quad I_1 \geq I_0). \qquad (16a)$$

20. Note that

$$\frac{d \, \text{slope}}{dI_0} = \frac{d}{dI_0} \left[\frac{p U_0'}{(1-p) U_1'} \right]$$

subject to $I_1 = \gamma I_0$ is $\gtreqqless 0$ as $-(U_1''/U_1') \, \gamma \gtreqqless -(U_0''/U_0')$; the latter defines increasing, constant, or decreasing relative risk aversion. Similarly

$$\frac{d}{dI_0} \left[\frac{p U_0'}{(1-p) U_1'} \right]$$

subject to $I_1 - I_0 = L$ is $\gtreqqless 0$ as $-(U_1''/U_1') \gtreqqless -(U_0''/U_0')$; the latter defines increasing, constant, or decreasing absolute risk aversion (see Pratt 1964; Arrow 1965). (Diagrammatically, constant absolute risk aversion implies that the slopes of the indifference curves are constant along any 45° line joining two equilibrium positions—the indifference curves are like EPF and IQ_2J in fig. 3.) Equation (16a) in n.19 implies that increasing relative risk aversion, $\eta_0 > 1$, is compatible with decreasing absolute risk aversion, $\epsilon_{se} < 0$, only if $\eta_0 < W/I_0(1 + \pi)$.

21. Since the slopes of the indifference curves necessarily are constant along the "certainty line" and by assumption become increasingly steep toward I_0 along other rays from the origin, a given percentage deviation of the price of insurance from the fair price results in smaller percentage changes in the ratio I_1/I_0 at higher indifference levels. That is, $\sigma = (d \log I_1/I_0)/d \log \pi$ decreases at higher indifference levels when π equals the fair price.

22. This result appears to contradict one by Lees and Rice (1965) because they define the loading factor in terms of the gross rather than net amount paid in claim; that is by λ' in $\pi = [(1 + \lambda') p]/[1 - (1 + \lambda') p]$. A reduction in p, λ' held constant, would reduce λ—our definition of the loading factor—and thus would increase the incentive to insure.

23. Some evidence is presented in Lees and Rice (1965).

24. Let the amount a that is spent processing and investigating each claim be the only administrative cost of providing insurance. In a zero profit equilibrium position, the unit price of insurance would equal the ratio of the total amount collected in premiums in state 1 (including administration costs) to the difference between the net amount paid in claims in state 0 and administration costs: $\pi = (pd + pa)/[d(1 - p) - pa]$, where d is the amount covered by insurance. The degree of loading defined by $\lambda = [(1 - p)/p]\pi - 1 = (d + a)/[d - pa/(1 - p)] - 1 = a/[d - p(d + a)]$ would be larger the larger p was if d were fixed (d would tend to decrease as p increased, and this would increase λ even further).

25. Generally, the effect of an increase in p on the optimal values of I_0 and I_1, assuming that $\pi = [(1 + \lambda) p]/(1 - p)$ and that λ, I_0^e, and I_1^e are constant, is given by

$$\frac{\partial I_0}{\partial p} = \frac{1}{D}\left[U_1'' s\pi \frac{1 + \lambda}{1 - p} \right] < 0$$

$$\frac{\partial I_1}{\partial p} = \frac{1}{D}\left[U_0'' s\pi \frac{1}{1 - p} \right] < 0$$

provided $U'' < 0$. An increase in p would then lower the optimal amount of insurance $s = I_0 - I_0^e$ and increase the optimal expenditure on insurance $b = I_1^e - I_1$.

26. These have been called "loss protection" and "loss prevention," respectively (see Mehr and Commack 1966, 28–29).

27. For analytical convenience we assume that I_0^e alone is affected by c, although, of course, both endowments may be affected. Moreover, the assumption that $\partial L/\partial c \leq 0$ is not always true: an individual could increase I_1^e and reduce I_0^e by deliberately exposing himself to hazards; for example, by committing a crime or engaging in a risky legal occupation (see Ehrlich 1970). The condition $\partial L/\partial c > 0$ can be said to define "negative self-insurance."

28. See equation (A5). Note that the transformation curve may be kinked at the endowment point.

29. If the opposite were true, there would be an incentive to increase the loss by increasing I_1 and reducing I_0 (see n. 27 above).

30. Although c denotes the expenditure on self-insurance rather than the reduction in the size of the loss, there is a one-to-one relationship between expenditure and insurance because $-L'(c) > 1$.

31. By differentiating equation (19) with respect to α—p, I_0^e and I_1^e held constant—one obtains $\partial c^0/\partial \alpha = (pU_0'/U_{ee}^*) \, (\partial L'/\partial \alpha) = (+)/(-) < 0$, where $U_{ee}^* = \partial^2 U^*/\partial c^2 < 0$ (see Appendix A), and by assumption $\partial L'/\partial \alpha > 0$.

32. By differentiating equation (19) with respect to $I_0^e - I_1^e$, p and L' held constant, one obtains $-\partial c^0/\partial I_0^e = \partial c^0/\partial L^e = -\{pU_0''\,[L'(c)+1]/U_{cc}^*\}\,\partial L/\partial L^e = (-)/(-) > 0$, where by assumption $\partial L/\partial L^e > 0$.

33. The price of self-insurance is given by $\pi = -1/[L'(c) + 1]$, where $L'(c)$ presumably does not depend on p. The loading factor is then given by $\lambda = -\{1/[L'(c)+1]\}\,[(1-p)/p] - 1$. Hence $\partial \lambda/\partial p < 0$.

34. That is, not only would $\partial I_i^e/\partial E > 0 \; i = 0, 1$ where E is the stock of human capital, but probably also $\partial^2 L/\partial c\partial E < 0$.

35. A mathematical proof can be found in Appendix A.

36. Equation (26) can be derived by maximizing $(1-p) \, (I_1^e - c) + p \, [I_1^e - L(L^e, c) - c]$ with respect to c.

37. Equation (25) can be derived by maximizing $W = (I_1^e - c) + \pi[I_1^e - L(L^e, c) - c]$ with respect to c. We are indebted to Jacques Drèze for emphasizing this point.

38. The only explicit discussion is by Hirshleifer (1970, 217).

39. This example is discussed by Hirshleifer (1970).

40. The effect of the introduction of self-protection on the variance of income, $p(1-p) \, (I_1^e - I_0^e)^2$, can be found by differentiation $v'(r) \equiv \partial \, \text{Var} \, (I^e)/\partial r = (1 - 2p) \, (I_1^e - I_0^e)^2 p'(0)$, where r is the expenditure on self-protection. Clearly $v'(r) \gtreqless 0$ as $p \gtreqless 1/2$.

41. An equal proportional increase in endowments ($I_1^e = \gamma I_0^e$) would increase the demand for self-protection if $(dr^0/dI_0^e) = (1/U_{rr}^*)[p'(r^0) \, (U_1'\gamma - U_0') + (1-p) U_1''\gamma + pU_0''] > 0$. A sufficient condition if $U'' < 0$ is $(U_1'/U_0') \, (I_1^e/I_0^e) \geq 1$, or that the "average relative risk aversion" between I_0^e and I_1^e be sufficiently greater than one.

42. That is, $-\partial r^0/\partial I_0^e = [p'(r^0)U_0' - pU_0'']/U_{rr}^* \gtreqless 0$ as $-[p' (r^0)]/p \gtreqless -U_0''/U_0'$.

43. That is, $\partial r^0\partial \beta = [(U_1 - U_0)/U_{rr}^*] \, (\partial p'/\partial \beta) = (+)/(-) > 0$, where by assumption $\partial p'/\partial \beta < 0$.

44. See, for example, Arrow (1962, 612, 613, 616; 1963, 945, 961). Some writers have viewed moral hazard, in part, as a moral phenomenon related to fraud in the collection of benefits (see, for example, Mehr and Commack 1966, 174): a fire insurance policy, for example, may create an incentive for arson as well as for carelessness. Our analysis deals explicitly only with the effects of market insurance on self-protection, although implicitly it applies also to the effects on fraud.

45. If $U = aI + bI^2$, with $b < 0$, equation (35) becomes $[p - (1/2)] I_1^c - [p - (1/2)] I_0^c > 0$. Since $I_1^c > I_0^c$, this implies that $p > 1/2$.

46. If $\pi'(r) = 0$, the optimality condition for r, given the value of s, is from equation (32): $-p'(r^*) [U(I_1^c - r^* - s\pi) - U(I_0^c - r^* + s)] - (1 - p) U'(I_1^c - r^* - s\pi) - pU'(I_0^c - r^* + s) = 0$. Self-protection would be discouraged by market insurance if an exogenous increase in the latter always reduced the optimal value of r^*; that is, if $dr^*/ds < 0$, or $dr^*/ds = \{p'(r^*) [U_1'(-\pi) - U_0'] + [(1 - p) U_1''(-\pi) + pU_0'']\}/U_{rr}^* < 0$, where $U_{rr}^* < 0$. The first term in the numerator is necessarily positive since $p'(r^*)$ is negative and π, U_0' and U_1' are all positive. Therefore, a sufficient condition for the inequality to hold is that the second term be nonnegative, or since $\pi = [(1 + \lambda) p]/(1 - p)$, that $U_0'' \geq (1 + \lambda) U_1''$. If $\lambda \geq 0$—no negative loading—this latter inequality necessarily holds provided U'' and $U''' \leq 0$; for example, if U were the quadratic function $aI + bI^2$, with $b \leq 0$. Of course, it might hold even if $U''' > 0$.

47. According to equations (B2) and (B9) and the condition $U'' < 0$, $U_1'[1 + s^* \pi'(r^*)] < U_0'$ if $\pi \geq p/(1 - p)$.

48. One can write $\lambda'(r) = (\partial\lambda/\partial p) (\partial p/\partial r)$, where $\partial p/\partial r < 0$. Hence $\lambda'(r) > 0$ only if $\partial\lambda/\partial p < 0$. (But see our discussion on pages 126–27.)

49. According to equation (B7), an increase in λ due to an exogenous factor θ would not change $\pi'(r)$ if, and only if, $[p'(r)/(1 - p)] [\partial\lambda(r, \theta)/\partial\theta] = -p[\partial\lambda'(r, \theta)/\partial\theta]$. This assumption is made to separate an autonomous change in the price of insurance from an autonomous change in the effect of self-protection on the price of insurance.

50. Using equations (B8) and (B9) and the second-order optimality conditions discussed above, it follows that $U_{rr}^* = (1 - p) U_1''\pi^2 + pU_0'' + 2U_1'/s^* - (1 - p) U_1's^*\pi''(r) < 0$; $U_{s,r}^* = -(1 - p) U_1''\pi^2 - pU_0'' > 0$; and

$$\Sigma = U_{ss}^* \left[\frac{2U_1'}{s^*} - (1 - p) U_1' s^* \pi''(r) \right] > 0.$$

Since by equation (B4) $U_{ss}^* < 0$, $2U_1'/s^* - (1 - p) U_1' s^* \pi''(r)$ must be negative in order for Σ to be positive.

51. See equation (B4) and the footnote following equation (B10).

REFERENCES

Arrow, K. J. "Economic Welfare and the Allocation of Resources for Invention." In *The Rate and Direction of Inventive Activity: Economic and Social Factors*, edited by National Bureau Committee for Economic Research (NBER). Princeton, N.J.: NBER, 1962.

———. "Uncertainty and the Welfare Economics of Medical Care." *AER* 53 (December 1963): 941–73.

————. "The Role of Securities in the Optimal Allocation of Risk Bearing." *Rev. Econ. Studies* (April 1964): 91–96.

————. *Aspects of the Theory of Risk Bearing.* Helsinki: Yrgö Jahnssonin Säätio, 1965.

Becker, G. S. "Uncertainty and Insurance, a Few Notes." Unpublished paper, 1968.

Becker, G. S., and Michael, R. T. "On the Theory of Consumer Demand." Unpublished paper, March 1970.

Demsetz, H. "Information and Efficiency: Another Viewpoint." *J. Law and Econ.* 12, no. 1 (April 1959): 1–22.

Ehrlich, I. "Participation in Illegitimate Activities: An Economic Analysis." Ph.D. dissertation, Columbia Univ., 1970.

Hirshleifer, J. "Investment Decision under Uncertainty: Applications of the State Preference Approach." *QJE* 80 (May 1966): 252–77.

————. *Investment, Interest and Capital.* Englewood Cliffs, N.J.: Prentice-Hall, 1970.

Lees, D. S., and Rice, R. G. "Uncertainty and the Welfare Economics of Medical Care: Comment." *AER* 55 (March 1965): 140–54.

Mehr, R. I., and Commack, E. *Principles of Insurance.* 4th ed. Homewood, Ill.: Irwin, 1966.

Mossin, J. "Aspects of Rational Insurance Purchasing." *JPE* 76 (July/August): 1968): 553–68.

Pratt, J. W. "Risk Aversion in the Small and in the Large." *Econometrica* 32, nos. 1–2 (January–April 1964): 122–36.

Smith, V. L. "Optimal Insurance Coverage." *JPE* 76 (January/February 1968): 68–77.

A THEORY OF
SOCIAL INTERACTIONS

· 6 ·

This essay uses simple tools of economic theory to analyze interactions between the behavior of some persons and different characteristics of other persons. Although these interactions are emphasized in the contemporary sociological and anthropological literature, and were considered the cornerstone of behavior by several prominent nineteenth-century economists, they have been largely ignored in the modern economic literature. The central concept of the analysis is "social income," the sum of a person's own income (his earnings, etc.) and the monetary value to him of the relevant characteristics of others, which I call his social environment. By using the concept of social income, I can analyze the effect on these expenditures of changes in different sources of income and in different prices, including the "price" of the social environment. Interactions among members of the same family receive the greatest attention. The "head" of a family is defined not by sex or age, but as that member, if there is one, who transfers general purchasing power to all other members because he cares about their welfare. A family with a head is a highly interdependent organization that has the following properties: A redistribution of income among members does not affect

First published in the *Journal of Political Economy* 82, no. 6 (November–December 1974): 1063–93. © 1974 by The University of Chicago. All rights reserved.

the consumption or welfare of any member because it simply induces offsetting changes in transfers from the head. Not only the head but other members too act "as if" they "loved" all members, even when they are really selfish, in the sense that they maximize not their own income alone but family income. Transfers from parents to children in the form, say, of schooling, gifts, and bequests tend to be negatively related to what the income of children would be relative to their parents in the absence of these transfers. Therefore, the relative income of children inclusive of transfers could be unrelated or even negatively related to these transfers. Consequently, one cannot infer anything about the stability across generations of economic or social positions simply from knowing the relation between parental position and the amount transferred.

"No Man Is an Island."

John Donne, *Devotions upon Emergent*

"Man is a social animal."

Seneca, *De beneficiis*

I. INTRODUCTION

Before the theory of consumer demand began to be formalized by Jevons, Walras, Marshall, Menger, and others, economists frequently discussed what they considered to be the basic determinants of wants. For example, Bentham (1789, chap. 5) discusses about 15 basic kinds of pleasures and pains—all other pleasures and pains are presumed to be combinations of the basic set—and Marshall (1962, bk. 3, chap. 2) briefly discusses a few basic determinants of wants before moving on to his well-known presentation of marginal utility theory. What is relevant and important for present purposes is the prominence given to the interactions among individuals.

Bentham mentions "the pleasures . . . of being on good terms with him or them," "the pleasures of a good name," "the pleasures resulting from the view of any pleasures supposed to be possessed by the beings who may be the objects of benevolence," and "the pleasures resulting from the view of any pain supposed to be suffered by the beings who may become the objects of malevolence." Nassau Senior said that "the desire for distinction . . . is a feeling which if we consider its universality, and its constancy, that it affects all men and at all times, that it comes with us from the cradle and never leaves us till we go into the grave, may be pronounced to be the most powerful of all human passions" (quoted by Marshall 1962, 87). Marshall also stresses the desire for distinction and illustrates its influence by discussing food, clothing, housing, and productive activities.[1]

As greater rigor permeated the theory of consumer demand, variables like distinction, a good name, or benevolence were pushed further and further out of sight. Each individual or family generally is assumed to have a utility function that depends directly on the goods and services it consumes. This is not to say that interactions between individuals have been completely ignored. Pigou (1903), Fisher (1926, 102), and Panteleoni (1898)[2] included attributes of others in utility functions (but did nothing with them). In recent literature, "demonstration" and "relative income" effects on savings and consumption,[3] "bandwagon" and "snob" influences on ordinary consumption theory,[4] and the economics of philanthropic contributions[5] have been discussed. But these efforts have not been unified and, more significantly, have not captured the dominance attributed to social interactions by nineteenth-century economists.

Of course, sociologists have for a long time emphasized the central role of interactions and their importance in the basic structure of wants or personality. Veblen's conspicuous consumption and conspicuous leisure (if for this purpose he is classified as a sociologist) have entered ordinary discourse. At one point he said: "But it is only when taken in a sense far removed from its naive meaning that the consumption of goods can be said to afford the incentive from which accumulation invariably proceeds. The motive that lies at the root of ownership is emulation," and "the usual basis of self-respect is the respect accorded by one's neighbors" (Veblen 1934, 25, 30). Interactions were also emphasized by Durkheim, Simmel, Freud, and Weber, as well as in modern discussions of "social exchange" and the "theory of action" (see Blau 1968; Parsons 1968).

My interest in interactions can probably be traced to a study of discrimination and "prejudice" where I analyzed discriminatory behavior by incorporating the race, religion, sex, or other personal characteristics of employees, fellow workers, customers, dealers, neighbors, etc., into utility functions (Becker 1971 [1st ed., 1957]). Subsequently, in order to provide a theoretical framework for a study of philanthropy by the National Bureau of Economic Research, I incorporated the standard of living of "poorer" persons into the utility functions of "richer" ones (Becker 1961). Further reflection gradually convinced me that the emphasis of earlier economists deserved to be taken much more seriously because social interactions had significance far transcending the special cases discussed by myself[6] and others.

This essay incorporates a general treatment of interactions into the modern theory of consumer demand. In Section II, various characteristics of different persons are assumed to affect the utility functions of some persons, and the behavioral implications are systematically explored. Section III develops further implications and applications in the context of analyzing intrafamily relations, charitable behavior, merit goods and multiperson interactions, and envy and hatred. The variety and significance of these applications is persuasive testimony not only to the importance of social interactions but also to the feasibility of incorporating them into a rigorous analysis.

II. Theoretical Framework

Equilibrium for a Single Person

According to the modern (and very old!) theory of household behavior,[7]

$$U_i = U_i(Z_1, \ldots, Z_m) \qquad (1)$$

is the utility function of the *i*th person, and $Z_1, \ldots, Z_m$ are the basic wants or commodities. As indicated earlier, Bentham mentions about 15 basic wants, whereas Marshall and Senior stress an even smaller number. Each person also has a set of production functions that determine how much of these commodities can be produced with the market goods, time, and other resources available to him:

$$Z_j = f_j^i(x_j, t_j, E^i, R_j^1, \ldots, R_j^r), \qquad (2)$$

where x_j are quantities of different market goods and services; t_j are quantities of his own time; E^i stands for his education, experience, and "environmental" variables; and $R_j^1, \ldots, R_j^r$ are characteristics of other persons that affect his output of commodities. For example, if Z_1 measures *i*'s distinction in his occupation, $R_1^1, \ldots, R_1^r$ could be the opinions of *i* held by other persons in the same occupation. Presumably, characteristics of others affect the production of a significant fraction of commodities.

If the R_j were completely outside *i*'s control—that is, unaffected by what he does with his resources—*i* would maximize U taking the R_j as given. This is one way to justify the usual neglect of interactions. They are considered beyond the control of the persons being studied and are therefore taken as given when one is analyzing their reactions to changes in resources and prices.

The point of departure of my approach is to assume the contrary, namely, that *i* can change R_j by his own efforts. For example, he can avoid social opprobrium and perhaps ostracism by not engaging in criminal activities;

achieve distinction by working diligently at his occupation, giving to charities, or having a beautiful house; or relieve his envy and jealousy by talking
meanly about or even physically harming his neighbors. These effects can be
formalized in a production function for the $(R^1_j, \ldots, R^r_j)$ that depends partly
on the efforts of i and partly on other variables.

To simplify the discussion,[8] I follow Senior and assume only a single
commodity (distinction?) that is produced with a single good (the input of
time is ignored) and a single characteristic of others. Then maximizing utility
is equivalent to maximizing the output of this commodity, and one can write

$$U_i = Z(x, R). \qquad (3)$$

I assume also (until the section on Merit Goods and Multiperson Interactions) that the effect of other variables (including the efforts of others) on
this characteristic is not dependent on i's own efforts. Therefore, R can be
written as the additive function

$$R = D_i + h, \qquad (4)$$

where h measures the effect of i's efforts, and D_i the level of R when i makes
no effort; that is, D_i measures i's "social environment."

His budget constraint for money income can be written as

$$p_x x + p_R h = I_i, \qquad (5)$$

where I_i is his money income, $p_R h$ is the amount he spends on R, and p_R is
the price to him of a unit of R. Substitute $R - D_i$ for h in equation (5) to get

$$p_x x + p_R R = I_i + p_R D_i = S_i. \qquad (6)$$

The right-hand side gives the sum of i's money income and the value to him
of his social environment, and will be called his social income. The left-
hand side shows how his social income is "spent": partly on his "own" goods
(x) and partly on the characteristics of others (R).[9]

If i maximizes the utility-output function given by equation (3) subject
to the constraint on social income given by equation (6), the equilibrium
condition is[10]

$$\frac{\partial U_i}{\partial x} \bigg/ \frac{\partial U_i}{\partial R} = \frac{p_x}{p_R}. \qquad (7)$$

If I did not want to purchase any R, p_R would be a "shadow" price, measured
by the monetary equivalent of the marginal utility (equal to the marginal
product) of R to i when $R = D_i$ (or when $h = 0$).

FIGURE I

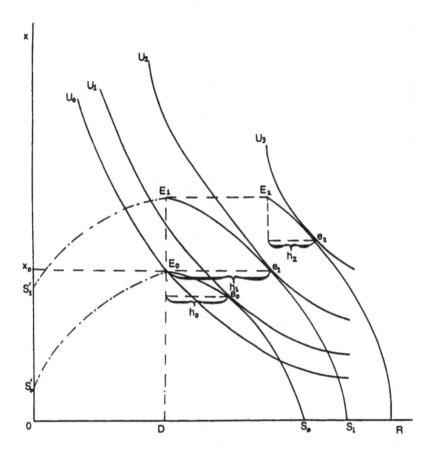

His equilibrium position is shown in figures 1 and 2. The first figure assumes that R has a positive marginal product in the production of Z (a positive marginal utility); that R refers, for example, to the respect accorded i rather than to his envy of others. The quantity OD measures his social environment, and $0x_0$ his own income (measured in terms of x), so that the "endowed" point E_o gives his utility when he spends nothing on R. If E_oS_o measures the opportunities available for purchasing additional R,[11] he would maximize his utility by moving along E_oS_o to point e_o, where the slope of this opportunity curve equaled the slope of his indifference curve. His equilibrium purchase of R is measured by the line segment h_o.

Figure 2 assumes that R has a negative marginal product (or utility)

FIGURE 2

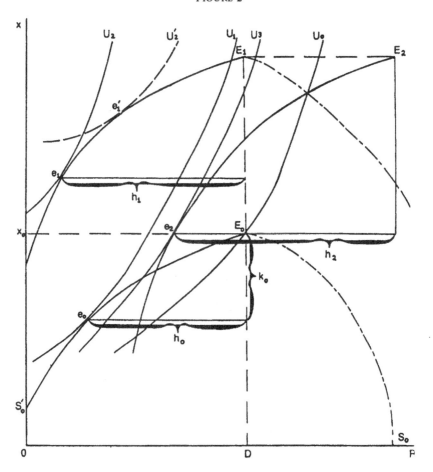

because, say, it measures the income or prestige of persons that i envies. The section of the opportunity curve to the southeast of point E_o is now irrelevant, and he moves along the southwest section $E_o S_o'$ to point e_o. He is willing to give up resources to reduce R because his utility is raised by a reduction in R; at point e_o, he spends enough resources to reduce R by h_o.

Note that since the marginal (and average) price of R is negative in figure 2, i's social income is *less* than his own income because the value of his social environment is subtracted from his own income. That is, he is made worse off by his social environment if it is dominated by characteristics of others that are distasteful to him. Note too that as long as the marginal utility of R is not zero at the socially endowed position, his social income would differ from his own income even if he did not want to spend anything on R. He would add to (or subtract from) his own income the product of D and the (monetary equivalent of the) marginal utility of R at the endowed position E_o. In other words, the traditional income concept is incomplete even when no resources are spent trying to influence the attitudes or situation of others.

The analysis developed for social interactions in these figures and in equations (3), (6), and (7) is also applicable whenever there is a physical environment that either can be altered directly or can have its effects augmented or diminished. For example, the human capital of a person is the sum of the amount inherited and that acquired through investments; moreover, the amount invested is partly determined by the inheritance. Or the temperature in a house is determined by the weather and expenditures on fuels, insulation, etc., that reinforce or offset the natural environment.

A more general analysis, therefore, would assume that every term entering the utility function has both an environmental and acquired component. The general analysis could readily be developed, but I have chosen to simplify the discussion by ignoring the nonsocial environment. The results are consistent with those from the general analysis as long as the contribution of the social environment is, on the whole, significantly more important than that of the physical environment. This is assumed to be true. (I am indebted to Gilbert Ghez and especially Robert Barro for stressing the general nature of the analysis.)

Income and Price Effects

An increase in i's own income alone—without any change in prices or the social environment—would increase both x and R unless one were inferior. The average percentage response in x and R per 1 percent change in his own income is not unity, but is less by the fraction α, where α is the share of the social environment in his social income.[12] Therefore, the effect of a change in his own income on his utility output is smaller the more important his social environment is.

Put differently, the greater the contribution of his social environment to his social income, the more his welfare is determined by the attitudes and behavior of others rather than by his own income. Traditional models of choice by economists assume that own efforts and access to property income and transfer payments determine welfare. On the other hand, those who stress the social environment, its normative requirements and sanctions for compliance and noncompliance, and the helplessness of the individual in the face of his environment naturally see society dominating individual efforts and, consequently, see little scope for important choices by individuals.

The relative importance of the social environment, as well as other implications of the theory of social interactions, can be empirically estimated from information on expenditures motivated by these interactions. If i's social environment did not change when his own income changed, the induced absolute change in the characteristics of others would equal the change in his contribution to these characteristics. However, the relative change in his contribution would differ from the relative change in these characteristics because the level of the latter is partly determined by the social environment.

Consider again figures 1 and 2, where an increase in i's own income with no change in the environment is shown by a vertical increase in the endowed position from E_o to E_1. Since his equilibrium position changes from e_o to e_1, the change in R is exactly equal to $h_1 - h_o$, the change in i's contribution to R. The percentage change in R in figure 1 is clearly less than that in h, since R is the sum of h and (a fixed) D. Since the percentage change in R in figure 2 is negative, it is also less than the percentage change in h, which is positive (since h is negative). However, if R had been increased by the increase in i's own income—if, say, the new equilibrium position was at point e_1'—the percentage change in R would be positive and would clearly exceed in algebraic value the negative percentage change in h.

The own-income elasticity of demand for contributions is related to the elasticity of demand for characteristics by the following formula:[13]

$$n_h \equiv \frac{dh}{dI_i} \cdot \frac{I_i}{h} = \frac{n_R}{\bar{n}(= 1 - \alpha)} \left[1 + \alpha\left(\frac{1}{\beta} - 1\right) \right], \qquad (8)$$

where $0 \leq \beta \leq 1$ is the fraction of own income that is spent on contributions to R. If $\alpha > 0$, if the social environment adds to i's social income, then clearly $n_h > n_R$.[14] Moreover, if $n_R \geq \bar{n} = 1 - \alpha < 1$, necessarily $n_h > 1$ even when $n_R < 1$; that is, contributions to the characteristics of others could have a "high" income elasticity even when the characteristics themselves had a "low" elasticity. Of course, if $n_h > 1$, the own-income elasticity of demand for own consumption (n_x) would be less than unity. That is, social interaction implies a relatively *low* income elasticity for own consumption even without introducing transitory changes in income, errors in variables, and the like.

Equation (8) further implies that an increase in α, an increase in the social environment, with no change in the own-income elasticity of demand for characteristics relative to the average elasticity $(n_R/\bar{n})$,[15] would increase the own-income elasticity of demand for contributions.[16] In other words, the more that i's social income was determined by his social environment, the greater would be the percentage change in his contributions to the characteristics of others as his own income changed.

If, on the other hand, $\alpha < 0$—the social environment subtracted from i's social income—then equation (8) implies that $n_h < n_R$ when $n_R > 0$, and $n_h > n_R$ when $n_R < 0$ (these different cases are shown in fig. 2). His demand for characteristics would probably be reduced by an increase in his own income (i.e., $n_R < 0$) if these characteristics have a negative marginal utility to him. Again, an increase in α, with $n_R/\bar{n}$ held constant, would raise n_h (the argument in n. 16 fully applies).

Since the social environment to any person cannot be readily observed, an indirect method of estimating at least its sign would be useful. If $n_R/\bar{n}$ were known, that is, if the relative income elasticity of demand for characteristics were known, the sign of α could be estimated simply from information on the own-income elasticity of demand for contributions to the environment, and its magnitude from additional information on the fraction of own income spent on these contributions. Equation (8) implies that

$$\alpha = \frac{n_h(\bar{n}/n_R) - 1}{1/\beta - 1}. \tag{9}$$

Therefore, $\alpha \gtreqless 0$ as $n_h(\bar{n}/n_R) \gtreqless 1$, and information on n_h, $\bar{n}/n_R$, and β would be sufficient to estimate α.

An increase in a social environment that adds to i's social income would increase his demand for own goods if they had positive income elasticities. If his own income were unchanged, his increased expenditure on own goods would have to be "financed" by reduced contributions to the characteristics of others. Similarly, an increase in a social environment that subtracts from his social income would increase his expenditures on others and reduce his expenditures on own goods. Consequently, the effect of a change in the environment is always (i.e., as long as own goods are not inferior) partly offset by induced changes in i's contributions in the opposite direction, regardless of whether the environment adds to or subtracts from i's social income.

Geometrically, a change in the social environment is shown by a horizontal movement of the endowed position. An increase in the environment shifts the endowment in figure 1 from point E_1 to E_2; the equilibrium position is changed from point e_1 to a point on a higher indifference curve (e_2), and i's contribution declines from h_1 to h_2. In figure 2, the equilibrium is changed from point e_1 to a point on a lower indifference curve (e_2), and i's contribution increases from h_1 to h_2.[17]

If both the own and environment incomes of i changed, the effect would be a combination of those when each alone changed. For example, if both incomes increased, the effect on his contributions of the increase in the environment would at least partly offset the effect of the increase in his own income. In particular, if both incomes increased by the same percentage, the percentage change in contributions would be greater than, equal to, or smaller than that percentage as his demand for characteristics exceeded, equaled, or was less than unity.

Through the assumption that p_R is constant, I have been assuming, in effect, that expenditures and the social environment are perfect substitutes in producing characteristics of others. However, the qualitative implications of this assumption can also be derived if they are simply better substitutes for each other than for own consumption—if p_R rises as h rises, but not "too" rapidly. For example, a rise in the environment would reduce contributions, and a rise in own income would increase contributions by a relatively large percentage if the environment and expenditures on these characteristics are simply relatively close direct substitutes.

A rise in the cost of changing the characteristics of others (p_R) would induce the usual substitution (and perhaps income) effects away from these characteristics. If the environment were given, the absolute change in contributions would equal the absolute change in these characteristics, while the percentage changes would differ according to equation (8) in the following way:

$$E_h = -\frac{dh}{dp_R}\frac{p_R}{h} = E_R\left[\frac{1+\alpha(1/\beta-1)}{1-\alpha}\right] \qquad (10)$$

(same proof as in n. 13 above). Therefore, when $\alpha > 0$, E_h would exceed E_R by an amount that would be greater, the greater α and the smaller β. Similarly, when $\alpha < 0$, E_h would be less than E_R[18] by an amount that would be greater, the greater the absolute value of α and the smaller β.

III. Applications

Three specific applications of the general analysis of social interaction are now considered: interactions among members of the same family, charity, and envy and hatred. These applications not only provide empirical support for the income and price implications just derived, but also bring out a number of other implications of social interaction.

The Family

Assume that i cares about his spouse j in the sense that i's utility function depends on j's welfare.[19] I assume until much later in this section that j does not care positively or negatively about i. For simplicity, define the variable measuring this dependence, R_i, as follows:

$$R_i = \frac{I_j + h_{ij}}{p_x} = \frac{S_i}{p_x} = x_j, \tag{11}$$

where I_j is j's own income, h_{ij} are the contributions from i to j, S_j is j's social income, and x_j are the goods consumed by j. The social income of i can be derived by substituting equation (11) into equation (6):

$$p_x x_i + p_R R_i = S_i = I_i + \frac{p_R I_j}{p_x}, \tag{12}$$

where p_R is the price to i of transferring resources to j. If i can transfer resources to j without any "transactions" costs—presumably, these costs are reduced by sharing a common household—and if i cares sufficiently about j to have $h_{ij} > 0$, then $p_R = p_x$, and

$$S_i = p_x x_i + p_x x_j = I_i + I_j = I_{ij}. \tag{13}$$

The social income of i equals the combined own incomes of i and j, or the "family's" own income. Moreover, the equilibrium condition given by equation (7) implies that

$$\frac{\partial U_i}{\partial x_i} \bigg/ \frac{\partial U_i}{\partial (R_i = x_j)} = \frac{p_x}{p_R} = 1, \tag{14}$$

or i would receive equal marginal utility from j's and his own consumption.

Conditions (13) and (14) are shown in figure 3. Resources can be transferred from i to j by moving along i's budget line in a southeast direction from the endowed position at point E_0. The equilibrium position is at point e, where the slope of i's indifference curves equals the slope of his budget line ($=$ to -1) . The vertical (or horizontal) intercept gives the family's own income—i's social income—deflated by the price of x.

An important implication of this analysis is that a change in the distribution of family income between i and j has no effect at all on the consumption or welfare of either, as long as i continues to transfer resources to j. A change in the distribution would be on the same budget line as E_0 if total family income is unchanged: the change from E_0 to E_1 is nominally more favorable to j, whereas the change to E_2 is nominally more favorable to i. Since there is only one point of tangency between i's budget line and an

FIGURE 3

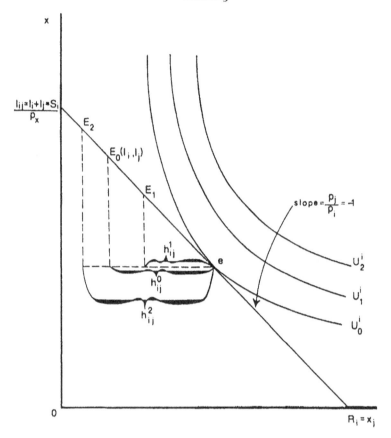

indifference curve, the equilibrium position must be unchanged at e. A shift in favor of j's income to E_1 simply induces an equal reduction in i's contributions to j (from h_{ij}^0 to h_{ij}^1 in the figure), whereas a shift against j's income to E_2 induces an equal increase in his contributions (from h_{ij}^0 to h_{ij}^2).[20]

This discussion has assumed a two-person family but is equally applicable to larger families that include grandparents, parents, children, uncles, aunts, or other kin. If one member, call him the "head," cares sufficiently about all other members to transfer general resources to them,[21] redistribution of income among members would not affect the consumption of any member, as long as the head continues to contribute to all.

The head's concern about the welfare of other members provides each, including the head, with some insurance against disasters. If a disaster reduced the income of one member alone, k, by say 50 percent, the head would increase his contributions to k, and thereby offset to some extent the decline in k's income. The head would "finance" his increased contribution to k by reducing his own consumption and his contributions to other members; in effect each member shares k's disaster by consuming less. If k's share of family income were negligible, he would essentially be fully insured against his own disasters because even a 50 percent decline in his income would have a negligible effect on family income, and thus on the consumption of each member. Since the share contributed by any member would tend to be inversely related to family size, large families, including the extended kinship family found in certain societies, can provide self-insurance especially when old-age, health, and other kinds of market insurance are not available or are very costly.[22] Note that insurance is automatically provided when resources are voluntarily transferred, without the need for any member to have dictatorial control over the family's allocation of resources.

The result on the unimportance of the distribution of income among persons linked by transfers can also be used to understand the interaction among generations.[23] Suppose that the resources of the present generation are changed at the expense of or to the benefit of the resources accruing to future generations. For example, increased government debt or social security payments are financed by increased taxes on future generations, or increased public investment, perhaps in schools, with benefits accruing to future generations is financed by taxes on the present generation. If present and future generations are fully connected by a series of intergenerational transfers, called "bequests," then each of these apparent changes in the relative resources of present and future generations would tend to be offset by equal but opposite changes in bequests. In particular, increased public debt would not raise the real wealth or consumption of the present generation or reduce that of future generations because increased taxes on future generations would be matched by increased bequests to them. Similarly, increased public investment in education would be matched by reduced private investment in education.[24]

The budget constraint of the head is determined by total family income, not his own income alone—equation (13) for a two-person family can be readily generalized to many persons. Since the head maximizes his utility subject to his budget constraint, anything that increased family income would increase his utility. Therefore, the head would consider the effect on total family income of his different actions, and would forfeit own income if the incomes of other family members were increased even more. For example, he would not move to another city if his spouse's or children's income would be decreased by more than his own income would be increased. Or, although children usually eventually set up their own households and fully control their own incomes, the head would guide and help finance their investments in education and other human capital to maximize the present value of the real income yielded by these investments.[25]

Put differently, the head automatically internalizes the "external" effects of his actions on other family members.[26] Indeed, because the head maximizes family income, he *fully* internalizes these externalities not only when the income of different members but also when their consumption, the other side of the budget constraint, is directly affected. He would take an action directly affecting consumption only when either the value of any increase in his consumption exceeded the value (to him) of any decrease in other members' consumption, or when any decrease in his own was less valuable than the increase in theirs.[27]

For example, he would read in bed at night only if the value of reading exceeded the value (to him) of the loss in sleep suffered by his wife, or he would eat with his fingers only if its value exceeded the value (to him) of the disgust experienced by his family. The development of manners and other personal behavior "rules" between family members well illustrates how apparent "external" effects can be internalized by social interaction between members.

Note too that not only is the head better off when his utility is raised, but so too are other members of his family, even if his actions directly reduce their consumption or increase their discomfort and disgust. For if his utility is raised and if their welfare has a positive income elasticity to him, he would increase his contributions to them by more than enough to offset their initial losses. For example, if he benefits from reading at night, his wife does too because he more than compensates her for her loss of sleep.[28]

The head maximizes a utility function that depends on the consumption of all family members subject to a budget constraint determined by family income and family consumption. Therefore, the effect of a change in relative prices of goods, or in aggregate family income (as well as in its distribution) on a family's consumption of different goods, could be predicted solely from the head's utility function and a budget constraint on family variables. The usual substitution and income effects of demand theory would be fully applicable.

In this sense, then, a family with a head can be said to maximize "its" consistent and transitive utility function of the consumption of different members subject to a budget constraint defined on family variables. The "family's" utility function is identical with that of one member, the head, because his concern for the welfare of other members, so to speak, integrates all the members' utility functions into one consistent "family" function.

That is, a "family's" utility function is the same as that of one of its members not because this member has dictatorial power over other members, but because he (or she!) cares sufficiently about all other members to transfer resources voluntarily to them. Each member can have complete freedom of action; indeed, the person making the transfers would not change the consumption of any member even with dictatorial power! For example, if i had dictatorial power, he could move the equilibrium position e in figure 3 to the vertical axis (or anywhere else), but would not choose to move it because his utility partly depends on j's consumption.[29]

Nothing much has yet been said about the preferences of members who are not heads. The major, and somewhat unexpected, conclusion is that if a head exists, *other members also are motivated to maximize family income and consumption, even if their welfare depends on their own consumption alone*. This is the "rotten kid" theorem (I owe this name to the Barro family). For consider a selfish member j who can take an action that would reduce his income by b, but increase that of another member k by c. Initially, j would be worse off by b, since the gain to k is of no direct concern to him. However, if $c = b$, the head would transfer enough additional resources to j from k to leave him (and k) equally well off, since intrafamily reallocations of income do not affect the consumption of any member. Moreover, if $c > b$—if family income were raised by j's action—and if j's welfare were a superior "good" to the head, then he would transfer enough additional resources to j to make j better off. Consequently, even a selfish j would only undertake actions that raised family income or consumption, regardless of the initial impact on him.

In other words, when one member cares sufficiently about other members to be the head, all members have the same motivation as the head to maximize family opportunities and to internalize fully all within-family "externalities," regardless of how selfish (or, indeed, how envious) these members are. Even a selfish child receiving transfers from his parents would *automatically* consider the effects of his actions on other siblings as well as on his parents. Put still differently, sufficient "love" by one member guarantees that all members act as if they loved other members as much as themselves. As it were, the amount of "love" required in a family is economized: sufficient "love" by one member leads all other members by "an invisible hand" to act as if they too loved everyone.

Armed with this theorem, I do not need to dwell on the preferences of nonheads. Of course, just as there may be no head if all members are sufficiently selfish, so there may be none if they are all sufficiently altruistic. Each would want to transfer resources to other members, but no one would want to accept transfers. Aside from that, mutual interaction or mutual interdependence of welfare raises no particular problems.[30]

By assuming in figure 3 and in the formal development given by equations (11)–(14) that only a single good is consumed by each person, I eliminated any distinction between transferring general purchasing power and transferring particular goods to another member. If each member consumes many goods, the conclusions in this section about family utility functions, internalization of within-family externalities, and so on fully hold only if the head is content to transfer general purchasing power. He would transfer in this form if his utility function depended on the utility of other members—that is, if his utility function could be written in the form

$$U_h = U_h[x_{h1}, \ldots, x_{hm}, g_1(x_{21}, \ldots, x_{2m}), \ldots, g_n(x_{n1}, \ldots, x_{nm})], \quad (15)$$

where x_{ij} is the quantity of the jth good consumed by the ith person, and

$$dg_i = 0 \left(= \sum_{j=1}^{m} \frac{\partial g_i}{\partial x_{ij}} dx_{ij} \right)$$

implies that the utility of the ith person is unchanged. If he is concerned not about the utility of other members but about their consumption of particular "merit" goods, the conclusions can be quite different. The systematic discussion of merit goods is postponed to pages 166–69.

If parents are transferring resources to their children in the form, say, of gifts and expenditures on education and other human capital or after they die in the form of bequests, then an increase in the income of parents by a given percentage would tend to increase contributions to children by a still larger percentage, certainly by one exceeding the increased welfare of their children (see the discussion in Section II). In other words, contributions to children can be very responsive to a change in parental income without the welfare of children being so responsive.

Empirical evidence on bequests, gifts, and many other transfers to children is seriously deficient. The general impression is, however, that bequests have a very high income elasticity. Moreover, the elasticity of expenditures on children's education with respect to parental income does appear to be above unity (Schultz 1967, 9), which is consistent with the implications of the theory.

The responsiveness of expenditures on children's education and other training and skills to parental income has often been noted, and lamented as evidence of immobility and rigid "class" structure. Yet my analysis implies that the welfare of children—a measure of their "class"—rises by a smaller percentage than parent expenditures on them, and possibly even by a smaller percentage than parental income. Put differently, considerable regression toward the mean across generations—that is, the expected income or other measure of the position of children would be much closer to the average position than is that of their parents—can be observed at the same time that contributions to children are very responsive to parental income.[31]

The crucial point is that considerable regression toward the mean across generations would occur partly because of genetic factors and luck if all parents spent an equal amount on their children. As a result of this, and given interdependent preferences, higher-income parents tend to spend considerably more on their children than lower-income ones. However, these expenditures would only tend to dampen but not eliminate the regression toward the mean. Therefore, the elastic response of contributions to children can give a very biased picture of the degree of immobility or inheritance of "class" position. Indeed, contributions would be more responsive to parental income the stronger are the basic forces producing mobility because parents attempt to offset these forces. In other words, an elastic response of contributions to parental income may be evidence of sizable *mobility*![32]

Charity

If someone makes contributions of time or goods to unrelated persons or to organizations, he is said to be "charitable" or "philanthropic." The discussion of contributions within a family indicates that charitable behavior can be motivated by a desire to improve the general well-being of recipients.[33] Apparent "charitable" behavior can also be motivated by a desire to avoid the scorn of others or to receive social acclaim. Not much generality is sacrificed, however, by only considering charity motivated by a desire to improve well-being.[34]

The numerous implications about family behavior developed in the previous section fully apply to the synthetic "family" consisting of a charitable person i and all recipients of his charity. For example, no member's well-being would be affected by a redistribution of income among them, as long as i continued to give to all of them. For he would simply redistribute his giving until everyone losing income was fully compensated and everyone gaining was fully "taxed." Moreover, all members, not simply i, would try to maximize "family" opportunities and "family" consumption, instead of their own income or consumption alone. In addition, each member of a synthetic "family" is at least partly "insured" against catastrophes because all other members, in effect, would increase their giving to him until at least part of his loss were replaced. Therefore, charity is a form of self-insurance that is a substitute for market insurance and government transfers. Presumably, the rapid growth of these latter during the last 100 years discouraged the growth of charity.

According to the analysis in Section II, an increase in the income of a charitable person would increase his charitable giving by a greater percentage than the increase in the well-being of recipients. Indeed, his income elasticity of demand for giving would exceed unity, possibly by a substantial amount, as long as his elasticity of demand for their well-being (which I will call his demand for charity) was not much below his average income elasticity. The available evidence on charitable giving clearly supports this implication of the theory: income elasticities estimated by Taussig (1965) from giving in different income classes in 1962 are all well above unity, ranging from a low of +1.3 in the under $25,000 class to a high of +3.1 in the $100,000–$200,000 class.[35]

A crucial implication of charitable giving in terms of social interaction between the giver and others is that an increase in the incomes of recipients would reduce giving. Therefore, an increase in the incomes of both recipients and givers should not increase giving by as much as an increase in the incomes of givers alone. These implications are tested and confirmed by Schwartz (1970), who analyzes aggregate time series on incomes and charitable giving in the United States between 1929 and 1966 and also compares his findings with the cross-sectional findings of Taussig (1965) reported above.[36]

The usual theory of consumer choice ignores social interactions, and would consider charitable giving simply as a "good" that enters the giver's utility function along with his other goods:

$$U_i^! = U_i(x_i, h), \qquad (16)$$

where h measures the amount given by i, and x_i are the other goods that he consumes. This "conventional" approach does not imply that an increase in i's income would increase his giving by a particularly large percentage, or that an increase in the incomes of recipients would lower his giving. Therefore, considerable ad hocery would be required if the "conventional" approach were to explain the evidence on charitable giving that is more readily explained by an approach that incorporates social interactions.

These findings can be used to make very crude, but instructive, calculations of the share of recipient's own incomes in the social incomes of contributors. If the own-income elasticity of demand for giving is taken from Taussig as +2.0, the share of own income spent on giving as 0.04 (see Schwartz 1970, 1278), and the income elasticity of demand for charity as equal to the average income elasticity (actually, Schwartz's findings suggest that it may be lower than the average), then, according to equation (9), charity's share in social income would be $(2-1)/(1/0.04-1) \cong 0.4$. If the own-income elasticity of giving were taken as +3.0 rather than +2.0, charity's share would double to 0.08; if, in addition, the income elasticity of charity were only four-fifths of the average elasticity, its share would increase further to 0.11 (a tithe?).

Merit Goods and Multiperson Interactions

Contributors are content to transfer general purchasing power to recipients if they are concerned about the general welfare or utility of recipients—

as seen by recipients. They want to restrict or earmark their transfers, on the other hand, if they are concerned about particular "merit" goods consumed by recipients. For example, parents may want transfers to their children spent on education or housing, or only the money incomes rather than "full" incomes of children may be of concern to parents, or contributors to beggars may not want their giving spent on liquor or gambling.

Assume, therefore, that i transfers resources to j that are earmarked for particular goods consumed by j because the utility function of i depends not only on his own goods but also on these goods of j. If j were permitted to spend his own income as he wished, an assumption modified shortly, he would spend less on these goods as a result of the earmarked transfers from i. Clearly, the reduction in his own spending would be greater, the greater the transfer, the smaller the fraction of his social income spent on these goods, and the smaller their income elasticity. For example, if they take 20 percent of his social income and have an income elasticity equal to 2.0, he would reduce his own spending by $0.60 for each dollar earmarked by i.[37]

As long as j continues to spend on the merit goods, earmarked transfers are worth as much to j as a transfer of general purchasing power with equal monetary value. Moreover, i would not have a greater effect on j's consumption of these goods with earmarked transfers than with general transfers. Therefore, as long as j continues to spend on these goods, earmarked transfers are equivalent to general transfers; and the results derived for the latter fully hold for the former. For example, a redistribution of income between i and j would have no effect on the consumption of either as long as both continue to spend on the merit goods, or both i and j want to maximize their combined incomes, not their own incomes alone.

On the other hand, if j did not want to spend anything on the merit goods because earmarked transfers were sufficiently large, such transfers would be worth less to j and more to i than would general transfers with equal money value. Moreover, various results derived for general transfers no longer hold: for example, a redistribution of income to j and away from i would reduce j's consumption of merit goods and increase his consumption of other goods.

If i were aware that j reduced his spending on merit goods when transfers increased, i would be discouraged from giving because j's reaction raises i's private price of merit goods to

$$p_m^i = p_m \frac{1}{1 - r_j} = p_m \frac{1}{v_m n_m},^{38}$$ (17)

where p_m is the market price of merit goods, and the other terms are defined in note 37. Similarly, if j were aware that i reduced his transfers when j

increased his spending on merit goods, j would also be discouraged from spending because i's reaction raises the price to j. Indeed, j could end up consuming fewer merit goods than he would if i were not concerned! That these induced reactions are not simply hypothetical or always minor is persuasively shown in a recent study of higher education (Peltzman 1973). States earmark transfers to higher education mainly through highly subsidized public institutions. Private spending was apparently reduced by (at least) $0.75 per dollar of public spending in 1966–67; private spending may have been reduced by more than $1.00 per dollar of public spending in 1959–60, so that *total* spending on higher education in that year would have been reduced by public spending.

Both i and j want to limit the induced reactions of the other because such reactions reflect the incentive to "underreveal" preferences about merit goods and "free-ride" in their consumption. Since equation (17) shows that these reactions raise the price of merit goods to i and j, in effect, both want to lower these prices. Indeed, it is well known from the theory of public goods, and a merit good is a particular kind of "public" good, that efficient prices to i and j would be less than the market price; indeed, these efficient prices would *sum* to the market price of the merit good.[39] Efficient prices might be achieved, for example, by i and j matching each other's spending in specified proportions, or each might be given a spending quota.

I intentionally say "might" be achieved because any agreement has to be "policed" to ensure that each lives up to his commitment. Policing is relatively easy for the consumer of the merit goods, j, since he usually automatically knows how much is spent by i, but is much more difficult for i, since he does not automatically know how much is spent by j.[40] Parents may use their children's grades in school to measure the input of time and effort by children that presumably "matches" the money contribution by the parents.[41] Or parents may save a large part of their total transfer to children for a bequest when they die in order to provide an incentive for children to spend "appropriately," at least while their parents are alive.[42] This may explain why the inheritance tax on bequests apparently has induced relatively little substitution toward gifts to children (see Shoup 1966; Adams 1974).

The "underrevealing," "free-riding," coordination of efforts, and "policing" discussed for merit goods are common to all multiperson interactions—that is, all situations where two or more persons are affected by the consumption, attitudes, or other behavior of the same person. The analytical issues for multiperson interactions are the same as for other "public" goods: is public intervention desirable—for example, should charitable giving be deductible from personal income in arriving at tax liabilities in order to lower the private price of giving—and do private equilibria without government intervention more closely approximate joint maximization, a Nash noncooperative game solution, or something quite different? Since space is limited, I refrain from discussing further these and related issues.

Envy and Hatred

An envious or malicious person presumably would feel better off if some other persons become worse off in certain respects. He could "harm" himself (i.e., spend his own resources) in order to harm others: in figure 2, he gives up k_0 units of his own consumption in order to harm others by h_0 units. The terms of trade between his own harm and the harm to others, given by the curve $E_0 S_0^1$ in figure 2, is partly determined by his skill at "predatory" behavior and partly by public and private expenditures to prevent crime, libeling, malicious acts, trespass, and other predatory behavior. Since an increase in these expenditures would increase the cost to him of harming others, he would be discouraged from harming them. The limited evidence available on predatory expenditures supports this implication of the theory. Crimes against persons provide some evidence on predatory behavior, since most assaults and murders probably are motivated by the harm to victims.[43] The frequency of assaults and murder (and also crimes against property) apparently is strongly negatively related to the probability of conviction, punishment, and other measures of the cost of committing these crimes (see Ehrlich 1973).

Section II suggests that a rise in own income would tend to reduce predatory expenditures. An increase in the social environment,[44] on the other hand, would necessarily increase these expenditures, unless own consumption were an inferior good. Therefore, a rise in the social environment and own income by the same percentage would reduce predatory expenditures by less than would a rise in own income alone, and might even increase them.

Again, the implications of the theory can be tested with evidence on crimes against persons. Since assaults and murders have been more frequent at lower income levels,[45] an increase in own income appears to reduce crimes against persons, if differences in own income alone are measured by differences in the incomes of individuals at a moment in time (as in the discussion of charity on pages 165–66). As predicted by the theory, an increase in own income that is accompanied by an increase in the social environment (as measured by the income of others) does not have such a negative effect on these crimes. Indeed, the frequency of assaults and murders has not been reduced by the sizable growth in aggregate incomes during the last 40 years, nor do higher-income states presently have fewer crimes against persons than other states.[46]

Over the years, even acute observers of society have differed radically in their assessment of the importance of envy and hatred. Two hundred years ago, for example, Adam Smith recognized these "passions" but shunted them aside with the comment: "Envy, malice, or resentment, are the only passions which can prompt one man to injure another in his person or reputation. But the *greater part of men are not very frequently under the influence of those passions*, and the very worst men are so only occasionally. As their gratification too, how agreeable soever it may be to certain characters, is not attended with any real or permanent advantage it is in the greater part of men commonly restrained by prudential considerations. Men may live together in society with some tolerable degree of security, though there is no civil magistrate *to protect them from the injustice of those passions*" (Smith 1937; my italics).[47] To Thorstein Veblen, on the other hand, writing many years later, their motives are the very stuff of life that dominate everything else: "The desire for wealth can scarcely be satiated in any individual instance, and evidently a satiation of the average or general desire for wealth is out of the question. However widely, or equally, or 'fouly,' it may be distributed, no general increase of the community's wealth can make any approach to satiating this need, the ground of which is the desire of everyone to excel everyone else in the accumulation of goods" (Veblen 1934, 32).[48]

In principle, the importance of envy and hatred can be measured using equation (9) by the contribution of the relevant social environment to social income; this is done in a crude way on pages 165–66 for charity. Unfortunately, not enough information is available either on the own-income elasticity of demand or on the fraction of own income spent on "predatory" behavior to make even crude estimates of the relative contribution of envy and hatred.

Still, it may be useful to note several implications of the differing views about the significance of envy and hatred. For example, Veblen's belief that the welfare of a typical person primarily depends on his relative income position implies that social income essentially is zero: that the value of the social environment causing envy would exactly offset the value of own income.[49] For then, and only then, would a rise in this social environment and own income by the same percentage, prices held constant, not affect social income or welfare. That is, a rise in all incomes in a community by the same percentage would not improve anyone's welfare in Veblen's world.[50]

If social income were negative, if the environment causing envy were more important than own income, a rise in the environment and own income by the same percentage would lower social income and welfare. That is, a general rise in incomes in a more extreme Veblenian world would actually lower welfare![51]

On the other hand, Smith's belief that envy is a relatively minor determinant of welfare implies that social income is positive: the environment causing envy is less important than own income. A rise in the environment and own income by the same percentage would then raise social income and welfare. That is, Veblen's general rise in the community's income would raise the welfare of the typical person.

IV. Summary

This essay uses simple tools of economic theory to analyze interactions between the behavior of some persons and different characteristics of other persons. Although these interactions are emphasized in the contemporary sociological and anthropological literature, and were considered the cornerstone of behavior by several prominent nineteenth-century economists, they have been largely ignored in the modern economic literature.

The central concept of the analysis is "social income," the sum of a person's own income (his earnings, etc.) and the monetary value to him of the relevant characteristics of others, which I call his social environment. The optimal expenditure of his own income to alter these characteristics is given by the usual marginal conditions. By using the concept of social income, I can analyze the effect on these expenditures of changes in different sources of income and in different prices, including the "price" of the social environment. Perhaps the most important implication is that a change in own income alone would tend to cause a relatively large change in these expenditures; in other words, the own-income elasticity of demand for these expenditures would tend to be "large," certainly larger than the elasticity resulting from equal percentage changes in own income and the social environment.

Interactions among members of the same family receive the greatest attention. The "head" of a family is defined not by sex or age, but as that member, if there is one, who transfers general purchasing power to all other members because he cares about their welfare. A family with a head is a highly interdependent organization that has the following properties:

A redistribution of income among members does not affect the consumption or welfare of any member because it simply induces offsetting changes in transfers from the head. As a result, each member is at least partially insured against disasters that may strike him.

Not only the head but other members too act "as if" they "loved" all members, even when they are really selfish, in the sense that they maximize not their own income alone but family income. As it were, the existence of a head economizes on the amount of true love required in a family.

A family acts "as if" it maximized a consistent and transitive utility function subject to a budget constraint that depended only on family variables. This utility function is the same as the head's not because he has dictatorial power, but because his concern for the welfare of other members integrates all their utility functions into one consistent "family" function.

Transfers from parents to children in the form, say, of schooling, gifts, and bequests tend to be negatively related to what the income of children would be relative to their parents in the absence of these transfers. Therefore, the relative income of children *inclusive* of transfers could be unrelated or even negatively related to these transfers. Consequently, one cannot infer anything about the stability across generations of economic or social positions simply from knowing the relation between parental position and the amount transferred.

More briefly treated are charity and envy, with special attention to the effects of different kinds of income change on charitable contributions and expenditures to alleviate envy. For example, the much higher income elasticity of demand for charitable contributions estimated from differences in individual incomes at a moment in time than from aggregate changes in incomes over time is shown to be implied by this theory of social interactions, but not readily by the traditional theory of choice.

From a methodological viewpoint, the aim of the paper is to show how another relation considered important in the sociological and anthropological literature can be usefully analyzed when incorporated into the framework provided by economic theory. Probably the main explanation for the neglect of social interactions by economists is neither analytical intractability nor a preoccupation with more important concepts, but excessive attention to formal developments during the last 70 years. As a consequence, even concepts considered to be important by earlier economists, such as social interactions, have been shunted aside.

Notes

Over the years I have received helpful comments on a succession of drafts from numerous persons, especially my colleagues at the University of Chicago and the National Bureau of Economic Research (NBER). I received very useful comments on the draft prepared for publication from Robert Barro, Isaac Ehrlich, Sam Peltzman, and George Stigler, and valuable research assistance from Walter Wessels. My research has been supported by a grant to the NBER from the National Institute of Child Health and Human Development, National Institutes of Health, U.S. Department of HEW; but the paper is not an official NBER publication since it has not been reviewed by the NBER Board of Directors.

1. He limits his discussion of consumer demand to the largely formal theory of

marginal theory because of the importance he attaches to the interaction between activities, consumer behavior, and the basic wants: "Such a discussion of demand as is possible at this stage of our work must be confined to an elementary analysis of an almost purely formal kind" (1962, 90). He never developed the more complicated and less formal analysis.

2. I owe this reference to George Stigler.

3. See, e.g., Brady and Friedman (1947), Duesenbery (1949), or Johnson (1952).

4. See Leibenstein (1950).

5. See Vickery (1962), Schwartz (1970), Alchian and Allen (1967, 135–42), and Boulding (1973).

6. Other drafts that were also circulated include Becker (1968).

7. For an exposition of this theory, see Michael and Becker (1973).

8. I have also developed the analysis assuming many commodities and many characteristics.

9. Sociologists sometimes assert that variables like social approval and respect "do not have any material value on which a price can be put" (see Blau 1968). But prices measure only scarcity and have nothing intrinsically to do with "material value"; p_R, for example, only measures the resource cost to i of changing social approval, respect, etc.

10. I assume for simplicity in this formula that p_R measures the marginal as well as average price of R.

11. If he can also reduce R by giving up own goods, the curve E_0S_0 would continue in the southwest direction (see ES_0' in the figure). However, this section would be irrelevant if R had positive marginal utility.

12. By differentiating equation (6) with respect to I_i alone, $\bar{n} \equiv w_x n_x + w_R n_R = 1 - \alpha$, where

$$w_x = \frac{p_x x}{S_i}, \, w_R = \frac{p_R R}{S_i} = 1 - w_x, \, n_x = \frac{dx}{dI_i} \cdot \frac{I_i}{x}, \, n_R = \frac{dR}{dI_i} \cdot \frac{I_i}{R}, \, \alpha = \frac{p_R D_i}{S_i},$$

and I am assuming that p_R is given (not dependent on h, x, etc.). Of course, the weighted average of income elasticities with respect to a change in S_i must equal unity, as in the usual analysis.

13. Since $dh/dI_i = dR/dI_i$,

$$n_h = \frac{dh}{dI_i} \cdot \frac{I_i}{h} = \frac{dR}{dI_i} \cdot \frac{I_i}{R} \cdot \frac{R}{h} = n_R \cdot \frac{R}{h}. \tag{8'}$$

But

$$\frac{R}{h} = \frac{p_R R}{p_R h} = 1 + \frac{p_R D_i}{p_R h} = 1 + \frac{S_i - I_i}{\beta I_i} = 1 + \frac{1/(1-\alpha) - 1}{\beta} = \frac{(1-\alpha) + \alpha/\beta}{1-\alpha}.$$

Since $1 - \alpha = \bar{n}$ (see n. 12 above), $n_h = (n_R/\bar{n}) (\alpha/\beta + 1 - \alpha)$.

14. For $[1 + \alpha(1/\beta - 1)]/(1 - \alpha) > 1$, since $1/\beta > 1$, and $1 - \alpha < 1$.

15. An increase in α lowers $\bar{n}$ because the relative contribution of own income to social income is reduced.

16. $$\frac{dn_h}{d\alpha}\left(\frac{n_R}{\bar{n}} = \text{constant}\right) = \frac{n_R}{\bar{n}}\left(\frac{1}{\beta} - 1\right) - \frac{n_R}{\bar{n}}\alpha\,\beta^{-2}\frac{d\beta}{d\alpha}.$$

Both terms are greater than zero because $\beta < 1$, and $d\beta/d\alpha < 0$ (this is shown shortly); therefore, $dn_h/d\alpha > 0$.

17. The endowment-income elasticity of demand for contributions can easily be shown to equal

$$N_h = \frac{dh}{dD}\cdot\frac{D}{h} = (N_R - 1)\left\{\frac{1}{1-\alpha}\left[1 + \alpha\left(\frac{1}{\beta} - 1\right)\right]\right\} + 1.$$

Clearly, when $\alpha > 0$, $N_h < 0$ if $N_R \leq \alpha = \bar{N}$, the average endowment-income elasticity of demand; and when $\alpha < 0$, $N_h > 0$ if $N_R \geq \alpha$.

18. I assume that an increase in the absolute value of p_R reduces the demand for R, so that $E_h > 0$.

19. Caring is not simply a deus ex machina introduced to derive the following implications, since I have shown elsewhere (Becker 1974) that the marriage market is more likely to pair a person with someone he cares about than with an otherwise similar person that he does not care about.

20. If the utility of i also partly depended directly on the amounts he transferred to j, perhaps because i's "prestige" or "approval" partly depended on these transfers, then redistribution of family income would have a net effect on the consumption of both i and j.

21. A somewhat weaker assumption is that the family is "fully connected" through a series of transfers between members; for example, a transfers resources to b because a cares about b, b transfers to c because b cares about c, and so on until m transfers to the last member, n, and n transfers to no one (this assumption is made in an intergenerational context by Barro 1974). Indirectly, a (or any other member but n) would be transferring to all members because an increase in his contributions to b would induce an increase in the contributions to all other members.

22. The interaction between self- and market insurance is analyzed in Ehrlich and Becker (1972).

23. This application is taken from the detailed discussion in Barro (1974).

24. The empirical evidence does strongly suggest that most of the investment in higher education by state governments has been offset by reduced private investment (see Peltzman 1973; McPherson, in preparation).

25. The incentive that parents have to invest in their children is discussed in several places (see, e.g., De Tray 1973; Parsons 1974).

26. The Coase theorem proves that when "bargaining costs" are negligible, each family member could always be induced to maximize family opportunities through bargaining with and side payments from other members. I have proved that the head (and, as shown later, other members too) has this incentive and, in effect, makes or

receives "side payments" without bargaining with other members. The word "automatically" is used to distinguish this theorem from the Coase Theorem.

27. Although this is a rather immediate implication of his interest in maximizing family opportunities, a direct proof may be instructive. Suppose that a particular action changed the utility of the head by

$$dU_h = mu^h dx_h + \sum_{j=1, \neq h}^{n} mu^j dx_j, \tag{1'}$$

where $mu^j = \partial U_h/\partial x_j$, and dx_j measures the change in consumption of the jth family member. If the head can transfer resources to other members dollar for dollar, in equilibrium,

$$mu^j = \lambda_h p_j \quad \text{all } j, \tag{2'}$$

where λ_h is the marginal utility of income to the head, and p_j is the cost of x_j. Substitution of eq. (2') into (1') gives

$$dU^h = \lambda_h(p_h dx_h + \sum_{j=1, \neq h}^{n} p_j dx_j) = \lambda_h \sum_{\text{all } j} p_j dx_j. \tag{3'}$$

Since the head takes an action if and only if $dU_h > 0$, eq. (3') implies (since $\lambda_h > 0$) that he takes an action if, and only if,

$$\sum_{\text{all } j} p_j dx_j > 0, \tag{4'}$$

which was to be proved.

28. Recall that I have been assuming that only a single good is consumed by each person, although this analysis presupposes many goods. The transition to many goods is straightforward if the head's utility depends on a function of the various goods consumed by another member that is monotonically related to the utility function of that member (see the discussion later in this section).

29. It is difficult to contrast my derivation of a "family" utility function with a traditional derivation, since explicit derivations are rare. The most explicit appears to be in a well-known article on social indifference curves by Samuelson (1956). He considers the problem of relating individual and family utility functions, but his discussion is brief and the arguments sometimes are not spelled out. Without sufficient elaboration, he refers to a consistent "family welfare function" being grafted onto the separate utility functions of different family members (p. 10). In addition, he says that a family member's "preferences among his own goods have the special property of being independent of the other members' consumption. But since blood is thicker than water, the preferences of the different members are interrelated by what might be called a 'consensus' or 'social welfare function' which takes into account the deservingness or ethical worths of the consumption levels of each of the members." How are these preferences interrelated by a "consensus," and should not the "deservingness" of the consumption levels of different members simply be incorporated into different members' preferences (as in my approach)? Incidentally, at one

point (p. 9), Samuelson appears to believe that if the family utility function is the same as the head's, he must have sovereign power, which I have shown is not necessary. He later (p. 20) says that "if within the family there can be assumed to take place an optimal reallocation of income so as to keep each member's dollar expenditure of equal ethical worth, then there can be derived for the whole family a set of well-behaved indifference contours relating the totals of what it consumes: the family can be said to *act as if* it maximizes such a group preference function" (italics in original). In my analyses, the "optimal reallocation" results from interdependent preferences and voluntary contributions, and the "group preference function" is identical with that of the "head."

30. It frequently has been alleged to me that mutual interaction of the form

$$U_i = U_i[x_i, g_i(U_j)]$$

$$U_j = U_j[x_j, g_j(U_i)],$$

where x_i and x_j are the own consumption of i and j, and g_i and g_j are monotonic functions of the utility indexes U_i and U_j, results in instability and unbounded utility levels. For it is argued, an increase in x_i by one unit directly raises i's utility, which raises j's utility through g_j, which in turn further raises i's utility, and so on, until U_i and U_j approach infinity. Mathematically, there is an infinite regress, since, by substitution,

$$U_i = U_i[x_i, g_i\{x_j, g_j\{x_i, g_i\{x_j, g_j\{\ldots\}\}].$$

However, with appropriate restrictions on the magnitude of the interactions, the infinite regress has a finite effect, and the "reduced forms" of U_i and U_j on x_i and x_j are well defined. Consider, for example, the Cobb Douglas functions

$$U_i = x_i^{a_i} U_j^{b_i}$$

$$U_j = x_j^{a_j} U_i^{b_j},$$

where a_i and a_j presumably are greater than zero, and b_i and b_j can either be greater than or less than zero. By substitution,

$$U_i = x_i^{a_i/(1-b_ib_j)} x_j^{a_jb_i/(1-b_ib_j)} = x_i^{\alpha_i} x_j^{\beta_i}$$

$$U_j = x_i^{a_ib_j/(1-b_ib_j)} x_j^{a_j/(1-b_ib_j)} = x_i^{\alpha_j} x_j^{\beta_j},$$

where b_ib_j is independent of monotonic transformations on U_i and U_j. A finite sum to the regress requires that $|b_ib_j| < 1$; essentially, that the marginal utilities or disutilities due to interdependence are less than unity. Note that although it is possible for $a_i = b_i$ and $a_j = b_j$, for own consumption and the welfare of the other person to be equally "important," the condition $|b_ib_j| < 1$ implies that either $|\alpha_i| > |\beta_i|$, or $|\beta_j| > |\alpha_j|$, or both; that is, for at least one of the persons, own consumption has to be more important than the other person's consumption in the "reduced forms."

31. In one study, the elasticity of children's years of schooling with respect to parental income is a sizable $+1.2$, at the same time that the elasticity of children's

income with respect to parental income is only +0.3, or a 70 percent regression toward the mean (unpublished calculations by Jacob Mincer from the Eckland Sample). Note in this regard, however, that parents cannot easily prevent considerable regression toward the mean by investing in their children. For let the relation between the human capital invested in children and parental income be

$$S_c = a + b \log I_p + u,$$

where b is the elasticity of parental response, and u represents other determinants of S_c. According to the theory of investment in human capital (Mincer 1974; Becker 1975),

$$\log I_c = \alpha + r S_c + v,$$

where r is the rate of return on human capital, and v represents other determinants of $\log I_c$. Then by substitution,

$$\log I_c = (\alpha + ra) + rb \log I_p + (ru + v).$$

Even if r were as large as 0.2, and b as large as 2.0, rb would only be 0.4: the regression toward the mean would be 60 percent. If $v = c \log I_p + v'$, where $1 - c$ measures the degree of "intrinsic" regression to the mean, then by substitution,

$$\log I_c = (\alpha + ra) + (rb + c) \log I_p + (ru + tv').$$

Since the analysis in the text implies that b would be positively related to $1 - c$ as parents try to offset the "intrinsic" regression, the "observed" regression to the mean,

$$1 - \gamma = 1 - (c + rb) = (1 - c) - rb,$$

may be only weakly related to and also is less than the "intrinsic" regression $1 - c$. I am indebted to discussions with Jacob Mincer on the issues sketchily covered in this footnote.

32. It is generally believed that the United States has a more mobile "open" society than European countries do; yet (admittedly crude) comparisons of occupational mobility between fathers and sons do not reveal large differences between the United States and several Western European countries (Lipset and Bendix 1959). Since the analysis in this paper suggests that parents' contributions to their children's education and other training is more responsive to parental position in "open" societies, more responsive parental contributions are probably offsetting the greater "openness" of American society.

33. *The Random House Dictionary of the English Language* (unabridged, 1967) defines charity as "the benevolent feeling, especially toward those in need or in disfavor."

34. The utility function of a charitable person who desires to improve the general well-being of recipients can be written as

$$U_i = U_i \left[x_i, x_j \left(= \frac{l_j + h}{p_j} \right) \right],$$

where h is his charitable giving, x_j measures the well-being of recipients, and $\partial U_i / \partial I_j$ = $\partial U_i | \partial h > 0$; that is, a unit increase in the own income of recipients has the same effect on the utility of a charitable person as a unit increase in his giving. The utility function of a person who makes "charitable" contributions to win social acclaim can be written as

$$U_i = U_i\left(x_i, \frac{I_i}{p_i}, \frac{h}{p_j}\right),$$

where still $\partial U_i/\partial h > 0$—an increase in his contributions would increase his acclaim— but now the sign of $\partial U_i / \partial I_j$ is not so obvious. If, however, contributions and the income of recipients were much closer substitutes for each other than for the own consumption of the contributor, which is plausible, then these utility functions have similar implications. Not much generality is sacrificed, therefore, by only considering charity motivated by a desire to improve the well-being of recipients.

35. These estimates are net of differences in tax rates. Note, however, that charitable giving is estimated from itemized deductions in personal income tax returns. Since only giving to (certain) institutions and not to individuals can be deducted, since many taxpayers, especially with lower incomes, do not itemize their deductions, and since others inflate their deductions, the response of tax-reported giving may not accurately describe the response of actual giving.

36. Schwartz's study, like Taussig's, is based on personal income tax returns. Both studies also estimate the price elasticity of giving, where price is measured by one minus the marginal tax rate. Schwartz finds considerable response to price, elasticities generally exceeding -0.5, which is consistent with the implications of the theory of social interactions. Taussig, on the other hand, finds only a weak response to price; but Schwartz argues that Taussig's findings are biased downward.

37. It is easily shown that $r_j = 1 - v_m n_m$, where v_m is the share spent on merit goods; n_m, their income elasticity; and r_j, the reduction in j's own spending per unit increase in i's contribution. Therefore, if $v_m = 0.2$, and $n_m = 2.0$, $r_j = 0.6$.

38. For example, if j spent \$0.60 less for each dollar transferred by i, the price to i would be $p_m^i = p_m(1/0.4) = 2.5 p_m$, or more than twice the market price.

39. A proof of this well-known summation formula can be found in Samuelson (1954).

40. The difficulty of policing "merit" goods is shown amusingly in a recent Wizard of Id cartoon. Two drunks meet, and one says, "Could you spare a buck for a bottle of wine?" The other answers, "How do I know you won't buy food with it?"

41. I owe this example to Lisa Landes.

42. This conclusion about the incentives provided by large bequests is a special case of a more general result proven elsewhere (see Becker and Stigler 1974) that relatively large pensions discourage employees from acting contrary to the interests of their employers (a bequest serves the same purpose as a pension).

43. Most robberies, burglaries, and larcenies, on the other hand, probably are motivated by the prospects of material gain.

44. That is, in that part of the social environment that motivates predatory expenditures.

45. Persons committing crimes against other persons as well as against property are much more likely to live in low-income areas (see Crime Commission 1967a, table 9).

46. The rate of assaults grew significantly from 1933 to 1965 in the United States, and the murder rate remained about the same (Crime Commission 1967b, figs. 3, 4). Higher-income states do not have fewer crimes against persons even when the probability of conviction, the punishment, and several other variables are held constant (Ehrlich 1973, tables 2–5). Note that Ehrlich's study, unlike the evidence from the Crime Commission, holds the "price" of crime constant when estimating the effects of income (and holds income constant when estimating the effects of price).

47. Not much later, Jeremy Bentham reached a similar conclusion: "The pleasure derivable by any person from the contemplation of pain suffered by another, is in no instance so great as the pain so suffered" (Bentham 1952–54).

48. Similarly, a sociologist recently has argued that envy is a powerful motive in primitive as well as advanced societies, communist as well as capitalist ones, and is critical in determining economic progress and public policy (see Schoeck 1966).

49. "Own" income here includes the value of other aspects of the social environment.

50. If $U_i = U_i(I_i / \bar{I})$, where $\bar{I}$ is the average community income, then $S_i = I_i - p_r\bar{I}$, where S_i is i's social income, and p_r is the price of $\bar{I}$ in terms of I_i. If i did not engage in predatory behavior, p_r would simply equal the slope of his indifference curve: slope $= dI_i / d\bar{I} = I_i/\bar{I} = p_r$. Hence $S_i = I_i - I_i / \bar{I} \cdot \bar{I} = 0$.

51. When envy is so important, economic development is undesirable because it lowers welfare. See Schoeck's (1966) discussion of what he calls "the envy-barrier of the developing countries."

References

Adams, James D. "Asset Transfers at Deathtime." Dept. Econ., Univ. Chicago, February 1974.

Alchian, A. A., and Allen, W. R. *University Economics.* 2d ed. Belmont, Calif.: Wadsworth, 1967.

Barro, R. "Are Government Bonds Net Wealth?" *JPE* 82, no. 6 (November/ December 1974): 1095–1117.

Becker, G. S. "Notes on an Economic Analysis of Philanthropy." Nat. Bur. Econ. Res., April 1961.

———. "Interdependent Preferences: Charity, Externalities, and Income Taxation." Univ. Chicago, March 1968.

———. *The Economics of Discrimination.* 2d ed. Chicago: Univ. Chicago Press, 1971.

———. "A Theory of Marriage: Part II." *JPE* 82, no. 2, pt. 2 (March/April 1974): 11–26.

———. *Human Capital.* 2d ed. New York: Columbia Univ. Press, 1975.

Becker, G. S., and Stigler, G. J. "Law Enforcement, Malfeasance, and Compensation of Enforcers." *J. Legal Studies* 3, no. 1 (January 1974): 1–18.

Bentham, J. *Principles of Morals and Legislation.* Oxford: Clarendon, 1789.

———. "The Philosophy of Economic Science." In *Jeremy Bentham's Economic Writings*, edited by W. Stark. 3 vols. New York: Franklin, 1952–54.

Blau, P. M. "Social Exchange." In *International Encyclopedia of the Social Sciences*, edited by D. E. Sills. Vol. 7. New York: Macmillan, 1968.

Boulding, K. *The Economy of Love and Fear.* Belmont, Calif.: Wadsworth, 1973.

Brady, D., and Friedman, R. D. "Savings and the Income Distribution." In *Studies in Income and Wealth*, Conference on Research in Income and Wealth. Vol. 10. New York: Nat. Bur. Econ. Res., 1947.

Crime Commission. *Crime and Its Impact: An Assessment.* Task Force Report. Washington: Government Printing Office, 1967a.

———. *The Challenge of Crime in a Free Society.* Task Force Report. Washington: Government Printing Office, 1967b.

DeTray, D. "Child Quality and the Demand for Children." *JPE* 81, no. 2, pt. 2 (March/April 1973): 70–95.

Duesenberry, J. S. *Income, Savings, and the Theory of Consumer Behavior.* Cambridge, Mass.: Harvard Univ. Press, 1949.

Ehrlich, I. "Participation in Illegitimate Activities: A Theoretical and Empirical Investigation." *JPE* 81, no. 3 (May/June 1973): 521–65.

Ehrlich, I., and Becker, G. S. "Market Insurance, Self-Insurance, and Self-Protection." *JPE* 80, no. 4 (July/August 1972): 623–48.

Fisher, I. *Mathematical Investigations in the Theory of Value and Price.* New Haven, Conn.: Yale Univ. Press, 1926.

Johnson, H. "The Effect of Income-Redistribution on Aggregate Consumption with Interdependence of Consumers' Preferences." *Economica* (May 1952).

Leibenstein, H. "Bandwagon, Snob, and Veblen Effects in the Theory of Consumers' Demand." *QJE* 64 (May 1950): 183–207.

Lipset, S. M., and Bendix, R. *Social Mobility in Industrial Societies.* Berkeley: Univ. California Press, 1959.

McPherson, M. "The Effects of Public on Private College Enrollment." Ph.D. dissertation, Univ. Chicago, 1974.

Marshall, A. *Principles of Economics.* 8th ed. London: Macmillan, 1962.

Michael, R. T., and Becker, G. S. "On the New Theory of Consumer Behavior." *Swedish J. Econ.* 75, no. 4 (1973).

Mincer, J. *Schooling, Experience, and Earnings.* New York: Columbia Univ. Press, 1974.

Panteleoni, M. Pure Economics. Clifton, N.J.: Kelley, 1898.

Parsons, D. O. "Intergenerational Wealth Transfers and the Educational Decisions of Male Youth." Ohio State Univ., 1974.

Parsons, T. "Social Interactions." In International Encyclopedia of the Social Sciences, edited by D. S. Sills. Vol. 7. New York: Macmillan, 1968.

Peltzman, S. "The Effect of Government Subsidies-in-Kind on Private Expenditures: The Case of Higher Education." JPE 81, no. 1 (January/February 1973): 1–27.

Pigou, A. C. "Some Remarks on Utility." Econ. J. 13 (1903): 19–24.

Samuelson, P. A. "The Pure Theory of Public Expenditures." Rev. Econ. and Statis. (November 1954).

———. "Social Indifference Curves." QJE (February 1956).

Schoeck, H. Envy. New York: Harcourt, Brace & World, 1966.

Schultz, T. W. The Economic Value of Education. New York: Columbia Univ. Press, 1967.

Schwartz, R. "Personal Philanthropic Contributions." JPE 78, no. 6 (November/ December 1970): 1264–91.

Shoup, C. Federal Estate and Gift Taxes. Washington: Brookings Inst., 1966.

Smith, A. The Wealth of Nations. New York: Modern Library, 1937.

Taussig, M. "The Charitable Contribution in the Federal Personal Income Tax." Ph.D. dissertation, Massachusetts Inst. Tech., 1965.

Veblen, T. The Theory of the Leisure Class. New York: Modern Library, 1934.

Vickery, W. S. "One Economist's View of Philanthropy." In Philanthropy and Public Policy, edited by F. Dickinson. New York: Nat. Bur. Econ. Res., 1962.

DE GUSTIBUS NON
EST DISPUTANDUM

George J. Stigler
Gary S. Becker

· 7 ·

The venerable admonition not to quarrel over tastes is commonly interpreted as advice to terminate a dispute when it has been resolved into a difference of tastes, presumably because there is no further room for rational persuasion. Tastes are the unchallengeable axioms of a man's behavior: he may properly (usefully) be criticized for inefficiency in satisfying his desires, but the desires themselves are *data*. Deplorable tastes—say, for arson—may be countered by coercive and punitive action, but these deplorable tastes, at least when held by an adult, are not capable of being changed by persuasion.

Our title seems to us to be capable of another and preferable interpretation: that tastes neither change capriciously nor differ importantly between people. On this interpretation one does not argue over tastes for the same reason that one does not argue over the Rocky Mountains—both are there, will be there next year, too, and are the same to all men.

The difference between these two viewpoints of tastes is fundamental. On the traditional view, an explanation of economic phenomena that reaches a difference in tastes between people or times is the terminus of the argument: the problem is abandoned *at this point* to whoever studies and

First published in the *American Economic Review* 67, no. 2 (March 1977): 76–90. Reprinted by permission of the American Economic Association.

explains tastes (psychologists? anthropologists? phrenologists? sociobiologists?). On our preferred interpretation, one never reaches this impasse: the economist continues to search for differences in prices or incomes to explain any differences or changes in behavior.

The choice between these two views of the role of tastes in economic theory must ultimately be made on the basis of their comparative analytical productivities. On the conventional view of inscrutable, often capricious tastes, one drops the discussion as soon as the behavior of tastes becomes important—and turns his energies to other problems. On our view, one searches, often long and frustratingly, for the subtle forms that prices and incomes take in explaining differences among men and periods. If the latter approach yields more useful results, it is the proper choice. The establishment of the proposition that one may usefully treat tastes as stable over time and similar among people is the central task of this essay.

The ambitiousness of our agenda deserves emphasis: we are proposing the hypothesis that widespread and/or persistent human behavior can be explained by a generalized calculus of utility-maximizing behavior, without introducing the qualification "tastes remaining the same." It is a thesis that does not permit of direct proof because it is an assertion about the world, not a proposition in logic. Moreover, it is possible almost at random to throw up examples of phenomena that presently defy explanation by this hypothesis: Why do we have inflation? Why are there few Jews in farming?[1] Why are societies with polygynous families so rare in the modern era? Why aren't blood banks responsible for the quality of their product? If we could answer these questions to your satisfaction, you would quickly produce a dozen more.

What we assert is not that we are clever enough to make illuminating applications of utility-maximizing theory to all important phenomena—not even our entire generation of economists is clever enough to do that. Rather, we assert that this traditional approach of the economist offers guidance in tackling these problems—and that no other approach of remotely comparable generality and power is available.

To support our thesis we could offer samples of phenomena we believe to be usefully explained on the assumption of stable, well-behaved preference functions. Ultimately, this is indeed the only persuasive method of supporting the assumption, and it is legitimate to cite in support all of the existing corpus of successful economic theory. Here we shall undertake to give this proof by accomplishment a special and limited interpretation. We take categories of behavior commonly held to demonstrate changes in tastes or to be explicable only in terms of such changes, and show both that they are reconcilable with our assumption of stable preferences and that the reformulation is illuminating.

1. The New Theory of Consumer Choice

The power of stable preferences and utility maximization in explaining a wide range of behavior has been significantly enhanced by a recent reformulation of consumer theory.[2] This reformulation transforms the family from a passive maximizer of the utility from market purchases into an active maximizer also engaged in extensive production and investment activities. In the traditional theory, households maximize a utility function of the goods and services bought in the marketplace, whereas in the reformulation they maximize a utility function of objects of choice, called commodities, that they produce with market goods, their own time, their skills, training, and other human capital, and other inputs. Stated formally, a household seeks to maximize

$$U = U(Z_1, \ldots Z_m) \qquad (1)$$

with

$$Z_i = f_i(X_{1i}, \ldots X_{ki}, t_{1i}, \ldots t_{\ell i}, S_1, \ldots S_\ell, Y_i), i = 1 \ldots m \qquad (2)$$

where Z_i are the commodity objects of choice entering the utility function, f_i is the production function for the ith commodity, X_{ji} is the quantity of the jth market good or service used in the production of the ith commodity, t_{ji} is the jth person's own time input, S_j the jth person's human capital, and Y_i represents all other inputs.

The Z_i have no market prices since they are not purchased or sold, but do have "shadow" prices determined by their costs of production. If f_i were homogeneous of the first degree in the X_{ji} and t_{ji}, marginal and average costs would be the same and the shadow price of Z_i would be

$$\pi_i = \sum_{j=1}^{k} \alpha_{ji}\left(\frac{p}{w_1}, \frac{w}{w_1}, S, Y_i\right) p_j + \sum_{j=1}^{l} \beta_{ji}\left(\frac{p}{w_1}, \frac{w}{w_1}, S, Y_i\right) w_j \qquad (3)$$

where p_j is the cost of X_j, w_j is the cost of t_j, and α_{ji} and β_{ji} are input-output coefficients that depend on the (relative) set of p and w, S, and Y_i. The numerous and varied determinants of these shadow prices give concrete expression to our earlier statement about the subtle forms that prices take in explaining differences among men and periods.

The real income of a household does not simply equal its money income deflated by an index of the prices of market goods, but equals its full income (which includes the value of "time" to the household)[3] deflated by an index of the prices, π_i, of the produced commodities. Since full income and commodity prices depend on a variety of factors, incomes also take subtle forms. Our task in this paper is to spell out some of the forms prices and full income take.

II. STABILITY OF TASTES AND "ADDICTION"

Tastes are frequently said to change as a result of consuming certain "addictive" goods. For example, smoking of cigarettes, drinking of alcohol, injection of heroin, or close contact with some persons over an appreciable period of time often increases the desire (creates a craving) for these goods or persons, and thereby cause their consumption to grow over time. In utility language, their marginal utility is said to rise over time because tastes shift in their favor. This argument has been clearly stated by Alfred Marshall when discussing the taste for "good" music:

> There is however an implicit condition in this law [of diminishing marginal utility] which should be made clear. It is that we do not suppose time to be allowed for any alteration in the character or tastes of the man himself. It is therefore no exception to the law that the more good music a man hears, the stronger is his taste for it likely to become. (p. 94)

We believe that the phenomenon Marshall is trying to explain, namely, that exposure to good music increases the subsequent demand for good music (for some persons!), can be explained with some gain in insight by assuming constant tastes, whereas to assume a change in tastes has been an unilluminating "explanation." The essence of our explanation lies in the accumulation of what might be termed "consumption capital" by the consumer, and we distinguish "beneficial" addiction like Marshall's good music from "harmful" addiction like heroin.

Consider first beneficial addiction, and an unchanging utility function that depends on two produced commodities:

$$U = U(M, Z) \qquad (4)$$

where M measures the amount of music "appreciation" produced and consumed, and Z the production and consumption of other commodities. Music appreciation is produced by a function that depends on the time allocated to music (t_m), and the training and other human capital conducive to music appreciation (S_m) (other inputs are ignored):

$$M = M_m(t_m, S_m) \qquad (5)$$

We assume that

$$\frac{\partial M_m}{\partial t_m} > 0, \frac{\partial M_m}{\partial S_m} > 0$$

and also that

$$\frac{\partial^2 M_m}{\partial t_m \partial S_m} > 0$$

An increase in this music capital increases the productivity of time spent listening to or devoted in other ways to music.

In order to analyze the consequences for its consumption of "the more good music a man hears," the production and consumption of music appreciation has to be dated. The amount of appreciation produced at any moment j, M_j, would depend on the time allocated to music and the music human capital at j: t_{m_j} and S_{m_j}, respectively. The latter in turn is produced partly through "on-the-job" training or "learning by doing" by accumulating the effects of earlier music appreciation:

$$S_{m_j} = h\,(M_{j-1}, M_{j-2}, \ldots, E_j) \tag{6}$$

By definition, the addiction is beneficial if

$$\frac{\partial S_{m_j}}{\partial M_{j-v}} > 0, \text{ all } v \text{ in (6)}$$

The term E_j measures the effect of education and other human capital on music appreciation skill, where

$$\frac{\partial S_{m_j}}{\partial E_j} > 0$$

and probably

$$\frac{\partial^2 S_{m_j}}{\partial M_{j-v} \partial E_j} > 0$$

We assume for simplicity a utility function that is a discounted sum of functions like the one in equation (4), where the M and Z commodities are dated, and the discount rate determined by time preference.[4] The optimal allocation of consumption is determined from the equality between the ratio of their marginal utilities and the ratio of their shadow prices:

$$\frac{MU_{m_j}}{MU_{z_j}} = \frac{\partial U}{\partial M_j} \bigg/ \frac{\partial U}{\partial Z_j} = \frac{\pi_{m_j}}{\pi_{z_j}} \tag{7}$$

The shadow price equals the marginal cost of adding a unit of commodity output. The marginal cost is complicated for music appreciation M by the positive effect on subsequent music human capital of the production of music appreciation at any moment j. This effect on subsequent capital is an investment return from producing appreciation at j that reduces the cost of production at j. It can be shown that the marginal cost at j equals[5]

$$\pi_{m_j} = \frac{w\partial t_{m_j}}{\partial M_j} - w \sum_{i=1}^{n-j} \frac{\partial M_{j+i}}{\partial S_{m_{j+i}}} \bigg/ \frac{\partial M_{j+i}}{\partial t_{m_{j+i}}} \cdot \frac{dS_{m_{j+i}}}{dM_j} \cdot \frac{1}{(i+r)^i}$$

$$= \frac{w\partial t_{m_j}}{\partial M_j} - A_j = \frac{w}{MP_{t_{m_j}}} - A_j \quad (8)$$

where w is the wage rate (assumed to be the same at all ages), r the interest rate, n the length of life, and A_j the effect of addiction, measures the value of the saving in future time inputs from the effect of the production of M in j on subsequent music capital.

With no addiction, $A_j = 0$ and equation (8) reduces to the familiar marginal cost formula. Moreover, A_j is positive as long as music is beneficially addictive, and tends to decline as j increases, approaching zero as j approaches n. The term w/MP_{t_m} declines with age for a given time input as long as music capital grows with age. The term A_j may not change so much with age at young ages because the percentage decline in the number of remaining years is small at these ages. Therefore, π_m would tend to decline with age at young ages because the effect on the marginal product of the time input would tend to dominate the effect on A. Although π_m might not always decline at other ages, for the present we assume that π_m declines continuously with age.

If π_z does not depend on age, the relative price of music appreciation would decline with age; then by equation (7), the relative consumption of music appreciation would rise with age. On this interpretation, the (relative) consumption of music appreciation rises with exposure not because tastes shift in favor of music, but because its shadow price falls as skill and experience in the appreciation of music are acquired with exposure.

An alternative way to state the same analysis is that the marginal utility of time allocated to music is increased by an increase in the stock of music capital.[6] Then the consumption of music appreciation could be said to rise with exposure because the marginal utility of the time spent on music rose with exposure, even though tastes were unchanged.

The effect of exposure on the accumulation of music capital might well depend on the level of education and other human capital, as indicated by equation (6). This would explain why educated persons consume more "good" music (i.e., music that educated people like!) than other persons do.

Addiction lowers the price of music appreciation at younger ages without any comparable effect on the productivity of the time spent on music at these ages. Therefore, addiction would increase the time spent on music at younger ages: some of the time would be considered an investment that increases future music capital. Although the price of music tends to fall with age, and the consumption of music tends to rise, the time spent on music need not rise with age because the growth in music capital means that the consumption of music could rise even when the time spent fell with age. The time spent would be more likely to rise, the more elastic the demand curve for music appreciation. We can express this result in a form that will strike many readers as surprising; namely, that the time (or other inputs) spent on music appreciation is more likely to be addictive—that is, to rise with exposure to music—the more, not less, elastic is the demand curve for music appreciation.

The stock of music capital might fall and the price of music appreciation rise at older ages because the incentive to invest in future capital would decline as the number of remaining years declined, whereas the investment required simply to maintain the capital stock intact would increase as the stock increased. If the price rose, the time spent on music would fall if the demand curve for music were elastic. Consequently, our analysis indicates that the observed addiction to music may be stronger at younger than at older ages.

These results for music also apply to other commodities that are beneficially addictive. Their prices fall at younger ages and their consumption rises because consumption capital is accumulated with exposure and age. The time and goods used to produce an addictive commodity need not rise with exposure, even though consumption of the commodity does; they are more likely to rise with exposure, the more elastic is the demand curve for the commodity. Even if they rose at younger ages, they might decline eventually as the stock of consumption capital fell at older ages.

Using the same arguments developed for beneficial addiction, we can show that all the results are reversed for harmful addiction,[7] which is defined by a negative sign of the derivatives in equation (6):

$$\frac{\partial S_j}{\partial H_{j-v}} < 0, \text{ all } v \text{ in (6)} \qquad (9)$$

where H is a harmfully addictive commodity. An increase in consumption at any age reduces the stock of consumption capital available subsequently, and this raises the shadow price at all ages.[8] The shadow price would rise with age and exposure, at least at younger ages, which would induce consumption to fall with age and exposure. The inputs of goods and time need not fall with exposure, however, because consumption capital falls with exposure;

indeed, the inputs are likely to rise with exposure if the commodity's demand curve were inelastic.

To illustrate these conclusions, consider the commodity "euphoria" produced with input of heroin (or alcohol or amphetamines). An increase in the consumption of current euphoria raises the cost of producing euphoria in the future by reducing the future stock of "euphoric capital." The effect of exposure to euphoria on the cost of producing future euphoria reduces the consumption of euphoria as exposure continues. If the demand curve for euphoria were sufficiently inelastic, however, the use of heroin would grow with exposure at the same time that euphoria fell.

Note that the amount of heroin used at younger ages would be reduced because of the negative effect on later euphoric capital. Indeed, no heroin at all might be used only because the harmfully addictive effects are anticipated, and discourage any use. Note further that if heroin were used even though the subsequent adverse consequences were accurately anticipated, the utility of the user would be greater than it would be if he were prevented from using heroin. Of course, his utility would be still greater if technologies developed (methadone?) to reduce the harmfully addictive effects of euphoria.[9]

Most interestingly, note that the use of heroin would grow with exposure at the same time that the amount of euphoria fell, if the demand curve for euphoria and thus for heroin were sufficiently inelastic. That is, addiction to heroin—a growth in use with exposure—is the *result* of an inelastic demand for heroin, *not*, as commonly argued, the *cause* of an inelastic demand. In the same way, listening to music or playing tennis would be addictive if the demand curves for music or tennis appreciation were sufficiently elastic; the addiction again is the result, not the cause, of the particular elasticity. Put differently, if addiction were surmised (partly because the input of goods or time rose with age), but if it were not clear whether the addiction were harmful or beneficial, the elasticity of demand could be used to distinguish between them: a high elasticity suggests beneficial and a low elasticity suggests harmful addiction.[10]

We do not have to assume that exposure to euphoria changes tastes in order to understand why the use of heroin grows with exposure, or why the amount used is insensitive to changes in its price. Even with constant tastes, the amount used would grow with exposure, and heroin is addictive precisely *because* of the insensitivity to price changes.

An exogenous rise in the price of addictive goods or time, perhaps due to an excise tax, such as the tax on cigarettes and alcohol, or to restrictions on their sale, such as the imprisonment of dealers in heroin, would have a relatively small effect on their use by addicts if these are harmfully addictive goods, and a relatively large effect if they are beneficially addictive. That is, excise taxes and imprisonment mainly transfer resources away from addicts if the goods are harmfully addictive, and mainly reduce the consumption of addicts if the goods are beneficially addictive.

The extension of the capital concept to investment in the capacity to consume more efficiently has numerous other potential applications. For example, there is a fertile field in consumption capital for the application of the theory of division of labor among family members.

III. Stability of Tastes and Custom and Tradition

A "traditional" qualification to the scope of economic theory is the alleged powerful hold over human behavior of custom and tradition. An excellent statement in the context of the behavior of rulers is that of John Stuart Mill:

> It is not true that the actions even of average rulers are wholly, or anything approaching to wholly, determined by their personal interest, or even by their own opinion of their personal interest. . . . I insist only on what is true of all rulers, viz., that the character and course of their actions is largely influenced (independently of personal calculations) by the habitual sentiments and feelings, the general modes of thinking and acting, which prevail throughout the community of which they are members; as well as by the feelings, habits, and modes of thought which characterize the particular class in that community to which they themselves belong. . . . They are also much influenced by the maxims and traditions which have descended to them from other rulers, their predecessors; which maxims and traditions have been known to retain an ascendancy during long periods, even in opposition to the private interests of the rulers for the time being. (p. 484)

The specific political behavior that contradicts "personal interest" theories is not clear from Mill's statement, nor is it much clearer in similar statements by others applied to firms or households. Obviously, stable behavior by (say) households faced with stable prices and incomes—or more generally a stable environment—is no contradiction since stability then is implied as much by personal interest theories as by custom and tradition. On the other hand, stable behavior in the face of changing prices and incomes might contradict the approach taken in this essay that assumes utility maximizing with stable tastes.

Nevertheless, we believe that our approach better explains when behavior is stable than do approaches based on custom and tradition, and can at the same time explain how and when behavior does change. Mill's "habits and modes of thought," or his "maxims and traditions which have descended," in our analysis result from investment of time and other resources in the accumulation of knowledge about the environment, and of skills with which to cope with it.

The making of decisions is costly, and not simply because it is an activity which some people find unpleasant. In order to make a decision one requires information, and the information must be analyzed. The costs of searching for information and of applying the information to a new situation are such that habit is often a more efficient way to deal with moderate or temporary changes in the environment than would be a full, apparently utility-maximizing decision. This is precisely the avoidance of what J. M. Clark termed the irrational passion for dispassionate rationality.

A simple example of economizing on information by the habitual purchase from one source will illustrate the logic. A consumer buys one unit of commodity X in each unit of time. He pays a price p_t at a time t. The choices he faces are

1. To search at the time of an act of purchase to obtain the lowest possible price $\hat{p}_t$ consistent with the cost of search. Then $\hat{p}_t$ is a function of the amount of search s (assumed to be the same at each act of purchase):

$$\hat{p}_t = f(s), f'(s) < 0 \qquad (10)$$

where the total cost of s is $C(s)$.

2. To search less frequently (but usually more intensively), relying between searches upon the outcome of the previous search in choosing a supplier. Then the price p_t will be higher (relative to the average market price), the longer the period since the previous search (at time t_0),

$$p_t = g(t - t_0), g' > 0$$

Ignoring interest, the latter method of purchase will have a total cost over period T determined by

1. K searches (all of equal intensity) at cost $K\,C(s)$.

2. Each search lasts for a period T/K, within which $r = T/K$ purchases are made, at cost $r\bar{p}$, where $\bar{p}$ is the average price. Assume that the results of search "depreciate" (prices appreciate) at rate δ. A consumer minimizes his combined cost of the commodity and search over the total time period; the minimizing condition is[11]

$$r = \sqrt{\frac{2C}{\delta\hat{p}}} \qquad (11)$$

In this simple model with r purchases between successive searches, r is larger the larger the amount spent on search per dollar spent on the commodity ($C/\hat{p}$), and the lower the rate of appreciation of prices (δ). If there were full search on each individual act of purchase, the total cost could not be less than the cost when the optimal frequency of search was chosen, and might be much greater.

When a temporary change takes place in the environment, perhaps in prices or income, it generally would not pay to disinvest the capital embodied in knowledge or skills, or to accumulate different types of capital. As a result, behavior will be relatively stable in the face of temporary changes.

A related situation arises when an unexpected change in the environment does not induce a major response immediately because time is required to accumulate the appropriate knowledge and skills. Therefore, stable preferences combined with investment in "specific" knowledge and skills can explain the small or "inelastic" responses that figure so prominently in short-run demand and supply curves.

A permanent change in the environment, perhaps due to economic development, usually causes a greater change in the behavior of young than of old persons. The common interpretation is that young persons are more readily seduced away from their customs and traditions by the glitter of the new (Western?) environment. On our interpretation, young and old persons respond differently, even if they have the same preferences and motivation. To change their behavior drastically, older persons have to either disinvest their capital that was attuned to the old environment, or invest in capital attuned to the new environment. Their incentive to do so may be quite weak, however, because relatively few years remain for them to collect the returns on new investments, and much human capital can only be disinvested slowly.

Young persons, on the other hand, are not so encumbered by accumulations of capital attuned to the old environment. Consequently, they need not have different preferences or motivation or be intrinsically more flexible in order to be more affected by a change in the environment: they simply have greater incentive to invest in knowledge and skills attuned to the new environment.

Note that this analysis is similar to that used in the previous section to explain addictive behavior: utility maximization with stable preferences, conditioned by the accumulation of specific knowledge and skills. One does not need one kind of theory to explain addictive behavior and another kind to explain habitual or customary behavior. The same theory based on stable preferences can explain both types of behavior, and can accommodate both habitual behavior and the departures therefrom.

IV. Stability of Tastes and Advertising

Perhaps the most important class of cases in which "change of tastes" is invoked as an explanation for economic phenomena is that involving advertising. The advertiser "persuades" the consumer to prefer his product, and often a distinction is drawn between "persuasive" and "informative" advertising.[12] John Kenneth Galbraith is the most famous of the economists who argue that advertising molds consumer tastes:

> These [institutions of modern advertising and salesmanship] cannot be reconciled with the notion of independently determined desires for their central function is to create desires—to bring into being wants that previously did not exist. This is accomplished by the producer of the goods or at his behest.—Outlays for the manufacturing of a product are not more important in the strategy of modern business enterprise than outlays for the manufacturing of demand for the product. (pp. 155–56)

We shall argue, in direct opposition to this view, that it is neither necessary nor useful to attribute to advertising the function of changing tastes.

A consumer may indirectly receive utility from a market good, yet the utility depends not only on the quantity of the good but also on the consumer's knowledge of its true or alleged properties. If he does not know whether the berries are poisonous, they are not food; if he does not know that they contain vitamin C, they are not consumed to prevent scurvy. The quantity of information is a complex notion: its degree of accuracy, its multidimensional properties, its variable obsolescence with time are all qualities that make direct measurement of information extremely difficult.

How can this elusive variable be incorporated into the theory of demand while preserving the stability of tastes? Our approach is to continue to assume, as in the previous sections, that the ultimate objects of choice are commodities produced by each household with market goods, own time, *knowledge*, and perhaps other inputs. We now assume, in addition, that the knowledge, whether real or fancied, is produced by the advertising of producers and perhaps also the own search of households.

Our approach can be presented through a detailed analysis of the simple case where the output x of a particular firm and its advertising A are the inputs into a commodity produced and consumed by households; for a given household:

$$Z = f(x, A, E, y) \qquad (12)$$

where $\partial Z/\partial x > 0$, $\partial Z/\partial A > 0$. E is the human capital of the household that affects these marginal products, and y are other variables, possibly including advertising by other firms. Still more simply,

$$Z = g(A, E, y)\, x \qquad (13)$$

where $\partial g/\partial A = g' > 0$ and $\partial^2 g/\partial A^2 < 0$. With A, E, and y held constant, the amount of the commodity produced and consumed by any household is assumed to be proportional to the amount of the firm's output used by that household.[13] If the advertising reaching any household were independent of its behavior, the shadow price of Z, the marginal cost of x, would simply be the expenditure on x required to change Z by one unit. From equation (13), that equals

$$\pi_z = \frac{p_x}{g} \qquad (14)$$

where p_x is the price of x.

An increase in advertising may lower the commodity price to the household (by raising g), and thereby increase its demand for the commodity and change its demand for the firm's output, because the household is made to believe—correctly or incorrectly—that it gets a greater output of the commodity from a given input of the advertised product. Consequently, advertising affects consumption in this formulation not by changing tastes, but by changing prices. That is, a movement along a stable demand curve for commodities is seen as generating the apparently unstable demand curves of market goods and other inputs.

More than a simple change in language is involved: our formulation has quite different implications from the conventional ones. To develop these implications, consider a firm that is determining its optimal advertising along with its optimal output. We assume initially that the commodity indirectly produced by this firm (equation [12]) is a perfect substitute to consumers for commodities indirectly produced by many other firms. Therefore, the firm is perfectly competitive in the commodity market, and could (indirectly) sell an unlimited amount of this commodity at a fixed commodity price. Observe that a firm can have many perfect substitutes in the commodity market even though few other firms produce the same physical product. For example, a firm may be the sole designer of jewelry that contributes to the social prestige of consumers, and yet compete fully with many other products that also contribute to prestige: large automobiles, expensive furs, fashionable clothing, elaborate parties, a respected occupation, etc.

If the level of advertising were fixed, there would be a one-to-one correspondence between the price of the commodity and the price of the firm's output (see equation [14]). If π_z were given by the competitive market, p_x would then also be given, and the firm would find its optimal output in the conventional way by equating marginal cost to the given product price. There is no longer such a one-to-one correspondence between π_z and p_x, however, when the level of advertising is also a variable, and even a firm faced with a fixed commodity price in a perfectly competitive commodity market could sell its product at different prices by varying the level of advertising. Since an increase in advertising would increase the commodity output that consumers receive from a given amount of this firm's product, the price of its product would then be increased relative to the fixed commodity price.

The optimal advertising, product price, and output of the firm can be found by maximizing its income

$$I = p_x X - TC(X) - Ap_a \tag{15}$$

where X is the firm's total output, TC its costs of production other than advertising, and p_a the (constant) cost of a unit of advertising. By substituting from equation (14), I can be written as

$$I = \pi_z^0 g(A)X - TC(X) - Ap_a \tag{15'}$$

where π_z^0 is the given market commodity price, the advertising-effectiveness function (g) is assumed to be the same for all consumers,[14] and the variables E and y in g are suppressed. The first-order maximum conditions with respect to X and A are

$$p_x = \pi_z^0 g = MC(X) \tag{16}$$

$$\frac{\partial p_x}{\partial A} X = \pi_z^0 X g' = p_a \tag{17}$$

Equation (16) is the usual equality between price and marginal cost for a competitive firm, which continues to hold when advertising exists and is a decision variable. Not surprisingly, equation (17) says that marginal revenue and marginal cost of advertising are equal, where marginal revenue is determined by the level of output and the increase in product price "induced" by an increase in advertising. Although the commodity price is fixed, an increase in advertising increases the firm's product price by an amount that is proportional to the increased capacity (measured by g') of its product to contribute (at least in the minds of consumers) to commodity output.

In the conventional analysis, firms in perfectly competitive markets gain nothing from advertising and thus have no incentive to advertise because they are assumed to be unable to differentiate their products to consumers who have perfect knowledge. In our analysis, on the other hand, consumers have imperfect information, including misinformation, and a skilled advertiser might well be able to differentiate his product from other apparently similar products. Put differently, advertisers could increase the value of their output to consumers without increasing to the same extent the value of the output even of perfect competitors in the *commodity* market. To simplify, we assume that the value of competitors' output is unaffected, in the sense that the commodity price (more generally, the commodity demand curve) to any firm is not affected by its advertising. Note that when firms in perfectly competitive commodity markets differentiate their products by advertising, they still preserve the perfect competition in these markets. Note, moreover, that if different firms were producing the same physical product in the same competitive commodity market, and had the same marginal cost and advertising-effectiveness functions, they would produce the same output, charge the same product price, and advertise at the same rate. If, however, either their marginal costs or advertising effectiveness differed, they would charge different product prices, advertise at different rates, and yet still be perfect competitors (although not of one another)!

Not only can firms in perfectly competitive commodity markets—that is, firms faced with infinitely elastic commodity demand curves—have an incentive to advertise, but the incentive may actually be greater, the more competitive the commodity market is. Let us consider the case of a finite commodity demand elasticity.

The necessary conditions to maximize income given by equation (15'), if π_z varies as a function of Z, are

$$\frac{\partial I}{\partial X} = \pi_z g + X \frac{\partial \pi_z}{\partial Z} \frac{\partial Z}{\partial X} g - MC(X) = 0, \tag{18}$$

or since $Z = gX$, and $\partial Z/\partial X = g$,

$$\pi_z g \left(1 + \frac{1}{\epsilon_{\pi_z}} \right) = p_x \left(1 + \frac{1}{\epsilon_{\pi_z}} \right) = MC(X) \tag{18'}$$

where ϵ_{π_z} is the elasticity of the firm's commodity demand curve. Also

$$\frac{\partial I}{\partial A} = X \frac{\partial p_x}{\partial A} - p_a = \pi_z \frac{\partial Z}{\partial A} + \frac{\partial \pi_z}{\partial Z} \cdot \frac{\partial Z}{\partial A} \cdot Z - p_a = 0 \tag{19}$$

or

$$X \frac{\partial p_x}{\partial A} = \pi_z g' X \left(1 + \frac{1}{\epsilon_{\pi_z}} \right) = p_a \tag{19'}$$

Equation (18') is simply the usual maximizing condition for a monopolist that continues to hold when there is advertising.[15] Equation (19') clearly

FIGURE 1

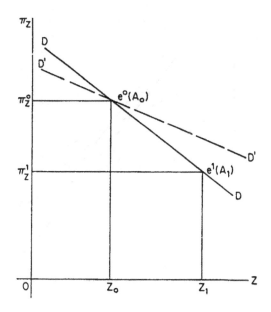

shows that, given $\pi_{zg}'X$, the marginal revenue from additional advertising is greater, the greater is the elasticity of the commodity demand curve; therefore, the optimal level of advertising would be positively related to the commodity elasticity.

This important result can be made intuitive by considering figure 1. The curve DD gives the firm's commodity demand curve, where π_z is measured along the vertical and commodity output Z along the horizontal axis. The firm's production of X is held fixed so that Z varies only because of variations in the level of advertising. At point e^0, the level of advertising is A_0, the product price is p_x^0, and commodity output and price are Z_0 and π_z^0, respectively. An increase in advertising to A_1 would increase Z to Z_1 (the increase in Z is determined by the given g' function). The decline in π_z induced by the increase in Z would be negatively related to the elasticity of the commodity demand curve: it would be less, for example, if the demand curve were $D'D'$ rather than DD. Since the increase in p_x is negatively related to the decline in π_z,[16] the increase in p_x, and thus the marginal revenue from the increase in A, is directly related to the elasticity of the commodity demand curve.[17]

The same result is illustrated with a more conventional diagram in figure 2: the firm's product output and price are shown along the horizontal and

FIGURE 2

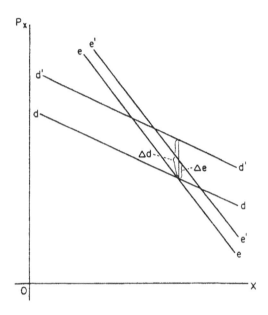

vertical axes. The demand curve for its product with a given level of advertising is given by *dd*. We proved earlier (fn. 15) that with advertising constant, the elasticity of the product demand curve is the same as the elasticity
of its commodity demand curve. An increase in advertising "shifts" the
product demand curve upward to *d'd'*, and the marginal revenue from additional advertising is directly related to the size of the shift; that is, to the
increase in product price for any given product output. Our basic result is
that the shift is itself directly related to the elasticity of the demand curve.
For example, with the same increase in advertising, the shift is larger from
dd to *d'd'* than from *ee* to *e'e'* because *dd* is more elastic than *ee*.

This role of information in consumer demand is capable of extension in
various directions. For example, the demand for knowledge is affected by the
formal education of a person, so systematic variations of demand for advertisements with formal education can be explored. The stock of information
possessed by the individual is a function of his age, period of residence in a
community, and other variables, so systematic patterns of purchase of heavily
and lightly advertised goods are implied by the theory.

V. FASHIONS AND FADS

The existence of fashions and fads (short episodes or cycles in the consumption habits of people) seems an especially striking contradiction of our thesis of the stability of tastes. We find fashions in dress, food, automobiles, furniture, books, and even scientific doctrines.[18] Some are modest in amplitude, or few in their followers, but others are of violent amplitude: who now buys a Ouija board, or a bustle? The rise and fall of fashions is often attributed to the fickleness of people's tastes. Herbert Blumer, the distinguished sociologist, gave a characteristic expression of this view:

> Tastes are themselves a product of experience, they usually develop from an initial state of vagueness to a state of refinement and stability, but once formed they may decay and disintegrate. . . .
>   The fashion process involves both a formation and an expression of collective taste in the given area of fashion. The taste is initially a loose fusion of vague inclinations and dissatisfactions that are aroused by new experience in the field of fashion and in the larger surrounding world. In this initial state, collective taste is amorphous, inarticulate, and awaiting specific direction. Through models and proposals, fashion innovators sketch possible lines along which the incipient taste may gain objective expression and take definite form. (p. 344).

The obvious method of reconciling fashion with our thesis is to resort again to the now familiar argument that people consume commodities, and only indirectly do they consume market goods, so fashions in market goods are compatible with stability in the utility function of commodities. The task here, as elsewhere, is to show that this formulation helps to illuminate our understanding of the phenomena under discussion; we have some tentative comments in this direction.

The commodity apparently produced by fashion goods is social distinction: the demonstration of alert leadership, or at least not lethargy, in recognizing and adopting that which will in due time be widely approved. This commodity—it might be termed *style*—sounds somewhat circular, because new things appear to be chosen simply because they are new. Such circularity is no more peculiar than that which is literally displayed in a race—the runners obviously do not run around a track in order to reach a new destination. Moreover, it is a commendation of a style good that it be superior to previous goods, and style will not be sought intentionally through less functional goods. Indeed, if the stylish soon becomes inferior to the unstylish, it would lose its attractiveness.

Style, moreover, is not achieved simply by change: the newness must be of a special sort that requires a subtle prediction of what will be approved novelty, and a trained person can make better predictions than an untrained person. Style is social rivalry, and it is, like all rivalry, both an incentive to individuality and a source of conformity.

The areas in which the rivalry of fashion takes place are characterized by public exposure and reasonably short life. An unexposed good (automobile pistons) cannot be judged as to its fashionableness, and fashions in a good whose efficient life is long would be expensive. Hence fashion generally concentrates on the cheaper classes of garments and reading matter, and there is more fashion in furniture than in housing.

Fashion can be pursued with the purse or with the expenditure of time. A person may be well-read (i.e., have read the recent books generally believed to be important), but if his time is valuable in the marketplace, it is much more likely that his spouse will be the well-read member of the family. (So the ratio of the literacy of wife to that of husband is positively related to the husband's earning power, and inversely related to her earning power.)

The demand for fashion can be formalized by assuming that the distinction available to any person depends on his social environment, and his own efforts: he can be fashionable, give to approved charities, choose prestigious occupations, and do other things that affect his distinction. Following recent work on social interactions, we can write the social distinction of the ith person as

$$R_i = D_i + h_i \qquad (20)$$

where D_i is the contribution to his distinction of his social environment, and h_i is his own contribution. Each person maximizes a utility function of R and other commodities subject to a budget constraint that depends on his own income and the exogenously given social environment.[19] A number of general results have been developed with this approach (see Becker), and a few are mentioned here to indicate that the demand for fashion (and other determinants of social distinction) can be systematically analyzed without assuming that tastes shift.

An increase in i's own income, prices held constant, would increase his demand for social distinction and other commodities. If his social environment were unchanged, the whole increase in his distinction would be produced by an increase in his own contributions to fashion and other distinction-producing goods. Therefore, even an average income elasticity of demand for distinction would imply a high income elasticity of demand for fashion (and these other distinction-producing) goods, which is consistent with the common judgment that fashion is a luxury good.[20]

If other persons increase their contributions to their own distinction, this may lower i's distinction by reducing his social environment. For distinction is scarce and is to a large extent simply redistributed among persons: an increase in one person's distinction generally requires a reduction in that of other persons. This is why people are often "forced" to conform to new fashions. When some gain distinction by paying attention to (say) new fashions, they lower the social environment of others. The latter are induced to increase their own efforts to achieve distinction, including a demand for these new fashions, because an exogenous decline in their social environment induces them to increase their own contributions to their distinction.

Therefore, an increase in all incomes induces an even greater increase in i's contribution to his distinction than does an increase in his own income alone. For an increase in the income of others lowers i's social environment because they spend more on their own distinction; the reduction in his environment induces a further increase in i's contribution to his distinction. Consequently, we expect wealthy countries like the United States to pay more attention to fashion than poor countries like India, even if tastes were the same in wealthy and poor countries.

VI. Conclusion

We have surveyed four classes of phenomena widely believed to be inconsistent with the stability of tastes: addiction, habitual behavior, advertising, and fashions, and in each case offered an alternative explanation. That alternative explanation did not simply reconcile the phenomena in question with the stability of tastes, but also sought to show that the hypothesis of stable tastes yielded more useful predictions about observable behavior.

Of course, this short list of categories is far from comprehensive: for example, we have not entered into the literature of risk aversion and risk preference, one of the richest sources of ad hoc assumptions concerning tastes. Nor have we considered the extensive literature on time preference, which often alleges that people "systematically undervalue . . . future wants."[21] The taste for consumption in say 1984 is alleged to continue to shift upward as 1984 gets closer to the present. In spite of the importance frequently attached to time preference, we do not know of any significant behavior that has been illuminated by this assumption. Indeed, given additional space, we would argue that the assumption of time preference impedes the explanation of life cycle variations in the allocation of resources, the secular growth in real incomes, and other phenomena.

Moreover, we have not considered systematic differences in tastes by wealth or other classifications. We also claim, however, that no significant behavior has been illuminated by assumptions of differences in tastes. Instead, they, along with assumptions of unstable tastes, have been a convenient crutch to lean on when the analysis has bogged down. They give the appearance of considered judgment, yet really have only been ad hoc arguments that disguise analytical failures.

We have partly translated "unstable tastes" into variables in the household production functions for commodities. The great advantage, however, of relying only on changes in the arguments entering household production functions is that *all* changes in behavior are explained by changes in prices and incomes, precisely the variables that organize and give power to economic analysis. Addiction, advertising, etc. affect not tastes with the endless degrees of freedom they provide, but prices and incomes, and are subject therefore to the constraints imposed by the theorem on negatively inclined demand curves, and other results. Needless to say, we would welcome explanations of why some people become addicted to alcohol and others to Mozart, whether the explanation was a development of our approach or a contribution from some other behavioral discipline.

As we remarked at the outset, no conceivable expenditure of effort on our part could begin to exhaust the possible tests of the hypothesis of stable and uniform preferences. Our task has been oddly two-sided. Our hypothesis is trivial, for it merely asserts that we should apply standard economic logic as extensively as possible. But the self-same hypothesis is also a demanding challenge, for it urges us not to abandon opaque and complicated problems with the easy suggestion that the further explanation will perhaps someday be produced by one of our sister behavioral sciences.

NOTES

We have had helpful comments from Michael Bozdarich, Gilbert Ghez, James Heckman, Peter Pashigian, Sam Peltzman, Donald Wittman, and participants in the Workshop on Industrial Organization.

1. Our lamented friend Reuben Kessel offered an attractive explanation: since Jews have been persecuted so often and forced to flee to other countries, they have not invested in immobile land, but in mobile human capital—business skills, education, etc.—that would automatically go with them. Of course, someone might counter with the more basic query: but why are they Jews, and not Christians or Muslims?

2. An exposition of this reformulation can be found in Robert Michael and Becker. This exposition emphasizes the capacity of the reformulation to generate many implications about behavior that are consistent with stable tastes.

3. Full income is the maximum money income that a household could achieve by an appropriate allocation of its time and other resources.

4. A consistent application of the assumption of stable preferences implies that the discount rate is zero; that is, the absence of time preference (see the brief discussion in Section VI).

5. The utility function

$$V = \sum_{j=1}^{n} a^j\, U(M_j, Z_j)$$

is maximized subject to the constraints

$$M_j = M(t_{m_j}, S_{m_j}); Z_j = Z(x_j, t_{z_j})$$

$$S_{m_j} = h(M_{j-1}, M_{j-2}, \ldots, E_j)$$

$$\sum \frac{px_j}{(1+r)^j} = \sum \frac{wt_{w_j} + b_j}{(i+r)^j}$$

and $t_{w_j} + t_{m_j} + t_{z_j} = t$, where t_{w_j} is hours worked in the jth period, and b_j is property income in that period. By substitution one derives the full wealth constraint:

$$\sum \frac{px_j + w(t_{m_j} + t_{z_j})}{(1+r)^j} = \sum \frac{wt + b_j}{(1+r)^j} = W$$

Maximization of V with respect to M_j and Z_j subject to the production functions and the full wealth constraint gives the first-order conditions

$$\alpha^j \frac{\partial U}{\partial Z_j} = \frac{\lambda}{(1+r)^j}\left(\frac{pdx_j}{dZ_j} + \frac{wdt_{z_j}}{dZ_j}\right) = \frac{\lambda}{(1+r)^j}\,\pi_{z_j}$$

$$\alpha^j \frac{\partial U}{\partial M_j} = \frac{\lambda}{(1+r)^j}\cdot\left(\frac{w\partial t_{m_j}}{\partial M_j} + \sum_{i=1}^{n-j} \frac{wdt_{m_{j+i}}}{dM_j}\cdot\frac{1}{(1+r)^i}\right) = \frac{\lambda}{(1+r)^j}\,\pi_{m_j}$$

Since, however,

$$\frac{dM_{j+i}}{dM_j} = 0 = \frac{\partial M_{j+i}}{\partial S_{m_{j+i}} + i}\frac{dS_{m_{j+i}}}{dM_j} + \frac{\partial M_{j+i}}{\partial t_{m_{j+i}}}\frac{dt_{m_{j+i}}}{dM_j}$$

then

$$\frac{dt_{m_{j+1}}}{dM_j} = -\frac{\partial M_{j+i}}{\partial S_{m_{j+i}}}\bigg/\frac{\partial M_{j+i}}{\partial t_{m_{j+i}}}\cdot\frac{dS_{m_{j+i}}}{dM_j}$$

By substitution into the definition of π_{m_j}, equation (8) follows immediately.

6. The marginal utility of time allocated to music at j includes the utility from the increase in the future stock of music capital that results from an increase in the

time allocated at j. An argument similar to the one developed for the price of music appreciation shows that the marginal utility of time would tend to rise with age, at least at younger ages.

7. In some ways, our analysis of beneficial and harmful addiction is a special case of the analysis of beneficial and detrimental joint production in Michael Grossman.

8. Instead of equation (8), one has

$$\pi_{h_j} = \frac{w}{MP_{t_j}} + A_j.$$

where $A_j \geq 0$.

9. That is, if new technology reduced and perhaps even changed the sign of the derivatives in equation (9). We should state explicitly, to avoid any misunderstanding, that "harmful" means only that the derivatives in (9) are negative, and not that the addiction harms others, nor, as we have just indicated, that it is unwise for addicts to consume such commodities.

10. The elasticity of demand can be estimated from the effects of changes in the prices of inputs. For example, if a commodity's production function were homogeneous of degree one, and if all its future as well as present input prices rose by the same known percentage, the elasticity of demand for the commodity could be estimated from the decline in the inputs. Therefore the distinction between beneficial and harmful addiction is operational: these independently estimated commodity elasticities could be used, as in the text, to determine whether an addiction was harmful or beneficial.

11. The price of the ith purchase within one of the K search periods is $p_i = \hat{p}(1 + \delta)^{i-1}$. Hence

$$\bar{p} = \frac{1}{r}\sum_{i=1}^{r} \hat{p}(1 + \delta)^{i-1} = \hat{p}\frac{(1 + \delta)^r - 1}{r\delta}$$

The total cost to be minimized is

$$TC = Kr\bar{p} + KC(s) = K\hat{p}\frac{(1 + \delta)^r - 1}{\delta} + KC$$

By taking a second-order approximation to $(1 + \delta)^r$, we get

$$TC = T\left\{ \hat{p}\left[1 + \frac{(r - 1)\delta}{2} \right] + \frac{C}{r}\right\}$$

Minimizing with respect to r gives

$$\frac{\partial TC}{\partial r} = 0 = T\left(\frac{\hat{p}\delta}{2} - \frac{C}{r^2}\right)$$

or

$$r = \sqrt{\frac{2C}{\delta \hat{p}}}$$

12. The distinction, if in fact one exists, between persuasive and informative advertising must be one of purpose or effect, not of content. A simple, accurately stated fact ("I offer you this genuine $1 bill for 10 cents") can be highly persuasive; the most bizarre claim ("If Napoleon could have bought our machine gun, he would have defeated Wellington") contains some information (machine guns were not available in 1814).

13. Stated differently, Z is homogeneous of the first degree in x alone.

14. Therefore,

$$p_x X = \pi_z^0 g \sum_{i=1}^{n} x_i$$

where n is the number of households.

15. If the level of advertising is held constant, Z is proportional to X, so

$$\epsilon_{\pi_z} = \frac{dZ}{Z} \bigg/ \frac{d_{\pi_z}}{\pi_z} = \epsilon_{px} = \frac{dX}{X} \bigg/ \frac{dp_x}{p_x}$$

16. Since $\pi_z g = p_x$,

$$\frac{\partial p_x}{\partial A} = \pi_z g' + g \frac{\partial \pi_z}{\partial A} > 0$$

The first term on the right is positive and the second term is negative. If g, g', and π_z are given, $\partial p_x / \partial A$ is linearly and negatively related to $\partial \pi_z / \partial A$.

17. Recall again our assumption, however, that even firms in perfectly competitive markets can fully differentiate their products. If the capacity of a firm to differentiate itself were inversely related to the elasticity of its commodity demand curve, that is, to the amount of competition in the commodity market, the increase in its product price generated by its advertising might not be directly related to the elasticity of its commodity demand curve.

18. "Fashion," indeed, does not necessarily refer only to the shorter-term preferences. Adam Smith says that the influence of fashion "over dress and furniture is not more absolute than over architecture, poetry, and music" (p. 283).

19. The budget constraint for i can be written as

$$\Pi_{R_i} R + \Pi_z Z = I_i + \Pi_{R_i} D_i = S_i$$

where Z are other commodities, Π_{R_i} is his marginal cost of changing R, I_i is his own full income, and S_i is his "social income."

20. Marshall believed that the desire for distinction was the most powerful of passions and a major source of the demand for luxury expenditures (see pp. 87–88, 106).

21. This quote is taken from the following longer passage in Böhm-Bawerk:

We must now consider a *second* phenomenon of human experience—one that is heavily fraught with consequence. That is the fact that we feel less concerned about future sensations of joy and sorrow simply because they do lie in the future, and the lessening of our concern is in proportion to the remoteness of that future. Consequently we accord to goods which are intended to serve future ends a value which falls short of the true intensity of their future marginal utility. *We systematically undervalue our future wants and also the means which serve to satisfy them.* (p. 268)

REFERENCES

Becker, G. S. "A Theory of Social Interaction." *J. Polit. Econ.* 82 (Nov./Dec. 1974): 1063–93.

Blumer, H. C. "Fashion." In *Int. Encyclo. Soc. Sci.* Vol. V. New York: 1968.

Böhm-Bawerk, Eugen von. *Capital and Interest.* Vol 2. South Holland, Ill.: 1959.

Galbraith, John K. *The Affluent Society*, Boston 1958.

Grossman, M. "The Economics of Joint Production in the Household." Rep. 7145. Center Math. Stud. Bus. Econ. Univ. Chicago: 1971.

Marshall, Alfred. *Principles of Economics.* 8th ed. London: 1923.

Michael, R. T., and G. S. Becker. "On the New Theory of Consumer Behavior." *Swedish J. Econ.* 75, (Dec. 1973): 378–96.

Mill, John S. *A System of Logic.* 8th ed. London: 1972.

Smith, Adam. *Theory of Moral Sentiments.* New Rochelle: 1969.

A NOTE ON RESTAURANT PRICING AND OTHER EXAMPLES OF SOCIAL INFLUENCES ON PRICE

· 8 ·

This note tries to explain why many successful restaurants, plays, sporting events, and other activities do not raise prices even with persistent excess demand. My approach assumes that demand by a typical consumer is positively related to quantities demanded by other consumers. This can explain not only the puzzle about prices but also why consumer demand is often fickle, why it is much easier to go from being "in" to being "out" than from "out" to "in," and why supply does not increase to reduce the excess demand.

A popular seafood restaurant in Palo Alto, California, does not take reservations, and every day it has long queues for tables during prime hours. Almost directly across the street is another seafood restaurant with comparable food, slightly higher prices, and similar service and other amenities. Yet this restaurant has many empty seats most of the time.

Why doesn't the popular restaurant raise prices, which would reduce the queue for seats but expand profits? Several decades ago I asked my class at Columbia to write a report on why successful Broadway theaters do not raise prices much; instead they ration scarce seats, especially through delays in

First published in the *Journal of Political Economy* 99, no. 5 (October 1991): 1109–16. © 1991 by the University of Chicago. All rights reserved.

FIGURE I

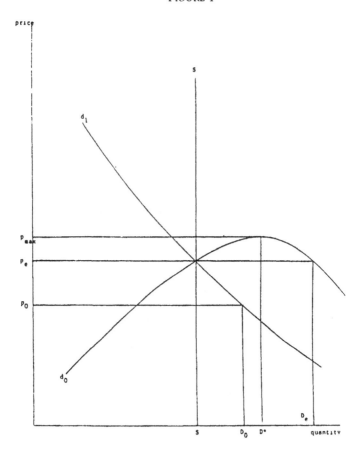

seeing a play. I did not get any satisfactory answers, and along with many others, I have continued to be puzzled by such pricing behavior. The same phenomenon is found in the pricing of successful sporting events, such as the World Series and Super Bowls, and in a related way in the pricing of best-selling books. This note suggests a possible solution to the puzzle based on social interactions.

The puzzle is easily shown in a supply-demand diagram, in which S in figure 1 is the number of restaurant tables, theater seats, and so forth, and d_1 is the usual negatively inclined demand curve. At a price of p_0, the S units sold must be rationed, with $D_0 - S$ being the excess demand at that price. Clearly, profits increase if price is raised to p_e since S units are still sold, but at a higher price. The profit-maximizing price is even higher if d_1 is inelastic at p_e.

Many explanations have been suggested for apparently nonmaximizing prices such as p_0. It could be a tax dodge if speculators who sell tickets at a higher price than p_0 share profits with owners or employees that are not reported as taxable income. A similar story applies to the maître d' who provides scarce tables to customers willing to pay "under the table." However, it is unclear why such tax evasion or principal-agent conflicts should be more common with successful plays and restaurants than with the sale of steel or oranges. Moreover, nonprice rationing apparently existed on Broadway long before tax considerations were important.

Price increases will be discouraged if consumers believe that they are unfair (see Kahneman, Knetsch, and Thaler 1986). This may sometimes help explain why prices do not rise to take advantage of temporary shortfalls in supply, but it is not plausible when rationing is more permanent. A series of gradual price increases could eliminate the gap in figure 1 without causing serious complaints about unfair pricing.

In this note I provide a different explanation, which assumes that a consumer's demand for some goods depends on the demands by other consumers. The motivation for this approach is the recognition that restaurant eating, watching a game or play, attending a concert, or talking about books are all social activities in which people consume a product or service together and partly in public.

Suppose that the pleasure from a good is greater when many people want to consume it, perhaps because a person does not wish to be out of step with what is popular or because confidence in the quality of the food, writing, or performance is greater when a restaurant, book, or theater is more popular. This attitude is consistent with Groucho Marx's principle that he would not join any club that would accept him.

Formally, I propose that the demand for a good by a person depends positively on the aggregate quantity demanded of the good:

$$D = \sum d^i (p, D) = F(p, D), \quad F_p < 0, F_d > 0, \qquad (1)$$

where $d^i(p, D)$ is the demand of the ith consumer, and D is the market demand. For each value of D, the equilibrium price solves $D = F(p, D)$. Since $F_p < 0$, there is a unique price for each feasible level of demand, given by the inverse demand function, $p = G(D)$. There are formal similarities between the effects of social interactions and the gains from standardization (see, e.g., Farrell and Saloner 1988).

Social interactions imply that $\partial G/\partial D$ may not be negative. As is well known, $F_d > 0$ can lead to a positive relation between price and aggregate demand. By differentiating equation (1), we get

$$\frac{dp}{dD} = G_d = \frac{1 - F_d}{F_p}. \qquad (2)$$

If the social interaction is strong enough—if $F_d > 1$—an increase in aggregate demand would increase the demand price. If $F_d > 1$ for all $D < D^*$, $F_d = 1$ for $D = D^*$, and $F_d < 1$ for $D > D^*$, the demand price rises as D increases for $D < D^*$, it hits a peak when $D = D^*$, and then it falls as D increases beyond D^* (see d_0 in fig. 1).

Since d_0 is rising at the market-clearing price p_e, it obviously pays to raise price above p_e: no less is sold and each unit fetches more. Indeed, profits are maximized when the price equals p_{max}, the peak demand price. The positively inclined demand curve in the vicinity of S explains why popular restaurants remain popular despite "high" prices. Obviously, demand must be rationed at p_{max} since D^* exceeds S. To simplify the discussion, I assume that the method used to ration demand is costless, such as a pure lottery system, so that the money price is the full cost to consumers.

Since a firm that charges p_{max} has a permanent gap measured by the difference between D^* and S, shouldn't it raise price still further, cut the gap, and make even more profits? The answer from figure 1 is clear: demand is discontinuous at p_{max} for price increases and falls to zero even for trivial increases. The reason for the discontinuity is clear. If demand fell only a little (say to D_1) at $p = p_{max} + \epsilon$, there would be multiple demand prices at D_1: p_1 and $p_{max} + \epsilon$. We know that demand price is unique at D_1 and at all other values of D. Hence demand must fall to zero when $\epsilon > 0$, no matter how small ϵ is.

Of course, demand curves like d_0 that first rise and then fall are not the only possible outcome of the positive effect of market demand on the quantities demanded by each consumer. The net effect could be a demand curve that is negatively inclined (when F_d is always less than one, as d_1 in fig. 1), or it could be the demand d in figure 2 that is first negatively sloped, becomes positively sloped for some D, and then becomes negatively sloped again. The firm would like to charge p^* in figure 2 and sell all S units, with demand at D_g^* and the gap being sizable. This equilibrium is similar to the equilibrium at p_{max} in figure 1.

However, if the firm simply chooses the price p^*, demand may be at D_b^* rather than at D_g^* since demand has two values at p^*. Moreover, D_b^* is not an attractive equilibrium since the excess capacity $(S - D_b^*)$ is substantial. If the firm must have an inferior equilibrium, it prefers p_e to p^* since marginal revenue is zero when $p = p_e < p^*$ and $D = D_e < S$.

FIGURE 2

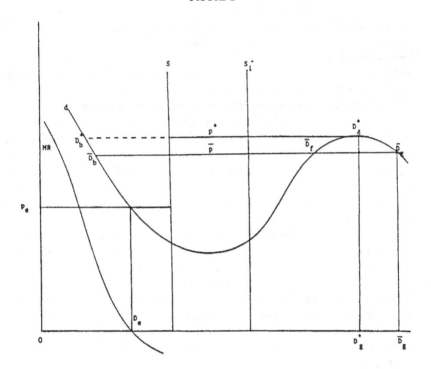

Consequently, there are two competing locally profit-maximizing equilibria: one has excess capacity and a low price ($S - D_e$, p_e), and the other has excess demand and a high price ($D_g^* - S, p^*$). The difference between these equilibria corresponds to the difference between a struggling restaurant or play with excess tables or seats and a highly successful one that is "in" and turns away would-be customers.

Obviously, producers prefer the excess demand equilibrium, but how can they help bring that about? Since each consumer demands more when others do, producers can try to coordinate consumers to induce them to raise their demands together.

Advertising and publicity may help, for these have a multiplier effect when consumers influence each other. Advertising that raises the demands of some consumers also indirectly raises the demands of other consumers since higher consumption by those vulnerable to publicity campaigns stimulates the demands of others. This explains the promotion of new books, and it suggests that goods with bandwagon properties tend to be heavily advertised.

The distinctive equilibria at $D = D_e$ and $D = D_g^*$ are a formal recognition of the well-known fact mentioned at the beginning that one restaurant may do much better than another one, even though they have very similar food and amenities. The success or failure of new books is an equally good example. Stephen Hawking's *A Brief History of Time* was on the *New York Times* best-seller list for over 100 weeks and sold more than 1.1 million hardcover copies. Yet I doubt if 1 percent of those who bought the book could understand it. Its main value to purchasers has been as a display on coffee tables and as a source of pride in conversations at parties.

The inequality in book sales is large: the coefficients of variation in total sales to August 1989 of books issued in 1987–88 by one publisher exceeded 129 percent and 177 percent for hardcover fiction and nonfiction books, respectively (the data were supplied to me by Eugene Kandel). The success or failure of trade books—like that of restaurants, plays, and other events—often depends on fortuitous factors that help sales snowball when they catch on and sink when they flop.

Figure 2 can explain an important characteristic of book pricing: the price of the hardcover edition almost never increases when a book turns out to succeed, nor until remaindering does it fall so much if it flops (see the analysis and evidence in Kandel [1990]). The reason is that p^* is more or less the optimal price whether the book flops or not, assuming that demand is quite inelastic for $p < p^*$ (so that p_e is close to p^*). Publishers set a price of p^* and hope for success, but they recognize that they may end up with many unsold copies $(S - D_b^*)$ that are mainly useful in the remainder market and for the paper content.

The "fickleness" of consumers evident in the shift of restaurants between "in" and "out" categories is also captured by this analysis. Although the equilibrium at (p_e, D_e) is locally stable, the one at (p^*, D_g^*) is not stable for shocks that reduce demand, and neither equilibrium is stable for large changes. If consumers at (p^*, D_g^*) lose confidence that other consumers want the good, demand will drop all the way to D_b^*.

This analysis explains too another commonly noted phenomenon: it is much easier to go from being "in" to being "out" than from being "out" to being "in." Since the equilibrium at (p_e, D_e) is locally stable in *both* directions, only a large upward shock to demand could shift that "out" equilibrium to the more profitable one at (p^*, D_g^*).

The partial instability of the profitable equilibrium at (p^*, D_g^*) may also explain a puzzle about supply. If price is not raised when demand exceeds supply, why doesn't output expand to close the gap? That does happen for best-sellers, where unexpected heavy demand is usually met by additional printings. Sometimes, too, restaurants faced with excess demand expand seating capacity, but often they do not. One explanation for why they do not expand is that restaurants know customers are fickle and a booming business is very fragile. They might be reluctant to expand capacity if demand at p^* could suddenly fall from D_g^* to D_b^*. The cost of an expansion in capacity from, say, S to S_1 could then drive a restaurant into bankruptcy.

Another possible explanation of why supply does not grow is that aggregate demand depends not only on price and aggregate demand but also positively on the gap between demand and supply:

$$D = \sum d^i\left(p, D, \frac{D}{S}\right) = F\left(P, D, \frac{D}{S}\right), \frac{\partial F}{\partial d/s} > 0. \tag{3}$$

Greater supply might not pay because that lowers the gap and, hence, the optimal price available to a producer.

This may explain why customers who have trouble getting into the popular Palo Alto restaurant mentioned at the beginning of this note do not switch to the nearby unpopular one. When I suggest doing this to my wife, she usually answers that she prefers the amenities at the popular restaurant. But the main difference in "amenities" is that one restaurant is crowded and has queues, while the other one is partially empty and provides immediate seating!

The gap between what is demanded and what is supplied affects demand when consumers get utility from competing for goods that are not available to everyone who wants them—such as an exclusive club—or when the camaraderie on a queue itself delivers utility. Of course, entering the gap into the demand function to explain why supply does not increase appears to be an ad hoc invention of a "good" to solve a puzzle. Therefore, I do not want to overemphasize the importance of the gap between demand and supply, although I do believe that it is sometimes relevant.

In an insightful comment, Ted Bergstrom was disturbed by the leftward instability of the equilibrium at (p^*, D_g^*) and proposed a somewhat different approach. In his model, typical consumers prefer a larger aggregate demand only up to some fraction of capacity; beyond that they find a restaurant, theater, and so forth "too crowded." He shows that this can lead to a locally *stable* high-price profit-maximizing equilibrium in which demand equals capacity. Bergstrom's suggestion is valuable for some problems, but the model in this note seems better suited to the best-seller phenomenon, persistent excess demand, and the much greater fragility of being an "in" activity than an "out" activity.

Moreover, a restaurant could increase the leftward stability of a high-price equilibrium by lowering price in figure 2 below p^*, say to $\bar{p} < p^*$, which has a demand at $\bar{D}_g > \bar{D}^*_g$. The seller might be willing to trade off a lower price than p^* for a more stable equilibrium: the point $(\bar{p}, \bar{D}_g)$ is stable not only for increases in demand but also for some shocks that lower demand.

However, $\bar{p}$ does not avoid but magnifies the multiple equilibrium problem since there is the unstable equilibrium at $\overline{D}_f$ as well as the excess capacity locally stable equilibrium at $i\overline{D}_b$.

It may strike some readers as ad hoc to make a person's demand depend on the demands of others in order to explain why restaurants, theaters, publishers, and others do not raise price when demand exceeds supply. But economists have paid insufficient attention to direct social influences on behavior. Fortunately, social interactions finally are being incorporated into economic models to explain residential segregation and neighborhood "tipping," custom, pay structure, gambling, and other behavior (for some examples, see Becker [1974]; Schelling [1978]; Akerlof [1980]; Brenner [1983]; Jones [1984]; Frank [1985]; Granovetter [1985]; Bond and Coulson [1989]). Therefore, the analysis in this note fits well into a growing economic literature that recognizes the influence on consumers and workers of the social world they live in.

NOTE

I am indebted for helpful comments to Ted Bergstrom, Bruno Frey, David Friedman, Milton Harris, Eugene Kandel, Edward Lazear, Kevin M. Murphy, Sherwin Rosen, and George Stigler and to the participants in a Seminar on Rational Choice in the Social Sciences at the University of Chicago and to the Lynde and Harry Bradley Foundation and the Hoover Institution for support.

REFERENCES

Akerlof, George A. "A Theory of Social Custom, of Which Unemployment May Be One Consequence." *QJE* 94 (June 1980): 749–75.

Becker, Gary S. "A Theory of Social Interactions." *JPE* 82 (November/ December 1974):1063–93.

Bond, Eric W., and N. Edward Coulson. "Externalities, Filtering and Neighborhood Change." *J. Urban Econ.* 26 (September 1989): 231–49.

Brenner, Reuven. *History: The Human Gamble.* Chicago: Univ. Chicago Press, 1983.

Farrell, Joseph, and Garth Saloner. "Coordination through Committees and Markets." *Rand J. Econ.* 19 (Summer 1988): 235–52.

Frank, Robert H. *Choosing the Right Pond: Human Behavior and the Quest for Status.* New York: Oxford Univ. Press, 1985.

Granovetter, Mark. "Economic Action and Social Structure: The Problem of Embeddedness." *American J. Sociology* 91 (November 1985): 481–510.

Jones, Stephen R. C. *The Economics of Conformism.* Cambridge, Mass.: Blackwell, 1984.

Kahneman, Daniel, Jack L. Knetsch, and Richard Thaler. "Fairness as a Constraint on Profit Seeking: Entitlements in the Market." *AER* 76 (September 1986): 728–41.

Kandel, Eugene. "Intertemporal Pricing in the Book Publishing Industry." Manuscript. Rochester, N.Y.: Univ. Rochester, Simon School Management, 1990.

Schelling, Thomas C. *Micromotives and Macrobehavior.* New York: Norton, 1978.

HABITS, ADDICTIONS, AND TRADITIONS

· 9 ·

The past casts a long shadow on the present through its influence on the formation of present preferences. The past influences present preferences through habitual, addictive, and traditional behavior, and in other ways. These have profound implications for the analysis of economic and social phenomena, including short- and long-run changes in the amount of smoking due to higher taxes on a pack of cigarettes, and the effects of taxes on effort and work habits in the long run. The link between the past and present choice may also explain why and how parents influence the formation of children's preferences, how people get committed to future decisions, and the formation and support of institutions and culture.

I. INTRODUCTION

The usual assumption in most discussions of behavior over time is that choices today are not directly dependent on choices in the past. J. R. Hicks expressed strong disapproval of this assumption:

First published in *Kyklos* 45, no. 3 (1992): 327–46. Reprinted by permission of Helbing & Lichtenhahn Verlag AG, Basle and Frankfurt/M.

It is nonsense that successive consumptions are independent; the normal condition is that there is a strong complementarity between them (1965, page 261).

It is ironic that this sentence comes at the end of a rather lengthy monograph on economic growth that relies throughout on the independence assumption. The assumption of independence is not "nonsense," for it usefully simplifies many problems that are not crucially affected by dependencies over time. But the assumption has discouraged economists from grappling with other issues of considerable significance—including addictions, work habits, preference formation, why children support their elderly parents, preference solutions to the problem of future commitments, and the evolution and stability of institutions. These are the kinds of questions I address in this paper.

A growing literature during the past two decades has assumed instead of independence that current consumption is affected by past consumption. The most influential work has been by Boyer (1978), Houthakker and Taylor (1966), Kydland and Prescott (1982), Philips (1974), Pollak (1970), Ryder and Heal (1973), Spinnewyn (1981), von Weizsacker (1971), and various colleagues and students at Chicago: Iannaccone, Murphy, Hansen, Stigler, Constantinides, Heaton, and Hotz. I will not try to review, summarize, or reference these contributions, but will concentrate on the issues that have interested me.

II. HABITS

Some influences of past consumption on present behavior are obvious. If I just ate a filling dinner, I do not want to eat another dinner in the near future —not even a Persian delight cooked by my wife. Essentially all goods are substitutes if the time intervals are sufficiently close and the quantities consumed are big enough. Even lovers of potato chips or those most hooked on crack do not want any more now if they consumed large quantities during the past hour.

But for many goods, when the time periods compared are not very close, greater consumption earlier stimulates greater, not lesser, consumption later. Following common usage, I define *habitual* behavior as displaying a positive relation between past and current consumption; economists call these goods complements. Well-known examples include smoking, using heroin, eating ice cream or Kellogg's Corn Flakes, jogging, attending church, telling lies, and often intimacy with a lover.

A full discussion needs to consider both short-term substitutions in consumption and the longer-term complementarities. Murphy and I (1988) present a model of cycles or binges in the amount of eating that has both substitutions and complementarities over time in food consumption, and Heaton (1991) finds both types of relations in the time series on aggregate consumption in the United States. This paper concentrates on the complementary relations because these are responsible for the habitual behavior I want to highlight.

Of course, there are vast differences in the degree of habituation to the same activity: most people can drink or work regularly without ever becoming alcoholics or workaholics. And the likelihood that a person becomes habituated to any activity varies with circumstances and age. Soldiers who became addicted to drugs while in Vietnam usually stopped the habit soon after returning to civilian life, while former smokers and alcoholics often resume their habits after becoming unemployed or when their marriages break up.

Habits are *harmful* or "bad" if greater present consumption lowers future utility, as in the detrimental effects on future health of heavy smoking or drinking. Similarly, habits are *beneficial* if greater present consumption raises future utility; regular swimming or regular church attendance may be examples. It is natural that bad habits get more attention than good ones, but as we will see, rational behavior also implies that the observed strong habits are more likely to be harmful than beneficial.

If greater past consumption of a good increased the marginal utility of present consumption, myopic persons who do not consider the future consequences of their actions would increase their present consumption. But higher current utility does not guarantee that rational forward-looking persons consume more than in the past. Rational consumers also consider how greater current consumption affects the marginal utilities or disutilities in the future.

Murphy and I provide a necessary and sufficient condition for a rational forward-looking consumer to develop a habit (1988); for earlier derivations, see Ryder and Heal (1973) and Iannaccone (1986). It is indeed necessary for greater past consumption to raise the marginal utility from present consumption—this corresponds to what is called "reinforcement" in the addiction literature. But several other parameters are also important, including the rate of discount on future utilities, and the rate of decay or depreciation in the contribution of past consumption to current utility. The larger the rate at which either the future or past is discounted, the more likely that a good with a given amount of reinforcement is habitual, and the stronger is the habit (see section 1 of the Appendix). This conclusion is intuitive, for the bigger are these discount rates, the smaller are the effects on future utility of greater present consumption. Then reinforcement has the more dominating effect.

An *addiction* is defined simply as a strong habit. Technically, a habit becomes an addiction when the effects of past consumption on present consumption are sufficiently strong to be destabilizing (see section 1 of the Appendix). Therefore, a shock to an individual, such as unemployment, may lead for a while to larger and larger increases over time in the amount consumed of addictive goods. Demand for addictive goods tends to be bifurcated: people either consume a lot, or they abstain because they anticipate that they will come "hooked" if they begin to consume. Smoking is a good example of bifurcation, for 70 percent of adults in the United States do not smoke, while persons who do smoke generally consume at least half a pack a day.

A habit may be raised into an addiction by exposure to the habit itself. Certain habits, like drug use and heavy drinking, may reduce the attention to future consequences—there is no reason to assume discount rates on the future are just given and fixed (elsewhere I have developed an analysis of endogenous discount rates [Becker 1990]). Since an increase in the discount rate strengthens the commitment to all habits, there would be further induced increases in discount rates. The result may be an explosive expansion of certain habits into powerful addictions.

The presumption from the theory that addictions are partly caused by heavy decay rates on past consumption in a way is consistent with the medical evidence. For the damage to lungs, liver, and other organs declines rather quickly after a person stops heavy drinking or smoking, unless the point of no return had been reached.

Since people who heavily discount the future and past would place little weight on the future consequences of their behavior, they are less likely to be deterred from "harmful" activities that reduce future utility, even when these are not habitual. And they would be less attracted by "beneficial" activities that raise utility in the future, even when these are not habitual, such as limiting cholesterol intake. But since high discount rates on the future and past also foster strong habits and addiction, people with high rates would be *especially* attracted by harmful activities that are addictive, or at least highly habitual.

Therefore, we expect addictions to be associated with harmful activities. This can explain why addictions usually cause duress—declines in well-being over time. It can also explain why drug addictions and crime tend to go together, and why religious people tend to be law-abiders, even if drug use and religion do not affect the propensity to engage in crime, and even if crime and religion are not addictive.

Nothing in the analysis of forward-looking utility-maximizing behavior presumes that people know for sure whether they will become habituated or addicted to a substance or activity, although that is sometimes claimed by critics of this approach. An individual may have considerable uncertainty about whether she would become an alcoholic if she begins to drink regularly. A troubled teenager who begins to experiment with drugs may expect, but not be certain, that his life will begin to straighten out, perhaps because of a good job or marriage, before he becomes addicted. Since these and other choices are made under considerable uncertainty, some persons become addicted simply because events turn out to be less favorable than was reasonable to anticipate—the good job never rescued the drug user. Persons who become addicted because of bad luck may regret their addictions, but that is no more a sign of irrational behavior than is any regret voiced by big losers at a race track that they bet so heavily.

I define *traditional* behavior as habits that are sensitive to choices in the more distant past—including sometimes choices made by parents and others in the past—because the effects of the past decay slowly. Tradition-related habits are unlikely to be addictive because low depreciation rates reduce the strength of a habit. Such habits are especially important for understanding culture and institutions, as I will try to show later.

III. Invidious Comparisons

Economists usually do not consider why preferences are what they are, but it is advisable to discuss habit formation since many writers have claimed that habitual behavior is not fully rational. Although little is known about the mechanisms behind the development of habits, it is not obvious to me that they are less rational than other preferences.

Alcohol, heroin, cocaine, smoking, and certain other drugs have well-documented biological-pharmacological effects on consumers that raise their desire for the drugs. Habit helps economize on the cost of searching for information, and of applying the information to a new situation (see Stigler and Becker [1977, 81–83]). And most people get mental and physical comfort and reassurance in continuing to do what they did in the past. Thomas Jefferson was surely right when he asserted in a letter to an acquaintance that "He who permits himself to tell a lie once, finds it much easier to do it a second and third time, till at length it becomes habitual" (1785).

Another promising lead in understanding the formation of habit comes from recognizing that the utility of many goods depends on how present consumption of these goods compares with the amounts consumed in the past. For example, a given standard of living usually provides less utility to persons who had grown accustomed to a higher standard in the past. It is the decline in health, rather than simply poor health, that often makes elderly persons depressed. And what appeared to be a wonderful view from a newly occupied house may become boring and trite after living there for several years.

Goods that involve such invidious comparisons with the past are "harmful" in the sense I am using this term because greater consumption now lowers future utility by raising the future standard of comparison. What is more interesting for present purposes and less obvious is that such goods also tend to be habitual: current consumption is encouraged by greater past consumption in order to come closer to the standard set by past behavior.

Indeed, a good *must* be habitual if utility from the good depends on the difference between current consumption and a weighted sum of the amounts consumed in the past. Note that in such cases the effect of comparisons with the past is so powerful that a good must be habitual *regardless* of the discount rate on future utilities or the decay rate on past consumption. The habit is stronger when past consumption has a bigger weight, and it is an addiction when past consumption is weighted more heavily than present consumption (see section 2 of the Appendix).

If utility depends on comparisons between present and past consumption, it would be highest just after consumption rose to a permanently higher level, and it would decline over time as the person became accustomed to that level. Similarly, utility would be lowest just after consumption fell to a permanently lower level.

If the standard of living itself involved such comparisons with the past, the nouveau riche would tend to be the happiest of people, the new poor the most miserable, and the long-term rich may not be so much happier than the long-term poor. Indeed, the long-term rich are only a little happier than the long-term poor when the weight on past consumption almost equals the weight on present consumption (see section 2 of the Appendix, and Ryder and Heal [1973]). Suicides might be more closely related to declines in the living standard—perhaps due to a loss of wealth or health—than to the level itself.

Adam Smith (1976) has a few wonderful paragraphs in *The Theory of Moral Sentiments* on the transitory gains in utility from a higher standard of living:

> The poor man's son, whom heaven in its anger has visited with ambition . . . pursues the idea of a certain artificial and elegant repose . . . which, if in the extremity of old age he should at last attain to it, he will find to be in no respect preferable to that humble security and contentment which he has abandoned for it (pages 299–300). (I owe this reference to George Stigler.)

Rapid economic growth raises the level of happiness partly by increasing the number of new rich and reducing the number of new poor. Indeed, a mere slowing of the growth rate could lower utility even when incomes continue to rise if the habitual component to the standard of living were sufficiently powerful.

IV. Price and Wealth Effects

It is often claimed that habitual and traditional behavior, especially addictions, do not respond much to changes in prices and wealth. The explanation sometimes offered is that habits influence behavior in ways that are independent of calculation, or that habits are locked in by the past. I will consider only the responses of rational habitual behavior since I am claiming in this paper that habitual behavior does not imply a reluctance to "calculate."

An unexpected fall in the price of a habitual good may have only a slight impact on demand as long as past consumption has not changed much. This is probably the basis for the claim that habits get locked in by the past. But the magnitude of the response to say a permanent fall in price would grow over time as consumption continues to increase, even if it only increased slightly at first. By the definition of highly habitual goods, each increase in consumption of these goods raises future consumption by relatively large amounts. Therefore, it is not surprising that the long-run price elasticity of demand between steady states is *larger*, not smaller, for the more strongly habitual goods (see Becker and Murphy [1988]). Moreover, short-run changes in demand are misleading since the ratio of short-run to long-run elasticities is smaller for the stronger habits (see Becker, Grossman, and Murphy [1991]).

Grossman, Murphy, and I [1990] recently used the rational habit model to study empirically the demand for cigarettes in the United States. We find cigarette demand to be rather strongly habitual, a not very surprising conclusion. The responses to price changes are not small: a 10 percent permanent fall in the price of a pack of cigarettes increases smoking by 4 percent one year later, and by almost 8 percent after a few years. Perhaps more surprising is the evidence that smokers are not myopic—they do try to anticipate the future, as measured by the effects of future prices on current consumption.

There are strong differences of opinion in the United States about whether drug use should be legalized, differences that cut across political labels of liberal or conservative. Everyone agrees that legalization would greatly reduce the retail price of drugs, but much of the disagreement comes from different views about how legalization will affect the demand for drugs.

Since many drugs are strongly habitual and even addictive, the analysis of rational addiction suggests that the demand for drugs may not increase much shortly after legalization, but that it would increase by a lot in the long run—especially by the poor (see Becker, Grossman, and Murphy [1991])—unless legalization has other effects than simply lowering price.

One important other effect concerns peer pressure, which induces some teenagers to smoke, drink heavily, and experiment with drugs. Although I do not know of convincing reasons why strongly habitual and addictive behavior is *generally* more subject to pressure from peers than other behavior, it is straightforward to show that habitual behavior is more *vulnerable*, in the sense that a given level of peer pressure has an especially large effect on habitual behavior. Strong peer pressure can convert moderately habitual behavior into what appears to be a strong habit or even an addiction.

Consider a fall in price of a habitual good subject to peer pressure. Each consumer would increase his demand, partly because price is lower, and partly because other consumers have raised their demands. Habit increases demand over time, and so too does the pressure to consume more when peers also do. This synergy between peer pressure and habit implies that peer pressure has a larger effect on the elasticity of demand when the habit is stronger; similarly, a stronger habit has more of an effect on the long-run elasticity where there is greater peer pressure (see section 3 of the Appendix). Consequently, it may only appear that peer pressure is stronger for habitual behavior since such pressure has greater effects on demand when habits are stronger.

The importance of peer pressure in the market for drugs generally strengthens the conclusion that legalization would greatly increase the use of drugs. One qualification would be if pressure to use drugs declined when they became legal. Another would be if the synergy between peer pressure and habits produced sections of positively sloped demand curves (see section 3 of the Appendix), and hence multiple equilibria in the drug market. Legalization might then lower both price and drug use by shifting the market to a wholly different equilibrium. As yet, however, there is no evidence that the drug market is characterized by such multiple equilibria.

Econometric studies usually find that high taxes on incomes and other taxes on work effort do not have large effects on the hours worked by men. Yet more than fifty years of weak work incentives under communist rule in Eastern Europe and elsewhere had a shattering effect on work effort in these countries. The commitment to hard work apparently has also eroded in countries like Sweden that greatly raised the effective tax on work effort during the past quarter century.

The econometric findings can be reconciled with these other observations by recognizing that work is a tradition-habit that builds up very slowly over time, perhaps partly under the influence of examples set by parents and others. As Victor Hugo said, "Nothing is more dangerous than discontinued labor—it is habit lost. A habit easy to abandon, difficult to resume" (1909, Vol. II, p. 159). The long time it takes for high taxes and other policies to break down slowly accumulated work habits is not easily captured by econometric studies, even by studies that use a few years of panel data to discover some effects of work habits (see, e.g., Bover [1991]).

Countries can take advantage of the slow decay of good work habits by imposing heavy *temporary* taxes on effort. But the pessimistic side of the story is that Eastern Europe and the Soviet Union will have difficulty rebuilding the good work habits eroded during the many decades of mismanagement and weak work incentives.

Being on welfare may create a bad habit if children and parents lose their initiative by becoming dependent on government handouts. Then many families may refuse to go on welfare, even when eligible—as is the case in the United States—because the cost of dependency exceeds the value of the payments. Although a sizable fall in welfare payments might greatly increase the number who decline to go on, it could *initially* have only a minor impact on the number of families who remain on welfare since they have become habituated to the welfare payments (see Sanders [1991]).

The permanent income model explains why total consumption often does not respond much to income shocks by assuming that many shocks have a large temporary component. Yet some critics have argued that aggregate consumption in the United States is too stable—the excess stability issue—to be explained by the permanent income story because aggregate shocks are alleged to have a small transitory component. Even if they are right about aggregate shocks, and there is considerable disagreement, the problem is not with the permanent income concept—which is surely basically correct—but with the assumption that preferences are separable over time. If current consumption depends on past consumption, even a permanent shock to income may initially have only a small effect on consumption.

Habit-driven responses to permanent shocks can explain most of the behavior usually explained since Friedman's work (1957) by nonhabitual responses to transitory shocks. For example, Friedman showed that higher-income groups would save a larger fraction of their incomes than lower-income groups if only because these groups contain relatively many persons who received positive transitory income shocks. However, higher-income groups save a lot also because they contain relatively many persons who are *newly* rich. I believe that the effects of habits as well as the distinction between permanent and transitory income are needed for a satisfactory explanation of aggregate consumption behavior (see Heaton [1991] and Ferson and Constantinides [1991]).

V. Preference Formation

Each person is born perhaps not as a tabula rasa—an empty slate—but with limited experiences that get filled in by childhood and later experiences. These experiences influence teenage and adult desires and choices partly by creating habits, addictions, and traditions. The habits acquired as a child or young adult generally continue to influence behavior even when the environment changes radically. For example, Indian adults who migrate to the United States often eat the same type of cuisine they had in India, and continue to wear the same style of clothing. A woman who was badly sexually abused as a child may forever fear and dislike men, including those who would treat her with consideration and respect. A person may remain an alcoholic until he dies mainly because he started drinking heavily as a teenager.

Childhood experiences can greatly influence behavior over a person's entire life because it may not pay to try to greatly change habits when the environment changes. Childhood-acquired habits then continue, even though these would not have developed if the environment when growing up had been the same as the environment faced as an adult.

The Freudian emphasis on the crucial influence of early childhood on later behavior would be consistent with utility-maximizing forward-looking behavior if behavior were highly habitual. For then experiences while a child could have a very large effect on adult preferences and choices.

Children spend their early years under the care of parents and close relatives who determine what they eat, read, observe, and hear. The enormous influence this has on children's preferences explains the close link between parents and children in many attitudes and choices, including religious and political party affiliations, the propensities to smoke, eat breakfast, or divorce, and the taste for Chinese, Iranian, or Southern-style cuisine.

A natural way in a utility-maximizing framework to model the influence of parents on children is to assume that the preferences of children and adults evolve from early childhood and later experiences under the influence of habitual, including addictive and traditional, behavior. Indeed, some of my remarks will go well beyond habitual behavior to other recursive influences of early childhood and other past experiences on present and future preferences.

Altruistic parents maximize their own utility in part by maximizing their children's. They would try to direct the evolution of children's preferences toward raising the utility of children. For example, parents may refrain from smoking even when that gives them much pleasure because their smoking raises the likelihood that the children will smoke. Or they may take their children to church, even when not religious, because they believe exposure to religion is good for children. Indeed, many parents stop going after their children leave home.

Selfish parents do not care about the welfare of children, but they too are often concerned about the evolution of children's preferences. They may want to be taken care of when old or ill, but cannot have a contract with their children to help out. However, they can try to shape the formation of children's preferences to raise the chances their children will help voluntarily.

The preferences children get when young, in effect, can *precommit* them to helping out much later when they are adults and their parents are elderly. Parents can help make the children altruistic, or can make grown children feel "guilty" when they do not help. Propensities toward guilt may lower the lifetime utility of children—selfish parents do not care—but helping out of guilt may raise the utility of adult children, *conditional on their past experiences.*

Therefore, even selfish parents do not necessarily neglect or abuse children, for they might spend considerable time, money, and emotional resources on children to rig the evolution of preferences in their own favor. This sounds calculating and selfish. It is. Yet the opportunity to "commit" children to helping out when parents need it can induce selfish parents to treat their children much better than they would if adult preferences and behavior did not evolve from childhood experiences and treatment. It also implies that selfish parents become meaner when they need not rely on their children, perhaps because the government becomes committed to helping out the elderly in need.

Children carry along into adulthood the baggage of experiences they had only a limited role in shaping. Therefore, a rational person can meaningfully state that she does not "like" her preferences in the sense that she doesn't like the inherited baggage: the guilt, the sexual fears, the propensity to smoke or drink heavily, and so forth. She can change the stock of experiences over time, but how much a rational person wants to change depends on how long she expects to live, the strength of the influence of the past on present choices, and other factors. We all are to some extent prisoners of experiences we wish we never had.

Economists are so conditioned to identifying rational choice with separable preferences that we often call "irrational" quite rational behavior that is the result of past experiences. We have trouble understanding the people who take good care of elderly parents even when not forced by social norms or altruism—I have tried to indicate why this can be utility-maximizing behavior once the importance of guilt and other results of past experiences is recognized.

A prominent example is the literature on "endowment" effects (see Kahneman, Knetsch, and Thaler [1990]). A family may refuse to sell for half a million dollars the house it has lived in for twenty years, even though it would be unwilling to spend anywhere near that amount for an otherwise equivalent house. Of course, the qualifier "otherwise" is crucial since twenty years in the same house presumably built up memories and attachments to *that* particular house, not to a seemingly "equivalent" house that is really not equivalent.

A more difficult example of the endowment effect concerns a person like Sherwin Rosen who stores a young bottle of wine that cost a few bucks. By luck the bottle turns out to be worth several hundred dollars after ten years. But Sherwin refuses to sell, even though he would never contemplate paying that much for an otherwise equivalent bottle. Irrational? Or like the family that refuses to sell its house, a case where the experience of "consuming" a particular bottle for a long time raised the value attached to *that* bottle, not to an otherwise equivalent bottle?

Other "rational" interpretations of the refusal are possible; e.g., Sherwin may get pleasure from bragging about his shrewdness in acquiring such a bottle. And an interpretation that uses the effects of owning the bottle for ten years on present demand for it may seem forced since the bottle was not "consumed" during the decade. But such a reaction partly reflects the economist's narrow conception of "consumption." People consume paintings, and old rugs and coins simply by looking at them occasionally, and they may value such objects more over time as they grow attached to them.

VI. Commitment, Institutions, and Culture

Game theory has shown the crucial importance of commitment in the strategic interactions over time of two or more participants. The equilibria that emerge are often highly sensitive to whether players can commit to future behavior. Yet it may be difficult to enforce commitment since people can renege on promises or slip out of contractual obligations. Still, I believe the difficulty of obtaining binding commitments has been exaggerated because of the common assumption that preferences are independent of the past, so that a person's utility-maximizing choices at any moment do not directly depend on past choices.

For habits, addictions, traditions, and other preferences that are directly contingent on past choices partly control, and hence commit, future behavior in predictable ways. Indeed, habits and the like may be very good substitutes for long-term contracts and other explicit commitment mechanisms.

Consider, for example, a firm that would charge consumers a lower price now if they agree to buy more of the good for some time into the future. Unfortunately, it is not possible to write a contract that ensures future purchases. But a contract may not be necessary if the good is habitual since habituated consumers are automatically committed to buying more in the future when they buy more now.

A firm may help finance investments in a worker's general skills if the worker will remain with the firm. A written contract that commits the worker to stay is not enforceable, but the firm may know that the worker is likely to remain after he has been there for a while since the job becomes a habit.

I have already shown how parents may be reasonably confident that their children will help out when they become adults and the parents are elderly because the parents help structure the children's adult preferences by controlling childhood experiences.

Such influences of habitual and other recursive preference relations on behavior get incorporated into the optimal strategies of players in sequential games. For example, a parent may save less to support herself when elderly if her children are conditioned to help out. A boss may exploit his workers' attachments to their jobs, or society may punish crimes more severely now because that raises social support for punishments in the future.

Elsewhere, Grossman, Murphy, and I (1990) consider the optimal pricing of a monopolist who sells a habitual good. We show that wealth-maximizing prices are below the prices where current marginal revenue equals marginal cost since a lower price now, in effect, "commits" consumers to increase their future consumption (for a more complete analysis of optimal pricing, see Fethke and Jagannathan [1991]). Therefore, the optimal prices will be higher if consumers are prevented from raising their future consumption.

This analysis can explain the rise in price-cost margins, and hence "profits," of cigarette companies during the past few years. The continuing growth in legislation that restricts smoking is a major observable obstacle to future increases in the demand for cigarettes. Producers are induced to raise cigarette prices and current "profits," even though they are obviously hurt by legislated restrictions on smoking.

These examples of the effects of preferences on commitment are rather straightforward, although some of you may be dubious. You will then be far more dubious of the following examples, which extend the analysis of habits and traditions to include institutions and culture. I was led to this line of argument by reading in the *Federalist Papers* James Madison's criticisms of Jefferson's proposal for temporary constitutions that are rewritten by each succeeding generation. Madison did more than just claim that a constitution protects fundamental rights and helps commit the actions of future generations. He recognized that a basic problem is whether people are willing to obey a constitution: the world is strewn with wonderful constitutions that are ignored or evaded.

Madison argued in effect that a constitution is more likely to be followed out of habit and tradition the longer it has been around. The frequent changes advocated by Jefferson would deprive a constitution of—I can do no better than quote Madison's words—

> that veneration, which time bestows on everything, and without which perhaps the wisest and freest governments would not possess the requisite stability

and

> when the examples which fortify opinion are ancient as well as numerous, they are known to have a double effect. (Madison [1787]).

Madison and others—he apparently was following Hume (1748)—claim that preferences are formed not simply by what a person did in the past, what his parents did, and what contemporary peers are doing, but also by the behavior of past generations of "peers." This extensive influence of the past on present beliefs and behavior helps stabilize older institutions and cultures. As Madison argued in rejecting Jefferson's suggestion for frequent change, the ultimate strength of the support for an institution depends on whether there is time to cumulate the support over several generations.

Sometimes, support for an institution or ethic—such as the belief in honesty—is called "unthinking" attachment to a culture or ethic. Wordsworth claimed that "habit rules the unreflecting herd" (1822). But this is no more "unthinking" than other preferences that are formed by what happened in the past.

Obedience to institutions often can be utilized in social decision making. The armed forces try to instill the habit of obedience to commands during fighting by emphasizing military traditions, rigid rules, and response to peer pressure. Young people asked to contribute heavily to social security may not have to worry that the next generation will refuse to support them when they become elderly, even though it might *appear* to be in the next generation's self-interest to do so. Indeed, this generation's support of the elderly may well strengthen the tradition-habit that will induce the next generation to support the elderly.

I readily admit that I do not know how far one can push this point of view. And the stress on institutions influenced by tradition-habits and peer pressure may seem to be an ad hoc trick invented to solve intractable commitment and collective choice problems. But this approach does come out of an attention to more straightforward problems, such as heavy drinking, drug use, and brand preferences. And the evolution of preferences out of past experiences seems far more intuitive, even when extended to institutions and culture, than the opposite assumption so dominant in economics that preferences are independent of the past.

Some of you might be surprised to hear a coauthor of the *de gustibus* point of view, with its emphasis on stable preferences, waxing enthusiastically about the formation of preferences. But what *de gustibus* assumes is that *metapreferences* are stable. Metapreferences include past choices and choices by others as arguments in a person's current utility function. In fact, addictive behavior and social interactions were two of the major examples analyzed by Stigler and myself (1977).

The message of that paper is not that preferences at time *t* for different people depend in the same way on their consumption at *t*. Rather, it is that common rules determine the way different variables and experiences enter the metapreferences that motivate most people at most times. And that forward-looking rational actors maximize the utility from their metaprefer-ences, not from current preferences alone, because they recognize that choices today affect their utilities in the future.

VII. Conclusion

My concluding remarks can be brief. I have tried to show that the past casts a long shadow on the present through its influence on the formation of present preferences and choices. These links between the past and the present do not simply provide a technical generalization of the independence as-sumption regarding preferences that permits a few more wiggles in the data to be explained.

The systematic analysis of habitual, addictive, and traditional behavior, and of other ways the past influences present preferences, has profound implications for the analysis of many kinds of economic and social phenom-ena. These surely include the demand for branded goods, how income shocks affect aggregate consumption, and short- and long-run changes in smoking due to higher taxes on a pack of cigarettes. They also include a better understanding of how legalization would change drug use, the effect of income and other taxes on effort and work habits in the long run, and why the nouveau riche and new poor are so different from the long-term rich and long-term poor.

With a still bolder vision and a lot of luck, the link between the past and present choices may also explain why and how parents influence the formation of children's preferences, how people get committed to future decisions, and the formation and support of institutions and culture.

Appendix

1. Let the utility function at time t be

$$U(t) = U(y(t), c(t), S(t)), \qquad (1.1)$$

where y is a nonhabitual good, c is habitual, and $S = c(t) - \delta S(t)$, where δ is the depreciation rate on past consumption of c. The overall utility function at $t = 0$ is the discounted value of the $U(t)$, where σ is the rate of discount. I assume that overall utility is maximized subject to a wealth constraint, where the amount of wealth is given.

A good is *habitual* if

$$\frac{dc(t)}{dS(t)} > 0 \qquad (1.2)$$

when the marginal utility of wealth is held constant. That is, when a "compensated" increase in past consumption raises present consumption. Since at a steady state, $c = \delta S$, it is natural to define an *addiction* as a habit strong enough that

$$\frac{dc(t)}{dS(t)} > \delta \qquad (1.3)$$

This implies that a steady state is unstable if c is addictive near this state.

Becker and Murphy (1988) show that a necessary and sufficient condition for a good to be habitual near a steady state is that

$$(\sigma + 2\delta)U_{cs} > -U_{ss}, \qquad (1.4)$$

where $U_{cs} = \partial^2 U / \partial c \partial S$, and $U_{ss} = \partial^2 U / \partial S^2$.

2. Let utility from the habitual good c at time t be separable from the other goods (y), and expressible as

$$V(t) = V[c(t) - \alpha \delta S(t)], \qquad (2.1)$$

where α is a constant > 0. Since δ is the depreciation rate on past consumption of c, $\delta S(t) = \bar{c}(t)$, a weighted average of past consumption. Then

$$V_{cc} = V''$$

$$V_{cs} = \alpha\delta V''$$

$$V_{ss} = (\alpha\delta)^2 V''$$

and

$$2\delta V_{cs} = -2\alpha\delta^2 V'' > -V_{ss} = -\alpha^2\delta^2 V'' \qquad \text{for all } \alpha < 2.$$

Therefore, for all σ and $\delta > 0$, the modified Stone-Geary utility function in equation (2.1) satisfies the condition in equation (1.4) for c to be a habit. It can be shown that the habit is stronger when α is greater, and it is an addiction when $\alpha > 1$.

Equation (2.1) implies that in a steady state where $c = \delta S = \bar{c}$,

$$V = V[\bar{c}(1 - \alpha)],$$

and   (2.2)

$$V_c = V'(1 - \alpha).$$

Therefore, a rise in c between steady states has a smaller effect on utility when the habit (α) is stronger (given the value of V').

The effect on steady-state consumption of a permanent change in the price of c compensated to hold the marginal utility of wealth (λ) constant is

$$\frac{dc}{dp_c} \cong \frac{\lambda}{V''(1 - \alpha)^2} \qquad \text{if } \sigma \cong 0 \qquad (2.3)$$

(This is a special case of equation [18] in Becker and Murphy [1988].) Clearly, the effect on c is greater when α—the strength of the habit—is bigger.

3. I now expand the utility function in equation (2.1) to include peer pressure:

$$V(t) = [c(t) - \alpha\delta S(t) - \gamma\bar{C}(t)], \qquad (3.1)$$

where $\gamma > 0$ measures the strength of the pressure, and $\bar{C} = \sum\frac{c_i}{N} = c$ when all N consumers are identical. Peer pressure alters the effects of a change in the price of c on its steady-state consumption to

$$\frac{dc}{dp_c} \cong \frac{\lambda}{V''(1 - \alpha)(1 - \alpha - \gamma)} \qquad \text{if } \sigma \cong 0. \qquad (3.2)$$

A proof is straightforward. The first-order condition for each consumer near a steady state is

$$V_c + \frac{V_s}{\sigma + \delta} = \lambda p_c \, .$$

Differentiating with respect to p_c while holding λ constant, assuming $c = \delta S$, and $\overline{C} = c$, we get

$$\left\{ V_{cc} + \frac{V_{cs}}{\delta} + V_{c\bar{c}} + (\frac{V_{ss}}{\delta} + V_{sc} + V_{s\bar{c}}) \frac{1}{\sigma + \delta} \right\} \cdot \frac{dc}{dp_c} = \lambda \, .$$

Substituting $V'' = V_{cc}$, $-\alpha\delta V'' = V_{cs}$, $\alpha^2\delta^2 V'' = V_{ss}$, $-\gamma V'' = V_{c\bar{c}}$, and $\alpha\gamma\delta V'' = V_{sc}$, and setting $\sigma = 0$, we get

$$V''(1 - 2\alpha - \gamma + \alpha^2 + \alpha\gamma) \frac{dc}{dp_c} = \lambda \, ,$$

which is equation (3.2)

Clearly, $[d/d(\gamma)] [(dc)/(dp_c)]$ is greater in absolute value when α is greater. Moreover, the demand curve becomes unstable $[(d_c)/(dp_c) > 0]$ when $\alpha + \gamma > 1$.

NOTE

An earlier version was given as the Nancy Schwartz Lecture at Northwestern University, May 15, 1991. I have had helpful comments from Joseph Hotz, Kevin Murphy, Richard Posner, and Sherwin Rosen, and useful assistance from David Meltzer, and M. Rebecca Kilburn. I am indebted to a grant from the Lynde and Harry Bradley Foundation to the Center for the Study of the Economy and the State, to the National Institute of Child Health and Development (Grant 5 R17HD22054), and to the National Science Foundation (Grant SES-9010748) for support.

REFERENCES

Becker, Gary S. "Optimal Discounting of the Future." Department of Economics, University of Chicago, April 1990.

Becker, Gary S., Michael Grossman, and Kevin M. Murphy. "An Empirical Analysis of Cigarette Addiction." NBER Working Paper No. 3322, April 1990.

Becker, Gary S., Michael Grossman, and Kevin M. Murphy. "Rational Addiction and the Effect of Price on Consumption." *American Economic Review Papers and Proceedings* 81 (1991): 237–241.

Becker, Gary S. and Kevin M. Murphy. "A Theory of Rational Addiction." *Journal of Political Economy* 96 (1988): 675–700.

Boyer, Olympia. "Relaxing Intertemporal Separability: A Rational Habits Model of Labor Supply Estimated from Panel Data." *Journal of Labor Economics* 9 (1991): 85–100.

Ferson, Wayne, and George Constantinides. "Habit Persistence and Durability in Aggregate Consumption: Empirical Tests.'" *Journal of Financial Economics*. Forthcoming.

Fethke, Gary, and Raj Jagannatham. "Monopoly Pricing with Habit Formation." Working Paper series 91–10. University of Iowa, April 1991.

Friedman, Milton. *A Theory of the Consumption Function*. Princeton, N.J.: Princeton University Press, 1957.

Heaton, John. "An Empirical Investigation of Asset Pricing with Temporally Dependent Preference Specifications." Massachusetts Institute of Technology, February 1991.

Hicks, John R. *Capital and Growth*. Oxford: Clarendon Press, 1965.

Houthhakker, H. S., and Lester D. Taylor. *Consumer Demand in the United States 1929–1970*. Cambridge, Mass.: Harvard University Press, 1966.

Hugo, Victor. *Les Miserables* (1862), *Saint Denis*, Book II, Chapter I. Translated by Charles E. Wilbour. New York: J.M. Dent & Sons, 1909.

Hume, David. *An Enquiry Concerning Human Understanding*. 1748.

Iannaccone, Laurence R. "Addiction and Satiation." *Economics Letters* 21 (1986): 95–99.

Jefferson, Thomas. Letter to Peter Carr, August 19, 1785.

Kahneman, Daniel, Jack Knetsch, and Richard Thaler. "Experimental Tests of the Endowment Effect and the Coase Theorem." *Journal of Political Economy* 98 (1990): 1325–48.

Kydland, Finne E. and Edward C. Prescott. "Time to Build and Aggregate Fluctuations." *Econometrica* 50 (1982): 1345–1370.

Madison, James. *Federalist Papers*, No. 49. 1787.

Philips, Louis. *Applied Consumption Analysis*. Amsterdam: North-Holland, 1974.

Pollak, Robert A. "Habit Formation and Dynamic Demand Functions." *Journal of Political Economy* 78 (1970): 745–763.

Ryder, Harl E., Jr. and Geoffrey M. Heal. "Optimum Growth with Intertemporally Dependent Preferences." *Review of Economic Studies* 40 (1973): 1–33.

Sanders, Seth. "A Dynamic Model of Welfare Participation." Ph.D. thesis, Department of Economics, University of Chicago, 1991.

Smith, Adam. *The Theory of Moral Sentiments*, Indianapolis, Ind.: Liberty Classics, 1976.

Spinnewyn, Frans. "Rational Habit Formation." *European Economic Review* 15 (1981): 91–109.

Stigler, George J., and Gary S. Becker. "De Gustibus Non Est Disputandum." *American Economic Review* 67 (1977): 76–99.

von Weizsacker, Carl C. "Notes on Endogenous Changes of Tastes." *Journal of Economic Theory* 3 (1971): 345–372.

Wordsworth, William. *Ecclesiastical Sonnets*, pt. II, Sonnet 28, "Reflections." 1822.

FAMILY, MARRIAGE, AND FERTILITY

◆ ◆

◆ PART ◆ TWO ◆

AN ECONOMIC ANALYSIS
OF FERTILITY

· 10 ·

The inability of demographers to predict Western birthrates accurately in the postwar period has had a salutary influence on demographic research. Most predictions had been based either on simple extrapolations of past trends or on extrapolations that adjusted for changes in the age-sex-marital composition of the population. Socioeconomic considerations are entirely absent from the former and are primitive and largely implicit in the latter. As long as even crude extrapolations continued to give fairly reliable predictions, as they did during the previous half century, there was little call for complicated analyses of the interrelation between socioeconomic variables and fertility. However, the sharp decline in birthrates during the thirties coupled with the sharp rise in rates during the postwar period swept away confidence in the view that future rates could be predicted from a secularly declining function of population compositions.

Malthus could with some justification assume that fertility was determined primarily by two primitive variables, age at marriage and the frequency of coition during marriage. The development and spread of knowledge about contraceptives during the last century greatly widened the scope of family size decision making, and contemporary researchers have been forced to pay

First published in Ansley Coale et al., *Demographic and Economic Change in Developed Countries: A Conference of the Universities–National Bureau Committee for Economics. A Report of the National Bureau of Economic Research* (Princeton, N.J.: Princeton University Press, 1960), pp. 209–40. Reprinted by permission of the National Bureau of Economic Research.

greater attention to decision making than either Malthus or the forecasters did. Psychologists have tried to place these decisions within a framework suggested by psychological theory; sociologists have tried one suggested by sociological theory, but most persons would admit that neither framework has been particularly successful in organizing the information on fertility.

Two considerations encouraged me to analyze family size decisions within an economic framework. The first is that Malthus's famous discussion was built upon a strongly economic framework; mine can be viewed as a generalization and development of his. Second, although no single variable in the Indianapolis survey[1] explained more than a small fraction of the variation in fertility, economic variables did better than others. Section I develops this framework and sets out some of its implications. Section II uses this framework to analyze the actual effects of income on fertility. Section III speculates about some further implications of the discussion in I and II.

I. The Economic Framework

General Considerations

In societies lacking knowledge of contraception, control over the number of births can be achieved either through abortion or abstinence, the latter taking the form of delayed marriage and reduced frequency of coition during marriage. Since each person maintains some control over these variables, there is room for decision making even in such societies. Other things the same, couples desiring small families would marry later and have more abortions than the average couple. Yet the room for decision making would be uncomfortably small, given the taboos against abortion, the strong social forces determining the age of marriage, and the relative inefficiency of reductions in the frequency of coition. Chance would bulk large in determining the distribution of births among families.[2]

The growth of knowledge about contraception has greatly widened the scope of decision making, for it has separated the decision to control births from the decision to engage in coition. Presumably, such a widening of the scope of decision making has increased the importance of environmental factors, but which of the numerous environmental factors are most important? To simplify the analysis of this problem I assume initially that each family has perfect control over both the number and spacing of its births.

For most parents, children are a source of psychic income or satisfaction, and, in the economist's terminology, children would be considered a consumption good. Children may sometimes provide money income and are then a production good as well. Moreover, neither the outlays on children nor the income yielded by them are fixed but vary in amount with the child's age, making children a durable consumption and production good. It may seem strained, artificial, and perhaps even immoral to classify children with cars, houses, and machinery. This classification does not imply, however, that the satisfactions or costs associated with children are morally the same as those associated with other durables. The satisfaction provided by housing, a "necessity," is often distinguished from that provided by cars, a "luxury," yet both are treated as consumer durables in demand analysis. Abstracting from the kind of satisfaction provided by children makes it possible to relate the "demand" for children to a well-developed body of economic theory. I will try to show that the theory of the demand for consumer durables is a useful framework in analyzing the demand for children.

Tastes

As consumer durables, children are assumed to provide "utility." The utility from children is compared with that from other goods via a utility function or a set of indifference curves. The shape of the indifference curves is determined by the relative preference for children, or, in other words, by "tastes." These tastes may, in turn, be determined by a family's religion, race, age, and the like. This framework permits, although it does not predict, fertility differences that are unrelated to "economic" factors.

Quality of Children

A family must determine not only how many children it has but also the amount spent on them—whether it should provide separate bedrooms, send them to nursery school and private colleges, give them dance or music lessons, and so forth. I will call more expensive children "higher-quality" children, just as Cadillacs are called higher-quality cars than Chevrolets. To avoid any misunderstanding, let me hasten to add that "higher quality" does not mean morally better. If more is voluntarily spent on one child than on another, it is because the parents obtain additional utility from the additional expenditure and it is this additional utility which we call higher "quality."

Income

An increase in income must increase the amount spent on the average good, but not necessarily that spent on each good. The major exceptions are goods that are inferior members of a broader class, as a Chevrolet is considered an inferior car, margarine an inferior spread, and black bread an inferior bread. Since children do not appear to be inferior members of any broader class, it is likely that a rise in long-run income would increase the amount spent on children.[3]

For almost all other consumer durables, such as cars, houses, or refrigerators, families purchase more units as well as better-quality units at higher income levels, with the quantity income elasticity usually being small compared to the quality elasticity.[4] If expenditures on children responded in a similar way, most of the increased expenditures on children would consist of an increase in the quality of children. Economic theory does not guarantee that the quantity of children would increase at all, although a decease in quantity would be an exception to the usual case. Thus an increase in income should increase both the quantity and quality of children, but the quantity elasticity should be small compared to the quality elasticity.

Malthus, on the other hand, concluded that an increase in income would lead to a relatively large increase in family size. His argument has two major components. First, an increase in income would cause a decline in child mortality, enabling more children to survive childhood. If a decrease in births did not offset the decrease in child mortality, the number of children in the average family would increase. His second argument is less mechanical and takes greater account of motivation. An increase in income increases fertility by inducing people to marry earlier and abstain less while married.

My analysis has generalized that of Malthus by relating the quantity of children to the quality of children and by permitting small (even negative) quantity income elasticities as well as large ones. My conclusion that in modern society the quantity elasticity is probably positive but small differs from his for the following reasons. First, child mortality has fallen so low that the ordinary changes in income have little effect on the number of survivors out of a given birth cohort. Moreover, it is doubtful that even a large decline in child mortality would have much effect on family size, for parents are primarily interested in survivors, not in births per se. Therefore, a decline in child mortality would induce a corresponding decline in births.[5] Second, births can now be controlled without abstinence and this has greatly reduced the psychic costs of birth control. "Human nature" no longer guarantees that a growth in income appreciably above the subsistence level results in a large inadvertent increase in fertility.

Cost

In principle the net cost of children can be easily computed. It equals the present value of expected outlays plus the imputed value of the parents' services, minus the present value of the expected money return plus the imputed value of the child's services. If net costs were positive, children would be on balance a consumer durable and it would be necessary to assume that psychic income or utility was received from them. If net costs were negative, children would be a producer durable and pecuniary income would be received from them. Children of many qualities are usually available, and the quality selected by any family is determined by tastes, income, and price. For most families in recent years the net expenditure on children has been very large.[6]

Real incomes per capita in the United States have increased more than threefold in the last 100 years, which must have increased the net expenditure on children. It is possible that in the mid–nineteenth century children were a net producer's good, providing rather than using income. However, the marginal cost of children must have been positive in families receiving marginal psychic income from children; otherwise, they would have had additional children. Even in 1850, the typical family in the United States was producing fewer children than was physically possible. Some more direct inferences can be drawn from the data on Negro slaves, an extreme example of a human producer's good. These data indicate a positive net expenditure on male slaves during their first eighteen years.[7] Slave raising was profitable because the high price that an eighteen-year-old could bring more than offset the net cost during the first eighteen years. Presumably, in most families expenditures on white children during their first eighteen years were greater than those on slaves. Moreover, after eighteen, white children became free agents and could decide whether to keep their income or give it to their parents. The amount given to parents may have been larger than the costs before eighteen, but it is more likely that costs before eighteen dominated returns after eighteen. This conclusion does not imply that monetary returns from children were unimportant, and indeed, they are stressed at several points in this paper. It does imply, however, that a basic framework which treats children as a consumer's good is relevant not only for the present, but also for some time in the past.

A change in the cost of children is a change in the cost of children of *given quality*, perhaps due to a change in the price of food or education. It is well to dwell a little on this definition for it is widely misunderstood. One would not say that the price of cars has risen over time merely because more people now buy Cadillacs and other expensive cars. A change in price has to be estimated from indexes of the price of a given quality. Secular changes in real income and other variables have induced a secular increase in expenditures on children, often interpreted as a rise in the cost of children. The cost of children may well have risen (see p. 257) but the increase in expenditure on children is no evidence of such rise since the quality of children has risen. Today children are better fed, housed, and clothed, and in increasing numbers are sent to nursery schools, camps, high schools, and colleges. For the same reason, the price of children to rich parents is the same as that to poor parents even though rich parents spend more on children.[8] The rich simply choose higher-quality children as well as higher qualities of other goods.[9]

It is sometimes argued that social pressures "force" richer families to spend more on children, and that this increases the cost of children to the rich. This higher cost is supposed to explain why richer families have fewer children than others and why richer societies have fewer children than poorer ones. However, since the cost of different goods is given in the marketplace, social pressures cannot change this, but can only change the basket of goods selected. That is, social pressures influence behavior by affecting the indifference curve structure, not by affecting costs. To put this differently, social pressures may affect the income elasticity of demand for children by rich (and poor) families, but not the price elasticity of demand. Therefore, the well-known negative relationship between cost (or price) and quantity purchased cannot explain why richer families have had relatively few children. Moreover, nothing in economic analysis implies that social pressures would make the quantity income elasticity of demand for children negative. Thus my conclusion that the quantity income elasticity is relatively small but positive and the quality elasticity relatively large is entirely consistent with an analysis which emphasizes social pressures.

Suppose there was an equal percentage decline in the price of all qualities of children, real income remaining constant. Although economic theory suggests that the "amount" of children consumed would increase, it does not say whether the amount would increase because of an increase in quantity, quality, or both—the last, however, being most likely. It also has little to say about the quantitative relationship between price and amount. There are no good substitutes for children, but there may be many poor ones.[10]

Supply

By and large, children cannot be purchased on the open market but must be produced at home. Most families are no longer self-sufficient in any major commodity other than children. Because children are produced at home, each uncertainty in production is transferred into a corresponding uncertainty in consumption, even when there is no uncertainty for all families taken together. Although parents cannot accurately predict the sex, intelligence, and height of their children, the distribution of these qualities is relatively constant for the country as a whole. This uncertainty makes it necessary to distinguish between actual and expected utility. Thus suppose a group of parents received marginal utility equal to U_m from a male child and

U_f from a female child. The expected utility from an additional child equals $EU = PU_m + (1 - P)U_f \cong \dfrac{U_m + U_f}{2}$, where P, the probability of a male, is approximately equal to $1/2$. They would have additional children whenever the expected utility per dollar of expected cost from an additional child were greater than that from expenditures elsewhere. The actual utility is either U_f or U_m, which differs from EU as long as $U_f \neq U_m$. In fact, if U_f (or U_m) were negative, some parents would receive negative utility.

A second important consequence of uniting consumption and production is that the number of children available to a family is determined not only by its income and prices but also by its ability to produce children. One family can desire three children and be unable to produce more than two, while another can desire three and be unable to produce fewer than five.[11] The average number of live births produced by married women in societies with little knowledge of contraception is very high. For example, in nineteenth-century Ireland, women marrying at ages 20–24 averaged more than 8 live births.[12] This suggests that the average family more frequently had excess rather than too few children.

Relatively effective contraceptive techniques have been available for at least the last 100 years, but knowledge of such techniques did not spread rapidly. Religious and other objections prevented the rapid spread of knowledge that is common to other technological innovations in advanced countries. Most families in the nineteenth century, even in advanced Western countries, did not have effective contraceptive information. This information spread slowly from upper socioeconomic groups to lower ones.[13]

Each family tries to come as close as possible to its desired number of children. If three children are desired and no more than two are available, two are produced; if three are desired and no fewer than five are available, five are produced. The marginal equilibrium conditions would not be satisfied for children but would be satisfied for other goods, so the theory of consumer's choice is not basically affected.[14] Families with excess children consume less of other goods, especially of goods that are close substitutes for the quantity of children. Because quality seems like a relatively close substitute for quantity, families with excess children would spend less on each child than other families with equal income and tastes. Accordingly, an increase in contraceptive knowledge would raise the quality of children as well as reduce their quantity.

II. An Empirical Application

Having set out the formal analysis and framework suggested by economic theory, we now investigate its usefulness in the analysis of fertility patterns.

It suggests that a rise in income would increase both the quality and quantity of children desired; the increase in quality being large and the increase in quantity small. The difficulties in separating expenditures on children from general family expenditures notwithstanding, it is evident that wealthier families and countries spend much more per child than do poorer families and countries. The implication with respect to quantity is not so readily confirmed by the raw data. Indeed, most data tend to show a negative relationship between income and fertility. This is true of the census data for 1910, 1940, and 1950, where income is represented by father's occupation, mother's education, or monthly rental; the data from the Indianapolis survey; the data for nineteenth-century Providence families; and several other studies as well.[15] It is tempting to conclude from this evidence either that tastes vary systematically with income, perhaps being related to relative income, or that the number of children is an inferior good. Ultimately, systematic variations in tastes may have to be recognized; but for the present it seems possible to explain the available data within the framework outlined in Section I, without assuming that the number of children is an inferior good. First, it is well to point out that not all the raw evidence is one way. In some studies, the curve relating fertility and income flattens out and even rises at the higher-income classes, while in other studies the curve is positive throughout.[16] Second, tastes are not the only variable that may have varied systematically with income, for there is a good deal of general evidence that contraceptive knowledge has been positively related to income. Himes, in his history of contraception, indicates that the upper classes acquired this knowledge relatively early.[17] If such knowledge spread gradually from the upper classes to the rest of society, fertility differentials between classes should have first increased and then narrowed. This was clearly the pattern in England and was probably the pattern in the United States.[18]

Such evidence does little more than suggest that differential knowledge of contraceptive techniques might explain the negative relationship between fertility and income. Fortunately, the Indianapolis survey makes it possible, at least for 1941, to assess its quantitative importance. Table 1 presents some data from this study. In column (1) the native-white Protestant couples in the sample are classified by the husband's income, and column (2) gives the number of children born per 100 couples in each income class. The lowest-income class was most fertile (2.3 children per couple) and a relatively high class least fertile (1.5 children per couple), but the highest class averaged slightly more children than the next highest. This relationship between economic level and fertility was about the same as that shown by the 1940 census.[19] Sterility did not vary systematically with income, so column (3), which is restricted to relatively fecund families, differs only slightly from column (2).

TABLE 1

CHILDREN EVER BORN PER 100 COUPLES IN INDIANAPOLIS
CLASSIFIED BY HUSBAND'S INCOME AND PLANNING STATUS
(NATIVE-WHITE PROTESTANTS)

Income (1)	All Couples (2)	Relatively Fecund (3)	Number and Spacing Planners (4)	All Planners (5)	Desires of Relatively Fecund (6)
$3,000 +	159	180	149	175	171
2,000–2,999	149	176	182	161	170
1,600–1,999	163	194	91	126	153
1,200–1,599	189	229	97	144	175
1,200 and less	227	266	68	146	193

SOURCE: *Social and Psychological Factors Affecting Fertility*, P. K. Whelpton and C. V. Kiser, eds., N.Y., Milbank Memorial Fund, 1951, Vol. 2, part 9. Columns (2) and (3) from Table 4; columns (4) and (5) computed from Figure 8; column (6) computed from Figures 8 and 21.

It is well known that rich families use contraception earlier and more frequently than poor families. It has been difficult to determine whether poor families are ignorant of contraceptive methods or whether they desire more children than richer ones. The Indianapolis survey tried to separate ignorance from tastes by classifying couples not only by use of contraception but also by control over births. Column (4) gives the average number of children for "number and spacing planning" couples, including only couples who had planned all their children. A positive pattern now emerges, with the richest families averaging more than twice as many children as the poorest families. The income elasticity is about $+0.42$. Column (5) presents data for "number planned" couples, including all couples that planned their last child. These data also show a positive pattern, with an elasticity of $+0.09$, lower than that for number and spacing planners.

Fecund couples having excess children were asked questions about the number of such children. Column (6) uses this information and that in column (5) to relate income to the number of children desired by all fecund couples. The elasticity is negative, being about -0.07.[20] After an intensive study, however, Potter found evidence that the number of desired children was overestimated; his own estimates of desired fertility show a positive relationship with income.[21] Thus evidence from the Indianapolis survey indicates that differential knowledge of contraception does convert a positive relation between income and *desired* fertility into a negative relation between income and *actual* fertility.[22]

Several other surveys provide information on desired fertility. For example, in 1954 a group at Michigan asked Detroit area families: "In your opinion what would be the ideal number of children for a young couple to have, if their standard of living is about like yours?" There was a distinct positive relationship between the ideal number of children and income of the family head.[23]

If knowledge of contraceptive techniques did not vary with income, the relation between actual fertility and income would equal that between desired fertility and income. Contraceptive knowledge is said to be diffused among all income classes in Stockholm, and the fertility of Stockholm families from 1917 to 1930 was positively related to income.[24] Contraceptive knowledge was said to be very primitive in *all* income classes of prewar China, and a positive relation between fertility and income also seemed to prevail there.[25] Graduates in the same college class are probably relatively homogeneous in contraceptive knowledge and values as well as in formal education. I have the impression that income and fertility of these graduates tend to be positively related, but I have been able to examine only one sample. Some graduates from Harvard and Yale were classified by occupation and "degree of success." Within each occupation, the more successful graduates usually had more children.[26]

Information has been obtained on the family income, education, earners, and dependent children of a sample of the subscribers to Consumers Union.[27] This sample is particularly valuable for our purposes since it primarily consists of families with a keen interest in rational, informed consumption. If my analysis is at all relevant, fertility and income should be more positively related in this group than in the U.S. population as a whole. Table 2 presents the average number of dependent children for single-earner families with the head aged 35–44, each family classified by its income and by the education of the head. There is a substantial positive relationship between income and children within each educational class; education per se has relatively little effect on the number of children. The income elasticity is about 0.09 and 0.14 for graduates of a four-year college and of a graduate school respectively. These data, then, are very consistent with my analysis, and indicate that well-informed families do have more children when their income increases.

Contraceptive knowledge in the United States spread rapidly during World War II, largely fostered by the military in its effort to limit venereal disease and illegitimacy. We would expect this to have reduced the relative fertility of low-income classes, and Census Bureau studies in 1952 and 1957 confirm this expectation. Table 3 presents the data for urban and rural

TABLE 2

AVERAGE NUMBER OF DEPENDENT CHILDREN FOR SINGLE-EARNER FAMILIES
WITH HEAD AGE 35–44 IN A SAMPLE OF SUBSCRIBERS TO CONSUMERS UNION,
APRIL 1958

| | AVERAGE NUMBER OF DEPENDENT CHILDREN BY EDUCATION CLASS OF HEAD | | | |
Income Class	High School Graduate or Less	Some College	Graduate of Four-Year College	Graduate Degree
Less than $3,000	2.43	1.61	2.50	2.17
3,000–3,999	2.15	2.47	2.18	2.23
4,000–4,999	2.70	2.40	2.04	2.18
5,000–7,499	2.68	2.73	2.88	2.67
7,500–9,999	2.80	2.94	3.00	3.03
10,000–14,999	2.89	3.03	3.12	3.23
15,000–24,999	2.85	3.04	3.04	3.31
25,000 and over	3.12	3.23	3.28	3.60

SOURCE: Unpublished data from consumer purchases study by Thomas Juster at the National
Bureau of Economic Research.

nonfarm families for 1952 and all families for 1957 with column (1) giving
husband's income, column (2) the age-standardized number of children
under 5 per 100 men aged 20 to 59, column (3) the age-standardized number
of children ever born per 100 wives aged 15 to 44, and column (4) the
number ever born per 100 wives aged 45 and older. Columns (2) and (3) deal
primarily with childbearing since 1940 and show a much weaker negative
relationship between fertility and income than does column (4), which deals
primarily with childbearing before 1940.

The relationship between fertility and income can be investigated not
only with cross-sectional income differences but also with time series differences. Cyclical fluctuations in income have regularly occurred in Western
nations, and, if our analysis is correct, a change in income would induce a
change in fertility in the same direction. For our purpose cyclical fluctuations
in fertility can be measured by the cyclical fluctuations in births (although
see p. 256–57). Some earlier studies presented evidence that births do
conform positively to the business cycle, even when adjusted for fluctuations
in the marriage rate.[28]

I have related some annual figures since 1920 on first and higher-order
birthrates—brought forward one year—to the National Bureau annual busi-

TABLE 3

FERTILITY BY HUSBAND'S INCOME

Husband's Income (1)	Children under 5 per 100 Married Men 20–59 (age standardized) (2)	Children Born per 100 Wives 15–44 Years Old (age standardized) (3)	Children Born per 100 Wives over 45 (4)
Part I: In Urban and Rural Nonfarm Areas in the United States in 1952			
$7,000 +	53	189	194
6,000–6,999	52	188	210
5,000–5,999	50	188	210
4,000–4,999	52	177	217
3,000–3,999	52	184	240
2,000–2,999	51	189	256
1,000–1,999	40	181	279
1,000 and less	40	211	334
Part II: For the United States in 1957			
$7,000 +	—	216	213
5,000–6,999	—	220	230
4,000–4,999	—	221	240
3,000–3,999	—	236	279
2,000–2,999	—	247	304
1,000–1,999	—	289	341
1,000 and less	—	—	383

SOURCES: I. U.S. Bureau of the Census, *Current Population Reports*, Wash., Government Printing Office, 1953, no. 46, p. 20.
II. U.S. Bureau of the Census, *Current Population Reports*, Wash., Government Printing Office, 1958, no. 84, p. 12.

ness cycle dates. Column (3) of table 4 gives the percentage change per year in first and higher-order birthrates from the beginning of one phase to the beginning of the next phase. The strong secular decline in births before World War II makes most of these entries negative before that time and hence obscures the effect of cyclical fluctuations in economic conditions. If economic conditions affected births they should have declined more rapidly (or risen less rapidly) during a downswing than during an upswing. This can be detected from the first differences of the entries in column (3), which are shown in column (4). Aside from the wartime period, 1938–1948, second and higher-order births conform perfectly in direction to the reference dates and first births conform almost as well. So reference cycle analysis strongly indicates that business conditions affect birthrates. This effect is not entirely

TABLE 4

REFERENCE CYCLE PATTERN OF BIRTHRATES FOR U.S. SINCE 1920

FIRST BIRTHS							
REFERENCE CYCLE DATES[1]		Birthrates per 1,000 Women 15–44, Brought Forward One Year at Reference Cycle Dates[2]		Annual Percentage Change During a Business		Excess of Annual Percentage Change During Business Expansion Over	
Peak	Trough	At Peak	At Trough	Expansion	Contraction	Preceding Contraction	Succeeding Contraction
(1)		(2)		(3)		(4)	
1920		39					
	1921		34		−12.82		
1923		34		0.00		+12.82	
	1924		34		0.00		0.00
1926		32		−2.94		−2.94	
	1927		30		−6.25		−3.31
1929		30		0.00		+.6.25	
	1932		25		−5.57		−5.57
1937		31		4.80		+10.37	
	1938		31		0.00		−4.80
1944		29		−1.06		−1.06	
	1946		46		28.33		+29.39
1948		36		−10.87		−39.20	
	1949		33		−8.33		+2.54
1953		34		0.76		+9.09	
	1954		33		−2.94		−3.70
1957		33•		0.00		+2.94	

dependent on cyclical fluctuations in the marriage rate since second and higher-order births conform exceedingly well.

The next step is to relate the magnitude of the movement in births to that in general business, and to compare this with corresponding figures for other consumer durables. Time series giving net national product and purchases of consumer durables were analyzed in the same way as birthrates were. The figures for birthrates in column (4) of table 4 and corresponding figures for purchases of consumer durables were divided by corresponding figures for national product to obtain cyclical income elasticities for births and con-

TABLE 4 (continued)

HIGHER-ORDER BIRTHS							
REFERENCE CYCLE DATES[1]		Birthrates per 1,000 Women 15–44, Brought Forward One Year at Reference Cycle Dates[2]		Annual Percentage Change During a Business		Excess of Annual Percentage Change During Business Expansion Over Preceding Succeeding Contraction	
Peak	Trough	At Peak	At Trough	Expansion	Contraction	Preceding Contraction	Succeeding Contraction
(1)		(2)		(3)		(4)	
1920		82					
	1921		78		− 4.88		
1923		78		0.00		+ 4.88	
	1924		74		− 5.13		− 5.13
1926		68		− 4.05		+ 1.08	
	1927		64		− 5.88		− 1.83
1929		60		− 3.12		+ 2.76	
	1932		52		− 4.45		− 1.33
1937		48		− 1.53		+ 2.92	
	1938		47		− 2.08		− 0.55
1944		57		3.46		+ 5.54	
	1946		67		8.47		+ 5.01
1948		71		2.98		− 5.49	
	1949		73		2.81		− 0.17
1953		84		3.77		+ 0.96	
	1954		85		1.19		− 2.58
1957		88*	·	3.53		+ 2.34	

*Last figure is for 1956. SOURCE: [1] See National Bureau of Economic Research Standard Reference Dates for Business Cycles. [2] See Dudley Kirk, Appendix to "The Influence of Business Cycles on Marriage and Birth Rates."

sumer durables. These figures, shown in table 5, are positive for almost all phases, and this indicates that cyclical changes in births and purchases of consumer durables have been in the same direction as those in national output. The cyclical change in first births was usually greater than that in higher-order births, and both were usually less than the change in output. Changes in first and higher-order births were, however, far from insignificant, averaging 74 and 42 percent of the corresponding change in output.

Cyclical changes in births are small compared to those in consumer

TABLE 5

CYCLICAL INCOME ELASTICITIES FOR BIRTHS AND
CONSUMER DURABLE PURCHASES DURING REFERENCE CYCLE PHASES

Reference Cycle Phases (1)		First Births (2)	Higher-Order Births (3)	Purchases of Consumer Durables (4)
1920–1921	Down	0.81	0.31	2.48
1921–1923	Up	0.00	.58	2.96
1923–1924	Down	− 1.55	.57	6.63
1924–1926	Up	.87	.48	5.26
1926–1927	Down	2.05	.90	4.05
1927–1929	Up	.37	.09	1.40
1929–1932	Down	.47	.13	1.51
1932–1937	Up	.26	.03	1.96
1937–1938	Down	− .09	.46	1.38
1938–1944	Up	4.26	.73	9.20
1944–1946	Down	3.89	.54	5.33
1946–1948	Up	− .44	.03	0.11
1948–1949	Down	.88	.09	0.01
1949–1953	Up	.78	.54	1.78
1953–1954	Down	1.19	.95	3.23
1954–1957	Up			
Simple average excluding 1938–1948		.56	.42	2.84
and negative figures		.77	.42	2.84

SOURCE: Birthrates from column (4) of Table 4; similar figures were computed for consumer durable purchases and net national product. The durable figures were from Raymond W. Goldsmith, A Study of Savings in the United States, Vol. 1, Tables Q-6 and A-25 for 1920–1949 and from U.S. Dept. of Commerce, Survey of Current Business, July 1958, Table 2, for 1949–1957. Net national product figures were from Simon Kuznets, Technical Tables (mimeo), T-5, underlying series in Supplement to Summary Volume on Capital Formation and Financing for 1920–1955 and from U.S. Dept. of Commerce, Survey of Current Business, July 1958 Table 4, for 1955–1957.

durables. The latter averaged about 2.84 times the change in output, or about 4 and 7 times the change in first and higher-order births respectively. This is consistent with our emphasis on inadequate knowledge of birth control; inadequate knowledge seems to explain much but not all of the difference between the average cyclical change in higher-order births and in purchases of durables.[29] Some would be explained by the fact that the data for children include only fluctuations in numbers, while those for durables include both fluctuations in numbers and in quality. The rest may be explained by other differences between children and consumer durables.

For example, to purchase a consumer durable it is necessary to make a down payment with one's own resources and to finance the remainder either with one's own or with borrowed resources. The economic uncertainty generated by a depression increases the reluctance to use own or borrowed resources and induces creditors to raise standards and screen applicants more carefully.[30] Therefore some purchases of durables would be postponed until economic conditions improved. The "purchase" of children, however, is less apt to be postponed than the purchase of other durables. The initial cost of children (physician and delivery charges, nursery furniture, expenses, and so on) is a smaller fraction of its total cost than is the initial cost of most other durables because expenditures on children are more naturally spread over time. Hence children can be "purchased" with a smaller down payment and with less use of borrowed funds than can most other durables.

There is still another reason why the "purchase" of children is less apt to be postponed. Ceteris paribus, the demand for a good with a lengthy construction period is less sensitive to a temporary economic movement than the demand for more readily constructed goods, since delivery is likely to occur when this movement has passed. The construction and delivery period is very short for durables like cars and quite long for children. It takes about ten months on the average to produce a pregnancy and this period combined with a nine-month pregnancy period gives a total average construction period of nineteen months. This period is sufficiently long to reduce the impact on the demand for children of temporary movements in income.

There are also some reasons why the "purchase" of children is more apt to be postponed. For example, since children cannot be bought and sold they are a less "liquid" asset than ordinary durables, and the economic uncertainty accompanying a depression would increase the community's preference for liquid assets. A more complete analysis would also have to take account of other factors, such as the accelerator and the permanent income concept, which may have produced different cyclical responses in fertility and consumer durables. Our aim here, therefore, is not to present a definitive explanation of the relative cyclical movement in fertility but only to suggest that economic analysis can be useful in arriving at such an explanation.

Although the data on cyclical movements in fertility appears consistent with our analysis, another piece of time series data is in apparent conflict with it. Over time per capita incomes in the United States have risen while fertility has declined, suggesting a negative relationship between income and fertility. Of course, many other variables have changed drastically over time and this apparent conflict in the secular movements of fertility and income should not be taken too seriously until it can be demonstrated that these other changes were not responsible for the decline in fertility. Three changes seem especially important: a decline in child mortality; an increase in con-traceptive knowledge; and a rise in the cost of children.

The number of children in the average completed urban white family declined by about 56 percent from 1870 to 1940. The decline in child mortality explains about 14 percentage points or 25 percent of this decline.[31] Some evidence already presented indicates that a large secular increase in contraceptive knowledge occurred in the United States. It is not possible, however, to estimate its magnitude precisely enough to compare it to the decline in fertility.

I have emphasized that the increase over time in expenditures on chil-dren is not evidence that the cost of children has increased since the quality of children has also increased. Changes in the relative cost of children have to be assessed from indexes of the relative cost of given quality children. There are several reasons why the relative cost of a given quality child may have changed over time. The decline in child mortality decreased the cost of a given quality child, although it may have only a small effect. The growth of legislation prohibiting child labor and requiring education may have raised the cost of children, but largely made compulsory only what was being done voluntarily by most parents.[32] This is another aspect of the increase in quality of children and does not imply any increase in their cost. If such legislation raised costs at all, it did so primarily for the poorest families since they would be less apt to give their children much education. Therefore, legislation may have been partly responsible for the narrowing of fertility differentials by income class in the last fifty years.[33] The movement from farm to urban communities raised the average cost of children to the population as a whole since it is cheaper to raise children on a farm, but did not appreciably affect the cost within urban communities. Because technological advance has probably been more rapid in the marketplace than in the home, the imputed cost of time and effort spent on children probably rose, perhaps by a substan-tial amount. This discussion suggests that there was a secular rise in the cost of children which also contributed to the secular decline in fertility.

Secular changes in educational attainment, religious attachment, dis-crimination against women, and so on, may also have decreased fertility, and presumably there were changes other than the growth of income which increased fertility. It would take a major study—and even that might be inconclusive—to determine whether the factors decreasing fertility were sufficiently strong to produce a secular decline in fertility in spite of the secular rise in income. At present, it seems that the negative correlation between the secular changes in fertility and income is not strong evidence against the hypothesis that an increase in income would cause an increase in fertility—tastes, costs, and knowledge remaining constant.

III. Some Further Implications

Section II tries to show that the economic analysis of Section I is very useful in understanding the effect of income on fertility. This section sketches some additional implications. Our understanding of temporal fluctuations in births would be deepened if it were more widely recognized that births are "flows" to the "stock" of children, just as new car purchases are flows to the stock of cars. Flows are determined not only by variables determining stocks, but also by depreciation rates, acceleration, savings, and, as shown in our discussion of cyclical movements in births, by considerations of timing. The recent work relating births to parity shows that demographers as well as economists are beginning to stress the interaction between stocks and flows.[34] This work needs to be extended in a systematic fashion.

The discussion in Section I made it clear that the quantity and quality of children are intimately related. An increase in income or a decline in the cost of children would affect both the quantity and quality of children, usually increasing both. An increase in contraceptive knowledge would also affect both, but would increase quality while decreasing quantity. The quality of children is very important in its own right, for it determines the education, health, and motivation of the future labor force. It is a major contribution of an economic framework to bring out the mutual interaction of quantity and quality—an interaction that has been neglected all too often in writings both on population and on the quality of the labor force.

It is often said that farm families are larger than urban families because of a difference in tastes. Since farmers have a comparative cost advantage in raising children as well as in raising foodstuffs, they would tend to be more fertile even without any difference in tastes. The rural advantage may not be the same at all qualities and, indeed, presumably is less at higher qualities where child labor and food are less important. Over time, rural as well as urban families have moved to higher-quality children, and this may have contributed to the narrowing of urban-rural fertility differentials in recent decades. The influence of differences in the cost of children deserves much more systematic study, for it may partly explain not only these urban-rural fertility differences but also the secular decline in fertility up to World War II and the apparent secular narrowing of fertility differentials among urban economic classes.

In the Western world, birthrates in the early postwar period were well
above rates of the thirties. In some countries, including the United States
and Canada, they have remained at about the early postwar level; in others,
including Great Britain and Sweden, they have drifted down to about their
1940 level; in still others, including France, they have drifted down to a
position intermediate between their immediate pre- and postwar levels. The
analysis in this paper does not readily explain these differences, but it does
explain why birthrates in all these countries are well above levels predicted
from their secular trends. The secular decline in child mortality and the
secular increase in contraceptive knowledge were important causes of the
secular decline in births. By 1945 the level of child mortality was so low that
little room remained for a further improvement. Although contraceptive
knowledge was not well spread throughout every layer of society, the room
for its further improvement was also more limited than it had been. With
the weakening of these forces, much of the steam behind the secular decline
in birthrates has been removed. Positive forces like the growth in income are
now opposed by weaker negative forces, and it is not too surprising that
fertility has ceased to decline and even has risen in some countries.

Several recent studies of consumption have used a measure of family size
as an independent variable along with measures of income and price.[35] This
procedure is justifiable if family size were a random variable or completely
determined by "noneconomic" factors.[36] If, on the other hand, family size
were partly determined by economic factors, this procedure would result in
misleading estimates of the regression coefficients for the other independent
variables. Thus, suppose family size were positively related to income, and
food consumption varied with income only because family size did. The
regression coefficient between food consumption and income, holding family
size constant, would be zero, an incorrect estimate of the long-run effect of
an increase in income on food consumption. One would not estimate the
effect of income on gasoline consumption by finding the regression coefficient
between gasoline consumption and income, holding the number of cars
constant. For gasoline consumption might increase with income largely because the number of cars does, just as food consumption might increase
because family size does. This discussion, brief as it is, should be sufficient to
demonstrate that students of consumption economics need to pay more
attention to the determinants of family size than they have in the past.

IV. Summary

This paper employs an economic framework to analyze the factors determining fertility. Children are viewed as a durable good, primarily a consumer

durable, which yields income, primarily psychic income, to parents. Fertility is determined by income, child costs, knowledge, uncertainty, and tastes. An increase in income and a decline in price would increase the demand for children, although it is necessary to distinguish between the quantity and quality of children demanded. The quality of children is directly related to the amount spent on them.

Each family must produce its own children since children cannot be bought or sold in the marketplace. This is why every uncertainty in the production of children (such as their sex) creates a corresponding uncertainty in consumption. It is also why the number of children in a family depends not only on its demand but also on its ability to produce or supply them. Some families are unable to produce as many children as they desire and some have to produce more than they desire. Therefore, actual fertility may diverge considerably from desired fertility.

I briefly explored some implications of this theory. For example, it may largely explain the postwar rise in fertility in Western nations, the relatively small cyclical fluctuation in fertility compared to that in other durables, some observed relations between the quantity and quality of children, and why rural women are more fertile than urban women.

I tested in more detail one important implication, namely that the number of children desired is directly related to income. Crude cross-sectional data show a negative relationship with income, but the crude data do not hold contraceptive knowledge constant. When it is held constant, a positive relationship appears. This view is supported by the positive correspondence between cyclical movements in income and fertility. The secular decline in fertility may also be consistent with a positive relationship since the secular decline in child mortality and the secular rise in both contraceptive knowledge and child costs could easily have offset the secular rise in income.

COMMENT
James S. Duesenberry, Harvard University

1. For many years economists have taken variations in rates of population growth, and in family size, as *data* which help to explain various economic phenomena but which cannot themselves be explained in terms of economic theory. Becker has done us a real service in bringing economic analysis to bear on the problem once more. He has not only worked out the implications of traditional economic theory for demographic theory but has also gone some distance in testing those implications against the empirical data.

Becker argues that those couples with sufficient contraceptive knowledge to control births have to decide how many children to have. For most people, children produce certain satisfactions and have a net cost. In those circumstances we expect (with some qualifications) that the number of children per family will rise with income just as we expect the number of cars or chairs or cubic feet of housing space per family to rise with income. But just as in those cases we expect the quality of cars or chairs or houses to rise with income as well as the number, we also expect the quality of children to rise with income as well as the number. That is, we expect the children of the rich to be better housed, fed, and educated than those of the poor.

Becker then qualifies the argument by taking into account the fact that in some circumstances children may yield their parents a net income instead of having a net cost. In that case the theory of investment is relevant as well as the theory of consumption. He has brought in a number of other considerations which I need not review but which lead to only minor qualifications of his main arguments.

After reviewing the implications of economic theory, Becker then faces the fact that for many years the raw data on differential fertility have shown a fairly strong negative relationship between variations in income and variations in numbers of children per family. Moreover, until recently the average number of children per completed family has been declining although average family income has been rising secularly.

Becker maintains that the negative correlation between income and family size is due to the negative association between income and knowledge of contraceptive methods. I think that most of us would agree that differential knowledge does explain a large part of the apparent negative relation between income and family size.

The evidence of the Indianapolis study certainly supports that conclusion. Becker, however, tries to use the study to support his conclusion that there should be a positive association between income and family size. I must say that the evidence he cites did not strike me as exactly overwhelming.

The empirical evidence offers, I would say, rather ambiguous support for Becker's hypothesis. That may be because we have only a limited amount of the right kind of data but there are, I think, some reasons for thinking that Becker's theoretical case may not be so open and shut as appears. Those reasons have to do with the nature of the "cost" of children and with the limitations on the possibility of substitution between quantity and quality of children.

II. Becker has taken the occasion to correct the simple-minded who fail to distinguish between the cost of children of given quality and expenditure per child. Now, of course, it is correct to regard changes in prices (or relative prices) of a given quality of a good as changes in the cost of that good and

changes in amount or quality of the good purchased (at a given price schedule) as changes in expenditure not involving changes in cost. But not all of
those who say that the cost of children rises with income are so simple-
minded as Becker suggests, though their language may not be exact. What
Leibenstein, for example, appears to mean is that the expenditure per child
which the parents consider to be necessary rises with income.

Questions of semantics aside, there is an important substantive difference
between Becker's approach and that taken by economists whose approach is,
if he will excuse the expression, more sociological.

I used to tell my students that the difference between economics and
sociology is very simple. Economics is all about how people make choices.
Sociology is all about why they don't have any choices to make.

Becker assumes that any couple considers itself free to choose any combination it wishes of numbers of children and expenditure per child (prices
of particular goods and services being given). I submit that a sociologist
would take the view that given the educational level, occupation, region,
and a few other factors, most couples would consider that they have a very
narrow range of choice. To take only one example, I suggest that there is no
one in the room, not even Becker, who considers himself free to choose
either two children who go to university or four children who stop their
education after high school. It may be said that that still leaves lots of room
for variation, but I think it can be said that no one in this room considers
seriously having, say, four children who attend third-rate colleges at low cost
per head or three who attend better ones.

For this audience I need not go through the whole routine about roles,
goals, values, and so on. It will be sufficient to remark that there is no area
in which the sociological limitations of freedom of choice apply more strongly
than to behavior in regard to bringing up children.

Effective freedom of choice between quantity and quality of children is
also limited by more mundane and mechanical considerations. The principle
of substitution which is at the basis of Becker's argument suggests that if the
parents have low-quality children, as he puts it, they can spend more of their
income on something else. Quality of children means, in Becker's terminology, nothing more than expenditure per child (with a given price schedule).
But in many respects the standard of living of the children is mechanically
linked to that of the parents. Is it possible to have crowded housing conditions for the children and uncrowded conditions for the parents? As the
father of four I am in a position to answer with an unqualified negative.
Children may eat a different menu from their parents, but if so, it is because
they *like* peanut butter sandwiches. I could go on but I am sure it's unnecessary. A final point in this connection is the noncash cost of improving quality

in children. Becker has used the term quality as though it were just another expression for expenditure at constant prices. But in the more ordinary sense of the term, quality has to be bought with time as well as money. Most parents think (probably mistakenly) that their children are better off if the parents spend time with them. Now time can be bought in the sense that domestic help and appliances can be bought to free time for other things. But even if one had nothing else to do, the marginal disutility of Cub Scout and PTA meetings rises rapidly. These noncash costs must certainly be of some importance in determining family size.

Becker will say that this is merely an aspect of the diminishing marginal utility of numbers of children. He is correct, of course, but the investment of time in children is not a matter of individual choice any more than the investment of money. The time which parents spend on children is largely determined by social conventions. Those conventions differ among social classes. Since social class is often associated with income, the noncash costs I have mentioned will influence the apparent relation between income and family size in many cross sections.

Those considerations lead me to the following conclusions: (1) the effect of income on family size which Becker expects will be greatly weakened by the tendency for the standard of living for children to advance more or less proportionately with that of the parents, and (2) standards of education and of expenditure of time on children will vary with social class. Social class in turn will be associated with income but not in a unique way. In some societies it may turn out that the "cost" of children rises faster than income, in others more slowly.

To put it more generally, economic factors are certainly likely to influence the number of children born to those who are able to plan births. But I do not feel that we are likely to find out much about their influence by simply drawing an analogy between children and durable goods.

Bernard Okun, Princeton University

Rupert Vance, in his presidential address before the Population Association of America at Princeton in 1952, prescribed for demographers "a good stiff dosage of theory, adequately compounded."[37] Gary Becker has heeded Vance's prescription, and in addition has presented us with an interesting and challenging paper.

The essence of Becker's theory of the demand for children can be reduced to two propositions. First, as family income increases, parents will provide their children with a higher level of living. Second, as income increases, parents will probably increase the number of children which they demand.

My comments will strongly concur with the first proposition, but will question the second.

In his economic theory, Becker treats children like consumer durables. His justification for treating children in this fashion is that, like automobiles, children are a source of utility and require a considerable outlay of expenditures. It is then contended that the nature of the demand for children is similar to that for automobiles—higher-income families demand more automobiles and better-quality automobiles; similarly, they demand more children and spend more per child.

In his analysis, Becker distinguishes two components in the expenditures on a child. The first relates to the size and nature of the basket of goods and services which the child consumes. The second relates to the prices of the goods and services which the child consumes. Expenditures per child can change either because of a change in the composition of the child's consumption basket, or because of a change in the prices of the components of the basket. Becker equates the additional utility received by the parents resulting from an increase in expenditures of the first kind, that is, expenditures directed toward an improvement in the composition of the basket, with the increase in the "quality" of the child. Such expenditures shall be referred to as quality expenditures. Becker defines a change in expenditures per child resulting simply from a change in the prices of one or more components of the basket, that is, the second kind of change, as a change in the "cost" of a child. Thus, in Becker's framework, the concept of a change in the cost of a child is a very narrow one. It refers only to a change in expenditures per child, where the child continues to consume a fixed basket of goods and services.

A word of caution is necessary here. Becker has related quality expenditures to the amount of utility that children provide for their parents. This relation, however, is valid only within a given family unit. One cannot conclude that the family which purchases less for their child derives less total utility from him in comparison with the family which purchases more. Such a conclusion implies an unwarranted interpersonal comparison of utility. If the Jones boy is paying for dancing lessons while the Smith boy is reading a borrowed copy of Marshall's *Principles*, one cannot conclude that the Joneses are deriving more utility than the Smiths with regard to these alternative pursuits of their respective sons.

Becker has imputed much theoretical significance to his distinction between the concepts of quality expenditures and cost expenditures. For example, in his conclusion, it is suggested that a secular increase in the "cost" component contributed to a secular decline in fertility. Nothing is said about the effect of a secular change in the "quality" component. We shall return to this point shortly.

Becker's paper suggests a second distinction between the quality and cost components. The cost of a child, which depends on the prices of commodities and services, is determined by the market forces of supply and demand. Cost, therefore, is not a family decision variable, and is independent of family income. On the other hand, quality expenditures are a family decision variable and are positively related to income. Becker stresses that higher-income families have higher-quality children (spend more per child), and that this is a voluntary decision. According to Becker, "The rich simply choose higher-quality children."

Is the quality expenditure component purely a decision variable? Do the rich really have a choice? To a large extent, I submit that they do not. It is almost impossible to conceive of a child who is raised at a much lower level of living than that of his parents. He lives where they live, tends to eat what they eat, and in general, as a matter of course, shares about the same standard of living that they do, by virtue of his living with them. Surely, the child cannot be sent to live in the slums of the Lower East Side while his parents dwell in a penthouse on Park Avenue. Thus, automatically, when parents raise their own level of living, their child's is also raised, and quality expenditures per child *must* rise.

When demographers, economists, or anybody, for that matter, speak of a decline in the birthrate, they are referring to a decline in the number of children born divided by either total population or some component of population (for example, women of childbearing age). The total number of children born is not weighted by a quality index—every child is given a weight of unity. Thus, if we are to turn to economic theory for an explanation of the decline in the birthrate, one must argue that *expenditures* (as opposed to "cost") per child have risen over time. It is theoretically irrelevant to distinguish between quality expenditures and "cost" expenditures. Becker's conclusion that an increase in "cost" expenditures per child contributed to the decline in the birthrate is useful only if he is referring to a decline in the birthrate of children of homogeneous quality. But since quality expenditures per child have increased over time, this is not the case. Therefore, in explaining birthrate trends or fertility differences by income, where quality expenditures per child vary in a systematic way, although not reflected in the measurement of the birthrate, Becker's distinction between quality and "cost" expenditures is not useful. The relevant economic variable is simply expenditures per child.

It is for the reasons cited above that I wish to defend Harvey Leibenstein against Becker's criticism. I might add that I have a vested interest in doing so since an argument similar to Leibenstein's appears in one of my own writings.[38] Becker quotes Leibenstein as follows: "The conventional costs of child maintenance increase as per capita income increases. The style in which a child is maintained depends on the position and income of the parents; therefore, we expect such costs to rise as incomes rise."[39]

Although Becker is correct in noting that Leibenstein failed to make the statistical distinction between quality and "cost" expenditures, this is not the relevant distinction that should be made in a theory of the demand for children which attempts to link income and fertility. The relevant distinction, if any, is voluntary expenditures versus involuntary expenditures. To a large extent, the higher income and social position of the family *require* that it spend more per child. In this sense, a rise in income necessarily results in a relative increase in expenditures per child. This, economic theory suggests, would have a depressing effect on the quantity of children demanded. Consequently, the quantity income elasticity of demand for children is quite low. Indeed, for most of the income range, the quality income elasticity may be so high that it contributes to a negative quantity income elasticity of demand.

On the other hand, the quantity income elasticity for consumer durables is generally much higher. Several distinctions between children and consumer durables account for this. One distinction has already been alluded to in the preceding discussion. The quality of a child as a function of income is less of a decision variable than, for example, the quality of an automobile. This may tend to cause the quality income elasticity of consumer goods to be less than that for children, and this would allow a higher quantity income elasticity for consumer goods.

For consumer goods, quantity appears to be a closer substitute for quality than in the case of children. Two lower-price cars may be considered equivalent to one high-priced car for the high-income family. But is it just as likely that this family would be indifferent toward having two children who are untrained or not well educated, or having one well-educated child? Probably not. In fact some parents may derive disutility if their children fall below their quality standards.

Probably a more common occurrence among higher-income two-car families is that they will own one high-priced car, and also own a lower-quality second car. Are they apt to follow a similar policy with regard to children—that is, we already have one son who is a Princeton graduate, so we can plan to finance our second son only through high school? I think not. This unwillingness to diminish the quality of successive children tends to diminish the quantity income elasticity of demand for children, relative to that for commodities.

For reasons cited above, it is suggested here that unlike the typical case for consumer durables, the quantity income elasticity of demand for children may well be negative, or if positive, be very low. Briefly restated, our main point is that as income increases, quality expenditures per child do—and in a large measure must—increase to such an extent that parents tend to reduce their demand for children. Note, however, an exception to this proposition—in the very high income families, where family size tends to be larger than in the middle-income families, it seems evident that parents can satisfy their quality requirements without having to restrict the quantity of children by the same degree as the somewhat lower income families.

The weight of the empirical evidence presented at this National Bureau conference as well as that of other studies supports the proposition that, for most of the income range, fertility varies inversely with income. Becker contends that these data do not apply to his theory because lower-income people have inadequate knowledge of birth control. If all families had perfect control over family size, Becker contends that the relationship would be reversed. In this fashion, he defends the position that the quantity income elasticity is positive.

Becker notes correctly that knowledge of birth control is ever-increasing. If the quantity income elasticity of the demand for children is positive, one would expect the inverse birthrate differentials by income to be ever-narrowing as birth control knowledge continuously spreads. While a narrowing trend has occurred, it has been far from persistent. For example, Clyde Kiser found, in comparing family size and income in the United States in 1952 and 1957, that "the apparent enlargement of the differentials by income was quite pronounced."[40] This is a finding which clearly weakens Becker's point that differentials in birth control knowledge are the factor accounting for the inverse relation between income and family size.

There is also strong evidence to suggest that where social or economic forces prevail which tend to diminish the size of family desired, the lack of knowledge of modern birth control techniques is not an obstacle in the path of declining family size. For example, according to Whelpton's figures, in the southern United States, which was largely rural in 1800 as well as in 1870, the fertility rate declined by more than 50 percent from 1800 to 1870—a period long before modern birth control methods were known.[41] A similar experience occurred in France after 1800. This evidence tends to weaken the contention that an improvement in birth control knowledge explained a significant share in the secular decline in fertility.

Becker also attempts to support his thesis that income and the demand for children are positively related by pointing to the positive conformity of the birthrate to fluctuation in the business cycle. I feel that during a business cycle, the time period may be too short for parents' views and standards regarding quality of children to change significantly as a result of a change in income. During the downswing, parents will strive to maintain their standard of living and the quality of their children. Faced with this economic pressure, they will postpone having more children. During the peak stages, income may be rising faster than child-quality standards, and couples can think in terms of having more children without encroaching on their accustomed level of living and their child-quality standards.

The well-known "making-up" theory may partly account for the positive association between fluctuations in income and fertility over the business cycle. This theory holds that the business cycle mainly affects the timing of the arrival of children, but has no or but negligible effect on completed family size. For all these reasons, a positive association between changes in income and the birth rate over the cycle is readily explained.

In the long run, however, standards of living and child-quality standards adjust to a secular rise in income. The secular rise in income causes an increase in the quality of children, and therefore expenditures per child rise. This tends to diminish the quantity of children demanded, and the well-known empirical inverse relation between income and the birthrate reasserts itself.

Notes

I am indebted to Richard A. Easterlin and Eugenia Scandrett for helpful comments, and to many others, especially Cornelius J. Dwyer, who commented on the draft prepared for the conference.

1. *Social and Psychological Factors Affecting Fertility*, ed. by P. K. Whelpton and C. V. Kiser, Milbank Memorial Fund, Vols. 1–4.

2. The effect of chance will be fully discussed in a subsequent paper.

3. This is also suggested by another line of reasoning. It is known that $\Sigma k_i n_i \equiv 1$, where k_i is the fraction of income spent on the ith commodity, and n_i is the income elasticity of the amount spent on the ith commodity. Other things the same, the larger k_i is, the less likely it is that n_i is either very small or very large. In particular, the less likely it is that n_i is negative. In most families the fraction of income spent on children is quite large and this decreases the likelihood that the income elasticity for children is negative.

4. Chow estimated the total income elasticity for automobiles at about $+2$. Cf. G. C. Chow, *Demand for Automobiles in the United States*, Amsterdam: North Holland Publishing Co., 1951; however, the quantity elasticity is only about -0.31. Cf. *Federal Reserve Bulletin*, August 1956, p. 820.

5. This will be discussed more fully in a future publication.

6. See J. D. Tarver, "Costs of Rearing and Educating Farm Children," *Journal of Farm Economics*, February 1956, pp. 144–153, and L. I. Dublin and A. J. Lotka, *The Money Value of a Man*, Ronald Press, 1946, ch. 4. Most studies consider only the costs and returns before age eighteen. It is possible that returns bulk larger than costs at later ages; but because these ages are heavily discounted and because costs are so

large before age eighteen, there is little chance that a correction of this bias would substantially reduce the net cost of children.

7. See A. H. Conrad and J. R. Meyer, "The Economics of Slavery in the Ante Bellum South," *Journal of Political Economy*, April 1958, p. 108. At an 8 percent discount rate (about the estimated rate of return on slaves), the present value of the net costs is +$35, or about one-third of the present value of gross costs. The data are subject to considerable error and are at best a rough indication of the magnitudes involved.

8. One qualification is needed because the rich may impute a higher value than the poor to the time spent on children. The same qualification is needed in analyzing the demand for other goods.

9. As an example of how prevalent this error is, even among able economists, we refer to a recent discussion by H. Leibenstein in *Economic Backwardness and Economic Growth*, John Wiley, 1957, pp. 161–70. He tries to relate cost of children to level of income, arguing, among other things, that "The relation between the value of a child as a contributor to family income and changes in per capita income is fairly clear. As per capita income increases, there is less need to utilize children as sources of income. At the same time the level of education and the general quality of the population implied by a higher income per head mean that more time must be spent on child training, education, and development, and, therefore, less time is available to utilize the child as a productive agent. Therefore, the higher the income, the less the utility to be derived from a prospective child as a productive agent" and "The conventional costs of child maintenance increase as per capita income increases. The style in which a child is maintained depends on the position and income of the parents; therefore, we expect such costs to rise as incomes rise" (ibid., pp. 163–64).

By trying to relate cost to income Leibenstein confused cost and quality, and succeeded only in inadvertently relating quality to income. His technique would imply that the relative price of almost every group of goods rose over time because the quality chosen rose, an obvious impossibility. This flaw in his procedure greatly weakens his analysis of the secular decline in birthrates.

Bernard Okun also applied economic analysis to the population area, and explicitly assumed that the cost of children is higher to rich people because they spend more on children (see *A Rational Economic Model Approach to the Birth Rate*, Rand Corp. Series, P1458, August 1958). His argument, like Leibenstein's, would imply that the cost of many (if not most) goods is greater to richer families than to poorer ones. Also see S. H. Coontz, *Population Theories and the Economic Interpretation*, London: Routledge, 1957, Part II.

10. Let x be the quantity of children, p an expenditure measure of the quality of x, y an index of other goods, I money income, U a utility function, α a parameter shifting the cost of each quality of x by the same percentage, and π the price of y. A consumer maximizes $U(x, y, p)$ subject to the constraint $\alpha px + \pi y = I$. This leads to the equilibrium conditions

$$\frac{Ux}{\alpha p} = \frac{Up}{\alpha x} = \frac{Uy}{\pi}$$

The marginal utility from spending a dollar more on the quantity of children must equal the marginal utility from spending a dollar more on their quality.

After a draft of this paper was written I came across an article by H. Theil, "Qualities, Prices, and Budget Inquiries," *The Review of Economic Studies*, 19, pp. 129–47, which treats the interaction of quality and quantity in an elegant manner. Also see, in the same issue, H. S. Houthhakker, "Compensated Changes in Quantities and Qualities Consumed," pp. 155–64. Theil differentiates equations like these and shows that a compensated decrease in the price of a good of given quality must increase either the quantity of goods or the quality, or both.

11. There is some ambiguity in the last part of this sentence since abstinence enables a family to produce as few children as desired. The terms "unplanned," "excess," or "unwanted" children refer to children that would not be conceived if there were perfect mechanical control over conception. No children are unplanned in terms of the contraceptive knowledge and techniques actually known.

12. See D. V. Glass and E. Grebenik, *The Trend and Pattern of Fertility in Great Britain*, Paper of the Royal Commission on Population, Vol. VI, p. 271.

13. For evidence supporting the statements in this paragraph see the definitive work by N. A. Himes, *Medical History of Contraception*, Baltimore: The Williams and Wilkins Company, 1936.

14. A consumer maximizes a utility function $U = u(x_1, \ldots x_n)$ (neglecting quality considerations) subject to the constraints $\sum_{i=1}^{n} p_i x_i \equiv Y$, and $x_1 \geq$ or $\leq c$, where p_i is the price of the ith commodity, Y is money income, and x_1 refers to children. If the second constraint were effective, x_1 would equal c. Then the consumer would maximize $U = U(c, x_2, \ldots x_n)$ subject only to $\sum_{i=2}^{n} p_i x_i \equiv Y' \equiv Y - p_1 c$, and this gives the usual marginal conditions for $x_2, \ldots, x_n$.

15. U.S. Bureau of the Census, Census of Population, 1940; Washington: *Differential Fertility 1910 and 1940*, Washington: Government Printing Office, 1945; U.S. Bureau of the Census, Census of Population, 1950; *Fertility*, Washington: Government Printing Office, 1955; *Social and Psychological Factors Affecting Fertility*, by P. K. Whelpton and C. V. Kiser, eds., Millbank Memorial Fund, 1951; A. J. Jaffe, "Differential Fertility in the White Population in Early America," *Journal of Heredity*, August 1940, pp. 407–11.

16. K. A. Edin and E. P. Hutchinson, *Studies of Differential Fertility*, London, 1935; W. H. Banks, "Differential Fertility in Madison County, New York, 1865," *Milbank Memorial Fund Quarterly*, Vol. 33, April 1955, pp. 161–86.

17. Himes, op. cit.

18. See the papers by C. V. Kiser and G. Z. Johnson in *Demographic and Economic Change in Developed Countries* (Princeton, N.J.: Princeton University Press, 1960).

19. Whelpton and Kiser, eds., op. cit., Vol. 2, p. 364.

20. These elasticities are estimates of the slope of the regression of the logarithm of fertility on the logarithm of income. The mean of the open-end income class is assumed to be $4,000, and the mean of the other classes is assumed to be at their midpoints.

21. R. G. Potter, "The Influence of Primary Groups on Fertility," Ph.D. dissertation, Department of Social Relations, Harvard University, 1955, Appendix A, pp. 277–304.

22. This conclusion must be qualified to allow for the possibility that tastes and costs also varied with income. Since all couples lived in the same city the cost of children was presumably the same. Age, religion, color, and nativity were held constant in an attempt to limit the systematic variation in tastes. Education did vary with income, but for number and spacing planners it was possible to separate the effect of income from the effect of education. The simple correlation coefficient between fertility and income is +0.24 and between fertility and education −0.17, with both significant at the 1 percent level. The partial correlation coefficient between fertility and income, holding education constant, is +0.23, about the same as the simple coefficient, and is also significant at the 1 percent level. The partial correlation between fertility and education is only +0.04, not significant even at the 10 per cent level. (For these correlations see Whelpton and Kiser, eds., op. cit., Vol. 3.) Holding education constant has little effect on the relationship between income and fertility.

23. See R. Freedman, D. Goldberg, and H. Sharp, "'Ideals' about Family Size in the Detroit Metropolitan Area, 1954," *Milbank Memorial Fund Quarterly*, Vol. 33, April 1955, pp. 187–97. An earlier survey asked about the ideal family size for the average American couple, and found a negative relationship between ideal size and income of the head. But ideal size should be related to the income *assumed* by a respondent, rather than to his own income; and there is no way to do this. R. G. Potter has criticized both surveys because of their tendency to show larger ideal than realized families. See his "A Critique of the Glass-Grebenik Model for Indirectly Estimating Desired Family Size," *Population Studies*, March 1956, pp. 251–70. It is not possible to determine whether this bias is systematically related to income.

24. See Edin and Hutchinson, op. cit.

25. See H. D. Lamson, "Differential Reproductivity in China," *The Quarterly Review of Biology*, Vol. 10, no. 3, September 1933, pp. 308–21. Abstinence, which is equally available to lower and upper classes, is the major form of birth control when contraceptive knowledge is limited.

26. See E. Huntington and L. F. Whitney, *The Builders of America*, New York: Morrow, 1927, ch. XV. Although they did not clearly define "success," it appears that income was a major factor in ranking persons within an occupation and a less important factor in ranking occupations.

27. This is part of a study by Thomas Juster on buying plans, and I am indebted to him for making the data available to me.

28. V. L. Galbraith and D. S. Thomas, "Birth Rates and the Interwar Business Cycles," and D. Kirk, "The Relation of Employment Levels to Births in Germany,"

both in *Demographic Analysis*, J. J. Spengler and O. D. Duncan, eds., Glencoe: Free Press, 1956.

29. An estimate of the desired change in births of planned families can be readily obtained if we assume that the distribution of contraceptive knowledge among U.S. whites is the same as among families in the Indianapolis study, that for planned families the actual change in births equals the desired change, and that for other families the actual change is nil. Then the desired change equals the actual change (averaging 42 percent of the change in output) divided by the fraction of all births in planned families (31 percent), or about 136 percent of output. This is about half of the change for consumer durables.

30. For evidence relating credit conditions to cyclical fluctuations in the demand for housing, see J. Guttentag, *Some Studies of the Post-World War II Residential Construction and Mortgage Markets*, Ph.D. dissertation, Department of Economics, Columbia University, 1958.

31. Taken from my unpublished paper "Child Mortality, Fertility, and Population Growth."

32. See G. J. Stigler, *Employment and Compensation in Education*, National Bureau of Economic Research, Occasional Paper 33, 1950, Appendix B.

33. This analysis casts doubt on the view that the sharp decline in British fertility during the 1870s and 1880s resulted from the introduction of compulsory education. The decline was greatest in the upper classes which were least affected by this legislation.

34. Both economists and demographers found that wartime effects on stocks had important consequences for postwar flows.

35. See, for example, Theil, op. cit., S. J. Prais and H. S. Houthhakker, *The Analysis of Family Budgets*, Cambridge: Cambridge University Press, 1955. Measures of family size often include not only the inner core of parents and their children but also other relatives living in the same household. My discussion refers only to the inner core; a somewhat different discussion is required for "other relatives."

36. Prais and Houthhakker appear to believe that family size is determined by noneconomic factors when they say "It might be thought that since household size is, in a sense, a noneconomic factor." ibid., p. 88.

37. Rupert B. Vance, "Is Theory for Demographers?" *Social Forces*, Vol. 31, 1952, p. 13.

38. See Bernard Okun, *Trends in Birth Rates in the United States Since 1870*, Baltimore: The Johns Hopkins Press, 1958, pp. 177–80.

39. Harvey Leibenstein, *Economic Backwardness and Economic Growth*, John Wiley, 1957, pp. 163–64.

40. Clyde V. Kiser, "Differential Fertility in the United States," in *Demographic and Economic Change in Developed Countries*.

41. P. K. Whelpton, *Forecasts of the Population of the United States 1945–1975*, Bureau of the Census, 1947, p. 16.

A Theory of Marriage: Part I

· 11 ·

I present in this paper the skeleton of a theory of marriage. The two basic assumptions are that each person tries to do as well as possible and that the "marriage market" is in equilibrium. With the aid of several additional simplifying assumptions, I derive a number of significant implications about behavior in this market. For example, the gain to a man and woman from marrying compared to remaining single is shown to depend positively on their incomes, human capital, and relative difference in wage rates. The theory also implies that men differing in physical capital, education or intelligence (aside from their effects on wage rates), height, race, or many other traits will tend to marry women with like values of these traits, whereas the correlation between mates for wage rates or for traits of men and women that are close substitutes in household production will tend to be negative. The theory does not take the division of output between mates as given, but rather derives it from the nature of the marriage market equilibrium. The division is determined here, as in other markets, by marginal productivities, and these are affected by the human and physical capital of different persons, sex ratios (that is, the relative numbers of men and women), and some other variables.

First published in the *Journal of Political Economy* 81, no. 4 (July–August 1973): 813–46.

I. Introduction

In recent years, economists have used economic theory more boldly to explain behavior outside the monetary market sector, and increasing numbers of noneconomists have been following their examples. As a result, racial discrimination, fertility, politics, crime, education, statistical decision making, adversary situations, labor-force participation, the uses of "leisure" time, and other behavior are much better understood. Indeed, economic theory may well be on its way to providing a unified framework for *all* behavior involving scarce resources, nonmarket as well as market, nonmonetary as well as monetary, small group as well as competitive.

Yet, one type of behavior has been almost completely ignored by economists,[1] although scarce resources are used and it has been followed in some form by practically all adults in every recorded society. I refer to marriage. Marital patterns have major implications for, among other things, the number of births and population growth, labor-force participation of women, inequality in income, ability, and other characteristics among families, genetical natural selection of different characteristics over time, and the allocation of leisure and other household resources. Therefore, the neglect of marriage by economists is either a major oversight or persuasive evidence of the limited scope of economic analysis.

In this essay, it is argued that marriage is no exception and can be successfully analyzed within the framework provided by modern economics. If correct, this is compelling additional evidence on the unifying power of economic analysis.

Two simple principles form the heart of the analysis. The first is that, since marriage is practically always voluntary, either by the persons marrying or their parents, the theory of preferences can be readily applied, and persons marrying (or their parents) can be assumed to expect to raise their utility level above what it would be were they to remain single. The second is that, since many men and women compete as they seek mates, a *market* in marriages can be presumed to exist. Each person tries to find the best mate, subject to the restrictions imposed by market conditions.

These two principles easily explain why most adults are married and why sorting of mates by wealth, education, and other characteristics is similar under apparently quite different conditions. Yet marital patterns differ among societies and change over time in a variety of ways that challenge any single theory. In some societies divorce is relatively common, in others, virtually impossible, and in Western countries it has grown rapidly during the last half century. Some societies adjust to legal difficulties in receiving divorces by delaying marriage, whereas others adjust by developing more flexible "consensual," "common-law," or "trial" marriages. In many the bride brings a dowry, in others the groom pays a bride-price, and in still others couples marry for "love" and disdain any financial bargaining. In some the newly married usually set up their own household, in others they live with one set of parents.

I do not pretend to have developed the analysis sufficiently to explain all the similarities and differences in marital patterns across cultures or over time. But the "economic" approach does quite well, certainly far better than any available alternative.[2] It is hoped that the present essay will stimulate others to carry the analysis into these uncharted areas.

Section II considers the determinants of the gain from marriage compared to remaining single for one man and one woman. The gain is shown to be related to the "compatibility" or "complementarity" of their time, goods, and other inputs used in household production.

Section III considers how a group of men and women sort themselves by market and nonmarket characteristics. Positive assortive mating—a positive correlation between the values of the traits of husbands and wives—is generally optimal, one main exception being the sorting by the earning power of men and women, where a negative correlation is indicated. Empirically, positive assortive mating is the most common and applies to IQ, education, height, attractiveness, skin color, ethnic origin, and other characteristics.

Section IV considers how the total output of a household gets divided between the husband and wife. The division is not usually fixed, say at 50-50, or determined mechanically, but changes as the supply of and demand for different kinds of mates changes.

Part II (chapter 12, this volume) develops various extensions and modifications of the relatively simple analysis in this part. "Caring" is defined, and some of its effects on optimal sorting and the gain from marriage are treated. The factors determining the incidence of polygamous marital arrangements are considered. The assumption that the characteristics of potential mates are known with certainty is dropped, and the resulting "search" for mates, delays in marriage, trial marriage, and divorce are analyzed. Divorce and the duration of marriage are also related to specific investments made during marriage in the form of children, attachments, and other ways. We also briefly explore the implications of different marital patterns for fertility, genetical natural selection, and the inequality in family incomes and home environments.

II. The Gain from Marriage

This section considers two persons, M and F, who must decide whether to marry each other or remain single. For the present, "marriage" simply means that they share the same household. We assume that marriage occurs if, and only if, both of them are made better off—that is, increase their utility.[3]

Following recent developments in the theory of household behavior, we assume that utility depends directly not on the goods and services purchased in the marketplace, but on the commodities produced "by" each household.[4] They are produced partly with market goods and services and partly with the own time of different household members. Most important for present purposes, commodities are not marketable or transferable among households, although they may be transferable among members of the same household.

Household-produced commodities are numerous and include the quality of meals, the quality and quantity of children, prestige, recreation, companionship, love, and health status. Consequently, they cannot be identified with consumption or output as usually measured: they cover a much broader range of human activities and aims. We assume, however, that all commodities can be combined into a single aggregate, denoted by Z. A sufficient condition to justify aggregation with fixed weights is that all commodities have constant returns to scale, use factors in the same proportion, and are affected in the same way by productivity-augmenting variables, such as education. Then different commodities could be converted into their equivalent in terms of any single commodity by using the fixed relative commodity prices as weights.[5] These weights would be independent of the scale of commodity outputs, the prices of goods and the time of different members, and the level of productivity.

Maximizing utility thus becomes equivalent for each person to maximizing the amount of Z that he or she receives. Moreover, our concentration on the output and distribution of Z does not presuppose transferable utilities, the same preference function for different members of the same household, or other special assumptions about preferences.

Each household has a production function that relates its total output of Z to different inputs:

$$Z = f(x_1, \ldots, x_m; t_1, \ldots, t_k; E), \tag{1}$$

where the x_i are various market goods and services, the t_j are the time inputs of different household members, and E represents "environmental" variables The budget constraint for the x_i can be written as:

$$\sum_{i}^{m} p_i x_i = \sum^{k} w_j l_j + v, \qquad (2)$$

where w_j is the wage rate of the jth member, l_j the time he spends working in the market sector, and v property income. The l_j and t_j are related by the basic time constraint

$$l_j + t_j = T \quad \text{all } j, \qquad (3)$$

where T is the total time of each member. By substituting equation (3) into (2), the goods and time constraints can be combined into a single "full" income constraint:

$$\sum^{m} p_i x_i + \sum^{k} w_j t_j = \sum^{k} w_j T + v = S, \qquad (4)$$

where S stands for full income, the maximum money income achievable, if the w_j are constants.

We assume that a reduction in the household's total output of Z makes no member better off and some worse off.[6] Consequently, each member would be willing to cooperate in the allocation of his time and goods to help maximize the total output of Z. Necessary conditions to maximize Z include

$$\frac{MP_{t_i} \equiv (\partial Z / \partial t_i)}{MP_{t_j} \equiv (\partial Z / \partial t_j)} = \frac{w_i}{w_j}, \qquad \text{for all } 0 < t < T. \qquad (5)$$

If the household time of the kth member $= T$, then

$$\frac{MP_{t_k}}{MP_{t_j}} = \frac{\mu_k}{w_j}, \qquad (6)$$

Where $\mu_k \geq w_k$ is the "shadow" price of the time of k. Also

$$\frac{MP_{x_i}}{MP_{t_j}} = \frac{p_i}{w_j} \qquad \text{for all } x_i > 0 \text{ and } 0 < t_j < T. \qquad (7)$$

Each member must cooperate and allocate his time between the market and nonmarket sectors in the appropriate proportions.

If M and F are married, their household is assumed to contain only the two time inputs t_m and t_f; for simplicity, the time of children and others living in the same household is ignored. As long as they remain married, $T_m = T_f$ = 24 hours per day, 168 hours per week, and so forth, and conditions (5) to (7) determine the allocation of the time of M and F between the market and nonmarket sectors. More time would be allocated to the market sector by M than by F (less to the nonmarket sector) if $w_m > w_f$ and if $MP_{t_f} \geq MP_{t_m}$ when $t_f = t_m$. Indeed, F would specialize in the nonmarket sector ($l_f = 0$) if either w_m/w_f or MP_{t_f}/MP_{t_m} were sufficiently large.

A singles household is taken to be exactly the same as a married one except that $T_f = 0$ when M is single and $T_m = 0$ when F is single. A singles household allocates only its own time between the market and nonmarket sectors to satisfy equation (7). Single persons generally allocate their time differently than married persons because the former do not have time and goods supplied by a mate. These differences depend partly on the elasticities of substitution among the x_i, t_f, and t_m, and partly on the differences between the market wage rates w_m and w_f. For example, single F are more likely to "work" more than married F and single M less than married M, the greater the percentage excess of w_m over w_f. Empirically, single women clearly "work" more than married women and single men less than married men.[7]

If Z_{m0} and Z_{0f} represent the maximum outputs of single M and F, and m_{mf} and f_{mf} their incomes when married, a necessary condition for M and F to marry is that

$$m_{mf} \geq Z_{m0}$$

$$f_{mf} \geq Z_{0f}. \qquad (8)$$

If $m_{mf} + f_{mf}$, the total income produced by the marriage, is identified with the output of the marriage,[8] a necessary condition for marriage is then that

$$m_{mf} + f_{mf} \equiv Z_{mf} \geq Z_{m0} + Z_{0f}. \qquad (9)$$

Since most men and women over age 20 are married in all societies, equation (9) must generally hold because of fundamental reasons that are not unique to time or place. We have a useful framework for discovering these reasons.

The obvious explanation for marriages between men and women lies in the desire to raise own children and the physical and emotional attraction between sexes. Nothing distinguishes married households more from singles households or from those with several members of the same sex than the presence, even indirectly, of children. Sexual gratification, cleaning, feeding, and other services can be purchased, but not *own* children:[9] both the man and woman are required to produce their own children and perhaps to raise them. The physical and emotional involvement called "love" is also primarily between persons of the opposite sex. Moreover, persons in love can reduce the cost of frequent contact and of resource transfers[10] between each other by sharing the same household.

Economies of scale may be secured by joining households, but two or more males or females could equally well take advantage of these economies and do so when they share an apartment and cooking. Consequently, the explanation of why men and women live together must go beyond economies of scale.

The importance of own children and love implies that, even with constant returns to scale, M (now standing for a man) and F (now standing for a woman) gain from marriage because t_m and t_f are not perfect substitutes for each other or for goods and services supplied by market firms or households. When substitution is imperfect, single persons cannot produce small-scale equivalents of the optimal combination of inputs achieved by married couples.

Consequently, the "shadow" price of an hour of t_f to a single M—the price he would be willing to pay for t_f—would exceed w_f, and the "shadow" price of t_m to a single F—the price she would be willing to pay for t_m—would exceed w_m. Both gain from marriage because M then, in effect, can buy an hour of t_f at w_f and F can buy an hour of t_m at w_m, lower prices they then would be willing to pay. Of course, this is also why married households use positive amounts of t_f and t_m.

Our explanation of the gain from marriage focuses on the complementarity between M and F. The gain from complementarity can be illustrated in much-exaggerated measure by assuming that the production function relating Z to t_m, t_f, and x has the Cobb-Douglas form

$$Z = kx^a t_m^b t_f^c. \tag{10}$$

Clearly, $Z_{m0} = Z_{0f} = 0$ since both t_m and t_f are needed to produce Z (Z = 0 if t_m or t_f = 0), whereas Z_{mf} can take any value. Other functions have less extreme "complementarity" and permit positive production when some inputs are absent but less "efficiently" than when all are present.

Some sociological literature also suggests that complementarity between men and women is the major source of the gain from marriage (Winch 1958, 1967; Goode 1963), but the meaning of "complementarity" is left rather vague and ill defined. By building on the substantial economic literature that analyzes complementarity and substitution in production, we have shown how "complementarity" determines the gain from marriage.

Can this analysis also explain why one man is typically married to one woman, rather than one man to several women, several men to one woman, or several men to several women? The importance of own children is sufficient to explain why marriages of several men to one or several women are uncommon since it would be difficult to identify the father of a child if many men had access to the same woman, whereas the identity of the mother is always known. The marriage of several women to one man does not suffer from this defect, and, indeed, such marriages have been more common. However, if the sex ratio equaled about unity, each household having several women and one man would have to be balanced by households having only men. If we assume that all men and all women are identical, and if we make the rather plausible assumption of "diminishing returns" from adding persons to a household having one man and one woman, the total output from say

two single male households and one household with three women and one
man would be smaller than the total output from three households each
having one man and one woman.[11] Consequently, monogamous unions—
one man married to one woman—predominate because it is the most efficient
marital form. Polygamy is encouraged when the sex ratio is significantly
different from unity and when men or women differ greatly in wealth, ability,
or other attributes.[12]

Our definition of marriage in terms of whether a man and a woman share
the same household differs from the legal definition because our definition
includes persons in "consensual" and casual unions and excludes legally
married persons who are separated. However, our analysis does have useful
implications about the choice between legally recognized and other unions
(Kogut 1972), as well as about the decisions to remain married, divorce,
remarry legally, remarry "consensually," remain single, and so forth, that must
be made in the course of a lifetime (see Part II, chapter 12).

The gain from marriage has to be balanced against the costs, including
legal fees and the cost of searching for a mate, to determine whether marriage
is worthwhile. The larger gain is relative to costs, the larger the net gain
from marriage; presumably, therefore, the larger too is the fraction of persons
who marry. We now consider the more important determinants of this net
gain.

The gain is greater the more complementary are the inputs: the time of
spouses and market goods. Since we have argued that these inputs are complementary in good part because of the desire to raise own children, the gain
would be positively related to the importance of children. Hence, persons
desiring relatively few or low-"quality" children either marry later, end their
marriages earlier, or do both.[13]

The gain from marriage also depends on market opportunities. The effect
of a change in opportunities can be analyzed most easily by equating the
maximum output of any household to its full income deflated by the average
cost of producing a unit of output. For example, with constant returns to
scale, the output of a married household with both members participating in
the labor force can be written as

$$Z_{mf} = \frac{\text{full income}}{\text{average cost of production}} \equiv \frac{S_{mf}}{C_{mf}(w_m, w_f, p)} \equiv \frac{S_m + S_f}{C_{mf}}, \quad (11)$$

where C_{mf} depends on the wage rates of t_m and t_f and the price of x.[14] The
output of a singles household can be written in the same form except that
only one price of time enters the average cost functions C_m and C_f.[15]

What is the effect of an increase in income on the incentive to marry?
If only the property incomes of M and F, v_m and v_f, rose exogenously by the

same percentage, and if $v_m/S_m = v_f/S_f$, then S_m, S_f, and S_{mf} would all rise by the same percentage. With constant returns to scale, Z_{m0}, Z_{0f}, and Z_{mf}, and thus the absolute gain from marriage, would also rise by the same percentage as full income since neither C_{mf}, C_m, nor C_f would be affected by the rise in property incomes, as long as both M and F continue to participate in the labor force,[16] and assuming that property income is unaffected by the allocation of time.[17] Since a rise in property income should not greatly affect the cost of getting married, the incentive to marry would also rise.

The effect of a rise in wage rates alone[18] on the incentive to marry is less clear-cut. A rise in the wage rates of M and F by the same percentage would increase outputs by smaller percentages than full incomes, even with constant returns to scale, because costs of production also rise.[19] Moreover, the cost of getting married rises to the extent that the own time of M and F enters into search and other marital costs. Consequently, the effect on the net gain from marriage is not clear a priori and depends on the relative importance of own time in marriage costs and in the production of output in single and married households.

Consequently, our analysis predicts that a rise in property income, necessarily, and a rise in wage rates, possibly, increase the incentive to marry. This implication runs counter to the popular opinion that poor persons marry earlier and divorce less than rich persons but is consistent with the empirical evidence. In the United States, at least, the probability of separation and divorce is negatively related to income (U.S., Bureau of the Census 1971). Keeley (1972) finds too that when years of schooling and a few other variables are held constant, higher-wage persons appear to marry earlier than others.

Our analysis implies that a rise in w_f relative to w_m, F's wage rate relative to M's, with the productivity of time in the nonmarket sector held constant, would decrease the gain from marriage if w_f were less than w_m: the gain from substituting M's time in the market for F's time (and F's time in the household for M's time) is greater the lower w_f is relative to w_m. As a proof, consider an increase in w_f "compensated" by a sufficient decrease in w_m to maintain constant the combined output of the two singles households. The increase in w_f would not increase married output as much as the decrease in w_m would decrease it if married F worked sufficiently fewer hours in the market sector than single F, and married M worked at least as much as single M. Since married women do work much less than single women and married men work more than single men, an increase in the wage rate of women relative to men would decrease the incentive to marry.[20] As supporting evidence, note that American states that have higher wage rates of women relative to men also have smaller fractions of men and women who are married (Santos 1970; Freiden 1972).

The gain from marriage also depends on traits, such as beauty, intelligence, and education, that affect nonmarket productivity as well, perhaps, as market opportunities. The analysis of sorting in Section III implies that an increase in the value of traits that have a positive effect on nonmarket productivity, market productivity held constant, would generally increase the gain from marriage. Presumably this helps explain why, for example, less attractive or less intelligent persons are less likely to marry than are more attractive or more intelligent persons.[21]

III. The Marriage Market and Sorting of Mates

Optimal Sorting

We now consider not one M and F who must decide whether to marry or remain single, but many Ms and Fs who must decide whom to marry among numerous potential candidates, as well as whether to marry. If there are n Ms and n Fs (unequal numbers of M and F are discussed in Section IV), each is assumed to know all the relevant[22] entries in an $n + 1 \times n + 1$ payoff matrix showing the maximum household commodity output that can be produced by any combination of M and F:

$$
\begin{array}{c|cccc}
 & F_1 & \cdots & F_n & \\
\hline
M_1 & Z_{11} & \cdots & Z_{1n} & Z_{10} \\
 & & Z_{ij} & & \\
M_n & Z_{n1} & \cdots & Z_{nn} & Z_{n0} \\
 & Z_{01} & \cdots & Z_{0n} &
\end{array}
\tag{12}
$$

The last row and column give the output of single M and F. Each person has $n + 1$ possibilities and the $2n$ persons together have $n^2 + 2n$ possibilities. We assume that each person gains from marriage, so that the singles row and column of the payoff matrix can be ignored.

There are $n!$ different combinations that permit each M to marry one F and vice versa; that is, there are $n!$ ways to select one entry in each married row and column. The total output over all marriages produced by any one sorting can be written as

$$
Z^k = \sum_{i \in M, j \in F} Z_{ij}, \qquad k = 1, \ldots, n!.
\tag{13}
$$

Number one of the sortings that maximizes total output so that its entries lie along the diagonal and write

$$Z^* = \sum_{i=1}^{n} Z_{ii} = \max_k Z^k \geq Z^k \quad \text{all } k. \tag{14}$$

If the total output of any marriage is divided between the mates,

$$m_{ij} + f_{ij} = Z_{ij}, \tag{15}$$

where m_{ij} is the income of the ith M from marriage to the jth F, and similarly for f_{ij}. If each chooses the mate who maximizes his or her "income," the optimal sorting must have the property that persons not married to each other could not marry and make one better off without making the other worse off. In game theoretic language, the optimal sorting is in the "core" since no "coalition" outside the core could make any of its members better off without making some worse off.

Persons entering noncore marriages could not produce more together than the sum of their incomes in the core. For, if they could, and if any division of output between mates were feasible, they could find a division of their output that would make each better off, a contradiction of the definition of the core. If the sorting along the diagonal were in the core, this condition states that

$$m_{ii} + f_{jj} \geq Z_{ij} \quad \text{all } i \text{ and } j. \tag{16}$$

Conditions (15) and (16) immediately rule out any sorting that does not maximize the total output of commodities over all marriages, for at least one M and one F would then be better off with each other than with their mates.[23] Moreover, the theory of optimal assignments, which has the same mathematical structure as the sorting of persons by marriage, implies the existence of a set of incomes that satisfy conditions (15) and (16) for sortings that maximize total output.[24]

The solution can be illustrated with the following 2×2 matrix of payoffs:

$$\begin{array}{c} \quad\quad F_1 \quad F_2 \\ \begin{array}{c} M_1 \\ M_2 \end{array} \begin{bmatrix} 8 & 4 \\ 9 & 7 \end{bmatrix} . \end{array} \tag{17}$$

Although the maximum output in any marriage is between M_2 and F_1, the optimal sorting is M_1 to F_1 and M_2 to F_2. For, if $m_{11} = 3$, $f_{11} = 5$, $m_{22} = 5$, and $f_{22} = 2$, M_2 and F_1 have no incentive to marry since $m_{22} + f_{11} = 10 > 9$, and neither do M_1 and F_2 since $m_{11} + f_{22} = 5 > 4$. In other words, the marriage market chooses not the maximum household commodity output of any single marriage but the maximum sum of the outputs over all marriages, just as competitive product markets maximize the sum of the outputs over all firms.

Let us stress again that the commodity output maximized by all households is not to be identified with national output as usually measured, but includes conversation, the quantity and quality of children, and other outputs that never enter or enter only imperfectly into the usual measures. Put still differently, the marriage market acts as if it maximizes not the gain from marriage compared to remaining single for any particular marriage, but the average gain over all marriages.[25]

Each marriage can be considered a two-person firm with either member being the "entrepreneur" who "hires" the other at the "salary" m_{ij} or f_{ij} and receives residual "profits" of $Z_{ij} - m_{ij}$ or $Z_{ij} - f_{ij}$. Another interpretation of the optimal sorting is that only it enables each "entrepreneur" to maximize "profits" for given "salaries" of mates because only the optimal sorting satisfies condition (16). With all other sortings, some "entrepreneurs" could do better by "hiring" different mates than those assigned to them.

Assortive Mating

We now consider the optimal sorting when M and F differ in a trait, or set of traits, such as intelligence, race, religion, education, wage rate, height, aggressiveness, tendency to nurture, or age. Psychologists and sociologists have frequently discussed whether likes or unlikes mate, and geneticists have occasionally assumed positive or negative assortive mating instead of random mating. But no systematic analysis has developed that predicts for different kinds of traits when likes or unlikes are motivated to mate.[26] Our analysis implies that likes or unlikes mate when that maximizes total household commodity output[27] over all marriages, regardless of whether the trait is financial (like wage rates and property income), or genetical (like height and intelligence), or psychological (like aggressiveness and passiveness).

Assume that M differs only in the quantitative trait A_m, and F only in A_f, that each trait has a monotonic effect on the output of any marriage, and that higher values have the larger effect:

$$\frac{\partial Z_{ij}(A_m, A_f)}{\partial A_m} > 0, \qquad \frac{\partial Z_{ij}}{\partial A_f}(A_m, A_f) > 0. \tag{18}$$

If increasing both A_m and A_f adds the same amount to output as the sum of the additions when each is increased separately, all sortings of M and F would give the same total output. On the other hand, if increasing both adds more to output than the sum of the separate additions, a sorting of large A_m with large A_f and small A_m with small A_f would give the greatest total output since an increase in A_m reinforces the effect of an increase in A_f. The converse holds if increasing both adds less to output than the sum of the separate additions. Mathematically, this states that positive or negative assortive mating—mating of likes or unlikes—is optimal as

$$\frac{\partial^2 Z(A_m, A_f)}{\partial A_m\, \partial A_f} \gtreqless 0 \tag{19}$$

(proofs in Appendix, section 1).

Consider, as an example, a matrix of outputs when $n = 2$:

$$
\begin{array}{cc}
 & \begin{array}{cc} A_1 & A_2 \end{array} \\
\begin{array}{c} A_1 \\ A_2 \end{array} &
\begin{bmatrix} Z_{11} & Z_{12} \\ Z_{21} & Z_{22} \end{bmatrix},
\end{array}
\qquad \text{with } A_2 > A_1. \tag{20}
$$

If $Z_{22} - Z_{12} > Z_{21} - Z_{11}$, if equality (19) is positive, then obviously $Z_{11} + Z_{22} > Z_{12} + Z_{22}$, and a positive correlation between A_m and A_f maximizes total output, as predicted from (19).

One tradition in production theory distinguishes substitution from complementarity by the sign of the cross-derivative of output with respect to different inputs into a production function. Although condition (19) is not defined in terms of household production functions, duality theory implies that the same condition holds when A_m and A_f are treated as inputs into these production functions.[28] Condition (19) says, therefore, that the association of likes is optimal when traits are complements and the association of unlikes is optimal when they are substitutes, a plausible conclusion since high values of different traits reinforce each other when they are complements, and offset each other when they are substitutes.

Economists have generally considered the sorting of different *quantities* of different traits, such as labor and capital, not different *qualities* of the same trait. Although sorting by quantity and quality are related analytically, many applications of sorting by quality are also directly available in economics, such as the optimal sorting of more able workers and more able firms,[29] more "modern" farms and more able farmers, or more informed customers and more honest shopkeepers. As already mentioned (n. 26), some sociologists have considered "complementarity" to be an important determinant of sorting, but have not given a rigorous analysis of the effects of "complementarity" or embedded their discussions in the context of a functioning marriage market.

Mating of likes—positive assortive mating—is extremely common, whether measured by intelligence, height, skin color, age, education, family background, or religion, although unlikes sometimes also mate, as measured, say, by an inclination to nurture or succor, to dominate or be deferential. This suggests that traits are typically but not always complements.

The determinants of complementarity and substitutability are best discovered by going explicitly to the household production function and the maximization process. All households are assumed to have the same production *function*; that is, if the inputs of time, goods, and *all* traits were exactly the same, the output of commodities would be exactly the same. Different families can, of course, produce different outputs from the same input of goods and time if their education, ability, and so forth, differ.

We consider a number of determinants in turn. First, if M and F differ *only* in their market wage rates—each M and each F are identical in all other market and in nonmarket traits—according to equation (11), the optimal output between M and F who are both participating in the labor force can be written as

$$Z = \frac{S}{C(w_m, w_f, p)},\tag{21}$$

where the subscripts on Z, S, and C have been omitted and constant returns to scale assumed. Then, by differentiation and by using equation (4),

$$
\left.
\begin{array}{c}
Z^m = \dfrac{T}{C} - \dfrac{S}{C^2}C^m, \\[2mm]
Z^m = \dfrac{\partial Z}{\partial w_m} \quad \text{and} \quad C^m \equiv \dfrac{\partial C}{\partial w_m}
\end{array}
\right\}
\tag{22}
$$

where

Since

$$C^m = t_m Z^{-1},\tag{23}$$

where t_m is the time spent by M in the household,

$$Z^m = l_m C^{-1} > 0\tag{24}$$

if l_m, the time spent at work, is greater than zero. Similarly,

$$Z^f = \frac{T}{C} - \frac{S}{C^2}C^f = l_f C^{-1} > 0.\tag{25}$$

Positive or negative assortive mating by wage rates is optimal as

$$\frac{\partial^2 Z}{\partial w_m \, \partial w_f} \equiv Z^{mf} \equiv Z^{fm} \gtrless 0.\tag{26}$$

Differentiate Z^f with respect to w_m to get

$$Z^{fm} = -C^{-2}C^m l_f + C^{-1}\frac{\partial l_f}{\partial w_m}.\tag{27}$$

The first term on the right is clearly negative, so Z^{fm} will be negative if the second term, $\partial l_f / \partial w_m \leq 0$, is nonpositive, that is, if t_m and t_f are not gross complements, as these terms are usually defined.[30] Consequently, a perfectly negative rank correlation between w_m and w_f would maximize total commodity output if the time of M and F were not such gross complements as to swamp the first term in (27). Considerable empirical evidence supports the conclusion that t_m and t_f are not gross complements (Ofek 1970; Smith 1972).

A negative correlation between w_m and w_f maximizes total output because the gain from the division of labor is maximized. Low-wage F should spend more time in household production than high-wage F because the forgone value of the time of low-wage F is lower; similarly, low-wage M should spend more time in household production than high-wage M. By mating low-wage F with high-wage M and low-wage M with high-wage F, the cheaper time of both M and F is used more extensively in household production, and the expensive time of both is used more extensively in market production.

All persons have been assumed to participate in the labor force. During any year, however, most married women in the United States do not participate, and a significant number never really participate throughout their married life. Our analysis does predict that many women would have only a weak attachment to the labor force since low-wage women would be discouraged from participation both by their low wage and by the high wage of their husbands.[31]

If some women are not in the labor force, however, the wage rates of men and women need not be perfectly negatively correlated to maximize total output. For assume that all women with wage rates below a certain level would not participate in the labor force with a perfectly negative correlation between the wage rates of men and women. These women have $\partial Z / \partial w_f = 0$,[32] and, thus, $Z^{fm} = 0$; therefore, up to a point, they could switch mates without lowering total output. Consequently, other sortings having weaker negative, and conceivably even positive, correlations would also maximize total output; that is, many sortings would be equally good, and wage rates would not be a decisive determinant of the optimal sorting.

If M and F differ only in their stock of nonhuman capital, K_m and K_f, and if everyone participates in the labor force, $\partial C / \partial K_m = \partial C / \partial K_f = 0$ since the value of time is measured by the market wage rates. If the rate of return on K, denoted by r, depended positively on the amount of time allocated to "portfolio management," r would be positively related to K.[33] It then follows that

$$\frac{\partial Z}{\partial K_m} = \frac{\partial Z}{\partial K_f} = rC^{-1} > 0$$

and

$$\frac{\partial^2 Z}{\partial K_m \partial K_f} = \frac{dr}{dK}C^{-1} > 0$$

$\Bigg\}$.[34]   (28)

A perfectly positive correlation between the nonhuman capital of M and F would be optimal, an implication that is consistent with evidence on sorting by, say, parental wealth.

If some F did not participate in the labor force, the value of their time would be measured by a "shadow" price that exceeded their wage rate and was not constant but positively related to the sum of their nonhuman capital.[35] Moreover, a perfectly positive correlation of this capital is no longer necessarily optimal because of diminishing returns to an increase in the time of M and goods for a given amount of the time of F (for proof, see Appendix, section 2).

All differences in the output of commodities, by assumption the only determinant of behavior, not related to differences in wage rates or nonhuman capital are, by definition, related to differences in nonmarket productivity.[36] The widespread differences between men and women in nonmarket productivity are caused by differences in intelligence, education, health, strength, height, personality, religion, and other traits. We now consider the optimal sorting of traits that affect nonmarket productivity, while assuming that wage rates and nonhuman capital are the same for all M and for all F.

To demonstrate the tendency toward complementarity of nonmarket traits in the context of household commodity outputs, rewrite the optimal output equation given by (21) as

$$Z = \frac{S}{C(w_m, w_f, p, A_m, A_f)},$$ (29)

where A_m and A_f are the traits of M and F. Then using the assumption that w_m, w_f, and the rate of return on nonhuman capital are independent of A_m and A_f,

$$\left.\begin{array}{l}\frac{\partial C}{\partial A_m} \equiv C_{a_m} \\ \frac{\partial C}{\partial A_f} \equiv C_{a_f}\end{array}\right\} < 0 \quad \text{and} \quad \frac{\partial S}{\partial A_f} = \frac{\partial S}{\partial A_m} = 0.$$ (30)

Then,

$$\left.\begin{array}{l} \dfrac{\partial Z}{\partial A_m} = -SC^{-2}C_{a_m} \\[2mm] \dfrac{\partial Z}{\partial A_f} = -SC^{-2}C_{a_f} \end{array}\right\} > 0, \qquad (31)$$

and

$$\frac{\partial^2 Z}{\partial A_m \partial A_f} > 0 \qquad \text{if } 2C^{-1}C_{a_m}C_{a_f} > C_{a_m,a_f} . \qquad (32)$$

Since the term on the left is positive, equation (32) necessarily holds if A_m and A_f have either independent or reinforcing effects on productivity, for then $C_{a_m,a_f} \le 0$; moreover, (32) might hold even if they had offsetting effects. Therefore, perfectly positive assortive mating is definitely optimal if the traits have reinforcing effects; less obvious and more impressive, however, is the conclusion that positive assortive mating is also optimal if they have independent effects because C enters inversely in the equation for Z, or even if they have offsetting effects if these are weaker than a multiple of the direct ones.[37]

The reasons for the prevalence of a complementary relation between traits that raise nonmarket productivity can be seen more transparently by considering a couple of special cases. If the percentage effect on output of a trait were independent of the quantities of goods and time, the optimal output equation could be written as

$$Z = \frac{S}{b(A_m, A_f) \, K \, (w_m, w_f, p)} , \qquad (33)$$

where $\partial b / \partial A_m \equiv b_{a_m} < 0$, and $\partial b / \partial A_f \equiv b_{a_f} < 0$. Hence,

$$\frac{\partial^2 Z}{\partial A_m \partial A_f} > 0 \qquad \text{as } 2b^{-1}b_{a_m}b_{a_f} > b_{a_m,a_f}, \qquad (34)$$

which must hold if $b_{a_m,a_f} \le 0$ and can easily hold even if $b_{a_m,a_f} > 0$. Positive assortive mating is optimal even when these productivity effects are independent because productivity is raised multiplicatively: higher A_m (or A_f) have bigger *absolute* effects when combined with higher A_f (or A_m). A fortiori, this multiplicative relation encourages the mating of likes when the effects are reinforcing and can do so even when they are offsetting.[38]

The effect of most traits on nonmarket output is not independent of goods and time, but generally operates through the time supplied to the household; for example, if the time supplied became zero, so would the effect. A simple way to incorporate this interaction is to assume that each trait affects outputs only by augmenting the effective amount of own household time. It is shown in section 3 of the Appendix that positive assortive mating would still be optimal as long as the elasticity of substitution between the household time of M and F was not very high.[39] Negative assortive mating can be expected for own-time-augmenting traits only if they augment dimensions that are easily substitutable between M and F. Dominant and deferential persons tend to marry each other (Winch 1958), perhaps, therefore, because the dominant person's time can be used when households encounter situations calling for dominance and the deferential person's time can be used when they call for deference.

Note that it is shown in Section II that the gain from marriage is also greater when substitution between the time of M and F is more difficult. Therefore, the mating of likes should be more common when marriage is more attractive, an important and subtle implication of the analysis.

How do the nonmarket traits of one sex combine with the market traits of the other? In particular, does our analysis justify the popular belief that more beautiful, charming, and talented women tend to marry wealthier and more successful men? Section 4 of the Appendix shows that a positive sorting of nonmarket traits with nonhuman wealth always, and with earning power usually,[40] maximizes commodity output over all marriages. The economic interpretation is basically that nonmarket productivity and money income tend to combine multiplicatively, so that higher values of a trait have larger absolute effects when combined with higher income.

Scattered references have been made to the empirical evidence on sorting, and this evidence is now considered a little more systematically. The simple correlations between the intelligence, education, age, race, nonhuman wealth, religion, ethnic origin, height, and geographical propinquity of spouses are positive and strong.[41] A small amount of evidence suggests that the correlations between certain psychological traits, such as a propensity to dominate, nurture, or be hostile, are negative.[42] The correlation by intelligence is especially interesting since, although intelligence is highly inheritable, the correlation between mates is about as high as that between siblings (Alstrom 1961). Apparently, the marriage market, aided by coeducational schools, admissions tests, and the like, is more efficient than is commonly believed.

This evidence of positive simple correlations for a variety of traits, and of negative correlations for some, is certainly consistent with our theory of sorting. A more powerful test of the theory, however, requires evidence on partial correlations, when various other traits are held constant. For example, how strong is the correlation by intelligence, when years of schooling and family background are held constant? We do not yet have results on partial correlations by intelligence, but do have some on years of schooling, wage rates, and age, for samples of white and black families.[43] Even when age and wage rates are held constant, the correlation between years of schooling is high, +.53 for whites and virtually the same (+.56) for blacks. Although the partial correlations between wage rates are much lower, they are also positive, +.32 for whites and a bit lower (+.24) for blacks.

The strong positive partial correlation between years of schooling is predicted by the theory, but the positive correlation between wage rates is troublesome since the theory predicts a negative correlation when nonmarket productivity is held constant. Note, however, that the sample is biased because it is restricted to women in the labor force in a particular year. Since the higher the husband's wage rate the higher must be his wife's wage rate to induce her to enter the labor force, a negative correlation across all mates is consistent with a positive one for those having wives in the labor force.[44] Indeed, Gregg Lewis has shown[45] that a correlation of about +.3 for mates who are participating almost certainly implies a negative one (about −.25) for all mates, given the relatively small fraction of married women who participate. If his calculations hold up, this would be striking confirmation of our theory since it is counter to common impressions and is one of the few examples (and a predicted one!) of negative associative mating.

Other evidence, probably less affected by unobserved differences in non-market productivity, does suggest that the gain from marriage is greater when differentials between male and female wage rates are greater. For example, a larger percentage of persons are married in American states that have higher wages of males and lower wages of females, even when age, years of schooling, the sex ratio, the fraction Catholic, and other variables are held constant (Santos 1970; Frieden 1972). Or a larger fraction of black households are headed by women in metropolitan areas with higher earnings of black women relative to black men (Reischauer 1970) .

Quantitative evidence on the association of traits that affect nonmarket productivity with earnings and other income is scarce. The evidence we put together and referred to earlier indicates that husband's wage rate and wife's education are significantly positively correlated, even when husband's education and wife's wage rate are held constant.[46] One interpretation, stressed in Benham's (1972) paper, is that a wife's education contributes to her husband's earnings, just as a mother's education is said to contribute to her children's earnings (Leibowitz 1972). An alternative suggested by our theory of sorting is that a wife's education is a proxy for traits affecting her nonmarket productivity, especially when her wage rate is held constant[47] and that women with higher nonmarket productivity marry men with higher earning power. Although the relative importance of these alternative interpretations has not been determined, Benham (1972) does find that hours worked by husbands are positively related to wife's education, a sufficient condition for positive sorting (see n. 40).

Our analysis of mating and sorting has assumed perfect certainty in the production of household commodities. Uncertainty surrounds the production of many commodities, but our concern here is only with uncertainty about the "quality" of own children since children are a major source of the gain from marriage. An important result in population genetics is that positive assortive mating of inheritable traits, like race, intelligence, or height, increases the correlation of these traits among siblings; the increase would be greater the more inheritable the trait is and the greater the degree of assortive mating (Cavalli-Sforza and Bodmer 1971, chap. 9, sec. 7). Therefore, inheritable traits of M and F can be said to be complements in reducing the uncertainty about one's children. Positive assortive mating of inheritable traits would increase the utility of total output if more certainty about the "quality" of children is desirable—perhaps because friction between siblings or the cost of raising them is increased by uncertainty.

Our analysis of sorting is based on several other simplifying assumptions that ought to be modified in a fuller treatment. For example, the conclusion in Section II, that the gain from marriage is independent of preferences, assumes, among other things, no joint production and constant returns to scale in households. With beneficial joint production[48] or increasing returns, mating of persons with similar preferences would be optimal and conversely with detrimental production or decreasing returns. Similarly, the conclusion in Section II, that a monogamous union is always optimal, which is taken for granted in the discussion of sorting, should be modified to consider polygamy (we do this in Part II) and remaining single (see the discussion of search in Part II). Further, we have considered only one trait at a time, holding all other traits constant. But since people differ in many interdependent traits, optimal sortings should be determined for a set of traits, perhaps using the canonical correlation coefficient or related statistics as the measure of association.

Probably the assumption that would be most questioned is that any division of output between mates is feasible. Some of the output may not be divisible at all and may constitute a "public," or better still, a "family" commodity. Children might be said to be largely a family commodity, and, as shown in Part II, "caring" can convert the whole output into family commodities. Or some divisions may not be feasible because they are not enforceable. For example, even though the marriage market might dictate a 2/5 share for a particular husband, he may receive a 3/5 share because his wife cannot "police" the division perfectly.

Although the rigidities resulting from family commodities and enforcement problems can often be overcome (through dowries and other capital transfers), it is instructive to consider a model of sorting that incorporates these rigidities in an extreme fashion. How robust are the conclusions about optimal sorting when complete rigidity in the division of output replaces the assumption of complete negotiability?

Rigidity is introduced by assuming that M_i would receive a constant fraction e_i of commodity output in *all* marriages, and F_j receive d_j. Note that e_i and e_k ($k \neq i$) or d_j and d_k ($k \neq j$) need not be equal, and that

$$e_i + d_j \gtrless 1, \tag{35}$$

as family commodities or enforcement costs were dominant. The matrix showing the incomes for all combinations of M and F would then be

$$
\begin{array}{c|ccc}
 & F_1 & F_j & F_n \\
\hline
M_1 & e_1 Z_{11}, d_1 Z_{11} & \cdots\cdots & e_1 Z_{1n}, d_n Z_{1n} \\
M_i & & e_i Z_{ij}, d_j Z_{ij} & \\
M_n & e_n Z_{n1}, d_1 Z_{n1} & \cdots\cdots & e_n Z_{nn}, d_n Z_{nn}
\end{array}
\tag{36}
$$

If

$$\hat{Z}_1 \equiv Z_{st} > Z_{ij}, \quad \text{all } i \neq s, \text{all } j \neq t, \tag{37}$$

were the maximum output in any possible marriage and if each person tried to maximize his commodity income, M_s would marry F_t since they could not do as well in any other marriage.[49] Now exclude M_s and F_t from consideration, and if

$$\hat{Z}_2 = Z_{uv} > Z_{ij}, \quad \text{all } i \neq u \text{ or } s, \text{all } j \neq v \text{ or } t, \tag{38}$$

were the maximum output in all other marriages, M_u would marry F_v. This process can be continued through the $\hat{Z}_3, \ldots, \hat{Z}_n$ until all the M and F are sorted.

How does this sorting, which combines the various maxima, compare with that obtained earlier, which maximizes total output? As the example in (17) indicates, they are not necessarily the same: combining the maxima in that example sorts M_2 with F_1 and M_1 with F_2, whereas maximizing total output sorts M_1 with F_1 and M_2 with F_2. Yet, in perhaps the most realistic cases, they are the same, which means that the sum of the maxima would equal the maximum of the sums.

Assume that an increase in trait A_m or A_f always increases output and that M and F are numbered from lower to higher values of these traits. Then, $\hat{Z}_1$ is the output of M_n with F_n, $\hat{Z}_2$ is that of M_{n-1} with F_{n-1}, and $\hat{Z}_n$ that of M_1 with F_1. Consequently, when traits have monotonic effects on output, the most common situation, combining the various maxima implies perfectly positive assortive mating.

We showed earlier that, in a wide variety of situations, namely, where traits are "complementary," maximizing total output also implies perfectly positive assortive mating. In these situations, permitting the market to determine the division of output and imposing the division a priori gives exactly the same sorting. Therefore, the implication of the theory about the importance of positive assortive mating is not weakened, but rather strengthened, by a radical change in assumptions about the determinants of the division of output.

When maximizing total output implies negative assortive mating, as it does between wage rates (with nonmarket productivity held constant), and between own-time-augmenting traits that are close substitutes, these assumptions about the division of output have different implications. The empirical evidence on sortings cannot yet clearly choose between these assumptions, however, because positive sortings are so common: perhaps the positive correlation between observed wage rates is evidence of rigidities in the division, but several alternative interpretations of this correlation have been suggested that are consistent with a negative "true" correlation, and some psychological traits are apparently negatively correlated. Moreover, dowries and other capital transfers (discussed in Part II) provide more effective fluidity in the division than may appear to the casual observer.

IV. The Division of Output between Mates

With complete negotiability the division of output is given by conditions (15) and (16). The m_{ii} and f_{ii} are determined by their marginal productivity in the sense that if $Z_{ki} > Z_{kk}$, necessarily $f_{ii} > f_{kk}$,[50] and similarly for the m_{ii}. Also, if $f_{ii} > f_{kk}$, necessarily $Z_{ii} > Z_{ik}$.[51] The following limits are easily derived:

$$\left.\begin{array}{l} Z_{ii} - \text{Max}_k\,(Z_{ki} - Z_{kk}) \geq m_{ii} \geq \text{Max}_k\,(Z_{ik} - Z_{kk}) \\ Z_{ii} - \text{Max}_k\,(Z_{ik} - Z_{kk}) \geq f_{ii} \geq \text{Max}_k\,(Z_{ki} - Z_{kk}) \end{array}\right\}_{.52} \quad (39)$$

The division of output resulting from conditions (15) and (16) is not unique, however. For if a set of m_{ii} and f_{ii} satisfies these conditions with all $0 < m_{ii} < Z_{ii}$, a positive quantity λ exists, such that $m_{ii} + \lambda$ and $f_{ii} - \lambda$ also satisfy these conditions. The range of indeterminacy in the division would narrow as the sum of $\text{Max}_k\,(Z_{ik} - Z_{kk})$ and $\text{Max}_k\,(Z_{ki} - Z_{kk})$ approached closer to Z_{ii}.

Clearly, the indeterminacy would vanish if the distribution of Z_{ik} became

FIGURE 1

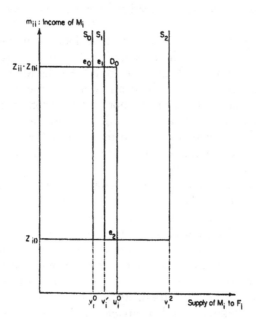

continuous. It could also vanish in a second case to which we turn. Assume v_i identical M_i and u_i identical F_i; by identical is meant that they would produce the same output with any mate or while single, so that they would receive the same income in market equilibrium. If the number of v_i were sufficiently large for a competitive equilibrium, there would be a supply curve of M_i to the marriage market: it would be horizontal at the singles income Z_{i0} until all v_i^0 were married, and then would rise vertically (see S_0 in fig. 1). Similarly, if the number of u_i were sufficiently large, there would be a market supply curve of F_i: it would be horizontal at Z_{0i} until all u_i^0 were married, and then would rise vertically. If initially we assume, for simplicity, that the M_i and F_i either marry each other or remain single, the supply curve of F_i would also be a derived demand curve for M_i that would be horizontal at $Z_{ii} - Z_{0i}$ until all u_i^0 were married, and then would fall vertically (D_0 in fig. 1); moreover, the supply curve of M_i to the market would be its supply curve to F_i.

The equilibrium income to each M_i is given by point e_0, the intersection of S_0 and D_0. If the sex ratio (v_i^0/u_i^0) were less than unity, the equilibrium position is necessarily on the horizontal section of the derived demand curve, as is e_0. All the M_i would marry and receive the whole difference between their married output and the singles output of F_i. All the F_i would receive their singles output and, therefore, would be indifferent between marrying and remaining single, although market forces would encourage v_i^0 of them to marry.

An increase in the sex ratio due to an increase in the number of M_i would lengthen the horizontal section of the supply curve and shift the equilibrium position to the right, say, to e_1. All the M_i would continue to marry and a larger fraction of the F_i also would. If the sex ratio rose above unity, equilibrium would be on the horizontal section of the supply rather than the derived demand curve (see e_2). Now all the F_i would marry and receive the whole difference between their married output and the singles output of M_i; market forces would induce u_i^0 of the M_i to marry, and $v_i^2 - u_i^0$ to remain single.

The importance of sex ratios in determining the fraction of men and women who marry has been verified by numerous episodes and in several studies. An aftermath of a destructive war is many unmarried young women pursuing the relatively few men available, and men usually either marry late or not at all in rural areas that have lost many young women to cities. Statistical studies indicate that the fraction of women currently married at different ages is positively related to the appropriate sex ratio.[53]

I know of only highly impressionistic evidence on the effects of the sex ratio, or for that matter any other variable, on the division of output between mates. This division usually has not been assumed to be responsive to market forces, so that no effort has been put into collecting relevant evidence. Admittedly, it is difficult to separate expenditures of goods and time into those that benefit the husband, the wife, or both, but with enough will something useful could be done. For example, the information giving the separate expenditures on husband's and wife's clothing in some consumer surveys, or on the "leisure" time of husbands and wives in some time budget studies could be related to sex ratios, wage rates, education levels, and other relevant determinants of the division of output.

If we drop the assumption that all the M_i and F_i must either marry each other or remain single, M_i's supply curve to F_i would differ from its market supply curve because marriage to other persons would be substituted for marriage to F_i; similarly, F_i's supply curve to M_i would differ from its market supply curve. To demonstrate this, suppose that at point e_0 in figure 1, M_i does better by marrying F_i than by marrying anyone else; that is, condition (16) is a strict inequality for M_i. If M_i's income from marrying F_i were less than at e_0, the difference between the sum of M_i's income and that of other $F_j \neq F_i$, and what they could produce together would be reduced. At some income, this difference might be eliminated for an F, say, F_k: then all the M_i would be indifferent between marrying F_i and F_k.

At lower values of M_i's income from marrying F_i, some of the M_i would

FIGURE 2

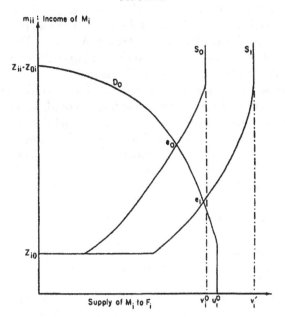

try to marry F_k. The increase in the supply of mates to F_k would raise M_i's income and reduce that of M_i's mates. In equilibrium, just enough M_i would marry F_k to maintain equality between the income M_i receives with F_i and F_k. The important point is that if some M_i marry F_k, the number marrying F_i would be less than the number supplied to the marriage market (v_i). Moreover, the number marrying F_i might fall still further as M_i's income with F_i fell further because some might marry, say, F_p, if they could then do as well with F_p as with F_i or F_k.

The net effect of these substitutions toward other F is a rising supply curve of M_i to F_i, shown by S_0 in figure 2, with an elasticity determined both by the distribution of substitute F and by the effect on the income of these F of a given increase in the number of M_i available to marry them. Since F_i would also substitute toward other M, its derived demand curve for M_i would also fall, as D_0 does in figure 2. The equilibrium position e_0 determines both the division of output between M_i and F_i and the number marrying each other. The difference between the total number of M_i, v_i^0, and the number marrying F_i no longer measures the number of M_i remaining single, since at e_0 all M_i marry, but rather it measures the number marrying other F and receiving the same income as the M_i marrying F_i; similarly, for the F_i.

An increase in the number of M_i from v_i^0 to v_i' would shift their supply

298 • FAMILY, MARRIAGE, AND FERTILITY

curve to F_i to the right and lower the equilibrium position to e_1 in figure 2. The reduction in M_i's income (equal to the increase in F_i's income) is negatively related to the elasticities of the demand and supply curves, which are determined by the availability of substitute M and F. The additional M_i all marry, some to F_i and some to other F; a larger fraction of the F_i are induced to marry M_i by the increase in F_i's income.

An increase in the sex ratio between M_i and F_i would not necessarily increase the fraction of F_i or decrease the fraction of M_i who marry since all can marry if some marry other F or M. However, if all F_i and M_i married, an increase in their sex ratio would tend to decrease the number of other M or increase the number of other F who marry, if the quantity of other M and F were fixed. For an increase in the ratio of M_i to F_i not only lowers M_i's and raises F_i's income, but also lowers the incomes of substitute M and raises those of substitute F. Some of these M would thereby be induced not to marry because their gain from marriage would be eliminated, and some F would be induced to marry because a gain from marriage would be created. Consequently, an increase in the ratio of M_i to F_i would still decrease the fraction of M and increase the fraction of F marrying, if substitute M and F as well as M_i and F_i were considered.

To illustrate these effects, assume an autonomous increase (perhaps due to selective immigration) in the size of a group of identical men, aged 24, who initially were indifferent between marrying women aged 22 and those slightly older or younger, although most married 22-year-olds. The increase in their numbers would decrease their income and the proportion marrying women aged 22. For if the percentage increase in the number marrying women aged 22 were as large as the increase in the number marrying other women, the income of those marrying 22-year-olds would fall by more than others, since men aged 24 are a larger fraction of all men marrying women aged 22 than of all men marrying women of other ages. Moreover, the income of women aged 22 would increase and more of them would marry men aged 24; the income of older or younger men marrying women aged 22 would fall and they would be encouraged to marry women of other ages; the income of women somewhat older or younger than 22 would increase too, and so on.[54]

V. Summary and Concluding Remarks

I have presented in this paper only the skeleton of a theory of marriage. The two basic assumptions are that each person tries to do as well as possible and that the "marriage market" is in equilibrium. With the aid of several additional simplifying assumptions, I am able to derive a number of significant implications about behavior in this market.

For example, the gain to a man and woman from marrying compared to remaining single is shown to depend positively on their incomes, human capital, and relative difference in wage rates

The theory also implies that men differing in physical capital, education or intelligence (aside from their effects on wage rates), height, race, or many other traits will tend to marry women with like values of these traits, whereas the correlation between mates for wage rates or for traits of men and women that are close substitutes in household production will tend to be negative.

My theory does not take the division of output between mates as given, but rather derives it from the nature of the marriage market equilibrium. The division is determined here, as in other markets, by marginal productivities, and these are affected by the human and physical capital of different persons, sex ratios, that is, the relative numbers of men and women, and some other variables.

In Part II I put some flesh on the skeleton by incorporating into the analysis love in marriage, the incidence and viability of polygamy, and separations, divorce, remarriage, and other life-cycle marital decisions. If my present plans materialize, subsequent papers will deal more quantitatively with the marriage market, including an empirical analysis of separation and divorce, and of married households as producers of market and nonmarket skills.

MATHEMATICAL APPENDIX

1. Optimal Sorting

Given a function $f(x, y)$, we first show that if $\partial^2 f/\partial x \partial y < 0$,

$$\frac{\partial[f(x_2, y) - f(x_1, y)]}{\partial y} \equiv \frac{\partial Q(x_2, x_1, y)}{\partial y} < 0 \qquad \text{for } x_1 < x_2. \quad \text{(A1)}^{55}$$

Since $\partial Q/\partial y = (\partial f/\partial y)(x_2, y) - \partial f/\partial y(x_1, y)$, $\partial Q/\partial y = 0$ for $x_2 = x_1$. By assumption, $(\partial/\partial x_2)(\partial Q/\partial y) = (\partial^2 f/\partial x \partial y)(x_2, y) > 0$. Since $\partial Q/\partial y = 0$ for $x_2 = x_1$ and $\partial Q/\partial y$ decreases in x_2, $\partial Q/\partial y < 0$ for $x_2 > x_1$; hence (A1) is proved. It follows immediately from (A1) that if $y_2 > y_1$,

$$f(x_2, y_1) - f(x_1, y_1) > f(x_2, y_2) - f(x_1, y_2). \quad \text{(A2)}$$

A similar proof shows that if $\partial^2 f/\partial x \partial y > 0$,

$$f(x_2, y_1) - f(x_1, y_1) < f(x_2, y_2) - f(x_1, y_2). \quad \text{(A3)}$$

We now are prepared to prove the following theorem: Let $f(x, y)$ satisfy $\partial^2 f / \partial x \partial y > 0$. Suppose $x_1 < x_2 < \cdots < x_n$ and $y_1 < y_2 < \cdots < y_n$. Then,

$$
\left.
\begin{array}{c}
\displaystyle\sum_{j=1}^{n} f(x_j, y_{i_j}) < \sum_{i=1}^{n} f(x_i, y_i) \\[2ex]
\text{for all permutations} \\[1ex]
(i_1, i_2, \ldots i_n) \neq (1, 2, \ldots n)
\end{array}
\right\} \quad . \qquad (A4)
$$

Assume the contrary; namely, that the maximizing sum for a permutation $i_1 \ldots i_n$, not satisfying $i_1 < i_2 < \cdots < i_n$. Then there is (at least) one j_0 with the property $i_{j_0} > i_{j_0+1}$. Therefore,

$$
f(x_{j_0}, y_{i_{j_0}}) + f(x_{y_{n+1}}, y_{i_{j_0+1}}) < f(x_{j_0}, y_{i_{j_0+1}}) + f(x_{j_0+1}, y_{i_{j_0}}), \qquad (A5)
$$

by (A3) since $y_{i_{j_0+1}} < y_{i_{j_0}}$. But this contradicts the optimality of $i_1, \ldots i_n$. QED.

A similar proof shows that if $\partial^2 f / \partial x \partial y < 0$, then

$$
\left.
\begin{array}{c}
\displaystyle\sum_{j=1}^{n} f(x_j, y_{i_j}) < \sum_{i=1}^{n} f(x_i, y_{n+1-i}) \\[2ex]
\text{for all permutations} \\[1ex]
(i_1, i_2, \ldots i_n) \neq (n, n-1, \ldots, 1)
\end{array}
\right\} \quad . \qquad (A6)
$$

2. Women Not in the Labor Force

If F did not participate in the labor force,

$$
S = T w_m + T \hat{w}_f + r(l_{pm}, l_{pf})(K_m + K_f) - l_{pm} w_m - l_{pf} \hat{w}_f, \qquad (A7)
$$

where $\hat{w}_f$, the "shadow" price of F, is greater than w_f, her market wage rate, unless F is at the margin of entering the labor force,[56] and l_{pm} and l_{pf} are the time allocated to portfolio management by M and F, respectively. If the production function for Z were homogeneous of the first degree in time and goods, $Z = S/C(p, w_m, \hat{w}_f, A_f A_m)$. Then,

$$
\frac{\partial Z}{\partial K_i} = C^{-1} \left[r + K \left(\frac{\partial r}{\partial l_{pm}} \frac{\partial l_{pm}}{\partial K_i} + \frac{\partial r}{\partial l_{pf}} \frac{\partial l_{pf}}{\partial K_i} \right) - \frac{\partial l_{pm}}{\partial K_i} w_m - \frac{\partial l_{pf}}{\partial K_i} \hat{w}_f \right]
$$
$$
+ TC^{-1} \frac{d\hat{w}_f}{dK_i} - SC^{-2} C^f \frac{d\hat{w}_f}{dK_i} - C^{-1} l_{pf} \frac{\partial \hat{w}_f}{\partial K_i} \qquad (A8)
$$
$$
= r C^{-1} > 0, \qquad i = m \quad \text{or} \quad f \qquad (A9)
$$

since $C^f = t_f Z^{-1} = (T - l_{pf}) Z^{-1}$, $K_m + K_f = K$, and $\hat{w}_f = (\partial r / \partial l_{pf}) K$ and $w_m = (\partial r / \partial l_{pm}) K$ with an optimal allocation of time. Similarly,

$$\frac{\partial Z}{\partial w_m} = TC^{-1} + \frac{TC^{-1}d\hat{w}_f}{dw_m} + C^{-1}\left(\frac{\partial r}{\partial l_{pm}}\frac{\partial l_{pm}}{\partial w_m}K + \frac{\partial r}{\partial l_{pf}}\frac{\partial l_{pf}}{\partial w_m}K\right.$$

$$\left. - l_{pm} - \frac{\partial l_{pm}w_m}{\partial w_m} - l_{pf}\frac{d\hat{w}_f}{\partial w_m} - \frac{\partial l_{pf}}{\partial w_m}\hat{w}_f\right) - SC^{-2}C^m \qquad (A10)$$

$$- SC^{-2}C^f\frac{\partial\hat{w}_f}{\partial w_m} = l_m C^{-1} > 0,$$

and

$$\frac{\partial Z}{\partial A_i} = -SC^{-2}C_{a_i} + TC^{-1}\frac{\partial\hat{w}_f}{\partial A_i} - SC^{-2}C^f\frac{\partial w_f}{\partial A_i} - C^{-2}l_{pf}\frac{\partial\hat{w}_f}{\partial A_i}$$

$$+ \text{ terms whose sum is zero} \qquad (A11)$$

$$= -SC^{-2}C_{a_i} > 0 \quad i = m \quad \text{or} \quad f,$$

if A_i does not directly affect r. Note that equations (A9)–(A11) are exactly the same as those when F does participate—equations (24), (28), and (31). Then,

$$\frac{\partial^2 Z}{\partial K_f \partial K_m} = C^{-1}\left|\frac{\partial r}{\partial l_{pm}}\frac{\partial l_{pm}}{\partial K_m} + \frac{\partial r}{\partial l_{pf}}\frac{\partial l_{pf}}{\partial K_m}\right| - rC^{-2}C^f\frac{\partial\hat{w}_f}{\partial K_m}. \qquad (A12)$$

The first term is positive, but the second one is negative since

$$\frac{\partial w_f}{\partial K_m} > 0, \quad \frac{\partial\hat{w}_f}{\partial K_f} > 0, \quad \left(\text{and}\frac{\partial\hat{w}_f}{\partial w_m} > 0\right). \qquad (A13)$$

A proof of (A13) follows from the derived demand equation for t_f. Of course,

$$\frac{\partial^2 Z}{\partial w_m\,\partial w_f} = 0. \qquad (A14)$$

Moreover,

$$\frac{\partial^2 Z}{\partial K_m\,\partial A_f} = -rC^{-2}C_{a_f} - C^{-2}C^f\frac{\partial\hat{w}_f}{\partial A_f}. \qquad (A15)$$

The first term is necessarily positive and the second would be nonnegative if $\partial\hat{w}_f/\partial A_f \le 0$. It can easily be shown that $\partial\hat{w}_f/\partial A_f = 0$ if A_f has a factor-neutral effect on output and $\partial\hat{w}_f/\partial A_f < 0$ if A_f is own-time augmenting. Consequently, there is some presumption that

$$\frac{\partial^2 Z}{\partial K_m\,\partial A_f} > 0. \qquad (A16)$$

The general expression for the cross-derivative of Z with respect to A_m and A_f can be found by differentiating equation (A11). We consider here only the case where the effects of factor-neutral, so that

$$Z = g(A_m, A_f) \, f \, (x, t_m, t_f), \qquad (A17)$$

or the optimal Z is $Z = gS/ \, [K \, (p, w_m, \hat{w}_f)]$, with

$$g_i = \frac{\partial g}{\partial A_i} > 0, \quad \text{and} \quad g_{mf} = \frac{\partial^2 g}{\partial A_m \, \partial A_f} > 0. \quad i = m, f. \quad (A18)$$

By substituting into (A11),

$$\frac{\partial Z}{\partial A_i} = Z \frac{g_i}{g} > 0. \qquad (A19)$$

Therefore,

$$\frac{\partial^2 Z}{\partial A_m \, \partial A_f} = \frac{g_m}{g^2} g_f Z + \frac{g_{mf} Z}{g} - \frac{g_m g_f Z}{g^2} = \frac{g_{mf} Z}{g} > 0. \qquad (A20)$$

3. Own-Time-Augmenting Effects

By own-time augmenting is meant that the household production function can be written as $Z = f(x, t_f', t_m')$, where $t_f' = g_f(A_f)t_f$, and $t_m' = g_m(A_m)t_m$ are the time inputs of F and M in "efficiency" units, and

$$\frac{dg_f}{dA_f} = g_f' > 0, \quad \text{and} \quad \frac{dg_m}{dA_m} = g_m' > 0, \qquad (A21)$$

indicates that an increase in the trait raises the number of efficiency units. The optimal Z can be written as $Z = S/C(p, w_m', w_f')$, where $w_m' = w_m/g_m$ and $w_f' = w_f/g_f$ are wage rates in efficiency units. Therefore,

$$\frac{\partial Z}{\partial A_m} = -t_m' C^{-1} \frac{\partial w_m'}{\partial A_m} > 0, \qquad (A22)$$

since $\partial w_m'/\partial A_m < 0$. Hence,

$$\frac{\partial^2 Z}{\partial A_m \, \partial A_f} = -\frac{\partial w_m'}{\partial A_m} C^{-1} \left(\frac{\partial t_m'}{\partial A_f} - \frac{\partial w_f'}{\partial A_f} t_m' t_f' S^{-1} \right) \cdot \qquad (A23)$$

The term outside the parenthesis and the second term in it are positive. The first term in the parenthesis might well be negative,[57] but Gregg Lewis has shown in an unpublished memorandum that $\partial^2 Z/\partial A_m \partial A_f$ is necessarily positive if the elasticity of substitution between the time of M and F is less than 2.

4. Sorting by Income and Nonmarket Productivity

If M differed only in K_m and F only in A_f, and if all M and F participated in the labor force, $\partial Z/\partial K_m = rC^{-1} > 0$, and

$$\frac{\partial^2 Z}{\partial K_m \, \partial A_f} = -rC^{-2}C_{a_f} > 0 \quad \text{since } C_{a_f} < 0. \tag{A24}$$

If M differed only in w_m, $\partial Z/\partial w_m = C^{-1}l_m > 0$, and

$$\frac{\partial^2 Z}{\partial w_m \, \partial A_f} = -C^{-2}C_{a_f}l_m + C^{-1}\frac{\partial l_m}{\partial A_f}. \tag{A25}$$

The first term on the right is positive, and the second would also be if $\partial l_m/\partial A_f \geq 0$, that is, if an increase in A_f does not reduce the time M spends in the market sector. Even if it does, the cross-derivative is still positive if the first term dominates. In particular, equation (A25) is necessarily positive if the effect of A_f is independent of the input of goods and time. For, if A_f were independent, $C = b(A_f)K(p, w_m, w_f)$. Since $l_m = (\partial C/\partial w_m) Z = (\partial K/\partial w_m)SK^{-1}$, then,

$$\frac{\partial l_m}{\partial A_f} = 0. \tag{A26}$$

NOTES

Submitted for publication October 1, 1972. Final version received December 21, 1972.

I have benefited from the discussion of several earlier drafts at the Workshop in Applications in Economics of the University of Chicago and in seminars at the National Bureau of Economic Research, Northwestern University, and the Population Council. Very helpful comments were received from H. Gregg Lewis, George J. Stigler, T. W. Schultz, William Brock, Marc Nerlove, Alan Frieden, and two referees. Michael Keeley provided valuable research assistance. My research has been supported by the National Bureau of Economic Research but this paper is not an official NBER publication since it has not been reviewed by the NBER board of directors.

1. To the best of my knowledge, the only exception prior to my own work is an unpublished paper by Gronau (1970). His paper helped stimulate my interest in the subject.

2. Some of the best work has been done by Goode (1963), but there is no systematic theory in any of his fine work.

3. More precisely, if they *expect* to increase their utility, since the latter is not

known with certainty. Part II discusses some consequences of this uncertainty, especially for the time spent searching for an appropriate mate and the incidence of
divorce and other marital separations.

4. An exposition of this approach is given in Michael and Becker (1972).

5. One serious limitation of these assumptions is that they exclude the output of
commodities from entering the production functions of other commodities. With
such "joint production," the relative price of a commodity would depend partly on
the outputs of other commodities (Grossman 1971). Joint production can result in
complementarity in consumption, and thereby affect the gain from marriage and the
sorting of mates. See the brief discussion in Section III.

6. This assumption is modified in Section III and in Part II.

7. See, e.g., *Employment Status and Work Experience* (U.S., Bureau of the Census
1963), tables 4 and 12.

8. Income and output can differ, however, because some output may be jointly
consumed. See the discussion in Section III and Part II.

9. The market in adoptions is used primarily by couples experiencing difficulties
in having their own children and by couples paid to raise other persons' children.

10. The relation between love and such transfers is discussed in Part II.

11. For example, assume that singles households have an output of 5 units of Z,
one man and one woman 13 units, one man and two women 20 units, and one man
and three women 26 units. Three households each with one man and one woman
would produce 39 units, whereas two single male households and one household
having three women and one man would produce only 36 units.

12. See the more extensive discussion of polygamy in Part II.

13. A further discussion can be found in Keeley (1972).

14. Duality theory shows that C is the dual of the production function.

15. Or, alternatively, the shadow price of F to M enters C_m, and the shadow price
of M to F enters C_f.

16. Even if married F did not participate in the labor force, the percentage rise in
Z_{mf} would still equal the share of property income in full income (see section 2 of the
Appendix).

17. The gain from marriage would increase even more if the income from nonhuman capital, i.e., property income, was positively related to the time allocated to
"portfolio management" (see the discussion in Section III).

18. By alone is meant in particular that the productivity of time in household
production or marital search is unchanged.

19. The percentage rise in output equals the percentage rise in wage rates multiplied by the ratio of total earnings to full income. Although this relation holds
whether or not married F is in the labor force (see section 2 of the Appendix), the
ratio of total earnings to full income can depend—positively or negatively—on her
participation.

20. A fortiori, if married women were not in the labor force, a compensated

increase in their wage rate would decrease the incentive to marry since an increase in their wage rate would not affect married output, whereas a decrease in the male wage rate would decrease output. This footnote as well as the text assumes that compensated changes in w_f and w_m do not much affect the cost of getting married.

21. Evidence on marriage rates by intelligence can be found in Higgins, Reed, and Reed (1962) and Bajema (1963). The statement on marriage rates by attractiveness is not based on any statistical evidence.

22. That is, all the entries relevant to their decisions. This strong assumption of sufficient information is relaxed in Part II, where "search" for a mate is analyzed.

23. If M_i married F_j and F_i married M_p in an optimal sorting that did not maximize total output, condition (16) requires that $m_{ij} + f_{pi} \geq Z_{ii}$, all ij, pi, or, by summation,

$$Z_p = \sum_{\text{all } ij, \, pi}^{n} m_{ij} + f_{pi} \geq \sum_i Z_{ii} = Z^* .$$

Since Z^* is the maximum total output, it must exceed Z_p, by assumption less than the maximum. Hence, a contradiction, and a proof that the optimal sorting cannot produce less than the maximum total output.

24. For a proof, see Koopmans and Beckman (1957).

25. Clearly,

$$\left[\sum_i^n Z_{ii} - \sum_{j=1}^n (Z_{0j} + Z_{j0}) \right] \Big/ n = \left\{ \sum_i [Z_{ii} - (Z_{0j} + Z_{j0})] \right\} \Big/ n$$

is maximized if

$$\sum Z_{ii}$$

is, since Z_{0j} and Z_{j0} are given and independent of the marital sorting.

26. Winch (1958) essentially assumes that each person tries to maximize utility ("In mate selection each individual seeks within his or her field of eligibles for that person who gives the greatest promise of providing him or her with maximum need gratification" [pp. 88–89]) and stresses complementary needs as a prerequisite for mating (especially in chap. 4), but he only considers psychological traits, brings in "eligibles" as a deus ex machina, and nowhere shows how mating by complementary needs brings equilibrium into the marriage market.

27. Let me emphasize again that commodity output is not the same as national product as usually measured, but includes children, companionship, health, and a variety of other commodities.

28. Wage rates or other monetary variables, however, cannot be treated as productive inputs.

29. This sorting is discussed for Japanese firms by Kurantani (1972). Hicks, (1948, chap. 2, sec. 3) asserts that more able workers work for more able firms without offering any proof. Black (1926) discusses the sorting of workers and firms with a few numerical examples.

30. This definition is different from the one given earlier in terms of the sign of the cross-derivative of profit or production functions. The definition in equation (28) is preferable, at least as a predictor of responses to changes in input prices. By "gross" rather than "net" complements is meant in the usual way that the income effect is included along with the substitution effect. Even if t_m and t_f were net complements they could still be gross substitutes since the income effect of an increase in w_m would tend to increase t_f.

31. Low-wage men also would be encouraged to work less both because of their low wage and the relatively high wage of their wives. They would not leave the labor force in large numbers, however, partly because average wage rates of men are so much higher than those of women and partly because the nonmarket productivity of women is higher than that of men.

32. As long as they are not indifferent at the margin to working in the market sector.

33. For this result and a more complete analysis of the allocation of time to portfolio management, see Ben-Zion and Ehrlich (1972).

34. If time is allocated to portfolio management, $S = wT + Kr(\ell_p) - w\ell_p$, where ℓ_p is the time so allocated. Then $\partial S/\partial K = r + (Kdr/d\ell_p)(d\ell_p/dK) - w(d\ell_p/dK) = r + d\ell_p/dK [(Kdr/d\ell_p) - w]$. Since, however, $Kdr/d\ell_p = w$ is one of the first-order maximization conditions, then $\partial S/\partial K = r$.

35. See the discussion in section 2 of the Appendix.

36. Differences in the earning power of children are assumed to be derived from differences in either the nonmarket productivity or incomes of their parents, and are not considered separately.

37. Equation (32) can be written as

$$2|\epsilon_{c_{a_m}}| > \epsilon_{c_{af,a_m}},$$

where $\epsilon_{c_{a_m}} = (C_{a_m} \cdot A_m)/C < 0$, and $\epsilon_{c_{a_m,a_f}} = C_{a_f,a_m} \cdot A_m/C_{a_f} > 0$ if the effects are offsetting. The cross-elasticity must be smaller than twice the absolute value of the direct elasticity.

38. Section 3 of the Appendix shows that positive assortive mating of A_m and A_f is still optimal even when F do not participate in the labor force.

39. The elasticity estimates of Ofek (1970) and Smith (1972) are only of modest size.

40. By "usually" is meant that a positive sorting with earnings always maximizes total output when an increase in a trait does not decrease the spouses' hours worked in the market sector and *could* maximize output even when they do decrease.

41. Many of the relevant studies are listed in Winch (1958, chap. 1).

42. See Winch (1958, chap. 5). Deference is treated as negative values of dominance, succorance as negative values of nurturance, and abasement as negative values of hostility.

43. A 20 percent random sample of the approximately 18,000 married persons in the 1967 Survey of Economic Opportunity was taken. Families were included only if

the husband and wife both were less than age 65 and were employed, the wife for at least 20 hours in the survey week.

44. Also, nonmarket productivity varies even when years of schooling and age are held constant. If investments that raise nonmarket productivity also raise, somewhat, market earning power (Heckman [1972] finds that the education of women raises their nonmarket productivity almost as much as their market earning power), the positive correlation between wage rates may really be picking up the predicted positive correlation between husband's wage rate and wife's nonmarket productivity.

45. Via an unpublished memorandum extending some work of Gronau (1972).

46. In a more detailed analysis, Benham (1972) finds similar results, after several additional variables are also held constant. Note, however, that the husband's wage rate is much more strongly related to his own than to his wife's education.

47. We argued earlier that her wage rate also is a proxy for such traits, when her education is held constant.

48. Grossman (1971) distinguishes beneficial from detrimental production by the effect of an increase in output of one commodity on the cost of producing others.

49. Clearly, $e_s Z_{st} > e_s Z_{sj}$, all $j \neq t$, and $d_t Z_{st} > d_t Z_{it}$, all $i \neq s$ by condition (37).

50. Since $f_{kk} + m_{kk} = z_{kk}$, all k, and $f_{ii} + m_{kk} \geq z_{ki}$, all i and k, then $f_{ii} - f_{kk} \geq z_{ki} - z_{kk} > 0$ by assumption.

51. That is, if $f_{ii} > f_{kk}$, then $Z_{ii} = m_{ii} + f_{ii} > m_{ii} + f_{ii} \geq Z_{ik}$.

52. Given conditions (15) and (16), $m_{ii} - m_{kk} \geq Z_{ik} - Z_{kk}$, all k, or, since $m_{kk} \geq 0$, $m_{ii} \geq Z_{ik} - Z_{kk}$, all k. The other conditions in (39) can be proved in a similar way.

53. See the studies essentially of whites by Santos (1970) and Freiden (1972), of blacks by Reischauer (1970), of Puerto Rico by Nerlove and Schultz (1970), and of Ireland by Walsh (1972). By "appropriate" is meant that a group of women must be matched with the men they are most likely to marry, e.g., college-educated women with college-educated men, or women aged 20–24 with men aged 25–29.

54. The permanence of these effects depends on whether the immigration continues or is once and for all.

55. I owe the proofs in this section to William Brock.

56. An earlier draft of this section developed the analysis using the shadow price of F, but contained some errors. I owe the present formulation to H. Gregg Lewis.

57. There is some evidence suggesting, e.g., that men with more educated wives generally work more hours (Benham 1972).

REFERENCES

Alstrom, C. H. "A Study of Inheritance of Human Intelligence." *Acta Psychiatrica et Neurologica Scandinavica* (1961).

Bajema, C. J. "Estimation of the Direction and Intensity of Natural Selection in

Relation to Human Intelligence by Means of the Intrinsic Rate of Natural Increase." *Eugenics Q.* 10 (December 1963): 175–87.

Benham, L. "Benefits of Women's Education within Marriage." Mimeographed. Univ. Chicago, 1972.

Ben-Zion, U., and Ehrlich, I. "A Model of Productive Saving." Mimeographed. Univ. Chicago, 1972.

Black, J. D. *Introduction to Production Economics.* New York: Henry Holt, 1926.

Cavalli-Sforza, L. L., and Bodmer, W. F. *The Genetics of Human Populations.* San Francisco: Freeman, 1971.

Freiden, Alan N. "A Model of Marriage and Fertility." Ph.D. dissertation, Univ. Chicago, 1972.

Goode, W. *World Revolution and Family Patterns.* New York: Free Press, 1963.

Gronau, R. "An Economic Approach to Marriage: The Intrafamily Allocation of Time." Paper presented at the Second World Congress of the Econometric Society, Cambridge, England, 1970.

―――. "The Wage Rate of Women: A Selectivity Bias." Mimeographed. Nat. Bur. Econ. Res., 1972.

Grossman, M. "The Economics of Joint Production in the Household." Report 7145, Center Math. Studies Bus. and Econ., 1971.

Heckman, J. "Shadow Prices, Market Wages, and Labor Supply." Mimeographed. Nat. Bur. Econ. Res., 1972.

Hicks, J. R. *The Theory of Wages.* New York: Peter Smith, 1948.

Higgins, J. V.; Reed, W. E.; and Reed, S. C. "Intelligence and Family Size: A Paradox Resolved." *Eugenics Q.* 9 (March 1962): 84–90.

Keeley, M. C. "A Model of Marital Formation: The Determinants of the Optimal Age of First Marriage and Differences in Age of Marriage." Mimeographed. Univ. Chicago, 1972.

Kogut, E. L. "An Economic Analysis of Demographic Phenomena: A Case Study of Brazil." Ph.D. dissertation, Univ. Chicago, 1972.

Koopmans, T. C., and Beckman, M. "Assignment Problems and the Location of Economic Activities." *Econometrica* 25 (January 1957): 53–76.

Kurantani, M. "Earnings Distribution and Specific Training: The Case of Japan." Mimeographed. Univ. Chicago, 1972.

Liebowitz, A. "Women's Allocation of Time to Market and Non-Market Activities." Ph.D. dissertation, Columbia Univ. 1972.

Michael, R., and Becker, G. S. "On the Theory of Consumer Behavior." Mimeographed. Nat. Bur. Econ. Res., 1972.

Nerlove, M., and Schultz, T. P. "Love and Life between the Censuses: A Model of Family Decision Making in Puerto Rico 1950–1960." RM-6322-AID, RAND (Santa Monica, Calif.), 1970.

Ofek, H. "Allocation of Goods and Time in a Family Context." Ph.D. dissertation, Columbia Univ., 1970.

Reischauer, R. "The Impact of the Welfare System on Black Migration and Marital Stability." Ph.D. dissertation, Columbia Univ., 1970.

Santos, F. P. "Marital Instability and Male-Female Complementarity." Ph.D. dissertation, Columbia Univ., 1970.

Smith, J. "The Life Cycle Allocation of Time in a Family Context." Ph.D. dissertation, Univ. Chicago, 1972.

U.S., Bureau of the Census. *U.S. Census of Population: 1960*. Washington : Government Printing Office, 1963.

―――. *Social and Economic Variations in Marriage, Divorce, and Remarriage: 1967*. Current Population Reports, Series P-20, no. 223. Washington: Government Printing Office, 1971.

Walsh, B. M. "Trends in Age at Marriage in Postwar Ireland." *Demography* 9 (May 1972): 187–202.

Winch, R. F. *Mate Selection*. New York: Harper, 1958.

―――. "Another Look at the Theory of Complementary Needs in Mate Selection." *J. Marriage and Family* 29 (November 1967): 756–62.

A Theory of Marriage:
Part II

· 12 ·

I. Introduction

In "A Theory of Marriage: Part I" (chapter 11, this volume), I presented an analysis of the "marriage market." This paper extends the analysis in that paper to include caring between mates, polygamous marital arrangements, genetic selection related to assortive mating, and separation, divorce, and remarriage. Its purpose is both to enrich the discussion in Part I and to show the power of this approach in handling different kinds of marital behavior.

In Part I I offered a simplified model of marriage that relies on two basic assumptions: (1) each person tries to find a mate who maximizes his or her well-being, with well-being measured by the consumption of household-produced commodities, and (2) the "marriage market" is assumed to be in equilibrium, in the sense that no person could change mates and become better off. I argued that the gain from marriage compared to remaining single for any two persons is positively related to their incomes, the relative difference in their wage rates, and the level of nonmarket-productivity-augmenting variables, such as education or beauty.

The optimal association between mates with respect to different traits, such as ability, education, race, income, and height, was analyzed. I showed

First published in the *Journal of Political Economy* 82, no. 2, pt. 2 (March–April 1974): S11–S26.

that positive associations, matings of likes, are usually optimal, although with respect to some traits mating of unlikes is optimal, for example, with wage rates. The division of the total "output" produced by mates is not assumed to be given a priori, but is determined by the nature of the marriage market equilibrium.

The simplified analyses in Part I have now been extended in several directions. The effect of "love" and caring between mates on the nature of equilibrium in the marriage market is considered. Polygamy is discussed, and especially the relation between its incidence and the degree of inequality among men and the inequality in the number of men and women. The implications of different sorting patterns for inequality in family resources and genetic natural selection are explored. The assumption of complete information about all potential mates is dropped and I consider the search for information through dating, coeducational schools, "trial" marriages, and other ways. This search is put in a life-cycle context that includes marriage, having children, sometimes separation and divorce, remarriage, and so forth.

II. Love, Caring, and Marriage

In Part I, I ignored "love," that cause of marriage glorified in the American culture. At an abstract level, love and other emotional attachments, such as sexual activity or frequent close contact with a particular person, can be considered particular nonmarketable household commodities, and nothing much need be added to the analysis, in the earlier paper, of the demand for commodities. That is, if an important set of commodities produced by households results from "love," the sorting of mates that maximizes total commodity output over all marriages is partly determined by the sorting that maximizes the output of these commodities. The whole discussion in Part I would continue to be relevant.

There is a considerable literature on the effect of different variables, such as personality, physical appearance, education, or intelligence, on the likelihood of different persons loving each other. Since I do not have anything to add to the explanation of whether or why one person would love another, my discussion concentrates on some effects of love on marriage. In particular, since loving someone usually involves caring about what happens to him or her,[1] I concentrate on working out several implications, for marriage, of "caring."

An inclusive measure of "what happens" is given by the level of commodity consumption, and the natural way for an economist to measure "caring" is through the utility function.[2] That is, if M cares about F, M's

FIGURE I

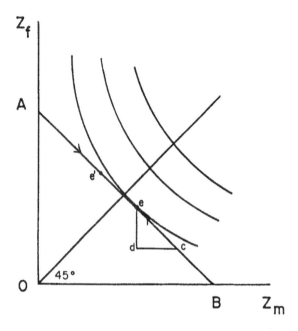

utility would depend on the commodity consumption of F as well as on his own; graphically, M's indifference curves in figure 1 are negatively inclined with respect to Z_m and Z_f, the commodities consumed by M and F respectively.[3] If M cared as much about F as about himself (I call this "full" caring), the slopes of all the indifference curves would equal unity (in absolute value) along the 45° line;[4] if he cared more about himself, the slopes would exceed unity, and conversely if he cared more about F.

Point c in figure 1 represents the allocation of commodities to M and F that is determined by equilibrium in the marriage market. Only if M were married to F could he transfer commodities to F, since household commodities are transferable within but not between households. If the terms of transfer are measured by the line AB, he moves along AB to point e: he transfers cd and F receives de. Presumably commodities can be transferred within a household without loss, so that AB would have a slope of unity. Then the equilibrium position after the transfer would be on the 45° line with full caring, and to the right of this line if M preferred his own consumption to F's.

Most people no doubt find the concept of a market allocation of commodities to beloved mates strange and unrealistic. And, as we have seen, caring can strikingly modify the market allocation between married persons. For example, the final allocation (point e) after the transfer from M to F has more equal shares than does the market allocation (point c).[5] Moreover, if F also cared about M, she would modify the market allocation by transferring resources to M from anywhere in the interval Ae' until she reached a point e',[6] generally to the left of e. The market completely determines the division of output only in the interval e'e: positions in Be are modified to e, and those in Ae' are modified to e'. Furthermore, if each fully cares for the other, points e and e' are identical and on the 45° line. Then the total amount produced by M and F would be shared equally, regardless of the market-determined division. This concept of caring between married persons, therefore, does imply sharing—equal sharing when the caring is full and mutual—and is thus consistent with the popular belief that persons in love "share."

Sharing implies that changes in the sex ratio or other variables considered in Section IV of Part I would not modify the actual distribution of output between married M and F (unless the market-mandated distribution were in the interval ee'). This is another empirical implication of caring that can be used to determine its importance.

I indicated in the earlier paper that total income would be less than total output in a marriage if resources were spent "policing" the market-mandated division of output, whereas total income would exceed total output if some output were a "family" commodity, that is, were consumed by both mates. Caring raises total income relative to total output both by reducing policing costs and by increasing the importance of family commodities.

Consider first the effect of caring on policing costs. "Policing" reduces the probability that a mate shirks duties or appropriates more output than is mandated by the equilibrium in the marriage market.[7] Caring reduces the need for policing: M's incentive to "steal" from his mate F is weaker if M cares about F because a reduction in F's consumption also lowers M's utility. Indeed, caring often completely eliminates the incentive to "steal" and thus the need to police. Thus, at point e in the figure, M has no incentive to "steal" from F because a movement to the right along AB would lower M's utility.[8] Therefore, if M cares about F sufficiently to transfer commodities to her, F would not need to "police" M's consumption.[9] Consequently, marriages with caring would have fewer resources spent on "policing" (via allowances or separate checking accounts?) than other marriages would.

M's income at e exceeds his own consumption because of the utility he gets from F's consumption. Indeed, his income is the sum of his and F's consumption, and equals OB (or OA), the output produced by M and F. Similarly, F's income exceeds her own consumption if she benefits from M's consumption.[10] Caring makes family income greater than family output because some output is jointly consumed. At point e, all of F's and part of

FAMILY, MARRIAGE, AND FERTILITY

M's consumption would be jointly consumed. Since both e and e' are on the 45° line with mutual and full caring, the combined incomes of M and F would then be double their combined output: all of M's and all of F's consumption would be jointly consumed.

Love and caring between two persons increase their chances of being married to each other in the optimal sorting. That love and caring cannot reduce these chances can be seen by assuming that they would be married to each other in the optimal sorting even if they did not love and care for each other. Then they must also be married to each other in the optimal sorting if they do love and care for each other because love raises commodity output and caring raises their total income by making part of their output a "family" commodity. Hence, their incomes when there is love and caring exceed their incomes when there is not. Consider the following matrix of outputs:

$$
\begin{array}{cc}
 & \begin{array}{cc} F_1 & \quad F_2 \end{array} \\
\begin{array}{c} M_1 \\ \\ M_2 \\ \\ \end{array}
& \left[\begin{array}{cc}
8 & 4 \\
(3, 5) & \\
9 & 7 \\
& (5, 2)
\end{array}\right]
\end{array} \quad . \qquad (1)
$$

With no caring, this is also the matrix of total incomes,[11] and $M_1 F_1$ and $M_2 F_2$ would be the optimal sorting if incomes were sufficiently divisible to obtain, say, the division given in parentheses. With mutual and full caring between M_1 and F_1, m'_{11}, the income of M_1, would equal $8 > 3$, and $\hat{f}'_{11}$, the income of F_1, would equal $8 > 5$;[12] clearly, M_1 would still be married to F_1 in the optimal sorting.

That love and caring can bring a couple into the optimal sorting is shown by the following matrix of outputs:

$$
\begin{array}{c}
\begin{array}{ccc} F_1 & \quad F_2 & \quad F_3 \end{array} \\
\begin{array}{c} M_1 \\ \\ M_2 \\ \\ M_3 \\ \\ \end{array}
\left[\begin{array}{ccc}
10 & 6 & 5 \\
(4, 6) & & \\
9 & 10 & 4 \\
& (6, 4) & \\
2 & 3 & 10 \\
& & (5, 5)
\end{array}\right]
\end{array} \quad . \qquad (2)
$$

Without love and caring the optimal sorting is $M_1 F_1$, $M_2 F_2$, and $M_3 F_3$, with a set of optimal incomes given in parentheses. If, however, M_1 and F_2 were in love and had mutual and full caring, the optimal sorting would become $M_1 F_2$, $M_2 F_1$, and $M_3 F_3$ because the incomes resulting from this sorting, $m_{12} = f_{21} = k > 6$,[13] and, say, $m_{21} = f_{21} = 4\frac{1}{2}$, and $m_{33} = f_{33} = 5$, can block the sorting along the diagonal.

Does caring per se—that is, as distinguished from love—encourage marriage: for example, couldn't M_1 marry F_1 even though he receives utility from F_2's consumption, and even if he wants to transfer resources to F_2? One incentive to combine marriage and caring is that resources are more cheaply transferred within households: by assumption, commodities cannot be transferred between households, and goods and time presumably also are more readily transferred within households. Moreover, caring partly results from living together,[14] and some couples marry partly because they anticipate the effect of living together on their caring.

Since, therefore, caring does encourage (and is encouraged by) marriage, there is a justification for the economist's usual assumption that even a multiperson household has a single well-ordered preference function. For, if one member of a household—the "head"—cares enough about all other members to transfer resources to them, this household would act *as if* it maximized the "head's" preference function, even if the preferences of other members are quite different.[15]

Output is generally less divisible between mates in marriages with caring than in other marriages[16] because caring makes some output a family commodity, which cannot be divided between mates. One implication of this is that marriages with caring are less likely to be part of the optimal sorting than marriages without caring that have the same total *income* (and thus have a greater total output).[17]

Another implication is that the optimal sorting of different traits can be significantly affected by caring, even if the degree of caring and the value of a trait are unrelated. Part I shows that when the division of output is so restricted that each mate receives a given fraction of the output of his or her marriage, beneficial traits are always strongly positively correlated in the optimal sorting. A negative correlation, on the other hand, is sometimes optimal when output is fully divisible. Caring could convert what would be an optimal negative correlation into an optimal positive one because of the restrictions it imposes on the division of output.

For example, assume that a group of men and women differ only in wage rates, and that *each* potential marriage has mutual and full caring, so that the degree of caring is in this case uncorrelated with the level of wage rates; then the optimal correlation between wage rates would be positive, although I showed in Part I that it is negative when there is no caring.[18] The (small amount of) evidence in that paper indicating that wage rates are negatively correlated suggests, therefore, that caring does not completely determine the choice of marriage mates.

III. Polygamy

Although monogamous unions predominate in the world today, some societies still practice polygamy, and it was common at one time. What determines the incidence of polygamous unions in societies that permit them, and why have they declined in importance over time?

I argued in Part I that polyandrists—women with several husbands— have been much less common than polygynists—men with several wives— because the father's identity is doubtful under polyandry. Todas of India did practice polyandry, but their ratio of men to women was much above one, largely due to female infanticide.[19] They mitigated the effects of uncertainty about the father by usually having brothers (or other close relatives) marry the same woman.

I showed in Part I that if all men and all women were identical, if the number of men equaled the number of women, and if there were diminishing returns from adding an additional spouse to a household, then a monogamous sorting would be optimal, and therefore would maximize the total output of commodities over all marriages.[20] If the plausible assumption of diminishing returns is maintained, inequality in various traits among men or in the number of men and women would be needed to explain polygyny.

An excess of women over men has often encouraged the spread of polygyny, with the most obvious examples resulting from wartime deaths of men. Thus, almost all the male population in Paraguay were killed during a war with Argentina, Brazil, and Uruguay in the nineteenth century,[21] and apparently polygyny spread afterward.

Yet, polygyny has occurred even without an excess of women; indeed, the Mormons practiced polygyny on a sizable scale with a slight excess of men.[22] Then inequality among men is crucial.

If the "productivity" of men differs, a polygynous sorting could be optimal, even with constant returns to scale and an equal number of men and women. Total output over all marriages could be greater if a second wife to an able man added more to output than she would add as a first wife to a less able one. Diminishing marginal products of men or women within each household do not rule out that a woman could have a higher marginal product as a second wife in a more productive household than as the sole wife in a less productive household.

Consider, for example, two identical women who would produce 5 units of output if single, and two different men who would each produce 8 and 15 units, respectively, if single. Let the married outputs be 14 and 27 when each man has one wife, and 18 and 35 when each has two.[23] Clearly, total output is greater if the abler man takes two wives and the other remains single than if they both take one wife: $35 + 8 = 43 > 14 + 27 = 41$. If the abler man received, say, 21 units and each wife received, say, 7 units, no one would have any incentive to change mates.

Our analysis implies generally that polygyny would be more frequent among more productive men—such as those with large farms, high positions, and great strength—an implication strongly supported by the evidence on polygyny. For example, only about 10–20 percent of the Mormons had more than one wife,[24] and they were the more successful and prominent ones. Although 40 percent of the married men in a sample of the Xavante Indians of Brazil were polygynous, "it was the chief and the heads of clans who enjoyed the highest degree of polygyny" (Salzano, Neel, and Maybury-Lewis 1967, 473). About 35 percent of the married men in sub-Saharan Africa were polygynous (Dorjahn 1959, 98–105), and they were generally the wealthier men. Fewer than 10 percent of the married men in Arab countries were polygynous, and they were the more successful, especially in agriculture (Goode 1963, 101–4).

I do not have a satisfactory explanation of why polygyny has declined over time in those parts of the world where it was once more common.[25] The declines in income inequality and the importance of agriculture presumably have been partly responsible. Perhaps the sex ratio has become less favorable, but that seems unlikely, wartime destruction aside. Perhaps monogamous societies have superior genetic and even cultural natural selection (see the next section). But since more successful men are more likely to be polygynous, they are more likely to have relatively many children.[26] If the factors responsible for success are "inherited," selection over time toward the "abler" might be stronger in polygynous than in monogamous societies. I have even heard the argument that Mormons are unusually successful in the United States because of their polygynous past! However, if the wives of polygynous males were not as able, on the average, as the wives of equally able monogamous males, selection could be less favorable in polygynous societies.

The decline in polygyny is usually "explained" by religious and legislative strictures against polygyny that are supposedly motivated by a desire to prevent the exploitation of women. But the laws that prevent men from taking more than one wife no more benefit women than the laws in South Africa that restrict the ratio of black to white workers (see Wilson 1972, 8) benefit blacks. Surely, laws against polygyny reduce the "demand" for women, and thereby reduce their share of total household output and increase the share of men.[27]

IV. ASSORTIVE MATING, INEQUALITY,
AND NATURAL SELECTION

I pointed out in Part I that positive assortive mating of different traits reduces the variation in these traits between children in the same family (and this is one benefit of such mating). Positive assortive mating also, however, increases the inequality in traits, and thus in commodity income, between families. Note that the effects on inequality in commodity and money incomes may be very different; indeed, if wage rates, unlike most other traits, are negatively sorted (as argued in Part I), assortive mating would reduce the inequality in money earnings and increase that in commodity income.

Positive sorting of inherited traits, like intelligence, race, or height, also increases the inequality in these traits among children in different families, and increases the correlation between the traits of parents and children (see proofs in Cavalli-Sforza and Bodmer [1971, chap. 9]). Moreover, positive sorting, even of noninherited traits such as education, often has the same effect because, for example, educated parents are effective producers of "education-readiness" in their children (see Leibowitz [1972] and the papers by her and Benham [JPE 2 (1982)]). The result is an increase in the correlation between the commodity incomes of parents and children, and thereby an increase in the inequality in commodity income among families spanning several generations. That is, positive assortive mating has primary responsibility for noncompeting groups and the general importance of the family in determining economic and social position that is so relevant for discussions of investment in human capital and occupational position.

Since positive assortive mating increases aggregate commodity income over all families, the level of and inequality in commodity income are affected in different ways. Probably outlawing polygyny has reduced the inequality in commodity income among men at the price of reducing aggregate commodity income. Perhaps other restrictions on mating patterns that reduce inequality would be tolerated, but that does not seem likely at present.

Since positive assortive mating increases the between-family variance, it increases the potential for genetic natural selection, by a well-known theorem in population genetics.[28] The actual amount of selection depends also on the inheritability of traits, and the relation between the levels of the traits of mates and the number of their surviving children (called "fitness" by geneticists). For example, given the degree of inheritability of intelligence, and a positive (or negative) relation between number of children and average intelligence of parents, the rate of increase (or decrease) per generation in the average intelligence of a population would be directly related to the degree of positive assortive mating by intelligence.

Moreover, the degree of assortive mating is not independent of inheritability or of the relation between number of children and parental traits. For example, the "cost" of higher-"quality" children may be lower to more-intelligent parents, and this affects the number (as well as quality) of children desired.[29] In a subsequent paper I expect to treat more systematically the interaction between the degree of assortive mating and other determinants of the direction and rate of genetic selection.

V. Life-Cycle Marital Patterns

Life-cycle dimensions of marital decisions—for instance, when to marry, how long to stay married, when to remarry if divorced or widowed, or how long to stay remarried—have received little attention in my earlier paper or thus far in this one. These are intriguing but difficult questions, and only the broad strokes of an analysis can be sketched at this time. A separate paper in the not-too-distant future will develop a more detailed empirical as well as theoretical analysis.

A convenient, if artificial, way to categorize the decision to marry is to say that a person first decides when to enter the marriage market and then searches for an appropriate mate.[30] The age of entry would be earlier the larger the number of children desired, the higher the expected lifetime income, and the lower the level of education.[31]

Once in the marriage market, a person searches for a mate along the lines specified in the now rather extensive search literature.[32] That is, he searches until the value to him of any expected improvement in the mate he can find is no greater than the cost of his time and other inputs into additional search. Some determinants of benefits and costs are of special interest in the context of the marriage market.

Search will be longer the greater the benefits expected from additional search. Since benefits will be greater the longer the expected duration of marriage, people will search more carefully and marry later when they expect to be married longer, for example, when divorce is more difficult or adult death rates are lower. Search may take the form of trial living together, consensual unions, or simply prolonged dating. Consequently, when divorce becomes easier, the fraction of persons legally married may actually *increase* because of the effect on the age at marriage. Indeed, in Latin America, where divorce is usually impossible, a relatively small fraction of the adult population is legally married because consensual unions are so important (see Kogut

1972); and, in the United States, a smaller fraction of women have been married in those states having more-difficult divorce laws (see Freiden [1972] and [JPE 2 (1982)]).[33]

Search would also be longer the more variable potential mates were because then the expected gain from additional "sampling" would be greater. Hence, other determinants being the same, marriage should generally be later in dynamic, mobile, and diversified societies than in static, homogeneous ones.

People marry relatively early when they are lucky in their search. They also marry early, however, when they are unduly pessimistic about their prospects of attracting someone better (or unduly optimistic about persons they have already met). Therefore, early marriages contain both lucky and pessimistic persons, while later marriages contain unlucky and optimistic ones.

The cost of search differs greatly for different traits: the education, income, intelligence, family background, perhaps even the health of persons can be ascertained relatively easily, but their ambition, resiliency under pressure, or potential for growth are ascertained with much greater difficulty.[34] The optimal allocation of search expenditures implies that marital decisions would be based on fuller information about more-easily searched traits than about more-difficult-to-search traits. Presumably, therefore, an analysis of sorting that assumes perfect information (as in Part I would predict the sorting by more-easily searched traits, such as education, better than the sorting by more-difficult-to-search traits, such as resiliency.[35]

Married persons also must make decisions about marriage: should they separate or divorce, and if they do, or if widowed, when, if ever, should they remarry? The incentive to separate is smaller the more important are investments that are "specific" to a particular marriage.[36] The most obvious and dominant example of marriage-specific investment is children, although knowledge of the habits and attitudes of one's mate is also significant. Since specific investments would grow, at least for quite a while, with the duration of marriage, the incentive to separate would tend to decline with duration.

The incentive to separate is greater, on the other hand, the more convinced a person becomes that the marriage was a "mistake." This conviction could result from additional information about one's mate or other potential mates. (Some "search" goes on, perhaps subconsciously, even while one is married!) If the "mistake" is considered large enough to outweigh the loss in marriage-specific capital, separation and perhaps divorce will follow.

The analysis in Part I predicts sorting patterns in a world with perfect information. Presumably, couples who deviate from these patterns because they were unlucky in their search are more likely than others to decide that they made a "mistake" and to separate as additional information is accumulated during marriage. If they remarry, they should deviate less from these patterns than in their first marriage. For example, couples with relatively large differences in education, intelligence, race, or religion, because they were unlucky searchers, should be more likely to separate,[37] and should have smaller differences when they remarry. In the subsequent paper referred to earlier, I plan to develop more systematically the implications of this analysis concerning separation, divorce, and remarriage, and to test them with several bodies of data.

VI. Summary

The findings from this extension of my earlier paper on "The Theory of Marriage" include:

a. An explanation of why persons who care for each other are more likely to marry each other than are otherwise similar persons who do not. This in turn provides a justification for assuming that each family acts as if it maximizes a single utility function.

b. An explanation of why polygyny, when permitted, has been more common among successful men and, more generally, why inequality among men and differences in the number of men and women have been important in determining the incidence of polygyny.

c. An analysis of the relation between natural selection over time and assortive mating, which is relevant, among other things, for understanding the persistence over several generations of differences in incomes between different families.

d. An analysis of which marriages are more likely to terminate in separation and divorce, and of how the assortive mating of those remarrying differs from the assortive mating in their first marriages.

The discussion in this paper is mainly a series of preliminary reports on more extensive studies in progress. The fuller studies will permit readers to gain a more accurate assessment of the value of our economic approach in understanding marital patterns.

Mathematical Appendix

1. Formally, M (or F) maximizes his utility function

$$U_m = U_m(Z_m, Z_f) \qquad \text{(A1)}$$

subject to the constraints

$$\left.\begin{array}{l} Z_m^0 - C_m = Z_m \\ Z_f^0 + C_m = Z_f \\ C_m \geq 0 \end{array}\right\}, \qquad (A2)$$

where Z_m^0 and Z_f^0 are the market allocations of output to M and F, and C_m is the amount transferred by M to F. If $C_m > 0$, these constraints can be reduced to a single income constraint by substitution from the Z_f into the Z_m equation:

$$m_{mf} = Z_{mf} = Z_f^0 + Z_m^0 = Z_m + Z_f, \qquad (A3)$$

where Z_{mf} is the output produced by M and F, and m_{mf} is M's income. Maximization of U_m subject to this single income constraint gives

$$\frac{\partial U_m}{\partial Z_m} = \frac{\partial U_m}{\partial Z_f}. \qquad (A4)$$

If $C_m = 0$, U_m is maximized subject to the two constraints $Z_m^0 = Z_m$ and $Z_f^0 = Z_f$. The equilibrium conditions are $\partial U_m/\partial Z_m = \lambda_m$, $\partial U_m/\partial Z_f = \mu_m$, where λ_m and μ_m are the marginal utilities of additional Z_m^0 and Z_f^0, respectively. The income of M would then be

$$m_{mf} = Z_m^0 + (\mu_m / \lambda_m) Z_f^0, \qquad (A5)$$

where μ_m/λ_m is the "shadow" price of Z_f to M in terms of Z_m.

Since $\mu_m/\lambda_m < 1$ (otherwise $C_m > 0$),

$$Z_m^0 + \frac{\mu_m}{\lambda_m} Z_f^0 < Z_{mf} = Z_m^0 + Z_f^0. \qquad (A6)$$

If $C_m > 0$, the "family" consisting of M and F would act as if it maximized the single "family" utility function U_m subject to the single family budget constraint given by (A3), even if F's utility function were quite different from U_m. In effect, transfers between members eliminate the conflict between different members' utility functions.

2. Total income in a marriage between M and F is

$$m_{mf} + f_{mf} = I_{mf} = Z_{mf} + p_m Z_{mf}^f + p_f Z_{mf}^m,$$

where I_{mf} is the total income in the marriage, Z_{mf}^m and Z_{mf}^f are the outputs allocated to M and F, Z_{mf} ($Z_{mf}^f + Z_{mf}^m$) is total output, p_m is the shadow price to M of a unit of Z_m^f, and p_f is a shadow price to F of a unit of Z_{mf}^m. Their incomes must be in the intervals

$$Z_{mf}^m + p_m Z_{mf}^f = m_{mf} \leq p_f Z_{mf},$$

$$Z_{mf}^f + p_f Z_{mf}^m = f_{mf} \leq Z_{mf}. \qquad (A7)$$

If $p_m = p_f = 0$—no caring—m_{mf} and f_{mf} can be anywhere between 0 and Z_{mf}. But if $p_m = p_f = 1$—mutual and full caring—then $m_{mf} = f_{mf} = Z_{mf}$. And, more generally, if p_m and $p_f > 0$, then

$$Z_{mf}^m < m_{mf} \leq Z_{mf} < I_{mf},$$
$$Z_{mf}^m < f_{mf} \leq Z_{mf} < I_{mf}. \qquad (A8)$$

Consider the following matrix of total *incomes*:

$$
\begin{array}{c}
 \\
M_1 \\
\\
M_2
\end{array}
\begin{array}{cc}
F_1 & F_2 \\
\left[\begin{array}{cc}
8 & 8 \\
 & (4,4) \\
7 & 7 \\
(3,4) &
\end{array}\right]
\end{array}
\quad . \qquad (A9)
$$

On the surface, both sortings are equally optimal, but this is not so if only M_1 and F_2 have a marriage with caring, say full and mutual, so that $m_{12} = f_{12} = 4$.[38] The sorting $M_1 F_2$ and $M_2 F_1$ is not as viable as the sorting $M_1 F_1$ and $M_2 F_2$ because income is more divisible between M_1 and F_1 than between M_1 and F_2.[39] For if, say, $m_{11} = 4\frac{1}{2}$, $f_{11} = 3\frac{1}{2}$, $m_{22} = 4\frac{1}{2}$, and $f_{22} = 2\frac{1}{2}$, no two persons have an incentive to change mates and marry each other.[40] On the other hand, since $M_{12} = f_{12} = 4$, unless $M_{21} = 3$ and $f_{21} = 4$, either M_1 and F_1, or M_2 and F_2 would be better off by marrying each other. If $m_{21} = 3$ and $f_{21} = 4$, M_1 and F_1, and M_2 and F_2 could be just as well off by marrying each other. Therefore, this sorting is not as viable as the sorting that does not have any marriages with caring.

3. Assume that the gain from marriage of a particular person M is positively related to the expected values of two traits of his mate, as in $m = g(A_1, A_2)$, with $\partial g/\partial A_i = g_i > 0$, $i = 1, 2$. If the marginal costs of search were c_1 and c_2 for A_1 and A_2, respectively, equilibrium requires that

$$\frac{g_1}{g_2} = \frac{c_1}{c_2}. \qquad (A10)$$

The lower c_1 is relative to c_2, the higher generally would be the equilibrium value of A_1 relative to A_2, since convexity of the isogain curves is a necessary condition for an internal maximum.

If g_1 and g_2 were invariant when search costs changed to all participants in the marriage market, not an innocuous assumption, then A_1^{max} and A_2^{max} would be the equilibrium values of A_1 and A_2 to M when everyone had perfect information about all traits. A reduction in the cost of searching A_1, therefore, would move the equilibrium value of A_1 to M closer to A_1^{max}, its value with perfect information.

Notes

I am indebted for helpful comments to Isaac Ehrlich, Robert T. Michael, Richard Posner, T. W. Schultz, George J. Stigler, and members of the Workshop in Applications of Economics at the University of Chicago. This research has been supported by a grant from the Ford Foundation to the National Bureau of Economic Research for the study of the economics of population. This paper is not an official NBER publication, since it has not been reviewed by the NBER Board of Directors.

1. The *Random House Dictionary of the English Language* includes in its definitions of love, "affectionate concern for the well-being of others," and "the profoundly tender or passionate affection for a person of the opposite sex."

2. This formulation is taken from my paper, "A Theory of Social Interactions" (1969).

3. Since there is only a single aggregate commodity, saying that M's utility depends on F's consumption is equivalent to saying that M's utility depends on F's utility (assuming that F does not care about M). If many commodities $Z_1, \ldots, Z_q$, were consumed, M's utility would depend on F's utility if $U^m = U^m[Z_{1m}, \ldots, Z_{qm}, g(Z_{1f}, \ldots, Z_{qf})]$ where g describes the indifference surface of F. Hence $(\partial U^m / \partial Z_{if}) / (\partial U^m / \partial Z_{jf}) = (\partial g / \partial Z_{if}) / (\partial g / \partial Z_{jf})$; this ratio is F's marginal rate of substitution between Z_i and Z_j.

4. "Full" caring might also imply that the indifference curves were straight lines with a slope of unity, that Z_f was a perfect substitute for Z_m.

5. Provided it were in the interval Ae, M would not modify the market allocation.

6. We assume that AB also given the terms of transfer for F, and that e' is the point of tangency between AB and her indifference curves.

7. Policing is necessary in any partnership or corporation, or, more generally, in any cooperative activity (see Becker 1971, 122–23; Alchian and Demsetz 1972).

8. A fortiori, a movement along any steeper line—the difference between AB and this line measuring the resources used up in "stealing"—would also lower M's utility.

9. With mutual and full caring, neither mate would have to "police." On the other hand, if each cared more about the other than about himself (or herself), at least one of them, say M, would want to transfer resources that would not be accepted. Then F would "police" to prevent undesired *transfers from* M. This illustrates a rather general principle; namely, that when the degree of caring becomes sufficiently great, behavior becomes similar to that when there is no caring.

10. F's income equals the sum of her consumption and a fraction of M's consumption that is determined by the slope of F's indifference curve at point e. See the formulation in section 1 of the Mathematical Appendix.

11. We abstract from other kinds of "family" commodities because they can be analyzed in exactly the same way that caring is.

12. The output of love raises these incomes even further.

13. The difference between k and 6 measures the output of love produced by M_1 and F_2.

14. So does negative caring or "hatred." A significant fraction of all murders and assaults involve members of the same household (see Ehrlich 1970).

15. For a proof, see section 1 of the appendix; further discussions can be found in Becker (1969).

16. See the proof in section 2 of the appendix.

17. See the example discussed in section 2 of the appendix.

18. As an example, let the matrix of outputs from different combinations of wage rates be

$$
\begin{array}{c}
 & F_{w1} \quad\quad F_{w2} \\
M_{w1} \\
M_{w2}
\end{array}
\begin{bmatrix}
5 & 10 \\
(5, 5) & (10, 10) \\
12 & 15 \\
(12, 12) & (15, 15)
\end{bmatrix}.
$$

If outputs were fully divisible, the optimal sorting would be $M_{w_1}F_{w_2}$ and $M_{w_2}F_{w_1}$ since that maximizes the combined output over all marriages. With mutual and full caring in all marriages, the income of each mate equals the output in his or her marriage; these incomes are given in parentheses. Clearly, the optimal sorting would now be $M_{w_2F_{w_2}}$ and $M_{w_1F_{w_1}}$.

19. See Rivers (1906). Whether the infanticide caused polyandry, or the reverse, is not clear.

20. An optimal sorting has the property that persons not married to each other could not, by marrying, make some better off without making others worse off. I show in Part 1 that an optimal sorting maximizes total output of commodities.

21. After the war, males were only 13 percent of the total population of Paraguay (see Encyclopaedia Britannica, 1973 ed., s.v. "Paraguay"). I owe this reference to T. W. Schultz.

22. See Young (1954, 124). The effective number of women can exceed the number of men, even with an equal number at each age, if women marry earlier than men and if widowed women remarry. The number of women married at any time would exceed the number of men married because women would be married longer (to different men—they would be sequentially polyandrous!). This apparently was important in sub-Saharan Africa, where polygyny was common (see Dorjahn 1959).

23. These numbers imply diminishing marginal products, since $18 - 14 = 4 < 6$, and $35 - 27 = 8 < 12$.

24. Young (1954, 441) says that "in some communities it ran as high as 20–25 percent of the male heads of families," but Arrington (1958, 238) says about 10 percent of all Mormon families were polygynous.

25. Polygyny was more common in Islamic and African societies than in Western and Asian ones, although in China and Japan concubines had some of the rights and obligations of wives (see Goode 1963, chap. 5).

26. Salzano, Neel, and Maybury-Lewis (1967, 486) found evidence among the Xavante Indians of "similar means but significantly greater variance for number of surviving offspring for males whose reproduction is completed than for similar fe-

males." This indicates that polygynous males (the more successful ones) have more children than other males.

27. An alternative interpretation of the religious and legislative strictures against polygyny is that they are an early and major example of discrimination *against* women, of a similar mold to the restrictions on their employment in certain occupations, such as the priesthood, or on their ownership of property. This hypothesis has been well stated by (of all people!) George Bernard Shaw: "Polygamy when tried under modern democratic conditions as by the Mormons, is wrecked by the revolt of the mass of inferior men who are condemned to celibacy by it; for the maternal instinct leads a woman to prefer a tenth share in a first rate man to the exclusive possession of a third rate." See his "Maxims for Revolutionists" appended to *Man and Superman* (Shaw 1930, 220). Shaw was preoccupied with celibacy; he has three other maxims on celibacy, one being "any marriage system which condemns a majority of the population to celibacy will be violently wrecked on the pretext that it outrages morality" (1930, 220).

28. This theorem was proved by Fisher (1958, 37–38) and called "the fundamental theorem of natural selection." For a more recent and extensive discussion, see Cavalli-Sforza and Bodmer (1971, sec. 6.7).

29. For a discussion of the interaction between the quantity and quality of children, see Becker and Lewis (1973).

30. This categorization is made in an important paper by Coale and McNeil, "The Distribution by Age of the Frequency of First Marriage in a Female Cohort" (1973). They show that the frequency distribution of the age at first marriage can be closely fitted in a variety of environments by the convolution of a normal distribution and two or three exponential distributions. The normal distribution is said to represent the distribution of age at entry into the marriage market, and the exponential distributions, the time it takes to find a mate.

31. For a theoretical and empirical study of these and other variables, see Keeley (1973).

32. The pioneering paper is by Stigler (1961). For more recent developments, see McCall (1970) and Mortensen (1970).

33. These results are net of differences in income, relative wages, and the sex ratio.

34. In the terminology of Nelson (1970), education, income, and intelligence are "search" traits, whereas resiliency and growth potential are "experience" traits.

35. See the discussion in section 3 of the Appendix.

36. The distinction between general and specific investment is well known, and can be found in Becker (1964, chap. 11). Children, for example, would be a specific investment if the pleasure received by a parent were smaller when the parent was (permanently) separated from the children.

37. If they have relatively large differences because they were less efficient searchers, they may be less likely to separate.

38. The *output* between M_1 and F_2 also equals four, half that between M_1 and F_1.

39. Or, put differently, the output between M_1 and F_1 exceeds that between M_1 and F_2.

40. F_2 would prefer to marry M_1, but could not induce M_1 to do so because m_{12} cannot exceed four, the output produced by M_1 and F_2 (see eq. [A7]), which is less than $m_{11} = 4\frac{1}{2}$.

References

Alchian, Armen A., and Harold Demsetz. "Production, Information Costs, and Economic Organization." AER 62 (December 1972): 777–95.

Arrington, Leonard J. Great Basin Kingdom. Lincoln: University of Nebraska Press, 1958.

Becker, Gary S. Human Capital. New York: Columbia University Press (for Nat. Bur. Econ. Res.), 1964.

———. "A Theory of Social Interactions." Unpublished paper. University of Chicago, September 1969.

———. Economic Theory. New York: Knopf, 1971.

Becker, Gary S., and Gregg H. Lewis. "On the Interaction between the Quantity and Quality of Children." JPE 81, no. 2, suppl. (March/April 1973): S279–88.

Cavalli-Sforza, L. L., and W. Bodmer. The Genetics of Human Populations. San Francisco: Freeman, 1971.

Coale, A. S., and D. R. McNeil. "The Distribution by Age of the Frequency of First Marriage in a Female Cohort." J. American Statistics Assoc. 67 (December 1972): 743.

Dorjahn, V. R. "The Factor of Polygyny in African Demography." In Continuity and Change in African Cultures, edited by W. R. Bascom and M. J. Huskovity. Chicago: University of Chicago Press, 1959.

Ehrlich, Isaac. "Participation in Illegitimate Activities: An Economic Analysis." Ph.D. dissertation, Columbia University, 1970.

Fisher, R. A. The Genetical Theory of Natural Selection. 2d ed. New York: Dover, 1958.

Freiden, Alan. "A Model of Marriage and Fertility." Ph.D. dissertation, University of Chicago, 1972.

Goode, William J. World Revolution and Family Patterns. New York: Free Press, 1963.

Keeley, Michael C. "A Model of Marital Formation: The Determinants of the Optimal Age at First Marriage and Differences in Age at Marriage." Ph.D. dissertation, University of Chicago, 1973.

Kogut, Edy L. "The Economic Analysis of Demographic Phenomena: A Case Study of Brazil." Ph.D. dissertation, University of Chicago, 1972.

Leibowitz, Arleen. "Women's Allocation of Time to Market and Nonmarket Activities: Differences by Education." Ph.D. dissertation, Columbia University, 1972.

McCall, J. J. "Economics of Information and Job Search." *QJE* 84 (February 1970): 113–26.

Mortensen, D. T. "Job Search, the Duration of Unemployment and the Phillips Curve." *AER* 60 (December 1970): 847–62.

Nelson, P. J. "Information and Consumer Behavior." *JPE* 78 (March/April 1970): 311–29.

Rivers, W. H. *The Todas.* London: Macmillan, 1906.

Salzano, F. M., J. V. Neel, and D. Maybury-Lewis. "Further Studies on the Xavante Indians." *American J. Human Genetics* 19 (July 1967): 463–89.

Shaw, George Bernard. *Man and Superman.* In *The Collected Works of Bernard Shaw.* Vol. 10, Ayot St. Lawrence ed. New York: Wise, 1930.

Stigler, George J. "The Economics of Information." *JPE* 69 (June 1961): 213–25.

Wilson, Frances. *Labour in the South African Gold Mines, 1911–1969.* Cambridge: Cambridge University Press, 1972.

Young, Kimball. *Isn't One Wife Enough?* New York: Holt, 1954.

Altruism, Egoism, and Genetic Fitness: Economics and Sociobiology

· 13 ·

I. Introduction

Economists generally take tastes as "given" and work out the consequences of changes in prices, incomes, and other variables under the assumption that tastes do not change. When pressed, either they engage in ad hoc theorizing or they explicitly delegate the discussion of tastes to the sociologist, psychologist, or anthropologist. Unfortunately, these disciplines have not developed much in the way of systematic usable knowledge about tastes.

Although economists have been reluctant to discuss systematically changes in the structure of tastes, they have long relied on assumptions about the basic and enduring properties of tastes. Self-interest is assumed to dominate all other motives,[1] with a prominent place also assigned to benevolence toward children[2] (and occasionally others), and with self-interest partly dependent on distinction and other aspects of one's position in society.[3] The dominance of self-interest and the persistence of some benevolence have usually been explained by "human nature," or an equivalent evasion of the problem.

The development of modern biology since the mid–nineteenth century and of population genetics in the twentieth century made clear that "human

First published in the *Journal of Economic Literature* 14, no. 3 (September 1976): 817–26. Reprinted by permission of the American Economic Association.

nature" is only the beginning, not the end of the answer. The enduring traits of human (and animal) nature presumably were genetically selected under very different physical environments and social arrangements as life on earth evolved during millions of years. It is not difficult to understand why self-interest has high survival value under very different circumstances,[4] but why should altruistic behavior, sometimes observed among animals as well as human beings, also survive?

This kind of question has been asked by some geneticists and other biologists especially during the last two decades. Their work has recently been christened "sociobiology" by Edward Wilson in an important book that organizes and develops further what has been done. According to Wilson, "the central theoretical problem of sociobiology [is]: how can altruism, which by definition reduces personal fitness, possibly evolve by natural selection?" (1975, 3).

Sociobiologists have tried to solve their central problem by building models with "group selection"; these models can be illustrated with the particular variant called "kin selection." Suppose that a person is altruistic toward his brother and is willing to lower his own genetic fitness[5] in order to increase his brother's fitness. If he lowers his own fitness by b units as a result of his altruistic behavior, he increases his brother's fitness by say c units. Since they have about one half of their genes in common, his altruism would increase the expected fitness of his own genes if $c > 2b$. In particular, it would then increase the expected fitness of the genes that contribute to his altruism. Therefore, altruism toward siblings, children, grandchildren, or anyone else with common genes could have high survival value, which would explain why altruism toward kin is one of the enduring traits of human and animal "nature."

The approach of sociobiologists is highly congenial to economists, since they rely on competition, the allocation of limited resources—of say food and energy—efficient adaptation to the environment, and other concepts also used by economists. Yet sociobiologists have stopped short of developing models having rational actors who maximize utility functions subject to limited resources. Instead they have relied solely on the "rationality" related to genetic selection: the physical and social environment discourages ill-suited behavior and encourages better-suited behavior. Economists, on the other hand, have relied solely on individual rationality and have not incorporated the effects of genetic selection.[6]

I believe that a more powerful analysis can be developed by joining the individual rationality of the economist to the group rationality of the socio-biologist. To illustrate the potential, the central problem of sociobiology, the biological selection of altruistic behavior, is analyzed using recent work by economists on social interactions (see Becker [1974] and Becker and Tomes

[1976]). I will show that models of group selection are unnecessary, since altruistic behavior can be selected as a consequence of individual rationality.

II. An Economic Model of Altruism

Consider first the effect of altruism on consumption and wealth, the usual focus of economists. Essentially by definition, an altruist is willing to reduce his own consumption in order to increase the consumption of others. Two considerations suggest that the own consumption of egoistic persons (or animals) would exceed that of equally able altruistic persons (or animals).[7] The own consumption of egoists would be greater if the wealth of egoists and altruists were equal because altruists give away some of their wealth to be consumed by others. Moreover, the wealth of egoists apparently also would tend to be greater because egoists are willing to undertake all acts that raise their wealth, regardless of the effects on others, whereas altruists voluntarily forgo some acts that raise their wealth because of adverse effects on others.

These forces are potent, but they are not the whole story, and a fuller analysis shows that the consumption and wealth of altruistic persons could exceed that of egoistic persons, even without bringing in social controls on the behavior of egoistic persons. Let us consider systematically the behavior of h who is altruistic toward an egoist i. By definition of altruism, h is willing to give some of his wealth to i, but how much is he willing to give? That surely depends on his degree of altruism, his and i's wealth, the "cost" of giving, and other considerations.

The economic approach assumes that all behavior results from maximizing utility functions that depend on different commodities. If, to simplify, the allocation and transfer of time is neglected, and both h and i consume a single aggregate of market goods and services, the utility function of an altruist h can be written as

$$U^h = U^h(X_h, X_i),[8]$$

(1)

where X_h and X_i are the own consumptions of h and i respectively. The budget constraint of h can be written as

$$pX_h + h_i = I_h,$$

(2)

where h_i is the dollar amount transferred to i, and I_h is h's own income. If h transfers to i without any monetary loss or gain—"dollar for dollar"—the amount received by i equals the amount transferred by h, and i's budget constraint would be

$$pX_i = I_i + h_i,$$

(3)

where I_i is i's own income. By substitution of (3) into (2), the basic budget constraint for h is derived:

$$pX_h + pX_i = I_h + I_i = S_h, \qquad (4)$$

where S is called h's "social income."[9]

The equilibrium condition for maximizing the utility function given by equation (1) subject to the social income constraint given by (4) is

$$\frac{\partial U^h / \partial X_h}{\partial U^h / \partial X_i} = \frac{MU_h}{MU_i} = \frac{P}{P} = 1. \qquad (5)$$

Then h would transfer just enough resources to i so that h would receive the same utility from increments to his own or to i's consumption. Put differently, h would suffer the same loss in utility from a small change in his own or i's consumption.

Clearly, h's altruism is relevant not only to transfers of income, but also to the production of income. He would pursue all actions that raised his (real) social income and refrain from all that lowered it because his utility would be increased by all increases in his social income. Since the latter is the sum of his own and i's own income, he would, in particular, refrain from actions that raised his own income at the expense of a greater reduction in i's own income. This was referred to earlier when it was said that altruists have lower personal income (or wealth) than egoists because altruists do not take advantage of all opportunities to raise their own income.

Note, however, that some actions of altruistic h could increase his utility and own consumption while reducing his own income, a combination that is impossible for an egoist. Suppose that h could increase his social income by actions that lowered his own income and raised i's even more. Since h's utility would increase, he would increase both his own and i's consumption, as long as neither were an inferior good. He could increase his own consumption only by reducing his transfers to i because his own income declined; this is consistent with an increase in i's consumption because i's own income increased. Therefore, h's own consumption would increase even though his own income declined, and i's own consumption would increase even though transfers from h declined. Consequently, if an egoist and altruist began with the same consumption—the own income of the altruist necessarily being greater—events could raise the consumption of the altruist above that of the egoist at the same time that they lowered the difference in their incomes.

The most important consideration benefiting altruists, however, and one that seems puzzling and paradoxical at first, is that egoistic i has an incentive to act "as if" he too were altruistic—toward h—in the sense that it would be to i's advantage to raise the combined incomes of i and h. In particular, i

would refrain from actions that lowered h's own income unless i's was raised even more, and i would lower his own income if h's were raised even more. Why should egoist i act as if he were altruistic? Consider the consequences to him (all that he cares about) of doing the contrary; for example, let i raise his own income at the expense of lowering h's even more. Since h's social income and utility decline because the sum of his own and i's income declines, h would want to reduce his own and i's own consumption. Then h would have to reduce his transfers to i by more than the increase in i's income. Therefore, as long as h's transfers remained positive, i's own consumption and welfare would be reduced by h's response. If i anticipated correctly h's reaction, i would refrain from these actions. A similar argument shows that i would benefit from his own actions even if they lowered his income as long as they raised h's income even more: for h would increase his transfers to i by more than the reduction in i's income.

In other words, by linking i's consumption with his own, the altruistic h discourages egoistic i from actions that lower h's consumption because then i's consumption would also be lower. Moreover, i would not refrain from harming other egoistic persons not linked to h. Therefore, the intuitively appealing conclusion that the own consumption of egoistic persons exceeds that of equally able altruistic persons is seriously qualified when interaction with others is incorporated. Even though an altruist gives away part of his income and refrains from some actions that raise his own income, his own consumption might not be less than that of an egoist because the beneficiaries of his altruism would consider the effect of their behavior on his consumption. These beneficial indirect effects on the behavior of others may dominate the direct "disadvantages" of being altruistic. Moreover, these indirect effects need not be minor and could greatly exceed the amount transferred to i. For example, assume that h transfers \$1,000 and that i could increase his own income by \$800 at the cost of harming h by \$5,000. Since i would not take these actions, h's altruism has increased his income by \$5,000, or by five times the amount transferred to i.

The analysis is easily extended to incorporate altruism by h toward egoistic persons j, k, . . . , as well as i. Then h would transfer resources to j, k, . . . , as well as i, and maximize a utility function of all these consumptions subject to a social income constraint equal to the sum of all these own incomes. Following the previous analysis, it can be shown that h would refrain from actions that raised his own income if the combined incomes of i, j, k, . . . were lowered even more. Moreover, he would lower his own income if their combined incomes were raised even more.

Furthermore, not only i but each of the others would lower his own income if h's were raised more and would refrain from raising his own income if h's were lowered still more. Therefore, h may give away more of his income, and refrain from more actions that raise his own income, yet he would benefit more too because more people would consider the effects of their behavior on him. Consequently, although the direct effects reducing his own consumption are stronger for an altruist toward many persons than toward a single person, the indirect effects are also stronger. The own consumption of an altruist toward many persons also need not be less than that of an equally able egoist.

The most important new consequence of multiperson altruism relates to the behavior of recipients toward each other. Although i, j, k, . . . are all egoistical and do not give or receive transfers from each other, each has an incentive to consider the effects of his behavior on the others. For example, j would not raise his own income if the sum of the incomes of i, k, . . . were reduced still more, and j would lower his own income if their incomes were raised still more. Elsewhere I have called this the "rotten kid theorem" (see Becker [1974]), although its applicability is not restricted to interaction among siblings.

To prove this theorem, assume the contrary; for example, let j raise his income and lower k's still more. Then h's social income (and utility) would be reduced because it is the sum of j's, k's, and the others' own incomes. Consequently, h would reduce the consumption of both j and k, assuming that these consumptions are superior goods to him, and would reduce his transfers to j by more than j's increase in income and raise his transfers to k by less than k's decrease in income. In the end j as well as k (and everyone else) would be worse off; if j could anticipate h's reaction, he would refrain from raising his income at greater expense to k.

Even though i, j, k, . . . are completely egoistical, they are linked together through h's altruism. Their own interest, not altruism, motivates them to maximize the sum of their own and h's incomes—that is, to maximize h's social income. This provides another reason why an altruist's own consumption may not be less than an egoist's consumption: beneficiaries of his altruism consider all indirect as well as direct effects of their behavior on his own consumption. They do not consider the effect of their behavior on the consumption of other persons not linked to this altruist.

Note that a sufficiently large redistribution of income away from h and toward i, j, k, . . . would make h unwilling to transfer resources to some of these persons, say to k. Then k and h would continue to be interested in maximizing the same social income only if the income redistribution induced k to transfer resources to h (or induced someone else, like j, to transfer to k). That is, k's (or someone else's) altruism—h's altruism toward k and k's toward h is an example of "reciprocal altruism"[10]—would increase the robustness of the conclusions with respect to large redistributions of income within the group initially related through h's altruism.

Each person in the group linked by an altruist's transfers has an incentive to maximize the group's total income, even if most are egoistical. The group's income could be maximized in the absence of altruism if the "government" imposed appropriate taxes and subsidies, or if members bargained with each other only to take actions that benefited the group as a whole. However, appropriate voluntary agreements and government action often are not achieved, especially when governments are primitive or subject to many pressure groups, contract law is not well developed, or other private transaction costs are sizable. Therefore, whereas the private behavior induced by the rotten kid theorem in an altruistic situation *automatically* maximizes group income, government responses or the Coase theorem (on private bargaining)[11] do not.

Recipients of *h*'s transfers are encouraged to act "as if" they are altruistic to each other and to *h* by the adverse reaction from *h* when they act egoistical. Therefore, the rotten kid theorem is essentially a theorem about the incentive that egoists have to *simulate* altruism when they benefit from someone else's altruism. More generally, an egoist has an incentive to try to simulate altruism whenever altruistic behavior increases his own consumption through its effect on the behavior of others. For example, egoist *n* may have an incentive to act as if he were altruistic toward *j*, in the sense that he would voluntarily transfer resources to *j*, maximize their combined own incomes, reduce his transfers when their combined own income fell, etc., if this discourages *j* from actions that harm *n*.

If egoists can always perfectly simulate altruism whenever altruistic behavior raises their own consumption, then, of course, the own consumption of true altruists would not exceed that of true egoists; they would be equal when egoists perfectly simulated altruism. We could still conclude, however, that "apparent" altruistic behavior—either true or simulated altruism—could increase own consumption, and that is important. Moreover, if altruism could be perfectly simulated, transactions and negotiation costs must be sufficiently small so that the Coase theorem could prevail. Conversely, if the Coase theorem broke down, say because of sizable bluffing and other bargaining costs, altruism could not be perfectly simulated, for otherwise the Coase theorem would prevail. When altruism cannot be perfectly simulated, the own consumption of altruists could exceed, perhaps by a good deal, the consumption of equally able egoists.

III. GENETIC FITNESS AND THE ECONOMIC MODEL OF ALTRUISM

Since sociobiologists are more concerned with selection and genetic fitness than with consumption and wealth per se, I can bring out sharply the relationship between this economic analysis of altruism and the central problem of sociobiology by reformulating the utility function to depend only on genetic fitness. Then altruistic h would have the function

$$U^h = U^h(f_h, f_i), \tag{6}$$

where f_h and f_i measure the fitness of h and i respectively, and the utility function of egoist i would depend only on his own fitness. Since genetic fitness depends directly on birth and death rates of offspring and on own life expectancy only to the extent that it influences the number of offspring, even an egoist must be somewhat concerned about the well-being of mates and children.

In the language of the household production approach to consumer behavior,[12] genetic fitness is a commodity produced by households using their own time and goods, their skills, experience, and abilities, and the physical and social environment. For example, the fitness of h would be produced according to

$$f_h = f_h(X_h, t_h; S_h, E_h), \tag{7}$$

where t_h is the time he directly[13] uses to produce fitness—as in the care and protection of children—S_h is his stock of skills and other human capital, and E_h is the environment.

If t, S, and E were exogenous, fitness could be changed only by changing the input of goods. With the exception of a small part of the human population during the last 100 years or so, access to food and perhaps some other goods has been the main determinant of fitness throughout the biological world. The close relation between fitness and goods can be made transparent by writing the production function for fitness as

$$f = aX, \tag{8}$$

where a depends on the biological species, and the parameters t, S, and E.[14] Fitness does not have a market price, since it is not directly purchased, but does have a "shadow" price, defined as the value of the goods used in changing fitness by one unit:

$$\pi = \frac{\partial(pX)}{\partial f} = \frac{p}{a}, \tag{9}$$

where p is the (constant) price or cost of X.

Altruistic h is willing to transfer some of his goods to i because he is willing to reduce his own fitness in order to improve i's fitness. This is precisely the definition of altruism in sociobiology: "When a person (or animal) increases the fitness of another at the expense of his own fitness, he can be said to have performed an act of *altruism*" (Wilson 1975, 117).

The budget constraint for h can be derived by substituting equation (8) into equation (4):

$$\frac{pf_h}{a_h} + \frac{pf_i}{a_i} = I_h + I_i = S_h,$$

or by equation (9),

$$\pi_h f_h + \pi_i f_i = S_h. \tag{10}$$

The social income of h is partly spent on his own and partly on i's fitness: the sum of the shadow values placed on their fitnesses equals his social income.

The equilibrium condition for maximizing h's utility function (6) subject to his budget constraint (10) is, with positive transfers,

$$\frac{\partial U^h}{\partial f_h} \bigg/ \frac{\partial U^h}{\partial f_i} = \frac{\pi_h}{\pi_i} = \frac{a_i}{a_h}. \tag{11}$$

If h and i were equally efficient producers of fitness, $a_h = a_i$, and h would transfer goods to i until he was indifferent between equal increments to his own and to i's fitness. If h were a more efficient producer of fitness, $a_h > a_i$, and he would be discouraged from promoting i's fitness: he would receive more utility from an increment to i's fitness than from an equal increment to his own fitness because his own fitness is cheaper to produce.

The important point is that all the earlier results on the consumption of goods apply equally to this analysis of fitness. Both the altruist h and the egoistical recipient i maximize the *sum* of their real incomes and would raise one of them only when the other were not reduced even more. In terms of fitness, they maximize the sum of the values placed on fitness and would increase the fitness of one only if the shadow value of its increase was not less than the shadow value of the decrease in the other's fitness:

$$\pi_h df_h + \pi_i df_i \geq 0. \tag{12}$$

For example, if $\pi_i > \pi_h$ because h is more efficient at producing fitness, any increase in h's fitness would have to be at least π_i / π_h times as large as the decrease in i's fitness.

I concluded earlier that although an altruist forgoes some own consumption to raise the consumption of others and forgoes some opportunities to raise his own income to avoid lowering the income of others, his own consumption may exceed that of an equally able egoist because the beneficiaries of his altruism are discouraged from harming him. Reasoning along the same lines, the same conclusion can be reached for altruism with regard to genetic fitness: although an altruist forgoes some own fitness to raise the fitness of others, and so forth, his own fitness may exceed that of an equally able egoist because the beneficiaries of his altruism are discouraged from harming him.

Therefore, two apparently equivalent statements about altruism by Wilson are in fact quite different. He says, "altruism . . . *by definition* reduces personal fitness" (1975, 3, my italics), yet simply defines an act of altruism "[w]hen a person (or animal) increase the fitness of another at the expense of his own fitness" (1975, 117). Using the latter definition, I have shown that altruism may actually increase personal fitness because of its effect on the behavior of others. Consequently, altruism does not by (Wilson's or my) definition necessarily reduce personal fitness.

This conclusion is highly relevant in answering the central question of sociobiology: "how can altruism . . . evolve by natural selection?" (Wilson 1975, 3). If altruism, on balance, raises own genetic fitness, then natural selection would operate in its favor. A central focus of sociobiology would be to identify when biological and social conditions have a sufficient effect on the behavior of the beneficiaries of altruism so that own fitness is increased by altruism.

Note that the extensive evidence among animals of what appears to be altruistic behavior[15]—for example, baboons expose themselves to danger to protect relatives—is not inconsistent with altruism increasing personal fitness because the effects of altruism on the behavior of beneficiaries have not been considered. Note, moreover, the incentive to try to simulate altruism whenever true altruism raises personal fitness, and sociobiologists have found it difficult to distinguish simulated altruism from true altruism.[16]

Even if altruism lowers fitness, and the sociobiologist's group selection must be used to explain how altruism evolves by selection, the actual trade-off between an altruist's and a beneficiary's fitness may be much more favorable to selection of altruism than the apparent trade-off. For example, if h were altruistic toward a brother i with about half his genes in common, kin selection would favor h's altruistic (and other) genes only if he could increase i's fitness by at least two units for every unit reduction in his own fitness. Since according to equation (12) he would be willing to exchange a unit of his own fitness for at least π_h/π_i units of i's, apparently his altruistic genes can be selected only if $\pi_h > 2\pi_i$, or only if his brother is more than twice as efficient in producing fitness as he is.

Yet when all the effects of his altruism on i are considered, his genes may be strongly selected even when i is much less than twice as efficient as he is. Assume, for example, that the total loss in h's fitness from his altruism would be 5 units if he and i were equally efficient producers of fitness. Assume further that the total gain to his brother would be 15 units—the gain to his brother *must* be at least as large as his own loss since his altruism cannot decrease their combined fitness (by equation (12) when $\pi_h = \pi_i$). Instead of the apparent rate of exchange of one unit of his brother's fitness for one unit of his own, or the 2 to 1 minimum rate required to select his altruistic genes, he adds three units to his brother's fitness for each unit of his own loss.

The utility function (6) and the analysis can again be generalized to include altruism by *h* toward *j*, *k*, . . . as well as *i*. He would try to maximize the sum of his own and their real incomes, and would affect different fitnesses only if the sum of the shadow values of the changes were nonnegative:

$$\pi_h df_h + \pi_i df_i + \pi_j df_j + \pi_k df_k + \cdots \geq 0. \qquad (13)$$

Each beneficiary of *h*'s altruism also maximizes the group's total real income and is constrained in his behavior by equation (13); in particular, each would reduce the fitness of another member of the group only if the value of the reduction were less than the value of the increase in his own fitness.

The sociobiological literature contends that a major conflict arises between parents and children because the altruism of parents toward children exceeds the altruism of children toward each other: "there is likely to evolve a conflict between parents and offspring in the attitudes toward siblings: the parents will encourage more altruism than the youngster is prepared to give" (Wilson 1975, 343), or "Conflict during socialization need not be viewed solely as conflict between the culture of the parent and the biology of the child; it can also be viewed as conflict between the biology of the parent and the biology of the child" (quoted in Wilson [1975, 343] from Robert L. Trivers [1974]). My analysis denies that such a conflict exists when parents are altruistic because children have an incentive to act as altruistically toward each other as their parents want them to, even if children are really egoistical. This application of the more general result on the simulation of altruism by beneficiaries led to the name the "rotten kid theorem.".

Of course, the substitution between the fitness of parents and children that is due to the parent's altruism might not maximize the selection of his altruistic genes. However, the actual substitution may be much more favorable to the selection of his genes than substitution given by the shadow prices of fitness. For example, if these prices were equal, a parent would be willing to give up a unit of his fitness to increase the fitness of each child by a unit; yet his altruism might be strongly selected: both his and his children's fitness might actually exceed what they would be if he were not altruistic or the reduction in his fitness might be much less than the increase in theirs.[17]

IV. Conclusion

Sociobiologists have explained the strong survival throughout most of the biological world of altruism toward children and other kin by group selection operating through the common genes of kin. Using an economic model of altruism, I have explained its survival by the advantages of altruism when there is physical and social interaction: kin have had much interaction with each other because they have usually lived with or near each other. Since the economic model requires interaction, not common genes, it can also explain the survival of some altruism toward unrelated neighbors or co-workers, and these are not explained by the kin selection models of socio-biologists (but perhaps can be explained by their other models of group selection).

I have argued that both economics and sociobiology would gain from combining the analytical techniques of economists with the techniques in population genetics, entomology, and other biological foundations of socio-biology. The preferences taken as given by economists and vaguely attributed to "human nature" or something similar—the emphasis on self-interest, altruism toward kin, social distinction, and other enduring aspects of prefer-ences—may be largely explained by the selection over time of traits having greater genetic fitness and survival value.[18] However, survival value is in turn partly a result of utility maximization in different social and physical environ-ments. To demonstrate this I have shown how the central problem of socio-biology, the natural selection of altruism, can be resolved by considering the interaction between the utility-maximizing behavior of altruists and egoists.

Notes

I am indebted to Jack Hirshleifer, Guity Nashat, George J. Stigler, and Edward O. Wilson for very helpful comments.

1. For example, Adam Smith said, "We are not ready to suspect any person of being defective in selfishness" (1969, 446), and "it is not from the benevolence of the butcher, the brewer, or the baker, that we expect our dinner, but from their regard to their own interest" [1937, 14].

2. According to Alfred Marshall, "men labor and save chiefly for the sake of their families and not for themselves" (1920, 228).

3. Nassau Senior said, "the desire for distinction . . . may be pronounced to be the most powerful of human passions" (1938, 12).

4. Ronald Coase argues convincingly that Adam Smith, especially in his *Moral Sentiments*, was groping toward an explanation of the importance of self-interest in terms of its contribution to viable social and economic arrangements (see Coase [1976]).

5. Genetic selection is defined as "the change in relative frequency in genotypes due to differences in the ability of their phenotypes to obtain representation in the

next generation" (Wilson 1975, 67). Genetic fitness is the relative contribution of one genotype to the next generation's distribution of genotypes, where a genotype is "the genetic constitution of an organism," and a phenotype is "the observable properties of an organism"(Wilson 1975, 585, 591).

6. Of course, economic analysis has sometimes been related to biological evolution: Alfred Marshall believed that economic systems evolve in the same way as biological systems do, and maximizing behavior has been said to be prevalent essentially because of the selection and survival of maximizers (see Armen A. Alchian [1950]). However, biological selection has not been integrated into and combined with the main body of economic analysis: it has been an occasional appendage rather than an integral part.

7. Although the following discussion might be as applicable to animals as to persons, I simplify the presentation by referring only to persons.

8. With many market goods and services, his utility function can be written as

$$U^h = U^h\{X_{h_1}, \ldots, X_{h_m}, g(X_{i_1}, \ldots, X_{i_m})\},$$

where X_{h_j} and X_{i_j} are the consumptions of the jth good by h and i respectively, and g is a function that would have the same indifference curves as i's utility function if h's welfare partly depended on i's welfare.

9. See Becker (1974). The essentials of the economic analysis of altruism in the present section are taken from that paper.

10. The term "reciprocal altruism" is used in a different and misleading way in sociobiology. It refers not to true altruism, but to one type of simulated altruism: a person helps others in the expectation or hope that he will be helped by them in the future (see Wilson [1975, 120–21]). This is more appropriately called "social exchange" by sociologists (see Peter M. Blau [1968]).

11. The rotten kid theorem, therefore, is a powerful substitute for the Coase theorem when there is altruism.

12. An exposition can be found in Michael and Becker (1973).

13. A brief but suggestive discussion of the allocation of time (and energy) in the biological world can be found in Wilson (1975, 143).

14. A more appropriate formulation might be

$$f = \alpha X,$$

where α depends on the species, and X is produced by the function

$$X = \psi(t, S, E).$$

For present purposes, however, this formulation and the one in the text are essentially equivalent.

15. See Wilson (1975, 121–28).

16. The literature on altruism among animals reveals how difficult it is to distinguish true from simulated and other apparent altruism (see Wilson [1975, 123–25]).

17. If $\pi_h = \pi_i = \pi_j = \pi_k, \ldots$, then necessarily by equation (13)

342   •   FAMILY, MARRIAGE, AND FERTILITY

$$G_c + L_h \geq 0,$$

where L_h is the total change in the parent's (h) fitness that results from his altruism, and G_c is the total change in his children's fitness. It could also be that

$$G_c > -2L_h,$$

or even that L_h as well as $G_c > 0$.

18. A few years ago Robert T. Michael and I already suggested that "if genetical natural selection and rational behavior reinforce each other in producing speedier and more efficient responses to changes in the environment, perhaps that common preference function has evolved over time by natural selection and rational choice as that preference function best adopted to human society" (1973, 392n. 2).

References

Alchian, Armen A. "Uncertainty, Evolution, and Economic Theory." *Journal of Political Economy* 58 (June 1950): 211–21.

Becker, Gary S. "A Theory of Social Interactions." *Journal of Political Economy*, 82, no. 6 (November/December 1974): 1063–93.

Becker, Gary S., and Nigel Tomes. "Child Endowments and the Quantity and Quality of Children." *Journal of Political Economy*. August 1976.

Blau, Peter M. "Interaction: Social Exchange." In *International Encyclopedia of the Social Sciences*. Vol. 7, ed. D. E. Sills. New York: Macmillan, Free Press, 1968, pp. 452–58.

Coase, Ronald H. "Adam Smith's View of Man." *Journal of Law Economics*. October 1976.

Marshall, Alfred. *Principles of Economics.* 8th ed. London: Macmillan, 1920.

Michael, Robert T., and Gary S. Becker. "On the New Theory of Consumer Behavior." *Swedish Journal of Economics* 75, no. 4 (December 1973): 378–96.

Senior, Nassau. *An Outline of the Science of Political Economy.* Library of Economics edition. New York: Farrar & Rinehart (1836), 1938.

Smith, Adam. *The Theory of Moral Sentiments.* Reprint of 1853 edition. Introduction to 1969 edition by E. G. West. New Rochelle, N.Y.: Arlington House (1759), 1969.

———. *The Wealth of Nations.* Modern Library edition of 1904 edition, "copied" from original fifth edition and edited by Edwin Cannan. New York: Random House (1789), 1937.

Trivers, Robert L. "Parent-Offspring Conflict." *American Zoologist* 14, no. 1 (Winter 1974): 249–64.

Wilson, Edward O. *Sociobiology.* Cambridge, Mass.: Harvard University Press, 1975.

HUMAN CAPITAL AND THE RISE AND FALL OF FAMILIES

Gary S. Becker
Nigel Tomes

· 14 ·

This paper develops a model of the transmission of earnings, assets, and consumption from parents to descendants. The model assumes utility-maximizing parents who are concerned about the welfare of their children. The degree of intergenerational mobility is determined by the interaction of this utility-maximizing behavior with investment and consumption opportunities in different generations and with different kinds of luck. We examine a number of empirical studies for different countries. Regression to the mean in earnings in rich countries appears to be rapid. Almost all the earnings advantages or disadvantages of ancestors are wiped out in three generations.

I. Introduction

Ever since Pareto discovered that the distribution of larger incomes and wealth is reasonably well approximated by a particular skewed distribution, since then called the "Pareto distribution," economists have continued to discuss inequality in the distribution of earnings, income, and wealth among individuals and families. However, they have paid little attention to the

First published in the *Journal of Labor Economics* 4, no. 3, pt. 2 (1986): S1–S39. © 1986 by the University of Chicago. All rights reserved.

inequality within families over generations as determined by the relation between the incomes or wealth of parents, children, and later descendants. Schumpeter is the only major economist who systematically considered intergenerational mobility with empirical evidence as well as with theoretical analysis (see Schumpeter 1951).

Sociologists and other social scientists, on the other hand, have presented considerable empirical evidence on the occupations, education, and other characteristics of children and parents. Blau and Duncan (1967), in the influential book *The American Occupational Structure*, consider the effect of family background on the achievements of children. As long ago as 1889, John Dewey wrote, "[U]pon the average, children of parents who are exceptional, or who deviate from the mean, will themselves deviate from the mean only one third of their parents' deviation. . . . It is not likely that children of the poor would be better off, and children of the wealthier poorer in anything like the ratio of 2/3" (Dewey [1889, 333–34]; this statement was brought to our attention by O. D. Duncan).

Although discussions of inequality among families have been almost entirely separate from discussions of inequality between generations of the same family, these inequalities are analytically closely related. In particular, regression away from the mean in the relation between, say, the incomes of parents and children implies large and growing inequality of income over time, while regression toward the mean implies a smaller and more stable degree of inequality. These statements are obvious in a simple Markov model of the relation between parents and children:

$$I_{t+1} = a + bII_t + \epsilon_{t+1}, \tag{1}$$

where I_t is the income of parents, I_{t+1} is the income of children, a and b are constants, and the stochastic forces affecting the income of children (ϵ_{t+1}) are assumed to be independent of the income of parents.

Inequality in income will continue to grow over time if b is greater than or equal to unity, while inequality in income will approach a constant level if b is smaller than unity in absolute value. Clearly, the size of b also measures whether children of richer parents tend to be less rich than their parents and whether children of poorer parents tend to be better off than their parents. This example implies that, even in rigid and caste-dominated societies, many of the elite and underprivileged families would change places over generations unless inequality continued to grow over time ($b \geq 1$).

The degree of regression toward or away from the mean in the achievements of children compared to those of their parents is a measure of the degree of equality of opportunity in a society. The purpose of this paper is to analyze the determinants of unequal opportunities, sometimes called "intergenerational mobility," or, as in the title of our paper, "the rise and fall of families." We use all these terms interchangeably.

The many empirical studies of mobility by sociologists have lacked a framework or model to interpret their findings. We try to remedy this defect and to fill a more general lacuna in the literature by developing a systematic model that relies on utility-maximizing behavior by all participants, equilibrium in different markets, and stochastic forces with unequal incidence among participants.

An analysis that is adequate to cope with the many aspects of the rise and fall of families must incorporate concern by parents for children as expressed in altruism toward children, investments in the human capital of children, assortative mating in marriage markets, the demand for children, the treatment by parents of exceptionally able or handicapped children, and expectations about events in the next or in even later generations. Although these and other aspects of behavior are incorporated into a consistent framework based on maximizing behavior, we do not pretend to handle them all in a satisfactory manner. However, our approach indicates how a more complete analysis can be developed in the future.

The next section has a lengthy discussion of investments in the human capital of children. The discussion is lengthy because the relation between the earnings of parents and children is the major determinant of the rise and fall of most families. Section III moves on to consider the interaction between investments in human capital, transfers of material wealth (gifts and bequests) from parents to children, and the evolution of consumption over generations.

Section IV considers the effect of the number of children on intergenerational mobility of consumption and wealth and also the effect on mobility of assortative mating in marriage markets.

Section V assembles about a dozen studies of the degree of regression to the mean between parents and children in income, earnings, and wealth. Available studies are few and are based on limited data, but the magnitudes of some basic parameters of our model are suggested by the evidence for the United States and other countries.

Much of our analysis of human capital is based on the model developed in Becker's Woytinsky Lecture (1967) to explain different investments among families. However, that lecture is mainly concerned with inequality and skewness in earnings and wealth and does not derive relations between the earnings and assets of parents and children. The approach in this paper is also based on a series of papers by us in the last decade that analyzes marriage, fertility, altruism of parents, and long-run equilibrium relations between parents and children (see esp. Becker 1974, 1981; Becker and Tomes 1976, 1979; Tomes 1981).

The present paper is closest in spirit to Becker and Tomes (1979), but these papers differ in important ways. We believe that the present discussion is a considerable improvement. We now distinguish human capital and earnings from other wealth, and we incorporate restrictions on the intergenerational transfer of debt. We assume now that parents' utility depends on the utility of children instead of on the permanent income of children. We also consider the effect of endogenous fertility on the relation between the wealth and consumption of parents and children. These improvements explain why the implications of the present paper are sometimes quite different from those of the earlier paper. In an essay devoted to critiquing parts of Becker (1981), Becker and Tomes (1984), and an earlier draft of this paper, Goldberger (1985) sometimes fails to see these differences between the current paper and our earlier work. We comment further on his critique elsewhere in this paper.

Since inequality over generations and inequality between families are closely related (as implied by eq. [1]), any adequate analysis of inequality must also consider marital patterns, fertility, expectations about future generations, and investments in human capital. Therefore, it is hardly surprising that a growing literature during the last 15 years has tried to integrate more realistic models of family behavior into models of the distribution of income and wealth.[1] Although this literature and our work have many similarities, the present paper is almost alone in relating the rise and fall of families to investments in human capital that interact with the accumulation of assets, the evolution of consumption, and the demand for children.

II. EARNINGS AND HUMAN CAPITAL

Perfect Capital Markets

Some children have an advantage because they are born into families with greater ability, greater emphasis on childhood learning, and other favorable cultural and genetic attributes. Both biology and culture are transmitted from parents to children, one encoded in DNA and the other in a family's culture. Much less is known about the transmission of cultural attributes than of biological ones, and even less is known about the relative contributions of biology and culture to the distinctive endowment of each family. We do not need to separate cultural from genetic endowments, and we will not try to specify the exact mechanism of cultural transmission. We follow our previous paper (Becker and Tomes 1979; see also, e.g., Bevan 1979) in assuming as a first approximation that both are transmitted by a stochastic-linear or Markov equation:

$$E_t^i = \alpha_t + hE_{t-1}^i + v_t^i, \tag{2}$$

where E_t^i is the endowment (or vector of endowments) of the ith family in the tth generation, h is the degree (or vector of degrees) of "inheritability" of these endowments, and v_t^i measures unsystematic components or luck in the transmission process. We assume that parents cannot invest in their children's endowment.

A priori restriction on the magnitude or even on the sign of the inheritability of endowments are unnecessary since the degree of inheritability can be estimated from accurate information on the earnings of parents and children (and perhaps also grandparents). Yet the assumption that endowments are only partially inherited, that h is less than unity and greater than zero, is a plausible generalization to cultural endowments of what is known about the inheritance of genetic traits. This assumption implies that endowments regress to the mean: children with well-endowed parents tend also to have above-average endowments but smaller relative to the mean than their parents', whereas children with poorly endowed parents tend also to have below-average endowments but larger relative to the mean than their parents'.

The term α_t can be interpreted as the social endowment common to all members of a given cohort in the same society. If the social endowment were constant over time, and if $h < 1$, the average endowment would eventually equal $1/(1-h)$ times the social endowment (i.e., $\lim \overline{E}_t = \alpha/[1-h]$). However, α may not be constant because, for example, governments invest in the social endowment.

Practically all formal models of the distribution of income that consider wages and abilities assume that abilities automatically translate into earnings, mediated sometimes by demands for different kinds of abilities (see, e.g., Roy 1950; Mandelbrot 1962; Tinbergen 1970; Bevan and Stiglitz 1979). This is useful in understanding certain gross features of the distribution of earnings, such as its skewness, but is hardly satisfactory for analyzing the effect of parents on their children's earnings. Parents not only pass on some of their endowments to children, but they also influence the adult earnings of their children by expenditures on their skills, health, learning, motivation, "credentials," and many other characteristics. These expenditures are determined not only by the abilities of children but also by the incomes, preferences, and fertility of parents as well as the public expenditures on education and other human capital of children and other variables. Since earnings are practically the sole income for most persons, parents influence the economic welfare of their children primarily by influencing their potential earnings.

To analyze these influences in a simple way, assume 2 periods of life, childhood and adulthood, and that adult earnings depend on human capital (H), partly perhaps as a measure of credentials, and market luck (ℓ):

$$Y_t = \gamma(T_t, f_t)H_t + \ell_t. \tag{3}$$

The earnings of 1 unit of human capital (γ) is determined by equilibrium in factor markets. It depends positively on technological knowledge (T) and negatively on the ratio of the amount of human capital to nonhuman capital in the economy (f). Since we are concerned with differences among families, the exact value of γ is not usually important because that is common to all families. Therefore, we assume that the measurement of H is chosen so that $\gamma = 1$.

Although human capital takes many forms, including skills and abilities, personality, appearance, reputation, and appropriate credentials, we further simplify by assuming that it is homogeneous and the same "stuff" in different families. Since much research demonstrates that investments during childhood are crucial to later development (see, e.g., Bloom 1976), we assume also that the total amount of human capital accumulated, including on-the-job training, is proportional to the amount accumulated during childhood. Then adult human capital and expected earnings are determined by endowments inherited from parents and by parental (x) and public expenditures (s) on his or her development:

$$H_t = \psi(x_{t-1}, s_{t-1}, E_t), \quad \text{with} \quad \psi_j > 0, \quad j = x, s, E. \tag{4}$$

Ability, early learning, and other aspects of a family's cultural and genetic "infrastructure" usually raise the marginal effect of family and public expenditures on the production of human capital; that is,

$$\frac{\partial^2 H_t}{\partial j_{t-1} \partial E_t} = \psi_{jE} > 0, \quad j = x, s. \tag{5}$$

The marginal rate of return on parental expenditures (r_m) is defined by the equation

$$\frac{\partial Y_t}{\partial x_{t-1}} = \frac{\partial H_t}{\partial x_{t-1}} = \psi_x = 1 + r_m(x_{t-1}, s_{t-1}, E_t), \tag{6}$$

where $\partial r_m / \partial E > 0$ by inequality (5).

Although the human capital of different persons may be close substitutes in production, each person forms a separate human-capital "market." Rates of return to him depend on the amount invested in him as well as on aggregate stocks of human capital. Marginal rates of return eventually decline as more is invested in a person because investment costs eventually rise as his forgone earnings rise. Also, benefits decline increasingly rapidly as his remaining working life shortens (see the more extended discussion in Becker [1975]).

Nonhuman capital or assets can usually be purchased and sold in relatively efficient markets. Presumably, therefore, returns on assets are less sensitive to the amount owned by any person than are returns on human capital. Little is known about the effect of abilities, other endowments, and wealth on returns from different assets, although some theory suggests a positive relation (see Ehrlich and Ben-Zion [1976]; see also the evidence in Yitzhaki [1984]). Our analysis only requires the reasonable assumption that returns on assets are much less sensitive to endowments and accumulations by any person than are returns on human capital (a similar assumption is made in Becker [1967, 1975]). A simple special case of this assumption is that the rate of return on assets is the same to all persons.

Much of the endowed luck of children (v_t) is revealed to parents prior to most of their investment in children. Therefore, we assume that rates of return on these investments are fully known to parents (as long as the social environment [α_t] and public expenditures [s_{t-1}] are known). Parents must decide how to allocate their total "bequest" to children between human capital and assets. We assume initially that parents can borrow at the asset interest rate to finance expenditures on children and that this debt can become the obligation of children when they are adults.

Parents are assumed to maximize the welfare of children when no reduction in their own consumption or leisure is entailed. Then parents borrow whatever is necessary to maximize the net income (earnings minus debt) of their children, which requires that expenditures on the human capital of children equate the marginal rate of return to the interest rate:

$$r_m = r_t, \quad \text{or} \quad \hat{x}_{t-1} = g(E_t, s_{t-1}, r_t), \tag{7}$$

$$\text{with } g_E > 0 \text{ (by eq. [6]),} \quad g_r < 0, \quad \text{and also with } g_s < 0 \tag{8}$$

if public and private expenditures are substitutes. Parents can separate investments in children (an example of the separation theorem) from their own resources and altruism toward children because borrowed funds can be made the children's obligation.

The optimal investment is given in figure 1 by the intersection of the horizontal "supply curve of funds," rr, with a negatively inclined demand curve (HH or $H'H'$). This figure clearly shows that better-endowed children accumulate more human capital; those with the endowment E accumulate ON units of expenditure, while those with $E' > E$ accumulate $ON' > ON$. Therefore, better-endowed children would have higher expected earnings because equation (3) converts human capital into expected adult earnings. The total effect of endowments on earnings, and the inequality and skewness

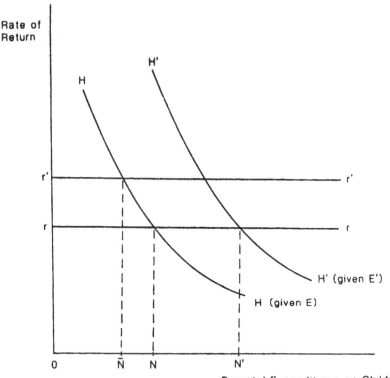

FIGURE I

RATES OF RETURN ON PARENTAL EXPENDITURES ON CHILDREN

in earnings relative to that in endowments, is raised by the positive relation between endowments and expenditures.

Clearly, an increase in the rate of interest reduces the investment in human capital and, hence, earnings. Compare ON and $O\overline{N}$ in figure 1. The effect of an increase in public expenditures is less clear. If public expenditures are perfect substitutes dollar for dollar for private expenditures, the production of human capital would be determined by their sum ($x + s$) and by E; an increase in public expenditures would then induce an equal decrease in private (parental) expenditures, and the accumulation of human capital would be unchanged. Even then, a sufficiently large increase in public expenditures would raise the accumulation of human capital because private expenditures cannot be negative.

Note that the human capital and earnings of children would not depend on their parents' assets and earnings because poor parents can borrow what is needed to finance the optimal investment in their children. However, the income of children would depend on parents because gifts and bequests of assets and debt would be sensitive to the earnings and wealth of parents. Indeed, wealthy parents would tend to self-finance the whole accumulation of human capital and to add a sizable gift of assets as well.

Although the earnings and human capital of children would not be directly related to parents' earnings and wealth, they would be indirectly related through the inheritability of endowments. The greater the degree of inheritability, the more closely related would be the human capital and earnings of parents and children. To derive the relation between the earnings of parents and children, substitute the optimal level of x given by equation (7) into the earnings-generating equation (3) to get

$$Y_t = \psi[g(E_t, s_{t-1}, r_t), s_{t-1}, E_t] + \ell_t = \phi(E_t, s_{t-1}, r_t) + \ell_t, \tag{9}$$

$$\text{where } \phi_E = \psi_g g_E + \psi_E = \left(\frac{\partial Y}{\partial x}\right)\left(\frac{\partial x}{\partial E}\right) + \frac{\partial Y}{\partial E} > 0.$$

Since this equation relates E to Y, ℓ, g, and r, E_t can be replaced by E_{t-1} from (2) and then Y_t can be related to Y_{t-1}, ℓ_t, v_t, ℓ_{t-1}, and other variables:

$$Y_t = F(Y_{t-1}, \ell_{t-1}, v_t, h, s_{t-1}, s_{t-2}, r_t, r_{t-1}, \alpha_t) + \ell_t. \tag{10}$$

Not surprisingly, the earnings of parents and children are more closely related when endowments are more inheritable (h). However, the relation between their earnings also depends on the total effect of endowments on earnings (ϕ_E). If this effect is independent of the level of endowments ($\phi_{EE} = 0$), then

$$Y_t = c_t + \alpha_t\phi_E + hY_{t-1} + \ell_t^*,$$
$$\text{where } \ell_t^* = \ell_t - h\ell_{t-1} + \phi_E v_t \tag{11}$$
$$\text{and } c_t = c(s_{t-1}, s_{t-2}, h, r_t, r_{t-1}).$$

The intercept c_t would differ among families if government expenditures (s_{t-1}, s_{t-2}) differed among them. The stochastic term ℓ_t^* is negatively related to the market luck of parents.

If the luck of adults and children (ℓ^*) is held constant, the earnings of children would regress to the mean at the rate of $1 - h$. However, the coefficient is biased downward by the "transitory" component of lifetime earnings of parents (ℓ_{t-1}) in OLS regressions of the actual lifetime earnings of children on the actual lifetime earnings of parents (Y_t on Y_{t-1}). If c_t is the same for all families, the expected value of the regression coefficient would equal

$$b_{t,t-1} = h\left(1 - \frac{\sigma_\ell^2}{\sigma_y^2}\right), \tag{12}$$

where σ_ℓ^2 and σ_y^2 are the variances of ℓ_t and Y_t. This coefficient is closer to the degree of inheritability when the inequality in the transitory component of lifetime earnings is a smaller fraction of the total inequality in lifetime earnings.

Families of particular races, religions, castes, or other characteristics who suffer from market discrimination earn less than do families without these characteristics. Persons with characteristics that are subject to discrimination earn less than do persons not subject to discrimination even when their parents' earnings are equal. Persons subject to discrimination would earn less—given the degree of inheritability—as long as discrimination reduces the earnings from given endowments, for discrimination then reduces the intercept in the equation that relates the earnings of parents and children ($c_t + \alpha_t \sigma_E$ in eq. [11]).

Imperfect Access to Capital

Access to capital markets to finance investments in children separates the transmission of earnings from the generosity and resources of parents. Economists have argued for a long time, however, that human capital is poor collateral to lenders. Children can "default" on the market debt contracted for them by working less energetically or by entering occupations with lower earnings and higher psychic income. Such "moral hazard" from the private nature of information about work effort and employment opportunities can greatly affect the earnings realized from human capital. Moreover, most societies are reluctant to collect debts from children that were contracted by their parents, perhaps because the minority of parents who do not care much about the welfare of their children would raise their own consumption by leaving large debts to children.

To bring out sharply the effect of imperfect access to debt contracted for children, we assume that parents must finance investments in children either by selling assets, by reducing their own consumption, by reducing the consumption by children, or by raising the labor force activities of children. Consider parents without assets[2] who would have to finance the efficient investment in human capital (say, ON in fig. 1) partly by reducing their own consumption because they cannot contract debt for their children. A reduction in their own consumption would raise its marginal utility relative to the marginal utility of resources invested in children. This would discourage some expenditure on children. Consequently, both the amount invested in children and parental consumption are reduced by limitations on the debt that can be left to children. Clearly, richer parents would tend to have both higher consumption and greater investments in children.

Therefore, expenditures on children by parents without assets depend not only on endowments of children and public expenditures, as in equation (7), but also on earnings of parents (Y_{t-1}), their generosity toward children (w), and perhaps now also on the uncertainty (ϵ_{t-1}) about the luck of children and later descendants, as in

$$\hat{x}_{t-1} = g^* (E_t, s_{t-1}, Y_{t-1}, \epsilon_{t-1}, w), \quad \text{with} \quad g^*_Y > 0. \quad (13)$$

Public and private expenditures would not be perfect substitutes if public expenditures affected rates of return on private expenditures, as when tuition is subsidized. However, if they are perfect substitutes, g^* would depend simply on the sum of s_{t-1} and Y_{t-1}: an increase in public expenditures is then equivalent to an equal increase in parental earnings. The effect of children's endowments on investments is now ambiguous ($g^*_E \gtreqless 0$) because an increase in their endowments raises the resources of children as well as the productivity of investments in their human capital. Expenditures on children are discouraged when children are expected to be richer because that lowers the marginal utility to parents of additional expenditures on children.

The demand curves for expenditures in figure 2 are similar to those in figure 1 and are higher in families with better-endowed children. The cost of funds to a family is no longer constant or the same to all families. Increased expenditures on children lower the consumption by parents, which raises their subjective discount rates (the shadow cost of funds). These discount rates are smaller to parents with higher earnings or more poorly endowed children. Expenditures on children in each family are determined by the intersection of supply and demand curves. An increase in parental earnings shifts the supply curve to the right and induces greater expenditures on children (compare S_1 and S_1' in fig. 2). The distribution of intersection points determines the distribution of investments and rates of return and, hence, as shown in Becker (1967, 1975), the inequality and skewness in the distribution of earnings.

By substituting equation (13) into the earnings-generating equations (3) and (4), we get

$$\begin{aligned} Y_t &= \psi[g^* [E_t, Y_{t-1}, k_{t-1}), s_{t-1}, E_t] + \ell_t \\ &= \phi^* (E_t, Y_{t-1}, k_{t-1}) + \ell_t, \end{aligned} \quad (14)$$

where k_{t-1} includes w, s_{t-1}, and ϵ_{t-1}. Earnings of children now depend directly on the earnings of parents as well as indirectly through the transmission of endowments. Some authors (e.g., Bowles 1972; Meade 1976; Atkinson 1983) argue for a direct effect because "contacts" of parents are said to raise the opportunities of children; others argue for a direct effect because parents are said to receive utility directly from the human capital of children.

FIGURE 2

PARENTAL EXPENDITURES ON CHILDREN, WITH CAPITAL CONSTRAINTS

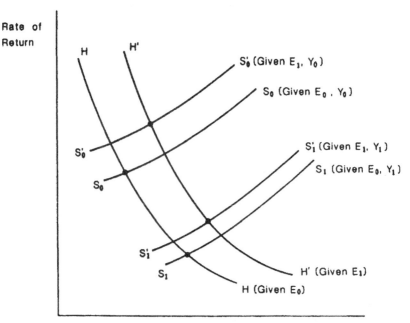

Parental Expenditures on Children

Fortunately, the effects of parent earnings on access to capital can be distinguished analytically from its effects on "contacts" and "utility."

The indirect effect of parents' earnings on the earnings of children operates through the transmission of endowments and can be found by substituting E_{t-1} for E_t and then using equation (14) for E_{t-1}:

$$Y_t = F(Y_{t-1}, Y_{t-2}, \ell_{t-1}, v_t, h, \alpha_t, k_{t-1}, k_{t-2}) + \ell_t. \qquad (15)$$

The sum of both the direct and the indirect effects of parents' earnings is

$$\frac{\partial Y_t}{\partial Y_{t-1}} = \phi^*_{Y_{t-1}} + \frac{h\phi^*_{E_t}}{\phi^*_{E_{t-1}}} > 0. \qquad (16)$$

The indirect effect of grandparents' earnings, holding parents' earnings constant, is

$$\frac{\partial Y_t}{\partial Y_{t-2}} = -h\phi^*_{Y_{t-2}}\left(\frac{\phi^*_{E_t}}{\phi^*_{E_{t-1}}}\right) < 0. \qquad (17)$$

Earnings of grandparents and grandchildren are indirectly linked through the constraints on financing investments in children. That is, the earnings of parents are not sufficient to describe the effects on children of both the resources and the endowments of parents. Equation (17) shows that an increase in the earnings of grandparents lowers the earnings of grandchildren when parents' earnings and grandchildren's luck are held constant. Constraints on financing investments in children introduce a negative relation between the earnings of grandparents and children and raise the positive effect of parents' earnings on children's earnings.[3]

If Y_t were approximately linearly related to E_t and Y_{t-1}, then[4]

$$Y_t \cong c_t' + (\beta^* + h) Y_{t-1} - \beta^* h Y_{t-2} + \ell_t^*, \quad \text{with} \quad \beta^* = \phi_Y^*. \quad (18)$$

The coefficient of parents' earnings exceeds the degree of inheritability by the marginal propensity to invest in the human capital of children (β^*). As in equation (12), OLS estimates of the coefficient of Y_{t-1} are biased downward by the transitory component of lifetime earnings. Ordinary least squares estimates of the relation between Y_t and Y_{t-1} tend toward[5]

$$\beta^* < b_{t,t-1}^* = \frac{b_{t,t-1 \cdot t-2}^*}{1 + h\beta^*} \leq \min(1, \beta^* + h, b_{t,t-1 \cdot t-2}^*), \quad (19)$$

where $b_{t,t-1 \cdot t-2}^*$ is the partial regression coefficient between Y_t and Y_{t-1}. Therefore, both partial and simple regression coefficients between the life-time earnings of parents and children provide upper limits of the effect of capital market constraints on the propensity to invest in children. The biases in these OLS estimates can sometimes be overcome by the use of instruments for the lifetime earnings of parents, such as the lifetime earnings of uncles or of great-grandparents (see Goldberger 1979; Behrman and Taubman 1985).

The direct relation between the earnings of parents and children in equation (14) is likely to be concave rather than linear because obstacles to the self-financing investments in children decline as parents' earnings increase. When investments in the human capital of children are sufficient to lower marginal rates of return to the market rate on assets, further increases in parents' earnings raise the assets bequeathed to children but have no effect on the amount invested in the human capital of children (if rates on assets are independent of parents' earnings). Presumably, "contacts" of parents and the direct utility to parents from the human capital of children are more important in richer families. Hence, capital constraints have different implications for the curvature of the relation between the earnings of parents and children than do these alternative explanations.

Becker and Tomes's (1979) discussion implies that, because β^* and h enter symmetrically, even knowledge of the true values of the coefficients attached to parents' and grandparents' incomes in an equation such as (18) could not identify β^* and h without other information, such as which coefficient is larger. Earnings in rich families not subject to capital constraints are related by the simple equation (11), which does not include β^*. Therefore, h would be known if the coefficient on parents' earnings in rich families is known. Then β^* and h could be distinguished in equation (18) by using this information on h.

In earlier drafts of the present paper we unwisely denote β^* by β, although β in Becker and Tomes (1979) refers to a different concept. Since the coefficient β^* measures the marginal propensity to invest in the human capital of children by capital-constrained parents who are prevented from making the wealth-maximizing investment in their children, β^* does not enter the earnings-generating equation for richer families (eq. [11]) who are not so constrained. Put differently, β^* is zero in richer families. There is no general presumption about the size of β^* relative to h even in low-income families because β^* depends on public transfers to children, incomes, and other variables.

The coefficient β in our earlier work (see, e.g., Becker and Tomes 1979) measures the marginal propensity to bequeath wealth to children when parents can leave debt to children and when human wealth is not distinguished from other wealth. Our earlier work and Section III of the present paper show that this propensity depends on the generosity of parents toward children and may not be sensitive to the level of income. However, it is likely to be large in most families (see Sec. III). Such a presumption motivated the assumption in our earlier work that $\beta > h$, an assumption used to identify β and h from the coefficients in an equation such as (18).

Goldberger (1985, 19–20) correctly states that we did not provide an independent way to evaluate this assumption. The present paper makes progress toward the goal of identification because h can be determined from knowledge of the coefficients in the equation for the earnings of parents and children in (richer) families who leave positive bequests to children. Given h, β^* (or a more general relation between β^* and parents' earnings) can be determined from knowledge of the coefficients on parents' or on grandparents' earnings in the earnings equation for poorer families who are capital constrained. Even β—the marginal propensity of parents to bequeath wealth to children—might be determined from information on the relation between the consumption of parents and children in richer families (see the next section).

Rich families can more readily self-finance a given investment in children than can poor and middle-level families. Richer families also have better than average endowments, which raises the wealth-maximizing investment in human capital by richer families above that by poorer families. Empirical observations strongly indicate that richer families come closer to financing the optimal investment in the human capital of children than do poorer families. This indicates that the wealth effect on investments in children dominates the endowment effect. The wealth effect would dominate if endowments regress strongly to the mean, for then the endowments of richer children would be much below those of their parents and the endowments of poorer children would be much above those of their parents. The evidence considered in Section VI does suggest that endowments relevant to earnings do regress strongly to the mean.

If returns on assets are not highly sensitive to earnings and endowments, the greater resources available to rich families to finance wealth-maximizing investments in children imply that equilibrium marginal rates of return on investments in children are lower in richer families than they are in more capital-constrained poor and middle-level families even though endowments and average rates of return are higher in richer families. Equilibrium marginal rates then tend to decline, perhaps not monotonically, as earnings of parents rise. Eventually, marginal rates on human capital would equal the rate of return on assets, and then marginal rates would be relatively constant as parents' earnings rose. Poorer children are at a disadvantage both because they inherit lower endowments and because capital constraints on their parents limit the market value of the endowments that they do inherit.

If marginal rates are lower in richer families, a small redistribution of human capital away from these families and toward children from poorer families would raise the average marginal rate of return across different families. This would raise efficiency even though endowments and the average productivity of investments in children are greater in richer families (see also Becker 1967, 1975). The usual conflict between "equity," as measured by inequality, and efficiency is absent because a redistribution of investments toward less advantaged children is equivalent to an improvement in the efficiency of capital markets.

Larger public expenditures on the human capital of children in families subject to capital constraints raise the total amount invested in these children even when public and private expenditures are perfect substitutes. The reason is that public expenditures increase the total resources of a family if taxes are imposed on other families. An increase in family resources in capital-constrained families is shared between parents and investments in children in a ratio determined by the marginal propensity to invest (β^*). If public and private expenditures are perfect substitutes, the fraction $1 - \beta^*$ of government expenditures on children is offset by compensatory responses of their parents. That is, to further equity toward other family members, even constrained parents redistribute some time and expenditures away from children who benefit from government expenditures to siblings and themselves. Compensatory responses of parents apparently greatly weaken the effects of public health programs, food supplements to poorer pregnant women, some head start programs, and social security programs (see the discussion in Becker (1981, 125–26, 251–53).

We saw in Section II that the total investment in children in families with positive bequests to children is unaffected by public expenditures on children that are perfect substitutes for parents' expenditures. Parents reduce their own expenditures to offset fully such public expenditures. However, public and private expenditures may not be perfect substitutes. If, for example, public expenditures raise rates of return on family expenditures, increased public expenditures could even raise family expenditures because a "substitution effect" works against the "redistribution effect."

Goldberger criticizes us (1985, 9–10; Simon [in press] repeats Goldberger's criticism) because we emphasize redistribution or income effects at the expense of substitution effects when discussing various public programs. Since our first joint paper we have explicitly noted that government programs may have substitution effects by changing rates of return on parental investments in children (see Becker and Tomes 1976, S156). However, we have emphasized the redistribution effects of many programs—including head start programs, welfare, aid to pregnant women, and social security—because the redistribution effects are clear, while substitution effects are not clear, even in direction. For example, what is the substitution effect of a social security program? Or is there evidence that head start programs raise rather than lower marginal rates of return on parents' expenditures? (See Becker 1981, 126.) Although tuition subsidies to education may appear to raise rates of return on parents' expenditures on education, actually they might lower marginal rates of return when combined with rationing of places (see Peltzman 1973).

Redistributions of expenditures within families induced by government subsidies can explain why many programs appear to have weak effects on participants (see the discussion in Becker [1981, 125–26, 251–53]). Of course, weak effects on participants do not imply that substitution effects are negligible or that they reinforce redistribution effects, but weak effects do imply that these programs do not have strong offsetting substitution effects.

Capital-constrained parents could finance expenditures on children by reducing their life-cycle savings if children could be counted on to care for elderly parents. In many societies, poorer and middle-income-level parents are supported during old age by children instead of by the sale of gold, jewelry, rugs, land, houses, or other assets that could be accumulated by parents at younger ages. Our analysis suggests that these parents choose to rely on children instead of on assets because rates of return on investments in children are higher than they are on other assets.

In effect, poorer and middle-level parents and children often have an implicit contract, enforced imperfectly by social sanctions, that parents invest in children in return for support during old age. Both parents and children would be made better off by such contracts if investments in children yield a high return, where included in the yield is any insurance provided by children against an unusually long old age.

III. Assets and Consumption

Our analysis implies that bequests and gifts of assets to children do not rise rapidly until marginal rates of return on investments in children are reduced to the rate on assets. Further increases in contributions from parents then mainly take the form of assets rather than of human capital because returns on assets are less sensitive to the amount accumulated. These conclusions imply that most bequests to children are found in a relatively small number of richer families and that the ratio of assets to human capital of children would rise as parents' wealth rose. The empirical evidence clearly indicates that assets and income from nonhuman capital are much more important in richer than in poorer families.

Empirical studies also indicate that the proportion of income saved remains reasonably constant or that it rises as income, including "permanent" income, increases (see the studies reviewed in Mayer [1972]). However, these studies provide flawed measures of savings because investments in human capital and "capital gains or losses" from intergenerational increases or decreases in endowments are not considered savings. Lower- and middle-income families invest primarily in their children's human capital. Endowments tend to increase from parents to children at lower income levels and to decrease from parents to children at higher levels because of regression to the mean in endowments. Therefore, empirical studies understate relative savings by lower- and middle-income families because both intergenerational capital gains and investments in human capital are relatively larger in these families. We believe that an appropriate concept of savings may well show that the fraction saved declines as permanent income rises. After all, this would be expected if equilibrium marginal rates of return on investments in children decline as income increases.

Our conclusion that most bequests of assets are found in a relatively small number of richer families does not presuppose "class" differences in altruism or other class differences in the propensity to save, as in Kaldor (1956) and Pasinetti (1962), or as used in Atkinson (1983). In our analysis, all families have the same intrinsic tendency to save and leave estates because they are assumed to have the same altruism toward children. Still, apparent "class" differences in savings would exist because poorer families save mainly in the human capital of children, which are not recorded as savings or bequests.

The assets of a person are determined by bequests from parents and by his own life-cycle accumulations. We assume that parents choose bequests by maximizing their expected utility, subject to the expected earnings and life-cycle asset accumulation of children. To develop further our analysis of bequests, we must turn to an explicit treatment of utility maximization by parents. We continue to assume, until the next section, that each adult has one child without marriage.

Suppose that the utility function of parents is additively separable in their own consumption and in various characteristics of children. Most of our analysis does not depend on a specific measure of these characteristics as long as they are positively related to the total resources of children. However, we can simplify the relation between the consumption by parents and children by assuming that parents' utility depends on the utility of children (U_c), as in

$$U_t = u(Z_t) + \delta U_{t+1}, \tag{20}$$

where Z_t is the consumption of parents and δ is a constant that measures the altruism of parents.

If the preference function given by equation (20) is the same for all generations and if consumption during childhood is ignored, then the utility of the parent indirectly would equal the discounted sum of the utilities from the consumption of all descendants:

$$U_t = \sum_{i=0}^{\infty} \delta^i u(Z_{t+i}). \tag{21}$$

The utility of parents depends directly only on the utility of children, but it depends indirectly on all descendants because children are concerned about their descendants.

We assume that parents succeed in maximizing their "dynastic" utility, as represented by equation (21). This rules out bargaining by children to obtain larger transfers than those that maximize parents' utility. A more general assumption is that parents maximize a weighted average of their own and their children's utility, with weights determined by bargaining power (see the normative use of this assumption in Nerlove, Razin, and Sadka [1984]); however, this generalization would not change any major conclusions.

With perfect certainty about rates of return and incomes in all generations, the first-order conditions to maximize utility are the usual ones. For example, with a constant elasticity of substitution in consumption,

$$u'(Z) = Z^{-}\sigma, \qquad (22)$$

where $\sigma > 0$, and

$$\ln Z_{t+1} = \frac{1}{\sigma}\ln(1 + r_{t+1})\delta + \ln Z_t, \qquad (23)$$

where r_{t+1} measures the marginal rate of return to investments in children in period t. With an exponential utility function,

$$u'(Z) = e^{-pZ}, \quad p > 0, \qquad (24)$$

and

$$Z_{t+1} = \frac{1}{p}\ln(1 + r_{t+1})\delta + Z_t. \qquad (25)$$

If parents could finance expenditures on their children with debt that becomes the obligation of children, the marginal cost of funds would equal the rate on assets in all families. Then equation (23) or equation (25) implies that the relative or absolute change in consumption between generations would be the same in all families that are equally altruistic (δ) and that have equal degrees of substitution (σ or p). Each family would maintain its relative or absolute consumption position over generations, and consumption would not regress to the mean. Stated differently, any degree of relative or absolute inequality in consumption in the parents' generation would then be fully transmitted to the children's generation.

Nevertheless, the earnings of children would still regress to the mean, regardless of the altruism of parents, as long as endowments are not fully inherited by children (see Sec. II). Consumption does not automatically regress to the mean when earnings do because parents can anticipate that their children would tend to earn less or more than they do. They can use debt and assets to offset the effect on wealth of the expected regression in earnings.

Therefore, although earnings may regress to the mean, well-being as measured by consumption would not regress at all if parents have full access to capital markets to finance investments in their children's human capital. The assets bequeathed to children would rise and the debt bequeathed would fall as parents' earnings rose. This crucial distinction between regression across generations in earnings and consumption appears to have been ignored in the extensive literature on the mobility of families.

Still, the main implication of equations such as (23) and (25) is disquieting, namely, that all initial differences among families in consumption and total resources are fully transmitted to future descendants. Surely, the resources of the current generation are essentially independent of the resources of their distant ancestors. Several forces are responsible for the decay over time in the influence of the past on consumption and total resources. These include difficulties in transmitting debt to children, uncertainty about the future, the effect of parents' wealth on fertility, and imperfect assortative mating. We consider these variables in turn.

Consumption is fully separated from earnings only when children can be obligated for debts created by parents. If debt cannot be created for children (see the discussion in Sec. II), parents without assets could not offset any upward regression in the endowments and earnings of their children. Parents would face a complicated maximization problem because capital constraints may be binding only for some descendants. The results of utility maximization can be summarized by endogenously determined subjective discount rates and marginal rates of return for each generation of a family that guide as well as reflect the decisions for that generation. These shadow prices exceed the rate on assets whenever constraints on access to debt prevent borrowing from children. Discount rates of (richer) parents with sufficient assets to raise or lower their bequests to children would equal the rate on assets.

We argue in Section II that equilibrium marginal rates of return of constrained parents tend to decline as their earnings become larger. Then equation (23) or equation (25) implies that the relative or absolute growth in consumption between generations would also decline as the earnings of parents rose. However, the relative or absolute growth in consumption between generations would be constant among richer families who receive a marginal rate of return equal to the rate on assets. Therefore, the consumption of children would regress more rapidly upward to the mean in poor families than downward to the mean in rich families. This produces a convex relation between the consumption of parents and children. At the same time, earnings regress more slowly upward in poor families than they regress downward in rich families.

Assets bequeathed to children in richer families act as a buffer to offset any regression to the mean in the earnings of children. The richest families could maintain their consumption over time compared to less rich families only by increasing their bequests sufficiently to offset the stronger downward regression in the earnings of the richest children. As a result, bequests could regress away from the mean.

Our analysis of consumption has assumed perfect certainty, although uncertainty about much of the luck of future generations is not fully insurable or diversifiable. If each generation knows the yields on investments in the human capital of children and in bequests to children, but may not have perfect certainty about the earnings of children and is still more uncertain about subsequent generations, then the first-order condition for maximization of expected utility is

$$\epsilon_t u'(Z_{t+1}) = \left(\frac{\delta^{-1}}{1 + r_{t+1}}\right) u'(Z_t), \tag{26}$$

where ϵ_t refers to expectations taken at generation t before any new information about earnings and other wealth of descendants is acquired between t and $t + 1$.

With the exponential function, this first-order condition becomes

$$Z_{t+1} = c + \frac{1}{p}\ln(1 + r_{t+1})\delta + Z_t + n_{t+1}, \tag{27}$$

where c is a positive constant and where n_{t+1}, the distribution of fluctuations in Z_{t+1} around $\hat{Z}_{t+1}$, does not depend on Z_t. If the capital market permitted all families to finance the wealth-maximizing investments in their children, $r_{t+1} = r_a$ in all families, where r_a is the asset rate. Then equation (27) implies that the growth in consumption follows a random walk with drift (Kotlikoff, Shoven, and Spivak [1986] derive a similar result when the length of life is uncertain). More generally, equation (27) shows that, if the utility function is exponential, uncertainty adds a random term to consumption but does not basically change the implications of our analysis concerning the degree of regression to the mean in consumption.

A second-order approximation to the left-hand side of equation (26) readily shows that the effect of uncertainty on the degree of regression toward the mean with a more general utility function than the exponential depends on the signs and magnitudes of second- and higher-order derivatives of the utility function.[6] Uncertainty could induce regression toward the mean in consumption even when there would be none with certainty. However, uncertainty could also induce regression away from the mean, or greater rates of regression toward the mean at higher rather than at lower levels of consumption, with utility functions that otherwise seem as empirically relevant as those having opposite implications. Consequently, we cannot make any strong statement concerning the effect of uncertainty on the degree of regression toward the mean in the consumption of parents and children.

IV. Fertility and Marriage

Regression toward the mean in marriage and the positive effect of wealth on fertility help explain why differences in consumption and total resources among richer families do not persist indefinitely into future generations. Here we only sketch out an analysis. The implications of fertility and marriage for consumption and bequests are also discussed in Becker and Tomes (1984) and Becker and Barro (1985).

Let us first drop the assumption that all parents have only one child and generalize the utility function in equation (20) to

$$U_p = u(Z_p) + a(n)nU_c, \qquad (28)$$

with $a' < 0$, where U_c is the utility of each of the n identical children and $a(n)$ is the degree of altruism per child. The first-order condition for the optimal number of children is that the marginal utility and marginal cost of children are equal. The marginal cost of children to parents equals net expenditures on children, including any bequests and other gifts. The marginal costs are determined by the circumstances and decisions of parents.

The previous section showed that the consumption and total resources of wealthy families may not regress down because these families can offset the downward regression in the earnings of their children by sufficiently large gifts and bequests. Fortunately, this unrealistic implication does not hold when the number of children can vary. Richer families tend to spend some of their greater resources on additional children. This reduces the bequest to each child below what it would be if they did not increase the number of children (see the proofs in Becker and Barro [1985]). A positive response of fertility to increases in wealth causes consumption and wealth per child to regress down, perhaps rapidly.

Poor and middle-income families without assets who are prevented from leaving debt to their children must trade off between earnings of each child, number of children, and parent consumption. The human capital invested in each child and, hence, the earnings of each child would then be negatively related to the number of children, as found in many studies (see, e.g., Blake 1981). The degree of regression to the mean in earnings among these families would be lower if fertility and parents' earnings are negatively related than if they are unrelated.

We do not have much to add to our previous analysis (see Becker and Tomes 1976; Becker 1981, chap. 6; Tomes 1981) of responses to differences between children. This analysis implies that richer families invest more human capital in better-endowed children and that they compensate other children with larger gifts and bequests. Poorer families who primarily invest in human capital face a conflict between the efficiency of greater investments in better-endowed children and the equity of greater investments in less well endowed children.

Despite the claim that observed differences between siblings in earnings is helpful in determining the degree of intergenerational mobility in earnings (see, e.g., Brittain 1977, 36–37), there is no necessary connection between the relation among siblings and the degree of intergenerational mobility. The reason is that differences in earnings between siblings is determined by characteristics within a single generation, such as the substitution between siblings in the utility function of parents, whereas intergenerational mobility in earnings is determined by differences across generations, such as the regression toward the mean of endowments (for a further discussion, see Tomes [1984]).

Regression to the mean in marriage—called imperfect positive assortative mating—also increases the degree of regression to the mean in earnings, consumption, and assets. However, the effect of marriage is less obvious than it may appear because parents often can anticipate the marital sorting of children. For example, wealthy parents would use gifts and bequests to offset some of the effects on the well-being of their children of the tendency for rich children to marry down, just as they use gifts and bequests to offset the effect of the regression downward in endowments. Although a full analysis of the interaction between the behavior of parents and expectations about the marriages of children is complicated by bargaining between in-laws on the gifts to be made to their children (some issues are discussed in Becker [1981, chap. 7] and Becker and Tomes [1984]), one cannot be satisfied with the many models that simply ignore expectations about children's marriages (see, e.g., Stiglitz 1969; Pryor 1973; Blinder 1976; Atkinson 1983).

Fertility and marriage have not been fully integrated into our analysis of intergenerational mobility—we only would insert "fully" into Goldberger's statement that "it's fair to say that [fertility and marriage are] not integrated into his intergenerational system" (1985, 13). However, the discussion in this section, the discussion of fertility in Becker and Barro (1985), and that of marriage in Becker and Tomes (1984) indicate to us that a utility-maximizing approach can integrate fertility, marriage, and intergenerational mobility into a common framework with useful implications.

V. Empirical Studies

Only a few empirical studies[7] link the earnings or wealth of different generations because of difficulties in gathering such information and because of insufficient interest by social scientists. Tables 1 and 2 present estimates from several studies of the degree of regression to the mean in earnings, income, and wealth, with coefficients of determination (when available), the number of observations, and notes about other variables (if any) included in each regression.

Table 1 has evidence on the earnings or incomes of sons and fathers from three studies based on separate data sets for the United States and one study each for England, Sweden, Switzerland, and Norway.[8] Although the average age of fathers and sons is quite different except in the Geneva study, both Atkinson (1981) and Behrman and Taubman (1983) present evidence that such differences in age do not greatly affect the estimated degree of regression to the mean.

The point estimates for most of the studies indicate that a 10 percent increase in father's earnings (or income) raises son's earnings by less than 2 percent. The highest point estimate is for York, England, where son's hourly earnings appear to be raised by 4.4 percent. However, the confidence intervals are sizable in all studies except Malmö because fathers' earnings "explain" a small fraction of the variation in the earnings of sons. Moreover, response errors and the transitory component in father's earnings (or income) may severely bias these regression coefficients.[9] Furthermore, the analysis in Section II indicates that transitory variations in lifetime earnings, and the omission of the earnings of grandparents, biases these regression coefficients downward. However, the error from omitting grandparents' earnings would be small if parents' earnings do not have a large effect (see eq. [18]) and if the transitory component in lifetime earnings is not large.

Hauser et al. (1975) reduce response errors and the transitory component by using a 4-year average of parents' income and a 3-year average of son's earnings, while Hauser (in press) uses a 4-year average of parents' income and a 5-year average of son's earnings during his initial period of labor force participation. Tsai (1983) not only averages incomes of parents over several years but also uses a retrospective report on their income in 1957. At Hauser's suggestion, we have corrected for the response errors in father's earnings by using the analysis in Bielby and Hauser (1977). Behrman and Taubman (1983) exclude sons who have less than 4 years of work experience because their earnings do not represent well their lifetime earnings. De Wolff and van Slijpe (1973) and Freeman (1981) reduce the importance of the transitory component by using the average income in father's occupation as an estimate of his lifetime earnings.

Despite these adjustments for response errors and transitory incomes, point estimates of the regression coefficients for earnings and incomes are rather low in all the studies (except for large incomes in Sweden). Moreover, a study in progress by Elizabeth Peters (1985) that uses data from the National Longitudinal Survey (the same survey used by Freeman [1981]) also finds a small coefficient (below .2) when a simple average of 4 years of son's earnings is regressed on a simple average of 5 years of father's earnings.

Some indirect evidence of sizable regression toward the mean in lifetime earnings is provided by life-cycle variations in earnings. By definition, en-

Table I
Regressions of Son's Income or Earnings on Father's Income or Earnings in Linear, Semilog, and Log-Linear Form

Location and Son's Year	Father's Year	Dependent	Independent	Other	Coefficient	t	R²	N	ε	Author
Wisconsin:										
1965–67	1957–62	E	IP	None	.15	8.5	.03	2069	.13	Hauser, Sewell, and Lutterman (1975)
·	1957–60	Log E	IP	None	.0006	10.6	.05	N.A.	.09	Hauser (in press)†
1974	1957–60	Log E	Log IP	None	.28‡	15.7	.09	2493	.28	Tsai (1983)†
United States, 1981–82	1981–82	Log E§	Log E§	None	.18	3.7	.02	722	.18	Behrman and Taubman (1983)
United States:										
1969 (young white)	When son was 14	Log H	Log I3	‖	.16	3.2	...	1607	.16	Freeman (1981)
1966 (older white)	When son was 14	Log H	Log I3	‖	.22	7.3	...	2131	.22	Freeman (1981)
1969 (young black)	When son was 14	Log H	Log I3	‖	.17	1.9	...	634	.17	Freeman (1981)
1966 (older black)	When son was 14	Log H	Log I3	‖	.02	0.4	...	947	.02	Freeman (1981)
York, England:										
1975–78	1950	Log H	Log W	None	.44	3.4	.06	198	.44	Atkinson (1981)
1975–78	1950	Log W	Log W	None	.36	3.3	.03	307	.36	Atkinson (1981)
Malmö, Sweden:										
1963	1938	Log I	ICD	None	.08	1.8	.19	545	.17*	de Wolff and van Slippe (1973)
					.12	2.4	.19	545	.13	
					.69	10.9	.19	545	.79	
Geneva, Switzerland, 1980	1950	IHH	IHH	None	.31	4.1	.02	801	.13	Girod (1984)
Sarpsborg, Norway, 1960	1960	Log I	Log I	None	.14	1.2	.01	115	.14	Soltow (1965)

NOTE: ε = elasticity of son's income or earnings with respect to father's income or earnings; E = earnings; H = hourly earnings; I = income; I3 = income in three-digit occupation; ICD = income-class dummy; IP = parents' income; IHH = household income; W = weekly earnings. * First 5 years in the labor force. † Also Robert M. Hauser (personal communication, October 2, 1984). ‡ Adjusted for response variability. § Adjusted for work experience. Sons with work experience of 4 years or less were excluded. The regression was weighted so that each father had equal weight. ‖ Work experience, three dummies for region of residence at age 14, five dummies for type of place of residence at age 14, and a dummy for living in one parent/female home at age 14. * The elasticities are values between pairs of income classes.

dowments are fixed over a lifetime. Therefore, earnings should be more closely related over the life cycle than across generations because endowments are imperfectly transmitted from parent to child (endowments are not a "fixed effect" across generations). Stated differently, relative to other members of his cohort, a person is usually much more similar to himself at different ages than is a father similar to his son when they are of the same age. The correlation coefficient between the "permanent" component of male earnings at different ages has been estimated from a 7-year panel to be about .7 in the United States (see Lillard and Willis 1978, table 1). The inheritability of endowments from fathers to sons is surely less, probably much less, than is the correlation between the permanent component of earnings at different ages.

The evidence in table 1 suggests that neither the inheritability of endowments by sons (h) nor the propensity to invest in children's human capital because of capital constraints (β^*) is large. For example, if the regression coefficient between the lifetime earnings of fathers and sons is $\leq .4$ and if the transitory variance in lifetime earnings is less than one-third of the iance in total lifetime earnings, then both h and β^* would be less than .28 if $h = \beta^*$; moreover, $h \leq .6$ if $\beta^* = 0$, and $h \leq 0$ if $\beta^* \geq .4$(see n. 4).

If capital constraints completely disappeared, would the same families dominate the best-paid and most prestigious occupations? (For this fear, see the often-cited article by Herrnstein [1971].) The answer is no: families in the best occupations would change frequently even in "meritocracies" because endowments relevant to earnings are not highly inheritable—h is less than .6 and may be much less. Another way to see this is by noting that, if the relation between the lifetime earnings of fathers and sons is no larger than .4, practically all the advantages or disadvantages of ancestors tend to disappear in only three generations: "from shirtsleeves to shirtsleeves in three generations." Parents in such "open" societies have little effect on the earnings of grandchildren and later descendants. Therefore, they have little incentive to try to affect the earnings of descendants through family reputation and other means,

In particular, any lifetime "culture of poverty" tends to disappear between generations because characteristics that determine earnings are variable between generations. For example, children of parents who earn only half the mean can expect to earn above 80 percent of the mean in their generation, and their own children can expect to earn only slightly below the mean.

Yet, family background is still important. For example, even if the degree of regression to the mean is 80 percent, children of parents whose earnings are twice the mean tend to earn 30 percent more than the children of parents whose earnings are only 50 percent of the mean. A 30 percent premium is large relative to the 10 percent–15 percent premium from union membership (see Lewis 1986) or to the 16 percent premium from 2 additional years of schooling (see Mincer 1974). Children from successful families do have a significant economic advantage.

Families who are poor partly because of discrimination against their race, caste, or other "permanent" characteristics may advance more slowly. Clearly, blacks in the United States have advanced much more slowly than have immigrants, partly because of public and private discrimination against blacks. Although many have studied changes over time in the average position of blacks relative to whites (see, e.g., the excellent recent study by Smith [1984]), few have studied the relation between earnings of sons and fathers in black families. The evidence in table 1 suggests that older blacks regress more rapidly to the mean than do older whites, although the evidence may be spurious because response errors are higher and apparently more complicated for blacks (see Bielby, Hauser, and Featherman 1977). Opportunities for younger blacks clearly have improved during the last 20 years. The evidence in table 1 that younger blacks regress more slowly suggests that discrimination raises the regression toward the mean in earnings (see the theoretical discussion in Sec. II).

Goldberger points out (1985, 29–30) that our earlier work uses much higher illustrative values for β than the values of β^* suggested by the empirical evidence in this section. But β and β^* are different: to repeat, β refers to the propensity to bequeath wealth to children by families who are not capital constrained. Therefore, low β^*s are not inconsistent with high βs. A low β^* combined with a low h does imply sizable intergenerational mobility in earnings, whereas a high β implies low intergenerational mobility in wealth and consumption among families that bequeath wealth to their children (we ignore the distinction between the wealth and consumption of children and the wealth and consumption per child; see Secs. III and IV).

We readily admit (see Sec. I) that the distinction in the present paper between earnings, wealth, and consumption as well as our attention to intergenerational capital constraints and fertility behavior have greatly clarified our thinking about intergenerational mobility. However, since a low β^* is not inconsistent with a high β, we see no reason why the empirical evidence of a low β^* "would occasion the tearing of [our] hair and the gnashing of [our] teeth" (Goldberger 1985, 29–30). Moreover, aside from fertility and marriage, we still expect high values for β (see Sec. III).

Table 2 presents evidence from three studies for the United States and Great Britain on the relation between the wealth of parents and children. Harbury and Hitchens (1979) and Menchik (1979) use probates of wealthy estates, while Wahl (1985) uses data on wealth from the 1860 and 1870 censuses. The estimated elasticity between the assets of fathers and sons is about .7 in the United States for probated assets in recent years but is less both for assets of living persons in the nineteenth century and for probated assets in Britain.

Wahl finds a small negative coefficient for grandparents' wealth when instruments are used for both parents' and grandparents' wealth but a positive coefficient for grandparents' wealth when their actual wealth is used. The theoretical analysis incorporated into equation (18) does imply a small negative coefficient for grandparents' wealth when the effect of parents' wealth is not large, as is the case in her study. However, Behrman and Taubman (1985) usually find small positive (but not statistically significant) coefficients on grandparents' schooling in their study of years of schooling for three generations. Their findings may be inconsistent with our theory, although equation (18) does imply a negligible coefficient for grandfathers' schooling when the coefficient on parents' schooling is small—it is less than .25 in their study.

The data in tables 1 and 2 are too limited to determine with confidence whether wealth or earnings regresses less rapidly to the mean, although wealth appears to regress less rapidly. Wealth would regress slowly if parents bequeath assets to children to buffer the total wealth and consumption of children against regression in their earnings. However, wealth would regress rapidly if wealthier parents have sufficiently more children than do poorer parents. Wahl (1985) does find a strong positive relation in the nineteenth century between the fertility and the wealth of parents.

Capital constraints on investments in children probably declined during this century in the United States and in many other countries because fertility declined, incomes rose, and government subsidies to education and to social security grew rapidly. Evidence in Goldin and Parsons (1984) is consistent with sizable capital constraints on poor families in the United States during the latter part of the nineteenth century. These families withdrew their children from school at early ages in order to raise the contribution of teenage children to family earnings. A weakening of capital constraints in the United States is also indicated by the decline over time in the inequality in years of schooling and by the declining influence of family background on education attainments of children (Featherman and Hauser 1976).

There is evidence that the influence of family background on the achievements of children is greater in less-developed countries than it is in the United States. For example, father's education has a greater effect on son's education in both Bolivia and Panama than in the United States. Moreover, the influence of father's education apparently declined over time in Panama as well as in the United States (see Kelley, Robinson, and Klein 1981, 27–66; Heckman and Hotz 1985).

TABLE 2
REGRESSIONS OF SON'S WEALTH ON FATHER'S AND GRANDFATHER'S WEALTH

Location and Son's Year	Father's Year	Notes	Coefficient for Father's Wealth	Coefficient for Grandfather's Wealth	R^2	N	Author
United States: Up to 1976	1930–46	*†	.69 (7.5)	...	.29	173	Menchik (1979)
1860	1860	†§	.76	...	.25	199	Menchik (1979)
		‡§	.21 (1.6)	.05 (2.0)	.46	45	Wahl (1985)
1860	1860	‖§	.26 (2.1)	−.008 (−1.6)	.14	106	Wahl (1985)
1870	1870	‡§	.30 (5.5)	.05 (2.4)	.27	46	Wahl (1985)
1870	1870	‖§	.46 (2.1)	−.03 (−1.6)	.10	125	Wahl (1985)
Great Britain 1934, 1956–57	1902, 1924–26	†	.48 (3.7)	...	...	...	Harbury and Hitchens (1979)
1956–57, 1965	1916, 1928	†	.48 (5.3)	...	...	...	Harbury and Hitchens (1979)
1973	1936	†	.59 (8.4)	...	...	...	Harbury and Hitchens (1979)

NOTE: t-statistics are in parentheses.

* Menchik also includes the following as explanatory variables: number of years between death of parents and child, number of child's siblings (plus one), and stepchild dummy.

† Log-linear regression.

‡ Wahl uses an instrument for parent's wealth. The following variables are used to create the instrument: age of household head (and age squared), occupational and regional dummies, residence farm/nonfarm, and whether parent is bloodline. Grandparent's wealth is actual wealth.

§ Wahl uses data for parents and maternal grandparents instead of for fathers and grandfathers.

‖ Wahl uses instruments for both parent's and grandparent's wealth. She creates the instruments by using the list given in the daggered note above.

VI. Summary and Discussion

This paper develops a model of the transmission of earnings, assets, and consumption from parents to children and later descendants. The model is based on utility maximization by parents concerned about the welfare of their children. The degree of intergenerational mobility, or the rise and fall of families, is determined by the interaction of utility-maximizing behavior with investment and consumption opportunities in different generations and with different kinds of luck.

We assume that cultural and genetic endowments are automatically transmitted from parents to children, with the relation between the endowments of parents and children determined by the degree of "inheritability." The intergenerational mobility of earnings depends on the inheritability of endowments. Indeed, if all parents can readily borrow to finance the optimal investments in children, the degree of intergenerational mobility in earnings essentially would equal the inheritability of endowments.

However, poor families often have difficulty financing investments in children because loans to supplement their limited resources are not readily available when human capital is the collateral. Such capital market restrictions lower investments in children from poorer families. Intergenerational mobility in earnings then depends not only on the inheritability of endowments but also on the willingness of poor families to self-finance investments in their children.

The degree of intergenerational mobility in earnings is also determined by the number of children in different families. Additional children in a family reduce the amount invested in each one when investments must be financed by the family. Consequently, a negative relation between family size and the earnings of parents also reduces the intergenerational mobility of earnings.

Assets act as a buffer to offset regression to the mean in the endowments and, hence, in the earnings of children. In particular, successful families bequeath assets to children to offset the expected downward regression in earnings.

Parents with good access to capital markets can transfer assets or debt to nullify any effect of regression to the mean in earnings on the consumption of children. This effectively separates the relation between the consumption by parents and children from inheritability of endowments and regression to the mean in earnings. Consumption in poorer and middle-level families who do not want to leave bequests tends to regress upward because equilibrium marginal rates of return on investments in the human capital of children tend to be higher in families with low earnings. Consumption and total resources in richer families that do leave bequests to children regress down to the mean, mainly because fertility is positively related to parents' wealth. In this way, larger families dilute the wealth bequeathed to each child. Imperfect assortative mating also tends to cause consumption and wealth to regress to the mean.

We have examined about a dozen empirical studies relating the earnings, income, and assets of parents and children. Aside from families victimized by discrimination, regression to the mean in earnings in the United States and other rich countries appears to be rapid, and the regression in assets is sizable. Almost all earnings advantages and disadvantages of ancestors are wiped out in three generations. Poverty would not seem to be a "culture" that persists for several generations.

Rapid regression to the mean in earnings implies that both the inheritability of endowments and the capital constraints on investments in children are not large. Presumably, these constraints became less important as fertility declined over time and as incomes and subsidies to education grew over time.

In this paper and in previous work we claim that a theory of family behavior is necessary to understand inequality and the rise and fall of families. In making the claim, however, we have not intended to downgrade the importance of empirically oriented studies. Indeed, we have always viewed them as a necessary complement to theoretical analysis. We apologize if our claims for maximizing theory could be interpreted as denying the value of empirical and statistical work that is not explicitly based on a model of maximizing behavior.

We still claim, however, that our model of family behavior is useful in understanding the effect of public policies and other events on inequality and the rise and fall of families. Here we part company with Goldberger (1985), who denies whether our theory adds much to formulations not based on a model of maximizing behavior. He claims (see esp. pp. 30–33) that our theory has few implications that differ from simple regressive models of the earnings or incomes of different generations of a family. Perhaps some perspective about the validity of his claim can be acquired through a brief summary of a few implications of our analysis.

1. Earnings regress more rapidly to the mean in richer than in poorer families. Moreover, even though endowments of children and earnings of parents are positively related, a small redistribution of investment in human capital from richer to poorer families would tend to raise the overall efficiency of investments. The reason is that investments by poorer families are constrained by limited access to funds.

2. Unlike earnings, consumption would regress more rapidly to the mean

374 ◆ FAMILY, MARRIAGE, AND FERTILITY

in poorer than in richer families if fertility is not related to parents' wealth. Indeed, consumption then would not tend to regress at all among rich families who leave gifts and bequests to their children.

3. However, our analysis also implies that fertility is positively related to the wealth of parents. This dilutes the wealth that can be left to each child and induces a regression to the mean among rich families in the relation between consumption per child and the consumption of parents.

We do not know of any other analysis of the family that has these implications, regardless of the approach used. The implications have not been tested empirically, but Goldberger (1985) mainly questions the novelty of the implications of our analysis, not their empirical validity. Additional implications are obtained by considering the effect of public programs.

Becker and Tomes (1979, 1175–78) show that a progressive income tax could raise the long-run relative inequality in after-tax income. The standard deviation clearly falls, but average incomes also fall eventually because parents reduce their bequests to children. Goldberger's useful calculations (1985, 24–25) support our analytical proof that an increase in the degree of progressivity could actually lead to an increase in after-tax inequality. His calculations suggest, however, that a couple of generations would elapse before relative inequality might even begin to increase. He overstates the delay before which inequality might begin to increase, and he understates the likelihood of an eventual net increase, by not considering the effect of greater progressivity on the contribution to inequality of the unsystematic component of the tax system (see Becker and Tomes 1979, 1177–78).[10]

We are not concerned with inequality in this paper, but we believe that the model developed here also implies that after-tax inequality might increase when the degree of progressivity increases. Income taxes alter behavior in our analysis partly by affecting the coefficients in equations such as (11), (18), and (27). Empirical or regressive models that start with such equations or with other equations not derived from an explicit model of behavior across generations would have difficulty in analyzing the effects of income taxes on the coefficients in these equations because such models usually provide insufficient guidance to how these coefficients are determined.

This conclusion applies to other policies as well and to various changes in the environment faced by families. Indeed, the issues are not special to inequality and intergenerational mobility but apply to efforts to understand all social behavior.

To illustrate with a different public program, consider the effects of public debt and social security on the consumption of different generations of a family. Barro (1974) uses a model of parent altruism that is similar to the model of altruism in this paper, when fertility is fixed, to question whether social security and public debt have significant effects on consumption. Parents who make positive bequests to children do not raise their consumption when they receive social security or revenue from the issue of public debt. Instead, they raise their bequests to offset the effect of these programs on the consumption of children. However, the consumption of altruistic parents who are constrained from leaving debt to children is raised by social security and public debt, and the consumption of their children is lowered (see Drazen 1978).

To avoid misunderstanding, we hasten to add that we do not claim that all public programs are neutralized through compensatory reductions within families. This is not true for poorer families in this example or for all families when fertility can vary (see Becker and Barro 1985). Moreover, we have shown that progressive income taxes reduce the incentive to invest in children. We claim not neutrality but that our analysis of family behavior is helpful in understanding the effects of various public programs on the rise and fall of families.

Systematic empirical evidence is necessary before this and other claims can be evaluated. We close by reiterating our belief that such evidence will confirm that the analysis of family behavior within a utility-maximizing framework provides many insights into the rise and fall of families in modern societies.

NOTES

Our research has been supported by National Science Foundation Grant no. 4S 8208260. We received valuable assistance from Gale Mosteller and Michael Gibbs. We appreciate the useful comments at the Conference on the Family and the Distribution of Economic Rewards and at seminars at Bar-Ilan University, Brigham Young University, the University of Chicago, the Hebrew University, Institute des Etudes Politiques, the University of Pennsylvania, Purdue University, Stanford University, and the University of Western Ontario. We especially thank Robert Willis for his helpful discussion at the Conference on the Family and the Distribution of Economic Rewards. We have also benefited from suggestions by Arthur Goldberger and Sherwin Rosen.

1. Among the important contributors to this literature are Stiglitz (1969), Blinder (1974), Conlisk (1974), Behrman and Taubman (1976), Meade (1976), Bevan (1979), Laitner (1979), Menchik (1979), Shorrocks (1979), Loury (1981), and Atkinson (1983).

2. Even parents who accumulate assets over their lifetime may lack assets while investing in children.

3. Goldberger (1985, 16–17) perhaps properly takes us to task for expressing too much "surprise" in our earlier work about a negative coefficient on grandparents' wealth (or income) because this is implied by our model (Becker and Tomes [1979] say that a negative coefficient "may seem surprising" [p. 1171]; Becker [1981] says "it is surprising" [p. 148]). However, we never claimed that an increase in grandparents' wealth would lower the wealth of grandchildren (Goldberger's discussion [1985, 2] is misleading about our claims). We have asked how persons who start with a presumed relation among the wealth of grandchildren, parents, and grandparents would interpret a negative coefficient on grandparents' wealth such as is found in Wahl's study (1985) reported in table 2.

4. A similar equation is derived in Becker and Tomes (1979, eq. [25]). However, the coefficient called β there refers to the propensity to bequeath all capital, including debt, to children, not to the propensity to invest in the human capital of children by parents who cannot leave debt. The approximation in eq. (18) would be linear in the logs of the earnings of children, parents, and grandparents if the endowment and earnings-generating equations are linear in logs. Then $\beta^* + h$ would give the percentage increase in the earnings of children per 1 percent increase in the earnings of fathers, and similarly for $-\beta^*h$.

5. Equation (18) implies that

$$b_{t,t-1} \cong \beta^* + h - h[b^*_{(\beta^* y_{t-2} + \ell_{t-1}) \cdot y_{t-1}}]$$

$$\cong \beta^* + h - \frac{h\sigma_\ell^2}{\sigma_y^2} - h\beta^* b^*_{t-1,\,t}.$$

If the economy is in long-run equilibrium (see Becker and Tomes 1979), then $b^*_{t,t-1} = b^*_{t-1,t}, \sigma^2_{y_{t-1}} = \sigma^2_{y_t}$, and the equality in eq. (19) follows. The relation between $b^*_{t,t-1}$ and the right-hand side of eq. (19) is derived in Becker and Tomes (1979, app. E).

6. If r_{t+1} is constant, a second-order approximation to u'_{t+1}, in eq. (26) gives

$$\frac{d\hat{Z}_{t+1}}{dZ_t} = \left(\frac{u''_t}{u'_t}\right)\left[\frac{u'_{t+1} + \dfrac{vu'''_{t+1}}{2}}{u''_{t+1} + \dfrac{vu''''_{t+1}}{2}}\right],$$

where u'''_{t+1} is the third derivative, u''''_{t+1} is the fourth derivative of utility from consumption in the $t + 1$ first generation, and v is the given variance of n_{t+1} around $\hat{Z}_{t+1}$. The term on the left-hand side is more likely to be less than one (regression toward the mean) when $(u)''''$ is large relative to $(u)'''$.

7. We are indebted to Robert Hauser for bringing to our attention several studies of intergenerational mobility that use the data on Wisconsin high school graduates and for guiding us through various adjustments that correct for response and measurement errors in these studies.

8. These studies have various limitations. Hauser et al. (1975) sample families in only one state (Wisconsin) and only include sons who graduated from high school; all fathers in the Behrman and Taubman (1983) sample are twins; fathers in the

Atkinson (1981) sample had modest earnings in the city of York; fathers in the de Wolff and van Slijpe (1973) study are from the city of Malmö; Soltow (1965) uses a very small sample from one city in Norway; and Girod (1984) surveys students in the canton of Geneva.

9. These estimates may also be biased (the direction is not clear) because information is not available on hours worked and nonpecuniary income from employment (see the discussion in Becker and Tomes [1984, n. 13]).

10. Although Goldberger admits that we only claim a possible long-run increase in inequality, he criticizes the statement that "perhaps this conflict between initial and equilibrium effects explains why the large growth in redistribution during the last fifty years has had only modest effects on after-tax inequality" (Becker [1981, 156]; a similar statement is in Becker and Tomes [1979, 1178]; Goldberger omits the "perhaps" in our statement and says we "conjecture"). He asks, "Is it true that over the past fifty years, the mean and variance of disposable income both fell? If not, what explanation has his model [i.e., Becker Tomes] provided?" (1985, 26–27). These are strange questions. We were not foolish enough to contend that only the tax system affected the growth of incomes during the past 50 years nor did we try to assess how other forces affected inequality. Since we could prove with our model that a progressive income tax need not lower inequality in the long run, and since inequality apparently did not decline significantly during the past 50 years, we speculated about whether progressive income taxes did lower inequality over this period. Surely, that speculation could be very relevant in forcing a reassessment of the common belief that progressive taxes lower inequality. Of course, other changes during this period could have masked a negative effect of income taxes on inequality, but this has to be proven rather than simply assumed.

References

Atkinson, A. B. "On Intergenerational Income Mobility in Britain." *Journal of Post Keynesian Economics* 3, no. 2 (1981): 194–217.

———. *Social Justice and Public Policy*. Cambridge, Mass.: MIT Press, 1983.

Barro, Robert J. "Are Government Bonds Net Wealth?" *Journal of Political Economy* 82, no. 6 (1974): 1096–1117.

Becker, Gary S. "Human Capital and the Personal Distribution of Income: An Analytical Approach." Woytinsky Lecture no. 1. Ann Arbor: University of Michigan, Institute of Public Administration, 1967.

———. "A Theory of Social Interactions." *Journal of Political Economy* 82, no. 6 (1974): 1063–93.

———. *Human Capital*. 2d ed. New York: Columbia University Press (for NBER), 1975.

——— *A Treatise on the Family*. Cambridge, Mass.: Harvard University Press, 1981.

Becker, Gary S. and Robert Barro. "A Reformulation of the Economic Theory of

Fertility." Discussion Paper no. 85–11. Chicago: Economics Research Center, NORC, October 1985.

Becker, Gary S., and Nigel Tomes. "Child Endowments and the Quantity and Quality of Children." Journal of Political Economy 84, no. 4, pt. 2 (1976): S143–S162

———. "An Equilibrium Theory of the Distribution of Income and Intergenerational Mobility." Journal of Political Economy 87, no. 6 (1979): 1153–89.

———. "Human Capital and the Rise and Fall of Families." Discussion Paper no. 84–10. Chicago: Economics Research Center, NORC, October 1984.

Behrman, Jere, and Paul Taubman. "Intergenerational Transmission of Income and Wealth." American Economic Review 66, no. 2 (1976): 436–40.

———. "Intergenerational Mobility in Earnings in the U.S." Mimeographed. Philadelphia: University of Pennsylvania, Center for Household and Family Economics, 1983.

———. "Intergenerational Earnings and Mobility in the United States: Some Estimates and a Test of Becker's Intergenerational Endowments Model." Review of Economics and Statistics 67, no. 1 (1985): 144–51

Bevan, D. L. "Inheritance and the Distribution of Wealth." Economica 46, no. 184 (1979): 381–402.

Bevan, D. L., and J. E. Stiglitz. "Intergenerational Transfers and Inequality." Greek Economic Review 1, no. 1 (1979): 6–26.

Bielby, William T., and Robert M. Hauser. "Response Error in Earnings Functions for Nonblack Males." Sociological Methods and Research 6, no. 2 (1977): 241–80.

Bielby, William T., Robert M. Hauser, and David I. Featherman. "Response Errors of Black and Nonblack Males in Models of the Intergenerational Transmission of Socioeconomic Status." American Journal of Sociology 82, no. 6 (1977): 1242–88.

Blake, Judith. "Family Size and the Quality of Children." Demography 18, no. 4 (1981): 421–42.

Blau, Peter M., and Otis Dudley Duncan. The American Occupational Structure. New York: Wiley, 1967.

Blinder, Alan S. Toward an Economic Theory of Income Distribution. Cambridge, Mass.: MIT Press, 1974.

———. "Inequality and Mobility in the Distribution of Wealth." Kyklos 29, no. 4 (1976): 607–38.

Bloom, Benjamin S. Human Characteristics and School Learning. New York: McGraw-Hill, 1976.

Bowles, Samuel. "Schooling and Inequality from Generation to Generation." Journal of Political Economy 80, no. 3, pt. 2 (1972): S219–S251.

Brittain, John A. The Inheritance of Economic Status. Washington, D.C.: Brookings Institution, 1977.

Conlisk, John. "Can Equalization of Opportunity Reduce Social Mobility?" American Economic Review 64, no. 1 (1974): 80–90.

Dewey, John. "Galton's Statistical Methods." *Publications of the American Statistical Association* 1, no. 7 (1889): 331–34.

Drazen, Allan. "Government Debt, Human Capital and Bequests in a Life-Cycle Model." *Journal of Political Economy* 86, no. 3 (1978): 505–16.

Ehrlich, Isaac, and Uri Ben-Zion. "Asset Management, Allocation of Time, and Returns to Saving." *Economic Inquiry* 14, no. 4 (1976): 558–86.

Featherman, David L., and Robert M. Hauser. "Changes in the Socioeconomic Stratification of the Races, 1962–1973." *American Journal of Sociology* 82, no. 3 (1976): 621–51.

Freeman, Richard B. "Black Economic Progress after 1964: Who Has Gained and Why?" In *Studies in Labor Markets*, edited by Sherwin Rosen. Chicago: University of Chicago Press (for NBER), 1981.

Girod, Roger. "Intra- and Intergenerational Income Mobility: A Geneva Survey (1950–1980)." Paper presented at the meeting of the International Sociological Association Research Committee on Stratification, Budapest, September 1984.

Goldberger, Arthur S. "Family Data Analysis: Assortment, Selection, and Transmission." Proposal to the National Science Foundation, Washington, D.C., 1979.

———. "Modeling the Economic Family." Woytinsky Lecture. Ann Arbor: University of Michigan, Institute of Public Administration, 1985.

Goldin, Claudia, and Donald O. Parsons. "Industrialization, Child Labor, and Family Economic Well-Being." Mimeographed. Philadelphia: University of Pennsylvania, Department of Economics, 1984.

Harbury, C. D., and D. M. W. N. Hitchens. *Inheritance and Wealth Inequality in Britain.* London: Allen & Unwin, 1979.

Hauser, Robert M. "Earnings Trajectories of Young Men." In *Social Stratification in Japan and the United States*, edited by D. J. Treiman and K. Tominaga. In press.

Hauser, Robert M., William H. Sewell, and Kenneth G. Lutterman. "Socioeconomic Background, Ability, and Achievement." In *Education, Occupation and Earnings*, edited by William H. Sewell and Robert M. Hauser. New York: Academic Press, 1975.

Heckman, James J., and V. Joseph Hotz. "The Labor Market Earnings of Panamanian Males." Mimeographed. Chicago: University of Chicago, 1985.

Herrnstein, Richard J. "I.Q." *Atlantic* 228, no. 3 (1971): 43–58.

Kaldor, Nicholas. "Alternative Theories of Distribution." *Review of Economic Studies* 23, no. 2 (1956): 83–100.

Kelly, Jonathan, Robert U. Robinson, and Herbert S. Klein. "A Theory of Social Mobility, with Data on Status Attainment in a Peasant Society." In *Research in Social Stratification and Mobility*, vol. 1, edited by Donald J. Treiman and Robert V. Robertson. Greenwich, Conn.: JAI, 1981.

Kotlikoff, Laurence J., John Shoven, and Avia Spivak. "The Effect of Annuity Insurance on Savings and Inequality." *Journal of Labor Economics* 4, no. 3, pt. 2(1986).

Laitner, J. P. "Household Bequests, Perfect Expectations, and the National Distribution of Wealth." *Econometrica* 47, no. 5 (1979): 1175–93.

Lewis, H. Gregg. *Union Relative Wage Effects: A Survey.* Chicago: University of
Chicago Press, 1986.

Lillard, Lee A., and Robert J. Willlis. "Dynamic Aspects of Earning Mobility."
Econometrica 46, no. 5 (1978): 985–1012.

Loury, Glenn C. "Intergenerational Transfers and the Distribution of Earnings."
Econometrica 49, no. 4 (1981): 843–67.

Mandelbrot, Benoit. "Paretian Distributions and Income Maximization." *Quarterly
Journal of Economics* 76, no. 1 (1962): 57–85.

Mayer, Thomas. *Permanent Income, Wealth, and Consumption.* Berkeley: University
of California Press, 1972.

Meade, J. E. *The Just Economy.* Albany: State University of New York Press, 1976.

Menchik, Paul L. "Inter-generational Transmission of Inequality: An Empirical Study
of Wealth Mobility." *Economica* 46, no. 184 (1979): 349–62.

Mincer, Jacob. *Schooling, Experience and Earnings.* New York: Columbia University
Press (for NBER), 1974.

Nerlove, Marc, Assaf Razin, and Efraim Sadka. "Some Welfare Theoretic Implications of Endogenous Fertility." Mimeographed. Philadelphia: University of Pennsylvania, Department of Economics, 1984.

Pasinetti, Luigi L. "Rate of Profit and Income Distribution in Relation to the Rate of
Economic Growth." *Review of Economic Studies* 29, no. 4 (1962): 267–79.

Peltzman, Sam. "The Effect of Government Subsidies-in-Kind on Private Expenditures: The Case of Higher Education." *Journal of Political Economy* 81, no. 1 (1973):
1–27.

Peters, Elizabeth. "Patterns of Intergenerational Mobility." Mimeographed. Boulder:
University of Colorado, 1985.

Pryor, F. L. "Simulation of the Impact of Social and Economic Institutions on the
Size Distribution of Income and Wealth." *American Economic Review* 63, no. 1
(1973): 50–72.

Roy, A. D. "The Distribution of Earnings and of Individual Output." *Economic Journal*
60, no. 239 (1950): 489–505.

Schumpeter, Joseph A. *Imperialism and Social Classes,* translated by Heinz Norden.
New York: Augustus M. Kelley, 1951.

Shorrocks, A. F. "On the Structure of Inter-Generational Transfers between Families." *Economica* 46, no. 184 (1979): 415–25.

Simon, Herbert. "Rationality in Psychology and Economics." *Journal of Business* (in
press).

Smith, James P. "Race and Human Capital." *American Economic Review* 74, no. 4
(1984): 685–98.

Soltow, Lee. *Toward Income Equality in Norway.* Madison: University of Wisconsin
Press, 1965.

Stiglitz, J. E. "Distribution of Income and Wealth among Individuals." *Econometrica* 37, no. 3 (1969): 382–97.

Tinbergen, Jan. "A Positive and a Normative Theory of Income Distribution." *Review of Income and Wealth* 16, no. 3 (1970): 221–34.

Tomes, Nigel. "The Family, Inheritance, and the Intergenerational Transmission of Inequality." *Journal of Political Economy* 89, no. 5 (1981): 928–58.

———. "Inequality within the Family and Regression to the Mean." Mimeographed. London: University of Western Ontario, Department of Economics, 1984.

Tsai, Shu-Ling. "Sex Differences in the Process of Stratification." Ph.D. dissertation, University of Wisconsin, 1983.

Wahl, Jenny Bourne. "Fertility in America: Historical Patterns and Wealth Effects on the Quantity and Quality of Children." Ph.D. dissertation, University of Chicago, 1985.

Wolff, P. de, and A. R. D. van Slijpe. "The Relation between Income, Intelligence, Education and Social Background." *European Economic Review* 4, no. 3 (1973): 235–64.

Yitzhaki, Shlomo. "On the Relation between Return and Income." Mimeographed. Jerusalem: Hebrew University, 1984.

THE FAMILY AND THE STATE

Gary S. Becker
Kevin M. Murphy

· 15 ·

I. INTRODUCTION

Children are incapable of caring for themselves during many years of physical
and mental maturation. Since their mental development is not sufficient to
trust any contractual arrangements they may reach with caretakers, laws and
social norms regulate the production and rearing of children. Laws punish
child abuse, the sale of children, and unauthorized abortions. They provide
compulsory schooling, welfare payments to families with dependent children,
stringent rules about divorce when young children are involved, and minimum ages of marriage.

Trades and contracts are efficient if no deviation from the terms would
raise the welfare of all participants. An alternative criterion for efficiency is
that the monetary gains to those benefiting from a deviation do not exceed
the monetary loss to those harmed. Unfortunately, the immaturity of children
sometimes precludes efficient arrangements between children and parents or
others responsible for child care.

This difficulty in establishing efficient relations within families provides
the point of departure for our interpretation of the heavy state involvement
in the family. We believe that a surprising number of state interventions

First published in the *Journal of Law & Economics* 31, no. 1 (April 1988): 1–18. © 1988 by
The University of Chicago. All rights reserved.

mimic the agreements that would occur if children were capable of arranging for their care. Stated differently, our belief is that many regulations of the family improve the efficiency of family activities. To be sure, these regulations raise the welfare of children, but they also raise the welfare of parents, or at least they raise the combined welfare of parents and children.

The efficiency perspective implies that the state is concerned with justice for children, if "justice" is identified with the well-being of children, for their well-being. is the prime factor in our analysis. The efficiency perspective does not imply, however, that the effect on children alone determines whether the state intervenes. The effect on parents is considered too. The state tends to intervene when both gain or when the gain to children exceeds the loss to their parents.

According to Richard Posner and others, the common law also improves efficiency when transaction costs are large. Richard Posner says, "In settings where the cost of allocating resources by voluntary market transactions is prohibitively high—where, in other words, market transactions are infeasible—the common law prices behavior in such a way as to mimic the market."[1]

We cannot *prove* that efficiency guides state involvement in the family. We will show, however, that state interventions in the market for schooling, the provision of old-age pensions, and access to divorce are consistent on the whole with the efficiency perspective.

The modern theory of regulation and public choice questions whether much government activity encourages efficiency and justice. Section VII sketches an analysis of interest-group behavior that can lead to government intervention to promote efficient family arrangements.

In order to interpret public policies, we develop an analysis of family behavior under different circumstances. The analysis greatly extends earlier work by Becker. His Woytinsky Lecture of more than twenty years ago shows that only parents who give their adult children gifts or bequests make optimal investments in children.[2] Becker and Tomes, and Becker's *A Treatise on the Family* develop this approach further.[3] Thompson and Ruhter reached the same conclusion while apparently unaware of this earlier literature.[4]

Our discussion of the gains from government intervention in family decisions generalizes the analysis of subsidies to schooling and other human capital found in Becker's Woytinsky Lecture and *Treatise*.[5] Thompson and Ruhter have a nice analysis with a similar interpretation of government intervention in families.[6] Also relevant is the discussion of fertility by Nerlove, Razin, and Sadka.[7]

II. Altruism toward Children

We assume that the large majority of parents are altruistic to their children in the sense that parental utility depends on the number of children and the utility of each child as well as on their own consumption. The altruism assumption is supported by the many sacrifices parents frequently make for children. Parents spend money, time, and effort on children through child care, expenditures on education and health, gifts, and bequests. More or less all parents spend on young children, but only some parents give sizable gifts to adult children or leave bequests.

Plato's *Republic* objects to the rearing of elite children by their parents. It advocates instead that "as soon as children are born, they will be taken in charge by officers appointed for this purpose . . . , while taking every precaution that no mother shall know her own child."[8] Plato's views attracted the attention of philosophers and stimulated experiments that invariably failed. Even the kibbutz movement has returned to giving parents responsibility for the care of children.

Parental altruism is the reason why essentially all societies have shown more common sense than Plato and give parents or other close relatives primary responsibility for child care. Altruistic parents are good caretakers because they consider the effects of their actions on the welfare of children. They sometimes sacrifice their own consumption and comfort to increase that of their children.

Of course, some parents abuse their children, as examples of battered children depressingly illustrate. But even contemporary Western countries display great confidence in parents as caretakers, at least relative to feasible alternatives. Despite the anguish over parental abuse of defenseless children, governments seldom remove children from their parents. Fewer than two children per 10,000 below age eighteen are under state care in either the United States or England and Wales.[9]

Sometimes cited against the importance of parents' altruism is that parents seldom insure the lives of their children. This evidence does not speak to the effect of a child's death on the utility of parents, however, because optimal insurance works to equalize the *marginal* utility of income in different states of the world. Even if a child's death enormously reduced parents' utility, it would not be insurable if it hardly raised and perhaps reduced the marginal utility of money to parents. Support for the importance of altruism comes from the time and effort parents devote to lowering the probability of accidents, illness, or other harm to children. These "self-protection" activities respond not to the effect of a child's mishap on the marginal utility of parents' income but, rather, to their effect on the *level* of parents' utility.

Our analysis recognizes that frequent contact among family members often raises the degree of altruism. That is to say, altruism may well have some of the properties of an addictive taste that is fostered by its consumption. [10] We believe that addictive aspects of altruism better explain the apparently larger bequests by parents to children who visit them more frequently than does the view that parents use bequests to "buy" visits. [11]

The "rotten kid theorem" states that, under certain conditions, both altruistic parents and their perhaps selfish children work out efficient relations that maximize the combined resources of the family as a whole. [12] If this theorem applies to most situations, state interventions in the family could not raise efficiency.

The rotten kid theorem fails to hold, however, when parents do not give children gifts or bequests. [13] They may not give because their altruism is weak, but even parents with strong altruism may not give gifts and bequests when they expect their children to be much better off than they are. Children are better off than parents when economic growth is rapid and when their endowments of ability and other qualities are higher than those of their parents.

Bequests are large in rich families, fairly common among the middle class, and unimportant in poor families. One reason is that endowments of children tend to exceed those of their parents in poor families and to be less than their parents in rich families. But whatever the reason, the evidence on bequests implies that certain types of efficient transactions with children are less common in poorer than in richer families. Nevertheless, bequests may cause other inefficiencies, as we will show in the next section.

III. Investments in the Human Capital of Children

Since parents must reduce their own consumption (including leisure) to raise the time and resources they spend on child care and children's education, training, and health, even altruistic parents have to consider the trade-off between their consumption and the human capital of children. But altruistic parents who plan to leave bequests can avoid this trade-off by using bequests to help finance their investments in children. In effect, they can force even selfish children to repay them for expenditures on the children's human capital. These parents would want to invest efficiently in children because that raises children's utility without costing them anything.

• FAMILY, MARRIAGE, AND FERTILITY

To make this clear, assume a 4 percent rate of return on assets accumulated over the life cycle to provide either old-age consumption or gifts and bequests. If the marginal rate of return on investments in children exceeds 4 percent, parents who give gifts and bequests could invest more in children without lowering their own consumption by accumulating fewer assets. For example, if the marginal rate on human capital is 7 percent, an additional $1,000 invested in children raises their adult earnings by about $70 per year. If parents finance this investment through reduced savings of $1,000 and by reducing annual gifts by $40, their consumption at all ages would be unaffected by greater investment, while their children's income increases by $30 per year.

Clearly, then, altruistic parents who leave bequests will invest until the marginal rate of return on human capital equals the rate on assets. They are better off with efficient investments because they can trade between bequests and investments.

Some altruistic parents do not leave bequests because they get less marginal utility from consumption by their adult children than from their own consumption when elderly. They would like to raise their own consumption at the expense of their children's, but they cannot do this if unable to leave debts to children. Although children have been responsible for parents' debts in some societies, that is uncommon nowadays. Selfish and weakly altruistic parents would like to impose a large debt burden on their children. Social pressures can discourage this in closely knit societies where elderly parents live with and depend on the care of children, but these pressures are not effective in mobile modern countries where the elderly do not live with children.

Parents who cannot leave debt can substitute their own consumption for their children's by investing less in the children's human capital and instead saving more for old age. Therefore, in families without bequests, the equilibrium marginal rate of return on investments in children must exceed the rate on assets saved for old age; otherwise, parents would reallocate some resources from children to savings. These parents underinvest in the human capital of children.

When the rate of return on savings is less than the marginal rate on human capital, both children and parents could be better off with a "contract" that calls for parents to raise investments to the efficient level in return for a commitment by children to repay their elderly parents. Unfortunately, young children cannot be a party to such contracts. Without government intervention, social norms, or "guilt" by parents and children, families without bequests would underinvest in children's human capital.

More generally, expenditures by an altruist are inefficient in the states of the world where he gives to a beneficiary if he does not give in other states.

When he does give, an altruist would get the same utility from equally small changes in his own and in his beneficiary's consumption. Therefore, he would be willing to give more in these states in return for a commitment by the beneficiary to give him even a little in the other states. The selfish beneficiary also gains from such an agreement since he would receive much more in some states than he gives up in the others. Unfortunately, the beneficiary's promises to give may not be credible, just as children's promises to support elderly parents may not be credible.

State intervention in the provision of education and other human capital could raise investments in children to the efficient levels. Since poor parents are least likely to make efficient investments, such intervention would also reduce the inequality in the opportunities between children from richer and poorer families. The compulsory schooling laws in the United States that began in the 1880s and spread rapidly during the subsequent thirty years tended to have this effect. A state usually set minimum requirements at a level that was already exceeded by all but the poorest families in that state.[14] These laws raised the schooling of poor children but did not tend to affect the schooling of other children.

Subsidies to public elementary schools in the United States also began to grow in the latter half of the nineteenth century, and subsidies to public high schools expanded rapidly during the twentieth century. These subsidies appear to have raised the schooling of poorer families relative to richer ones, for the effect of parental wealth and education on the education of children declined over time as public expenditures on schooling grew.[15]

Strong altruism of parents contributes to efficient investments in children by raising the likelihood that parents give gifts or bequests to adult children. Strong altruism may reduce efficiency in other ways, however, if children recognize that they will be rescued by parents when they get into trouble. For example, children who do not receive gifts now but expect gifts in the future from altruistic parents will save less and borrow more to increase their current consumption and reduce their future resources since altruistic parents tend to increase their gifts when children are poorer.[16] Similarly, children may have fun in school and neglect their studies if they expect greater future support from their parents when their earnings are lower. Or children who receive gifts from altruistic parents may take big risks because they expect large gifts if they fail and yet can keep most of their gains if they succeed since gifts cannot be negative.

Parents will not give children such perverse incentives if they can precommit the amount of future gifts and bequests. With precommitment, children cannot rely on parents to bail them out of bad gambles or other difficulties. Precommitment is unnecessary if parental altruism declines enough when they believe that children caused their own difficulties by gambling excessively, neglecting their studies, and so on. Parents may choose not to precommit, however, even when it is perfectly feasible. The rotten kid theorem gives one advantage of retaining flexibility in future transfers. Flexibility can discourage children from actions that help children but hurt parents even more. With flexible gifts and bequests, parents would reduce their transfers sufficiently to make children worse off if they take these actions.[17] Parents may choose not to precommit also because they want to help children who get into difficulties through no fault of their own.

When precommitment is either not feasible or not desirable, parents may take other actions to give children better incentives in the future. They would *overinvest* in education and other training if children cannot run down human capital as readily as marketable wealth. They would also invest more in other illiquid assets of children, such as their housing.

Public policies can also discourage children from inefficient actions. Many countries require parental approval when children want to marry early, drop out of school, get an abortion, or purchase alcoholic beverages. Presumably, one reason is to prevent children who do not anticipate delayed consequences from taking actions that will make them worse off in the future. Another reason, however, is that children may anticipate all too well the future help they will receive from parents if they get into trouble. The state then tries to reproduce the effects on children's behavior of an optimal degree of commitment by parents.

IV. Social Security and Other Old-Age Support

Throughout history, children have been a major help to elderly parents. The elderly frequently have lived with children who care for them when ill and provide food and other support. In the United States a mere thirty years ago, only about 25 percent of persons over age sixty-five lived alone.[18]

Richer families who leave bequests rely less on children because they are insulated from many risks of old age. For example, parents who live longer than expected can reduce bequests to finance consumption in the additional years. The opportunity to draw on bequests provides an annuity-like protection against an unusually long life and other risks of old age. If bequests are not a large part of children's assets, elderly parents get excellent protection against various hazards through the opportunity to reduce bequests, and yet this does not have much influence on children's welfare. In effect, children would help support their parents in old age, although their support is not fully voluntary.

Children in poorer and many middle-level families would be willing to help support parents who agree to invest the efficient amount in the children's human capital. Few societies have contracts or other explicit agreements between parents and children, but many societies have social "norms" that pressure children to support elderly parents. Although little is known about how norms emerge, it is plausible that norms are weaker in modern societies with anonymous cities and mobile populations. Public expenditures on the elderly together with public expenditures on children's education and other human capital can fill the void left by the breakdown in norms.

Expenditures on the elderly in Western countries have grown rapidly in recent decades. United States governments now spend more than $8,000 on each person aged sixty-five or over, largely in the form of medical and pension payments. Is the rapid growth in expenditures on the elderly mainly due to the political power of a growing elderly population? The media contains much discussion of generations fighting for a limited public purse.[19] Some economists support a balanced budget amendment to prevent present generations from heavy taxation of children and other future generations.[20] In a widely cited and stimulating presidential address to the American Population Association, Samuel Preston suggested that growing public support for the elderly has been partly at the expense of public expenditures on children.[21]

We would like to suggest the alternative interpretation that expenditures on the elderly are part of a "social compact" between generations. Taxes on adults help finance efficient investments in children. In return, adults receive public pensions and medical payments when old. This compact tries to achieve for poorer and middle-level families what richer families tend to achieve without government help; namely, efficient levels of investments in children and support to elderly parents.

Federal, state, and local expenditures on education, head start programs, welfare, and the like are large: in recent years they exceed $2,500 per child under age 22. Even though real expenditures per capita on the elderly in the United States grew at a rate exceeding 7 percent from 1950 to the 1980s, table 1 contradicts the impression that expenditures on the elderly grew at the expense of expenditures on children. Per capita public expenditures on the young hardly changed between 1950 and 1983 relative to per capita expenditures on the old.

As table 1 shows, public expenditures on education in the United States increased long before spending on the elderly did. If public spending on education and the elderly are both part of a social compact, then the first generation of parents taxed to finance investments in children would be the first to receive public old-age support. If education taxes start when a person is a young married adult, some thirty to forty years should elapse between the growth in spending on education and the introduction of social security.

390 • FAMILY, MARRIAGE, AND FERTILITY

TABLE I

REAL PER CAPITA PUBLIC EXPENDITURES IN THE UNITED STATES ON PERSONS
UNDER AGE TWENTY-TWO AND SIXTY-FIVE AND OVER (1980 DOLLARS)

	Children under Twenty-two, Including Higher Education ($) (1)	Persons Sixty-five and Over ($) (2)	Col. 1/Col. 2 (3)
1920	122	*	...
1930	293	126	2.33
1940	393	1,022	.38
1950	557	1,708	.33
1960	922	3,156	.29
1970	1,825	5,447	.34
1980	2,472	7,520	.33
1983	2,515	8,307	.30

Sources: U.S. Department of Health and Human Services, *Social Security Bulletin Annual Statistical Suppl.* (various years). U.S. Department of Education, National Center for Education Statistics, *Digest of Education Statistics* (various years). U.S. Department of Commerce, Bureau of the Census, *Statistical Abstract of the United States* (various years).
* Unable to estimate but apparently a small amount.

Perhaps the actual lag in the United States was longer because immigration was not really constrained until the early 1920s. A social security system introduced prior to that time might well have encouraged substantial immigration of older people.

The much greater per capita spending on the elderly ($8,300 vs. $2,500) seems difficult to reconcile with a social compact between the young and the old. But these numbers are deceiving: the young, if anything, actually do better than the old. To show this, suppose young adults pay $2,500 to finance public investments in the human capital of each child. When adults reach age sixty-five they receive $8,300 annually for the remainder of their lives. These expenditures on children and the elderly continue until possibly a last future generation. Which generations would be better off with these expenditures?

Since the net reproduction rate in the United States is now close to unity, we assume that the representative parent has one child at age twenty-five. We also ignore offsetting reductions in parents' spending on children in response to public expenditures on children and offsetting reductions in children's support of parents in response to social security payments (our analysis applies directly if reduced parental spending equals reduced child support). Currently in the United States, a twenty-five-year-old has a .79 probability of reaching age sixty-five, and a sixty-five-year-old can expect to live until age eighty-two. Therefore, each adult member of the initial generation would pay $2,500 annually from ages twenty-five to forty-six and expects to receive $6,557 (.79 x $8,300) from ages sixty-six to eighty-two. All subsequent generations receive a per capita government investment in their human capital of $2,500 until age twenty-two. The last generation does not invest in children, but it pays $6,557 from ages forty-one to fifty-seven to support the elderly of the prior generation. Each member of all in-between generations pays $2,500 from ages twenty-five to forty-six to support children of the succeeding generation, $6,557 from ages forty-one to fifty-seven to support the elderly of the prior generation, and expects to receive $6,557 from ages sixty-six to eighty-two.

Since estimated rates of return on schooling and other types of training exceed 5 percent,[22] and since most public expenditures on children are for schooling and other training, we assume conservatively that these have an average rate of return of 5 percent in the form of equal increases in earnings from ages twenty-three to sixty-five. Then $2,500 invested for twenty-two years would increase earnings each year by $5,939. The after-tax net earnings of each member of the last generation would increase by $5,939 from ages twenty-three to forty; they decrease by $618 ($6,557–$5,939) from ages forty-one to fifty-seven while they are taxed to support the elderly of the previous generation; and they increase again by $5,939 from ages fifty-eight to sixty-five. The present value of this net earnings stream is positive for all nonnegative interest rates. Therefore, the last generation clearly gains from this exchange of child support for old-age support.

Unlike the last generation, generations between the first and the last must also support children of the succeeding generation but receive support when old. The reader can work out the arithmetic of their complicated net earnings stream, but the bottom line is that the present value of this stream is positive for nonnegative interest rates. Therefore, all generations in between the first and the last also unambiguously benefit from the present combination of public spending on the young and old.

The initial generation of adults does the least well. Each member pays $2,500 on child care from ages twenty-five to forty-six and gains $6,557 in old-age support from ages sixty-six to eighty-two. The internal rate of return on this series of gains and losses is a little less than 2 percent. This rate is slightly higher than the average interest rate (1.8) on short-term U.S. government securities from 1948 to 1980 after adjustment for anticipated inflation,[23] but it is considerably lower than the 4 percent average rate of return on tangible business capital in the United States during the post–World War II period.[24] This generation does less well because their human capital is not augmented by public spending; however, they may still be better off even if this internal rate of return is less than the appropriate market rate of interest because their utility is higher when the welfare of the next generation is higher (assuming altruism toward children).

Whatever the conclusion about the initial generation, our results sharply contradict the view that government payments to the elderly in the United States are large relative to government spending on the young. Indeed, any generation that benefits from the current level of public investments in children can easily use the higher earnings created by these investments to provide current levels of support for the elderly, and they would still have a considerable profit left over. Therefore, children would be happy to enter into a social compact with their parents whereby the children support their parents when old at current levels in return for a commitment to the current level of public support on children.

Our theoretical analysis implies that an efficient compact between the young and the old raises the human capital of children from poorer and middle-class families in return for contributions to the health and incomes of older members of these families. We indicated earlier that public spending on education favored the poor and middle class. Public spending on medical care also favors poorer families: the rapid growth in public spending on medical care during the past twenty years sharply reduced the effect of family income on medical care.[25] In addition, poor and middle-level older persons are much more likely to live apart from their children than they were before social security became important.[26]

V. DIVORCE

Practically all societies forbid marriage prior to specified ages; many countries have banned marriages between men and women of different races, religions, and social classes; and Christian countries have not allowed polygamy. Regulation of divorce is equally common. The United States and other Western countries essentially did not allow divorce until the mid–nineteenth century. There were fewer than two(!) divorces per year in England from 1800 to 1850.[27] Gradually, divorce laws in the West liberalized toward allowing divorce when one party committed adultery, abandoned his or her spouse, or otherwise was seriously "at fault." Divorce by mutual consent also began to be possible, especially when there were no young children. About twenty years ago, the United States and other countries started to allow either spouse to divorce without proving fault or getting consent.

Although some divorces badly scar the children involved, little is known about the usual effects of divorce on children. Among other things, the available evidence cannot distinguish the effect of a divorce from the effect of having parents who do not get along.[28] All altruistic parents consider the interests of children and are less likely to divorce when their children would be hurt badly. Nevertheless, even if we ignore the conflict between divorced parents in determining how much time and money each spends on their children,[29] altruistic parents might still divorce when their children are harmed. Parents who do not leave bequests might divorce even when the money value of the cost to children exceeds the money value of the gain to parents. The reason is that children do not have a credible way to "bribe" their parents to stay if they cannot commit to old-age support or other future transfers to parents contingent on the parents not getting a divorce.

The story is different in families with bequests. If divorce does not change the degree of altruism toward children and if a divorce only affects future earnings and the value of other tradable resources, then children would also be made better off if their parents decide to divorce. The reason is that parents raise their gifts and bequests to compensate children for any losses from the divorce. This is an implication of the rotten kid theorem.[30]

On the other hand, children may suffer from a divorce even by parents who give bequests if the divorce reduces the nontradable goods consumed by children. For example, children may be unhappy after a divorce because they seldom see their fathers. Parents cannot directly compensate children for the effect of a divorce on their happiness or other consumption. Indeed, if the effect on nontradables lowers the marginal utility to children of tradable resources, altruistic parents who divorce would *reduce* their gifts of tradables to children and thereby make children still worse off.

We claimed earlier that the degree of altruism is not fixed but often responds to the frequency and intensity of contacts with beneficiaries. In particular, over time a divorced father might become less altruistic toward his children as his contact with them declines. This would explain why many divorced fathers are delinquent in child support payments,[31] and it strengthens our conclusion that a divorce may make children worse off even when their parents are quite altruistic prior to a divorce and even if they continue to give bequests after a divorce.

A divorce may greatly harm a wife who has many children and cannot earn much in the labor force or when her ex-husband fails to meet his financial and other obligations to the children. This is true even when divorce requires mutual consent because in many societies husbands could intimidate wives into agreeing to a divorce under unfavorable terms for them.

It does not seem farfetched to suggest that the state often regulates divorce to mimic the terms of contracts between husbands and wives and parents and children that are not feasible. Such contracts, for example, might greatly reduce the incidence of divorce when families have many children since the aggregate loss to children (and mothers) from divorce would rise with the number of children. Many countries did prohibit divorce when the typical family was large. Moreover, even when a divorce could not be easily obtained, marriages without children often could dissolve—could be "annulled." Divorce laws eased as birthrates began to decline in the nineteenth century. In recent decades, low birthrates and the much higher labor force participation of women stimulated a further easing toward no-fault divorce.

Some parents choose to separate from their children not through divorce but through the sale of their children. The universal ban on this practice strongly suggests that the sale of children lowers social utility. Young unmarried women and poor parents who need money are the two groups most likely to sell their children. Some children sold to prosperous families who want them may consider themselves better off than if they had remained with their parents. But even children who would suffer greatly might be sold because they have no way to compensate their parents for keeping them. Just as a ban on divorce may improve efficiency because certain contracts between parents and children are not feasible, so too may the ban on the sale of children improve efficiency. Nevertheless, Landes and Posner, and Posner could be correct that a very limited right to sell babies is better than the present controlled adoption system.[32] Note that subsidies to poor families with children through aid to families with dependent children and other programs encourage unmarried and other poor mothers to keep their children rather than give them up for adoption.

VI. Optimal Population

With a heroic amount of additional imagination, we can consider not only the relation between parents and actual children but also contracts between parents and *potential* children. Such a thought experiment provides a new way of determining optimal family size and optimal population. The literature on optimal population has lacked an attractive guiding principle.[33]

Suppose that a potential child could commit to compensating his parents eventually if he is born. This "contract" would be Pareto improving (we assume that third parties are not hurt by births) if the child would still prefer to be born after compensation to parents that makes them better off. Since such contracts are impossible, some children may not get born even when both parents and children could be better off. Both fertility and population growth are too low when compensation from unborn children to their parents would be Pareto improving.

The first-order utility-maximizing condition with respect to number of children implies that parents are indifferent to a small increase in numbers. Unborn children want to compensate parents to change indifference into a positive preference for additional children. All parents might appear to welcome compensation, regardless of their altruism, because compensation lowers the net cost of additional children. This conclusion is correct for parents who do not provide gifts and bequests to children since these parents would benefit from old-age support or other compensation from children (see Section III).

The surprising result is that compensation *lowers* the utility of parents who do provide children with gifts and bequests. Compensation from potential children, in effect, reduces the net gift to these children. But parents do not need compensation to reduce gifts since they may reduce them in any case if they so choose. Therefore, families with gifts and bequests to children do have the Pareto-efficient number of children (neglecting effects outside the family): compensation from unborn children makes the parents worse off rather than better off.

The seemingly bizarre thought experiment with unborn children has a very concrete implication. We have shown that poorer families are less likely than richer ones to leave bequests. If commitments for compensation from unborn children are not feasible, fertility in poorer families is too low, and fertility in richer families (who give bequests) is optimal. Therefore, our approach implies—with any third-party effects ignored—that the aggregate private fertility rate is below the Pareto-efficient rate.

A conclusion that poorer families may have too few children will shock some readers because poorer families already have larger families than richer ones. But other factors raise fertility by poorer families, including welfare programs, subsidies to education, and limited birth control knowledge.

Thompson and Ruhter also conclude that parents who do not leave bequests tend to have too few children,[34] but their argument, in contrast to ours, seems to depend on the underinvestment in the human capital of each child by these families. Such an argument is not correct since underinvestment in children may induce families to have too many rather than too few children. The suboptimal expenditure per child "artificially" lowers the effective cost of an additional child through the interaction between the quantity and quality of children.[35]

VII. Political Competition between Generations

Since public policy results from competition among interest groups, how does competition for political favors lead to efficiency-raising state interventions in the family? In this section we sketch out a possible answer when parental altruism is important.

Political competition between adults and children is hardly a contest since children cannot vote and do not have the means and maturity to organize an effective political coalition. If adults use their political power to issue bonds and other obligations, they can help support themselves when old by selling these obligations to the next generation of younger adults. Some economists support balanced government budgets and limits on debt issue to control such exploitation of the political weakness of children and later generations. Of course, this is not a problem if each generation can repudiate debt issues by previous generations. Since the issues involved in debt repudiation are beyond the scope of this article, we will just assume that debt is not repudiated.

Although present generations may be able to exploit future generations, altruism limits their desire to do so. Indeed, if all parents are altruistic and leave bequests, present generations have no desire to exploit future generations. After all, if they want to, they may take resources from future generations by leaving smaller bequests. Although families who do not leave bequests favor debt and other exploitation of the political weakness of future generations, their degree of altruism may greatly affect how they use their political power against future generations.

We showed in Section III that families who do not leave bequests underinvest in the human capital of their children. They can increase the wealth of the children's generation by using their political power to raise education and other training through state schools and subsidies to other investments in children. Then the present generation may, if it wishes, issue obligations to future generations that extract this increase in children's wealth.

Although selfish parents try to extract as much as they can from children, altruistic parents may prefer to share some of the increased wealth with children. This means that future generations may also benefit from the political power of present generations. Therefore, even if the altruism of many parents is not strong enough to lead to positive bequests and efficient investments in human capital, it could be strong enough to ensure that future generations also gain when the present generation uses its political power to issue debt and other obligations to future generations.

This overly simplified analysis of political power and political incentives may help explain why public expenditures in the United States on children are not small compared to public expenditures on the elderly. The discussion in Section IV indicates that the next generation gains enough from public expenditures on children by the current generation to pay social security and other help to the elderly of the current generation, and yet the next generation still has some profit left over from the public investment in their human capital.

VIII. Summary

We have tried to understand the widespread intervention by governments in families. We conclude that many public actions achieve more-efficient arrangements between parents and children. Clearly, parents and children cannot always make efficient arrangements because children are unable to commit to compensation of parents in the future.

Families who leave bequests can "force" children to repay parents for investments in human capital by reducing bequests. Therefore, these families do not underinvest in children's human capital. By contrast, families who do not leave bequests, often poorer families, do underinvest in children. The state may subsidize schools and other training facilities to raise investments in children by poorer families to efficient levels.

We consider not only subsidies to education and training but also social security and other old-age support, subsidies to births, laws that limit access to divorce and the sale of children, and laws that require parents' permission for early marriage and other choices of children. It is remarkable how many state interventions in family decisions appear to contribute to the efficiency of family arrangements.

Notes

This is the ninth Henry Simons Lecture, delivered by Becker to the University of Chicago Law School on February 25, 1987. We received valuable research assistance from Michael Gibbs and insightful comments on an earlier draft from David Friedman, Richard Posner, and Sam Preston. Our research was supported by National Science Foundation grant SES-8520258 and by National Institute of Child Health and Human Development grant SSP I R37 HD22054.

1. Richard A. Posner, *Economic Analysis of Law* 230 (3d ed. 1986).

2. Gary S. Becker, "Human Capital and the Personal Distribution of Income: An

Analytical Approach," W. S. Woytinsky Lecture (1967), reprinted in Gary S. Becker, *Human Capital* (2d ed. 1975).

3. Gary S. Becker and Nigel Tomes, "Human Capital and the Rise and Fall of Families," *J. Lab. Econ.* S1 (1986): 4; Gary S. Becker, *A Treatise on the Family* (1981).

4. Earl A. Thompson and Wayne E. Ruhter, "Parental Malincentives and Social Legislation" (unpublished paper, UCLA undated).

5. Becker, supra note 2; Becker, supra note 3.

6. Thompson and Ruhter, supra note 4.

7. Marc Nerlove, Assaf Razin, and Efraim Sadka, "Some Welfare Theoretic Implications of Endogenous Fertility" (unpublished paper, University of Pennsylvania 1987).

8. *The Republic of Plato*, 160 (Francis M. Cornford trans. 1951).

9. See Robert Dingewall and John Eckelaar, *Rethinking Child Protection*, in *State Law and the Family* 99 (M. D. A. Freeman ed. 1984); American Humane Ass'n, *Highlights of Official Child Neglect and Abuse Reporting* (1984).

10. On addiction, see Gary S. Becker and Kevin M. Murphy, "A Theory of Rational Addiction," *J. Pol. Econ.* (in press).

11. This view is developed in B. Douglas Bernheim, Andrei Schliefer, and Larry H. Summers, "The Strategic Bequest Motive," *J. Lab. Econ.* 4 (1986): S151.

12. Becker, supra note 3, ch. 8.

13. Other qualifications are discussed in Theodore Bergstrom, "Remarks on Public Goods Theory and the Economics of the Family" (unpublished paper, University of Michigan 1984).

14. See William M. Landes and Lewis C. Solmon, "Compulsory Schooling Legislation: An Economic Analysis of Law and Social Change in the Nineteenth Century," *J. Econ. Hist.* 32 (1972): 54.

15. David L. Featherman and Robert M. Hauser, "Changes in the Socioeconomic Stratification of the Races," *Am. J. Soc.* 92 (1976): 621.

16. Neil Bruce and Michael Waldman, "The Rotten-Kid Theorem Meets the Samaritan's Dilemma" (Working Paper No. 402, UCLA 1986); Asser Lindbeck and Jorgen W. Weibull, "Strategic Interaction with Altruism: The Economics of Fait Accompli" (unpublished paper, University of Stockholm 1987) develop similar arguments.

17. Becker, supra note 3, at 188–89; and Bruce and Waldman (1986).

18. Robert T. Michael, Victor Fuchs, and Sharon R. Scott, "Changes in the Propensity to Live Alone: 1950–76," *Demography* 17 (1980): 39.

19. See, for example, Philip Longman, "Justice between the Generations," *Atl. Monthly* 85 (1985): 73.

20. See James M. Buchanan and Richard E. Wagner, *Democracy in Deficit: The Political Legacy of Lord Keynes* (1977).

21. Samuel H. Preston, "Children and the Elderly: Divergent Paths for America's Dependents," *Demography* 21 (1984): 435.

22. See George Psacharopoulos, *Returns to Education: An International Comparison* (Keith Hinchcliffe asst. 1973).

23. See Robert J. Barro, *Macroeconomics* (2d ed. 1987), at ch. 7.

24. See Edward C. Prescott, *Response to a Skeptic* (Quarterly Review, Federal Reserve Bank of Minneapolis 1986).

25. Victor R. Fuchs, *Who Shall Live: Health, Economics, and Social Choice* (1975).

26. Michael et al., supra note 18.

27. Griselda Rowntree and Norman H. Camer, "The Resort to Divorce in England and Wales, 1858–1957," *Population Stud.* 11 (1958): 188.

28. See Robert E. Emery, "Interpersonal Conflict and the Children of Discord and Divorce," *Psychological Bull.* 92 (1982): 310.

29. This issue is well analyzed in Yoram Weiss and Robert J. Willis, "Children as Collective Goods and Divorce Settlements," *J. Lab. Econ.* 3 (1985): 268.

30. Becker, supra note 12.

31. Weiss and Willis, supra note 29, give other reasons.

32. Elisabeth M. Landes and Richard Posner, "The Economics of the Baby Shortage," *J. Legal Stud.* 7 (1978): 323; Richard A. Posner, "The Regulation of the Market in Adoptions," *B. U. L. Rev.* 67 (1987): 59.

33. See the criticisms of this literature in James E. Meade, "Population Explosion: The Standard of Living and Social Conflict," *Econ. J.* 77 (1967): 233; David Friedman, "What Does 'Optimum Population' Mean?" *Research Pop. Econ.* 3 (1981): 273.

34. Thompson and Ruhter, supra note 4.

35. See the analysis in Gary S. Becker and Kevin M. Murphy, "Incomplete Markets and Investment in Children" (unpublished paper, University of Chicago 1986); Nerlove et al., supra note 7.

DISCRIMINATION

◆ ◆ ◆

◆ *PART* ◆ *THREE* ◆

The Forces Determining Discrimination in the Marketplace

· 16 ·

In the sociopsychological literature on this subject one individual is said to discriminate against (or in favor of) another if his behavior toward the latter is not motivated by an "objective" consideration of fact.[1] It is difficult to use this definition in distinguishing a violation of objective facts from an expression of tastes or values. For example, discrimination and prejudice are not usually said to occur when someone prefers looking at a glamorous Hollywood actress rather than at some other woman; yet they are said to occur when he prefers living next to whites rather than next to Negroes. At best calling just one of these actions "discrimination" requires making subtle and rather secondary distinctions.[2] Fortunately, it is not necessary to get involved in these more philosophical issues. It is possible to give an unambiguous definition of discrimination in the marketplace and yet get at the essence of what is usually called discrimination.

I. The Analytical Framework

Money, commonly used as a measuring rod, will also serve as a measure of discrimination. If an individual has a "taste for discrimination," he must act

First published in Gary S. Becker, *The Economics of Discrimination*, 2d ed. (Chicago: University of Chicago Press, 1971). © 1971 by The University of Chicago. All rights reserved.

as if he were willing to pay something, either directly or in the form of a reduced income, to be associated with some persons instead of others. When actual discrimination occurs, he must, in fact, either pay or forfeit income for this privilege. This simple way of looking at the matter gets at the essence of prejudice and discrimination.

Social scientists tend to organize their discussion of discrimination in the marketplace according to their disciplines. To the sociologist, different levels of discrimination against a particular group are associated with different levels of social and physical "distance" from that group or with different levels of socioeconomic status; the psychologist classifies individuals by their personality types, believing that this is the most useful organizing principle. The breakdown used here is most familiar to the economist and differs from both of these: all persons who contribute to production in the same way, e.g., by the rent of capital or the sale of labor services, are put into one group, with each group forming a separate "factor of production." The breakdown by economic productivity turns out to be a particularly fruitful one, since it emphasizes phenomena that have long been neglected in literature on discrimination.

By using the concept of a *discrimination coefficient* (this will often be abbreviated to DC), it is possible to give a definition of a "taste for discrimination" that is parallel for different factors of production, employers, and consumers. The *money* costs of a transaction do not always completely measure *net* costs, and a DC acts as a bridge between money and net costs. Suppose an *employer* were faced with the money wage rate π of a particular factor; he is assumed to act as if $\pi(1 + d_i)$ were the *net* wage rate, with d_i as his DC against this factor. An *employee*, offered the money wage rate π_j for working with this factor, acts as if $\pi_j(1 - d_j)$ were the net wage rate, with d_j as his DC against this factor. A *consumer*, faced with a unit money price of p for the commodity "produced" by this factor, acts as if the net price were $p(1 + d_k)$, with d_k as his DC against this factor. In all three instances a DC gives the percentage by which either money costs or money returns are changed in going from money to net magnitudes: the employer uses it to estimate his net wage costs, the employee his net wage rate, and the consumer the net price of a commodity.

A DC represents a nonpecuniary element in certain kinds of transactions, and it is positive or negative, depending upon whether the nonpecuniary element is considered "good" or "bad." Discrimination is commonly associated with *disutility* caused by contact with some individuals, and this interpretation is followed here. Since this implies that d_i, d_j, and d_k are all greater than zero, to the employer this coefficient represents a nonmonetary cost of production, to the employee a nonmonetary cost of employment, and to the consumer a nonmonetary cost of consumption.[3] "Nepotism" rather than "discrimination" would occur if they were less than zero, and they would then represent nonmonetary *returns* of production, employment, and consumption to the employer, employee, and consumer, respectively.

The quantities πd_i, $\pi_j d_j$, and $p d_k$ are the exact money equivalents of these nonmonetary costs; for given wage rates and prices, these money equivalents are larger, the larger d_i, d_j, and d_k are. Since a DC can take on any value between zero and plus infinity, tastes for discrimination can also vary continuously within this range. This quantitative representation of a taste for discrimination provides the means for empirically estimating the quantitative importance of discrimination.

II. Tastes for Discrimination

The magnitude of a taste for discrimination differs from person to person, and many investigators have directed their energies toward discovering the variables that are most responsible for these differences. I also attempt to isolate and estimate the quantitative importance of some of these variables; the following discussion briefly describes several such variables.

The discrimination by an individual against a particular group (to be called N) depends on the social and physical distance between them and on their relative socioeconomic status. If he works with N in production, it may also depend on their substitutability in production. The relative number of N in the society at large also may be very important: it has been argued that an increase in the numerical importance of a minority group increases the prejudice against them, since the majority begins to feel their growing power; on the other hand, some argue that greater numbers bring greater knowledge and that this leads to a decline in prejudice. Closely related to this variable are the frequency and regularity of "contact" with N in different establishments and firms.

According to our earlier definition, if someone has a "taste for discrimination," he must act *as if* he were willing to forfeit income in order to avoid certain transactions; it is necessary to be aware of the emphasis on the words "as if." An employer may refuse to hire Negroes solely because he erroneously underestimates their economic efficiency. His behavior is discriminatory not because he is prejudiced against them but because he is ignorant of their true efficiency. Ignorance may be quickly eliminated by the spread of knowledge, while a prejudice (i.e., preference) is relatively independent of knowledge.[4] This distinction is essential for understanding the motivation of many organizations, since they either explicitly or implicitly assume that discrimination can be eliminated by a wholesale spread of knowledge.[5]

Since a taste for discrimination incorporates both prejudice and ignorance, the amount of knowledge available must be included as a determinant of tastes. Another proximate determinant is geographical and chronological location: discrimination may vary from country to country, from region to region within a country, from rural to urban areas within a region, and from one time period to another. Finally, tastes may differ simply because of differences in personality.

III. Market Discrimination

Suppose there are two groups, designated by W and N, with members of W being perfect substitutes in production for members of N. In the absence of discrimination and nepotism and if the labor market were perfectly competitive, the equilibrium wage rate of W would equal that of N. Discrimination could cause these wage rates to differ; the *market discrimination coefficient* between W and N (this will be abbreviated to "MDC") is defined as the proportional difference between these wage rates. If π_w and π_n represent the equilibrium wage rates of W and N, respectively, then

$$\text{MDC} = \frac{\pi_w - \pi_n}{\pi_n}.$$

If W and N are imperfect substitutes, they may receive different wage rates even in the absence of discrimination. A more general definition of the MDC sets it equal to the difference between the ratio of W's to N's wage rate with and without discrimination.[6] In the special case of perfect substitutes, this reduces to the simpler definition given previously, because π_w^0 would equal π_n^0:

It should be obvious that the magnitude of the MDC depends on the magnitude of individual DCs. Unfortunately, it is often implicitly assumed that it depends *only* on them; the arguments proceed as if a knowledge of the determinants of tastes was sufficient for a complete understanding of market discrimination. This procedure is erroneous; many variables in addition to tastes take prominent roles in determining market discrimination, and, indeed, tastes sometimes play a minor part. The abundant light thrown on these other variables by the tools of economic analysis has probably been the major insight gained from using them.

The MDC does depend in an important way on each individual's DC; however, merely to use some measure of the average DC does not suffice.

The complete distribution of DCs among individuals must be made explicit because the size of the MDC is partly related to individual *differences* in tastes. It also depends on the relative importance of competition and monopoly in the labor and product markets, since this partly determines the weight assigned by the market to different DCs. The economic and quantitative importance of N was mentioned as one determinant of tastes for discrimination; this variable is also an independent determinant of market discrimination. This independent effect operates through the number of N relative to W and the cost of N per unit of output relative to the total cost per unit of output. Both may be important, although for somewhat different reasons, in determining the weight assigned by the market to different DCs. Reorganizing production through the substitution of one factor for another is a means of avoiding discrimination; the amount of substitution available is determined by the production function.

The MDC is a direct function of these variables and an indirect function of other variables through their effect on tastes. Our knowledge of the economic aspects of discrimination will be considered satisfactory only when these relationships are known exactly.

IV. The Model

A framework has been proposed for analyzing discrimination in the marketplace because of race, religion, sex, color, social class, personality, or other nonpecuniary considerations. Individuals are assumed to act as if they have "tastes for discrimination," and these tastes are the most important immediate cause of actual discrimination. When an employer discriminates against employees, he acts as if he incurs nonpecuniary, psychic costs of production by employing them; when an employee discriminates against fellow employees or employers, he acts as if he incurs nonpecuniary, psychic costs of employment by working with them; when a consumer discriminates against products, he acts as if he incurs nonpecuniary, psychic costs of consumption by consuming them.

It is desirable to formulate these nonpecuniary costs or tastes in a way that is sufficiently specific to yield quantitative empirical insights and sufficiently general to incorporate new information as it becomes available. Both these desiderata are satisfied by the concept of a "discrimination coefficient." The discrimination coefficient of an employer against an employee measures the value placed on the nonpecuniary cost of employing him, since it represents the percentage difference between the money and the true or net wage rate "paid" to him. If π is the money wage rate paid, then $\pi(1+d)$ is the net wage rate, with d being the discrimination coefficient. Likewise, the discrimination coefficient of other employees against this employee measures the value placed on the nonpecuniary costs of working with him, since it represents the percentage difference between the money and the net wage rates received for working with him; and the discrimination coefficient of a consumer measures the value placed on the nonpecuniary costs of buying a product (partly) produced or sold by him, since it represents the percentage difference between the money and the net price paid for this product.

Although these coefficients are the proximate determinant of choices, they are in turn, like other tastes, influenced by more fundamental variables. In the past, those who attempted to establish a relation between discrimination and other variables usually employed rather direct techniques, as exemplified by the interpretation of answers to questionnaires. By relating discrimination coefficients to an economic analysis of price determination through the market mechanism, it is possible to infer indirectly some of these relationships from data giving incomes and other economic statistics for various groups. These inferences are usually restricted to whites and Negroes or whites and nonwhites because data are lacking for other groups.

V. Tastes for Discrimination

Since people discriminate little against those with whom they have only indirect "contact" in the marketplace, some direct contact must be necessary for the development of a desire to discriminate. This does not necessarily contradict the view that discrimination would be eliminated if people got to know one another sufficiently well through close contact. It merely emphasizes that, while certain kinds of contact may be a cure for discrimination, other may cause it. Several different kinds of contact were examined in an attempt to discover the most important ones.

Discrimination against Negroes seems to be positively correlated with their relative number. However, this relation is stronger for discrimination that does not go through the market (as illustrated by opportunities for formal education) than for discrimination that does. Moreover, while this relation can be measured in various ways, e.g., by using the relative number of Negroes in a plant, firm, city, or state, their (relative) number in a metropolitan area is the only one used in this study. The amount of contact between Negroes and whites can be measured not only by the relative numerical importance of Negroes but also by their relative economic importance. Various measures of economic importance were suggested, but it was not possible here to investigate any of them carefully.

Contact has other dimensions besides numerical and economic importance; among them are intensity, duration, and "level." There is some evidence that discrimination is less against Negroes in temporary than in permanent jobs, and this may occur because the duration of contact is less. There is also abundant evidence that discrimination by Negroes against one another is much less than is discrimination by whites against Negroes, and this may result from the more intense contact among Negroes (and among whites) than between Negroes and whites. Intense contact can be associated with little discrimination for at least three reasons: (1) discrimination may be caused by ignorance, and contact may eliminate this ignorance; (2) Negroes and whites may have different physical and social characteristics, and contact may lead Negroes and whites to value their own characteristics; (3) Negroes may discriminate less and have more contact with one another precisely because they value their own characteristics.

Evidence clearly shows that discrimination is greater against older and better-educated nonwhites. (This does not imply that older and better-educated whites discriminate more than those who are younger and less educated; none of the evidence examined has any direct bearing on this.) This greater discrimination may reflect, at least partly, a positive connection between discrimination and occupation, since older and better-educated nonwhites have higher and more responsible occupational positions. Whites in lower occupations may greatly discriminate against them because they have a relatively large amount of authority and decision-making powers. Data showing the incomes of whites and nonwhites in different occupations are extremely limited, but the crude evidence available does not contradict this hypothesis. An alternative, albeit related, interpretation is that discrimination is greater against older and better-educated nonwhites because their income is large relative to the persons with whom they are employed. This interpretation emphasizes that the level of contact can also be measured by income, and discrimination by whites may be a decreasing function of their income relative to nonwhites. It has been impossible to determine whether either relation between discrimination and "level" of contact is an important explanation of the increase in discrimination with age and education.

Within each region members of the same economic factor of production appear to have very similar tastes for discrimination; however, the reader should be cautious in accepting this conclusion, since the statistical procedures used probably overestimated this similarity.

In the last few decades much controversy and legislation have centered around regional differences in discrimination against Negroes and other nonwhites. By developing an analysis based on the concept of a discrimination coefficient, it was possible to make the first quantitative estimate of such regional differences. In 1940, tastes for discrimination in the South appear

410 • DISCRIMINATION

to have been, on the average, about twice those in the North. Although relatively more Negroes live in the South, this does not seem to explain much of the regional difference in discrimination, nor can other variables examined explain this difference, and at present it must be accepted as reflecting a regional difference in tastes.

How has the absolute and relative economic position of Negroes changed over time? Insight into this was obtained by examining the occupational position of Negroes and whites for several dates during the last half century. The average occupational position of Negroes has risen quite strikingly in both the North and the South, but their position relative to whites has been remarkably stable; in the North this was only slightly higher in 1950 than in 1910, and in the South it was slightly lower in 1950 than in 1910. While many important and relevant changes may have taken place in both regions, a very tentative conclusion from this stability would be that neither striking increases nor striking decreases in discrimination against Negroes have occurred during the last four decades.

VI. Market Discrimination and Segregation

Tastes for discrimination are an important part of the theory explaining actual discrimination, but there is no simple and unique way to go from one to the other. The theory incorporates all analysis of other variables which, so to speak, determine the observable form taken by tastes. Suppose one is interested in members of two groups, called N and W, respectively. Tastes for discrimination affect market relationships by causing market discrimination or market segregation or both against N or W.

Market discrimination against N exists if discrimination has reduced N's average net wage rate (or income) by a greater percentage than W's; the *market discrimination coefficient* (MDC) is defined as the difference between the actual ratio of W's average net wage rate (or income) to N's and the ratio that would exist if there were no discrimination. The MDC equals zero if there is no discrimination and is an increasing function of the amount of market discrimination against N. If N and W are perfect substitutes in production and if there is perfect competition in all markets, the MDC is simply the percentage difference between W's and N's actual average net wage rates (or incomes). Market segregation of members of N exists if they have more contact with one another than they would have if there were no discrimination; a *market segregation coefficient* (MSC) could be defined as the difference between a measure of actual contact and what it would be if there were no segregation. It is easy to confuse these two concepts, and yet a careful distinction between market segregation and market discrimination is essential for a clear understanding of the observable consequences of tastes for discrimination. Market discrimination was analyzed in individual labor and capital markets and in all markets combined. The latter analysis employed a model in which members of W and N owned various quantities of two homogeneous factors of production—labor and capital. Effective discrimination occurred against N if discrimination by either W or N reduced N's total net (i.e., net of psychic costs) income by a greater percentage than W's. By abstracting from government discrimination and monopolistic practices, it is possible completely to isolate the structural forces causing effective discrimination in a competitive economy.

Discrimination must decrease the total net incomes of both N and W; it decreases N's total net income by a greater percentage than W's if

$$\frac{Y_w}{Y_n} > \frac{l_n}{l_w},$$

where Y_n and Y_w are the aggregate incomes of N and W when there is no discrimination, and l_n and l_w are the amounts of labor supplied by N and W. Thus effective discrimination would occur against N if W was more of an "economic majority" than N was a "labor majority." This inequality is necessary as well as sufficient if W alone discriminates but is not necessary if N also does. Political discrimination is often strongest against political minorities, and this result shows that economic discrimination is strongest against economic minorities.

It was also shown that if $l_n < l_w$ and if N is relatively well supplied with labor, effective discrimination must occur against N. This explains, for example, why Negroes in the United States suffer more than whites from discrimination: even without monopolies, trade unions, and government discrimination, substantial discrimination by whites (and a fortiori by Negroes) would greatly reduce the net income of Negroes.

The MDC against members of N selling a particular kind of labor (or capital) clearly depends on the average tastes for discrimination of all groups—factors of production, employers, and consumers—working with N in the marketplace. However, it does not depend on this alone. A given taste for discrimination causes more market discrimination if the group is complementary to, rather than substitutable for, N, so that the distribution of tastes between substitutes and complements is important.

Differences among members of the same group may also be important. At each equilibrium position, some members of a group work with N and others with members of W that are selling the same labor (or capital); it is easy to show that those working with N have relatively small discrimination coefficients against N. An increase in the supply of N relative to W means that some of those working with W must be induced to work with N; since they have relatively large discrimination coefficients, they can be induced to do so only if the relative return for working with N increases, and an increase in this relative return must be accompanied by an increase in the MDC against N. Therefore, the MDC changes with all changes in the relative supply of N if there are differences in tastes within a group. As mentioned earlier, however, the evidence suggests that members of the same group usually have very similar tastes for discrimination against nonwhites.

The extent of concentration in the labor and output markets is also relevant to the extent of discrimination. Employer discrimination should, on the average, be less in competitive industries than in monopolistic ones. Monopolistic and competitive industries in the South were investigated for 1940. For all eight census occupational categories, the number of nonwhites employed by monopolistic industries relative to the number employed by competitive industries is quite consistent with our theory. Another theoretical implication is that employee discrimination is larger in unionized than in equivalent competitive labor markets, but the relevant empirical material has not been examined.

The analysis developed in this monograph implies—for fixed discrimination coefficients—a negative correlation between the market discrimination against N and N's relative economic importance in the productive process. All the evidence examined is consistent with this implication. For example, Negroes tend to be more numerous in occupations and industries in which they have relatively little contact with whites.

Segregation of (say) Negroes and whites occurs because Negroes want to discriminate less against other Negroes than whites do; some segregation is found throughout our social and economic system. Complete market segregation does not occur because the relative supply of factors owned by Negroes and whites differs, making it profitable for Negroes to "trade" with whites, even though there is substantial discrimination against them. As mentioned earlier, segregation and discrimination are often confused, and a good example of this confusion is found in the discussions of Negro housing. Many whites do not want to live near Negroes, and this is a primary cause of residential segregation, not of residential discrimination (as is often believed). The latter could occur only if many whites were willing to forfeit income in order to avoid renting or selling a dwelling to Negroes who would live near *other* whites. My own conjecture is that this kind of behavior is not very common and that the residential discrimination observed in many northern cities is a consequence of the in-migration of Negroes and the residential segregation in these cities.

Differentials between whites and nonwhites have been explained in terms of discrimination against nonwhites, although a theory based on nepotism in favor of whites would have almost exactly the same empirical implications. In other words a theory based on "hatred" of one group is not easily distinguished empirically from one based on "love" of the other group. Thus these two theories can be used interchangeably for most problems in positive economic analysis; at the same time, one's conclusions about normative issues may greatly depend on whether "hatred" or "love" is assumed to motivate decisions.

VII. SUGGESTIONS FOR FUTURE RESEARCH

Since the theoretical framework proposed in this monograph seems consistent with both general knowledge and the available quantitative evidence, it may not be amiss to point out some implications that can fruitfully be investigated further. Additional analysis of differentials between whites and nonwhites would be worthwhile, since data are relatively abundant and discrimination against nonwhites is currently a very pressing issue. The large regional difference in discrimination in 1940 could not be explained by the regional distribution of nonwhites. The 1950 census data should be subjected to a similar analysis; if like conclusions are reached, an attempt should be made to discover variables that can account for the difference. It would also be interesting to determine whether the traditionally greater unemployment of nonwhites than of whites is consistent with the analysis presented here.

Studies should be made of the relative importance of employer, employee, consumer, and government discrimination. One study could extend this work on the relative amount of employer discrimination in monopolistic and competitive industries; another could investigate the relative amount of employee discrimination in unionized and competitive labor markets. The latter would probably be especially fruitful, since too often the word has been taken for the deed; that is, union pronouncements have been considered synonymous with union behavior.

Data from the 1950 census could be used to determine the scope, magnitude, and causes of segregation and discrimination in housing. The literature on minority housing is sufficiently confused to make this an extremely promising field.

A more thorough study should be made of the relation between market discrimination against a group of nonwhites and their importance in the productive process. This relation has not previously received much attention in the literature.

There is abundant evidence that discrimination against nonwhites systematically increases with their age and education. Many barriers to the education of nonwhites will probably be taken down in the future, and this will increase their education relative to that of whites. This would also increase their income relative to that of whites if there were no discrimination; but, since discrimination rises with education, an increase in the education of nonwhites may increase only slightly their incomes relative to those of whites. Hence it is important to investigate the cause of the greater market discrimination against older and better-educated nonwhites.

The power of the analysis can be further tested by applying it to other groups, such as women, Jews, individuals with the same personality type, members of the same caste or social class, etc. Data limitations preclude a detailed study of most of the groups except women, for whom there is a large quantity of economic information. An analysis of income and occupational differentials between men and women should be very useful not only because much discrimination has occurred against women but also because it has long been recognized that "productivity" differences between men and women explain a significant part of these differentials. Discussions of other minorities usually reveal an unwillingness to admit that important differences in "productivity" and "taste" exist between them and the majority. I believe that these differences *are* important, although the discussion in this monograph is probably also biased toward underestimating them. An analysis of the relative returns to women should therefore add some perspective to discussions of discrimination against all minorities.

The analysis in this monograph can be viewed as a case study in the quantitative analysis of nonpecuniary variables. In recent years much emphasis has been placed on the importance of nonpecuniary variables in the choice of occupation, working conditions, etc.; yet little has been done toward *estimating* their quantitative importance. The present analysis of discrimination suggests a quantitative approach to these other nonpecuniary variables, and this may be its most useful by-product.

NOTES

1. Many references can be cited for definitions of this kind. In a discussion of the problems involved in defining prejudice, Gordon Allport arrives at this definition: "Ethnic prejudice is an antipathy based upon a faulty and inflexible generalization" (see his *The Nature of Prejudice* [Cambridge, Mass.: Addison-Wesley Press, 1955], p. 9).

2. The distinction drawn by Allport and others is that those discriminating against Negroes give "erroneous" answers to various questions about Negroes, while

those asked about Hollywood actresses do not. Let us waive the problem of determining whether some answers are erroneous and probe this distinction from another direction. Suppose that the answers given about Negroes violate no known facts, while those given about Hollywood actresses are in blatant conflict with the facts. Would persons drawing this distinction now agree that the preference for whites is not, and that for actresses is, discrimination?

3. Allport makes a distinction between negative and positive prejudice that is identical with my distinction between a taste for discrimination and a taste for nepotism. He agrees that negative prejudice is usually the motivating force behind behavior considered to be discriminatory (op. cit., pp. 6 and 7). He asserts later (p. 25) that "we hear so little about love [positive] prejudice" because "prejudices of this sort create no social problem." In this he is mistaken, since the social and economic implications of positive prejudice or nepotism are very similar to those of negative prejudice or discrimination.

4. Many prejudiced people often erroneously answer questions about groups they discriminate against; their "ignorance" about these groups, however, is of secondary importance for understanding and combating their discrimination, since their behavior is independent of all attempts to give them the facts. For a similar observation see ibid., chap. i.

5. Some advertisements are primarily devoted to spreading knowledge, while others are aimed at changing preferences or prejudices by creating pleasant, although logically irrelevant, associations with their products. Likewise, some organizations try to change tastes for discrimination by creating unpleasant, although similarly irrelevant, associations with discrimination.

6. That is, $MDC = \pi_w/\pi_n - \pi_w^0/\pi_n^0$, where π_w^0 and π_n^0 are the equilibrium wage rates without discrimination.

EFFECTIVE
DISCRIMINATION

· 17 ·

An MDC (market discrimination coefficient) between any two groups can be defined for a particular labor or capital market or for all markets combined; in the latter, interest would center on the effect of discrimination on the total incomes of these groups. For example, discrimination by whites presumably reduces the income of Negroes, but how does it affect their own incomes? Many writers have asserted that discrimination in the marketplace by whites is in their own self-interest; i.e., it is supposed to raise their incomes. If this were correct, it would be in the self-interest of Negroes to "retaliate" against whites by discriminating against them, since this should raise Negro incomes. If, on the other hand, discrimination by whites reduces their own incomes as well, is the percentage reduction in their incomes greater or less than that in Negro incomes? It is an implicit assumption of most discussions that minority groups like Negroes usually suffer more from market discrimination than do majority groups like whites, but no one has isolated the fundamental structural reasons why this is so. It is shown in the following that discrimination by any group W reduces their own incomes as well as N's, and thus retaliation by N makes it worse for N rather than better. It is also shown why minorities suffer much more from discrimination than do majorities.

First published in Gary S. Becker, *The Economics of Discrimination*, 2d Ed. (Chicago: University of Chicago Press, 1971). © by The University of Chicago Press. All rights reserved.

I. The Model

New insights are gained and the analysis made simpler if the discussion is phrased in terms of trade between two "societies," one inhabited solely by N, the other by W. Government and monopolies are ignored for the present, as the analysis is confined to perfectly competitive societies. Since our emphasis here is on the overall incomes of W and N, the multiplicity of factors of production will also be ignored, and the discussion will be confined to two homogeneous factors in each society—labor and capital—with each unit of labor and capital in N being a perfect substitute in *production* for each unit of labor and capital in W. These societies do not "trade" commodities but factors of production used in producing commodities. Each society finds it advantageous to "export" its relatively abundant factors: W exports capital, and N labor. The amount of labor exported by N at a given rate of exchange of labor for capital is the difference between the total amount of labor in N and the amount used "domestically"; the amount of capital exported by W is derived in a similar manner.

The following conditions would be satisfied in a full equilibrium with no discrimination: (a) payment to each factor would be independent of whether it was employed with N or W; (b) the price of each product would be independent of whether it was produced by N or W; and (c) the unit payment to each factor would equal its marginal value product. If members of W develop a desire to discriminate against labor and capital owned by N, they become willing to forfeit money income in order to avoid working with N. This taste for discrimination reduces the net return[1] that W capital can receive by combining with N labor, and this leads to a reduction in the amount of W capital exported. Since this, in turn, reduces the income that N labor can receive by combining with W capital, less N labor is also exported. In the new equilibrium, then, less labor and capital are exported by N and W, respectively. It can be shown that this change in resource allocation reduces the equilibrium net incomes of both N and W.[2] Since discrimination by W hurts W as well as N, it cannot be a subtle means by which W augments its net command of economic goods.[3]

II. Discrimination and Capitalists

Although the aggregate net incomes of W and N are reduced by discrimination, all factors are not affected in the same way: the return to W capital and

N labor decreases, but the return to W labor and N capital actually increases. There is a remarkable agreement in the literature on the proposition that capitalists from the dominant group are the major beneficiaries of prejudice and discrimination in a competitive capitalistic economic system.[4] If W is considered to represent whites or some other dominant group, the fallacious nature of this proposition becomes clear, since discrimination *harms* W capitalists and benefits W workers. The most serious non sequitur in the mistaken analyses is the (explicit or implicit) conclusion that, if tastes for discrimination cause N laborers to receive a lower wage rate than W laborers, the difference between these wage rates must accrue as "profits" to W capitalists.[5] These profits would exist only if this wage differential resulted from price discrimination (due to monopsony power), rather than from a taste for discrimination.

III. Discrimination and Segregation

Trade between two societies is maximized when there is no discrimination, and it decreases with all increases in discrimination. Tastes for discrimination might become so large that it would no longer pay to trade; each society would be in economic isolation and would have to get along with its own resources. Since members of each society would be working only with each other, complete economic isolation would also involve *complete* economic *segregation*. More generally, since an increase in discrimination decreases trade and since a decrease in trade means an increase in economic segregation, an increase in discrimination must be accompanied by an increase in segregation.

The total MDC against N is defined as the difference between the actual ratio of the incomes of W and N and this ratio without discrimination.[6] There is "effective discrimination" against N whenever this MDC is positive. If effective discrimination occurs against N at all levels of discrimination by W, the income of N relative to W must be less when completely isolated from W than when freely trading with W; under these circumstances, N gains more from trade than W does.

It is proved in the appendix to this chapter that if effective discrimination occurs against N at all levels of discrimination by W, the absolute and relative income of N declines continuously as discrimination increases. This is shown in figure 1, in which the horizontal axis measures W's and the vertical axis N's net income; p_0 represents their incomes when there is no discrimination, p_1 when there is complete segregation, and the curve $p_0 w p_1$ when there are

FIGURE I

THE EFFECT OF DISCRIMINATION ON INCOMES

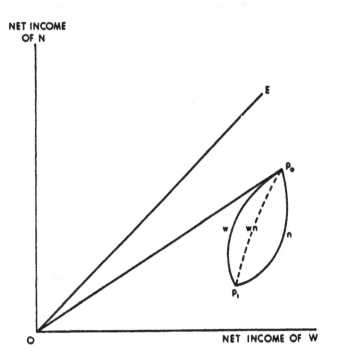

different amounts of discrimination by W. We have assumed that effective discrimination always occurs against N; therefore, $p_0 w p_1$ is never above the line op_0. The total MDC against N increases as discrimination increases; incomes reach a *minimum* and the total MDC a *maximum* when tastes for discrimination become sufficiently large to preclude any trade between W and N. This conclusion is very relevant to a proposal that has stimulated considerable discussion in the past, namely, that minority groups should avoid discrimination from the majority by completely segregating themselves, economically and otherwise.[7] If the minority is identified with N and the majority with W, this analysis demonstrates that complete segregation reduces the absolute and relative income of the minority and therefore increases, rather than decreases, the market discrimination against it. Effective discrimination occurs against a minority partly because it gains so much by "trading" with the majority; accordingly, complete segregation does not avoid the bad economic effects of discrimination but only multiplies them.

TABLE I
MEDIAN INCOME OF INDIANS AND NEGROES IN 1950
BY REGION AND URBAN-RURAL CLASSIFICATION

Region	Urban	Rural Farm	Rural Nonfarm	All
MEDIAN INCOME OF NEGROES (DOLLARS)				
Northeast	1,623	1,050	†	—
North-central	1,697	560	—	—
South	861	431	—	—
West	1,524	897	—	—
UNITED STATES	—	—	—	952
MEDIAN INCOME OF INDIANS (DOLLARS)				
Northeast	1,626	—	1,033	—
North-central	1,188	360	602	—
South	1,168	366	682	—
West	1,180	406	721	—
UNITED STATES	—	—	—	725

SOURCE: U.S. Bureau of the Census, *Census of Population, 1950: Special Report on Non-White Populations by Race* (Washington, D.C.: Government Printing Office, 1953), Tables 9 and 11.
† Data are not available.

IV. THE INCOME OF INDIANS AND NEGROES

The foregoing conclusion can be investigated empirically by comparing the income of two minority groups, one segregated from and the other trading with the dominant group. The American Indians are taken as a group that has been segregated from American whites (partly by choice and partly by force) and the American Negroes as a group that has been trading with these whites. Though Indians have had some economic contact with whites, they almost certainly have had less than Negroes. If, when the Negro slaves were freed, their per capita resources were no greater than the Indians' per capita resources, one can reasonably attribute some of the present difference between per capita Negro and Indian incomes to differences in their contact with whites. Data are presented in table 1, indicating that the median Indian net income in the United States in 1949 was only 76 percent of the median Negro net income.[8] Negro incomes were larger in five separate regions and urban-rural classes, smaller in one, and the same in one. Thus, for both the country as a whole and for smaller units, Negro incomes were substantially higher than Indian incomes in 1949.[9]

V. Discrimination and Economic Minorities

I have shown that a necessary and sufficient condition for effective discrimination to occur against N at all levels of discrimination by W is[10]

$$\frac{Y_0(W)}{Y_0(N)} > \frac{l_n}{l_w},\tag{1}$$

where l_n and l_w represent the amount of labor supplied by N and W, and $Y_0(W)$ and $Y_0(N)$ represent the aggregate incomes of W and N in the absence of discrimination. If N is a numerical minority, $l_n < l_w$[11] and $c_n < c_w$,[12] where c_n and c_w represent the amount of capital supplied by N and W. Therefore

$$\frac{Y_0(W)}{Y_0(N)} > 1,\tag{2}$$

and a fortiori that inequality (1) holds. Inequality (2) states that N's income is less than W's and hence that N is an economic minority. Therefore, if N is a numerical minority, it is also an economic minority, and effective discrimination must occur against it. If N is not a numerical minority, inequalities (1) and (2) no longer necessarily hold; they hold only if N is more of an economic minority than W is a numerical minority.[13]

It turns out, then, that a necessary condition for effective discrimination against N is that N be an economic minority; a sufficient condition is that N be a numerical minority; a necessary *and* sufficient condition is that N be more of an economic minority than a numerical majority. It has long been recognized that discrimination is closely connected with the minorities question, the emphasis being put on the inadequate political representation of numerical minorities. This analysis of discrimination in competitive free-enterprise societies also uses a minority-majority framework, but the concept of economic minorities is somewhat more important here than that of numerical ones. It seems reasonable that economic discrimination in competitive societies be related to economic minorities, and political discrimination to political minorities.

VI. Discrimination in the Real World

Negroes in the United States

Only about 10 percent of the total population of the United States is Negro; hence the amount of labor they supply is substantially less than the amount supplied by whites. Moreover, Negroes must be a net "exporter" of labor, since they clearly have more labor relative to capital than do the whites. These two conditions imply (by n. 12 and inequality [1]) that tastes for discrimination would produce—via the workings of a competitive economic system—effective discrimination against Negroes. There is evidence not only that effective discrimination occurs against Negroes but also that the total MDC is quite large. Negroes in the United States have owned an extremely small amount of capital, while whites have had a more balanced distribution of resources;[14] a substantial decline in the amount of white capital available to Negroes would greatly reduce the absolute and relative incomes of Negroes.

Estimates could be made of the economic loss to various groups resulting from discrimination in the marketplace if there were knowledge of the actual quantity of discrimination, the nature of production functions, and the amount of labor and capital supplied. A general technique for making these estimates will be illustrated by an example that also roughly indicates the magnitude of the economic loss to Negroes and whites in the United States resulting from discrimination in the marketplace by whites.

The production function is assumed to be of the following (Cobb-Douglas) form

$$X = kl^r c^{1-r},$$

with $r = \frac{2}{3}$. The amount of labor supplied by whites is taken as 9 times that supplied by Negroes, and of capital as 150 times.[15] Since units of measurement can be chosen at will, Negroes are assumed to have one unit of both labor and capital; these assumptions state that $l_n = 1$, $c_n = 1$, $l_w = 9$, and $c_w = 150$. If there were no discrimination, the incomes of Negroes and whites would be $Y_0(N) = 1.7$ and $Y_0(W) = 23.5$, and whites would export 14 units of capital; if discrimination were sufficiently large to cause complete segregation, their incomes would be $Y_1(N) = 1.0$ and $Y_1(W) = 23.2$ (see pp. 416–17). The maximum reduction in the income of Negroes is about 40 percent; the income of whites would be reduced by an almost imperceptible amount. With no discrimination, Negro per capita incomes would be about 66 percent of those of whites, and, with complete segregation, about 39 percent of those of whites.

The actual equilibrium position falls somewhere between these two extremes. If discrimination reduces the amount of capital exported by whites by about 40 percent, they would actually export 8 rather than 14 units of capital; Negro and white incomes would be 1.5 and 23.3, and thus per capita Negro incomes would be 57 percent of per capita white incomes. An MDC against Negro labor can be defined as the percentage difference between actual white and Negro net wage rates; an MDC against Negro capital as the percentage difference between actual white and Negro net rents on capital. These MDCs would be +0.21 and −0.31, respectively; hence the return to labor would be greater for whites, and the return to capital would be greater for Negroes. White labor and Negro capital gain from discrimination, and white capital and Negro labor lose from it; but, since the net loss of Negroes is greater than that of whites, total market discrimination occurs against Negroes. Discrimination in the marketplace by whites reduces Negro incomes by 13 percent, or, to put this in other words, Negro incomes would increase 16 percent if market discrimination ceased. Discrimination reduces the incomes of whites by a negligible amount because they gain very little from trading with Negroes.

The estimated economic loss to Negroes would be greater if the production function was more capital-intensive, if white capital was larger relative to Negro capital, or if discrimination reduced the amount of capital exported by more than 40 percent. Likewise, the estimated loss would be smaller if the opposite conditions were assumed. Inadequate knowledge of these variables makes it impossible to estimate this loss precisely, and 16 percent is an extremely rough estimate. The economic loss to Negroes seems substantial and important, although a far cry from the loss assumed in some discussions. [16]

It is often explicitly or implicitly assumed that the total MDC against Negroes is very large (to use the terms of this study); explanations have emphasized political discrimination, class warfare, monopolies, and market imperfections. My analysis shows that none of these influences is necessary, since substantial market discrimination against Negroes in the United States could easily result from the manner in which individual tastes for discrimination allocate resources within a competitive free-enterprise framework. The United States is often considered the best example of a country using competition to determine economic values. This implies that monopolies, political discrimination, and the like, are, at most, secondary determinants of market discrimination and that individual tastes for discrimination operating within a competitive framework constitute the primary determinant.

NonWhites in South Africa

In South Africa, nonwhites are about 80 percent of the total population; this is taken to mean that l_n is roughly four times l_w (see inequality [1] on p. 417). Since nonwhites are a numerical majority, effective discrimination does not *necessarily* occur against them; it would occur if aggregate white net incomes were at least four times aggregate nonwhite net incomes.[17] The very crude available evidence suggests that aggregate white net incomes are much more than four times those of nonwhites.[18] Therefore, tastes for discrimination in the private economic sector alone seem to have produced effective discrimination against nonwhites. The South African government has been active in regulating the economic activities of nonwhites. For this reason the market discrimination produced by the competitive economic sector *may* be less important than that produced by other sources; but it need not be, since it alone could be quite large.

VII. DISCRIMINATION BY MINORITIES

N may discriminate, in our model, by distinguishing between W and N capital; the money return for working with W capital must be sufficient to offset the psychic costs of doing so. A general analysis incorporating discrimination by both W and N could be developed, but there is no point in going into the details of this beyond stressing one important relationship. W's net income is uniquely determined by the amount of capital exported; discrimination determines this amount, and the latter alone determines W's income. N's net income depends on the amount of capital imported and its own taste for discrimination. For a given amount imported, N's net income is maximized if it is indifferent between indigenous and imported capital; the greater the preference for indigenuous capital, the smaller the net income. Hence, given W's net income and thus the amount of capital exported, N's net income is smaller, the greater the discrimination. Therefore, if both N and W discriminate, inequality (1) is sufficient but not necessary for effective discrimination always to occur against N; any necessary and sufficient condition would depend on the relative amount of discrimination by N. Consider figure 1 again. The curve p_0np_1 represents the incomes of N and W for different levels of discrimination by N, and it must be below p_0wp_1 at all points except p_0 and p_1. If both W and N discriminate, the point representing their incomes would be in the area bounded by p_0np_1w; the curve p_0wnp_1 summarizes a set of situations in which W discriminates more than N does.

Minority groups are often tempted to "retaliate" against discrimination from others by returning the discrimination. This is a mistake, since effective economic discrimination occurs against them, not because of the distribution of tastes but because of the distribution of resources. That is, majorities have a more balanced distribution of labor and capital than they do. Figure 1 clearly shows that, although N is hurt by W's discrimination, it is hurt even more by its own discrimination.

APPENDIX

Call the net (= money) return to domestic labor and capital in W, $\pi_c(W)$ and $\pi_c(W)$. In a competitive equilibrium position the return to each factor equals its marginal productivity; hence

$$\pi_c(W) = \frac{\partial f}{\partial c}(c = c_w - c_t; l = l_w) = \frac{\partial f}{\partial c}(c_w - c_t; l_w),$$

$$\pi_l(W) = \frac{\partial f}{\partial l}(c = c_w - c_t; l = l_w) = \frac{\partial f}{\partial l}(c_w - c_t; l_w),$$

where f is the production function in W; c_w and l_w are the total amount of labor and capital supplied by W; and c_t is the amount of capital exported. By footnote 1 of this chapter the equilibrium net income of W is

$$Y(W) = c_w \pi_c(W) + l_w \pi_l(W)$$

$$= c_w \frac{\partial f}{\partial c}(c_w - c_t; l_w) + l_w \frac{\partial f}{\partial l}(c_w - c_t; l_w).$$

N allocates its labor between W and N capital, with the intent of equalizing its marginal physical product in both uses. The equilibrium net income of N is

$$Y(N) = c_n \pi_c(N) + l_n \pi_l(N) = c_n \frac{\partial f'}{\partial c}(c_n + c_t; l_n) + l_n \frac{\partial f'}{\partial l}(c_n + c_t; l_n),$$

where f' is the production function in N, and c_n and l_n are the total amount of labor and capital supplied by N. The impact of discrimination on $Y(W)$ and $Y(N)$ could be determined by explicitly introducing tastes for discrimination; however, the analysis is simpler with another approach. An increase in discrimination by W decreases the quantity of capital exported, and therefore the latter is a monotonic function of W's taste for discrimination.

It can be shown that if f and f' are homogeneous of the first degree,

$$\frac{\partial Y(W)}{\partial c_t} > 0, \tag{A1}$$

$$\frac{\partial Y(N)}{\partial c_t} > 0, \tag{A1'}$$

and thus discrimination by W reduces the net incomes of both N and W. Inequality (A1) can be proved thus: If a function is homogeneous of the first degree, all first-order partial derivatives are homogeneous of zero degree; in particular, $\partial f/\partial c$ is homogeneous of zero degree. By Euler's theorem for homogeneous functions,

$$c\frac{\partial(\partial f/\partial c)}{\partial c} + l\frac{\partial(\partial f/\partial c)}{\partial l} \equiv 0,$$

or

$$c\frac{\partial^2 f}{\partial c^2} + l\frac{\partial^2 f}{\partial l\partial c} \equiv 0. \tag{A2}$$

According to a well-known theorem on the derivative of a function of a function,

$$\frac{\partial f}{\partial c_t} \equiv \frac{\partial f}{\partial c}\frac{\partial c}{\partial c_t}.$$

Since $c = c_w - c_t$, then $\partial c/\partial c_t = -1$, and

$$\frac{\partial f}{\partial c_t} \equiv -\frac{\partial f}{\partial c}. \tag{A3}$$

It follows from identity (A3) that

$$\frac{\partial Y(W)}{\partial c_t} \equiv l\frac{\partial^2 f}{\partial l\partial c_t} - c_w\frac{\partial^2 f}{\partial c_t^2}, \tag{A4}$$

and from identities (A2) and (A3) that

$$c\frac{\partial^2 f}{\partial c_t^2} \equiv l\frac{\partial^2 f}{\partial l\partial c_t}. \tag{A5}$$

By substituting identity (A5) in identity (A4), one obtains

$$\frac{\partial Y(W)}{\partial c_t} \equiv -c_t\frac{\partial^2 f}{\partial c_t^2}. \tag{A6}$$

If there is diminishing marginal productivity, $\partial^2 f/\partial c_t^2 < 0$. Since $c_t \geq 0$, it must follow that

$$\frac{\partial Y(W)}{\partial c_t} \geq 0. \qquad \text{QED}$$

Inequality (A1') can be proved in the same way.

By looking at the problem in a slightly different way, it is possible to acquire an intuitive understanding of this result. Suppose labor enters the United States from abroad and that some United States capital (c_t) is employed with this labor. A well-known economic theorem states that United States citizens must (economically) benefit from immigration as long as there is diminishing marginal productivity of labor, since intramarginal immigrants raise the productivity of American capital. The net income of United States citizens is an increasing function of the amount of immigration, which can be measured by c_t, the amount of capital employed with immigrants. This dicussion shows that treating discrimination as a problem in trade and migration is far from artificial, since they are closely and profoundly related.

Let us define

$$R = \frac{Y(N)}{Y(W)}.$$

Then

$$\frac{\partial R}{\partial c_t} = \frac{Y(W)\,[\partial Y(N)/\partial c_t] - Y(N)\,[\partial Y(W)/\partial c_t]}{[Y(W)]^2},$$

or, from identity (A6),

$$\frac{\partial R}{\partial c_t} = \frac{Y(W)\,[-c_t\,(\partial^2 f'/\partial c_t^2)] - Y(N)\,[-c_t\,(\partial^2 f/\partial c_t^2)]}{[Y(W)]^2}.$$

Hence

$$\frac{\partial R}{\partial c_t} \gtreqless 0 \qquad \text{as } Y(N)\frac{\partial^2 f}{\partial c_t^2} \gtreqless Y(W)\frac{\partial^2 f'}{\partial c_t^2}. \tag{A7}$$

If f were identical with f' and if there were no discrimination, the amount of capital exported would be just sufficient to equalize the equilibrium relative supply of factors "abroad" with the relative supply at "home." That is to say,

$$\frac{c_n + \hat{c}_t}{l_n} = \frac{c_w - \hat{c}_t}{l_w},$$

or

$$l_n = bl_w,$$

and

$$c_n + \hat{c}_t = b(c_w - \hat{c}_t).$$

Since $\partial f/\partial c_t$ is homogeneous of zero degree in c and l, $\partial^2 f/\partial c_t^2$ must be homogeneous of -1 degree in c and l,

$$\frac{\partial^2 f}{\partial c_t^2}(ac, al) = \frac{1}{a}\frac{\partial^2 f}{\partial c_t^2}(c, l),$$

where a is any number. If $c = c_w - \hat{c}_t$, $l = l_w$, and $a = b$, it follows that

$$\frac{\partial^2 f}{\partial c_t^2}(c_n + \hat{c}_t, l_n) = \frac{l_w}{l_n}\frac{\partial^2 f}{\partial c_t^2}(c_w - \hat{c}_t, l_w).$$

Substituting this in inequality (A7) and using the assumption of diminishing marginal productivity, we get the following simple condition:

$$\frac{\partial R}{\partial c_t/c_t = \hat{c}_t} \gtreqless 0 \quad \text{as} \quad \frac{Y(N)}{Y(W)} \gtreqless \frac{l_w}{l_n}, \tag{A8}$$

or

$$\frac{Y(W)}{Y(N)} \gtreqless \frac{l_n}{l_w}.$$

If in the absence of discrimination, N's relative income were less than W's relative supply of labor, a slight taste for discrimination by W would reduce N's income by a greater percentage than it would W's.

If $\partial R/(\partial c_t/c_t = \hat{c}_t) > 0$, $\partial R/\partial c_t$ would probably be greater than zero for all admissible values of c_t. For example, if

$$\frac{\partial R}{\partial c_t/c_t = \hat{c}_t} > 0 \quad \text{and} \quad \frac{\partial_f^3}{\partial c_t^3} > 0,$$

it would follow that

$$\frac{R}{c_t = \hat{c}_t - \epsilon} < \frac{R}{c_t = \hat{c}_t},$$

where ϵ is a small positive number, and

$$\frac{\partial^2 f/(\partial c_t^2/c_t = \hat{c}_t - \epsilon)}{\partial^2 f'/(\partial c_t^2/c_t = \hat{c}_t - \epsilon)} < \frac{\partial^2 f/(\partial c_t^2/c_t = \hat{c}_t)}{\partial^2 f'/(\partial c_t^2/c_t = \hat{c}_t)} = 1.$$

Accordingly, if

$$R < \frac{\partial^2 f' / \partial c_t^2}{\partial^2 f / \partial c_t^2},$$

when $c_t = \hat{c}_t$, it must a fortiori be true when $c_t = \hat{c}_t - \epsilon$. By continuing to reason along these lines, one would readily show that it must be true for all c_t.[19] This analysis is the basis for the assumption in this chapter and the rest of the appendix that an increase in discrimination by W must reduce N's net income relative to W's, if and only if

$$\frac{1}{R} = \frac{Y(W)}{Y(N)/c_t = \hat{c}_t} > \frac{l_n}{l_w}. \tag{A9}$$

If there are different tastes for discrimination among W (or N), some new problems enter the analysis. The unit money price of domestic W capital would not equal the unit net price of exported capital: capital on the margin between working with labor supplied by N and W would, of course, receive the same net return "abroad" and "domestically"; capital with smaller tastes for discrimination would find it advantageous to work with N. All capital working with W labor would receive the same net return, but capital with relatively small tastes for discrimination would receive a larger net return for working with N labor. It follows that net income as defined here would underestimate true net income, since it assumes that the net return to all capital is the same as the net return to marginal capital. The curve representing the net incomes of W and N for various levels of discrimination by W would touch $p_0 w p_1$ at p_0 and p_1 (in fig. 1) and would be to its right at intermediate positions.

Clearly, if inequality (A9) were satisfied, there still would be effective discrimination against N; but would it be a necessary condition even if W alone discriminates? Assume that the level of discrimination by W varies by proportionate changes in the average taste for discrimination and in the dispersion around the average. In a small neighborhood around the point p_0 the average would be of the same order of smalls as the dispersion. It is conjectured that in this neighborhood the difference between the net income of marginal and intramarginal capital would be of a higher order of smalls. If this were true, the curve representing net incomes of W and N for various levels of discrimination by W would be tangent to $p_0 w p_1$ at p_0, and inequality (A9) would be necessary, as well as sufficient.

NOTES

1. If W wants to discriminate, exported capital must receive a higher equilibrium money return than domestically used capital, to compensate for working with N labor. However, if all W has the same taste for discrimination, the equilibrium net return must be the same for all W capital. Net and money returns to domestic capital are identical, since there are no psychic costs to working with W labor; therefore, the equilibrium money return to domestic capital can be used as the equilibrium net return to all W capital. The money and net returns to all W labor are the same, since it works only with W capital.

2. See the appendix to this chapter.

3. If we compare discrimination with tariffs, we find that, although some of their effects are similar, other effects are quite different. Discrimination always decreases both the societies' net incomes, while a tariff of the appropriate size can, as Bickerdike long ago pointed out, increase the levying society's net income. A tariff operates by driving a wedge between the price a society pays for imported goods and the price each individual member pays; it does not create any distinction between net income and total command over goods. Discrimination does create such a distinction and does not drive a wedge between private and social prices. Discrimination has more in common with transportation costs than with tariffs.

4. Saenger, a psychologist, said: "Discriminatory practices appear to be of definite advantage for the representatives of management in a competitive economic system" (*The Social Psychology of Prejudice* [New York: Harper & Bros., 1953], p. 96). Allport, another psychologist, likewise said: "We conclude, therefore, that the Marxist theory of prejudice is far too simple, even though it points a sure finger at *one* of the factors involved in prejudice, viz., rationalized self-interest of the upper classes" (*The Nature of Prejudice* [Cambridge, Mass.: Addision-Wesley Press, 1955], p. 210). Similar statements can be found in A. Rose, *The Costs of Prejudice* (Paris: UNESCO, 1951), p. 7; and throughout O. C. Cox, *Caste, Class, and Race* (Garden City, N.Y.: Doubleday, 1948); J. Dollard, *Caste and Class in a Southern Town* (New Haven, Conn.: Yale University Press, 1937); C. McWilliams, *A Mask for Privilege: Anti-Semitism in America* (Boston: Little, Brown, 1948); H. Aptheker, *The Negro Problem in America* (New York: International Publishers, 1946); and many other books as well.

5. D. A. Wilkerson, in his introduction to Aptheker's book, said: "Precisely this same relationship between material interests and Negro oppression exists today. . . . The per capita annual income of southern Negro tenant farmers and day laborers in 1930 was about $71, as compared with $97 for similar white workers. Multiply this difference of $26 by the 1,205,000 Negro tenants and day laborers on southern farms in 1930, and it is seen that planters 'saved' approximately $31,000,000 by the simple device of paying Negro workers less than they paid white workers" (Aptheker, op. cit., p. 10).

6. Let Y (N) and Y (W) represent the actual incomes of N and W, and $Y_0(N)$ and $Y_0(W)$ their incomes without discrimination. The total MDC is defined as

$$MDC = \frac{Y(W)}{Y(N)} - \frac{Y_0(W)}{Y_0(N)}.$$

7. In the 1920s there was a large movement, under the leadership of Marcus Garvey, to take Negroes in America back to Africa to "escape from" discrimination. This conclusion is also helpful in understanding some effects of apartheid.

8. In using money income to measure net income it is implicitly assumed that the cost to Negroes of trading with whites is small relative to their total command over goods.

9. It is not clear that a region-urban-rural breakdown of the data is desirable, since some of the advantages of trading with whites stem from the possibility of moving to remunerative white urban areas or even to other regions.

These data might underestimate Indian male incomes if a larger proportion of the Indian than of the Negro labor force were female, since females generally earn less than males. However, only 20 percent of the Indian labor force was female in 1950, as against 35 percent of the Negro labor force (see U.S. Bureau of the Census, *Census of Population, 1950: Special Report on Non-White Populations by Race* [Washington, D.C.: Government Printing Office, 1953], Tables 9 and 10). Thus median Indian male incomes were probably *less* than the 76 percent of Negro male incomes cited in the text for 1949.

One might suspect that the Indian population had been increasing at a faster rate than the Negro, so that some of the increase in Indian income had been taken up in the form of a relatively larger population. Once again the contrary seems to be true. Estimates of the Indian population date from 1890; in that year Indian population was 3 percent of the Negro population, and in 1950 it was 2 percent (see U.S. Bureau of the Census, *Statistical Abstract of the United States, 1953* [Washington, D.C.: Government Printing Office, 1954], p. 38). Therefore, the Negro population has increased at a significantly faster rate than the Indian.

Nor are there very large differences in education between the two groups. The median number of years of schooling in 1950 was 6.9 for Negro males and 7.7 for Negro females; 7.3 for Indian males and 7.4 for Indian females (see U.S. Bureau of the Census, *Special Report on Non-White Populations by Race*, Table 9).

This comparison is intended to be suggestive and not conclusive. Much more detailed work is necessary to determine the income of Indians and Negroes in the late nineteenth century and to standardize these income data for 1949.

10. See the appendix to this chapter (pp. 425–29).

11. If N is a numerical minority, the amount of labor owned by N (l'_n) is less than that owned by W (l'_w). The amount supplied to the market is $l_n = a_n l'_n$ and $l_w = a_w l'_w$. If $a_n = a_w$, $l'_n < l'_w$ implies $l_n < l_w$. More generally, $l'_n < l'_w$ implies $l_n < l_w$ if, and only if, $a_n/a_w < l'_w/l'_n$. This seems like a plausible restriction and is implicit in the inferences drawn in the text.

12. N exports labor if, and only if $l_n/l_w > c_n/c_w$. If, $l_n < l_w$, then $c_n < c_w$.

13. This statement is completely rigorous only if $a_n = a_w$.

14. Some mutual interaction may have occurred here, since poverty is a cause, as well as a result, of an unbalanced distribution of resources. For example, poor individuals often find it very difficult to obtain funds for investments in themselves.

15. This considers capital invested in humans as capital and not labor. If it were considered as labor, the assumption that Negro and white labor were perfect substitutes in production would be untenable, since whites have more capital invested in themselves than Negroes have. Since the number of Negroes in the labor force is about one-ninth the number of whites, the assumption that white labor is nine times that of Negro labor is reasonable if the innate capacities of whites and Negroes are roughly the same. The ratio of white to Negro capital was arrived at essentially by a guess. Our model implies that Negroes in the United States "export" unskilled labor to whites and that whites "export" capital—including skilled labor—to Negroes.

16. I have come across only one clear and explicit attempt to estimate the economic costs of discrimination. The technique used is clearly stated in the following paragraph:

"The results of these calculations represent a shocking reminder of the real cost of discrimination to our country in production, expressed in dollars and cents terms. We found that the average annual income of the Negro family is $1043. The average income for Whites is $3062, or roughly three times that of Negroes. And, when the difference in income is multiplied by the number of Negro family units which could add to the productive wealth of the nation, we discovered the appalling loss of four billion dollars of real wealth annually because of discrimination against Negroes alone" (see E. Roper, "The Price Business Pays," in *Discrimination and the National Welfare*, ed. R. M. MacIver [New York: Harper & Bros., 1948], p. 18).

Roper's implicit assumption that Negroes and whites would receive the same income without discrimination is a mistake: whites would receive larger incomes than Negroes because they have much more capital per capita. In the example used here, eliminating all discrimination would raise per capita Negro incomes to only 66 percent of per capita white incomes. This mistake partly explains why Roper assumed that Negro incomes would increase by 200 percent, this being about ten times my estimated increase. On the other hand, his implicit assumption that whites suffer a negligible economic loss is correct.

17. Inequality (1) refers to white and nonwhite incomes in equilibrium without discrimination; yet the condition stated above is in terms of actual net income with discrimination. However, there is no contradiction between these statements, since this condition implies inequality (1). If there were effective discrimination against *whites*, their relative net income would be less with discrimination than without it; so that, if their actual net incomes were at least four times those of nonwhites, their incomes without discrimination would also be at least four times those of nonwhites. But, by inequality (1), this implies that there must be effective discrimination against nonwhites rather than against whites. Consequently, if white net incomes were at least four times those of nonwhites, there must be effective discrimination against nonwhites.

18. See the study of native income by D. H. Houghton and D. Philcox, "Family Income and Expenditure in a Ciskei Native Reserve," *South African Journal of Economics* 18 (December 1950): 418–38, and the data giving the national income of South Africa in the report of the United Nations Statistical Office, *National and per Capita Incomes in Seventy Countries, 1949* (1950). These income figures overestimate the net incomes of whites and nonwhites, since the nonmonetary costs of working with each other have not been netted out of the gross production figures. It is unlikely, although not impossible, that the true net incomes of whites are less than four times those of nonwhites.

19. Although production functions that are homogeneous of the first degree do not necessarily have positive third-order partial derivatives, a wide and important class of them does, e.g., all homogeneous Cobb-Douglas functions. In general, if f is homogeneous of the first degree, Euler's theorem states that

$$l \frac{\partial f}{\partial l} + c \frac{\partial f}{\partial c} \equiv X.$$

After twice differentiating this identity with respect to c, one gets

$$\frac{c \partial^3 f}{\partial c^3} + \frac{\partial^2 f}{\partial c^2} + \frac{l \partial^3 f}{\partial l \partial c^2} \equiv 0.$$

Since $\partial^2 f / \partial c^2 < 0$, $\partial^3 f / \partial c^3$ must be > 0 if $l \partial^3 f / \partial l \partial c^2 \leq 0$, and it may be > 0 if $\partial^3 f / \partial l \partial c^2 > 0$. It seems plausible that $\partial^3 f / \partial l \partial c^2 \leq 0$. In any case, the assumption that $\partial^3 f / \partial c^3 > 0$ is sufficient but not necessary for the conclusions reached above; it is necessary merely that $Y(W)/Y(N)$ increase at a faster rate than $(\partial^2 f / \partial c_t^2)/(\partial^2 f' / \partial c_t^2)$ as c_t decreases.

HUMAN CAPITAL, EFFORT, AND THE SEXUAL DIVISION OF LABOR

• 18 •

Increasing returns from specialized human capital is a powerful force creating a division of labor in the allocation of time and investments in human capital between married men and married women. Moreover, since child care and housework are more effort-intensive than leisure and other household activities, married women spend less effort on each hour of market work than married men working the same number of hours. Hence, married women have lower hourly earnings than married men with the same market human capital, and they economize on the effort expended on market work by seeking less demanding jobs. The responsibility of married women for child care and housework has major implications for earnings and occupational differences between men and women.

I. Introduction

The labor force participation of married women in Western countries has increased enormously during the last thirty years. Initially, the increase was concentrated among older women, but it eventually spread to younger

First published in the *Journal of Labor Economics* 3, no. 1, pt. 2 (1985): S33–S58. © 1985 by The University of Chicago. All rights reserved.

women with small children. Although this paper will not be primarily concerned with the causes of the increase, it will be useful first to sketch out briefly an "economic" explanation (based on Becker 1981, chap. 11) that can be tested against the evidence.

The major cause of the increased participation of married women during the twentieth century appears to be the increased earning power of married women as Western economies developed, including the rapid expansion of the service sector. The growth in their earning power raised the forgone value of their time spent at child care and other household activities, which reduced the demand for children and encouraged a substitution away from parental, especially mothers', time. Both of these changes raised the labor force participation of married women.

The gain from marriage is reduced, and hence the attractiveness of divorce raised, by higher earnings and labor force participation of married women, because the sexual division of labor within households becomes less advantageous. Consequently, this interpretation also implies the large growth in divorce rates over time. The decline in the gain from marriage is reflected also in the increased number of "consensual unions" (unmarried couples living together), the large increase in families headed by women, and even partly in the large growth in illegitimate birthrates relative to legitimate rates during recent decades.

Divorce rates, fertility, and labor force participation rates of women also interact in various other ways. For example, fertility is reduced when divorce becomes more likely, because child care is more difficult after a marriage dissolves. There is evidence that couples who anticipate relatively high probabilities of divorce do have fewer children (see Becker, Landes, and Michael 1977). The labor force participation of women is also affected when divorce rates increase, not only because divorced women participate more fully, but also because married women will participate more as protection against the financial adversity of a subsequent divorce.

One difficulty with this explanation is that economic progress and the growth in earning power of women did not accelerate in developed countries after 1950, yet both divorce rates and labor force participation rates of married women have risen far more rapidly since then. I tentatively suggest that threshold effects of increased female earning power on labor force participation rates, fertility, and divorce rates are responsible for much of the acceleration. As the earning power of women continued to grow, fertility continued to fall until the time spent in child care was reduced enough so that married women could anticipate spending appreciable time in the labor force prior to their first child and subsequent to their last child. Women then had much greater incentive to invest in market-oriented human capital, which accelerated the increase in their earning power, participation, and divorce rates, and accelerated the reduction in fertility.

The modest increase in the hourly earnings of women relative to men during the last thirty years in the United States and many other Western countries (but not all; see Gregory, McMahon, and Whittingham [1985]; Gustafsson and Jacobsson [1985]) has been an embarrassment to the human capital interpretation of sexual earnings differentials, since this interpretation seems to imply that increased participation of married women would induce increased investment in earnings-raising market human capital. However, the increased participation may have temporarily reduced the earnings of women because increased supply generally lowers price, the average labor force experience of working women would be initially reduced, and observed earnings are temporarily reduced by increased on-the-job investments (see O'Neill 1985; Smith and Ward 1985).

Nevertheless, the evidence still suggests, although it does not demonstrate, that the earnings of men and women would not be equal even if their participation were equal. Some have inferred substantial discrimination in the marketplace against women, perhaps supported by the evidence in Zabalza and Tzannatos (1983) for Great Britain. This paper argues that responsibility for child care, food preparation, and other household activities also prevents the earnings of women from rising more rapidly.

Child care and other housework are tiring and limit access to jobs requiring travel or odd hours. These effects of housework are captured by a model developed in this paper of the allocation of energy among different activities. If child care and other housework demand relatively large quantities of "energy" compared to leisure and other nonmarket uses of time by men, women with responsibilities for housework would have less energy available for the market than men would. This would reduce the hourly earnings of married women, affect their jobs and occupations, and even lower their investment in market human capital when they worked the same number of market hours as married men. Consequently, the housework responsibilities of married women may be the source of much of the difference in earnings and in job segregation between men and women.

Section II sets out a model of the optimal division of labor among intrinsically identical household members who invest in different kinds of activity-specific human capital. Increasing returns from investments in specific human capital encourage a division of labor that reinforces differences in market and household productivity of men and women due to other forces, including any discrimination against women.

Section III models an individual's optimal allocation of energy among different activities. Many implications are derived, including a measure of the value of time in different activities, the forces encouraging the production of energy, and especially a very simple equation for the optimal supply of energy per hour of each activity.

Section IV applies the analysis of specialized investment and of the allocation and production of energy to earnings and occupational differentials between married men and women. It shows that married women with responsibility for child care and other housework earn less than men, choose "segregated" jobs and occupations, and invest less in market human capital even when married men and women work the same number of market hours.

Section V provides a summary and concluding remarks.

II. HUMAN CAPITAL AND THE DIVISION OF LABOR

The human capital approach has recognized from the beginning that the incentive to invest in human capital specific to a particular activity is positively related to the time spent at that activity (see Becker 1964, 51–52, 100–102). This recognition was early used to explain empirically why married women have earned significantly less than married men since women have participated in the labor force much less than married men (see Oaxaca 1973; Mincer and Polachek 1974).

It was not recognized immediately, however, that investments in specialized human capital produce increasing returns and thereby provide a strong incentive for a division of labor even among basically identical persons. This is recognized in chapter 2 of my book on the family (1981), where economies of scale from investments in activity-specific human capital are shown to encourage identical members of a household to specialize in different types of investments and to allocate their time differently. I also suggest there that the advantages of specialized investments provide more insights into comparative advantage in international trade than does the conventional emphasis on differences in factor supplies. These increasing returns to scale and advantages of specialization are illustrated in this section with a simple model heavily influenced by discussions with and examples in Rosen (1982) and Gros (1983).

Assume that a person's earnings in each of m market activities are proportional to his time spent at the activity and to his stock of human capital specific to the activity:

$$I_i = b_i t_{w_i} h_i, \qquad i = 1, \ldots, m, \qquad (1)$$

where h_i is capital completely specific to activity i. To simplify further, assume that h_i is produced only with investment time (t_{h_i}):

$$h_i = a_i t_{h_i}, \qquad i = 1, \ldots, m. \qquad (2)$$

If the total time spent at all work and investment activities is fixed, then

$$\sum_{i=1}^{m}(t_{w_i} + t_{h_i}) = \sum t_i = T, \tag{3}$$

where $t_i = t_{w_i} + t_{h_i}$. By summing over earnings in all activities, and substituting from (2),

$$I = \sum I_i = \sum c_i t_{w_i} t_{h_i}, \tag{4}$$

where $c_i = a_i b_i$.

Since earnings in each activity are determined by the product of work and investment time, total earnings are maximized when these times are equal:

$$I = \frac{1}{4}\sum c_i t_i^2, \tag{5}$$

when $t_{h_i} = t_{w_i}$. The increasing returns from the total time allocated to an activity (t_i) arise from the independence between the cost of accumulating human capital and the amount of time spent using the capital. These increasing returns imply that earnings are maximized when all time is spent on just one activity:

$$I^* = \frac{c_k}{4} T^2, \tag{6}$$

where $c_k \geq c_i$, all i. Examples of complete specialization in human capital specific to a single "activity" include doctors, dentists, carpenters, economists, and so on.

The same formulation is applicable to time allocated among consumption activities produced under constant returns to scale, where the effective time input is proportional both to consumption-specific human capital and consumption time, as in

$$Z_i = b_i t_{z_i} h_i. \tag{7}$$

If $h_i = a_i t_{h_i}$, then

$$Z_i = c_i t_{z_i} t_{h_i}, \tag{8}$$

and the output of each commodity is maximized by equating the time spent on production and investment:

$$Z_i^* = \frac{c_i t_i^2}{4}, \tag{9}$$

where $t_i = t_{z_i} + t_{h_i}$.

If the utility function is a simple Leontief function of these commodities,

$$U = \min(Z_1, \ldots, Z_m), \tag{10}$$

and if $c_i = c$, for all i, utility would be maximized by allocating equal time to each commodity:

$$U^a = Z_i^* = \frac{cT^2}{4m^2}. \tag{11}$$

This indirect utility function depends positively on the total time available and negatively on the number of commodities produced and consumed in fixed proportion.

The link between production and consumption would be severed if other persons also produced these commodities. To eliminate any *intrinsic* comparative advantage, I assume that all persons are basically identical. Even though all commodity production functions have constant returns to scale in effective time, there is still a gain from trade because each person can concentrate his investment and production on a smaller number of commodities and trade for the others. By reducing the number of commodities produced, advantage can be taken of the increasing returns to the *total* time spent on a commodity (see eq. [9]). For example, if two persons each produce half the commodities and trade their excess production unit for unit, the output of each commodity would equal

$$Z_i^1 = \frac{cT^2}{4(m/2)^2}, \quad i = 1, \ldots, \frac{m}{2} \tag{12}$$
$$Z_j^2 = \frac{cT^2}{4(m/2)^2}, \quad j = \frac{m}{2} + 1, \ldots, m.$$

Since they trade half the production, the indirect utility function of each person becomes

$$U^t = \frac{1}{2}\frac{cT^2}{4(m/2)^2} > \frac{cT^2}{4m^2} = U^a. \tag{13}$$

Increasing returns from investments in specialized human capital are the source of the gains from increasing the "extent of the market." Trade permits a division of labor in investments that effectively widens the market and thereby raises the welfare even of basically identical traders. The gain from specialization and trade in this example is simply proportional to the number of traders; each of p traders, $p \leq m$, would specialize in m/p commodities, and produce

Figure i

The Gains from Specialization and Trade

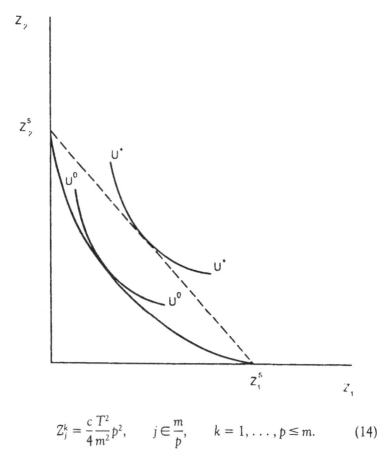

$$Z_j^k = \frac{c}{4}\frac{T^2}{m^2}p^2, \qquad j \in \frac{m}{p}, \qquad k = 1, \dots, p \le m. \qquad (14)$$

If $(p - 1)/p$th of the output were traded unit for unit, the level of utility would be proportional to the number of traders:

$$U^t = \frac{1}{p} Z_j^k = \frac{c}{4}\frac{T^2}{m^2}p, \qquad p \le m. \qquad (15)$$

The effect of specialization and trade on welfare is shown in figure 1 (suggested by John Muellbauer). A person without access to trade has a convex opportunity boundary between Z_1 and Z_2 because of increasing returns from specific investments; his utility is maximized at the point of tangency with an indifference curve (U^0). A market with many basically identical persons has better opportunities and can obtain by specialization and trade any point on the straight line joining the intercepts, Z_1^s and Z_2^s. If b persons specialize completely in Z_1 and $n - b$ specialize in Z_2, trading provides each person with $(b/n)Z_1^s$ units of Z_1 and $(1 - b/n)Z_2^s$ units of Z_2. This defines a straight-line opportunity boundary between Z_1^s and Z_2^s as b varies from zero to n. The improvement in welfare from trade (U^*/U^0) is determined by the degree of increasing returns or by the convexity of the opportunities for a person without trade.

The analysis is readily generalized to permit substitution among a continuum of commodities. The number of commodities consumed along with the degree of specialization in production by any trader would then also depend on the extent of the market (see the analysis in Gros [1983]). Moreover, goods and services as well as time can be inputs into the production of commodities and human capital. The following proposition survives all reasonable generalizations.

PROPOSITION. If n basically identical persons consume in equilibrium m $<<$ n commodities produced under constant or increasing returns to scale with specific human capital, each person will completely specialize in producing only one commodity and accumulate only the human capital specific to that commodity. The other $m - 1$ commodities will be acquired by trades with other specialized producers. If $n > 1$ is smaller or not much larger than m, or with decreasing returns to scale, specialization may be incomplete, but *some* commodities *must* be produced by only one person.[1]

This analysis is applicable to the division of labor and specialization within households and families because the production of children, many aspects of child care and investments in children, protection against certain risks, altruism, and other "commodities" are more efficiently produced and consumed within households than by trades among households (see Becker [1981] for a further discussion). Most societies in all parts of the world have had a substantial division of labor, especially by age and sex, in the activities of household members. Although the participation of women in agriculture, trade, and other nonhousehold activities varies greatly throughout different parts of the world, women are responsible for the lion's share of housework, especially child care and food preparation, in essentially all societies. Moreover, even when they participate in market activities, women tend to engage in different activities than men do (see Boserup [1970] for evidence from less-developed countries that supports these statements).

The advantages of investments in specific human capital encourage a sharp division of labor among household members but do not in and of themselves say anything about the *sexual* division of labor. I suggested in my book on the family that men and women have intrinsically different comparative advantages not only in the production of children, but also in their contribution to child care and possibly to other activities (Becker 1981, 21–25). Such intrinsic differences in productivity would determine the direction of the sexual division by tasks and hence sexual differences in the accumulation of specific human capital that reinforce the intrinsic differences.

Some have objected to the presumption that intrinsic differences in comparative advantage are an important cause of the sexual division of labor, and have argued instead that the sexual division is mainly due to the "exploitation" of women. Yet a sexual division of labor according to intrinsic advantage does not deny exploitation. If men have full power both to determine the division of labor and to take all household output above a "subsistence" amount given to women (a competitive marriage market would divide output more equally), men would impose an efficient division of labor because that would maximize household output, and hence their own "take." In particular, they would assign women to child care and other housework *only if* women have a comparative advantage at such activities.[2]

This argument is suggestive but not conclusive because it assumes that sexual differences in comparative advantage are independent of the exploitation of women. Yet exploited women may have an "advantage" at unpleasant activities only because the monetary value of the disutility tends to be smaller for exploited (and poorer) persons, or because exploited persons are not allowed to participate in activities that undermine their exploitation.[3]

No definitive judgment has to be made for the analysis in this paper (and in my book on the family), because it does not depend on the *source* of the comparative advantage of women at household activities, be it discrimination or other factors. It only requires that investment in specific human capital reinforce the effects of comparative advantage. Indeed, the analysis does not even require that the initial difference in comparative advantage between men and women be large: a small initial difference can be transformed into large observed differences by the reinforcing effects of specialized investments.

This conclusion is highly relevant to empirical decompositions of earnings differentials between men and women. Suppose, for example, that men and women have the same basic productivity, but that discrimination reduces the earnings of women 10 percent below their market productivity. Given the advantage of specialization, such discrimination would induce a sexual division of labor, with most women specialized to the household and most men specialized to the market. As a result, earnings of the average woman would be considerably less than those of the average man, say only 60 percent. A decomposition of the 40 percent differential would show that sexual differences in investments in human capital explain 30 percentage points, or 75 percent, and that only 25 percent remains to be explained by discrimination. Yet in this example, the average earnings of men and women would be equal without discrimination, because there would be no sexual division of labor. More generally, discrimination and other causes of sexual differences in basic comparative advantage can be said to explain the *entire* difference in earnings between men and women, even though differences in human capital may appear to explain most of it.

This magnification of small differences in comparative advantage into large differences in earnings distinguishes differences between men and women from those between blacks and whites or other groups. A little market discrimination against blacks would not induce a large reduction in their earnings, because there is no racial division of labor between the market and household sectors. (However, even slightly greater market discrimination against black men compared with black women could be magnified into much larger reductions in the earnings of black men than black women, because black women would be induced to spend more time in the labor force than white women, and black men would spend less time than white men.) Consequently, the empirical decomposition of earnings differences into discrimination and other sources should be interpreted more cautiously for men and women than for other groups because of the division of labor between men and women.

III. The Allocation of Effort

The huge increase in the labor force participation of married women in developed countries should have encouraged much greater investment by women in market capital, which, presumably, would raise their earnings relative to men's. Yet sexual differences in earnings are very large (perhaps 40 percent) in the Soviet Union, where women participate almost as much as men (see Ofer and Vinokur 1981), and they have not declined much in the United States. The persistence of these large differences may be evidence of substantial market discrimination against women (see the evidence for Great Britain in Zabalza and Tzannatos [1931]) or of a countervailing temporary depression in the earnings of women due to the entrance of many women with little market experience (see Mincer 1983; O'Neill 1985; Smith and Ward 1985).

An additional factor is the continuing responsibility of women for housework. For example, married women in the Soviet Union have responsibility for most of the child care and other housework even though they participate in the labor force almost as much as married men, and Ofer and Vinokur (1981) argue that the earnings of married Soviet women are much lower than

444 • DISCRIMINATION

the earnings of married men in good part because of these responsibilities. O'Neill (1983) has a similar argument regarding the lower earnings and segregated occupations of married women in the United States. Time budget studies clearly show that women have remained responsible for a large fraction of the child care and other housework even in advanced countries (see, e.g., Gronau [1976] for Israel, Stafford [1980] for the United States, and Flood [1983] for Sweden).

The earnings of women are adversely affected by household responsibilities even when they want to participate in the labor force as many hours as men, because they become tired, must stay home to tend to sick children or other emergencies, and are less able to work odd hours or take jobs requiring much travel. Although many effects of these responsibilities on the earnings and occupations of women have been frequently recognized, apparently the only systematic analysis is in my unpublished paper (Becker 1977). A model of the allocation of energy (or effort) among various household and market activities is developed there, and many implications are obtained, including some relating to differences in earnings and the allocation of time between husbands and wives.

This section further develops that model and shows how the allocation of energy is affected by the energy intensities of different activities, and also how its allocation interacts with the allocation of time and with investments in market and nonmarket human capital. The incentive to increase one's supply of energy is shown to depend positively on market human capital and other determinants of wage rates.

Firms buy a *package* of time and effort from each employee, with payment tied to the package rather than separate payments for units of time and effort. Earnings depend on the package according to

$$I = I(t_m, E_m) \qquad (16)$$

with $\partial I/\partial E_m$ and $\partial I/\partial t_m > 0$, and $I(0, t_m) = I(E_m, 0) = 0$, where E_m is effort and t_m is time. By entering E_m explicitly, I am assuming that firms can monitor the effort supplied by each employee, perhaps indirectly (see, e.g., Mirrlees 1976; Shavell 1979). If firms were indifferent to the distribution of hours among identical workers, earnings would be proportional to hours worked for a given effort per hour:

$$I = w(e_m)t_m, \qquad (17)$$

with $w' > 0$ and $w(0) = 0$, where $e_m = E_m/t_m$ is effort per hour. A simple function that incorporates these properties is

$$I = \alpha_m e_m^{\sigma_m} t_m = \alpha_m E_m^{\sigma_m} t_m^{1-\sigma_m} = \alpha_m t_m', \qquad (18)$$

with $t'_m = e_m^{\sigma_m} t_m$, and $\alpha_m = \beta_m h_m$, where h_m is market human capital, and σ_m, the effort intensity of work, is assumed to be constant and measures the elasticity of earnings with respect to effort per hour.

Clearly, an increase in hours would raise earnings when total effort (E_m) is held constant only when $\sigma_m < 1$. However, $\sigma_m < 1$ implies that equal effort (e_m) is used with each hour, because increases in effort per hour then have diminishing effects on earnings. Equation (18) implies that earnings are proportional to an "effective" quantity of time (t'_m) that depends on effort per hour as well as number of hours.

Each firm chooses σ_m and α_m to maximize its income, subject to production functions, competition from other firms, the methods used to monitor employees, and the effect of σ_m and α_m on the effort supplied by employees. An analysis of these decisions and of market equilibrium is contained in Becker (1977). Here I only indicate that the trade-off between α_m and σ_m depends on the cost to firms of monitoring effort (perhaps indirectly), and by the effect of these parameters on the effort supplied by employees.

Time and effort not supplied to firms are used in the household (or nonmarket) sector. Each household produces a set of commodities with market goods and services, time, and effort:

$$Z_i = Z_i(x_i, t_i, E_i), \quad i = 1, \ldots, n. \tag{19}$$

If time and effort in the household sector also combine to produce "effective" time, the production function for Z_i can be written as

$$Z_i = Z_i(x_i, t'_i), \tag{20}$$

with $t'_i = w_i(e_i)t_i = \alpha_i e_i^{\sigma_i} t_i = \alpha_i E_i^{\sigma_i} t_i^{1-\sigma_i}$, with $0 < \sigma_i < 1$, and $\alpha_i = \beta_i h_i$, where h_i is human capital that raises the productivity of time spent on the ith commodity, and σ_i is the effort intensity of that commodity. The sum of the time spent on each commodity and the time spent at market activities must equal the total time available:

$$\sum_{i=1}^{n} t_i + t_m = t_h + t_m = t, \tag{21}$$

where t_h is the total time spent in the household sector.

The total energy at the disposal of a person during any period can be altered by the production of energy and by reallocation of energy over the life cycle. I first assume a fixed supply of energy that must be allocated among activities during a single period:

$$\sum_{i=1}^{n} E_i + E_m = E, \tag{22}$$

where E is the fixed available supply. This equation can be written as

$$\sum_{i=1}^{n} e_i t_i + e_m t_m = \bar{e}t = E, \qquad (23)$$

where $\bar{e}$ is the energy spent per each of the available hours. Since the decision variables, e_j and t_j, enter multiplicatively rather than linearly, the allocation of time directly "interacts" with the allocation of energy.

Total expenditures on market goods and services must equal money income:

$$\sum p_i x_i = w_m(e_m)t_m + v = I + v = Y, \qquad (24)$$

where Y is money income and v is income from transfer payments, property, and other sources not directly related to earnings. Money income is affected not only by the time but also by the energy allocated to the market sector. Full income (S) is achieved when all time and energy is spent at work since earnings are assumed to be independent of the time and energy spent on commodities:

$$w_m(\bar{e})t + v = S. \qquad (25)$$

Full income depends on four parameters: property income (v), the wage rate function (w_m), the available time (t), and the supply of energy per unit of time $(\bar{e})$.

Each household maximizes a utility function of commodities

$$U = U(Z_1, \ldots, Z_n), \qquad (26)$$

subject to the full income constraint in equation (25) and to the production functions given by equation (20). The following first-order conditions are readily derived:

$$\frac{\partial U}{\partial x_i} \equiv U_{x_i} = \tau p_{x_i}$$

$$\frac{\partial U}{\partial t_i'} w_i \equiv U_{t_i} = \mu + \epsilon e_i$$

$$\tau w_m = \mu + \epsilon e_m \qquad (27)$$

$$\frac{\partial U}{\partial t_i'}\left[t_i \frac{dw_i}{de_i} \right] \equiv U_{e_i} = \epsilon t_i$$

$$\tau t_m \frac{dw_m}{de_m} = \epsilon t_m,$$

where τ, μ, and ϵ are the marginal utilities of income, time, and effort, respectively.

The interpretation of these conditions is straightforward. The second and third indicate that the marginal utility of an additional hour spent at any activity must equal the sum of the opportunity cost of this hour in both time (μ) and effort (ϵe_j). An additional hour has an effort as well as a time cost because some effort is combined with each hour. The fourth and fifth conditions simply indicate that the marginal utility of effort per hour must equal the opportunity cost of effort (ϵt_j).

Each household selects the combination of goods and effective time that minimizes the cost of producing commodities. Effective time can be substituted for goods by reallocating either time or effort from work to commodities. Costs of production are minimized when the marginal rate of substitution between goods and effective time equals the cost of converting either time or effort into market goods.

On substituting the third into the second condition, one obtains

$$U_{t_i} = \tau\left[w_m - \frac{\epsilon}{\tau}(e_m - e_i) \right] = \tau\hat{w}_i, \tag{28}$$

where $\hat{w}_i$ is the shadow price or cost of an additional hour at the ith activity. Another expression for the marginal cost of time is obtained by combining the last two conditions, and using the relation between U'_{t_i} and U_{t_i}:

$$U_{t_i} = \frac{\tau w'_m \cdot w_i}{w'_i} = \frac{\tau w_m(1 - \sigma_m)}{(1 - \sigma_i)} = \tau\hat{w}_i, \tag{29}$$

where $w'_j = \partial w_j/\partial e_j$.

The marginal cost of time is below the wage rate for all activities with effort intensities less than the effort intensity of work because the saving of energy from reallocating time away from work is also valued. Equation (29) shows that the marginal cost is the difference between the wage value and the money value of the saving in (or expenditure on) energy: e_m is the value of an additional unit of energy, and $e_m - e_i$ is the saving (or expenditure on) energy.

Consequently, the marginal cost of time would be least for commodities using the least energy per hour. Moreover, the marginal cost is not the same even for persons with the same wage rate, if the money value of energy and the saving in energy differ. Note also that the cost of time *exceeds* the wage rate for highly effort-intensive activities (e.g., the care of young children).

The second and fourth optimality conditions immediately imply that

$$e_i = \frac{\mu}{\epsilon} \frac{\sigma_i}{1 - \sigma_i} \qquad (30)$$

(I am indebted to John Muellbauer for pointing this out). The optimal amount of energy allocated to an hour of any activity is proportional to the marginal cost of time in terms of energy, and also is positively related to the effort intensity of the activity. The cost of time in terms of energy is a sufficient statistic for other variables, including effort intensities of other activities, investments in human capital, property income, and the allocation of time, because they can affect the energy allocation per hour of any activity only by affecting this statistic.

A remarkably simple relation for the ratio of the optimal allocation of energy to any two activities is immediately derived from (30), or from (29) and the fourth condition in (27):

$$\frac{e_j}{e_i} = \frac{\sigma_j(1 - \sigma_i)}{\sigma_i(1 - \sigma_j)}, \qquad (31)$$

for all i, j, including m. The optimal ratio of energy per hour in any two activities depends only on their effort intensities, and will be constant as long as these intensities are constant, regardless of changes in other intensities, the utility function, the allocation of time, and so on.

The ratio of efforts per hour in equation (31) does not depend on utility, the allocation of time, and other variables, because it is a necessary condition to produce efficiently, that is, to be on the production possibility frontier between commodities in the utility function. A change in the effort intensity of an activity might change the absolute amount of energy per hour in all activities, but would not change the ratio between the energies per hour in any two other activities. The simple relations in equations (30) and (31) are of great use in determining the effects of different parameters on the allocation of energy.

A few things can be surmised about the ordering of effort intensities in different activities. Sleep is obviously closely dependent on time but not energy; indeed, sleep is more energy producing than energy using. Listening to the radio, reading a book, and many other leisure activities also depend on the input of time but less closely on energy. By contrast, many jobs and the care of small children use much energy. Available estimates of the value of time are usually much below wage rates, one-half or less, which suggests by equation (29) that the effort intensity of work greatly exceeds the intensities of many household activities.[4]

A change in property income, human capital, the allocation of time, or other variables that do not change effort intensities would change the effort per hour in all activities by the same positive or negative proportion, equal to the percentage change in the energy value of time (see eq. [30]). This proportionality, and constant energy ratios in different activities, is a theorem following from utility maximization (and other assumptions of our model) and should not be confused with the assumption of a constant effort per hour in each activity (an assumption made, for example, by Freudenberger and Cummins [1976]).

A decrease in hours worked and an increase in "leisure," induced perhaps by a rise in property income, would save on energy and raise the energy value of time, because work is more effort-intensive than leisure.[5] Then the energy spent on each hour of work and other activities would increase by the same proportion, which would raise hourly earnings and the productivity of each hour spent on other activities. Conversely, a compensated increase in market human capital that raised hours worked would reduce the energy value of time, and hence also the energy spent on each hour of work.

The effect of increased market human capital on wage rates, a major determinant of the return to investments in market capital, is positively related to the energy spent on each hour of work. Therefore, the incentive to invest in market capital is greater when the energy per hour as well as number of hours of work (see Sec. II) is greater,[6] since costs of investing in human capital are only partly dependent on wage rates. The same conclusion applies to investment in capital specific to any other activity.

Earnings in some jobs are highly responsive to changes in the input of energy, while earnings in others are more responsive to changes in the amount of time. That is, some have larger effort intensities, and others have larger time intensities. Persons devoting much time to effort-intensive household activities like child care would economize on their use of energy by seeking jobs that are not effort-intensive, and conversely for persons who devote most of their household time to leisure and other time-intensive activities.

The stock of energy varies enormously from person to person, not only in dimensions like mental and physical energy,[7] but also in "ambition" and motivation. Although equation (30) implies that an increase in the stock of energy, and hence in the energy value of time, increases the energy per hour by the same percentage with all activities, the productivity of working time would increase by a larger percentage if work is more effort-intensive than the typical household activity. Then persons with greater stocks of energy would excel at work not only because their wage rates would be above average, but also because the productivity of their working time would be especially high.

If the (full) income effect of greater energy is weak,[8] persons with greater energy also tend to work longer hours and at more effort-intensive jobs because their time is relatively more productive at work than at household activities. Consequently, more-energetic persons would both work longer hours and earn more per hour.

Since the elasticity of output with respect to energy per hour is less than unity ($\sigma_m < 1$), a given increase in the stock of energy would raise output by a smaller percentage if hours worked were unchanged. However, the induced increase in hours would raise output by more than the increase in the stock of energy. Several experimental studies do find that an increase in the consumption of calories by workers doing physically demanding work, where calories are an important source of "energy," apparently raises their output by a larger percent (see U.N. Food and Agriculture Organization 1962, 14–15, 23–25).

Since a person's health affects his energy, ill health reduces hourly earnings (see the evidence in Grossman [1976]), because a lower energy level reduces the energy spent on each working (and household) hour. Ill health also reduces hours worked because work is relatively effort-intensive; that is, sick time is spent at home rather than at work because rest and similar leisure activities use less energy than work. Therefore, more-energetic persons can be said to work longer hours and earn more per hour partly because they are "healthier."

The energy available to a person changes not only because of illness and other exogenous forces, but also because of the expenditure of time, goods, and effort on exercise, sleep, physical check-ups, relaxation, proper diet, and other energy-producing activities. At the optimal rate of production, the cost of additional inputs equals the money value of additional energy:

$$w'_m = \beta_m \sigma_m e_m^{\sigma_m - 1} h_m = \frac{\epsilon}{\tau} = w'_m t_s \frac{de_s}{dE} + p_s \frac{dx_s}{dE} + w_m \frac{(1 - \sigma_m)}{1 - \sigma_s} \frac{dt_s}{dE}, \quad (32)$$

where e_s, x_s, and t_s are inputs into the production of energy.[9] The term on the right is the cost of inputs used to produce an additional unit of energy; the money value of an additional unit equals the effect on hourly earnings of an increase in energy per hour (see the last condition in [27]).

An increase in the marginal wage rate increases the optimal production of energy because marginal benefits increase relative to marginal costs. An increase in market human capital and a decrease in energy per hour of work (perhaps resulting from an increased number of working hours) both encourage the production of energy by raising benefits relative to cost of production; indeed, costs could decline when energy per hour decreased because the value of time would decrease. Increased production of energy would also improve health, given the positive relation between health and energy.

Many have argued that long hours of work substantially reduce produc-

among persons because more energetic persons work longer. Moreover, even if longer working hours by any given person directly reduce his energy (and productivity) per hour of work, longer hours also encourage his production of energy and of market human capital. Since more energy and market capital raise the productivity of each working hour, longer hours could even indirectly *raise* his productivity per hour.

The incentive to invest in energy varies over the life cycle as the stock of market human capital and other determinants of the value of energy vary. Therefore, hourly earnings rise at younger ages probably partly because of increased production of energy, and conversely for declines in earnings at older ages. The stock of energy at a particular age might also be augmentable by "borrowing" from other ages, perhaps with substantial penalty or interest. In extreme forms, borrowing and repayment of energy produce "overwork" and "burnout."[11]

IV. Division of Labor in the Allocation of Effort between Husbands and Wives

Since more energetic persons have a comparative advantage at effort-intensive activities, efficient marriage markets match more-energetic with less-energetic persons (i.e., negative sorting by energy). A larger fraction of the time of energetic spouses would be allocated to effort-intensive activities like work where they have a comparative advantage, and a larger fraction of the time of sluggish spouses would be allocated to the household activities where they have a comparative advantage.

The evidence is much too scanty to argue that a division of labor by energy level helps explain the division of labor between married men and women. Therefore, I assume that women have responsibility for child care and other housework for reasons unrelated to their energy or to the effort intensity of housework. Nevertheless, differences in effort intensities have important implications for sexual differences in earnings, hours worked, and occupations.

To demonstrate this, I follow the brief discussion in the previous section suggesting that housework activities like child care are much more effort-intensive than leisure-oriented activities and may be more or less effort-intensive than market activities. Married women with primary responsibility for child care and other housework allocate less energy to each hour of work than married men who spend equal time in the labor force. A simple proof uses the assumption that housework is more effort-intensive than leisure, and the implication of equation (31) that the ratio of the energy spent on each hour of any two activities depends only on the effort intensities of these activities.[12]

Since married women earn less per hour than married men when they spend less energy on each hour of work, the household responsibilities of married women reduce their hourly earnings below those of married men even when both participate the same number of hours and have the same market capital. These household responsibilities also induce occupational segregation because married women seek occupations and jobs that are less effort-intensive and otherwise are more compatible with the demands of their home responsibilities. The same argument explains why students who attend class and do homework have lower hourly earnings than persons not in school when both work the same number of hours and appear to have similar characteristics (see the evidence and discussion in Lazear [1977]).

Therefore, the traditional concentration on the labor force participation of women gives a misleading, perhaps a highly misleading, impression of the forces reducing the earnings and segregating the employment of married women. Nor is this all. Married women would invest less in market human capital than married men even when both spend the same amount of time in the labor force. Since the benefit from investment in market human capital is positively related to hourly earnings and hence to the energy spent on each hour of market work (see the previous section), the benefit is greater to married men even when they do not work longer hours than married women.

The lower earnings of married women due both to their lower energy spent on work and their lower investment in market human capital discourages their labor force participation relative to that of their husbands. Of course, their lower participation further discourages their investment in market capital (but see n. 6), and could even lower their energy spent on each hour of work if they substitute toward housework that is more effort-intensive than their market activities. A full equilibrium could involve complete specialization by wives in housework and other nonmarket activities.

Table 1 (brought to my attention by June O'Neill) shows that even married women employed full-time in the United States work much more at home than do unemployed or part-time employed married men, let alone full-time employed married men. Moreover, married women employed full-time work many fewer hours (about 9 hours per week) in the market than do married men employed full-time, although total hours worked are a little higher for these women. There is considerable other evidence that the occupations and earnings of women are also affected by their demand for part-time employment and flexible hours (see Mincer and Polachek 1974, table 7; O'Neill 1983).

This analysis implies that the hourly earnings of single women exceed

TABLE 1

TIME USE OF MARRIED MEN AND MARRIED WOMEN IN THE UNITED STATES
BY HOURS PER WEEK AT HOME AND AT MARKET WORK, 1975–76

Type of Activity	Employed Full-Time	Employed Part-Time	All*	Employed Full-Time	All†
	MARRIED WOMEN			MARRIED MEN	
Market work:	38.6	20.9	16.3	47.9	39.2
At job‡	35.7	18.9	15.0	44.0	36.0
Travel to/from job	2.9	2.0	1.3	3.9	3.2
Work at home:	24.6	33.5	34.9	12.1	12.8
Indoor housework	14.6	21.0	20.8	2.8	3.5
Child care	2.8	3.2	4.9	1.7	1.5
Repairs, outside work, gardening	1.6	1.7	2.2	3.8	3.9
Shopping, services	5.6	7.6	7.0	3.8	3.9
Leisure	21.0	25.5	26.7	23.0	27.1
Total work time	63.2	54.4	51.2	60.0	52.0
Sample size	101	51	220	236	307

SOURCE: Hill (1981), based on data from a national sample of U.S. households collected by the Survey Research Center of the University of Michigan.
* Includes married women with no market work.
† Includes married men with part-time work and no market work.
‡ Includes lunch and coffee breaks.

those of married women even when both work the same number of hours and have the same market capital because child care and other household responsibilities induce married women to seek more convenient and less energy-intensive jobs. The analysis also can explain why marriage appears to raise the health of men substantially and women's health only moderately (see Fuchs 1975). Since married men accumulate more market human capital and work longer hours than single men (see Kenny 1983), married men produce larger stocks of energy than single men, which improves their health. The effect of marriage on the energy of women is more ambiguous: the value of energy to women not working in the market is measured by the value of additional energy in the household, which can be sizable. However, the value of energy to working women is measured by its value at work, which has been below the value to men because women have invested less in market human capital and have chosen less energy-intensive work.

The large growth in the labor force participation of married women during the last thirty years has been accompanied by a steep fall in fertility and a sharp rise in divorce rates. The fall in fertility clearly raises the hourly earnings of married women because they have more energy and more flexible time to devote to market work instead of child care. The time spent in housework by married women in the United States apparently did decline significantly after 1965 (see Stafford 1980).

The effect of the growth in divorce on the hourly earnings of women is more ambiguous. On the one hand, married women invest more in market human capital when they anticipate working because they are likely to become divorced. On the other hand, since divorced women in the United States and other Western countries almost always retain custody of their children, the demands of child care on their energy and attention might exceed those of married women, for they have no husbands to share any of the housework.[13]

V. Summary and Concluding Remarks

This paper argues that increasing returns from specialized human capital is a powerful force creating a division of labor in the allocation of time and investments in human capital even among basically identical persons. However, increasing returns alone do not imply the traditional sexual division of labor, with women having primary responsibility for many household activities, unless men and women tend to differ in their comparative advantages between household and market activities. Whatever the reason for the traditional division—perhaps discrimination against women or high fertility—housework responsibilities lower the earnings and affect the jobs of married women by reducing their time in the labor force and discouraging their investment in market human capital.

This paper also develops a model of an individual's allocation of energy among different activities. More energy is spent on each hour of more-energy-intensive activities, and the ratio of the energy per hour in any two activities depends only on their effort intensities and not at all on the stock of energy, utility function, money income, allocation of time, or human capital. Other implications are derived about the cost of time to different activities, the effect of hours worked on hourly earnings, the effect of earnings on investment in health, and the effect of an increase in the energy spent on each hour of work on the benefits from investment in market human capital.

Since housework is more effort-intensive than leisure and other household activities, married women spend less energy on each hour of market work than married men working the same number of hours. As a result, married women have lower hourly earnings than married men with the same market human capital, and they economize on the energy expended on market work by seeking less demanding jobs. Moreover, their lower hourly earnings reduce their investment in market capital even when they work the same number of hours as married men.

Therefore, the responsibility of married women for child care and other housework has major implications for earnings and occupational differences between men and women even aside from the effect on the labor force participation of married women. I submit that this is an important reason why the earnings of married women are typically considerably below those of married men, and why substantial occupational segregation persists, even in countries like the Soviet Union where labor force participation rates of married men and women are not very different.

The persistence of these responsibilities in all advanced societies may only be a legacy of powerful forces from the past and may disappear or be greatly attenuated in the near future. Not only casual impressions, but also evidence from time budgets indicate that the *relative* contribution of married men to housework in the United States has significantly increased during the last decade (Stafford 1980; personal communication from Stafford about a 1981 survey). The frequency of partial or complete custody of children by divorced fathers has also increased. A continuation of these trends would increase the energy and time spent at market activities by women, which would raise their earnings and incentive to invest in market human capital. The result could be a sizable increase in the relative earnings of married women and a sizable decline in their occupational segregation during the remainder of this century.

Even if the process continued until married women no longer had primary responsibility for child care and other housework, married households would still greatly gain from a division of labor in the allocation of time and investments if specialized household and market human capital remained important, or if spouses differed in energy. This division of labor, however, would no longer be linked to sex: husbands would be more specialized to housework and wives to market activities in about half the marriages, and the reverse would occur in the other half.

Such a development would have major consequences for marriage, fertility, divorce, and many other aspects of family life. Yet the effect on the inequality in either individual or family earnings would be more modest since all persons specialized to housework would still earn less than their spouses, and the distribution of family earnings would still be determined by the division of labor between spouses, by the sorting of spouses by education and other characteristics, by divorce rates and the custody of children, and so forth.

However, a person's sex would then no longer be a good predictor of earnings and household activities. It is still too early to tell how far Western societies will move in this direction.

Notes

This research has been supported by grant no. HD 14256-03 from the National Institutes of Health and no. SES-8208260 from the National Science Foundation. I received very helpful comments from Robert Michael, Jacob Mincer, John Muellbauer, Sherwin Rosen, Yoram Weiss, and participants in the Applications of Economics Workshop of the University of Chicago. Much of Section III was worked out jointly with H. Gregg Lewis. Gale Mosteller provided valuable assistance.

1. This proposition essentially combines theorems 2.2, 2.3, and 2.4 in Becker (1981, chap. 2).

2. Presumably, the advantages to slave owners of an efficient division of labor explain why slaves have sometimes been assigned to highly skilled activities (see Finley 1980).

3. However, Guity Nashat pointed out to me that even slaves sometimes had major military responsibilities (see, e.g., Inalcik [1970] for a discussion of the Janissaries).

4. However, practically all estimates of the value of time refer to time spent on transportation. Beesley's estimates for commuting time (1965) rise from about 30 percent of hourly earnings for lower-income persons to 50 percent for higher-income persons; similar results were obtained by Lisco (1967) and McFadden (1974). Becker (1965) estimates the time spent in commuting at about 40 percent of hourly earnings. Gronau (1970) concludes that business time during air travel is valued at about the hourly earnings of business travelers, while personal air travel time is apparently considered free.

5. By equation (23), $e_m t_m + e_h t_h = E$, where $e_h = E_h/t_h$. If $e_h = \gamma e_m$, where $\gamma < 1$ because $\sigma_m > \sigma_h$, then

$$\frac{\partial e_m}{\partial t_m} = \frac{-e_m(1-\gamma)}{\gamma t + t_m(1-\gamma)} < 0.$$

6. These variables have opposite effects when hours of work change if work is more effort-intensive than the competing household activities. Since

$$MP = \frac{\partial I}{\partial h_m} = w_m t_m,$$

then

$$\frac{\partial MP}{\partial t_m} = (1 + n_m \sigma_m) w_m,$$

where

$$n_m = \frac{\partial e_m}{\partial t_m} \frac{t_m}{e_m}.$$

Given that $0 < \sigma_m < 1$, and that $-1 \leq n_m \leq 1$, then $0 < \partial MP/\partial t_m$ and $(\partial MP/\partial t_m) \gtrless w_m$ as $n_m \gtrless 0$. A change in hours worked always changes the marginal product of human capital in the same direction (as argued in the Section II), but the effect can be substantially attenuated if n_m is quite negative, because work is *much* more effort-intensive than the competing household activities, and conversely, if n_m is positive, because work is less effort-intensive than these activities.

7. The inequality in energy is dramatically conveyed in the following preface to a biography of Gladstone: "Lord Kilbracken, who was once his principal private secretary, said that if a figure of 100 could represent the energy of an ordinary man, and 200 that of an exceptional man, Gladstone's energy would represent a figure of at least 1,000" (see Magnus 1954, xi). I owe this reference to George Stigler.

8. The sign of the income effect is ambiguous even when leisure is a superior good. The elasticity of working hours with respect to an increase in the stock of energy equals

$$\frac{\partial t_m}{\partial E} \frac{E}{t_m} = \eta_{t_m} E = R[x\delta_c(\sigma_m - \sigma_h) - \sigma_m(x - v) N_t + x\sigma_h N_x],$$

where t_h and x are the total time and goods used in the household ($p_x = 1$), N_t and N_x are the *full* income elasticities of t'_h and x respectively, δ_t is the elasticity of substitution between x and t'_h in the utility function, and R is positive. The substitution effect is essentially given by $x\delta_c(\sigma_m - \sigma_h) > 0$ if $\sigma_m > \sigma_h$. The income effect is given by $x\sigma_h N_x - \sigma_m(x - v)N_t \gtrless 0$. It is greater than zero if $(\sigma_h/\sigma_m) > k_e(N_t/N_x)$, where k_e is the share of earnings in money income. This footnote is based on notes by H. Gregg Lewis.

9. I assume that inputs are devoted exclusively to the production of energy, but the analysis is readily extended to "joint production," where, say, a good diet produces both energy and commodities.

10. In his classic study of the sources of economic growth in the United States, Denison (1962) assumed that each hour of work beyond forty-three hours per week reduces productivity by at least 30 percent.

11. Bertrand Russell claims that he worked so hard on *Principia Mathematica* that "my intellect never quite recovered from the strain" (1967, 230).

12. By equation (31), $e_c = \gamma_1 e_m$ and $e_\ell = \gamma_2 e_m$, where $\gamma_1 > \gamma_2$ because $\sigma_t > \sigma_e$, where c refers to housework and ℓ to leisure. Since $e_m t_m + e_c t_c + e_\ell t_\ell = E$, then $e_m(t_m + \gamma_1 t_c + \gamma_2 t_\ell) = E$, and

$$\left. \frac{de_m}{dt_i} \right|_{dt_m = 0} = \frac{-e_m(\gamma_1 - \gamma_2)}{t_m + \gamma_1 t_c + \gamma_2 t_{c\ell}} < 0.$$

13. Dustin Hoffman lost his job in *Kramer vs. Kramer* after he became responsible for the care of his child.

REFERENCES

Becker, Gary S. *Human Capital*. New York: Columbia University Press (for NBER), 1964.

———. "A Theory of the Allocation of Time." *Economic Journal* 75 (1965): 493–517.

———. "A Theory of the Production and Allocation of Effort." NBER Working Paper no. 184. Cambridge, Mass.: NBER, 1977.

———. *A Treatise on the Family*. Cambridge, Mass.: Harvard University Press, 1981.

Becker, G. S., E. M. Landes, and R. T. Michael. "An Economic Analysis of Marital Instability." *Journal of Political Economy* 85 (1977): 1141–87.

Beesley, M. E. "The Value of Time Spent in Travelling: Some New Evidence." *Economica* 32 (1965): 174–85.

Boserup, Ester. *Women's Role in Economic Development*. London: Allen & Unwin, 1970.

Denison, E. *Sources of Economic Growth in the United States*. Washington, D.C.: Committee for Economic Development, 1962.

Finley, M. I. *Ancient Slavery and Modern Ideology*. New York: Viking, 1980.

Flood, L. "Time Allocation to Market and Non-Market Activities in Swedish Households." Department of Statistics Research Report. Göteborg: University of Göteborg, 1983.

Freudenberger, H., and G. Cummins. "Health, Work, and Leisure before the Industrial Revolution." *Explorations in Economic History* 13 (1976): 1–12.

Fuchs, V. R. *Who Shall Live?* New York: Basic, 1975.

Gregory, R., P. McMahon, and B. Whittingham. "Women in the Labor Force: Trends, Causes, and Consequences." *Journal of Labor Economics* 3, no. 1, pt. 2 (1985).

Gronau, R. "The Effect of Traveling Time on the Demand for Passenger Transportation." *Journal of Political Economy* 78 (1970): 377–94.

———. "The Allocation of Time of Israeli Women." *Journal of Political Economy* 84 (1976): S201–S220.

Gros, D. "Increasing Returns and Human Capital in International Trade." Thesis seminar paper. University of Chicago, Department of Economics, 1983.

Grossman, M. "The Correlation between Health and Schooling." In *Household Production and Consumption*, edited by N. E. Terleckyj. New York: Columbia University Press (for NBER), 1976.

Gustafsson, S., and R. Jacobsson. "Trends in Female Labor Force Participation in Sweden." *Journal of Labor Economics* 3, no. 1, pt. 2 (1985).

Hill, M. S. "Patterns of Time Use." Mimeographed. University of Michigan, Survey Research Center, 1981.

Inalcik, H. "The Rise of the Ottoman Empire." In *The Cambridge History of Islam*, vol. 1, edited by P. M. Holt, A. K. S. Lambton, and B. Lewis. Cambridge, Eng.: Cambridge University Press, 1970.

Kenny, L. W. "The Accumulation of Human Capital during Marriage by Males." *Economic Inquiry* 21 (1983): 223–31.

Lazear, E. P. "Schooling as a Wage Depressant." *Journal of Human Resources* 12 (1977): 164–76.

Lisco, T. E. "The Value of Commuters' Travel Time: A Study in Urban Transportation." Ph.D. dissertation, University of Chicago, 1967.

McFadden, D. "The Measurement of Urban Travel Demand." *Journal of Public Economics* 3 (1974): 303–28.

Magnus, P. *Gladstone*. London: Murray, 1954.

Mincer, J. "Comment on June O'Neill's 'The Trend in Sex Differential in Wages.'" Presented at the conference on Trends in Women's Work, Education and Family Formation, Sussex, England, May 31–June 3, 1983.

Mincer, J., and S. Polachek. "Family Investments in Human Capital: Earnings of Women." *Journal of Political Economy* 82 (1974): S76–S108.

Mirrlees, J. A. "The Optimal Structure of Incentives and Authority within an Organization." *Bell Journal of Economics* 7 (1976): 105–31.

Oaxaca, R. L. "Male-Female Wage Differentials in Urban Labor Markets." *International Economic Review* 14 (1973): 693–709.

Ofer, G., and A. Vinokur. "Earnings Differentials by Sex in the Soviet Union: A First Look." In *Economic Welfare and the Economics of Soviet Socialism*, edited by S. Rosefielde. Cambridge, Eng.: Cambridge University Press, 1981.

O'Neill, J. "The Determinants and Wage Effects of Occupational Segregation." Working Paper. Urban Institute, 1983.

———. "The Trend in the Male-Female Wage Gap in the United States." *Journal of Labor Economics* 3, no. 1, pt. 2 (1985).

Rosen, S. "The Division of Labor and the Extent of the Market." Mimeographed. University of Chicago, 1982.

Russell, B. *The Autobiography of Bertrand Russell, 1872–1914*. Boston: Little, Brown, 1967.

Shavell, S. "Risk Sharing and Incentives in the Principal and Agent Relationship." *Bell Journal of Economics* 10 (1979): 55–73.

Smith, J. P., and M. P. Ward. "Time-Series Growth in the Female Labor Force." *Journal of Labor Economics* 3, no. 1, pt. 2 (1985).

Stafford, F. P. "Women's Use of Time Converging with Men's." *Monthly Labor Review* 103 (1980): 57–59.

U.N. Food and Agriculture Organization. *Nutrition and Working Efficiency.* FFHC Basic Study no. 5. Rome: UNFAO, 1962.

Zabalza, A., and Z. Tzannatos. "The Effects of Britain's Anti-discriminatory Legislation on Relative Pay and Employment." Discussion Paper no. 155. London School of Economics, 1983.

LAW

◆ ◆ ◆ ◆

◆ *PART* ◆ *FOUR* ◆

CRIME AND PUNISHMENT: AN ECONOMIC APPROACH

· 19 ·

I. INTRODUCTION

Since the turn of the century, legislation in Western countries has expanded rapidly to reverse the brief dominance of laissez-faire during the nineteenth century. The state no longer merely protects against violations of person and property through murder, rape, or burglary but also restricts "discrimination" against certain minorities, collusive business arrangements, "jaywalking," travel, the materials used in construction, and thousands of other activities. The activities restricted not only are numerous but also range widely, affecting persons in very different pursuits and of diverse social backgrounds, education levels, ages, races, etc. Moreover, the likelihood that an offender will be discovered and convicted and the nature and extent of punishments differ greatly from person to person and activity to activity. Yet, in spite of such diversity, some common properties are shared by practically all legislation, and these properties form the subject matter of this essay.

In the first place, obedience to law is not taken for granted, and public and private resources are generally spent in order both to prevent offenses and to apprehend offenders. In the second place, conviction is not generally considered sufficient punishment in itself; additional and sometimes severe

First published in the *Journal of Political Economy* 76, no. 2 (March–April 1968): 169–217. © 1968 by The University of Chicago. All rights reserved.

punishments are meted out to those convicted. What determines the amount and type of resources and punishments used to enforce a piece of legislation? In particular, why does enforcement differ so greatly among different kinds of legislation?

The main purpose of this essay is to answer normative versions of these questions, namely, how many resources and how much punishment *should* be used to enforce different kinds of legislation? Put equivalently, although more strangely, how many offenses *should* be permitted and how many offenders *should* go unpunished? The method used formulates a measure of the social loss from offenses and finds those expenditures of resources and punishments that minimize this loss. The general criterion of social loss is shown to incorporate as special cases, valid under special assumptions, the criteria of vengeance, deterrence, compensation, and rehabilitation that historically have figured so prominently in practice and criminological literature.

The optimal amount of enforcement is shown to depend on, among other things, the cost of catching and convicting offenders, the nature of punishments—for example, whether they are fines or prison terms—and the responses of offenders to changes in enforcement. The discussion, therefore, inevitably enters into issues in penology and theories of criminal behavior. A second, although because of lack of space subsidiary, aim of this essay is to see what insights into these questions are provided by our "economic" approach. It is suggested, for example, that a useful theory of criminal behavior can dispense with special theories of anomie, psychological inadequacies, or inheritance of special traits and simply extend the economist's usual analysis of choice.

II. Basic Analysis

The Cost of Crime

Although the word "crime" is used in the title to minimize terminological innovations, the analysis is intended to be sufficiently general to cover all violations, not just felonies—like murder, robbery, and assault, which receive so much newspaper coverage—but also tax evasion, other so-called white-collar crimes, and traffic and other violations. Looked at this broadly, "crime" is an economically important activity or "industry," notwithstanding the almost total neglect by economists.[1] Some relevant evidence recently put together by the President's Commission on Law Enforcement and Administration of Justice (the "Crime Commission") is reproduced in table 1. Public expenditures in 1965 at the federal, state, and local levels on police, criminal

TABLE 1

ECONOMIC COSTS OF CRIMES

Type	Costs (millions of dollars)
Crimes against persons	815
Crimes against property	3,932
Illegal goods and services	8,075
Some other crimes	2,036
TOTAL	14,858
Public expenditures on police, prosecution, and courts	3,178
Corrections	1,034
Some private costs of combating crime	1,910
OVERALL TOTAL	20,980

SOURCE: President's Commission (1967d, 44).

courts and counsel, and "corrections" amounted to over $4 billion, while private outlays on burglar alarms, guards, counsel, and some other forms of protection were about $2 billion. Unquestionably, public and especially private expenditures are significantly understated, since expenditures by many public agencies in the course of enforcing particular pieces of legislation, such as state fair employment laws,[2] are not included, and a myriad of private precautions against crime, ranging from suburban living to taxis, are also excluded.

Table 1 also lists the Crime Commission's estimates of the direct costs of various crimes. The gross income from expenditures on various kinds of illegal consumption, including narcotics, prostitution, and mainly gambling, amounted to over $8 billion. The value of crimes against property, including fraud, vandalism, and theft, amounted to almost $4 billion,[3] while about $3 billion worth resulted from the loss of earnings due to homicide, assault, or other crimes. All the costs listed in the table total about $21 billion, which is almost 4 percent of reported national income in 1965. If the sizable omissions were included, the percentage might be considerably higher.

Crime has probably become more important during the last forty years. The Crime Commission presents no evidence on trends in costs but does present evidence suggesting that the number of major felonies per capita has grown since the early thirties (President's Commission 1967a, 22–31). Moreover, with the large growth of tax and other legislation, tax evasion and other kinds of white-collar crime have presumably grown much more rapidly than felonies. One piece of indirect evidence on the growth of crime is the large increase in the amount of currency in circulation since 1929. For sixty years prior to that date, the ratio of currency either to all money or to consumer expenditures had declined very substantially. Since then, in spite of further urbanization and income growth and the spread of credit cards and other kinds of credit,[4] both ratios have increased sizably.[5] This reversal can be explained by an unusual increase in illegal activity, since currency has obvious advantages over checks in illegal transactions (the opposite is true for legal transactions) because no record of a transaction remains.[6]

The Model

It is useful in determining how to combat crime in an optimal fashion to develop a model to incorporate the behavioral relations behind the costs listed in table 1. These can be divided into five categories: the relations between (1) the number of crimes, called "offenses" in this essay, and the cost of offenses, (2) the number of offenses and the punishments meted out, (3) the number of offenses, arrests, and convictions and the public expenditures on police and courts, (4) the number of convictions and the costs of imprisonments or other kinds of punishments, and (5) the number of offenses and the private expenditures on protection and apprehension. The first four are discussed in turn, while the fifth is postponed until a later section.

Damages. Usually a belief that other members of society are harmed is the motivation behind outlawing or otherwise restricting an activity. The amount of harm would tend to increase with the activity level, as in the relation

$$H_i = H_i(O_i),$$

with   (1)

$$H_i' = \frac{dH_i}{dO_i} > 0,$$

where H_i is the harm from the ith activity and O_i is the activity level.[7] The concept of harm and the function relating its amount to the activity level are familiar to economists from their many discussions of activities causing external diseconomies. From this perspective, criminal activities are an important subset of the class of activities that cause diseconomies, with the level of criminal activities measured by the number of offenses.

The social value of the gain to offenders presumably also tends to increase with the number of offenses, as in

$$G = G(O),$$

with (2)

$$G' = \frac{dG}{dO} > 0.$$

The net cost or damage to society is simply the difference between the harm and gain and can be written as

$$D(O) = H(O) - G(O). \qquad (3)$$

If, as seems plausible, offenders usually eventually receive diminishing marginal gains and cause increasing marginal harm from additional offenses, $G'' < 0$, $H'' > 0$, and

$$D'' = H'' - G'' > 0, \qquad (4)$$

which is an important condition used later in the analysis of optimality positions (see, for example, the Mathematical Appendix). Since both H' and $G' > 0$, the sign of D' depends on their relative magnitudes. It follows from (4), however, that

$$D'(O) > 0 \text{ for all } O > O_a \text{ if } D'(O_a) \geq 0. \qquad (5)$$

Until Section V the discussion is restricted to the region where $D' > 0$, the region providing the strongest justification for outlawing an activity. In that section the general problem of external diseconomies is reconsidered from our viewpoint, and there $D' < 0$ is also permitted.

The top part of table 1 lists costs of various crimes, which have been interpreted by us as estimates of the value of resources used up in these crimes. These values are important components of, but are not identical to, the net damages to society. For example, the cost of murder is measured by the loss in earnings of victims and excludes, among other things, the value placed by society on life itself; the cost of gambling excludes both the utility to those gambling and the "external" disutility to some clergy and others; the cost of "transfers" like burglary and embezzlement excludes social attitudes toward forced wealth redistributions and also the effects on capital accumulation of the possibility of theft. Consequently, the $15 billion estimate for the cost of crime in table 1 may be a significant understatement of the net damages to society, not only because the costs of many white-collar crimes are omitted, but also because much of the damage is omitted even for the crimes covered.

The Cost of Apprehension and Conviction

The more that is spent on policemen, court personnel, and specialized equipment, the easier it is to discover offenses and convict offenders. One can postulate a relation between the output of police and court "activity" and various units of manpower, materials, and capital, as in $A = f(m, r, c)$, where f is a production function summarizing the "state of the arts." Given f and input prices, increased "activity" would be more costly, as summarized by the relation

$$C = C(A)$$

and   (6)

$$C' = \frac{dC}{dA} > 0.$$

It would be cheaper to achieve any given level of activity the cheaper were policemen,[8] judges, counsel, and juries and the more highly developed the state of the arts, as determined by technologies like fingerprinting, wiretapping, computer control, and lie detecting.[9]

One approximation to an empirical measure of "activity" is the number of offenses cleared by conviction. It can be written as

$$A \cong pO,$$ (7)

where p, the ratio of offenses cleared by convictions to all offenses, is the overall probability that an offense is cleared by conviction. By substituting (7) into (6) and differentiating, one has

$$C_p = \frac{\partial C(pO)}{\partial p} = C'O > 0$$

and   (8)

$$C_O = C'p > 0$$

if $pO \neq 0$. An increase in either the probability of conviction or the number of offenses would increase total costs. If the marginal cost of increased "activity" were rising, further implications would be that

$$C_{pp} = C''O^2 > 0,$$
$$C_{OO} = C''p^2 > 0,$$ (9)

and

$$C_{pO} = C_{Op} = C''pO + C' > 0.$$

A more sophisticated and realistic approach drops the implication of (7) that convictions alone measure "activity," or even that p and O have identical elasticities, and introduces the more general relation

$$A = h(p, O, a). \tag{10}$$

The variable a stands for arrests and other determinants of "activity," and there is no presumption that the elasticity of h with respect to p equals that with respect to O. Substitution yields the cost function $C = C(p, O, a)$. If, as is extremely likely, h_p, h_O, and h_a are all greater than zero, then clearly C_p, C_O, and C_a are all greater than zero.

In order to ensure that optimality positions do not lie at "corners," it is necessary to place some restrictions on the second derivatives of the cost function. Combined with some other assumptions, it is *sufficient* that

$$C_{pp} \geq 0,$$
$$C_{OO} \geq 0, \tag{11}$$

and

$$C_{pO} \cong 0$$

(see the Mathematical Appendix). The first two restrictions are rather plausible, the third much less so.[10]

Table 1 indicates that in 1965 public expenditures in the United States on police and courts totaled more than $3 billion, by no means a minor item. Separate estimates were prepared for each of seven major felonies.[11] Expenditures on them averaged about $500 per offense (reported) and about $2,000 per person arrested, with almost $1,000 being spent per murder (President's Commission, 1967a, 26–65); $500 is an estimate of the average cost

$$AC = \frac{C(p, O, a)}{O}$$

of these felonies and would presumably be a larger figure if the number of either arrests or convictions were greater. Marginal costs (C_O) would be at least $500 if condition (11), $C_{OO} \geq 0$, were assumed to hold throughout.

The Supply of Offenses

Theories about the determinants of the number of offenses differ greatly, from emphasis on skull types and biological inheritance to family upbringing and disenchantment with society. Practically all the diverse theories agree, however, that when other variables are held constant, an increase in a person's probability of conviction or punishment if convicted would generally decrease, perhaps substantially, perhaps negligibly, the number of offenses he commits. In addition, a common generalization by persons with judicial experience is that a change in the probability has a greater effect on the number of offenses than a change in the punishment,[12] although, as far as I can tell, none of the prominent theories shed any light on this relation.

The approach taken here follows the economists' usual analysis of choice and assumes that a person commits an offense if the expected utility to him exceeds the utility he could get by using his time and other resources at other activities. Some persons become "criminals," therefore, not because their basic motivation differs from that of other persons, but because their benefits and costs differ. I cannot pause to discuss the many general implications of this approach,[13] except to remark that criminal behavior becomes part of a much more general theory and does not require ad hoc concepts of differential association, anomie, and the like,[14] nor does it assume perfect knowledge, lightning-fast calculation, or any of the other caricatures of economic theory.

This approach implies that there is a function relating the number of offenses by any person to his probability of conviction, to his punishment if convicted, and to other variables, such as the income available to him in legal and other illegal activities, the frequency of nuisance arrests, and his willingness to commit an illegal act. This can be represented as

$$O_j = O_j(p_j, f_j, u_j), \qquad (12)$$

where O_j is the number of offenses he would commit during a particular period, p_j his probability of conviction per offense, f_j his punishment per offense, and u_j a portmanteau variable representing all these other influences.[15]

Since only convicted offenders are punished, in effect there is "price discrimination" and uncertainty: if convicted, he pays f_j per convicted offense, while otherwise he does not. An increase in either p_j or f_j would reduce the utility expected from an offense and thus would tend to reduce the number of offenses because either the probability of "paying" the higher "price" or the "price" itself would increase.[16] That is,

$$O_{p_j} = \frac{\partial O_j}{\partial p_j} < 0$$

and (13)

$$O_{f_j} = \frac{\partial O_j}{\partial f_j} < 0,$$

which are the generally accepted restrictions mentioned above. The effect of changes in some components of u_j could also be anticipated. For example, a rise in the income available in legal activities or an increase in law-abidingness due, say, to "education" would reduce the incentive to enter illegal activities and thus would reduce the number of offenses. Or a shift in the form of the punishment, say, from a fine to imprisonment, would tend to reduce the number of offenses, at least temporarily, because they cannot be committed while in prison.

This approach also has an interesting interpretation of the presumed greater response to a change in the probability than in the punishment. An increase in p_j "compensated" by an equal percentage reduction in f_j would not change the expected income from an offense[17] but could change the expected utility, because the amount of risk would change. It is easily shown that an increase in p_j would reduce the expected utility, and thus the number of offenses, more than an equal percentage increase in f_j[18] if j has preference for risk; the increase in f_j would have the greater effect if he has aversion to risk; and they would have the same effect if he is risk neutral.[19] The widespread generalization that offenders are more deterred by the probability of conviction than by the punishment when convicted turns out to imply in the expected-utility approach that offenders are risk preferrers, at least in the relevant region of punishments.

The total number of offenses is the sum of all the O_j and would depend on the set of p_j, f_j, and u_j. Although these variables are likely to differ significantly between persons because of differences in intelligence, age, education, previous offense history, wealth, family upbringing, etc., for simplicity I now consider only their average values, p, f, and u,[20] and write the market offense function as

$$O = O(p, f, u). \tag{14}$$

This function is assumed to have the same kinds of properties as the individual functions, in particular, to be negatively related to p and f and to be more responsive to the former than the latter if, and only if, offenders on balance have risk preference. Smigel (1965) and Ehrlich (1967) estimate functions like (14) for seven felonies reported by the Federal Bureau of Investigation using state data as the basic unit of observation. They find that the relations are quite stable, as evidenced by high correlation coefficients; that there are significant negative effects on O of p and f; and that usually the effect of p exceeds that of f, indicating preference for risk in the region of observation.

A well-known result states that, in equilibrium, the real incomes of persons in risky activities are, at the margin, relatively high or low as persons are generally risk avoiders or preferrers. If offenders were risk preferrers, this implies that the real income of offenders would be lower, at the margin, than the incomes they could receive in less risky legal activities, and conversely if they were risk avoiders. Whether "crime pays" is then an implication of the

472 • LAW

attitudes offenders have toward risk and is not directly related to the efficiency of the police or the amount spent on combating crime. If, however, risk were preferred at some values of p and f and disliked at others, public policy could influence whether "crime pays" by its choice of p and f. Indeed, it is shown later that the social loss from illegal activities is usually minimized by selecting p and f in regions where risk is preferred, that is, in regions where "crime does not pay."

Punishments

Mankind has invented a variety of ingenious punishments to inflict on convicted offenders: death, torture, branding, fines, imprisonment, banishment, restrictions on movement and occupation, and loss of citizenship are just the more common ones. In the United States, less serious offenses are punished primarily by fines, supplemented occasionally by probation, petty restrictions like temporary suspension of one's driver's license, and imprisonment. The more serious offenses are punished by a combination of probation, imprisonment, parole, fines, and various restrictions on choice of occupation. A recent survey estimated for an average day in 1965 the number of persons who were either on probation, parole, or institutionalized in a jail or juvenile home (President's Commission 1967b). The total number of persons in one of these categories came to about 1,300,000, which is about 2 percent of the labor force. About one-half were on probation, one-third were institutionalized, and the remaining one-sixth were on parole.

The cost of different punishments to an offender can be made comparable by converting them into their monetary equivalent or worth, which, of course, is directly measured only for fines. For example, the cost of an imprisonment is the discounted sum of the earnings forgone and the value placed on the restrictions in consumption and freedom. Since the earnings forgone and the value placed on prison restrictions vary from person to person, the cost even of a prison sentence of given duration is not a unique quantity but is generally greater, for example, to offenders who could earn more outside of prison.[21] The cost to each offender would be greater the longer the prison sentence, since both forgone earnings and forgone consumption are positively related to the length of sentences.

Punishments affect not only offenders but also other members of society. Aside from collection costs, fines paid by offenders are received as revenue by others. Most punishments, however, hurt other members as well as offenders: for example, imprisonment requires expenditures on guards, supervisory personnel, buildings, food, etc. Currently about $1 billion is being spent each year in the United States on probation, parole, and institutionalization alone, with the daily cost per case varying tremendously from a low of $0.38 for adults on probation to a high of $11.00 for juveniles in detention institutions (President's Commission 1967b, 193–94).

The total social cost of punishments is the cost to offenders plus the cost or minus the gain to others. Fines produce a gain to the latter that equals the cost to offenders, aside from collection costs, and so the social cost of fines is about zero, as befits a transfer payment. The social cost of probation, imprisonment, and other punishments, however, generally exceeds that to offenders, because others are also hurt. The derivation of optimality conditions in the next section is made more convenient if social costs are written in terms of offender costs as

$$f' \equiv bf, \tag{15}$$

where f' is the social cost and b is a coefficient that transforms f into f'. The size of b varies greatly between different kinds of punishments: $b \cong 0$ for fines, while $b > 1$ for torture, probation, parole, imprisonment, and most other punishments. It is especially large for juveniles in detention homes or for adults in prisons and is rather close to unity for torture or for adults on parole.

III. Optimality Conditions

The relevant parameters and behavioral functions have been introduced, and the stage is set for a discussion of social policy. If the aim simply were deterrence, the probability of conviction, p, could be raised close to 1, and punishments, f, could be made to exceed the gain: in this way the number of offenses, O, could be reduced almost at will. However, an increase in p increases the social cost of offenses through its effect on the cost of combating offenses, C, as does an increase in f if $b > 0$ through the effect on the cost of punishments, bf. At relatively modest values of p and f, these effects might outweigh the social gain from increased deterrence. Similarly, if the aim simply were to make "the punishment fit the crime," p could be set close to 1, and f could be equated to the harm imposed on the rest of society. Again, however, such a policy ignores the social cost of increases in p and f.

What is needed is a criterion that goes beyond catchy phrases and gives due weight to the damages from offenses, the costs of apprehending and convicting offenders, and the social cost of punishments. The social welfare function of modern welfare economics is such a criterion, and one might assume that society has a function that measures the social loss from offenses. If

$$L = L(D, C, bf, O) \tag{16}$$

is the function measuring social loss, with presumably

$$\frac{\partial L}{\partial D} > 0, \qquad \frac{\partial L}{\partial C} > 0, \qquad \frac{\partial L}{\partial bf} > 0, \qquad (17)$$

the aim would be to select values of f, C, and possibly b that minimize L.

It is more convenient and transparent, however, to develop the discussion at this point in terms of a less general formulation, namely, to assume that the loss function is identical with the total social loss in real income from offenses, convictions, and punishments, as in

$$L = D(O) + C(p,O) + bpfO. \qquad (18)$$

The term $bpfO$ is the total social loss from punishments, since bf is the loss per offense punished and pO is the number of offenses punished (if there are a fairly large number of independent offenses). The variables directly subject to social control are the amounts spent in combating offenses, C; the punishment per offense for those convicted, f; and the form of punishments, summarized by b. Once chosen, these variables, via the D, C, and O functions, indirectly determine p, O, D, and ultimately the loss L.

Analytical convenience suggests that p rather than C be considered a decision variable. Also, the coefficient b is assumed in this section to be a given constant greater than zero. Then p and f are the only decision variables, and their optimal values are found by differentiating L to find the two first-order optimality conditions,[22]

$$\frac{\partial L}{\partial f} = D'O_f + C'O_f + bpfO_f + bpO = 0 \qquad (19)$$

and

$$\frac{\partial L}{\partial p} = D'O_p + C'O_p + C_p + bpfO_p + bfO = 0. \qquad (20)$$

If O_f and O_p are not equal to zero, one can divide through by them, and recombine terms, to get the more interesting expressions

$$D' + C' = -bpf\left(1 - \frac{1}{\epsilon_f}\right) \qquad (21)$$

and

$$D' + C' + C_p \frac{1}{O_p} = -bpf\left(1 - \frac{1}{\epsilon_p}\right), \qquad (22)$$

where

FIGURE I

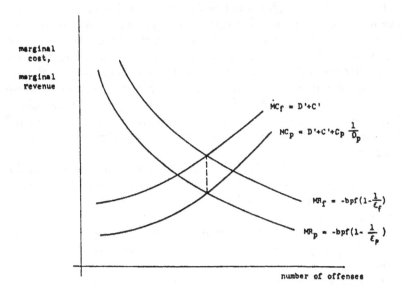

$$\epsilon_f = -\frac{f}{O}O_f$$

and   (23)

$$\epsilon_p = -\frac{p}{O}O_p.$$

The term on the left side of each equation gives the marginal cost of increasing the number of offenses, O: in equation (21) through a reduction in f and in (22) through a reduction in p. Since $C' > 0$ and O is assumed to be in a region where $D' > 0$, the marginal cost of increasing O through f must be positive. A reduction in p partly reduces the cost of combating offenses, and, therefore, the marginal cost of increasing O must be less when p rather than when f is reduced (see fig. 1); the former could even be negative if C_p were sufficiently large. Average "revenue," given by $-bpf$, is negative, but marginal revenue, given by the right-hand side of equations (21) and (22), is not necessarily negative and would be positive if the elasticities ϵ_p and ϵ_f were less than unity. Since the loss is minimized when marginal revenue equals marginal cost (see fig. 1), the optimal value of ϵ_f must be less than unity, and that of ϵ_p could only exceed unity if C_p were sufficiently large. This is a reversal of the usual equilibrium condition for an income-maximizing firm, which is that the elasticity of demand must exceed unity, because in the usual case average revenue is assumed to be positive.[23]

Since the marginal cost of changing O through a change in p is less than that of changing O through f, the equilibrium marginal revenue from p must also be less than that from f. But equations (21) and (22) indicate that the marginal revenue from p can be less if, and only if, $\epsilon_p > \epsilon_f$. As pointed out earlier, however, this is precisely the condition indicating that offenders have preference for risk and thus that "crime does not pay." Consequently, the loss from offenses is minimized if p and f are selected from those regions where offenders are, on balance, risk preferrers. Although only the attitudes offenders have toward risk can directly determine whether "crime pays," rational public policy indirectly ensures that "crime does not pay" through its choice of p and f.[24]

I indicated earlier that the actual ps and fs for major felonies in the United States generally seem to be in regions where the effect (measured by elasticity) of p on offenses exceeds that of f, that is, where offenders are risk preferrers and "crime does not pay" (Smigel 1965; Ehrlich 1967). Moreover, both elasticities are generally less than unity. In both respects, therefore, actual public policy is consistent with the implications of the optimality analysis.

If the supply of offenses depended only on pf—offenders were risk neutral—a reduction in p "compensated" by an equal percentage increase in f would leave unchanged pf, O, $D(O)$, and $bpfO$ but would reduce the loss, because the costs of apprehension and conviction would be lowered by the reduction in p. The loss would be minimized, therefore, by lowering p arbitrarily close to zero and raising f sufficiently high so that the product pf would induce the optimal number of offenses.[25] A fortiori, if offenders were risk avoiders, the loss would be minimized by setting p arbitrarily close to zero, for a "compensated" reduction in p reduces not only C but also O and thus D and $bpfO$.[26]

There was a tendency during the eighteenth and nineteenth centuries in Anglo-Saxon countries, and even today in many communist and under-developed countries, to punish those convicted of criminal offenses rather severely, at the same time that the probability of capture and conviction was set at rather low values.[27] A promising explanation of this tendency is that an increased probability of conviction obviously absorbs public and private resources in the form of more policemen, judges, juries, and so forth. Consequently, a "compensated" reduction in this probability obviously reduces expenditures on combating crime, and, since the expected punishment is unchanged, there is no "obvious" offsetting increase in either the amount of damages or the cost of punishments. The result can easily be continuous political pressure to keep police and other expenditures relatively low and to compensate by meting out strong punishments to those convicted.

Of course, if offenders are risk preferrers, the loss in income from offenses is generally minimized by selecting positive and finite values of p and f, even though there is no "obvious" offset to a compensated reduction in p. One possible offset already hinted at in footnote 27 is that judges or juries may be unwilling to convict offenders if punishments are set very high. Formally, this means that the cost of apprehension and conviction, C, would depend not only on p and O but also on f.[28] If C were more responsive to f than p, at least in some regions,[29] the loss in income could be minimized at finite values of p and f even if offenders were risk avoiders. For then a compensated reduction in p could raise, rather than lower, C and thus contribute to an increase in the loss.

Risk avoidance might also be consistent with optimal behavior if the loss function were not simply equal to the reduction in income. For example, suppose that the loss were increased by an increase in the ex post "price discrimination" between offenses that are not and those that are cleared by punishment. Then a "compensated" reduction in p would increase the "price discrimination," and the increased loss from this could more than offset the reductions in C, D, and $bpfO$.[30]

IV. Shifts in the Behavioral Relations

This section analyzes the effects of shifts in the basic behavioral relations—the damage, cost, and supply-of-offenses functions—on the optimal values of p and f. Since rigorous proofs can be found in the Mathematical Appendix, here the implications are stressed, and only intuitive proofs are given. The results are used to explain, among other things, why more damaging offenses are punished more severely and more impulsive offenders less severely.

An increase in the marginal damages from a given number of offenses, D', increases the marginal cost of changing offenses by a change in either p or f (see fig. 2a and b). The optimal number of offenses would necessarily decrease, because the optimal values of both p and f would increase. In this case (and, as shortly seen, in several others), the optimal values of p and f move in the same, rather than in opposite, directions.[31]

An interesting application of these conclusions is to different kinds of offenses. Although there are few objective measures of the damages done by most offenses, it does not take much imagination to conclude that offenses like murder or rape generally do more damage than petty larceny or auto theft. If the other components of the loss in income were the same, the optimal probability of apprehension and conviction and the punishment when convicted would be greater for the more serious offenses.

Table 2 presents some evidence on the actual probabilities and punish-

FIGURE 2

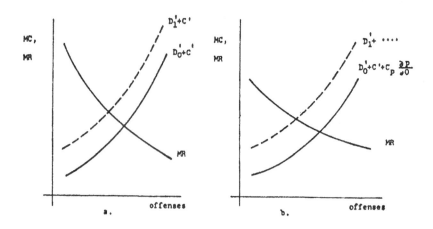

ments in the United States for seven felonies. The punishments are simply the average prison sentences served, while the probabilities are ratios of the estimated number of convictions to the estimated number of offenses and unquestionably contain a large error (see the discussions in Smigel 1965 and Ehrlich 1967). If other components of the loss function are ignored, and if actual and optimal probabilities and punishments are positively related, one should find that the more serious felonies have higher probabilities and longer prison terms. And one does: in the table, which lists the felonies in decreasing order of presumed seriousness, both the actual probabilities and the prison terms are positively related to seriousness.

Since an increase in the marginal cost of apprehension and conviction for a given number of offenses, C', has identical effects as an increase in marginal damages, it must also reduce the optimal number of offenses and increase the optimal values of p and f. On the other hand, an increase in the other component of the cost of apprehension and conviction, C_p, has no direct effect on the marginal cost of changing offenses with f and reduces the cost of changing offenses with p (see fig. 3). It therefore reduces the optimal value of p and only partially compensates with an increase in f, so that the optimal number of offenses increases. Accordingly, an increase in both C' and C_p must increase the optimal f but can either increase or decrease the optimal p and optimal number of offenses, depending on the relative importance of the changes in C' and C_p.

The cost of apprehending and convicting offenders is affected by a variety of forces. An increase in the salaries of policemen increases both C' and C_p, while improved police technology in the form of fingerprinting, ballistic

TABLE 2
PROBABILITY OF CONVICTION AND AVERAGE PRISON TERM FOR SEVERAL MAJOR FELONIES, 1960

	Murder and Nonnegligent Manslaughter	Forcible Rape	Robbery	Aggravated Assault	Burglary	Larceny	Auto Theft	All Three Felonies Combined
1. Average time served (months) before first release:								
a) Federal civil institutions	111.0	63.6	56.1	27.1	26.2	16.2	20.6	18.8
b) State institutions	121.4	44.8	42.4	25.0	24.6	19.8	21.3	28.4
2. Probabilities of apprehension and conviction (percent):								
a) Those found guilty of offenses known	57.9	37.7	25.1	27.3	13.0	10.7	13.7	15.1
b) Those found guilty of offenses charged	40.7	26.9	17.8	16.1	10.2	9.8	11.5	15.0
c) Those entering federal and state prisons (excludes many juveniles)	39.8	22.7	8.4	3.0	2.4	2.2	2.1	2.8

SOURCE: 1. Bureau of Prisons (1960, Table 3); 2 (*a*) and (*b*), Federal Bureau of Investigation (1960, Table 10); 2 (*c*), Federal Bureau of Investigation (1961, Table 2), Bureau of Prisons (n.d., Table A1; 1961, Table 8).

480 • LAW

FIGURE 3

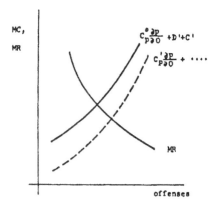

techniques, computer control, and chemical analysis, or police and court "reform" with an emphasis on professionalism and merit, would tend to reduce both, not necessarily by the same extent. Our analysis implies, there-fore, that although an improvement in technology and reform may or may not increase the optimal p and reduce the optimal number of offenses, it does reduce the optimal f and thus the need to rely on severe punishments for those convicted. Possibly this explains why the secular improvement in police technology and reform has gone hand in hand with a secular decline in punishments.

C_p, and to a lesser extent C', differ significantly between different kinds of offenses. It is easier, for example, to solve a rape or armed robbery than a burglary or auto theft, because the evidence of personal identification is often available in the former and not in the latter offenses.[32] This might tempt one to argue that the ps decline significantly as one moves across table 2 (left to right) primarily because the C_p's are significantly lower for the "personal" felonies listed to the left than for the "impersonal" felonies listed to the right. But this implies that the fs would increase as one moved across the table, which is patently false. Consequently, the positive correlation between p, f, and the severity of offenses observed in the table cannot be explained by a negative correlation between C_p (or C') and severity.

If $b > 0$, a reduction in the elasticity of offenses with respect to f increases the marginal revenue of changing offenses by changing f (see fig. 4a). The result is an increase in the optimal number of offenses and a decrease in the optimal f that is partially compensated by an increase in the optimal p. Similarly, a reduction in the elasticity of offenses with respect to p also increases the optimal number of offenses (see fig. 4b), decreases the optimal

FIGURE 4

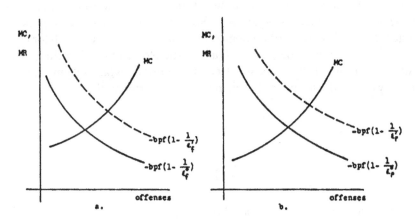

p, and partially compensates by an increase in f. An equal percentage reduction in both elasticities a fortiori increases the optimal number of offenses and also tends to reduce both p and f. If $b = 0$, both marginal revenue functions lie along the horizontal axis, and changes in these elasticities have no effect on the optimal values of p and f.

The income of a firm would usually be larger if it could separate, at little cost, its total market into submarkets that have substantially different elasticities of demand: higher prices would be charged in the submarkets having lower elasticities. Similarly, if the total "market" for offenses could be separated into submarkets that differ significantly in the elasticities of supply of offenses, the results above imply that if $b > 0$ the total loss would be reduced by "charging" *lower* "prices"—that is, lower ps and fs—in markets with *lower* elasticities.

Sometimes it is possible to separate persons committing the same offense into groups that have different responses to punishments. For example, unpremeditated murderers or robbers are supposed to act impulsively and, therefore, to be relatively unresponsive to the size of punishments; likewise, the insane or the young are probably less affected than other offenders by future consequences and, therefore,[33] probably less deterred by increases in the probability of conviction or in the punishment when convicted. The trend during the twentieth century toward relatively smaller prison terms and greater use of probation and therapy for such groups and, more generally, the trend away from the doctrine of "a given punishment for a given crime" is apparently at least broadly consistent with the implications of the optimality analysis.

An increase in b increases the marginal revenue from changing the number of offenses by changing p or f and thereby increases the optimal number of offenses, reduces the optimal value of f, and increases the optimal value of p. Some evidence presented in Section II indicates that b is especially large for juveniles in detention homes or adults in prison and is small for fines or adults on parole. The analysis implies, therefore, that other things the same, the optimal fs would be smaller and the optimal ps larger if punishment were by one of the former rather than one of the latter methods.

V. Fines

Welfare Theorems and Transferable Pricing

The usual optimality conditions in welfare economics depend only on the levels and not on the slopes of marginal cost and average revenue functions, as in the well-known condition that marginal costs equal prices. The social loss from offenses was explicitly introduced as an application of the approach used in welfare economics, and yet slopes as incorporated into elasticities of supply do significantly affect the optimality conditions. Why this difference? The primary explanation would appear to be that it is almost always implicitly assumed that prices paid by consumers are fully transferred to firms and governments, so that there is no social loss from payment.

If there were no social loss from punishments, as with fines, b would equal zero, and the elasticity of supply would drop out of the optimality condition given by equation (21).[34] If $b > 0$, as with imprisonment, some of the payment "by" offenders would not be received by the rest of society, and a net social loss would result. The elasticity of the supply of offenses then becomes an important determinant of the optimality conditions, because it determines the change in social costs caused by a change in punishments.

Although transferable monetary pricing is the most common kind today, the other is not unimportant, especially in underdeveloped and communist countries. Examples in addition to imprisonment and many other punishments are the draft, payments in kind, and queues and other waiting-time forms of rationing that result from legal restrictions on pricing (see Becker 1965) and from random variations in demand and supply conditions. It is interesting, and deserves further exploration, that the optimality conditions are so significantly affected by a change in the assumptions about the transferability of pricing.

Optimality Conditions

If $b=0$, say, because punishment was by fine, and if the cost of apprehending and convicting offenders were also zero, the two optimality conditions (21) and (22) would reduce to the same simple condition

$$D'(O) = 0. \qquad (24)$$

Economists generally conclude that activities causing "external" harm, such
as factories that pollute the air or lumber operations that strip the land,
should be taxed or otherwise restricted in level until the marginal external
harm equaled the marginal private gain, that is, until marginal net damages
equaled zero, which is what equation (24) says. If marginal harm always
exceeded marginal gain, the optimum level would be presumed to be zero,
and that would also be the implication of (24) when suitable inequality
conditions were brought in. In other words, if the costs of apprehending,
convicting, and punishing offenders were nil and if each offense caused more
external harm than private gain, the social loss from offenses would be
minimized by setting punishments high enough to eliminate all offenses.
Minimizing the social loss would become identical with the criterion of
minimizing crime by setting penalties sufficiently high.[35]

Equation (24) determines the optimal number of offenses, $\hat{O}$, and the
fine and probability of conviction must be set at levels that induce offenders
to commit just $\hat{O}$ offenses. If the economists' usual theory of choice is applied
to illegal activities (see Sec. II), the marginal value of these penalties has to
equal the marginal private gain:

$$V = G'(\hat{O}), \qquad (25)$$

where $G'(\hat{O})$ is the marginal private gain at $\hat{O}$ and V is the monetary value
of the marginal penalties. Since by equations (3) and (24), $D'(\hat{O}) = H'(\hat{O})$
$- G'(\hat{O}) = 0$, one has by substitution in (25)

$$V = H'(\hat{O}). \qquad (26)$$

The monetary value of the penalties would equal the marginal harm caused
by offenses.

Since the cost of apprehension and conviction is assumed equal to zero,
the probability of apprehension and conviction could be set equal to unity
without cost. The monetary value of penalties would then simply equal the
fines imposed, and equation (26) would become

$$f = H'(\hat{O}). \qquad (27)$$

Since fines are paid by offenders to the rest of society, a fine determined by

(27) would exactly compensate the latter for the marginal harm suffered, and the criterion of minimizing the social loss would be identical, at the margin, with the criterion of compensating "victims."[36] If the harm to victims always exceeded the gain to offenders, both criteria would reduce in turn to eliminating all offenses.

If the cost of apprehension and conviction were not zero, the optimality condition would have to incorporate marginal costs as well as marginal damages and would become, if the probability of conviction were still assumed to equal unity,

$$D'(\hat{O}) + C'(\hat{O}, 1) = 0. \qquad (28)$$

Since $C' > 0$, (28) requires that $D' < 0$ or that the marginal private gain exceed the marginal external harm, which generally means a smaller number of offenses than when $D' = 0$.[37] It is easy to show that equation (28) would be satisfied if the fine equaled the sum of marginal harm and marginal costs:

$$f = H'(\hat{O}) + C'(\hat{O}, 1).[38] \qquad (29)$$

In other words, offenders have to compensate for the cost of catching them as well as for the harm they directly do, which is a natural generalization of the usual externality analysis.

The optimality condition

$$D'(\hat{O}) + C'(\hat{O}, \hat{p}) + C_p(\hat{O}, \hat{p})\frac{1}{O_p} = 0 \qquad (30)$$

would replace equation (28) if the fine rather than the probability of conviction were fixed. Equation (30) would usually imply that $D'(\hat{O}) > 0$,[39] and thus that the number of offenses would exceed the optimal number when costs were zero. Whether costs of apprehension and conviction increase or decrease the optimal number of offenses largely depends, therefore, on whether penalties are changed by a change in the fine or in the probability of conviction. Of course, if both are subject to control, the optimal probability of conviction would be arbitrarily close to zero, unless the social loss function differed from equation (18) (see the discussion in Sec. III).

The Case for Fines

Just as the probability of conviction and the severity of punishment are subject to control by society, so too is the form of punishment: legislation usually specifies whether an offense is punishable by fines, probation, institutionalization, or some combination. Is it merely an accident, or have optimality considerations determined that today, in most countries, fines are the predominant form of punishment, with institutionalization reserved for the more serious offenses? This section presents several arguments which imply that social welfare is increased if fines are used *whenever feasible*.

In the first place, probation and institutionalization use up social resources, and fines do not, since the latter are basically just transfer payments, while the former use resources in the form of guards, supervisory personnel, probation officers, and the offenders' own time.[40] Table 1 indicates that the cost is not minor either: in the United States in 1965, about $1 billion was spent on "correction," and this estimate excludes, of course, the value of the loss in offenders' time.[41]

Moreover, the determination of the optimal number of offenses and severity of punishments is somewhat simplified by the use of fines. A wise use of fines requires knowledge of marginal gains and harm and of marginal apprehension and conviction costs; admittedly, such knowledge is not easily acquired. A wise use of imprisonment and other punishments must know this too, however, and, in addition, must know about the elasticities of response of offenses to changes in punishments. As the bitter controversies over the abolition of capital punishment suggest, it has been difficult to learn about these elasticities.

I suggested earlier that premeditation, sanity, and age can enter into the determination of punishments as proxies for the elasticities of response. These characteristics may not have to be considered in levying fines, because the optimal fines, as determined, say, by equations (27) or (29), do not depend on elasticities. Perhaps this partly explains why economists discussing externalities almost never mention motivation or intent, while sociologists and lawyers discussing criminal behavior invariably do. The former assume that punishment is by a monetary tax or fine, while the latter assume that nonmonetary punishments are used.

Fines provide compensation to victims, and optimal fines at the margin fully compensate victims and restore the status quo ante, so that they are no worse off than if offenses were not committed.[42] Not only do other punishments fail to compensate, but they also require "victims" to spend additional resources in carrying out the punishment. It is not surprising, therefore, that the anger and fear felt toward ex-convicts who in fact have *not* "paid their debt to society" have resulted in additional punishments,[43] including legal restrictions on their political and economic opportunities[44] and informal restrictions on their social acceptance. Moreover, the absence of compensation encourages efforts to change and otherwise "rehabilitate "offenders through psychiatric counseling, therapy, and other programs. Since fines do compensate and do not create much additional cost, anger toward and fear of appropriately fined persons do not easily develop. As a result, additional punishments are not usually levied against "ex-finees," nor are strong efforts made to "rehabilitate" them.

One argument made against fines is that they are immoral because, in effect, they permit offenses to be bought for a price in the same way that bread or other goods are bought for a price.[45] A fine *can* be considered the price of an offense, but so too can any other form of punishment; for example, the "price" of stealing a car might be six months in jail. The only difference is in the units of measurement: fines are prices measured in monetary units, imprisonments are prices measured in time units, etc. If anything, monetary units are to be preferred here as they are generally preferred in pricing and accounting.

Optimal fines determined from equation (29) depend only on the marginal harm and cost and not at all on the economic positions of offenders. This has been criticized as unfair, and fines proportional to the incomes of offenders have been suggested.[46] If the goal is to minimize the social loss in income from offenses, and not to take vengeance or to inflict harm on offenders, then fines should depend on the total harm done by offenders, and not directly on their income, race, sex, etc. In the same way, the monetary value of optimal prison sentences and other punishments depends on the harm, costs, and elasticities of response, but not directly on an offender's income. Indeed, if the monetary value of the punishment by, say, imprisonment were independent of income, the length of the sentence would be *inversely* related to income, because the value placed on a given sentence is positively related to income.

We might detour briefly to point out some interesting implications for the probability of conviction of the fact that the monetary value of a given fine is obviously the same for all offenders, while the monetary equivalent or "value" of a given prison sentence or probation period is generally positively related to an offender's income. The discussion in Section II suggested that actual probabilities of conviction are not fixed to all offenders but usually vary with their age, sex, race, and, in particular, income. Offenders with higher earnings have an incentive to spend more on planning their offenses, on good lawyers, on legal appeals, and even on bribery to reduce the probability of apprehension and conviction for offenses punishable by, say, a given prison term, because the cost to them of conviction is relatively large compared to the cost of these expenditures. Similarly, however, poorer offenders have an incentive to use more of their time in planning their offenses, in court appearances, and the like to reduce the probability of conviction for offenses punishable by a given fine, because the cost to them of conviction is relatively large compared to the value of their time.[47] The implication is that the probability of conviction would be systematically related to the earnings of offenders: negatively for offenses punishable by imprisonment and positively for those punishable by fines. Although a negative relation for felonies and other offenses punishable by imprisonment has been frequently observed and deplored (see President's Commission 1967c, 139–53), I do not know of any studies of the relation for fines or of any recognition that the observed negative relation may be more a consequence of the nature of the punishment than of the influence of wealth.

Another argument made against fines is that certain crimes, like murder or rape, are so heinous that no amount of money could compensate for the harm inflicted. This argument has obvious merit and is a special case of the more general principle that fines cannot be relied on exclusively whenever the harm exceeds the resources of offenders. For then victims could not be fully compensated by offenders, and fines would have to be supplemented with prison terms or other punishments in order to discourage offenses optimally. This explains why imprisonments, probation, and parole are major punishments for the more serious felonies; considerable harm is inflicted, and felonious offenders lack sufficient resources to compensate. Since fines are preferable, it also suggests the need for a flexible system of installment fines to enable offenders to pay fines more readily and thus avoid other punishments.

This analysis implies that if some offenders could pay the fine for a given offense and others could not,[48] the former should be punished solely by fine and the latter partly by other methods. In essence, therefore, these methods become a vehicle for punishing "debtors" to society. Before the cry is raised that the system is unfair, especially to poor offenders, consider the following.

Those punished would be debtors in "transactions" that were never agreed to by their "creditors," not in voluntary transactions, such as loans,[49] for which suitable precautions could be taken in advance by creditors. Moreover, punishment in any economic system based on voluntary market transactions inevitably must distinguish between such "debtors" and others. If a rich man purchases a car and a poor man steals one, the former is congratulated, while the latter is often sent to prison when apprehended. Yet the rich man's purchase is equivalent to a "theft" subsequently compensated by a "fine" equal to the price of the car, while the poor man, in effect, goes to prison because he cannot pay this "fine."

Whether a punishment like imprisonment in lieu of a full fine for offenders lacking sufficient resources is "fair" depends, of course, on the length of the prison term compared to the fine.[50] For example, a prison term of one week in lieu of a $10,000 fine would, if anything, be "unfair" to wealthy offenders paying the fine. Since imprisonment is a more costly punishment to society than fines, the loss from offenses would be reduced by a policy of leniency toward persons who are imprisoned because they cannot pay fines. Consequently, optimal prison terms for "debtors" would not be "unfair" to

them in the sense that the monetary equivalent to them of the prison terms
would be less than the value of optimal fines, which in turn would equal the
harm caused or the "debt."[51]

It appears, however, that "debtors" are often imprisoned at rates of
exchange with fines that place a low value on time in prison. Although I
have not seen systematic evidence on the different punishments actually
offered convicted offenders, and the choices they made, many statutes in the
United States do permit fines and imprisonment that place a low value on
time in prison. For example, in New York State, Class A Misdemeanors can
be punished by a prison term as long as one year or a fine no larger than
$1,000 and Class B Misdemeanors, by a term as long as three months or a
fine no larger than $500 (*Laws of New York* 1965, chap. 1030, Arts. 70 and
80).[52] According to my analysis, these statutes permit excessive prison sentences relative to the fines, which may explain why imprisonment in lieu of
fines is considered unfair to poor offenders, who often must "choose" the
prison alternative.

Compensation and the Criminal Law

Actual criminal proceedings in the United States appear to seek a mix-
ture of deterrence, compensation, and vengeance. I have already indicated
that these goals are somewhat contradictory and cannot generally be simultaneously achieved; for example, if punishment were by fine, minimizing the
social loss from offenses would be equivalent to compensating "victims" fully,
and deterrence or vengeance could only be partially pursued. Therefore, if
the case for fines were accepted, and punishment by optimal fines became
the norm, the traditional approach to criminal law would have to be significantly modified.

First and foremost, the primary aim of all legal proceedings would become
the same: not punishment or deterrence, but simply the assessment of the
"harm" done by defendants. Much of traditional criminal law would become
a branch of the law of torts,[53] say "social torts," in which the public would
collectively sue for "public" harm. A "criminal" action would be defined
fundamentally not by the nature of the action[54] but by the inability of a
person to compensate for the "harm" that he caused. Thus an action would
be "criminal" precisely because it results in uncompensated "harm" to others.
Criminal law would cover all such actions, while tort law would cover all
other (civil) actions.

As a practical example of the fundamental changes that would be
wrought, consider the antitrust field. Inspired in part by the economist's
classic demonstration that monopolies distort the allocation of resources and
reduce economic welfare, the United States has outlawed conspiracies and

other constraints of trade. In practice, defendants are often simply required to cease the objectionable activity, although sometimes they are also fined, become subject to damage suits, or are jailed.

If compensation were stressed, the main purpose of legal proceedings would be to levy fines equal to[55] the harm inflicted on society by constraints of trade. There would be no point to cease and desist orders, imprisonment, ridicule, or dissolution of companies. If the economist's theory about monopoly is correct, and if optimal fines were levied, firms would automatically cease any constraints of trade, because the gain to them would be less than the harm they cause and thus less than the fines expected. On the other hand, if Schumpeter and other critics are correct, and certain constraints of trade raise the level of economic welfare, fines could fully compensate society for the harm done, and yet some constraints would not cease, because the gain to participants would exceed the harm to others.[56]

One unexpected advantage, therefore, from stressing compensation and fines rather than punishment and deterrence is that the validity of the classical position need not be judged a priori. If valid, compensating fines would discourage all constraints of trade and would achieve the classical aims. If not, such fines would permit the socially desirable constraints to continue and, at the same time, would compensate society for the harm done.

Of course, as participants in triple-damage suits are well aware, the harm done is not easily measured, and serious mistakes would be inevitable. However, it is also extremely difficult to measure the harm in many civil suits,[57] yet these continue to function, probably reasonably well on the whole. Moreover, as experience accumulated, the margin of error would decline, and rules of thumb would develop. Finally, one must realize that difficult judgments are also required by the present antitrust policy, such as deciding that certain industries are "workably" competitive or that certain mergers reduce competition. An emphasis on fines and compensation would at least help avoid irrelevant issues by focusing attention on the information most needed for intelligent social policy.

VI. Private Expenditures against Crime

A variety of private as well as public actions also attempt to reduce the number and incidence of crimes: guards, doormen, and accountants are employed, locks and alarms installed, insurance coverage extended, parks and neighborhoods avoided, taxis used in place of walking or subways, and so on. Table 1 lists close to $2 billion of such expenditures in 1965, and this undoubtedly is a gross underestimate of the total. The need for private action is especially great in highly interdependent modern economies, where frequently a person must trust his resources, including his person, to the "care" of employees, employers, customers, or sellers.

If each person tries to minimize his expected loss in income from crimes, optimal private decisions can be easily derived from the previous discussion of optimal public ones. For each person there is a loss function similar to that given by equation (18):

$$L_j = H_j(O_j) + C_j(p_j, O_j, C, C_k) + b_j p_j f_j O_j. \tag{31}$$

The term H_j represents the harm to j from the O_j offenses committed against j, while C_j represents his cost of achieving a probability of conviction of p_j for offenses committed against him. Note that C_j not only is positively related to O_j but also is negatively related to C, public expenditures on crime, and to C_k, the set of private expenditures by other persons.[58]

The term $b_j p_j f_j O_j$ measures the expected[59] loss to j from punishment of offenders committing any of the O_j. Whereas most punishments result in a net loss to society as a whole, they often produce a gain for the actual victims. For example, punishment by fines given to the actual victims is just a transfer payment for society but is a clear gain to victims; similarly, punishment by imprisonment is a net loss to society but is a negligible loss to victims, since they usually pay a negligible part of imprisonment costs. This is why b_j is often less than or equal to zero, at the same time that b, the coefficient of social loss, is greater than or equal to zero.

Since b_j and f_j are determined primarily by public policy on punishments, the main decision variable directly controlled by j is p_j. If he chooses a p_j that minimizes L_j, the optimality condition analogous to equation (22) is

$$H'_j + C'_j + C_{jp_j}\frac{\partial p_j}{\partial O_j} = -b_j p_j f_j\left(1 - \frac{1}{\epsilon_{jp_j}}\right).^{60} \tag{32}$$

The elasticity ϵ_{jp_j} measures the effect of a change in p_j on the number of offenses committed against j. If $b_j < 0$, and if the left-hand side of equation (32), the marginal cost of changing O_j, were greater than zero, then (32) implies that $\epsilon_{jp_j} > 1$. Since offenders can substitute among victims, ϵ_{jp_j} is probably much larger than ϵ_p, the response of the total number of offenses to a change in the average probability, p. There is no inconsistency, therefore, between a requirement from the optimality condition given by (22) that $\epsilon_p < 1$ and a requirement from (32) that $\epsilon_{jp_j} > 1$.

VII. Some Applications

Optimal Benefits

Our analysis of crime is a generalization of the economist's analysis of external harm or diseconomies. Analytically, the generalization consists in introducing costs of apprehension and conviction, which make the probability of apprehension and conviction an important decision variable, and in treating punishment by imprisonment and other methods as well as by monetary payments. A crime is apparently not so different analytically from any other activity that produces external harm and when crimes are punishable by fines, the analytical differences virtually vanish.

Discussions of external economies or advantages are usually perfectly symmetrical to those of diseconomies, yet one searches in vain for analogues to the law of torts and criminality. Generally, compensation cannot be collected for the external advantages as opposed to harm caused, and no public officials comparable to policemen and district attorneys apprehend and "convict" benefactors rather than offenders. Of course, there is public interest in benefactors: medals, prizes, titles, and other privileges have been awarded to military heroes, government officials, scientists, scholars, artists, and businessmen by public and private bodies. Among the most famous are Nobel Prizes, Lenin Prizes, the Congressional Medal of Honor, knighthood, and patent rights. But these are piecemeal efforts that touch a tiny fraction of the population and lack the guidance of any body of law that codifies and analyzes different kinds of advantages.

Possibly the explanation for this lacuna is that criminal and tort law developed at the time when external harm was more common than advantages, or possibly the latter have been difficult to measure and thus considered too prone to favoritism. In any case, it is clear that the asymmetry in the law does not result from any analytical asymmetry, for a formal analysis of advantages, benefits, and benefactors can be developed that is quite symmetrical to the analysis of damages, offenses, and offenders. A function $A(B)$, for example, can give the net social advantages from B benefits in the same way that $D(O)$ gives the net damages from O offenses. Likewise, $K(B, p_1)$ can give the cost of apprehending and rewarding benefactors, where p_1 is the probability of so doing, with K' and $K_p > 0$; $B(p_1, a, v)$ can give the supply of benefits, where a is the award per benefit and v represents other determinants, with $\partial B/\partial p_1$ and $\partial B/\partial a > 0$; and b_1 can be the fraction of a that is a net loss to society. Instead of a loss function showing the decrease in social income from offenses, there can be a profit function showing the increase in income from benefits:

$$\Pi = A(B) - K(B, p_1) - b_1 p_1 aB. \tag{33}$$

If Π is maximized by choosing appropriate values of p_1 and a, the optimality conditions analogous to equations (21) and (22) are

$$A' - K' = b_1 p_1 a\left(1 + \frac{1}{e_a}\right) \tag{34}$$

and

$$A' - K' - K_p \frac{\partial p_1}{\partial B} = b_1 p_1 a\left(1 + \frac{1}{e_p}\right), \tag{35}$$

where

$$e_a = \frac{\partial B}{\partial a} \frac{a}{B}$$

and

$$e_p = \frac{\partial B}{\partial p_1} \frac{p_1}{B}$$

are both greater than zero. The implications of these equations are related to and yet differ in some important respects from those discussed earlier for (21) and (22).

For example, if $b_1 > 0$, which means that a is not a pure transfer but costs society resources, clearly (34) and (35) imply that $e_p > e_a$, since both $K_p > 0$ and $\partial p_1/\partial B > 0$. This is analogous to the implication of (21) and (22) that $\epsilon_p > \epsilon_f$, but, while the latter implies that, at the margin, offenders are risk *preferrers*, the former implies that, at the margin, benefactors are risk *avoiders*.[61] Thus, while the optimal values of p and f would be in a region where "crime does not pay"—in the sense that the marginal income of criminals would be less than that available to them in less risky legal activities—the optimal values of p_1 and a would be where "benefits do pay"—in the same sense that the marginal income of benefactors would exceed that available to them in less risky activities. In this sense it "pays" to do "good" and does not "pay" to do "bad."

As an illustration of the analysis, consider the problem of rewarding inventors for their inventions. The function $A(B)$ gives the total social value of B inventions, and A' gives the marginal value of an additional one. The function $K(B, p_1)$ gives the cost of finding and rewarding inventors; if a patent system is used, it measures the cost of a patent office, of preparing applications, and of the lawyers, judges, and others involved in patent litigation.[62] The elasticities e_p and e_a measure the response of inventors to changes in the probability and magnitude of awards, while b_1 measures the social cost of the method used to award inventors. With a patent system, the cost consists in a less extensive use of an invention than would otherwise occur, and in any monopoly power so created.

Equations (34) and (35) imply that with any system having $b_1 > 0$, the smaller the elasticities of response of inventors, the smaller should be the probability and magnitude of awards. (The value of a patent can be changed, for example, by changing its life.) This shows the relevance of the controversy between those who maintain that most inventions stem from a basic desire "to know" and those who maintain that most stem from the prospects of financial awards, especially today with the emphasis on systematic investment in research and development. The former quite consistently usually advocate a weak patent system, while the latter equally consistently advocate its strengthening.

Even if A', the marginal value of an invention, were "sizable," the optimal decision would be to abolish property rights in an invention, that is, to set $p_1 = 0$, if b_1 and K[63] were sufficiently large and/or the elasticities e_p and e_a sufficiently small. Indeed, practically all arguments to eliminate or greatly alter the patent system have been based either on its alleged costliness, large K or b_1, or lack of effectiveness, low e_p or e_a (see, for example, Plant 1934 or Arrow 1962).

If a patent system were replaced by a system of cash prizes, the elasticities of response would become irrelevant for the determination of optimal policies, because b_1 would then be approximately zero.[64] A system of prizes would, moreover, have many of the same other advantages that fines have in punishing offenders (see the discussion in Sec. V). One significant advantage of a patent system, however, is that it automatically "meters" A', that is, provides an award that is automatically positively related to A', while a system of prizes (or of fines and imprisonment) has to estimate A' (or D') independently and often somewhat arbitrarily.

The Effectiveness of Public Policy

The anticipation of conviction and punishment reduces the loss from offenses and thus increases social welfare by discouraging some offenders. What determines the increase in welfare, that is "effectiveness," of public efforts to discourage offenses? The model developed in Section III can be used to answer this question if social welfare is measured by income and if "effectiveness" is defined as a ratio of the maximum feasible increase in income to the increase if all offenses causing net damages were abolished by fiat. The maximum feasible increase is achieved by choosing optimal values of the probability of apprehension and conviction, p, and the size of punishments, f (assuming that the coefficient of social loss from punishment, b, is given).[65]

Effectiveness so defined can vary between zero and unity and depends essentially on two behavioral relations: the costs of apprehension and conviction and the elasticities of response of offenses to changes in p and f. The smaller these costs or the greater these elasticities, the smaller the cost of achieving any given reduction in offenses and thus the greater the effectiveness. The elasticities may well differ considerably among different kinds of offenses. For example, crimes of passion, like murder or rape, or crimes of youth, like auto theft, are often said to be less responsive to changes in p and f than are more calculating crimes by adults, like embezzlement, antitrust violation, or bank robbery. The elasticities estimated by Smigel (1965) and Ehrlich (1967) for seven major felonies do differ considerably but are not clearly smaller for murder, rape, auto theft, and assault than for robbery, burglary, and larceny.[66]

Probably effectiveness differs among offenses more because of differences in the costs of apprehension and conviction than in the elasticities of response. An important determinant of these costs, and one that varies greatly, is the time between commission and detection of an offense.[67] For the earlier an offense is detected, the earlier the police can be brought in and the more likely that the victim is able personally to identify the offender. This suggests that effectiveness is greater for robbery than for a related felony like burglary, or for minimum-wage and fair employment legislation than for other white-collar legislation like antitrust and public utility regulation.[68]

A Theory of Collusion

The theory developed in this essay can be applied to any effort to preclude certain kinds of behavior, regardless of whether the behavior is "unlawful." As an example, consider efforts by competing firms to collude in order to obtain monopoly profits. Economists lack a satisfactory theory of the determinants of price and output policies by firms in an industry, a theory that could predict under what conditions perfectly competitive, monopolistic, or various intermediate kinds of behavior would emerge. One by-product of our approach to crime and punishment is a theory of collusion that appears to fill a good part of this lacuna.[69]

The gain to firms from colluding is positively related to the elasticity of their marginal cost curves and is inversely related to the elasticity of their collective demand curve. A firm that violates a collusive arrangement by pricing below or producing more than is specified can be said to commit an "offense" against the collusion. The resulting harm to the collusion would depend on the number of violations and on the elasticities of demand and marginal cost curves, since the gain from colluding depends on these elasticities.

If violations could be eliminated without cost, the optimal solution would obviously be to eliminate all of them and to engage in pure monopoly pricing. In general, however, as with other kinds of offenses, there are two costs of eliminating violations. There is first of all the cost of discovering violations and of "apprehending" violators. This cost is greater the greater the desired probability of detection and the greater the number of violations. Other things the same, the latter is usually positively related to the number of firms in an industry, which partly explains why economists typically relate monopoly power to concentration. The cost of achieving a given probability of detection also depends on the number of firms, on the number of customers, on the stability of customer buying patterns, and on government policies toward collusive arrangements (see Stigler 1964).

Second, there is the cost to the collusion of punishing violators. The most favorable situation is one in which fines could be levied against violators and collected by the collusion. If fines and other legal recourse are ruled out, methods like predatory price-cutting or violence have to be used, and they hurt the collusion as well as violators.

Firms in a collusion are assumed to choose probabilities of detection, punishments to violators, and prices and outputs that minimize their loss from violations, which would at the same time maximize their gain from colluding. Optimal prices and outputs would be closer to the competitive position the more elastic demand curves were, the greater the number of sellers and buyers, the less transferable punishments were, and the more hostile to collusion governments were. Note that misallocation of resources could not be measured simply by the deviation of actual from competitive outputs but would depend also on the cost of enforcing collusions. Note further, and more important, that this theory, unlike most theories of pricing, provides for continuous variation, from purely competitive through intermediate situations to purely monopolistic pricing. These situations differ primarily because of differences in the "optimal" number of violations, which in turn are related to differences in the elasticities, concentrations, legislation, etc., already mentioned.

These ideas appear to be helpful in understanding the relative success of collusions in illegal industries themselves! Just as firms in legal industries have an incentive to collude to raise prices and profits, so too do firms producing illegal products, such as narcotics, gambling, prostitution, and abortion. The "syndicate" is an example of a presumably highly successful collusion that covers several illegal products.[70] In a country like the United

States that prohibits collusions, those in illegal industries would seem to have an advantage, because force and other illegal methods could be used against violators without the latter having much legal recourse. On the other hand, in countries like prewar Germany that legalized collusions, those in legal industries would have an advantage, because violators could often be legally prosecuted. One would predict, therefore, from this consideration alone, relatively more successful collusions in illegal industries in the United States, and in legal ones in prewar Germany.

VIII. Summary and Concluding Remarks

This essay uses economic analysis to develop optimal public and private policies to combat illegal behavior. The public's decision variables are its expenditures on police, courts, etc., which help determine the probability (p) that an offense is discovered and the offender apprehended and convicted, the size of the punishment for those convicted (f), and the form of the punishment: imprisonment, probation, fine, etc. Optimal values of these variables can be chosen subject to, among other things, the constraints imposed by three behavioral relations. One shows the damages caused by a given number of illegal actions, called offenses (O), another the cost of achieving a given p, and the third the effect of changes in p and f on O.

"Optimal" decisions are interpreted to mean decisions that minimize the social loss in income from offenses. This loss is the sum of damages, costs of apprehension and conviction, and costs of carrying out the punishments imposed, and can be minimized simultaneously with respect to p, f, and the form of f unless one or more of these variables is constrained by "outside" considerations. The optimality conditions derived from the minimization have numerous interesting implications that can be illustrated by a few examples.

If carrying out the punishment were costly, as it is with probation, imprisonment, or parole, the elasticity of response of offenses with respect to a change in p would generally, in equilibrium, have to exceed its response to a change in f. This implies, if entry into illegal activities can be explained by the same model of choice that economists use to explain entry into legal activities, that offenders are (at the margin) "risk preferrers." Consequently, illegal activities "would not pay" (at the margin) in the sense that the real income received would be less than what could be received in less risky legal activities. The conclusion that "crime would not pay" is an optimality condition and not an implication about the efficiency of the police or courts;

indeed, it holds for any level of efficiency, as long as optimal values of p and f appropriate to each level are chosen.

If costs were the same, the optimal values of both p and f would be greater, the greater the damage caused by an offense. Therefore, offenses like murder and rape should be solved more frequently and punished more severely than milder offenses like auto theft and petty larceny. Evidence on actual probabilities and punishments in the United States is strongly consistent with this implication of the optimality analysis.

Fines have several advantages over other punishments: for example, they conserve resources, compensate society as well as punish offenders, and simplify the determination of optimal ps and fs. Not surprisingly, fines are the most common punishment and have grown in importance over time. Offenders who cannot pay fines have to be punished in other ways, but the optimality analysis implies that the monetary value to them of these punishments should generally be less than the fines.

Vengeance, deterrence, safety, rehabilitation, and compensation are perhaps the most important of the many desiderata proposed throughout history. Next to these, minimizing the social loss in income may seem narrow, bland, and even quaint. Unquestionably, the income criterion can be usefully generalized in several directions, and a few have already been suggested in the essay. Yet one should not lose sight of the fact that it is more general and powerful than it may seem and actually includes more dramatic desiderata as special cases. For example, if punishment were by an optimal fine, minimizing the loss in income would be equivalent to compensating "victims" fully and would eliminate the "alarm" that so worried Bentham; or it would be equivalent to deterring all offenses causing great damage if the cost of apprehending, convicting, and punishing these offenders were relatively small. Since the same could also be demonstrated for vengeance or rehabilitation, the moral should be clear: minimizing the loss in income is actually very general and thus is *more useful* than these catchy and dramatic but inflexible desiderata.

This essay concentrates almost entirely on determining optimal policies to combat illegal behavior and pays little attention to actual policies. The small amount of evidence on actual policies that I have examined certainly suggests a positive correspondence with optimal policies. For example, it is found for seven major felonies in the United States that more damaging ones are penalized more severely, that the elasticity of response of offenses to changes in p exceeds the response to f, and that both are usually less than unity, all as predicted by the optimality analysis. There are, however, some discrepancies too: for example, the actual trade-off between imprisonment and fines in different statutes is frequently less, rather than the predicted more, favorable to those imprisoned. Although many more studies of actual policies are needed, they are seriously hampered on the empirical side by grave limitations in the quantity and quality of data on offenses, convictions, costs, etc., and on the analytical side by the absence of a reliable theory of political decision making.

Reasonable men will often differ on the amount of damages or benefits caused by different activities. To some, any wage rates set by competitive labor markets are permissible, while to others, rates below a certain minimum are violations of basic rights; to some, gambling, prostitution, and even abortion should be freely available to anyone willing to pay the market price, while to others, gambling is sinful and abortion is murder. These differences are basic to the development and implementation of public policy but have been excluded from my inquiry. I assume consensus on damages and benefits and simply try to work out rules for an optimal implementation of this consensus.

The main contribution of this essay, as I see it, is to demonstrate that optimal policies to combat illegal behavior are part of an optimal allocation of resources. Since economics has been developed to handle resource allocation, an "economic" framework becomes applicable to, and helps enrich, the analysis of illegal behavior. At the same time, certain unique aspects of the latter enrich economic analysis: some punishments, such as imprisonments, are necessarily nonmonetary and are a cost to society as well as to offenders; the degree of uncertainty is a decision variable that enters both the revenue and cost functions; etc.

Lest the reader be repelled by the apparent novelty of an "economic" framework for illegal behavior, let him recall that two important contributors to criminology during the eighteenth and nineteenth centuries, Beccaria and Bentham, explicitly applied an economic calculus. Unfortunately, such an approach has lost favor during the last hundred years, and my efforts can be viewed as a resurrection, modernization, and thereby I hope improvement on these much earlier pioneering studies.

MATHEMATICAL APPENDIX

This appendix derives the effects of changes in various parameters on the optimal values of p and f. It is assumed throughout that $b > 0$ and that equilibrium occurs where

$$\frac{\partial D}{\partial O} + \frac{\partial C}{\partial O} + \frac{\partial C}{\partial p}\frac{\partial p}{\partial O} = D' + C' + C_p\frac{\partial p}{\partial O} > 0;$$

the analysis could easily be extended to cover negative values of b and of this marginal cost term. The conclusion in the text (Sec. II) that $D'' + C'' > 0$ is relied on here. I take it to be a reasonable first approximation that the elasticities of O with respect to p or f are constant. At several places a sufficient condition for the conclusions reached is that

$$C_{pO} = C_{Op} = \frac{\partial^2 C}{\partial p \partial O} = \frac{\partial^2 C}{\partial O \partial p}$$

is "small" relative to some other terms. This condition is utilized in the form of a strong assumption that $C_{pO} = 0$, although I cannot claim any supporting intuitive or other evidence.

The social loss in income from offenses has been defined as

$$L = D(O) + C(O,p) + bpfO. \tag{A1}$$

If b and p were fixed, the value of f that minimized L would be found from the necessary condition

$$\frac{\partial L}{\partial f} = 0 = (D' + C')\frac{\partial O}{\partial f} + bpf(1 - E_f)\frac{\partial O}{\partial f}, \tag{A2}$$

or

$$0 = D' + C' + bpf(1 - E_f), \tag{A3}$$

if

$$\frac{\partial O}{\partial f} = O_f \neq 0,$$

where

$$E_f = \frac{-\partial f}{\partial O} \frac{O}{f}.$$

The sufficient condition would be that $\partial^2 L/\partial f^2 > 0$; using $\partial L/\partial f = 0$ and E_f is constant, this condition becomes

$$\frac{\partial^2 L}{\partial f^2} = (D'' + C'')O_f^2 + bp(1 - E_f)O_f > 0, \tag{A4}$$

or

$$\Delta \equiv D'' + C'' + bp(1 - E_f)\frac{1}{O_f} > 0. \tag{A5}$$

Since $D' + C' > 0$, and b is not less than zero, equation (A3) implies that

$E_f > 1$. Therefore Δ would be greater than zero, since we are assuming that $D'' + C'' > 0$; and $\hat{f}$, the value of f satisfying (A3), would minimize (locally) the loss L.

Suppose that D' is positively related to an exogenous variable α. The effect of a change in α on $\hat{f}$ can be found by differentiating equation (A3):

$$D_\alpha' + (D'' + C'')O_f \frac{d\hat{f}}{d\alpha} + bp(1 - E_f) \frac{d\hat{f}}{d\alpha} = 0,$$

or

$$\frac{d\hat{f}}{d\alpha} = \frac{-D_\alpha'(1/O_f)}{\Delta}. \tag{A6}$$

Since $\Delta > 0$, $O_f < 0$, and by assumption $D_\alpha' > 0$, then

$$\frac{d\hat{f}}{d\alpha} = \frac{+}{+} > 0. \tag{A7}$$

In a similar way it can be shown that, if C' is positively related to an exogenous variable β,

$$\frac{d\hat{f}}{d\beta} = \frac{-C_\beta'(1/O_f)}{\Delta} = \frac{+}{+} > 0. \tag{A8}$$

If b is positively related to γ, then

$$(D'' + C'')O_f \frac{d\hat{f}}{d\gamma} + bp(1 - E_f) \frac{d\hat{f}}{d\gamma} + pf(1 - E_f)b\gamma = 0,$$

or

$$\frac{d\hat{f}}{d\gamma} = \frac{-b_\gamma pf(1 - E_f)(1/O_f)}{\Delta}. \tag{A9}$$

Since $1 - E_f < 0$, and by assumption $b_\gamma > 0$,

$$\frac{d\hat{f}}{d\gamma} = \frac{-}{+} < 0 \tag{A10}$$

Note that since $1/E_f < 1$,

$$\frac{d(p\hat{f}O)}{d\gamma} < 0. \tag{A11}$$

If E_f is positively related to δ, then

$$\frac{d\hat{f}}{d\delta} = \frac{E_{f\delta}bpf(1/O_f)}{\Delta} = \frac{-}{+} < 0. \qquad \text{(A12)}$$

Since the elasticity of O with respect to f equals

$$\epsilon_f = -O_f\frac{f}{O} = \frac{1}{E_f},$$

by (A12), a reduction in ϵ_f would reduce $\hat{f}$.

Suppose that p is related to the exogenous variable r. Then the effect of a shift in r on $\hat{f}$ can be found from

$$(D'' + C'')O_f\frac{d\hat{f}}{dr} + (D'' + C'')O_p p_r + C_{pO} p_r$$

$$+ bp(1 - E_f)\frac{\partial\hat{f}}{\partial r} + bf(1 - E_f)p_r = 0,$$

or

$$\frac{d\hat{f}}{dr} = \frac{-(D'' + C'')O_p(1/O_f)p_r - bf(1 - E_f)p_r(1/O_f)}{\Delta}, \qquad \text{(A13)}$$

since by assumption $C_{pO} = 0$. Since $O_p < 0$, and $(D'' + C'') > 0$,

$$\frac{d\hat{f}}{dr} = \frac{(-) + (-)}{+} = \frac{-}{+} < 0. \qquad \text{(A14)}$$

If f rather than p were fixed, the value of p that minimizes L, $\hat{p}$, could be found from

$$\frac{\partial L}{\partial p} = \left[D' + C' + C_p\frac{1}{O_p} + bpf(1 - E_p) \right]O_p = 0, \qquad \text{(A15)}$$

as long as

$$\frac{\partial^2 L}{\partial p^2} = \left[(D'' + C'')O_p + C_p' + C_{pp}\frac{1}{O_p} + C_{pO} \right.$$

$$\left. + C_p\frac{\partial^2 p}{\partial O\partial p} + bf(1 - E_p) \right]O_p > 0. \qquad \text{(A16)}$$

Since $C_p' = C_{pO} = 0$, (A16) would hold if

$$\Delta' \equiv D'' + C'' + C_{pp}\frac{1}{O_p^2} + C_p\frac{1}{O_p}\frac{\partial^2 p}{\partial O \partial p}$$

$$+ bf(1 - E_p)\frac{1}{O_p} > 0. \quad (A17)$$

It is suggested in Section II that C_{pp} is generally greater than zero. If, as assumed,

$$D' + C' + C_p\frac{1}{O_p} > 0,$$

equation (A15) implies that $E_p > 1$ and thus that

$$bf(1 - E_p)\frac{1}{O_p} > 0.$$

If E_p were constant, $\partial^2 p/\partial O \partial p$ would be negative,[71] and, therefore, $C_p(1/O_p)$ $(\partial^2 p/\partial O \partial p)$ would be positive. Hence, none of the terms of (A17) are negative, and a value of p satisfying equation (A15) would be a local minimum.

The effects of changes in different parameters on $\hat{p}$ are similar to those already derived for $\hat{f}$ and can be written without comment:

$$\frac{d\hat{p}}{d\alpha} = \frac{-D_\alpha'(1/O_p)}{\Delta'} > 0, \quad (A18)$$

$$\frac{d\hat{p}}{d\beta} = \frac{-C_\beta'(1/O_p)}{\Delta'} > 0, \quad (A19)$$

and

$$\frac{d\hat{p}}{d\gamma} = \frac{-b_\gamma pf(1 - E_p)(1/O_p)}{\Delta'} < 0. \quad (A20)$$

If E_p is positively related to δ',

$$\frac{d\hat{p}}{d\delta'} = \frac{E_{p\gamma}'bpf(1/O_p)}{\Delta'} < 0. \quad (A21)$$

If C_p were positively related to the parameter s, the effect of a change in s on $\hat{p}$ would equal

$$\frac{d\hat{p}}{ds} = \frac{-C_{ps}(1/O_p^2)}{\Delta'} < 0. \quad (A22)$$

If f were related to the exogenous parameter t, the effect of a change in t on $\hat{p}$ would be given by

$$\frac{d\hat{p}}{dt}$$

$$= \frac{-(D''+C'')O_p f_t(1/O_p) - bf(1-E_p)f_t(1/O_p) - C_p(\partial^2 p/\partial O \partial f)f_t(1/O_p)}{\Delta'}$$

$$< 0 \quad \text{(A23)}$$

(with $C_{pO} = 0$), since all the terms in the numerator are negative.

If both p and f were subject to control, L would be minimized by choosing optimal values of both variables simultaneously. These would be given by the solutions to the two first-order conditions, equations (A2) and (A15), assuming that certain more general second-order conditions were satisfied. The effects of changes in various parameters on these optimal values can be found by differentiating both first-order conditions and incorporating the restrictions of the second-order conditions.

The values of p and f satisfying (A2) and (A15), $\hat{p}$ and $\hat{f}$, minimize L if

$$L_{pp} > 0, L_{ff} > 0, \quad \text{(A24)}$$

and

$$L_{pp}L_{ff} > L_{fp}^2 = L_{pf}^2. \quad \text{(A25)}$$

But $L_{pp} = O_p^2 \Delta'$, and $L_{ff} = O_f^2 \Delta'$, and since both Δ' and Δ have been shown to be greater than zero, (A24) is proved already, and only (A25) remains. By differentiating L_f with respect to p and utilizing the first-order condition that $L_f = 0$, one has

$$L_{fp} = O_f O_p [D'' + C'' + bf(1 - E_f)p_O] = O_f O_p \Sigma, \quad \text{(A26)}$$

where Σ equals the term in brackets. Clearly $\Sigma > 0$.

By substitution, (A25) becomes

$$\Delta \Delta' > \Sigma^2, \quad \text{(A27)}$$

and (A27) holds if Δ and Δ' are both greater than Σ. $\Delta > \Sigma$ means that

$$D'' + C'' + bp(1 - E_f)f_O > D'' + C'' + bf(1 - E_f)p_O, \quad \text{(A28)}$$

or

$$\frac{bfp}{O}(1 - E_f)E_f < \frac{bpf}{O}(1 - E_f)E_p. \quad \text{(A29)}$$

Since $1 - E_f < 0$, (A29) implies that

$$E_f > E_p, \quad \text{(A30)}$$

which necessarily holds given the assumption that $b > 0$; prove this by combining the two first-order conditions (A2) and (A15). $\Delta' > \Sigma$ means that

$$D'' + C'' + C_{pp}p_O^2 + C_p p_O p_{Op}$$

$$+ bf(1 - E_p)p_O > D'' + C'' + bf(1 - E_f)p_O. \quad (A31)$$

Since $C_{pp}p_O^2 > 0$, and $p_O < 0$, this necessarily holds if

$$C_p p p_{Op} + bpf(1 - E_p) < bpf(1 - E_f). \quad (A32)$$

By eliminating $D' + C'$ from the first-order conditions (A2) and (A15) and by combining terms, one has

$$C_p p_O - bpf(E_p - E_f) = 0. \quad (A33)$$

By combining (A32) and (A33), one gets the condition

$$C_p p p_{Op} < C_p p_O, \quad (A34)$$

or

$$E_{pO,p} = \frac{p}{p_O}\frac{\partial p_O}{\partial p} > 1. \quad (A35)$$

It can be shown that

$$E_{pO,p} = 1 + \frac{1}{E_p} > 1, \quad (A36)$$

and, therefore, (A35) is proven.

It has now been proved that the values of p and f that satisfy the first-order conditions (A2) and (A15) do indeed minimize (locally) L. Changes in different parameters change these optimal values, and the direction and magnitude can be found from the two linear equations

$$O_f \Delta \frac{\partial \tilde{f}}{\partial z} + O_p \Sigma \frac{\partial \tilde{p}}{\partial z} = C_1$$

and $\qquad\qquad\qquad\qquad\qquad\qquad\qquad\qquad$ (A37)

$$O_f \Sigma \frac{\partial \tilde{f}}{\partial z} + O_p \Delta' \frac{\partial \tilde{p}}{\partial z} = C_2.$$

By Cramer's rule,

$$\frac{\partial \tilde{f}}{\partial z} = \frac{C_1 O_p \Delta' - C_2 O_p \Sigma}{O_p O_f (\Delta \Delta' - \Sigma^2)} = \frac{O_p (C_1 \Delta' - C_2 \Sigma)}{+}, \tag{A38}$$

$$\frac{\partial \tilde{p}}{\partial z} = \frac{C_2 O_f \Delta - C_1 O_f \Sigma}{O_p O_f (\Delta \Delta' - \Sigma^2)} = \frac{O_f (C_2 \Delta - C_1 \Sigma)}{+} \tag{A39}$$

and the signs of both derivatives are the same as the signs of the numerators.

Consider the effect of a change in D' resulting from a change in the parameter α. It is apparent that $C_1 = C_2 = -D'_\alpha$, and by substitution

$$\frac{\partial \tilde{f}}{\partial \alpha} = \frac{-O_p D'_\alpha (\Delta' - \Sigma)}{+} = \frac{+}{+} > 0 \tag{A40}$$

and

$$\frac{\partial \tilde{p}}{\partial \alpha} = \frac{-O_p D'_\alpha (\Delta - \Sigma)}{+} = \frac{+}{+} > 0, \tag{A41}$$

since O_f and $O_p < 0$, $D'_\alpha > 0$, and Δ and $\Delta' > \Sigma$.

Similarly, if C' is changed by a change in β, $C_1 = C_2 = -C'_\beta$,

$$\frac{\partial \tilde{f}}{\partial \beta} = \frac{-O_p C'_\beta (\Delta' - \Sigma)}{+} = \frac{+}{+} > 0, \tag{A42}$$

and

$$\frac{\partial \tilde{p}}{\partial \beta} = \frac{-O_f C'_\beta (\Delta - \Sigma)}{+} = \frac{+}{+} > 0. \tag{A43}$$

If E_f is changed by a change in δ, $C_1 = E_{f\delta} bpf$, $C_2 = 0$,

$$\frac{\partial \tilde{f}}{\partial \delta} = \frac{O_p E_f bpf \Delta'}{+} = \frac{-}{+} < 0, \tag{A44}$$

and

$$\frac{\partial \tilde{p}}{\partial \delta} = \frac{-O_f E_f bpf \Sigma}{+} = \frac{+}{+} > 0. \tag{A45}$$

Similarly, if E_p is changed by a change in δ', $C_1 = 0$, $C_2 = E_{p\delta}' bpf$,

$$\frac{\partial \tilde{f}}{\partial \delta'} = -\frac{O_p E_{p\delta}' bpf \Sigma}{+} = \frac{+}{+} > 0, \tag{A46}$$

and

$$\frac{\partial \tilde{p}}{\partial \delta'} = \frac{O_f E_{p\delta}' bpf \Delta}{+} = \frac{-}{+} < 0. \tag{A47}$$

If b is changed by a change in γ, $C_1 = -b_\gamma pf(1-E_f)$, $C2 = -b_\gamma pf(1-E_p)$, and

$$\frac{\partial \bar{f}}{\partial \gamma} = \frac{-O_p b_\gamma pf[(1-E_f)\Delta' - (1-E_p)\Sigma]}{+} = \frac{-}{+} < 0, \qquad (A48)$$

since $E_f > E_p > 1$ and $\Delta' > \Sigma$; also,

$$\frac{\partial \bar{p}}{\partial \gamma} = \frac{-O_f b_\gamma pf[(1-E_p)\Delta - (1-E_f)\Sigma]}{+} = \frac{+}{+} > 0, \qquad (A49)$$

for it can be shown that $(1-E_p)\Delta > (1-E_f)\Sigma$.[72] Note that when f is held constant the optimal value of p is decreased, not increased, by an increase in γ.

If C_p is changed by a change in s, $C_2 = -p_O C_{ps}$, $C_1 = 0$,

$$\frac{\partial \bar{f}}{\partial S} = \frac{O_p p_O C_{ps}\Sigma}{+} = \frac{C_{ps}\Sigma}{+} = \frac{+}{+} > 0, \qquad (A50)$$

and

$$\frac{\partial \bar{p}}{\partial S} = \frac{-O_f p_O C_{ps}\Delta}{+} = \frac{-}{+} < 0, \qquad (A51)$$

NOTES

I would like to thank the Lilly Endowment for financing a very productive summer in 1965 at the University of California at Los Angeles. While there I received very helpful comments on an earlier draft from, among others, Armen Alchian, Roland McKean, Harold Demsetz, Jack Hirshliefer, William Meckling, Gordon Tullock, and Oliver Williamson. I have also benefited from comments received at seminars at the University of Chicago, Hebrew University, RAND Corporation, and several times at the Labor Workshop of Columbia; assistance and suggestions from Isaac Ehrlich and Robert Michael; and suggestions from the editor of the *Journal of Political Economy*.

1. This neglect probably resulted from an attitude that illegal activity is too immoral to merit any systematic scientific attention. The influence of moral attitudes on a scientific analysis is seen most clearly in a discussion by Alfred Marshall. After arguing that even fair gambling is an "economic blunder" because of diminishing marginal utility, he says, "It is true that this loss of probable happiness need not be greater than the pleasure derived from the excitement of gambling, and we are then thrown back upon the induction [sic] that pleasures of gambling are in Bentham's phrase 'impure'; since experience shows that they are likely to engender a restless,

feverish character, unsuited for steady work as well as for the higher and more solid pleasures of life" (Marshall 1961, note X, Mathematical Appendix).

2. Expenditures by the thirteen states with such legislation in 1959 totaled almost $2 million (see Landes 1966).

3. Superficially, frauds, thefts, etc., do not involve true social costs but are simply transfers, with the loss to victims being compensated by equal gains to criminals. While these are transfers, their market value is, nevertheless, a first approximation to the direct social cost. If the theft or fraud industry is "competitive," the sum of the value of the criminals' time input—including the time of "fences" and prospective time in prison—plus the value of capital input, compensation for risk, etc., would approximately equal the market value of the loss to victims. Consequently, aside from the input of intermediate products, losses can be taken as a measure of the value of the labor and capital input into these crimes, which are true social costs.

4. For an analysis of the secular decline to 1929 that stresses urbanization and the growth in incomes, see Cagan (1965, chap. iv).

5. In 1965, the ratio of currency outstanding to consumer expenditures was 0.08, compared to only 0.05 in 1929. In 1965, currency outstanding per family was a whopping $738.

6. Cagan (1965, chap. iv) attributes much of the increase in currency holdings between 1929 and 1960 to increased tax evasion resulting from the increase in tax rates.

7. The ith subscript will be suppressed whenever it is to be understood that only one activity is being discussed.

8. According to the Crime Commission, 85–90 percent of all police costs consist of wages and salaries (President's Commission 1967a, p. 35).

9. A task force report by the Crime Commission deals with suggestions for greater and more efficient usage of advanced technologies (President's Commission 1967e).

10. Differentiating the cost function yields $C_{pp} = C''(h_p)^2 + C'h_{pp}$; $C_{OO} = C''(h_O)^2 + C'h_{OO}$; $C_{pO} = C''h_O h_p + C'h_{pO}$. If marginal costs were rising, C_{pp} or C_{OO} could be negative only if h_{pp} or h_{OO} were sufficiently negative, which is not very likely. However, C_{po} would be approximately zero only if h_{pO} were sufficiently negative, which is also unlikely. Note that if "activity" is measured by convictions alone, $h_{pp} = h_{OO} = 0$, and $h_{pO} > 0$.

11. They are willful homicide, forcible rape, robbery, aggravated assault, burglary, larceny, and auto theft.

12. For example, Lord Shawness (1965) said, "Some judges preoccupy themselves with methods of punishment. This is their job. But in preventing crime it is of less significance than they like to think. Certainty of detection is far more important than severity of punishment." Also see the discussion of the ideas of C. B. Beccaria, an insightful eighteenth-century Italian economist and criminologist, in Radzinowicz (1948, I, 282).

13. See, however, the discussions in Smigel (1965) and Ehrlich (1967).

14. For a discussion of these concepts, see Sutherland (1960).

15. Both p_j and f_j might be considered distributions that depend on the judge, jury, prosecutor, etc., that j happens to receive. Among other things, u_j depends on the ps and fs meted out for other competing offenses. For evidence indicating that offenders do substitute among offenses, see Smigel (1965).

16. The utility expected from committing an offense is defined as

$$EU_j = p_j U_j(Y_j - f_j) + (1 - p_j)U_j(Y_j),$$

where Y_j is his income, monetary plus psychic, from an offense; U_j is his utility function; and f_j is to be interpreted as the monetary equivalent of the punishment. Then

$$\frac{\partial EU_j}{\partial p_j} = U_j(Y_j - f_j) - U_j(Y_j) < 0$$

and

$$\frac{\partial EU_j}{\partial f_j} = -p_j U_j'(Y_j - f_j) < 0$$

as long as the marginal utility of income is positive. One could expand the analysis by incorporating the costs and probabilities of arrests, detentions, and trials that do not result in conviction.

17. $EY_j = p_j(Y_j - f_j) + (1 - p_j)Y_j = Y_j - p_j f_j$.

18. This means that an increase in p_j "compensated" by a reduction in f_j would reduce utility and offenses.

19. From n. 16

$$-\frac{\partial EU_j}{\partial p_j}\frac{p_j}{U_j} = [U_j(Y_j) - U_j(Y_j - f_j)]\frac{p_j}{U_j} \gtreqless -\frac{\partial EU_j}{\partial f_j}\frac{f_j}{U_j} = p_j U_j'(Y_j - f_j)\frac{f_j}{U_j}$$

as

$$\frac{U_j(Y_j) - U_j(Y_j - f_j)}{f_j} \gtreqless U_j'(Y_j - f_j).$$

The term on the left is the average change in utility between $Y_j - f_j$ and Y_j. It would be greater than, equal to, or less than $U_j'(Y_j - f_j)$ as $U_j'' \gtreqless 0$. But risk preference is defined by $U_j'' > 0$, neutrality by $U_j'' = 0$, and aversion by $U_j'' < 0$.

20. We can be define p as a weighted average of the p_j, as

$$p = \sum_{j=1}^{n} \frac{O_j p_j}{\sum_{i=1}^{n} O_i},$$

and similar definitions hold for f and u.

21. In this respect, imprisonment is a special case of "waiting time" pricing that is also exemplified by queuing (see Becker 1965, esp. 515–16, and Kleinman 1967).

22. The Mathematical Appendix discusses second-order conditions.

23. Thus if $b < 0$, average revenue would be positive and the optimal value of ϵ_f would be greater than 1, and that of ϵ_p could be less than 1 only if C_p were sufficiently large.

24 If $b < 0$, the optimality condition is that $\epsilon_p < \epsilon_f$, or that offenders are risk avoiders. Optimal social policy would then be to select p and f in regions where "crime does pay."

25. Since $\epsilon_f = \epsilon_p = \epsilon$ if O depends only on pf, and $C = 0$ if $p = 0$, the two equilibrium conditions given by eqs. (21) and (22) reduce to the single condition

$$D' = -bpf\left(1 - \frac{1}{\epsilon}\right).$$

From this condition and the relation $O = O(pf)$, the equilibrium values of O and pf could be determined.

26. If $b < 0$, the optimal solution is p about zero and f arbitrarily high if offenders are either risk neutral or risk preferrers.

27. For a discussion of English criminal law in the eighteenth and nineteenth centuries, see Radzinowicz (1948, vol. I). Punishments were severe then, even though the death penalty, while legislated, was seldom implemented for less serious criminal offenses.

Recently South Vietnam executed a prominent businessman allegedly for "speculative" dealings in rice, while in recent years a number of persons in the Soviet Union have either been executed or given severe prison sentences for economic crimes.

28. I owe the emphasis on this point to Evsey Domar.

29. This is probably more likely for higher values of f and lower values of p.

30. If p is the probability that an offense would be cleared with the punishment f, then $1 - p$ is the probability of no punishment. The expected punishment would be $\mu = pf$, the variance $\sigma^2 = p(1 - p)f^2$, and the coefficient of variation

$$v = \frac{\sigma}{\mu} = \sqrt{\frac{1-p}{p}};$$

v increases monotonically from a low of zero when $p = 1$ to an infinitely high value when $p = 0$.

If the loss function equaled

$$L' = L + \psi(v), \qquad \psi' > 0,$$

the optimality conditions would become

$$D' + C' = -bpf\left(1 - \frac{1}{\epsilon_f}\right) \tag{21}$$

and

$$D' + C' + C_p\frac{1}{O_p} + \psi'\frac{dv}{dp}\frac{1}{O_p} = -bpf\left(1 - \frac{1}{\epsilon_p}\right).\qquad(22)$$

Since the term $\psi'(dv/dp)\,(1/O_p)$ is positive, it could more than offset the negative term $C_p(1/O_p)$.

31. I stress this primarily because of Bentham's famous and seemingly plausible dictum that "the more deficient in certainty a punishment is, the severer it should be" (1931, chap. ii of section entitled "Of Punishment," second rule). The dictum would be correct if p (or f) were exogenously determined and if L were minimized with respect to f (or p) alone, for then the optimal value of f (or p) would be inversely related to the given value of p (or f) (see the Mathematical Appendix). If, however, L is minimized with respect to both, then frequently they move in the same direction.

32. "If a suspect is neither known to the victim nor arrested at the scene of the crime, the chances of ever arresting him are very slim" (President's Commission 1967e, 8). This conclusion is based on a study of crimes in parts of Los Angeles during January 1966.

33. But see Becker (1962) for an analysis indicating that impulsive and other "irrational" persons may be as deterred from purchasing a commodity whose price has risen as more "rational" persons.

34. It remains in eq. (22), through the slope O_p, because ordinarily prices do not affect marginal costs, while they do here through the influence of p on C.

35. "The evil of the punishment must be made to exceed the advantage of the offense" (Bentham 1931, first rule).

36. By "victims" is meant the rest of society and not just the persons actually harmed.

37. This result can also be derived as a special case of the results in the Mathematical Appendix on the effects of increases in C'.

38. Since equilibrium requires that $f = G'(\hat{O})$, and since from (28)

$$D'(\hat{O}) = H'(\hat{O}) - G'(\hat{O}) = -C'(\hat{O}, 1),$$

then (29) follows directly by substitution.

39. That is, if, as seems plausible,

$$\frac{dC}{dp} = C'\frac{\partial O}{\partial p} + C_p > 0,$$

then

$$C' + C_p\frac{1}{\partial O/\partial p} < 0,$$

and

$$D'(\hat{O}) = -\left(C' + C_p\frac{1}{\partial O / \partial p}\right) > 0.$$

40. Several early writers on criminology recognized this advantage of fines. For example, "Pecuniary punishments are highly economical, since all the evil felt by him who pays turns into an advantage for him who receives" (Bentham 1931, chap. vi), and "Imprisonment would have been regarded in these old times [ca. tenth century] as a useless punishment; it does not satisfy revenge, it keeps the criminal idle, and do what we may, *it is costly*" (Pollock and Maitland 1952, 516; my italics).

41. On the other hand, some transfer payments in the form of food, clothing, and shelter are included.

42. Bentham recognized this and said, "To furnish an indemnity to the injured party is another useful quality in a punishment. It is a means of accomplishing two objects at once—punishing an offense and repairing it: removing the evil of the first order, and putting a stop to alarm. This is a characteristic advantage of pecuniary punishments" (1931, chap. vi).

43. In the same way, the guilt felt by society in using the draft, a forced transfer *to* society, has led to additional payments to veterans in the form of education benefits, bonuses, hospitalization rights, etc.

44. See Sutherland (1960, 267–68) for a list of some of these.

45. The very early English law relied heavily on monetary fines, even for murder, and it has been said that "every kind of blow or wound given to every kind of person had its price, and much of the jurisprudence of the time must have consisted of a knowledge of these preappointed prices" (Pollock and Maitland 1952, 451).

The same idea was put amusingly in a recent *Mutt and Jeff* cartoon which showed a police car carrying a sign that read: "Speed limit 30 M per H—$5 fine every mile over speed limit—pick out speed you can afford."

46. For example, Bentham said, "A pecuniary punishment, if the sum is fixed, is in the highest degree unequal. . . . Fines have been determined without regard to the profit of the offense, to its evil, or to the wealth of the offender. . . . Pecuniary punishments should always be regulated by the fortune of the offender. The relative amount of the fine should be fixed, not its absolute amount; for such an offense, such a part of the offender's fortune" (1931, chap. ix). Note that optimal fines, as determined by eq. (29), do depend on "the profit of the offense" and on "its evil."

47. Note that the incentive to use time to reduce the probability of a given prison sentence is unrelated to earnings, because the punishment is fixed in time, not monetary, units; likewise, the incentive to use money to reduce the probability of a given fine is also unrelated to earnings, because the punishment is fixed in monetary, not time, units.

48. In one study, about half of those convicted of misdemeanors could not pay the fines (see President's Commission 1967c, 148).

49. The "debtor prisons" of earlier centuries generally housed persons who could not repay loans.

50. Yet without any discussion of the actual alternatives offered, the statement is made that "the money judgment assessed the punitive damages defendant hardly seems comparable in effect to the criminal sanctions of death, imprisonment, and stigmatization" ("Criminal Safeguards" 1967).

51. A formal proof is straightforward if for simplicity the probability of conviction is taken as equal to unity. For then the sole optimality condition is

$$D' + C' = -bf\left(1 - \frac{1}{\epsilon_f}\right). \tag{1'}$$

Since $D' = H' - G'$, by substitution one has

$$G' = H' + C' + bf\left(1 - \frac{1}{\epsilon_f}\right), \tag{2'}$$

and since equilibrium requires that $G' = f$,

$$f = H' + C' + bf\left(1 - \frac{1}{\epsilon_f}\right), \tag{3'}$$

or

$$f = \frac{H' + C'}{1 - b(1 - 1/\epsilon_f)}. \tag{4'}$$

If $b > 0$, $\epsilon f < 1$ (see Sec. III), and hence by eq. (4'),

$$f < H' + C', \tag{5'}$$

where the term on the right is the full marginal harm. If p as well as f is free to vary, the analysis becomes more complicated, but the conclusion about the relative monetary values of optimal imprisonments and fines remains the same (see the Mathematical Appendix).

52. "Violations," however, can only be punished by prison terms as long as fifteen days or fines no larger than $250. Since these are maximum punishments, the actual ones imposed by the courts can, and often are, considerably less. Note, too, that the courts can punish by imprisonment, by fine, or by *both* (*Laws of New York* 1965, chap. 1030, Art. 60).

53. "The cardinal principle of damages in Anglo-American law [of torts] is that of *compensation* for the injury caused to plaintiff by defendant's breach of duty" (Harper and James 1956, 1299).

54. Of course, many traditional criminal actions like murder or rape would still usually be criminal under this approach too.

55. Actually, fines should exceed the harm done if the probability of conviction were less than unity. The possibility of avoiding conviction is the intellectual justification for punitive, such as triple, damages against those convicted.

56. The classical view is that $D'(M)$ always is greater than zero, where M measures the different constraints of trade and D' measures the marginal damage; the critic's

view is that for some M, $D'(M) < 0$. It has been shown above that if D' always is greater than zero, compensating fines would discourage all offenses, in this case constraints of trade, while if D' sometimes is less than zero, some offenses would remain (unless $C'[M]$, the marginal cost of detecting and convicting offenders, were sufficiently large relative to D').

57. Harper and James said, "Sometimes [compensation] can be accomplished with a fair degree of accuracy. But obviously it cannot be done in anything but a figurative and essentially speculative way for many of the consequences of personal injury. Yet it is the aim of the law to attain at least a rough correspondence between the amount awarded as damages and the extent of the suffering" (1956, 1301).

58. An increase in C_k—O_j and C held constant—presumably helps solve offenses against j, because more of those against k would be solved.

59. The expected private loss, unlike the expected social loss, is apt to have considerable variance because of the small number of independent offenses committed against any single person. If j were not risk neutral, therefore, L would have to be modified to include a term that depended on the distribution of $b_j p_j f_j O_j$.

60. I have assumed that

$$\frac{\partial C}{\partial p_j} = \frac{\partial C_k}{\partial p_j} = 0,$$

in other words, that j is too "unimportant" to influence other expenditures. Although usually reasonable, this does suggest a modification to the optimality conditions given by eqs. (21) and (22). Since the effects of public expenditures depend on the level of private ones, and since the public is sufficiently "important" to influence private actions, eq. (22) has to be modified to

$$D' + C' + C_p\frac{\partial p}{\partial O} + \sum_{i=1}^{n} \frac{dC}{dC_i}\frac{dC_i}{dp}\frac{\partial p}{\partial O} = -bpf\left(1 + \frac{1}{\epsilon_p}\right), \qquad (22')$$

and similarly for eq. (21). "The" probability p is, of course, a weighted average of the p_j. Eq. (22') incorporates the presumption that an increase in public expenditures would be partially thwarted by an induced decrease in private ones.

61. The relation $e_p > e_a$ holds if, and only if,

$$\frac{\partial EU}{\partial p_1}\frac{p_1}{U} > \frac{\partial EU}{\partial a}\frac{a}{U}, \qquad (1')$$

where

$$EU = p_1U(Y+a) + (1-p_1)U(Y) \qquad (2')$$

(see the discussion on pp. 464–65). By differentiating eq. (2'), one can write (1') as

$$p_1[U(Y+a) - U(Y)] > p_1aU'(Y+a), \qquad (3')$$

or

$$\frac{U(Y+a) - U(Y)}{a} > U'(Y+a). \tag{4'}$$

But (4') holds if everywhere $U'' < 0$ and does not hold if everywhere $U'' \geq 0$, which was to be proved.

62. These costs are not entirely trivial: for example, in 1966 the U.S. Patent Office alone spent $34 million (see Bureau of the Budget 1967), and much more was probably spent in preparing applications and in litigation.

63. Presumably one reason patents are not permitted on basic research is the difficulty (that is, cost) of discovering the ownership of new concepts and theorems.

64. The right side of both (34) and (35) would vanish, and the optimality conditions would be

$$A' - K' = 0 \tag{34'}$$

and

$$A' - K' - K_p\frac{\partial p_1}{\partial B} = 0. \tag{35'}$$

Since these equations are not satisfied by any finite values of p_1 and a, there is a difficulty in allocating the incentives between p_1 and a (see the similar discussion for fines in Sec. V).

65. In symbols, effectiveness is defined as

$$E = \frac{D(O_1) - [D(\hat{O}) + C(\hat{p}, (\hat{O}) + b\hat{p}\hat{f}\hat{O}}{D(O_1) - D(O_2)},$$

where $\hat{p}$, $\hat{f}$, and $\hat{O}$ are optimal values, O_1 offenses would occur if $p = f = 0$, and, O_2 is the value of O that minimizes D.

66. A theoretical argument that also casts doubt on the assertion that less "calculating" offenders are less responsive to changes in p and f can be found in Becker (1962).

67. A study of crimes in parts of Los Angeles during January 1966 found that "more than half the arrests were made within 8 hours of the crime, and almost two-thirds were made within the first week" (President's Commission 1967e, 8).

68. Evidence relating to the effectiveness of actual, which are not necessarily optimal, penalties for these white-collar crimes can be found in Stigler (1962, 1966), Landes (1966), and Johnson (1967).

69. Jacob Mincer first suggested this application to me.

70. An interpretation of the syndicate along these lines is also found in Schilling (1967).

71. If E_p and E_f are constants, $O = kp^{-a}f^{-b}$, where $a = 1/E_p$ and $b = 1/E_f$. Then

$$\frac{\partial p}{\partial O} = -\frac{1}{ka}\, p^{a\,+\,1} f^b,$$

and

$$\frac{\partial^2 p}{\partial O \partial p} = \frac{-(a+1)}{ka}\, p^a f^b < 0.$$

72. The term $(1 - E_p)\Delta$ would be greater than $(1 - E_f)\Sigma$ if

$$(D'' + C'')(1 - E_p) + bp(1 - E_f)(1 - E_p)f_O$$
$$> (D'' + C'')(1 - E_f) + bf(1 - E_f)^2 p_O,$$

or

$$(D'' + C'')(E_f - E_p) > -\frac{bpf}{O}(1 - E_f)\left[(1 - E_p)\frac{f_O O}{f} - (1 - E_f)\frac{p_O O}{p}\right],$$

$$(D'' + C'')(E_f - E_p) > -\frac{bpf}{O}(1 - E_f)[(1 - E_p)(E_f) - (1 - E_f)E_p],$$

$$(D'' + C'')(E_f - E_p) > -\frac{bpf}{O}(1 - E_f)(E_f - E_p).$$

Since the left-hand side is greater than zero, and the right-hand side is less than zero, the inequality must hold.

REFERENCES

Arrow, Kenneth J. "Economic Welfare and Allocation of Resources for Invention." In National Bureau Committee for Economic Research, *The Rate and Direction of Inventive Activity: Economic and Social Factors*. Princeton, N.J.: Princeton University Press (for the National Bureau of Economic Research), 1962

Becker, Gary S. "Irrational Behavior and Economic Theory." *Journal of Political Economy* 70 (February 1962).

———."A Theory of the Allocation of Time." *Economic Journal* 75 (September 1965).

Bentham, Jeremy. *Theory of Legislation*. New York: Harcourt Brace Co., 1931.

Bureau of the Budget. *The Budget of United States Government, 1968, Appendix.* Washington, D.C.: U.S. Government Printing Office, 1967.

Bureau of Prisons. *Prisoners Released from State and Federal Institutions.* ("National Prisoner Statistics.") Washington, D.C.: U.S. Dept. of Justice, 1960.

———. *Characteristics of State Prisoners, 1960.* ("National Prisoner Statistics.") Washington, D.C.: U.S. Dept. of Justice, n.d.

———. *Federal Prisons, 1960.* Washington, D.C.: U.S. Dept. of Justice, 1961.

Cagan, Phillip. *Determinants and Effects of Changes in the Stock of Money, 1875–1960.*

New York: Columbia University Press (for the National Bureau of Economic Research), 1965.

"Criminal Safeguards and the Punitive Damages Defendant." *University of Chicago Law Review* 34 (Winter 1967).

Ehrlich, Isaac. "The Supply of Illegitimate Activities." Unpublished manuscript, Columbia University, 1967.

Federal Bureau of Investigation. *Uniform Crime Reports for the United States*. Washington, D.C.: U.S. Dept. of Justice, 1960.

———. Ibid., 1961.

Harper, F. V., and F. James. *The Law of Torts*. Vol. II. Boston: Little Brown & Co., 1956.

Johnson, Thomas. "The Effects of the Minimum Wage Law." Ph.D. dissertation, Columbia University, 1967.

Kleinman, E. "The Choice between Two ' Bads'—Some Economic Aspects of Criminal Sentencing." Unpublished manuscript, Hebrew University, 1967.

Landes, William. "The Effect of State Fair Employment Legislation on the Economic Position of Nonwhite Males." Ph.D. dissertation, Columbia University, 1966.

Laws of New York. Vol. II (1965).

Marshall, Alfred. *Principles of Economics*. 8th ed. New York: Macmillan Co., 1961.

Plant, A. "The Economic Theory concerning Patents for Inventions." *Economica* (February 1934).

Pollock, F., and F. W. Maitland. *The History of English Law*. Vol. II. 2d ed. Cambridge: Cambridge University Press, 1952.

President's Commission on Law Enforcement and Administration of Justice. *The Challenge of Crime in a Free Society*. Washington, D.C.: U.S. Government Printing Office, 1967a.

———. *Corrections*. ("Task Force Reports.") Washington, D.C.: U.S. Government Printing Office, 1967b.

———. *The Courts*. ("Task Force Reports.") Washington, D.C.: U.S. Government Printing Office, 1967c.

———. *Crime and Its Impact—an Assessment*. ("Task Force Reports.") Washington, D.C.: U.S. Government Printing Office, 1967d.

———. *Science and Technology*. ("Task Force Reports.") Washington, D.C.: U.S. Government Printing Office, 1967e.

Radzinowicz, L. *A History of English Criminal Law and Its Administration from 1750*. Vol. I. London: Stevens & Sons, 1948.

Schilling, T. C. "Economic Analysis of Organized Crime." In President's Commission on Law Enforcement and Administration of Justice, *Organized Crime*. ("Task Force Reports.") Washington, D.C.: U.S. Government Printing Office, 1967.

Shawness, Lord. "Crime Does Pay Because We Do Not Back Up the Police." *New York Times Magazine*, June 13, 1965.

Smigel, Arleen. "Crime and Punishment: An Economic Analysis." M.A. thesis, Columbia University, 1965.

Stigler, George J. "What Can Regulators Regulate? The Case of Electricity." *Journal of Law and Economics* 5 (October 1962).

————. "A Theory of Oligopoly." *Journal of Political Economy* 72 (February 1964).

————. "The Economic Effects of the Antitrust Laws." *Journal of Law and Economics,* 9 (October, 1966).

Sutherland, E. H. *Principles of Criminology.* 6th ed. Philadelphia: J. B. Lippincott Co., 1960.

LAW ENFORCEMENT, MALFEASANCE, AND COMPENSATION OF ENFORCERS

Gary S. Becker
George J. Stigler

· 20 ·

The new economic approach to political behavior seeks to develop a positive theory of legislation, in contrast to the normative approach of welfare economics. The new approach asks why certain industries and not others become regulated or have tariffs imposed on imports or why income transfers take the form and direction they do, in contrast to asking which industries *should* be regulated or have tariffs imposed, or what transfers *should* be made.

Both the normative and positive approaches to legislation, however, generally have taken enforcement of laws for granted, and have not included systematic analyses of the cost of enforcing different kinds of laws. In separate studies[1] we recently formulated rules designed to increase the effectiveness of different laws. We proposed that offenders convicted of violating laws be punished by an amount related to the value of the damages caused to others, adjusted upward for the probability that offenders avoid conviction.

In and of itself, this rule says nothing about appropriations for enforcing laws, or the diligence and honesty of enforcers. We did discuss optimal enforcement through the introduction of enforcement cost functions, but did not seek to explore the detailed content of these functions. The purpose of the present essay is to inquire more closely into the enforcement problem.

Section I discusses the general circumstances that influence the vigor of

First published in the *Journal of Legal Studies* 3, no. 1 (January 1974): 1–18. © 1974 by The University of Chicago. All rights reserved.

enforcement and the frequency of violations. Section II considers the consequences of weak enforcement for the operation of the legal system. Section III makes two suggestions for improving the incentives given enforcers. Both utilize the price mechanism in related, yet somewhat different, ways: one penalizes malfeasance and other signs of weak enforcement; the other, which we think is preferable, rewards successful enforcement.

I. The Market in Enforcement

There is a powerful temptation in a society with established values to view any violation of a duly established law as a partial failure of that law. Even economists long trained in the harsh realities of a world in which wishes far outstrip resources will be found lamenting the moral laxity that leads to widespread violation of law. Yet it surely follows from basic economic principle that when some people wish to behave in a certain way very much, as measured by the amount they gain from it or would be willing to pay rather than forgo it, they will pursue that wish until it becomes too expensive for their purse and tastes. And in general it will not be inexpensive for society to make prohibited behavior expensive for the potential violator.

Thus the prohibitions of prostitution, gambling, and narcotics are widely held to be failures or at least very meager triumphs of enforcement. There is an obvious economic reason why violations should be extensive. These so-called victimless crimes are highly remunerative, if undetected, when entry into their performance is restricted by law. It is worth perhaps $500 a week to practice one of these trades in a neighborhood, and we must ask: to whom is it worth $500 a week to suppress the traffic? Indeed, a somewhat more effective enforcement of the prohibition would serve to increase the potential earnings. Unless the society has a preoccupation with this one goal to the exclusion of all others, it will not—it cannot—completely drive out the illegal activity, "whatever the cost."

Or reverse the viewpoint: how will the violator conduct himself? If a person violates a law carrying a punishment equivalent to[2] a fine of $10,000 he would be willing to spend up to $10,000 to avoid apprehension and conviction. He could, for example, bribe, intimidate, harass, or cultivate the police to avoid apprehension, and prosecutors or judges to avoid conviction if apprehended.

The same problem is encountered in the enforcement of noncriminal policies which bear heavily on particular people or enterprises. The recent, much publicized, episode of International Telephone and Telegraph's endeavors to obtain permission to remain merged to Hartford Insurance is a striking, but perhaps widely misinterpreted, illustration of our argument. ITT deployed extensive resources to obtain consent for the merger—clearly the company would have been delighted to spend $10 million in a legal manner to obtain the consent. To whom was it worth this sum to prevent the merger? (As an aside, we do not believe it was worth anything to society to prevent it.) The common misinterpretation, we suspect, is to assign a special significance to the episode: we are prepared to predict that an equally complex and expensive set of negotiations has dwelt behind the process of every major governmental decision of comparable consequence to a large company or labor union. Another illustration is the Knapp Commission's recent report of significant corruption in the New York City police department, a corruption which we confidently predict is not unique to the largest city's police department.

In fact the problem is encountered throughout the private sector. Every employer of a person who will have the opportunity to serve his own interests at the cost of his employer faces the problem of fidelity. The employee may commit torts for which there are legal remedies, as when the purchasing agent receives subsidies from a favored supplier. The employee may simply engage in nonfeasance: shirking or underperforming tasks which cannot be completely supervised.[3] (Even the professor must determine whether the term paper he is grading was written or purchased by the student!)

We should abandon all thoughts of judging enforcement of laws and rules as simply successes or failures, even if these categories are "realistically" defined. The society (or a person) buys the amount of enforcement which it deems appropriate to the statute or rule: more will be bought if the statute serves a more valuable goal (protects us from murder rather than assault) and if a given increase in enforcement is less expensive. So it is with all prudent conduct.

The level of enforcement will depend upon a variety of factors in addition to the effort (i.e., the amount of resources) that the society is prepared to devote to enforcement as a function of the amount of enforcement (reduction in probability of successful commission of the offense) that is obtained. There is, first of all, the degree of honesty of the enforcers: for a given bribe, some men will condone offenses that other men would prosecute. The honesty of enforcers will be dependent not only upon the supply of honesty in the population, but also on the amount spent to ascertain how honest a given person is. With an increasingly thorough and expensive investigation, one can determine with increasing precision the probable behavior of a given person.

There is, second, the structure of incentives to honesty embedded in the remuneration of enforcers. The correlation between the gain to enforcers from enforcing laws and the gain to violators from successful violation is almost certainly positive. But the variation in the gain to violators is often much greater than that to enforcers from preventing or punishing violations, so that the quality of enforcement would tend to decline as the gain to violators increased. This is one reason why effective enforcement against petty larcenists, muggers, or minor smugglers (once apprehended) is more common than it is against major antitrust or SEC violators, or wealthy murderers. The ITT case is in fact one illustration of this relation.

We do not mean that a highly profitable violation that is also flagrant and politically conspicuous can be committed without fear of apprehension and punishment. The penalty incurred by the enforcer—be he president, mayor, prosecuting attorney, or patrolman—from connivance would be sufficient to make it in his interest to enforce the law. Even so, would Leopold and Loeb, for example, have escaped the death penalty if their parents had been paupers?

The quality of enforcement depends, thirdly, on the temporal pattern of violations. It is difficult to bribe or even intimidate the enforcers who would be involved in a nonrepetitive violation. They are not easy to identify in advance—whose prowl car will be going by?—and not easy to negotiate with—how can negotiation be distinguished from entrapment? Repetitive violations, such as gambling, prostitution, or the sale of drugs, are otherwise. The substantial transactions costs of ascertaining that the other party is reliable (abides by contracts) become manageable for both violators and enforcers. In fact, the particular enforcers are no longer an independent variable: if the police chief is an unyielding saint, the mayor may be in greater need of cash.

This expectation of mutually profitable contracts between repetitive violators and enforcers is part of the logic behind the widely held view that prostitution or the regular sale of consumer goods cannot be successfully prohibited. It also helps explain the development of organized crime: an organization is engaged more continually in violations than its individual members are, and can, therefore, make arrangements with judges or police that would not be feasible for these members.

The quality of enforcement depends, fourthly, on whether a violation has a "victim," i.e., a particular person who largely bears the cost of the violation. The customer of the numbers game or of the prostitute or of the marijuana peddler is not, in his opinion, a loser by these activities, as contrasted (say) to the person who is burglarized or charged more than the permissible rent. Enforcement is generally more effective against violations with victims because victims have a stake in apprehending violators, especially when they receive restitution (as the recovery of a stolen television set or the excess paid over the legal rental). Consequently, victims, in effect, often do the enforcing themselves. The role of victims in enforcement is discussed more extensively in Section III.

II. The Quality of Enforcement and the Effectiveness of Laws

We have argued that the quality of enforcement depends on the magnitude and regularity of violations, and the interests of victims, but have not considered the relation between the quality of enforcement and the effectiveness of laws. We do this now for corruption, an extreme manifestation of apparently poor enforcement; a related analysis can be developed for intimidated or lackadaisical enforcement.

Consider enforcers with sufficient evidence to convict a person of a violation that is punishable by a $5,000 fine. The violator would be willing to bribe enforcers as much as $5,000 to ignore the evidence. If a $5,000 bribe were paid,[4] the violation would be punished as fully as it would be if the violator paid the fine; consequently, the deterrent effects of the bribe and the fine would be the same. Moreover, if the enforcers anticipated the bribe (and had no fear of detection), they would be willing to work for $5,000 less than they otherwise would. Then the state, rather than the enforcers, would in essence be collecting the bribe. The transaction between the violator and the enforcers is equivalent to the violator's paying the state $5,000 for his violation; i.e., it is equivalent to honest and diligent enforcement.

Effectiveness could actually be improved if a bribe of $5,000 were the alternative to punishment by a prison term with a monetary equivalent of a $5,000 fine. Again, one can show that the deterrence to violators would be the same, but with a bribe the state would collect as punishment not a prison term, but, in effect, a $5,000 fine. Since fines are preferable to other kinds of punishments,[5] the monetization of punishments by bribery would improve the operation of the punishment system.

Effectiveness is reduced if the amount paid in bribes is significantly less than the monetary equivalent of the punishment. Bribes may be less because competition among enforcers (for example, alternative examiners for auto licenses) lowers the market price of bribes, or because the marketable resources of violators are less than the monetary value of punishments. In these cases, bribery reduces punishment and thus deterrence.[6]

Whether a reduction in effectiveness is desirable or not obviously depends on whether laws are passed in the "social" interest or to reward special interest groups, to revert to the theme of the opening paragraph of this essay. For example, bribes that reduced the effectiveness of many housing codes,[7] of the laws in Nazi Germany against Jews, or of the laws restricting oil imports would improve, not harm, social welfare (although not as defined by the legislature). Some of the opposition we have encountered to our proposals (in Sec. III) to improve the quality of enforcement argues that more effective enforcement is often undesirable. Presumably this is based on the belief that many laws or the way they can be interpreted do not promote social welfare.

III. How to Improve Enforcement

Punishing Malfeasance

In this part we make two proposals for improving the quality of enforcement, our assumption being that better enforcement, on the whole, does more good than bad. The first proposal concerns punishment of enforcers for taking bribes or other acts of misfeasance or nonfeasance. We assume that enforcers discovered committing such acts are simply dismissed. Although occasionally imprisonment and fines are imposed on enforcers discovered in the most flagrant bribe taking, by far the most common sanction, if any, is dismissal.

If the state knew with certainty whenever enforcers did not perform adequately, and if dismissal always resulted, enforcers could be induced to perform adequately simply by being paid what they could get in other jobs requiring comparable skills, risk, effort, etc. To achieve certainty of detection, however, is extraordinarily expensive, partly because enforcers try to prevent detection. Since the state has its own enforcement budget constraint the effective probability of detection is invariably less than unity. How then can corrupt enforcement be discouraged when detection is uncertain?

The fundamental answer is to *raise* the salaries of enforcers above what they could get elsewhere, by an amount that is inversely related to the probability of detection, and directly related to the size of bribes and other benefits from malfeasance. A difference in salaries imposes a cost of dismissal equal to the present value of the difference between the future earnings stream in enforcement and in other occupations. This cost can more than offset the gain from malfeasance.

To develop the analysis formally in a simple model, let p be the probability of detecting malfeasance during any single time period. Although p is taken as given, it depends on the amounts spent by the state on detection. Let b be the monetary value of the gain to enforcers from bribery and other malfeasance; b is also taken as given, although it depends on p and other variables. Let r be the discount rate, and v_i the earnings that could be obtained by enforcers (aged i) in other occupations. The problem is to find the minimum salary (w_i) to enforcers, in each time period, that would discourage them from malfeasance.

We start from the final period of employment of a given enforcer, n, and work backward. He can either receive w_n with certainty, or, by engaging in malfeasance during this period, have the probability p of receiving v_n (he is dismissed at the beginning of the period and forfeits his gain from malfeasance), and $1-p$ of receiving $b+w_n$. If he is risk neutral and maximizes expected wealth, the minimum w_n that would discourage malfeasance is determined from the equation

$$w_n = pv_n + (1-p)(b+w_n),\qquad(1)$$

or

$$w_n = v_n + \frac{1-p}{p}b.\qquad(2)$$

Consider now his position at the beginning of period $n-1$. With no malfeasance in periods $n-1$ and n, the present value of his income stream would be $w_{n-1} + \frac{w_n}{1+r}$. With malfeasance in period $n-1$, he has the probability p of receiving a present value equal to $v_n + \frac{v_n}{(1+r)}$,[8] and a probability $1-p$ of receiving $b+w_{n-1}+\frac{w_n}{1+r}$.[9] By equating these present values, the minimum w_{n-1} can be determined:

$$w_{n-1} + \frac{w_n}{1+r} = p\left(v_{n-1}+\frac{v_n}{1+r}\right) + (1-p)\left(b+w_{n-1}+\frac{w_n}{1+r}\right);\qquad(3)$$

hence by using equation (2),

$$w_{n-1} = v_{n-1} + \frac{(1-p)b}{p}\frac{r}{1+r}.\qquad(4)$$

Similarly, by continuing to go backward in time one can derive the general expression

$$w_i = v_i + \frac{(1-p)b}{p}\frac{r}{1+r},\qquad i = 1,\ldots,n-1.\qquad(5)$$

The income as an enforcer in the first $n-1$ periods is higher than elsewhere by an amount that is inversely related to the probability of detection, and directly related to the gain from malfeasance and (approximately) to the interest rate. The term $\frac{(1-p)b}{p}$ can be considered a measure of the "temptation" of malfeasance.[10] The cost of dismissal is the present value of the excess income stream that would be forgone. The income in the last period is still higher to offset the increasing attractiveness of malfeasance as retirement nears because of the decline in the number of years of future income that must be forgone.

The excess of the premium in the last period over that in other periods can be considered the capital value of the "pension" at the beginning of the last period:

$$P = \frac{(1-p)b}{p} - \frac{(1-p)b}{p}\frac{r}{1+r} = \frac{(1-p)b}{p}\frac{1}{1+r}. \tag{6}$$

The prospect of losing the pension is an increasingly important deterrent to malfeasance as one gets closer and closer to retirement. The forgone interest on this capital value, rP, the pension "income," equals the annual premium in the first $n-1$ years:

$$rP = \frac{(1-p)b}{p}\frac{r}{1+r}. \tag{7}$$

Consequently, the pension income is also directly proportional to the gain from malfeasance and inversely proportional to the probability of detection. The ratio rP/w_i, of pension income to salary, clearly ranges from 0 to 1[11] and would be larger the more tempting malfeasance is relative to the incomes available elsewhere. Therefore, this ratio can serve as an indirect measure of the relative importance of bribes and other temptations available.

The present value of the lifetime salary to an enforcer is

$$V_w = \sum_{i=1}^{n}\frac{w_i}{(1+r)^{i-1}} = \sum_{i=1}^{n}\frac{v_i}{(1+r)^{i-1}} + \sum_{i=1}^{n-1}\frac{(1-p)b}{p}\frac{r}{(1+r)^i}$$
$$+ \frac{(1-p)b}{p}\frac{1}{(1+r)^{n-1}}, \tag{8}$$
$$= V_v + \frac{(1-p)b}{p}. \tag{9}$$

This present value would exceed the present value of salaries available elsewhere by the temptation of malfeasance. Consequently, the payments to each enforcer could be reduced by charging an "entrance fee" equal to $\frac{(1-p)b}{p}$; then enforcement would pay as well as the best alternative, no more and no less, and an appropriate number of persons would be available for employment as enforcers.

Malfeasance can be eliminated, therefore, even when the probability of detection is quite low, without lifetime payments to enforcers that exceed what they could get elsewhere. The appropriate pay structure has three components: an "entrance fee" equal to the temptation of malfeasance, a salary premium in each year of employment approximately equal to the income yielded by the "entrance fee,"[12] and a pension with a capital value approximately equal also to the temptation of malfeasance. As it were, enforcers post a bond equal to the temptation of malfeasance, receive the income on the bond as long as they are employed, and have the bond returned if they behave themselves until retirement. Put differently, they forfeit their bond if they are fired for malfeasance.[13]

As the probability of detecting malfeasance, p, is made smaller, resources spent on detection would be reduced with no effect on malfeasance if salaries and the entrance fee adjust according to equations (2), (5), and (9). Consequently, the optimum would appear to be a probability of detection arbitrarily close to zero, and earnings and the entrance fee indefinitely high. Then malfeasance would be discouraged at zero cost to the state!

As entrance fees become larger, the state appears to have more incentive to fire enforcers without cause since it could then pocket these fees. But if the probability, i, of being fired without cause (that is, if he is honest) were known to enforcers, their salaries would have to rise to take account of this, according to the formulas:

$$w_i = v_i + \frac{(1-p)b}{p-i}\frac{(r+i)}{1+r}, \tag{10}$$
$$w_n = v_n + \frac{(1-p)b}{p-i}.$$

As i increased, the salaries that must be paid enforcers to discourage them from malfeasance would also increase; hence, the state would not gain from increasing i.[14] (Note that i could also be viewed as including the probability that innocent enforcers would voluntarily quit their jobs.)

It is, however, costly to determine whether someone is being fired with or without cause. The greater their salary, the greater the stake of enforcers in litigating efforts to fire them by proving their innocence: they would try to arrange for compulsory hearings on dismissals, appeals procedures, and the like. The extent of the procedures, and hence their cost, would rise as the probability of detection went down and salaries went up. When these costs of litigation are included, the optimal probability of detecting malfeasance is not necessarily arbitrarily close to zero, but would depend on the increase in litigation expenditures as salaries rose (i.e., as the probability of detection fell). Of course, the optimal probability would not be zero if enforcers were unable to borrow a sufficiently large entrance "bond" because lenders were uncertain about being repaid.

Since eliminating malfeasance by raising salaries may not be costless, it may be preferable simply to permit malfeasance. If enforcers anticipate engaging in malfeasance they will be willing to accept a lower salary than they can get elsewhere: their gain from malfeasance is a "compensating differential." If their gain equals the loss to the state, the state would not suffer a net loss nor would enforcers obtain a net gain—by net is meant after account is taken of the compensating differential—from malfeasance. The gain to enforcers is likely, however, to be less than the loss to the state because of the time and effort that enforcers spend on malfeasance, because of transactions costs in disposing of stolen merchandise, and because of the other reasons discussed in Section II. Then if enforcers did not obtain a net gain from malfeasance, the state (and society) would suffer a net loss.

Formally, we have

$$v_i = w_i + b, \tag{11}$$

where $v_i - w_i = b$ is the compensating differential to enforcers, and

$$w_i + \alpha b = w_i^s, \tag{12}$$

where w_i^s is the total "wage" rate paid by the state, and α is the loss to the state for each dollar equivalent received by enforcers from malfeasance. Then, by substitution,

$$w_i^s - v_i = b(\alpha - 1). \tag{13}$$

The net cost to the state from malfeasance, the difference between w_i^s and v_i, is greater the greater the gain to enforcers (b), and the greater the net "social" or deadweight loss ($\alpha - 1$) per dollar of gain to enforcers.

Therefore, whether salaries should be raised and malfeasance eliminated (or lowered) and whether malfeasance should be permitted depend on the cost of the optimal probability of detecting malfeasance, and the deadweight loss from malfeasance. The higher the latter—the less that malfeasance resembles a transfer payment—the more likely that malfeasance should be eliminated.

Our analysis of malfeasance is applicable not only to enforcers but to all public and private employees who must be "trusted." By "trust" is meant the following. Assume that employees must choose between several actions, say, for simplicity, two, A and B: A makes them better off whereas B makes their employers better off. Employers could ensure that action B would be chosen if they always knew when A occurred, simply by paying employees as much as they could get elsewhere, and by firing them whenever A occurred. If, however, A could be detected only some of the time, employees would have to be "trusted" to take the appropriate (that is, B) action. They would do so if the pattern of compensation we developed for enforcers were adopted: a salary premium, pension, and "entrance fee" all determined by the tempta- tion of malfeasance

Clearly, therefore, the temptations seducing enforcers are also available to purchasing agents, sales personnel, soldiers, physicians, lawyers, manag- ers, and persons in many other occupations.[15] Trust calls for a salary premium not necessarily because better-quality persons are thereby attracted,[16] but because higher salaries impose a cost on violations of trust.

The extent of control by the stockholders over the conduct of the officers of large corporations has been a much-debated subject at least since the celebrated study by Berle and Means, *The Modern Corporation*.[17] The focus of attention has gradually shifted away from their main concern, the difficul- ties in using the proxy fight and the stockholders' suit to protect stockholder interests. The recent focus has been upon the takeover bid and the merger as devices to eliminate inefficient or corrupt management.

Throughout the period of discussion, however, one assumption of Berle and Means has been almost unquestioned: when one or a few stockholders have a controlling holding of voting stock, there is no serious problem of ownership control. Yet the incentives to malfeasance and nonfeasance are obviously present in all employment and agency arrangements, and these incentives are presumably important in the management of all large enter- prises. There is no entry in a corporate income statement, "profits that would have been attained with superb management," to guide even the single owner of all the stock of a corporation.

The cases of diffused and concentrated ownership of a corporation's stock differ in certain respects: the dominant owner has a larger incentive to monitor the performance, and offers a more accessible market to others with information to sell on the performance of management, than each of numer- ous part owners. These differences may not be very important, however, if specialists ("takeover artists" and merger-seeking companies) undertake the task of searching for mismanaged enterprises.

As we already indicated, the role of trust in an employment contract is larger, the less easily and quickly the quality of performance can be ascer- tained. The more diverse the activities of the enterprise, the more rapidly it is growing or declining, the more unstable the industries in which it is operating—in each case the greater the role for trust in one's managers. We would therefore expect to find the pattern of compensation we developed for enforcers to be especially prominent for managers in companies with these characteristics.

Rewarding Enforcement

Although the compensation structure we have developed could eliminate malfeasance, it would not automatically result in optimal enforcement. No guidance is provided to the optimal number of enforcers (or more generally to the optimal total expenditure on enforcement), as opposed to the optimal expenditure per enforcer. Moreover, considerable resources may be spent by the state in detecting malfeasance, by enforcers in hiding it, and, more generally, by the state and enforcers in protecting their own interests.

A highly promising method of compensating enforcers is suggested by the market in private transactions, which also has innumerable "rules" to be enforced. It is a rule that I am not to take a quart of milk from a store unless I pay 40 cents, or that I am not to receive wages from my employer unless I work 40 hours. Of course, there are reciprocal rules: the 40 cents is not paid unless the quart of milk is received; the wages must be paid if I have performed the work. The "rules"—which are what contracts embody—are enforced extensively and effectively: the escape rate on murders is higher than on 20-cent pencils in a variety store. The enforcement is good precisely because the incentives to enforcers are as large as the incentives to prospective violators.

The same method is often used, almost inadvertently, to enforce public statutes—namely, in the widespread reliance on victim enforcement. Persons charged in excess of the legal ceiling on rents report their landlords because they anticipate a reduction in their rents. Laws against shoplifting are enforced primarily by stores, often using private police, because the shopkeepers are the immediate beneficiaries. Similarly, libel laws are enforced by those libeled because they anticipate compensation. Private triple damage suits have become the only effective sanction of the antitrust laws. In the great electrical equipment conspiracy, General Electric was fined $400,000, and paid several hundred million dollars in damages The recently developed class action suits extend victim enforcement to include many situations where the damage is so widely diffused that no one victim alone has much incentive to enforcement.

The amount of victim enforcement would be optimal if successful enforcers were paid the amount that they had suffered in damages, excluding their enforcement costs, divided by the probability that they are successful (this assumes that victim enforcers are risk neutral). If this amount were levied in fines against convicted violators, so that, in effect, violators compensated victims, the gain to victims from enforcement would be the same as the punishment to violators; hence these enforcers could not be corrupted.

Of course, most victims would not literally become enforcers: they would hire lawyers, private investigators, and other specialized "enforcement firms" to gather evidence and argue their cases. Free competition among these firms would ensure that enforcement was provided at cost. Moreover, these firms would not wait passively until contacted by victims, but would seek out evidence and bring it to the attention of victims.[18]

The essence of victim enforcement is compensation of enforcers on performance, or by a "piece rate" or a "bounty," instead of by a straight salary. Why not then generalize this system, and let *anyone* enforce statutes and receive as compensation for performance the fines levied against convicted violators? Specialist enforcement firms would develop and would either compensate victims en masse (by appropriate division of penalties with, e.g., the motor vehicle fund), or retain all awards for themselves. Where victim cooperation aids enforcement, we would expect that, whatever the formal distribution of awards, victims would receive a share. Where victims had little to contribute to detection and conviction, it seems more appropriate to allow the enforcers, whoever they be, to retain the awards. The rule that *anyone* could enforce a statute would basically achieve this distribution.

Free competition among enforcement firms may seem strange, even terrifying, and much more radical than the method of compensation proposed earlier to eliminate malfeasance by salaried enforcers. But society does not pretend to be able to designate who the bakers should be—this is left to personal aptitudes and tastes. Why should enforcers of laws be chosen differently? Let anyone who wishes enter the trade, innovate, and prosper or fail. The method by which ditchdiggers, professors, and senators are obtained surely should supply us with health inspectors, antitrust inspectors, rent-control investigators, and even tax collectors.

The case for allowing rules to be enforced by normal market methods of recruitment is not simply a mechanical generalization of the case for competition, for it corrects a major error of the theory of rules. This error—or omission—is to assume that rules provide any guidance or incentive to their enforcement: on the contrary, rules usually provide neither the slightest hint of where to look for violations nor the incentive to convict violators. Nothing in the Sherman Act tells us where to look for collusion; nothing in the motor vehicle laws tells us who will be a speeder; nothing in a pure food law tells us who will be an adulterator. Moreover, as we have been arguing, often there is little incentive to convict the colluder, speeder, or adulterator.

Consider some additional advantages of this proposal. Society would use fewer resources to detect malfeasance because payment for performance reduces the gain from malfeasance. Moreover, society is more likely to use fines equal to damages divided by the probability of conviction[19] to punish offenders if it must pay this amount to successful enforcers. Although private enforcement of rules need not change the rules, we predict that they would gain currency and relevance because enforcement would then be much more efficient and transparent. In addition, the right amount of self-protection by potential victims is encouraged, not the excessive (wasteful) self-protection that results when victims are not compensated, or the inadequate self-protection that results when they are automatically compensated. Further, rewards of innovation will spur technical progress in private enforcement as in other economic callings.

Capricious or arbitrary enforcement is always possible, and is much encouraged under our present system by the policy of not compensating acquitted persons for the costs (of all sorts) that they had borne. If a man is falsely charged with a crime, or a federal regulatory body erroneously denounces a company, at present neither victim is compensated in general, and we consider this a shameful flaw in our system of enforcement. The proposed system would have full compensation of persons acquitted of charges paid by the enforcement firms bringing these charges. This proposal is equally relevant to public enforcement but is more easily adopted in a regime of private enforcement because of the legal tradition of governmental immunity.

As with our proposal to eliminate malfeasance, innumerable complications would be encountered by private enforcement in a world full of variety and ingenuity (and just a little fraud). Impoverished violators would pose a problem in restitution: where violators have no legally merchantable skills the state would be compelled to use nonmonetary punishments, such as imprisonment, and to compensate the persons apprehending them. Impoverished enforcers also pose a problem in restitution: perhaps enforcement firms should be required to post a bond or its equivalent ("malpractice" insurance) to guarantee their solvency if they are required to pay damages to persons they have falsely accused or harassed.[20] The state also would be compelled to assess more accurately the damage of numerous violations (adultery, assault, sale of a stock or commodity off an organized exchange, driving a truck without an ICC license), but one need not apologize for retracing Bentham's steps after almost two centuries. Violence unfortunately must often be met by violence; so it will be necessary to face the question of who should be permitted to use force in enforcing laws. At least limited use of licensed firms seems desirable here.

Since different enforcement firms would compete to eliminate any particular malfeasance, the concept of double jeopardy would need elaboration and rules would be needed to determine the docket order in courts of different enforcers, and, more generally, to determine the distribution of compensation when several enforcers were involved in a conviction.

If the probability of conviction implicit in the punishment levied against convicted violators and paid to successful enforcers were less than the actual probability, the state could eliminate the difference in probabilities by lowering the fines on offenders (rewards to enforcers). This would lower the actual probability because enforcers have less to gain from enforcement. By lowering fines sufficiently, the implicit and actual probabilities could be equalized. Similarly, if initially the implicit probability exceeded the actual one, fines could be raised until they were equalized.

One might question whether the equilibrium probability of conviction thus obtained with private enforcement would be socially optimal, for since the apprehension and conviction of violators consume real resources, society can conserve its resources by raising punishments and lowering probabilities.[21] Perhaps public enforcement could more readily achieve an optimal combination of punishments and probabilities, but note that the temptation of malfeasance by public enforcers and thus the cost of policing them would rise as the punishment rose, and that an appropriate tax on private enforcement could lower its equilibrium probability of conviction to any desired level.

CONCLUSION

We conclude by emphasizing that the view of enforcement and litigation as wasteful in whole or in part is simply mistaken. They are as important as the harm they seek to prevent, and are really only names for the orderly ascertainment of facts, resolution of doubts, and reduction of conflicts. In any event, the amount of enforcement is determined ultimately by the rules to be enforced and the quality of enforcement.

We have discussed different methods of improving the quality of enforcement. One discourages malfeasance by raising the salaries of public enforcers, whereas the other encourages results by paying private enforcers for performance, or on a piece-rate basis. Both methods have considerable advantages over much contemporary enforcement procedure, and the latter method in particular would unleash the powerful forces of competition.

APPENDIX

The analysis can be generalized by assuming that (1) the probability of detection depends on the experience of enforcers and other variables; (2) the income available at any age in other occupations depends on the age of entry into these occupations; (3) expected utility rather than expected wealth is maximized; and so forth. We here analyze the relation between the gain from malfeasance and the experience of enforcers; that is, the bribes and other gains available are assumed to increase as enforcers become more experienced and have more authority.

Let b_i be the monetary equivalent of the gain from malfeasance at age i. Then the minimum salaries that discourage malfeasance can be shown to be

$$w_n = v_n + \frac{(1-p)b_n}{p}, \qquad \text{(A.1)}$$

$$w_i = v_i + \left[\frac{(1-p)b_i}{p} - \frac{(1-p)b_{i+1}}{p(1+r)}\right], \qquad i = 1 \ldots n-1 \quad \text{(A.2)}$$

and the difference in present values is

$$V_w - V_v = \frac{(1-p)b_n}{p}. \qquad \text{(A.3)}$$

For the equivalent of equation (3) is

$$w_{n-1} + \frac{w_n}{1+r} = p\left(v_{n-1} + \frac{v_n}{1+r}\right)$$
$$+ (1-p)\left(b_{n-1} + w_{n-1} + \frac{w_n}{(1+r)}\right), \qquad \text{(3)}$$

which implies by using (A.1) that

$$w_{n-1} = v_{n-1} + \frac{(1-p)b_{n-1}}{p} - \frac{(1-p)b_n}{p(1+r)}; \qquad \text{(4')}$$

similarly for the other w_i. Moreover,

$$V_w = \sum_{i=1}^{n} \frac{w_i}{(1+r)^{i-1}}$$

$$= V_v + \sum_{i=1}^{n} \frac{\left[\dfrac{(1-p)b_i}{p} - \dfrac{(1-p)b_{i+1}}{p(1+r)}\right]}{(1+r)^{i-1}} + \frac{(1-p)b_n}{p(1+r)^{n-1}}, \qquad \text{(8')}$$

which implies equation (A.3).

If b increases over time, the earnings of enforcers would begin *below* alternative earnings, *equal* alternative earnings when b rises at the interest rate, and remain *above* alternative earnings thereafter. The effect is similar to that resulting from investment in human capital; indeed, analytically the problems are very close, with the growth in earnings due to the accumulation of human capital. For equation (A.2) can be written as

$$w_i = v_i + \frac{r(1-p)b_i}{p} - \frac{(1-p)}{p}\left(\frac{b_{i+1}}{(1+r)} - (1-r)b_i\right),$$

$$\cong v_i + \frac{r(1-p)b_i}{p} - \frac{(1-p)}{(1+r)p}(b_{i+1} - b_i) \text{ if} \frac{1-r}{1+r} = 1. \quad \text{(A.4)}$$

The term $\dfrac{r(1-p)b_i}{p}$ is the income yielded by the malfeasance "capital" accumulated to period i, and $\dfrac{(1-p)}{(1+r)p}(b_{i+1} - b_i)$ is the amount invested in additional capital in period i; the latter is subtracted from earnings capacity to arrive at "net" earnings.[22] The stock of malfeasance capital in period $i + 1$ is then the stock in i plus the value in $i + 1$ of the net investment in i or

$$C_{i+1} = \frac{(1-p)b_i}{p} + (1+r)\frac{(1-p)}{(1+r)p}(b_{i+1} - b_i) = \frac{(1-p)}{p}b_{i+1}. \quad \text{(A.5)}$$

Equation (A.1) indicates that that pension is largely determined by the temptation of malfeasance in the terminal year of employment, not the average temptation during the whole employment period. This may help explain why pension incomes are often geared to earnings shortly before retirement instead of average earnings during the whole employment period. The "entrance fee" (given by equation [A.3]), on the other hand, equals the temptation in the initial year of employment. Since this fee results from considering the difference between lifetime earnings streams, the initial temptation is important not because of myopia, but rather because enforcers pay for the growth in the gain from malfeasance through appropriate reductions in earnings.

Consequently, the "entrance fee" and the capital value of the pension are no longer similar when the gain from malfeasance grows with experience. Indeed, the fee might be only a small fraction of the pension or extra earnings. For example, if the gain (b) grew 20-fold from the initial to terminal year of employment—say from $500 to $10,000—and if the pension's capital value were 5 times average earnings, the entrance fee would be only about 1/20 of the pension, and 1/4 of average earnings.

NOTES

Our research has been supported by a grant from the National Science Foundation to the National Bureau of Economic Research. This paper is not an official Bureau publication, however, since it has not yet undergone the full critical review accorded National Bureau publications, including approval by the Bureau's board of directors.

1. See Gary S. Becker, "Crime and Punishment: An Economic Approach," *Journal of Political Economy* 76 (1968): 169; George J. Stigler, "The Optimum Enforcement of Laws," *Journal of Political Economy* 78 (1970): 526.

2. We say "equivalent to" because the punishment may be in the form of imprisonment, loss of business, probation, etc., instead of a fine.

3. See Armen A. Alchian and Harold Demsetz, "Production, Information on Costs, and Economic Organization," *American Economic Review* 62 (1972): 777; Gary S. Becker, *Economic Theory* (1971), pp. 122–23.

4. A bribe would not be less than the value to an enforcer of enforcing a law, nor would it be greater than the cost to a violator of punishment. Its location between these extremes is determined by bargaining between the parties. We are indebted to William M. Landes for comments on this point.

5. See Gary S. Becker, supra note 1, at 193–98; George J. Stigler, supra note 1, at 531–31.

6. Again, however, by monetizing punishment, bribery reduces the social cost of punishments.

7. This is apropos of the recent revelation in the *New York Times* of significant bribery in the enforcement of these codes in New York City.

8. We assume that if he is fired for malfeasance in any period, he cannot return in any future period.

9. Equation (1) ensures that his expected income in period n equals w_n both when he does and when he does not engage in malfeasance in that period.

10. We assume that enforcers plan their behavior using the expected value of the gain from malfeasance. Therefore, they would not be tempted to engage in malfeasance if the expected value did not justify it, even if an unexpected good opportunity for malfeasance came along, because they would not have planned their behavior ("covered their tracks") for malfeasance. We are indebted to Arnold Harberger for raising this point.

11. It approaches 1 as v_i gets smaller and smaller relative to $r\,P$.

12. This pay structure follows from our assumption that dismissal is the only punishment for malfeasance. However, if enforcers detected in malfeasance were fined, their salary should be equal to what they could get elsewhere, if fines equaled the temptation of malfeasance. The minimum value of the fine, F, that would just discourage malfeasance is given by:

$$(1-p)(w_i+b)+p(v_i-F) = w_i,$$

or

$$F = (v_i - w_i) + \frac{(1-p)b}{p}.$$

Then

$$F = \frac{(1-p)b}{p} \quad \text{if} \quad v_i = w_i.$$

13. The analysis is generalized somewhat in the appendix at the end of this paper.

14. For any undesired behavior, the efficiency argument against punishing innocent persons is that behavior depends on the *difference* between p and i, the probabilities of punishing guilty and innocent persons respectively. Any increase in i relative to p would increase the undesired behavior, even if p itself was also increasing.

15. Robert J. Barro analyzes these temptations for politicians in "The Control of Politicians: An Economic Model," *Public Choice* 12 (spring 1973). Truth is perhaps no stranger than fiction:

> It appeared that the firms [makers of safes] were fully alive to the possibility of fraud or theft on the part of their men. For this reason only old hands who had been with them for many years, and of whose honesty they were completely satisfied, were entrusted with the fitting of the keys. *These men, moreover, were paid a high rate of wages, so as to reduce temptations as far as possible.*
> Freeman Willis Crofts, *Crime at Guilford* (1935).

16. Adam Smith believed that occupations requiring trust paid higher wages in order to attract better-quality persons. "Such confidence [i.e. trust] could not safely be reposed in people of a very mean or low condition. Their reward must be such, therefore, as may give them that rank in the society which so important a trust requires." *The Wealth of Nations* (Modern Library ed.), p. 105.

17. Adolf Berle and Gardner Means, *The Modern Corporation and Private Property* (1933).

18. Some law firms now take the incentive in proving antitrust violations in class action suits.

19. The optimality of these fines is discussed in Gary S. Becker, supra note 1, at 191–193, and George J. Stigler, supra note 1, at 531.

20. We owe this point to Melvin Reder.

21. See the discussion in Gary S. Becker, supra note 1, at 183–84, 193.

22. See the related equations for human capital in Gary S. Becker, *Human Capital* (1964), chs. 2, 3.

POLITICS

◆ ◆ ◆ ◆ ◆

◆ PART ◆ FIVE ◆

COMPETITION AND DEMOCRACY

· 21 ·

Economists have often argued that if an industry acts as a monopolist it would
be desirable government policy either to break up the monopoly or, if this is
undesirable because of increasing returns, to regulate and perhaps even
nationalize it.[1] This proposition, although extremely well known and often
accepted as obvious, turns out upon close examination to be far from obvious,
and to involve several assumptions of doubtful validity. The argument supporting this proposition goes something as follows: Monopolies cause a mal-
distribution of resources, since the price charged by a monopolist exceeds
marginal costs and an optimal distribution requires price equal to marginal
cost. An optimal allocation would occur if the industry were made competitive, since price equals marginal costs in competitive industries. If the industry were a "natural" monopoly, price could be made equal to marginal cost
either indirectly by government regulation or directly by government administration. Therefore, the recommendation is an antitrust law to prevent or
break up contrived monopolies and government regulation or government
administration of natural monopolies.

The non sequitur in this argument is the sentence beginning with "therefore"; the recommendation of government intervention does not follow from
the demonstration that government intervention could improve matters.

First published in the *Journal of Law & Economics* 1, no. 3 (1958): 105–9. © 1958 by The
University of Chicago. All rights reserved.

Demonstrating that a set of government decisions would improve matters is not the same as demonstrating that actual government decisions would do so. This kind of inference is logically equivalent to identifying the actual workings of the market sector with its ideal workings.

In Section I a theory of the workings of a political democracy under ideal conditions is developed. It is shown that an ideal democracy is very similar to an ideal free enterprise system in the marketplace. That is, political decisions would be determined by the values of the electorate and the political sector would be run very efficiently. Section II tries to determine why actual democracies differ significantly from the ideal, and whether government regulation of private monopolies in actual democracies would improve matters.

I. Competition in Ideal Democracies

An ideal political democracy is defined as: *an institutional arrangement for arriving at political decisions in which individuals endeavor to acquire political office through perfectly free competition for the votes of a broadly based electorate.* [2] Three aspects of this definition warrant some discussion. No country could legitimately be called a political democracy unless a large fraction of its population could vote. Although "large" is a matter of degree, it is clear that countries have differed greatly; for example, seventeenth-century England had much too narrow a franchise to qualify as a political democracy.

It is often said that the transfer of activities from the marketplace to the political sector would reduce the role of competition in organizing activities. In a political democracy individuals (or parties) do compete for political office—in, say, periodic elections—by offering platforms to the electorate. In an ideal political democracy competition is free in the sense that no appreciable costs or artificial barriers prevent an individual from running for office, and from putting a platform before the electorate. The transfer of activities from the market to the state in a political democracy does not necessarily reduce the amount of competition, but does change its form from competition by enterprises to competition by parties. Indeed, perfect competition is as necessary to an ideal political democracy as it is to an ideal free enterprise system. This suggests that the analysis of the workings of a free enterprise economy can be used to understand the workings of a political democracy.

The immediate aim of any political party is to be chosen by the electorate, just as the immediate aim of any firm is to be chosen by consumers. This immediate aim of the firm is consistent with a wide range of ultimate aims, such as the desire to help consumers (altruism) or the desire for economic power; the one most consistent with available data and most frequently used is the desire to maximize income or "profits." Likewise this immediate aim of the political party is consistent with many ultimate aims, such as the desire to help one's country (altruism) or the desire for prestige and income; the one most frequently used[3] is the desire for power, which can be defined as the ability to influence behavior of others. Most of this paper requires only an assumption about the immediate aim of parties; at several points, however, the analysis is also related to some ultimate aims.

This definition has several important implications. First, it is easy to show that there must be freedom of speech and expression in ideal democracies. If an individual is free to offer a platform to the electorate, he is free to criticize the platform of others. Unless all possessed at least as much freedom as candidates they could increase their freedom merely by running for office. Since this situation is unstable they would ultimately have to possess as much freedom as candidates do.

Another important implication of this definition can be shown most simply by assuming that all voters have the same preferences. If the party in office did not adopt the policies preferred by the electorate, another party could gain more popular support by offering a platform closer to these preferences. Consequently, the only equilibrium platform would be one that perfectly satisfied these preferences. An ideal political democracy would be perfectly responsive to the "will" of the people. The ultimate aim of each party may be to acquire political power, but in equilibrium no one, including those "in power," has any political power.[4] There is no room for choice by political officials because political decisions are completely determined by electorate preferences. This theorem casts light on the controversy of whether a representative should vote according to his own dictates or according to the will of his constituents.[5] In an ideal democracy unless he follows the "will" of his constituents, he does not remain in office very long.

Third, in an ideally competitive free enterprise system, only the most efficient firms survive; for example, if the level of a firm's costs were independent of output and varied from firm to firm, only the firm with the lowest costs would survive. Similarly, in an ideal democracy only the most efficient parties survive; if the costs incurred by the state in operating an industry were independent of output and dependent on the party in office, only the party with the lowest costs could remain in office. An industry would be operated equally efficiently by the state and by the marketplace if the most efficient party had the same costs as the most efficient firm. This does not merely state—as the analysis by Lange of socialism does—that the political sector conceptually *could* reproduce the free enterprise equilibrium, but that it would do so. The costs of the most efficient party and most efficient firm may differ if different individuals are drawn into political and market activity. Private enterprise would operate an industry more efficiently than the state only if the most efficient firm had lower costs than the most efficient party, and vice versa.

II. COMPETITION IN ACTUAL DEMOCRACIES

There is relatively little to choose between an ideal free enterprise system and an ideal political democracy; both are efficient and responsive to preferences of the "electorate." Those advocating a shift of activities from the marketplace to the state must argue that the actual enterprise system is far from ideal because it contains numerous monopolies and other imperfections. Those advocating a minimum number of state activities must argue that the actual political system is even further from the ideal. Imperfections in the marketplace have elsewhere been discussed extensively, so we can concentrate on some important political imperfections.

Since each person has a fixed number of votes—either 1 or 0—regardless of the amount of information he has and the intelligence used in acting on this information, and since minorities are usually given no representation, it does not "pay" to be well informed and thoughtful on political issues, or even to vote. An efficient party may be unable to convince enough voters that it is more efficient than other parties. In the marketplace minorities have "representation" and the number of "votes" a person has is related to his "proportioned productivity," so the incentives to act wisely are greater here than in the political sector. Therefore, it is relatively easy for an efficient firm to survive since it need only gain the support of creditors and consumers who have a direct personal interest in making wise decisions.

Political competition is reduced by the large scale required for political organizations. Candidates for many offices, such as the presidency and state governorships, must have enough resources to reach millions of voters. Many groups that would like to compete for these offices do not have sufficient resources to reach large numbers of voters. Although it is sometimes necessary for a firm to organize on a national or state basis, this is clearly less important in the market sector than in the political sector. The scale of political activity is large, also, because many offices tie together numerous activities. A candidate who knows how to run the post office efficiently must convince voters that he knows something about immigration policy, public utility regulations, and a host of other problems in addition to post office administration. This tie-in of activities may prevent persons who are efficient at one activity only from running for office. Tie-ins are also found in the marketplace but since they cover relatively few activities, a firm can usually specialize in the product or process at which it is most efficient. Since an ideal democracy as well as an ideal enterprise system has an optimal separation of activities, it is somewhat puzzling that tie-ins are much more important in the political sector. I suspect that an electorate with a limited amount of political information finds it easier to place one person in charge of many activities than to choose one person for each activity.

Although ignorance and the large scale required of political organizations are perhaps the two most potent forces producing monopoly and other imperfections in democracies, periodic rather than continuous elections, and different preferences among members of the electorate also do so.[6] I am inclined to believe that monopoly and other imperfections are at least as important, and perhaps substantially more so, in the political sector as in the marketplace. If this belief is even approximately correct, it has important implications for the query which opened this essay; namely, does the existence of market imperfections justify government intervention? The answer would be no, if the imperfections in government behavior were greater than those in the market. It may be preferable not to regulate economic monopolies and to suffer their bad effects, rather than to regulate them and suffer the effects of political imperfections.

Notes

A draft of this paper was written in the summer of 1952, but pressure of other work prevented me from revising it for publication until the summer of 1957. In the interval, an article using a similar approach was published by Anthony Downs, "An Economic Theory of Political Action in a Democracy," *Journal of Political Economy* 67 (1957): 135; however, our work does not overlap too much, since Downs emphasizes somewhat different aspects of the political structure than I do here.

1. Henry Simons vigorously argued that all "natural" monopolies (i.e., monopolies caused by increasing returns) should be nationalized by the state; see his "A Positive Program for Laissez-Faire," reprinted in *Economic Policy for a Free Society* (1948).

2. For a similar definition, see J. Schumpeter, *Capitalism, Socialism and Democracy* (1942), p. 269.

3. See, for example, A. Kaplan and H. Lasswell, *Power and Society* (1950), p. 75.

4. Similarly, in a full market equilibrium no firm makes any "profits" although each may be motivated by a desire for profits.

5. The classic statement of one viewpoint is contained in Burke's speech to the electors of Bristol in 1774.

6. For relation between political tie-ins and different preferences among the electorate see my *The Economics of Discrimination* (1957), pp. 64–66.

PUBLIC POLICIES, PRESSURE GROUPS, AND DEADWEIGHT COSTS

· 22 ·

This paper presents a model of competition among special interest groups for political influence. Each active group exerts pressure to affect its taxes and subsidies, where activities of different groups are related by the equality between total tax collections and total tax subsidies. The deadweight costs and benefits of taxes and subsidies play a major role in our model. An increase in the deadweight cost of taxation encourages pressure by taxpayers, while an increase in the deadweight costs of subsidies discourages pressure by recipients. Various applications of the analysis are discussed.

I. INTRODUCTION

The activities of governments have grown remarkably rapidly in all Western countries during the twentieth century, especially during the last fifty years. This growth cannot be entirely explained by benevolent governments that maximize social welfare because subsidies to agriculture, restrictions on entry into the airline, trucking, and other industries, duties on Japanese imports,

First published in the *Journal of Public Economics* 28 (1985): 329–347. Reprinted with the kind permission of Elsevier Science S.A., Lausanne, Switzerland, publishers of the *Journal of Public Economics*.

and many other regulations and public activities are not consistent with any traditional social welfare function.

This failure of theories of benevolent government induced economists to join political scientists in searching for alternative ways to analyze actual government behavior. The usual alternative is a model of majority rule voting, either among the electorate or the legislature, as best illustrated by median voter theory. Another approach assumes that bureaucrats have the power to determine the enactment and implementation of many regulations and other legislation.

A third approach stresses the capacity of pressure groups to influence political outcomes as they jockey for political power. This approach received an early and vigorous formulation by Bentley (1908) that greatly affected the thinking of political scientists. I recently (Becker [1983]) published a paper that tries to model the competition among pressure groups for political influence in a more rigorous way. This paper extends the analysis and develops many implications. To concentrate on pressure groups, I ignore bureaucrats and politicians, and do not give much attention to voters, although, of course, I recognize that bureaucrats must be induced to implement policies, and votes and politicians are necessary to pass legislation.

The next section presents a generalized version of this model that permits pressure groups to be altruistic and envious as well as selfish. The "representative" member of a group maximizes his utility by spending resources on political activities to create pressure that affects his subsidies or taxes. These expenditures compete with expenditures by other pressure groups because of the budget constraint that the total amount collected in taxes (including taxes on future generations) must equal total government expenditures.

The optimal pressure by a group is determined by the effect of its political expenditures on the utility of members. The effect on utility is crucially related to the deadweight (or social) costs and benefits of taxes and subsidies. Section III uses this relation between utility and deadweight costs and benefits to reformulate the "Compensation Principle" of welfare economics as a major tool in the analysis of actual, as opposed to normative, public policies.

Sections IV and V consider various examples of the effect of dead weight costs and benefits on public policies. These include the deregulation and privatization "movements" in the United States and other countries, the effects of recessions and declines in demand on tariffs and trade barriers, the *apparent* lower efficiency of public firms than of private firms, the taxation of farmers in developing countries and their subsidization in rich countries, and the effect of altruism and envy on taxes and subsidies. Section VI contains a summary, and a brief discussion of the role of pressure groups in democracies and other political systems.

II. The Model

Any relevant model of the political sector must incorporate a political budget constraint because subsidies are obviously limited by taxes. Indeed, if all taxes (T) were explicit levies, as with property and income taxes, and if all subsidies (S) were explicit transfers, as with welfare payments and veterans' bonuses, the political budget constraint would simply be

$$S = T. \tag{1}$$

Implicit taxes and subsidies due to regulations of activities are also related, but less simply. Still, equality between taxes and subsidies provides a convenient point of departure to begin the formal analysis. If n_s identical persons are subsidized and n_t identical persons are taxed, this political budget constraint can be written as

$$S = n_s\sigma = n_t\tau = T, \tag{2}$$

where σ and τ are the subsidy per member of s, and the tax per member of t.

The term τ should be interpreted as the tax collected per member of t, net of any subsidy to t; similarly, σ is the subsidy per member of s, net of any tax paid by t. Since τ and σ can be negative as well as positive, I need not specify a priori which group on balance pays taxes or receives a subsidy. However, I do assume at this stage that the characteristics defining membership in a group—such as age, location, or occupation—are exogenously determined, so that a member of t cannot convert into a member of s, and vice versa.

Taxes and subsidies are influenced, but not fully determined, by constitutions and other aspects of political systems. A crucial assumption of my approach is that they are also influenced by taxpayers and recipients who exert pressure on voters, legislators, and others involved in political decisions to further their own interests through the political process. A simple way to incorporate political pressure is to relate the taxes levied and subsidies transferred to political pressure by different groups (and other variables):

$$S = T = I\left(p_s, p_t, \frac{n_s}{n_t}, x\right), \tag{3}$$

where I is the "influence function," p_s and p_t are pressures by recipients and taxpayers, n_s/n_t is the relative number of recipients, and x refers to the political system and other relevant considerations. My earlier paper (Becker [1983]) started with separate influence functions for taxes and subsidies, and showed that the equality between taxes and subsidies reduces these to a single influence function.

Since selfish taxpayers only exert pressure to lower taxes, and selfish recipients only exert pressure to raise subsidies, pressure from selfish groups would be positive only in regions where

$$\frac{\partial S}{\partial p_s} = \frac{\partial I}{\partial p_s} = I_s \geqq 0 \quad \text{and} \quad \frac{\partial T}{\partial p_t} = \frac{\partial I}{\partial p_t} = I_t \leqq 0. \quad (4)$$

The influence function presumably also directly depends on the ratio of recipients to taxpayers because an increase in that ratio would raise the number of votes in favor of subsidies to s. That is,

$$\frac{\partial I}{\partial (n_s / n_t)} \geqq 0. \quad (5)$$

However, this does not guarantee that an increase in the relative number of s raises subsidies because pressure exerted by s is negatively related to their relative number of members (see Section V).

More detailed properties of the influence function are determined by constitutions, judicial traditions, and other aspects of political structures. Fortunately, for the limited purposes of this paper, it is not necessary to examine further the "black box" of political structure. I only need to assume that the influence function, especially the derivatives specified in eqs. (3) and (4), is stable over time, so that the "contest" between s and t has a stable foundation. Even riots and other violence are permitted as a form of political pressure (see Mirani [1985]), as long as political outcomes are stably related to violence as well as to other kinds of pressure.

If payoffs from political activities do not distinguish between identical members of s and identical members of t, subsidies and taxes would be public goods. Recipients (and payers) then have strong incentives to share costs by exerting pressure collectively. To model the group exertion of pressure, I introduce a pressure production function for each group that depends on its total political expenditures and the number of members:

$$\left. \begin{array}{l} p^i = p^i(m_i, n_i) \quad \text{with} \quad m_i = a_i n_i, \\[2mm] \dfrac{\partial p^i}{\partial m_i} = p^i_m \geqq 0 \quad \text{and} \quad p^i_n \leqq 0, \end{array} \right\} \quad i = s, t, \quad (6)$$

where m_i is total expenditure of money, time, and effort by the ith group on campaign contributions, lobbying, advertisements, and other political activities, and a_i is their expenditure per member.

Free riding and shirking increase the cost of producing pressure. If the incentive to free ride increases with the number of members, the pressure produced by a given total expenditure (m) would decline as the number of members increased because the cost of "collecting" m would rise. The second inequality in (6) captures the effect of numbers on free riding and the cost of producing pressure.

The utility function of each person depends on his tax or subsidy, and his expenditure on the production of pressure:

$$U^s = U^s(\sigma, \tau, a_s) \quad \text{with} \quad \frac{\partial U^s}{\partial a_s} = U^s_a < 0 \quad \text{and} \quad \frac{\partial U^s}{\partial \sigma} = U^s_\sigma > 0$$

$$U^t = U^t(\tau, \sigma, a_t), \quad \text{with} \quad U^t_a < 0 \quad \text{and} \quad \frac{\partial U^t}{\partial \tau} = U^t_\tau < 0$$
(7)

Clearly, taxes hurt and subsidies benefit. Moreover, with altruism toward the other group, U^t also depends positively on σ, and U^s also depends negatively on τ; with envy, these signs would be reversed.

I assume that each group chooses its expenditure on political pressure to maximize the utility of its members, where optimal expenditures are conditional on the political budget equation and pressure production functions, including incentives to free ride. The interaction between groups is modeled simply as a Cournot-Nash noncooperative game in expenditures. Equilibrium for this game is determined by the utility maximizing condition for each group with respect to its expenditures on political pressure, that take as given expenditures by the other group:

$$\frac{dU^t}{da_t} = 0 = U^t_a + U^t_\tau \frac{\partial \tau}{\partial p_t} p^t_m n_t$$

$$\frac{dU^s}{da_s} = 0 = U^s_a + U^s_\sigma \frac{\partial \sigma}{\partial p_s} p^s_m n_s$$
(8)

or

$$-F(\tau, \sigma a_t) = -\frac{U^t_a}{U^t_\tau} = I_t p^t_m$$

$$G(\sigma, \tau a_s) = -\frac{U^s_a}{U^s_\sigma} = I_s p^s_m$$
(9)

The optimal expenditures on pressure, and hence the optimal levels of pressure, are determined by these equations (see Becker [1983] for a discussion of second-order and stability conditions). The equilibrium level of taxes and subsidies is then determined by the influence function in eq. (3). Optimal expenditures on pressure by a group would be zero, and the group would not organize politically, if the gain in lower taxes or higher subsidies were less than the cost of exerting pressure; one or both of these equations would then be replaced by inequalities.

The right-hand side of (9) measures the effect on influence of additional expenditures on pressure, while the left-hand side is determined by the monetary value of the change in utility from changes in taxes and subsidies, respectively. If s and t were both selfish, and if taxes and subsidies adversely affected the allocation of resources, the monetary value of the utility cost of taxes would exceed the amount paid ($F < 1$), and the monetary value of subsidies would be less than the amount received ($G > 1$). If taxes or subsidies improved the allocation of resources—perhaps by promoting public goods, reducing pollution, or because t were sufficiently altruistic toward s—then either $F > 1$, $G < 1$, or both.

The effect of taxes and subsidies on the allocation of resources can be brought out explicitly by writing

$$F = 1 - d^t(\tau, \sigma), \qquad G = 1 + d^s(\sigma, \tau), \qquad (10)$$

where d^t is the marginal deadweight or social cost to taxpayers from taxes equal to τ and subsidies equal to σ, and d^s is the marginal social cost to recipients from subsidies equal to σ and taxes equal to τ. If marginal taxes or subsidies raised efficiency, then d^t, d^s, or both would be less than zero. These functions depend on the level of taxes and subsidies because marginal distorting effects tend to rise, and marginal improving effects tend to fall, as the rate of taxation and subsidization increase. With altruism, envy, public goods, or externalities, d^t may depend on subsidies as well as taxes, and d^s may depend on taxes as well as subsidies.

Substitution of eq. (10) into the optimality conditions in eq. (9) immediately shows that expenditures on political pressure by taxpayers tend to be greater when the social cost of taxes is greater. This seems surprising and counterintuitive when taxpayers are selfish and not concerned about society as a whole. However, since pressure by taxpayers is assumed to reduce tax *collections* (by eqs. [3] and [4]), the effect of additional pressure on the utility of selfish recipients depends on the effect of lower taxes on their utility, which is positively related to the deadweight costs of taxation. Similarly, optimal expenditures on pressure even by selfish recipients are smaller when the social cost of subsidies is greater because the effect of subsidies on the utility of selfish recipients depends negatively on the deadweight cost of subsidies.

Since marginal social costs of subsidies tend to rise, and any marginal social benefits tend to fall, as subsidies increase, recipients would be discouraged from exerting additional pressure as subsidies increased, *even without any reactions by taxpayers.* Moreover, increased subsidies and taxes would encourage taxpayers to exert additional pressure by raising the marginal social cost of taxes. That is, higher subsidies and taxes tend to raise the "countervailing political power" of taxpayers.

If all taxes and subsidies adversely affect efficiency, taxing and subsidizing each group would involve inefficient "cross-hauling" because both could be made better off by equal reductions in their taxes and subsidies until one group were only subsidized and the other only taxed. Fortunately, a group does have an incentive to reduce the amount of cross-hauling because the incentive to exert pressure to lower taxes tends to exceed the incentive to exert pressure to raise subsidies. The reason is that the monetary equivalent of a dollar reduction in taxes paid exceeds a dollar because of the deadweight cost of taxes, whereas the monetary equivalent of a dollar increase in subsidies received is less than a dollar because of the deadweight cost of subsidies. If, as a result of the incentive to eliminate taxes first, s exerted enough pressure to eliminate its taxes, cross-hauling would be eliminated since the subsidy to t would also be eliminated. Cross-hauling could remain only if pressure by *both* groups were more productive in obtaining subsidies than in reducing taxes.[1]

Aggregate efficiency should be defined as not only net of deadweight costs and benefits of taxes and subsidies, but also net of expenditures on the production of political pressure ($m_s + m_t$) since these expenditures are only "rent-seeking" inputs into the determination of policies. Therefore, efficiency would be raised if all groups could agree to reduce their expenditures on political influence. Restrictions on campaign contributions, registration of and monitoring of lobbying organizations, limitations on total taxes and public expenditures, and other laws may be evidence of cooperative efforts to reduce "wasteful" expenditures on cross-hauling and political pressure. Unfortunately, little is known about the success of different kinds of political systems in reducing the waste from competition among pressure groups.

Cournot-Nash behavior is especially wasteful because each group is assumed to believe that pressure by other groups is fixed and independent of its own pressure, whereas in the model, increased pressure by one group tends to stimulate countervailing pressure from other groups by raising their taxes or reducing their subsidies; see the positively sloped reaction curves in Becker (1983). A more realistic model of behavior would be Cournot-Nash in *strategies*, and would permit each group to consider these reactions when determining its own "strategy" (its own reactions). A noncooperative equilibrium incorporating such reactions appears to have less pressure than a Cournot-Nash equilibrium in expenditures because each group would be discouraged from raising its pressure by the positive reactions of other groups. If so, fewer resources would then be wasted on the production of pressure. Mutually beneficial reductions in pressure might be expected also if competition among groups were modeled as repeated games. Such repetition may explain how even large groups manage to limit free riding by members (see Section V), and why groups may prefer to spread their subsidies and taxes over time (see Smith [1985]).

Although the equilibrium level of taxes and subsidies depends on how the interaction between groups is modeled, social costs of subsidies appear to discourage pressure by subsidized groups, and social costs of taxes encourage pressure by taxed groups, in very different models of this interaction. The apparent robustness of these effects suggests that costs and benefits are important determinants of *actual* taxes, regulations, and other public policies.

III. The Compensation Principle and Public Policy

The new welfare economics developed the compensation principle to determine whether public policies are socially beneficial. Some of the pioneers even claimed[2] that a policy is beneficial as long as gainers *could* compensate losers, regardless of whether compensation were actually paid. This view is untenable except when the political process has equalized the marginal social "worths" of gainers and losers, which begs the question of what determines *actual* policies. Nevertheless, distribution continues to be neglected by most assessments of the harm from monopoly and other "market failures," and by most evaluations of public policies; these essentially consider only whether gainers *could* compensate losers.

Yet, somewhat paradoxically, the potential to compensate is an important determinant of *actual* political behavior in a model of competing interest groups. To show why, assume that taxes on t are positive even when neither s nor t exert pressure ($I^0 = I(0, 0) > 0$) and that both must decide whether to exert pressure to change taxes by say \$100. Clearly, s would not be willing to spend more than $100/(1 + d_0^s)$ on pressure because this amount measures their monetary gain from an additional subsidy of \$100; for the same reason, t would not be willing to spend more than $100/(1 - d_0^t)$. Hence, the maximum that s would spend exceeds, equals, or is less than the maximum that t would spend as

$$\frac{100}{1 + d_0^s} \gtreqless \frac{100}{1 - d_0^t}, \qquad \text{or as } d_0^s + d_0^t \gtreqless 0. \qquad (11)$$

The second inequality is precisely the condition that determines whether gainers (s) could compensate losers (t). If both taxes and subsidies were socially costly (d_0^s and $d_0^t > 0$), gainers could not compensate losers, and the maximum expenditure by losers to block an increase in taxes would exceed the maximum expenditure by gainers to support the increase. Similarly, if both taxes and subsidies were socially beneficial (d_0^s and $d_0^t < 0$), gainers could compensate losers, and the maximum expenditure by gainers would exceed that by losers. More generally, the sign of $d_0^t + d_0^s$ determines whether gainers could compensate losers, and whether the maximum expenditure by gainers would exceed or would be less than that by losers.

Therefore, the maximum expenditure by gainers to support a policy would exceed the maximum expenditures by losers to oppose the policy if, and only if, the sum of the monetary equivalents of the gains and losses to all persons were positive. An increase in the sum of these monetary equivalents will be called an increase in "social output." The link between social output and incentives to exert pressure does not presume that pressure groups are altruistic, nor that compensation is paid to losers, nor that any social welfare function is politically relevant, for they are linked even in a non-cooperative game without side payments between competing and selfish pressure groups.

I have been careful to refer to the *maximum* expenditure on political pressure because actual expenditures depend also on the right-hand side of eq. (9): on the cost of producing pressure and the effect of pressure on political influence. If both groups were equally efficient at producing pressure when they spent equal amounts, recipients would spend more to raise subsidies (and taxes) than payers spend to reduce them if additional subsidies (and taxes) raised social output. If gainers did spend more, the value of the influence function would increase above its initial level, and subsidies and taxes would increase; conversely, the value of the influence function would decrease below its initial level if losers spent more because social output were reduced by subsidies to s.

The equilibrium conditions for both groups given by eqs. (9) and (10) imply that if the productivity of s and t in producing influence were equal, only policies that raised social output would be supported by pressure of s and t, although some policies that raised social output might be blocked by the countervailing pressure of t. Clearly, however, the effect on social output of some implemented policies could be negative *net* of the supporting and opposing (rent-seeking) expenditures by s and t.

Some policies might raise social output because of altruism by taxpayers or envy by recipients. Redistributions are Pareto-improving when altruistic taxpayers also benefit. Although altruists would be harmed by redistributions beyond the Pareto-efficient point, social output would be increased as long as the monetary value of the gains to beneficiaries exceeds the monetary value of the loss to altruists. If beneficiaries were no less efficient at producing political influence than altruists, expenditures by beneficiaries to support further redistribution would exceed the opposing expenditures by altruists. The amount redistributed would then go beyond the Pareto-efficient point (the same conclusion is reached by Roberts [1982]). A similar argument leads to the expectation of political redistributions to envious groups even when they are no more efficient at producing influence than envied groups.

Of course, policies that reduced social output would be supported if gainers were sufficiently effective at producing influence to offset their relatively small gains. Yet despite the complaints of economists and others about the social cost of various regulations and programs, policies with high social cost would not survive competition among pressure groups unless those benefiting were *exceedingly* powerful politically. More commonly, surviving policies have low social cost *relative* to the millions of proposals that fail to gain political support. Similarly, public goods with large social benefits, such as protection against crime, tend to survive the competition among pressure groups, but public goods with modest social benefits do not survive when those opposing are politically powerful.

The compensation principle also suggests some tendency for the political sector to use the most efficient methods available to redistribute to beneficiaries. However, a satisfactory analysis of the choice of methods must consider whether the influence function itself depends on the methods used—perhaps because some methods hide private and social costs. Moreover, apparently inefficient taxes and subsidies may be used to reduce free riding on the political expenditures of others; for example, acreage restrictions are used in agriculture to limit entry of additional farmers (see Gardner [1983] and the discussion at the end of Section V]) or subsidies may be spread over time rather than paid as a lump sum to permit retaliation against free-riding members (see Smith [1985]).

If the *intent* of public policies were fully known, I am confident that the public sector would be revealed to be a far more efficient producer and redistributor than is popularly believed. For example, casual impressions and systematic evidence (see Borcherding [1982]) both indicate that public and regulated enterprises appear to be less efficient than private enterprises producing the same products. Yet, since employees (and other inputs) in public and regulated industries are paid relatively well (see the evidence on earnings in regulated industry in Moore [1978] and Pergamit [1983]; the evidence in Robinson and Tomes [1984] on public enterprises is somewhat mixed), these enterprises may only *appear* to be less efficient because they are used to raise the income of employees (or others). Redistribution should be included among the measured "outputs" of public and regulated enterprises before one can conclude that they are less efficient than private enterprises.

IV. Regulation and Deregulation

Subsidies that affect prices of outputs and inputs cause small deadweight loss when supply elasticities are low, say because capital and labor are not very mobile. Short-run mobility is lower when more is invested in human and physical capital specific to a firm or industry. Therefore, workers and firms with sizable specific investments tend to have relatively large gains from lobbying for government protection against temporary and unexpected declines in demand because the deadweight cost of subsidies to them is relatively small. Several studies have found, indeed, that tariffs and other import restrictions do increase during recessions and at other times when output of domestic industries declines (see, for example, Hillman [1982] and Marvel and Ray [1983]). This explanation of why depressed firms and industries are often successful at obtaining political assistance does not require irrationality (or even altruism), and meets Bernholz's (1984) challenge to find an explanation consistent with rational political choice.

Workers and firms with specific investments are also vulnerable to taxes, such as "excess profits" taxes, when demand for their services rises temporarily or unexpectedly, since they have relatively small gains from lobbying against these taxes. The relatively low deadweight cost of taxes on factors with permanently inelastic supplies makes them good sources of revenue to finance public good and other public expenditures that raise social output because they offer less political resistance.[3] However, they are as likely to be subsidized at the expense of other groups as taxed to finance subsidies to others, unless they are more or less productive at political lobbying than others.

Small open economies have little international monopoly power because they face elastic supplies of imports and elastic demands for exports. Since the deadweight cost to countries imposing tariffs or export taxes is greater when these elasticities are greater, industries and consumers who benefit from tariffs and export taxes should have less political power in small open economies than in large self-sufficient economies, and less power in open regions of an economy than in self-sufficient regions (see Maloney, McCormick, and Tollison [1984]). Krueger (1983) uses a related argument to explain why Hong Kong, Taiwan, Singapore, South Korea, and some other small developing countries were among the earliest to reject the emphasis prevailing in the 1950s on import substitution and self-sufficiency in favor of international specialization.

Protection to firms and workers from adverse conditions is likely to be incomplete because marginal deadweight costs rise as the degree of protection increases. In my approach, rising deadweight costs curtail the power of firms and other subsidy recipients *even when* the political power of consumers and other *taxpayers* is *unchanged*. Although taxpayers are more likely to organize and exert pressure when deadweight costs are greater, additional pressure by subsidy recipients is discouraged by higher deadweight costs even when taxpayers remain unorganized (see Section II).

I have assumed active pressure groups with stable influence functions, but I have not restricted the analysis to democracies, or to societies that permit easy formation of pressure groups. Consequently, the analysis implies that regulations and other public programs are moderated by their social cost in *any* political system, no matter how totalitarian, where groups lobby for political influence. In particular, the trend in communist countries away from collective farms to private plots, and away from "sharing the same rice bowl" to "eating out of separate bowls" appears to be a response to the large (and perhaps growing) social cost of collectivization and sharing. Large social costs reduce the political feasibility of programs even when farmers, consumers, and others have no political power, as long as the incentive to exert pressure by bureaucrats, party members, and other beneficiaries declines as the social cost of their subsidies increases.

Deadweight costs of regulations and other policies often rise over time as labor and capital become more mobile, as substitutes develop for products that have been made more expensive, and as other costly methods of evading and avoiding the effects of particular regulations are discovered. For example, the deadweight cost of regulating security transactions rose significantly as institutional investors with elastic demands became important (see Jarrell [1984]), the cost of regulating airline travel rose as airline travel expanded into new and diverse markets (see Spiller [1983]), the cost of banking regulations grew as interest rates became higher and more variable, and new methods of intermediation were invented (Carron [1983]), and the cost of high marginal income tax rates grew as tax shelters, the underground econ-omy, and other "loopholes" were expanded.

Therefore, the recent deregulation of airlines, banks, security firms, and other industries in the United States—see the catalog in Noll and Owen (1983, table 1.1)—is consistent with the implication of my analysis that political support for a regulation withers when its deadweight cost becomes large. However, this catalog cannot yet be called a "movement" because the total amount of regulation in the United States has not declined appreciably. Expanded environmental, energy, safety, civil rights, labor, import, and other social regulations replaced the reduced regulation of particular industries.

I suspect that the appearance of a deregulation "movement" is partly an echo of the regulatory "movement" of the 1930s (itself a response to the

Great Depression), when the securities, airline, banking, and many other industries became regulated. If deadweight costs in these industries grew over time at not very different rates, their political influence would wane at similar times. The deregulations and privatizations in recent years are also related, I believe, to the rapid expansion of transfer payments during the 1960s and 1970s. This expansion raised the marginal deadweight burden of income and other taxes,[4] which stimulated pressure by taxpayers to prune more socially costly programs that could not muster enough political support after tax burdens rose.

V. Many Pressure Groups

Many countries have hundreds, and some have thousands, of active pressure groups; for example, over 3,000 Political Action Committees (PACs) are active in the United States (U.S. Federal Election Commission [1982]). The influence function that determines taxes and subsidies with only two pressure groups can be generalized to separate influence functions for the taxes and subsidies of each of many groups:

$$\left. \begin{array}{l} T^i = I^{t_i}(p_1, \ldots, p_k, n_1, \ldots, n_k) \\ S^i = I^{s_i}(p_1, \ldots, p_k, n_1, \ldots, n_k) \end{array} \right\}, i = 1, \ldots, k, \qquad (12)$$

where T^i and S^i are the taxes collected from and subsidies given to the ith group, and p_i is the pressure exerted by the ith group with n_i identical members. Cross-hauling of taxes and subsidies tends to increase as the number of distinct groups increases because a group may sometimes be subsidized along with some other groups, and taxed along with still different groups. An example is the subsidy to railroad conductors as a "by-product" of regulations that raise the price of air travel, and the tax on conductors as a "by-product" of subsidies to build highways.

Although taxes and subsidies need not be equal for each group, the total amount collected in taxes would be related to the total paid in subsidies. If taxes and subsidies are explicit levies and transfers, total taxes collected would equal total subsidies paid out:

$$\sum S^i = S = T = \sum T^i. \qquad (13)$$

This government budget equation implies that one of the influence functions in eq. (12) can be determined from the others, and that lower taxes or higher subsidies to one group would raise the taxes or lower the subsidies of all other groups.

If groups did not cooperate, pressures exerted by each, including perhaps no pressure, would be determined from conditions similar to those in eq. (9)

that depend on utility functions, pressure production functions, influence functions, and a government budget equation. Some groups may cooperate, however, through coordinated lobbying or log-rolling in the legislature to raise their subsidies and lower their taxes. I do not try to model political cooperation because the main implication of noncooperative behavior used in this paper—the effect of deadweight costs on subsidies, taxes, and political pressure—appears to be highly relevant also to cooperating groups who do not use side payments. Even when cooperating with other groups, the gain to a group from additional pressure is greater when the deadweight cost of its subsidies is smaller and when the dead weight cost of its taxes is larger.

Small groups might seem to have especially strong incentives to cooperate with others because they do not have enough members to support favorable referenda and legislation. This apparent disadvantage of small groups motivates models of the median voter, of legislative log-rolling (see Buchanan and Tullock [1962]), and of competition for votes in cooperative political games (see, for example, Aumann and Kurz [1977]).

I believe, however, that the political handicaps of small groups are exaggerated by models that assume voters are well informed and automatically vote in favor of their interests. As is well known, the same majority rule that motivates these models implies rational voters would not become well informed, and may be misled to vote against their interests (see, among others, Becker [1983], and Brennan and Buchanan [1984]). Therefore, small groups may be able to acquire political support by persuading misinformed voters to vote in their favor (Denzau and Munger [1983] develop an explicit model combining unorganized voters and expenditures on pressure). If many voters are vulnerable to persuasion, the size of a group would be less important than its capacity to persuade others.

Moreover, small groups have certain political advantages that may swamp any adverse effects of fewer voters.[5] They may control more easily free riding and shirking by members. In addition, if groups taxed to finance subsidies are much larger, those subsidized face less countervailing political pressure. An increase in the number of taxpayers lowers taxes per payer, and hence also lowers the marginal deadweight loss to each payer, which discourages countervailing pressure (see the proof in Becker [1983, 384–85]). Note that this conclusion is another example of the effect of deadweight costs, and does not assume small taxes and subsidies are neglected.

That *relatively* small groups are effective competitors for political influence is consistent with the evidence that farmers are more likely to be subsidized in countries where farming is less important, and are more likely to be taxed in countries where farming is more important (see Bates [1981], Binswanger and Scandizzo [1983], and Miller [1985]). This view also implies that the rapid aging of Western populations will *reduce* rather than raise social security and other subsidies to older persons, even though the old will have more voters.

Fear of universal suffrage has essentially been a fear that the numerous poor will outvote the rich and middle classes, and tax away much of their wealth. Yet the *net* redistribution to the poor appears to be modest, at least in the United States (see Reynolds and Smolensky [1977]). My analysis claims that the number of poor is also a political handicap because large redistributions to them impose a sizable excess burden on the less numerous middle class and rich.

Even without envy, the wealth of the rich is also a political handicap because a given amount collected in income or wealth taxes per person has a smaller deadweight cost when the payer is rich. The middle classes could provide an effective political compromise between numbers and wealth since they are less numerous than the poor and less wealthy than the rich. Perhaps this is the explanation of "Director's Law" of redistribution to the middle classes from the rich and poor (see Stigler [1970]).

Although I have assumed throughout that the size of each group is fixed, politically successful groups do attract additional members, e.g., farming became more attractive after being subsidized, or work became less appealing after welfare payments grew. Subsidized groups try to limit the entry of additional members because that dilutes the gains of established members. One way to limit entry is to lobby for subsidies that are less vulnerable to entry. For example, acreage restrictions encourage fewer new farmers than output subsidies do (see Gardner's [1983] comparison), and the Civil Aeronautics Board did not certify a single new trunk airline between 1938 and 1976 (see Meyer and Oster [1984]).

VI. SUMMARY AND DISCUSSION

A model has been presented of competition among special interest groups for political influence. Each active group exerts pressure to affect its subsidies and taxes, where activities of different groups are related by the equality between total tax collections and total subsidy payments. A group's political effectiveness depends on its control over free riding by members, as stressed in the extensive literature on collective choice.

This paper argues that political effectiveness is also determined by the deadweight (or social) costs and benefits of taxes and subsidies. An increase in the deadweight cost of taxation encourages pressure by taxpayers because they are then harmed more by tax payments. Similarly, an increase in the deadweight cost of subsidies discourages pressure by recipients because they then benefit less from subsidies received.

The "Compensation Principle" of welfare economics turns out to be a significant part of this theory of actual political policies. If the gain to groups that benefit exceeds the loss to groups that suffer, and if access to political influence were otherwise the same for all groups, gainers would exert more political pressure than losers, and a policy would tend to be implemented. Note that the criterion is whether gainers *could* compensate losers; actual compensation need not be paid to losers.

If gainers could not compensate losers, a policy would not be implemented unless gainers had much better access to political influence. Therefore, the Compensation Principle combined with an analysis of the production of political influence provides a unified approach to the political feasibility both of public goods and other policies that raise social output (where gainers could compensate losers), and of policies that redistribute to favored groups (where gainers could not compensate).

The emphasis in the theory on deadweight costs is reminiscent of Ramsey pricing and the theory of optimal taxation, where marginal deadweight costs are related to marginal "social worths." However, optimal tax theory uses deadweight costs to prescribe *optimal* public policies, whereas my analysis uses deadweight costs to explain *actual* policies in a world of competing and possibly selfish pressure groups. Still, if deadweight costs (and benefits) are important determinants of actual policies, the many calculations of deadweight cost in the applied welfare literature, and many analytical results of welfare economics and optimal tax theory, are relevant also to positive theories of political behavior.[6]

The almost universal condemnation of special interest groups includes the recent allegation by Olson (1982) that they are responsible for sluggish growth and the eventual decline of nations. Most of the condemnation is based on the many redistributions to special interest groups that reduce social output because of deadweight costs of taxes and subsidies.

Clearly, actual political systems do not have social welfare functions, benevolent dictators, or other political procedures that *automatically* choose the optimal production of public goods, optimal effluence taxes, and other public policies that raise output and efficiency. Therefore, the condemnation of special interest groups is excessive because competition among these groups contributes to the survival of policies that raise output: favorably affected groups tend to lobby more for these policies than unfavorably affected groups lobby against. Indeed, no policy that lowered social output would survive if all groups were equally large and skillful at producing political influence, for the opposition would always exert more influence than proponents. The condemnation of special interest groups is more justified when there is highly unequal access to political influence. Powerful groups then can secure the implementation of policies that benefit them while reducing social output, and can thwart policies that harm them while raising output.

If special interest groups are crucial to the political process, political systems would be largely defined by their activities and opportunities. Democracies have competition among groups with relatively equal political strength, while totalitarian and other nondemocratic systems have restricted competition among groups with highly unequal strength. Redistribution in democracies (and other systems) would be guided not by social welfare functions or other measures of social fairness, but mainly by the altruism, selfishness, envy, and morality of the more powerful interest groups.

In democracies so defined, a few pressure groups cannot easily obtain very large subsidies (although many groups may each obtain relatively small subsidies), since I have shown that large subsidies stimulate countervailing pressure by those taxed to finance the subsidies. In totalitarian systems, on the other hand, a few groups can more readily use the state to raise substantially their well-being because other groups are not permitted to form effective opposition.

I conclude by considering briefly the implications of the analysis in this paper for the theme of the Symposium: the expansion of government in Western democracies during the last hundred years. More efficient taxes (such as the income tax) and subsidies, and improved methods of collecting and distributing them, encouraged expansion by reducing the resistance of tax-payers and raising pressure from potential recipients. Industrialization and the accompanying division of labor multiplied separate interests, which permitted some special interests to acquire political influence because they were small relative to the number of taxpayers. The development of radio, television, and other methods of communication widened the opportunities to influence the revealed "preferences" of voters and legislators. Undoubtedly the decline in laissez-faire ideology contributed to the growth in government, but most of the decline was probably *induced* by the arguments and propaganda of the many groups seeking public largesse.

These changes facilitated government growth in all countries, but can they explain the details of growth documented in the papers by Bernholz (1984), Borcherding (1984), Lindbeck (1984), Musgrave (1984), and others, especially the rapid increase in transfer payments during the last twenty years? Although an answer is beyond the goals of this paper, I believe an important part of the answer is found in changes in the access to political influence of the old, ill, and other beneficiaries of transfer payments.

NOTES

Prepared for the Nobel Symposium on the Growth of Government, 15–17 August 1984. Let me express appreciation to the commentators, James Mirrlees and Ingemar Stahl, for excellent comments, and to other participants at the Symposium for a lively discussion. I had valuable assistance from Gale Mosteller, and useful comments from Robert Barro, Michael Munger, Richard Posner, and George Stigler. My research was supported by the Center for the Study of the Economy and the State at the University of Chicago.

1. Formally,

$$n_s\sigma_s = n_t\tau_t = I^t(p_s^0, p_t^1),$$
$$n_t\sigma_t = n_s\tau_s = I^s(p_s^1, p_t^0),$$

where σ_j and τ_j are the subsidies and taxes to each member of the jth group ($j = s, t$), p_j^0 and p_j^1 are the pressures by j to raise its subsidies and lower its taxes, respectively, and I^t and I^s are the influence functions for subsidies to s and t. Equilibrium conditions for t are

$$\frac{\partial I^t}{\partial m_t^1} \frac{\partial U^t}{\partial \tau_t} \lesseqgtr \frac{-\partial U^t}{\partial a_t^1}$$

and

$$\frac{\partial I^s}{\partial m_t^0} \frac{\partial U^t}{\partial \sigma_t} \lesseqgtr \frac{-\partial U^t}{\partial a_t^0},$$

with similar conditions applying to s. Since $-\partial U^t/\partial \tau_t > \partial U^t/\partial \sigma_t$ because of the deadweight cost of taxes and subsidies, expenditures to reduce taxes are more productive than expenditures to raise subsidies unless $-\partial I^t/\partial m_t^0$ is sufficiently larger than $\partial I^t/\partial m_t^1$.

2. For example, Kaldor wrote: "Whether the landlords, in the free-trade case, should in fact be given compensation or not, is a political question on which the economist, *qua* economist, could hardly pronounce an opinion. The important fact is that, in the argument in favour of free-trade, *the fate of the landlords is wholly irrelevant*: since the benefits of free-trade are by no means destroyed even if the landlords are fully reimbursed for their losses" (Kaldor [1939, 550–51], my italics). I owe this reference to Chipman and Moore (1978), who have an excellent review of the issues.

3. I am indebted to Robert Barro for reminding me of the literature on the optimal taxation of factors with inelastic supplies.

4. See, for example, estimates by Browning and Johnson (1984) and Stuart (1984) of the sizable burden of income taxes in the United States, and by Lindbeck (1983) of the huge burden of income taxes and transfer payments in Sweden.

5. A recent model of the politics of tariff formation by Wellisz and Wilson (1984) also implies (for somewhat different reasons) that small groups have political advantages.

6. For example, Barro (1986) uses optimal tax theory to explain actual government deficits.

References

Aumann, Robert J., and Mordecai Kurz. "Power and Taxes." *Econometrica* 50 (1977): 1137–1161.

Barro, Robert J. "The Behavior of U.S. Deficits." In: R. Gordon, ed., *The American Business Cycle: Continuity and Change*. Chicago: University of Chicago Press, 1986.

Bates, Robert H. *Markets and States in Tropical Africa*. Berkeley: University of California Press, 1981.

Becker, Gary S. "A Theory of Competition among Pressure Groups for Political Influence." *Quarterly Journal of Economics*, 98 (1983): 371–400.

Bentley, Arthur F. *The Process of Government*. Chicago: University of Chicago Press, 1908.

Bernholz Peter. "Growth of Government, Economic Growth, and Individual Freedom." Nobel Symposium on the Growth of Government, Stockholm, 1984.

Binswanger, Hans P., and Pasquale L. Scandizzo. "Patterns of Agricultural Protection." World Bank Discussion paper no. ARU15. Washington, D.C, 1983.

Borcherding, Thomas E. "Toward a Positive Theory of Public Sector Supply Arrangements." In *Public Enterprise in Canada*, R. Prichard, editor. Toronto: Butterworth, 1984.

Borcherding, Thomas E. "A Survey of Empirical Studies about Causes of the Growth of Government." Nobel Symposium on the Growth of Government, Stockholm, 1984.

Brennan, Geoffrey, and James M. Buchanan. "The Logic of Levers: The Pure Theory of Electoral Preference." Paper delivered at a conference on the Political Economy of Public Policy. Stanford Center for Policy Research, Stanford, Calif., 1984.

Browning, Edgar K., and William R. Johnson. "The Trade-off between Equality and Efficiency." *Journal of Political Economy* 92 (1984): 175–203.

Buchanan, James M., and Gordon Tullock. *The Calculus of Consent*, Ann Arbor, Mich.: University of Michigan Press, 1962.

Carron, Andrew S. "The Political Economy of Financial Regulation." In *The Political Economy of Deregulation*, edited by Roger G. Noll and Bruce M. Owen. Washington, D.C.: American Enterprise Institute, 1983, pp. 69–83.

Chipman, John S., and James C. Moore. "The New Welfare Economics, 1939–1974." *International Economic Review* 19 (1978): 547–84.

Denzau, Arthur T., and Michael C. Munger. "Legislators and Interest Groups: How Unorganized Interests Get Represented." Working Paper No. 81. (Washington University, Center for the Study of American Business, 1983

Gardner, Bruce. "Efficient Redistribution through Commodity Markets." *American Journal of Agricultural Economics* 65 (1983): 225–34.

Hillman, Arye L. "Declining Industries and Political-Support Protectionist Motives." *American Economic Review* 72 (1982): 1180–87.

Jarrell, Gregg A. "Change at the Exchange: The Causes and Effects of Deregulation." *Journal of Law and Economics* (1984): 273–312.

Kaldor, Nicholas. "Welfare Propositions of Economics and Interpersonal Comparisons of Utility." *Economic Journal* 49 (1939): 549–52.

Krueger, Anne O. "The Developing Countries' Role in the World Economy." ITT Key Issues Lecture Series, University of Chicago, 1983.

Lindbeck, Assar. "Interpreting Income Distributions in a Welfare State." *European Economic Review* 21 (1983): 227–56.

———. "Redistribution Policy and the Expansion of the Public Sector—The Political Economy of the Welfare State." Nobel Symposium on the Growth of Government, Stockholm, 1984.

Maloney, Michael T., Robert E. McCormick, and Robert D. Tollison. "Economic Regulation, Competitive Governments, and Specialized Resources." *Journal of Law and Economics* 27 (1984): 329–38.

Marvel, Howard P., and Edward J. Ray. "The Kennedy Round: Evidence on the Regulation of International Trade in the United States." *American Economic Review* 73 (1983): 190–97.

Meyer, John R., and Clinton V. Oster Jr. *Deregulation and the New Airline Entrepreneurs.* Cambridge, Mass.: Massachusetts Institute of Technology, 1984.

Miller, Tracy C. "A Political Interest Group Model of Agricultural Price Policy in Developing Countries." Agricultural Economics Workshop, University of Chicago, 1985.

Mirani, S. Kaveh. "Collective Political Violence and the Redistribution of Political Income." Ph.D. dissertation, University of Chicago, 1985.

Moore, Thomas Gale. "The Beneficiaries of Trucking Regulation." *Journal of Law and Economics* 21 (1978): 327–43.

Musgrave, Richard. "Excess Budget: Norms, Hypotheses, and Performance." Nobel Symposium on the Growth of Government, Stockholm, 1984.

Noll, Roger G., and Bruce M. Owen, editors. *The Political Economy of Deregulation.* Washington, D.C.: American Enterprise Institute, 1983, chapter 2.

Olson, Mancur, Jr. *The Logic of Collective Action.* (Cambridge, Mass.: Harvard University Press, 1965.

———. *The Rise and Decline of Nations.* New Haven, Conn.: Yale University Press, 1982.

Pergamit, Michael R. "Wages and Employment in Regulated Industries." Ph.D. disseration, University of Chicago, 1983.

Reynolds, Morgan, and Eugene Smolensky. *Public Expenditures, Taxes, and the Distribution of Income*. New York: Academic Press, 1977.

Roberts, Russell. *A Positive Model of Private Charity and Public Transfers*. New York: University of Rochester, 1982.

Robinson, Chris, and Nigel Tomes. "Union Wage Differentials in the Public and Private Sectors: A Simultaneous Equations Sepcification." *Journal of Labor Economics* 2 (1984): 106–27.

Smith, Rodney T. "An Economic Theory of Coalition Formation." Claremont Graduate School, Claremont, Calif., 1985.

Spiller, Pablo T. "The Differential Impact of Airline Regulation on Individual Firms and Markets: An Empirical Analysis." *Journal of Law and Economics* 26 (1983): 655–89.

Stigler, George J. "Director's Law of Public Income Redistribution." *Journal of Law and Economics* 13 (1970): 1–10.

Stuart, Charles. "Welfare Costs per Dollar of Additional Tax Revenue in the United States." *American Economic Review* 74 (1984): 352–62.

U.S. Federal Election Commission. *Reports on Financial Activities, 1979–1980*. Washington, D.C.: U.S. Government Printing Office, 1982.

Wellisz, Stanislaw, and John D. Wilson. "A Theory of Tariff Formation." Columbia University, 1984.

MONEY AND MACROBEHAVIOR

♦ ♦ ♦ ♦ ♦ ♦

♦ *PART* ♦ *SIX* ♦

THE CLASSICAL MONETARY THEORY: THE OUTCOME OF THE DISCUSSION

Gary S. Becker
William J. Baumol

· 23 ·

I. INTRODUCTORY

Recently a number of economists have shown a revived interest in the monetary theory of the classicists[1] and of the members of the Lausanne School and their successors.[2] It has been maintained that all of these authors held basically common views which have been called "the classical system." Moreover, it has been argued that this system suffers from serious formal shortcomings, in particular that either it is inconsistent or it must leave the absolute price level indeterminate.

We believe a summary of the results of the discussion is now appropriate, and that the conflicting views can be evaluated and to some extent reconciled. Moreover, the arguments can be stated rigorously without recourse to the mathematical apparatus which has been employed. A detailed restatement is therefore included in the belief that the discussion will become available to many who did not follow it before.

For our purposes we may consider the attack on the earlier writers to have been opened by Lange (13), although the discussion, as is indicated below, goes back much further. However, the immediate center of contention is Patinkin's restatement and refinement of the Lange position. We shall therefore describe the Lange-Patinkin version of the classical system and the

First published in *Economica* 19, no. 76 (November 1952): 355–76. All rights reserved.

difficulties which they have shown to be inherent in it. A more satisfactory structure which Patinkin has called "the modified classical system" will then be outlined. Finally, it will be argued through reexamination of some of the classical writings that most of the group probably never held views like those ascribed to them. Indeed, it will appear that "the modified classical system" is a considerably closer approximation to their analysis. No doubt it is true that "the classics," particularly as the term has been used in the discussion, denotes too heterogeneous a group to permit wholesale judgment to be passed on the basis of selections from several members alleged to be representative. Nevertheless, many of the members of that group, among them some of those specifically accused, have passages in their writings which explicitly contradict the charges against them. We do not mean that none of these writers ever expressed himself incorrectly or in a misleading manner on this subject, or that they were all in possession of a full analysis of the logical structure of the problem. It does, however, seem that in most cases where the problem was considered *explicitly*, it was analyzed in a manner which is at least formally valid.

II. The Classical System
according to Lange and Patinkin

Consider an exchange economy using (say) paper money as a medium of exchange. An individual who demands (supplies) a commodity gives up (receives) an equal value of the medium of exchange. If we call paper money a good and sum over all individuals, then by definition the total value of goods[3] (including money flow) demanded in this economy is identically equal to the total value of goods (including money flow) supplied. This result, which Lange calls Walras' Law,[4] has nothing whatsoever to do with equilibrium in the various markets, and holds for *all* price configurations.

Suppose that at *any* given set of prices people will supply commodities when and only when they use (and intend to use) the money received to demand other commodities "immediately," i.e., during the period under consideration. Again, by summing over all individuals, we see that at any set of prices the total money demand for *commodities* will be equal to the total money value of the quantity supplied of all *commodities*. It is this which Lange and Patinkin have identified with Say's Law. Because it is taken to hold no matter what the price structure and to distinguish it from other versions of the "Law" we shall refer to it as Say's Identity.

Patinkin in discussing his version of the classical system indicates[5] one particular set of circumstances which involves Say's Identity. He states that the classics, particularly the members of the Lausanne School, believed that money has no utility of its own, taking this to imply that in the static classical world there is no reason for any individual to desire any cash balances. Anyone who receives cash will try to exchange all his (useless) money for goods which have utility, so that, if there is a nonzero money supply, prices will rise indefinitely and the money market will be in equilibrium only with infinite prices.[6] Patinkin concludes that a classical economy can operate only if there are no stocks of money, and presents the paradox that this sort of "monetary" economy must in effect be a barter economy with a nonexistent money acting only as a unit of account! Moreover, if people have no money stocks and never add, or want to add, to them, Say's Identity clearly holds, as it must in a barter economy, since commodities will be demanded at once in any exchange.

An immediate implication of Say's Identity, or rather an equivalent way of stating it, is that the quantity of money demanded, considered either as a stock or a flow, is independent of the price structure and is always equal to the quantity of money supplied. For at any set of prices, the value of the total quantity of commodities supplied is equal to the total (nonreservation or flow) demand for money. Likewise the value of the total commodity demand is the quantity of money flow supplied. Thus with Say's Identity the quantity of money flow demanded must always equal the quantity supplied.

Moreover, the quantity of money stock supplied and demanded (cash balances) will be equal when and only when the demand for and supply of cash flows are equal, because if there is, e.g., an excess supply of cash, people will want to get rid of more money flow than is demanded. Thus, Say's Identity holds if and only if the quantity of money (stock or flow) is always equal to the quantity supplied.[7]

In our Say's Identity economy, let the money price of all commodities double (the quantity of money remaining unchanged or varying in an arbitrary manner). Since the relative prices of all commodities have remained the same we cannot expect buyers or sellers to make any substitutions among commodities. Only a substitution of money for commodities (an excess supply of commodities) is indicated, commodity prices having risen. But Say's Identity clearly precludes this too. Thus nothing will change with the change in price level.

It follows that the quantity demanded of each commodity will depend only on relative commodity prices. This is what is meant by the Leontief (15)-Lange-Patinkin contention that the classical supply and demand (excess demand) functions are homogeneous of degree zero *in prices alone*. In particular, this functional form requires that the quantity of any commodity demanded or supplied be unaffected by a proportional change in prices no matter what is happening to the stock of cash—even if the stock of cash remains constant. It also requires that quantities demanded or supplied, and relative prices and commodities, can never, even momentarily, be affected by the quantity of money.

The condition that equilibrium exists in all commodity markets can be sufficient at most to determine relative commodity prices. To determine absolute prices we must look at the remaining market—the money market. But the money market is *always* in equilibrium, no matter what the levels of the various prices. Hence, the condition that it be in equilibrium cannot be used to *determine* absolute prices. We conclude that in a Say's Identity economy, relative commodity prices are determinate, commodity quantities demanded and supplied depend only on relative commodity prices, and absolute (money) prices are indeterminate. Money is a "veil" since a good can have importance in the determination of equilibrium in the various markets of an economy only if the market for this good can conceivably be *out* of equilibrium.

In this version of the classical system the analysis of price determination is thus necessarily incomplete as it cannot specify (equilibrium) absolute prices.[8] According to Lange and Patinkin, the classics nevertheless sought to dichotomize the pricing process by determining relative prices in the "real sector" of the economy and absolute prices by introducing an additional relationship—the so-called Cambridge equation or its equivalent in a cash balance or other form of the quantity theory of money. This relates the quantity of money which people wish to hold to the price level by postulating that the quantity of cash the public demands will rise with absolute prices. Thus there would, ceteris paribus, be one and only one equilibrium price level corresponding to every level of the supply of cash—that at which people were willing to hold the amount of cash supplied. Clearly this contradicts Say's Identity which, as we have seen, requires that the quantity of cash demanded equal the supply *no matter what the price structure.*[9]

Thus, with the addition of a quantity theory or any other explanation of the absolute price level, this version of the classical system becomes self-contradictory. Without any such addition the system is incomplete in its explanation of the behavior of the economy.

III. "THE MODIFIED CLASSICAL SYSTEM"

The system just considered may be modified in a simple manner to eliminate the difficulties discussed. Patinkin[10] has called this revised model "the modified classical system." To accomplish this we need merely drop the obviously unrealistic assumption that the quantity of cash demanded is independent of the price structure. We may assume that the quantity of cash demanded will increase with the money value of transactions.

Suppose then that the prices of all commodities double, and that as a result, the quantity of money demanded doubles. Since the relative prices of commodities have remained unchanged, there will not be any substitution among commodities. People *will*, however, seek to increase their cash holdings by giving up commodities, i.e., by increasing the quantities of commodities (in money terms) they supply or decreasing the quantities they demand. We can conclude that when there is a significant money market, the demand for commodities cannot depend merely on relative commodity prices, but must also depend on absolute money prices. Thus, any attempt to dichotomize the pricing process by determining relative commodity prices in the commodity markets alone, is impossible (except in a very special sense indicated below) once a significant money market exists.[11]

The situation we are now considering is thus clearly inconsistent with Say's Identity—supply of all commodities does not necessarily equal total demand for all commodities. In particular, these will not be equal if the price structure is such as to cause the quantity of cash demanded to differ from the supply. Nevertheless, the present authors would like to point out that the ambiguous proposition called Say's Law can be interpreted in a way which makes it compatible with an economy in which the absolute price level does matter. This form of Say's Law, which we will call Say's Equality, states in effect that "supply will create its own demand," not despite the behavior of the price level but because of it. The comparative statics argument is that an excess supply of goods, obtained by disturbing a market equilibrium situation by a cash reduction, will cause the price level to fall to just that point where the excess demand for money is eliminated, since the price level will fall so long as and only so long as there is an excess demand for (insufficient supply of) cash. The foregoing is, in effect, the reasoning behind the cash balance forms of the quantity theory of money and, incidentally, the Pigou effect.

The Cambridge equation implies that for every relative price structure there exists a unique absolute price level at which the money market will be in equilibrium (Say's Equality). This is equivalent to stating that for every set of relative prices there exists a price level which brings about *overall* equilibrium in the commodity markets, i.e., the total quantity of money offered for commodities is equal to the total value of commodities supplied. Thus it is clear that this version of Say's Law is compatible with determinacy of an absolute price level.

Now assume that we start from a position of equilibrium in all markets. When all commodity prices and every stock of money doubles, the equilibrium is unaffected.[12] No substitutions take place since a proportionate change of commodity prices precludes substitution among commodities, and a substitution between commodities and money is rendered unnecessary, the doubled demand for money being satisfied by the augmented supply. This invariance is to be expected since in the models considered so far a doubling of the stock of money and all prices is strictly equivalent to a change in the unit of account (the "let's call fifty cents a dollar case") and, in effect, involves only a change in the name given the monetary unit.

If we assume that there never exists more than one set of prices compatible with equilibrium (the dangerous uniqueness assumption so often implicitly employed in comparative statics arguments) we arrive at the following comparative statics result: a doubling of the stock of cash *will* double equilibrium prices. Once again money is merely a veil. The phrase is, however, now used in the following comparative statics sense: the quantity of money in circulation affects only the equilibrium price level *and has no effect at all on equilibrium relative commodity prices*, and hence involves no intercommodity substitution once a new equilibrium is attained. Thus the price system can legitimately be dichotomized into a "real" sector and a monetary sector, but only in a discussion of *equilibrium* relative prices.

IV. The Role of Nonmonetary Assets

We already have all the material we need for an examination of the charges against the classics. However, it may be of some interest to digress briefly into a discussion of the role of assets which has played an important part in the models examined by Patinkin and the Keynesian systems

Hitherto we have explicitly assumed the absence of nonmonetary assets and, consequently, of an interest rate. We now drop this assumption to permit the existence of bonds. For the moment we also postulate an exchange economy, thus abstracting from production although, of course, this does not make economic sense if time is not also abstracted from. It may be assumed, because of the similarity in function between bond holding and money holding, that the community desires to hold the real value of its bonds constant,[13,14] so that now with a doubling of all cash stocks and all commodity prices[15] from initial equilibrium levels the asset market will not be kept in equilibrium. The quantity of bonds demanded will double (in money terms) without carrying the supply along with it. This yields a comparative statics result for an exchange economy with nonmonetary assets: a change in the supply of money cannot merely raise all commodity prices proportionately, leaving relative commodity prices and the interest rate unchanged. Necessarily relative commodity prices, the interest rate, or both of these, will change. Money is no longer a "veil" in any important sense.

Prior to the introduction of nonmonetary assets, our results held for a producing as well as for an exchange economy. To indicate one way in which production may affect an economy with real assets let us consider the following situation. Despite a zero net investment there exist capital goods which all wear out at the end of one production period (equal in length to the exchange period), and hence must be replaced. Bonds of one-period duration are issued to finance this gross investment, these being the only bonds in existence. A doubling of cash stocks and prices which were initially in equilibrium will still preclude intercommodity and commodity-money substitutions. In the asset market, the money value of the bonds issued must double to keep the real value of the capital goods constant.[16] But since the demand for bonds may also be expected to double, equilibrium is everywhere preserved. We may conclude that a change in the supply of money will (again using our uniqueness assumption) change all commodity prices proportionately, and leave relative commodity prices and the interest rate unchanged,[17] so that money will once again be a "veil" in a comparative statics sense.[18]

V. The Position of "the Classics"

We may sum up the allegations which have been made against the classics in the following three charges:

1. That they believed that cash has no utility of its own in the extreme sense that, in the static model which the classics (meaning in particular the members of the Lausanne School [cf. fn. 2 of this paper]) are alleged to have employed in their monetary analysis, people should, if consistently pursuing their own desires, seek to get rid of all their money as soon as possible.

2. That the classics believed that supplies of and demands for all commodities are homogeneous of degree zero in prices alone and so cannot be affected even momentarily by the quantity of money, and that they sought thus to dichotomize the pricing process, explaining the movement of (equilibrium and nonequilibrium) relative prices in the "real sector" alone, and the price level in the monetary sector by means of a quantity theory (illegitimately) superimposed on the system.[19]

3. Finally, that by Say's Law they meant Say's Identity which states that the supply of commodities will create its own demand irrespective of the behavior of the stock of cash and the price level.

Clearly these charges are not unrelated. Yet it may be worth investigating the attitude of "the classics" on each of these points simply because the authors may conceivably have failed to see the connection and illegitimately have accepted one of these and yet rejected one of the others which follows from it.

In the discussion we trust we have avoided reading too much into the classics in concluding that many of them held views more acceptable than those which have been attributed to them. Certainly we do not mean to imply that they always fully understood the perils they thereby avoided. It may be added that we began our investigation expecting considerably weaker results, and were most surprised to find how clearly many of the classics had expressed themselves on these matters.[20]

VI. The Utility of Cash

Here we may begin with no less an authority than J. B. Say who recapitulates his views on this question by stating, "I have . . . pointed out the various utility of gold and silver as articles of commerce, wherein originates their value; and considered their fitness to act as money, as part of that utility."[21] He had already noted that "paper (money) has a peculiar and inherent value," and, indeed, gone into this point at length.[22]

Ricardo was, of course, less interested in the question of the relation between utility and value. Nevertheless, Marget[23] takes this statement that its employment as money merely adds to the list of uses of bullion to imply that added utility is imparted to metal by its becoming money.

Senior can also be cited to this effect,[24] and Marget[25] points out that Jevons wrote of "the 'utility' of 'that quality of money' which a man 'will desire not to exchange.'" Wicksteed[26] speaks of the marginal significance of gold being raised by its use as a medium of exchange, as well as its use as a standard of value. And while Marshall, in speaking of the constancy of the marginal utility of money presumably referred to income rather than cash balances, there is at least one point in the Principles in which his money unmistakably means cash,[27] and in which he goes into detail on "the marginal utility of ready money."

Surely Patinkin is not justified in citing Walras as one of those to whom money has no utility. His only reference (indeed his only "damning" reference to Walras) is to the statement, "Soit (U) la monnaie que nous considérerons d'abord comme un objet sans utilité propre"[28] This is hardly conclusive, and it may well be meant to indicate no more than the author's intention at that point to deal only with monies like paper rather than, for example, gold. In any case, it includes the phrase "d'abord" (to begin with). Indeed it would be most strange for one who has been hailed as a mighty protagonist of the cash balance approach,[29] to find Walras denying utility to cash. But we have better evidence than this. In his *Théorie de la Monnaie* he makes it abundantly clear that he is most pleased that the theory of money provides such a fine and important application of the theory of marginal utility[30] and more than once speaks of the *rareté* of money[31] after having pointed out that this is the term he had appropriated from his father to designate marginal utility.[32]

Pareto is another of the only five "classics" (Walras, Pareto, Wicksell, Cassel and Divisia) whose work is specifically cited by Patinkin as an example of the mishandling of monetary theory. No doubt Pareto's monetary theory is considerably more superficial than that of Walras. Nevertheless even in his case the charges are questionable. As with Walras, Patinkin provides us with only one specific reference to prove that any of his charges apply to Pareto, and again this reference is intended to show that in the Paretan system money has no utility. But the choice of passage is here even more strange. The only reference to money on the page cited is the following: "La monnaie étant une marchandise doit avoir pour quelques individus une ophélimité propre; mais elle peut ne pas en avoir pour d'autres."[33] Surely this is the contradictory of Patinkin's allegation! Indeed, Pareto goes further—in effect reprimanding those others (?) who maintain that money has no utility.

> La monnaie remplit deux rôles principaux: 1° elle facilite l'échange des marchandises; 2° elle garantit cet échange. . . . C'est parce qu'on n'a pris parfois en considération que son premier rôle qu'on n'a vu dans la monnaie qu'un simple signe sans valeur intrinsèque.[34]

The list is by no means exhausted, but there seems little point in going on. "The classics" did not generally believe that the holding of cash balances adds nothing to utility beyond that which will eventually be derived by spending the money.

Of course there are those who might appear in some looser statements to have argued otherwise. J. S. Mill did argue that "money, as money, satisfies no want,"[35] but he wanted only to point out that money is valuable only because commodities can be bought for it,[36] a homily that should find few dissenters. Divisia more explicitly[37] and Knight by implication[38] have clearly denied a utility to money. In general, however, it seems rather difficult to find classicists taking the extreme form of the position attributed to them by Patinkin.

It may be remarked that the sort of statics which would be required to deprive money of utility in Patinkin's sense would be very special indeed. Transactions demand would be eliminated only if wage payments and all other receipts were staggered in time and amounts so as just to cover the transactions which the recipient desires to make at the moment he desires to make them. This would happen in particular if receipts and payments coincided in a steady stream.[39] Where these requisites do not hold, money derives a "utility" from the goods it can buy, it is true, but because it can buy them at the moment the buyer considers convenient.

VIII. Homogeneity of Demands and Supplies in Prices Alone

The "Pigou effect"[40] consists of a rise in the quantities of goods and services demanded with a fall in absolute prices, arising from the resulting increase in purchasing power of all cash holdings. This is a complete denial of the homogeneity postulate, for it permits the demands for goods to be affected by a change in the price level alone, relative prices remaining unchanged. If we are not to call the title of Professor Pigou's article misleading, this effect is part and parcel of the classical stationary state, and there is no more to be said upon the subject.

However, the homogeneity (dichotomization) allegation is really at the heart of the charges under examination, and so is worth some further investigation.[41] First it should be noted that even an unqualified statement that the quantity of money may not affect the quantities of the various commodities demanded and supplied need not mean that the author believes in homogeneity of supplies and demands in prices alone. This may merely be the following (comparative statics) assertion which has been argued above (following Patinkin[42]). If all cash stocks are raised in proportion all prices will rise in proportion, and thus there will be no change in quantities demanded or supplied once a new equilibrium is attained, even in the "modified" classical system. This is not the same as the homogeneity assumption which would never have permitted the quantities of the commodity demanded and supplied to vary even temporarily with the changed stock of cash (no matter how it is injected). What we must then disentangle is which of these, if either, approximates the views of the writers in question.

The literature is quite rich on the effect of an injection of cash, going back to Cantillon and Hume, both of whom make it abundantly clear that they are having no truck with "the homogeneity postulate." Thus Cantillon wrote,

> Through whatever hands the money which is introduced may pass it will naturally increase the consumption; but this consumption will be more or less great according to circumstances. It will be directed more or less to certain kinds of products or merchandise according to the idea of those who acquire the money. Market prices will rise more for certain things than for others however abundant the money may be.[43]

Similarly, Hume wrote,

> We find, that, in every kingdom, into which money begins to flow in greater
> abundance than formerly, everything takes a new face: labour and industry
> gain life; the merchant becomes more enterprising, the manufacturer more
> diligent and skillful, and even the farmer follows his plough with greater
> alacrity and attention.
>   . . . though the high price of commodities be a necessary consequence
> of the encrease of gold and silver, yet it follows not immediately upon that
> encrease . . . At first, no alteration is perceived; by degrees the price rises,
> first of one commodity, then of another; till the whole at last reaches a just
> proportion with the new quantity of specie.[44]

Malthus seems to have accepted Hume's analysis, and indeed to have
cited it with approbation, but Ricardo's attitude can at best be described as
lukewarm.[45] McCulloch felt that Hume had exaggerated the beneficial effects
of an influx of money, but nevertheless contested James Mill's out-and-out
denial of the validity of Hume's argument.[46] Note, however, that even if
McCulloch (like Walras, as Patinkin himself observes)[47] believed in "just a
little nonhomogeneity," e.g., believed that prices will rise sufficiently quickly
and close to proportionately to render nugatory the impact effects of an influx
of cash, he has escaped Patinkin's problems. He has accepted the "modified"
classical system, the argument with Hume being only over the time path
between the two equilibria which is irrelevant to the present discussion.

J. S. Mill also supported this sort of position,[48] but perhaps the clearest
statement is to be found in Marshall's testimony before the Gold and Silver
Commission to which the reader is referred.[49]

The case of Wicksell is worth special consideration, especially since he
is under particular attack by Patinkin on this point.[50] Wicksell in his writings
explicitly employed the device of proceeding from the (over) simple to the
complex. Hence it is dangerous to attribute lack of sophistication to him on
the basis of isolated passages, since these may be preceded by a warning and
adequately qualified later. Thus, as Patinkin points out, at several points[51]
Wicksell states that the demand functions for commodities will depend solely
on relative prices. But on each occasion the assumption provisionally made
is that money serves only as a unit of account and a medium of exchange,
and its function as a store of value is explicitly abstracted from.

However, he knew well enough how to deal with homogeneity:

> Let us suppose that for some reason or other commodity prices rise while
> the stock of money remains unchanged, or that the stock of money is
> diminished while prices remain temporarily unchanged. The cash balances
> will gradually appear to be *too small*. . . . I can rely on a higher level of

receipts in the future. But meanwhile I run the risk of being unable to meet my obligations punctually, and at best I may easily be forced by shortage of ready money to forgo some purchase that would otherwise have been profitable. I therefore seek to enlarge my balance . . . through a *reduction* in my *demand* for goods and services, or through an *increase* in the *supply* of my own commodity . . . the universal reduction in demand and increase in supply of commodities will necessarily bring about a continuous fall in all prices. This can only cease when prices have fallen to the level at which the cash balances are regarded as *adequate*.[52]

It is true that Cassel did commit himself to (the macroeconomic parts of) the model which Patinkin has called the classical system, and, indeed, the difficulties in which this involved him have been noted before.[53]

In sum there seems to be considerable ground for doubt about the validity of the attack on the classical system. Yet somehow Patinkin's argument is not completely pointless. Somewhere the impression seems to have arisen (and to have gotten into teaching) that this was indeed the nature of the classical system. Indeed, some of the classics themselves have, as we have seen, represented the contrary views as corrections of errors widely held. Keynes's polemics may have contributed considerably. One important source of confusion is, no doubt, the superficial resemblance between the valid comparative statics assertion that equilibrium relative prices may be unaffected by the quantity of cash (if injected into the system in an appropriate manner), and the position ascribed by Patinkin to the classics that relative prices can never be affected by the quantity of cash (however injected), even temporarily.

The nature of the mathematical notation employed may also partly be responsible. The demand and supply functions were usually written as functions of prices alone with no explicit cognizance taken of the quantity of cash or anything else, including money income, all of these having been held in abeyance via ceteris paribus. This may indicate merely that an author using this notation had for the moment not thought explicitly about the role of cash, or considered it unimportant at that point. Nevertheless, confusion about demands and supplies being homogeneous of degree zero in prices alone, may have arisen in this manner.

A particularly apt case in point is that of Lange himself who, as Patinkin shows, has gone wrong on just this point in the mathematical appendix to his book.[54] Yet much of the book itself is devoted to an examination of the effects of changes in the stock of cash and the price level on the quantities of individual commodities demanded and supplied, i.e., to a discussion of the effects of the absence of homogeneity in prices alone!

IX. SAY'S IDENTITY

This section will necessarily be the most inconclusive in our examination of the "classical views." This is largely because Say's Law seems to have been used ambiguously in most cases, the writers for the most part not having considered the relation between the law and the nature of the money market. Moreover, several different propositions have been referred to as Say's Law. Say himself, besides formulating the proposition[55] which has caused so much controversy, confused it with two different, considerably more innocuous, assertions.

The first is the tautological proposition that there will always be a market for all goods produced where we define a good to be something which can be sold at a price covering its costs.[56]

The second is the almost Keynesian view that demand will not exist without production since production creates the income with which goods can be bought.[57]

However, Say has also advocated the more familiar proposition, and at one place he makes it clear that he is thinking of the equality rather than the identity, but in a rather peculiar form.

> Sales cannot be said to be dull because money is scarce, but because other products are so. There is always money enough to conduct the circulation and mutual interchange of other values, when those values really exist. Should the increase of traffic require more money to facilitate it, the want is easily supplied, and is a strong indication of prosperity. . . . In such cases, merchants know well enough how to find substitutes for the product serving as the medium of exchange or money [by bills at sight, or after date, bank-notes, running-credits, write-offs, etc. as at London and Amsterdam] and money itself soon pours in, for this reason, that all produce naturally gravitates to that place where it is most in demand.[58]

Thus Say is operating with a nearly Wicksellian credit economy in which price level is indeed indeterminate. But this is so not because the quantity of money (and credit) has no influence, but rather because the quantity of circulating medium will vary by just the amount necessary to maintain any price level!

James Mill, on the other hand, makes a statement typical of many which were to follow, and which might be used to defend the view that most of the classics believed in Say's Identity: "When a man produces a greater quantity of any commodity than he desires for himself, it can only be on one account; namely, that he desires some other commodity."[59] Unless he here means money to be considered a commodity or unless, and this is a possibility we cannot rule out, he is assuming implicitly that the price level is adjusted to the quantity of cash, this would appear to imply acceptance of the identity. It is, of course, also possible that the problem did not occur to him.

If we compare this with McCulloch (who is sometimes considered the least subtle "classic") it becomes clear that it is not entirely far-fetched to argue that James Mill's statement need not mean that he believed in the identity rather than the equation. Thus McCulloch first argues very much like Mill, only more specifically excluding money: "It is, however, the acquisition of [other commodities] . . . and not of money, that is the end which every man has in view who carries anything to market."[60] He argues that therefore the redundance of individual produce must occur because production is misdirected and "is independent of the value of money." However, he at once makes it clear (and repeats this point in detail on the following page) that this is only a long-run equilibrium statement and is so *because the value of money has had time to adjust to the quantity*:

> It must, however, be borne in mind, that in the previous statements we have taken for granted that the value of money . . . has been invariable, or that, at all events, it has not been sensibly affected by sudden changes in its quantity and value. These changes may, as already stated, exert a powerful influence; and have frequently, indeed, occasioned the most extensive derangement in the ordinary channels of commercial intercourse . . . any sudden diminution of the quantity, and consequent rise in the value of money . . . may be such as materially to abridge the power of the society to make their accustomed purchases, and thus to occasion a glut of the market.[61]

Could there be a more forceful rejection of the identity?

J. S. Mill, in the *Principles*, speaks similarly of the "undersupply of money" during a commercial crisis,[62] this again in connection with a discussion of Say's Law, and after having just made the statement (quoted by Keynes in the *General Theory*) that "All sellers are inevitably, and by the meaning of the word, buyers" etc.[63] But the clearest statement on this point is that in J. S. Mill's second essay in his *Unsettled Questions*. We shall offer no quotations from there—it must be read in extenso. It is all there and explicitly—Walras' Law, Say's Identity which Mill points out holds only for a barter economy, the "utility of money" which consists in permitting purchases to be made when convenient, the possibility of (temporary) oversupply of commodities when money is in excess demand, and Say's Equality which makes this only a temporary possibility.[64] Indeed, in reading it one is led to wonder why so much of the subsequent literature (this paper included) had to be written at all.

It thus appears that the classics may have been taken too literally by Lange and Patinkin. As was the case in other connections, some of the classics may simply not have considered it worth the effort to point out that they were speaking about long-run equilibrium tendencies. Certainly the cases cited lend support to this view, and we have not found a "classic" who was explicit to the contrary.

The case of Wicksell is also particularly interesting in this connection because of Lange's comments. Lange himself points out that Wicksell (in our terminology) was driven to reject Say's Identity in favor of the Equality. After pointing out how Wicksell was forced to abandon the Identity in order to establish any monetary theory at all, he states,

> He finally appeased his conscience by stating that total demand and total supply must be equal only "ultimately" but may differ "in the first place." With this observation Wicksell, and with him all monetary theorists, gave up Say's law by substituting for the identity an equation which holds only in equilibrium. . . . But this tendency toward equilibrium . . . should not be confused with Say's law.[65]

NOTES

1. The authors are indebted to Professors Viner and Brunner for their comments and suggestions.

2. See references (1), (8), (12), (13), (14), (31)–(35), and cf. (17), (18) and (36). But note Patinkin's reservation: "To minimise this [the problem of textual interpretation] . . . I shall confine myself to the mathematical economists of this ['classical'] school" (31, p. 4).

3. "Commodities" are also considered "goods." Paper money is "a good" only.

4. Ref. 13, p. 50.

5. Ref. 34, pp. 140–45.

6. This equilibrium possibility is suggested by Brunner (1, footnote 20, pp. 167–68). Patinkin (32, footnote 7, p. 135) has argued that infinite prices are not economically meaningful. But surely they can be interpreted to mean that money is not wanted. For when money is worthless, the money price of any useful good must be infinite. Thus, economically, this is identical with the Phipps solution (see 35) which requires that the price of money be zero. In this case people will throw money away because it will buy nothing. This alone should already raise doubts as to whether any classic ever meant that money has no utility in this sense. But Knight (11, p. xxii)

does believe that money has no utility in a static economy and anticipates Patinkin in pointing out the consequences of this view. Cf. also, e.g., P. N. Rosenstein-Rodan (39, Part II).

7. The sufficiency of this condition was indicated earlier when Say's Identity was first introduced. Note that Say's Identity does not *require* that money have no utility, i.e., that demand (rather than *excess* demand) for money be zero.

8. Cf. Neisser (29).

9. See Lange (13, p. 65), Patinkin (31, pp. 12–16); (32, p. 138). Patinkin's contention goes somewhat further than this, pointing out that with Say's Identity no matter how the stock of cash behaves, the quantity of cash (flow) demanded and supplied must both increase in proportion with prices, i.e., they must both be homogeneous of degree one in absolute prices. This is true since the quantity of money (flow) supplied is the money demand for goods, which is the sum of the demands for the various goods each multiplied by its price. Since the quantity of each good demanded is unaffected by a proportionate change in prices, the sum of these demands each multiplied by its price, i.e., the quantity of money supplied, must change in proportion with the change in prices. The same argument holds for the demand for money, and hence for the excess supply of money. Now the Cambridge equation does not call for the excess supply of cash flows to behave in this manner *irrespective of the level of the stock of cash*. The *form* of the Cambridge relationship is thus in contradiction with the *form* assumed for the money excess supply function. It is this which Patinkin has called "Invalidity I" (32, p. 138). The next paragraph in this paper summarizes his "Invalidity II" (ibid., p. 141).

10. Ref. 31, pp. 23–26; 32, pp. 143–50; and 33.

11. Thus, if any equilibrium is possible, a Cambridge equation, or anything else implying that the quantities of money demanded and supplied are not equal at all price levels, requires that quantities of commodities supplied and demanded be not homogeneous of degree zero in prices alone. This can also be seen as follows: suppose prices, originally in equilibrium, are doubled, the stock of cash remaining constant, and that the quantities of cash stocks and flows demanded now (say) exceed the supply. By Walras' Law the quantity of some commodity supplied must exceed the demand. The demand for or the supply of that commodity must then have changed as a result of the change in price level alone, in violation of homogeneity. Hence, Hickman's system (8) which involves both a Cambridge equation and the assumption that the quantities demanded and supplied of all commodities are homogeneous of degree zero in prices alone, must be in error. What he has done, in effect, is assume that the quantity of cash stock demanded can differ from the supply (the Cambridge equation) whereas at the same time (Say's Identity) the quantity of cash flow demanded is identically equal to its supply, so that there are two separate conditions giving equilibrium in the monetary sector of the economy. Brunner has pointed out to us that this last sentence is not quite accurate—Say's Identity is not directly involved in Hickman's argument. However it comes close enough to the source of his difficulty for present purposes.

The argument of this footnote also indicates that the difficulty in the system attributed by Lange and Patinkin to the classics arises out of the homogeneity assumption, since this precludes inequality in money supply and demand. Say's Identity, since it implies homogeneity, provides a special case of this difficulty. Patinkin seems to have been the first to observe this point.

12. We require that *every* stock of cash doubles, and not just that the total quantity of cash in the system double, since the effects of an injection of cash will obviously vary with the method employed to introduce it. If given to the miser who sews it into a mattress, the effect will evidently be quite different from that of a gift to someone who spends it at once.

13. The Cambridge equation assumes that it desires to hold the real value of its money constant.

14. This assumption is related to that made by Patinkin (31, p. 18) and Brunner (1, passim).

15. The interest rate (thus the price of bonds) remaining constant.

16. Patinkin (31) fails to indicate how the bond supply behaves, and seems to conclude (p. 19) that because the demand for bonds will be homogeneous of degree one in prices, so will the excess demand for bonds.

17. In technical terminology we can say that the demand for and supply of each commodity is homogeneous of degree zero in commodity prices and the quantity of money. The supplies of and demands for bonds and money are homogeneous of degree one in the quantity of money and commodity prices.

18. Since the supply of money does not affect the interest rate, the explanation of the level of interest must be found in "real" factors. Cf. Patinkin (33).

19. This is what Brunner (1) has called "the complementarity property," meaning thereby that a separate money equation is superimposed on the system to complement the real sector.

20. The authors decidedly do not consider themselves experts in *Dogmengeschichte*, and so are forced to rely heavily on pilfered references coming largely from those extraordinary two volumes (19) where, conveniently, Professor Marget subjects closely related allegations to most painstaking examination (see esp. vol. II, pp. 8–124). No attempt has been made at an exhaustive survey of the literature.

21. Ref. 42, p. 228. He is arguing against Garnier, translator of the *Wealth of Nations*. Locke had said this by implication (16, pp. 578–82).

22. Ibid., p. 227, but cf. p. 133, esp. the footnote. It is noteworthy that in later French editions Say decided paper money was of sufficient importance to warrant a separate chapter (see the 6th edition, p. 256, and Chapter XXVI).

23. Ref. 19, vol. II, p. 31, footnote 81, where Turgot and Law are cited to the same effect. For the Ricardo references see (37), pp. 9–10.

24. Ref. 43, p. 23 ff. McCulloch argues that coins "exchange for other things, because they are desirable articles, and are possessed of real intrinsic value" (21, p. 135), but by this he may mean their value as metal, and is willing, though not without hesitation, to exempt drafts, checks and bills from this conclusion. Indeed, elsewhere (p. 217) he has sellers lend or spend their money immediately upon receipt.

25. Ref. 19, vol. II, p. 56, footnote 14.

26. Ref. 48, p. 600 (vol. II).

27. Ref. 24, p. 335 and footnote.

28. Ref. 44, p. 303.

29. See Marget (17) and esp. (18) for a spirited defense of Walras on these points written some twenty years before the Patinkin articles. After writing this the authors found that Professor Jaffé had, in a paper delivered at a meeting of the Econometric Society, pointed out Patinkin's misinterpretation of Walras on the utility of cash balances. For a summary see (10, pp. 327–28).

30. Ref. 45, esp. the introduction, pp. 65–70.

31. Ibid., esp. p. 102. He is presumably speaking of the utility of availability of cash which he distinguished from the utility of money per se.

32. Ibid., p. 66.

33. Ref. 30, p. 593. It is cited by Patinkin in (34, p. 140, footnote 5).

34. Ref. 30, p. 451.

35. Ref. 28, p. 6 (Preliminary Remarks). See also Hume (9, "Of Interest", p. 321) to the effect that money has "chiefly a fictitious value."

36. Thus compare (27, pp. 69–70).

37. Ref. 5, chapter XIX and the appendix.

38. Ref. 11, p. xxii.

39. This can to some extent be arranged artificially by investing money the moment it is received with provision for repayment the (perfectly foreseen) moment it will be needed. But this would only be done to the extent necessary to eliminate demand for cash completely if there were no transactions cost of making and then calling in the investment, and if, in addition, no effort were required in carrying out this transaction. Where these are not abstracted from, it will pay to hold at least small quantities of cash for payments planned for a time shortly after the money has been received, "perfectly" static world or no. It is true that if loans were perfectly safe (the outcomes perfectly foreseen) the distinction between cash and securities might disappear, but not the distinction between the "money-securities" and "real assets," and the latter would still have a positive yield because they are not convenient means of payment and so not perfectly liquid.

40. Ref. 36, pp. 349–50. Note the relation to Say's Equality.

41. Indeed, dichotomization accusations and denials always seem to have flown thick and fast. Locke (16, p. 582) and Say (42, p. 226) most emphatically insisted that dichotomization is illegitimate, arguing that, "money . . . is a commodity, whose value is determined by the same general laws, as that of all other commodities" (Say, op. cit., p. 226). Ricardo accuses Malthus and others (not completely specified) of saying that money is a commodity "subject to the same laws of . . . value . . . as other commodities," yet reasoning in an erroneous manner which showed "that they really consider money as something peculiar, varying from causes totally different from those which affect other commodities" (37, pp. 72–73). See also (38, p. 292), and (37, pp. 9–10). Yet this same charge is brought against Ricardo by Cannan (2, p.

182) and, in effect, Leontief (15). Similarly Senior attacked James Mill on this (43, pp. 8–9), while J. S. Mill explicitly affirmed that the value of money was determined like that of other commodities (28, Book III, chapter VII, Section 3, p. 488). To Walras the theory of money provided "une des premières et des plus décisives applications de mon système d'économie politique pure" (i.e., his marginal utility theory). (See 45, p. 69); while Ohlin has lauded Wicksell for "this 'new approach(!)' to monetary theory," for "Until then, and as matter of fact for long afterwards, it was regarded as self-evident that . . . a change in the general price level must be due to entirely different circumstances from a change in individual prices." (46, Ohlin's introduction, p. xiii).

42. Ref. 31, p. 23; 33, p. 53.

43. Ref. 3, p. 179.

44. Ref. 9, p. 313.

45. Ref. 38, pp. 387–88, and the reference to Malthus given there. For a case of nonhomogeneity in Ricardo, see (38, p. 179).

46. Ref. 21, pp. 556–57. But note that James Mill did not commit himself to homogeneity but argued rather that if the additional money were used to augment demand, prices would rise at once and rob this money of its value. See (26, pp. 160–61).

47. Ref. 31, p. 12, footnote 5.

48. Ref. 28, book III, chapter VIII, Section 2, and the second essay in (27).

49. Ref. 23, esp. pp. 38–52. It is noteworthy that at one point Marshall even included the stock of assets among the determinants of the demand for cash (22, p. 44, as cited by Hansen [7], p. 2). However, Marshall never seems to have done much with this.

50. Refs. 31, p. 12, footnote 5, and 32, p. 149, footnote 30.

51. Refs. 46, p. 23, and 47, vol. I, p. 67, and vol. II, p. 22.

52. Ref. 46, pp. 39–40 (Wicksell's italics).

53. See the excellent discussion by Marget (19, vol. II, pp. 338–41), also Wicksell (47, vol. I, pp. 224–55); Cassel (4, pp. 150–52).

54. See Lange (12, pp. 99–103). The Patinkin discussion of this point is in (31, pp. 18–20). This is not to deny that some recent mathematical theorists have adopted monetary analyses involving dichotomization of the real and monetary systems throughout their works. Indeed Brunner may well be right when he maintains in a letter to the authors that such an approach had recently become well entrenched.

55. Say's Law has been attributed to James Mill, but this judgment is not universally accepted. Though most of its components can be found there, the first edition of the *Traité* which appeared in 1803 had no well organized discussion of the "Law" (but McCulloch [20, p. 21]) seems not to have noticed this—note also the incorrect date given there). Before the second edition with its extended discussion of the Law appeared in 1814, James Mill had published his *Commerce Defended* (25) in which the argument is developed at length.

56. For references see Lange (13, p. 60, footnote 15), and Neisser (29, p. 385, footnote 4). In particular see Say's last two letters to Malthus (published posthu-

mously) and Malthus's reply to the first of these in (41, pp. 502–15, esp. pp. 504–05, 508 and 513).

57. This argument is found in many places in Say's discussions of the Law. See (42, pp. 136–37), reproduced in (40, pp. 340–42), and (41, p. 441).

58. Ref. 42, p. 134. The insertion in brackets is Say's footnote.

59. Ref. 26, p. 222.

60. Ref. 21, p. 217.

61. Ibid., pp. 218–19. The unabridged passage is even more forceful. He adds, "It is almost unnecessary to lay any examples of what is, unfortunately, so common before the reader."

62. Ref. 28, book III, chapter XIV, Section 4.

63. Ibid., Sections 2 and 3.

64. Ref. 27, pp. 46–74, esp. p. 69 ff. Mill remarks (p. 74) "these well-known facts . . . were equally well known to the authors of the doctrine (Say's Law) who, therefore, can only have adopted from inadvertence any form of expression which could to a candid person appear inconsistent with it."

Note that on p. 71 a general fall in commodity prices decreases the demand for cash not through the transactions demand, but via the expectation that the price fall will not be permanent.

65. Lange (13, p. 66), Wicksell (47, vol. II. pp. 159–60). See also the passage quoted above.

References

1. Brunner, Karl, "Inconsistency and Indeterminacy in Classical Economics." *Econometrica* 19 (April 1951).

2. Cannan, Edwin. *A Review of Economic Theory*. London: P. S. King, 1929.

3. Cantillon, Richard. *Essai Sur La Nature Du Commerce En Général*, Higgs translation. London: Macmillan, 1931.

4. Cassel, Gustav. *The Theory of Social Economy*, translated by Joseph McCabe. London: Unwin, 1923.

5. Divisia, F. *Économique Rationnelle*. Paris: Gaston Doin, 1917.

6. Fisher, Irving. *The Purchasing Power of Money*, revised edition. New York: Macmillan, 1911.

7. Hansen, Alvin. *Monetary Theory and Fiscal Policy*. New York: McGraw Hill, 1949.

8. Hickman, W. Braddock. "The Determinacy of Absolute Prices in Classical Economic Theory." *Econometrica* 18 (January 1950).

9. Hume, David. *Essays Moral, Political and Literary*. London: Longmans, Green and Co., 1875.

10. Jaffé, William. "The Éléments and its Critics," Abstract of a paper delivered before the Econometric Society, Chicago, December 27, 1950. *Econometrica* 19 (July 1951): 327–28.

11. Knight, F. H. *Risk, Uncertainty and Profit*. London School of Economics and Political Science Series of Reprints of Scarce Tracts in Economic and Political Science, No. 16. London, 1933.

12. Lange, Oscar. *Price Flexibility and Employment*. Cowles Commission Monograph No. 8. Bloomington, Ind.: Principia Press, 1944.

13. Lange, Oscar. "Say's Law: A Restatement and Criticsm." In *Studies in Mathematical Economics and Econometrics; in Memory of Henry Schultz*, edited by Oscar Lange, Francis McIntyre, and Theodore O. Yntema. Chicago: Chicago University Press, 1942.

14. Leontief, Wassily. "The Consistency of the Classical Theory of Money and Prices." *Econometrica* 18 (January 1950).

15. Leontief, Wassily. "The Fundamental Assumptions of Mr. Keynes' Monetary Theory of Employment." *Quarterly Journal of Economics* 51 (November 1936).

16. Locke, John. *An Essay on the Consequences of the Lowering of Interest and Raising the Value of Money*. London: Ward, Lock and Co. Edition of The Works of John Locke, (no date).

17. Marget, Arthur. "Léon Walras and the 'Cash Balance Approach' to the Problem of the Value of Money." *Journal of Political Economy* 39 (October 1931).

18. Marget, Arthur. "The Monetary Aspects of the Walrasian System," *Journal of Political Economy* 43 (April 1935).

19. Marget, Arthur. *The Theory of Prices*. New York: Prentice Hall, Vol. I, 1938, Vol. II, 1942.

20. McCulloch, J. R. *The Literature of Political Economy*. London, 1845.

21. McCulloch, J. R.. *Principles of Political Economy*, fourth edition. London, 1849.

22. Marshall, Alfred. *Money, Credit and Commerce*. London: Macmillan, 1923.

23. Marshall, Alfred. *Official Papers*. London: Macmillan, 1928.

24. Marshall, Alfred. *Principles of Economics*, 8th edition. London: Macmillan, 1920.

25. Mill, James. *Commerce Defended*, second edition. London, 1808.

26. Mill, James. *Elements of Political Economy*, second edition. London, 1824.

27. Mill, John S. *Essays on Some Unsettled Questions of Political Economy*. London, 1844. No. 7 in the Series of Reprints of Scarce Works on Political Economy, London School of Economics and Political Science, London, 1948.

28. Mill, John S. *Principles of Political Economy*, edited by W. S. Ashley. London: Longmans, Green, 1909.

29. Neisser, Hans. "General Overproduction." In *Readings in Business Cycle Theory*, Gottfried Haberler, editor. Philadelphia: American Economic Association, Blakiston, 1944.

30. Pareto, Vilfredo. *Manuel D'Économie Politique*, 2d edition. Paris: Giard, 1927.

31. Patinkin, Don. "The Indeterminacy of Absolute Prices in Classical Economic Theory." *Econometrica* 17 (January 1949).

32. Patinkin, Don. "The Invalidity of Classical Monetary Theory." *Econometrica* 19 (April, 1951).

33. Patinkin, Don. "A Reconsideration of the General Equilibrium Theory of Money." *Review of Economic Studies* 18 (1949–50).

34. Patinkin, Don. "Relative Prices, Say's Law, and the Demand for Money." *Econometrica* 16 (April 1948).

35. Phipps, Cecil G. "A Note on Patinkin's 'Relative Prices.'" *Econometrica* 18 (January, 1950).

36. Pigou, A. C. "The Classical Stationary State." *Economic Journal* 53 (December 1943).

37. Ricardo, David. *Letters of David Ricardo to Thomas Robert Malthus*, edited by James Bonard. London: Oxford, 1887.

38. Ricardo, David. *The Works of David Ricardo*. London: McCulloch-Edition, 1876.

39. Rosenstein-Rodan, P. N. "The Coordination of the General Theories of Money and Price." *Economica* 3 (August 1936).

40. Say, J. B. *Cours Complet D'Économie Politique Pratique*, third edition. Paris, 1852.

41. Say, J. B. *Oeuvres Diverses*. Paris, 1848.

42. Say, J. B. *A Treatise on Political Economy*. Prinsep translation. Philadelphia, 1853.

43. Senior, Nassau W. *Three Lectures on the Value of Money*, London 1840. London School of Economics and Political Science Reprints of Scarce Tracts in Economics and Political Science, No. 4, London, 1931.

44. Walras, Léon. *Éléments D'Économie Politique Pure*, édition définitive. Paris: Pichon et Durand-Auzias, 1926.

45. Walras, Léon. *Études D'Économie Politique Appliquée*, second edition. Paris: Pichon et Durand-Auzias, 1936.

46. Wicksell, Knut. *Interest and Prices*, translated by R. F. Kahn. London: Macmillan, 1936.

47. Wicksell, Knut. *Lectures on Political Economy*, translated by E. Classen, edited with an introduction by Lionel Robbins. London: Routledge, Vol. I, 1934, Vol. II, 1935.

48. Wicksteed, Philip H. *The Common Sense of Political Economy*, edited with an introduction by Lionel Robbins. London: Routledge, 1933.

FAMILY ECONOMICS AND MACROBEHAVIOR

· 24 ·

It is tempting to use the audience captured by a presidential address to pontificate about the sad state of economics. You probably will conclude that I have surrendered to the temptation. But I do recognize that my good luck in becoming president of our association does not automatically endow me with commanding wisdom over all of economics. I will do my best to stick to my knitting. And for many years much of my research has been directed toward investment in human capital and the understanding of family behavior.

Modern economists neglected the behavior of families until the 1950s. Since then economic analysis has been used to explain who marries whom and when (if ever) they divorce, the number of children and investments in each child's human capital, the extent and timing of labor force participation by married women, when elderly parents rely on children for support, and many other family choices. A fair conclusion, I believe (need I remind you of my biases?), is that the economic approach contributes important insights toward explaining the large decline in birthrates during the past 100 years, the rapid expansion in the labor force participation of married women after the 1950s, the explosive advance in divorce rates during the past two de-

First published in the *American Economic Review* 76, no. 1 (March 1988): 1–13. Reprinted by permission of the American Economic Association.

cades, and other major changes in the family. Family economics is now a respectable and growing field.

Yet perhaps because family economics is a new field, only a small literature considers the implications for other parts of economics. The family is such an important institution that progress in understanding how it behaves is justification enough for any discipline. But most economists, including the audience here, are not particularly concerned about family behavior. Your interest must be stimulated through a demonstration that its study helps in the analysis of other problems.

In this address I try to maintain your interest by exploring the contribution to macroeconomics from the progress in family economics. This is a challenge not only because macrobehavior is a central part of economics but also because its link to the family may seem remote and unimportant. By macroeconomics I mean the analysis of economywide behavior. Much of the time is spent on long-term economic growth, although I also discuss short and long cycles in economic activity, and the interaction between overlapping generations through social security, transmission of inequality, and in other ways.

Of course, one paper even by a macroexpert cannot do justice to these topics, and I do not pretend to be such an expert. My purpose is to help you recognize that many conclusions in these and presumably other macro areas change radically when family choices get the attention they deserve. I apologize for the technical nature of some of the discussion that may seem out of place in a presidential address.

I. The Malthusian and Neoclassical Models

In considering the relation between economic growth and the family, it is natural to begin with Thomas Malthus's great contribution. Although usually called the Malthusian theory of population growth, a more appropriate name is the Malthusian theory of wages and average income. His first monograph, subtitled "With Remarks on the Speculations of Mr. Godwin, M. Condorcet, and Other Writers," begins with an objection to the conclusion of these writers that the economic position of mankind will continue to improve over time. In the process of rebutting their arguments, Malthus develops his famous theory of population growth and reaches much more pessimistic conclusions about the long-term economic prospects of the average family.

You will recall that the Malthusian model assumes diminishing returns to increases in the level of population—that is, to increases in employment—when land and other capital are fixed. The analytical heart of his model (I am not concerned with the details of what he actually said) is consistent with constant returns to the scale of labor and capital, as long as the capital stock, including usable land, does not respond to changes in wages and interest rates.

The response of fertility and mortality to changes in income determine the Malthusian supply of population. Population grows more slowly when wages are low because the average person marries later and thereby has fewer children (the preventive check on population), and also because deaths increase when families are poorer (the positive check). Historical studies indicate that the effect of the economy on age at marriage was considerably greater, at least in Europe, than was its effect on death rates (see Ronald D. Lee 1987b, 450–51). Therefore, I will ignore the positive effect and consider only the preventive check through changes in the number of children.

The long-run equilibrium wage rate is found at the point on the positively inclined population supply curve where the average family has two children. The economy's production function then determines the stationary level of population that is consistent with this long-run wage rate. There is no presumption that this equilibrium wage is at the subsistence level, especially if the positive check through death rates is not important. In this model tastes for marriage and children, not vague notions of subsistence, determine long-run wages.

The long-run wage is stable in the Malthusian model when shocks push the system out of equilibrium. For example, if an infectious disease destroys much of the population, as the Black Death destroyed perhaps 25 percent of certain European populations during the fourteenth century, the decline in population raises the marginal productivity of labor. The resulting rise in wages encourages families to marry earlier and have more children. Population begins to grow and its increase over time lowers wage rates back toward equilibrium. Ultimately, this dynamic process restores both the wage rate and the level of population to their long-run levels.

If the amount of usable land increases, wages rise and that stimulates higher birthrates. Again, the growth in population continues to lower wage rates until eventually the long-run wage is restored. However, population is permanently higher because the amount of land is greater.

This example brings out that the equilibrium wage is more immune to shocks in the Malthusian system than is the level of population. Indeed, if tastes are stable over time—the Malthusian model, along with George Stigler and myself (1977), assumes *de gustibus non est disputandum*—and if technology does not continue to improve, the equilibrium wage rate remains fixed by the point on the stable supply curve where the typical couple has two surviving children. The Malthusian model does help some in explaining very long-term changes in European wage rates prior to the nineteenth century (Lee 1987b gives a good analysis of the evidence). People evidently married earlier when wages were above the equilibrium level and married later when they were below.

It is ironic that Malthus's first essay on population was published in 1798 at the close of the eighteenth century. Although his system was accepted by many leading economists of the nineteenth century (see John Stuart Mill 1848, Book I, ch. X), events after publication were not kind to the theory. Fertility eventually fell sharply rather than rose as wage rates and per capita incomes continued to advance during much of the nineteenth and twentieth centuries in the United States, Western Europe, and Japan.

The contradiction between the theory and events explains why most economists during the first half of this century showed little interest in explaining long-term trends in income and population. But the subject is too important to remain neglected, and Robert Solow, David Cass, and others developed the neoclassical growth model in the 1950s and early 1960s. This model incorporates two major advances over the Malthusian model. Each person maximizes utility that depends on present and future consumption. More important is the recognition that changes in the capital stock respond to rates of return on investments. Unfortunately, the neoclassical model also takes a sizable step backward from Malthus by assuming that fertility and other dimensions of population growth are independent of wages, incomes, and prices.

I trust that the basic properties of a simple neoclassical model are familiar. What may not be generally appreciated is that despite the different assumptions, the analytic structures of the neoclassical and Malthusian models are quite close and many of their implications are similar. If technology and preferences do not change over time, both models have stable steady-state levels of per capita income. The neoclassical equilibrating mechanism works through changes in the rate of investment, while the Malthusian mechanism works through changes in the rate of population growth. To illustrate, if the capital-labor ratio exceeds its steady-state level, the rate of return on capital is below and the wage rate is above their steady-state levels. In the neoclassical model this discourages investment, which lowers the capital-labor ratio over time (with exogenous population growth). In the Malthusian model this encourages population growth, which also lowers the capital-labor ratio over time (with exogenous investment in capital). We have seen that a shock to population in the Malthusian model has no effect on the level of population or per capita income in the long run. Similarly, in the neoclassical model a shock to the capital stock (perhaps wartime destruction of capital) has no long-run effect on the aggregate capital stock or per capita income.

The persistent growth in per capita incomes during the past two centuries is no easier to explain within the neoclassical framework than within the Malthusian. Of course, the neoclassical model postulates exogenous technological progress to "explain" continuing growth in per capita incomes, but the need to rely on "exogenous" progress is a confession of failure to explain growth within the model. Moreover, the Malthusian model can equally well postulate exogenous progress to "explain" persistent growth.

II. The Family and Economic Growth

After a short while the economics profession became disenchanted with the neoclassical model, presumably because it too did not help in understanding progress. The excitement reflected in hundreds of papers that extended and elaborated this model in the 1950s and 1960s gave way during the past fifteen years to a lack of interest in the analytics of growth that is a little reminiscent of the situation during the first half of the century.

Fortunately, a more relevant growth model is available through combining the best features of the neoclassical and Malthusian models and by adding a focus on investment in knowledge and skills. The neoclassicists are right to emphasize endogenous capital accumulation and utility maximization. Malthusians are right to stress the response of fertility and other components of population growth to changes in the economy, and that these responses can greatly influence economic change.

I will sketch out a modified neoclassical model where parents choose both the number of children and the capital (human or physical) bequeathed to each child. Parental altruism or "love" toward children provides a powerful framework for the analysis of both the quantity and so-called quality of children. Altruism means that the utility of parents depends on the utility of each child. The assumption of altruism is realistic for the vast majority of families, although parent-child interactions are determined also by other motives. Presumably, the altruism per child is negatively related to the number of children, so that an additional child lowers the utility per child to parents in the same way as (please excuse the analogy) an additional car lowers the utility per car.

Such altruism is easily grafted onto the neoclassical utility function by letting parents' utility depend on their own life-cycle consumption and separately on their degree of altruism per child, the number of children, and the utility of each child. This formulation has the important implication that preference for parents' relative to children's consumption (so-called time preference) is not exogenous but rises as the number of children increases.

The resources available to parents from the capital they inherit and labor earnings are spent either on own consumption, on the costs of rearing children, or on transfers to children of human and other capital. Since child rearing is time intensive, the cost of rearing children is positively related to the value of parents' time. Income per capita would rise between the parents' and the child's generations if the total capital bequeathed to each child exceeds the capital inherited by each parent.

Parents choose optimal values of their own consumption, the number of children, and capital transferred to each child while taking into account the cost of rearing children and the dependence of their utility on the utility of children. This analysis has many implications for the behavior of fertility that Robert Barro and I explore elsewhere (see 1987 and 1988). Here I concentrate on a few that alter implications of the neoclassical model about capital accumulation and growth.

If the number of children demanded by the typical family is positively related to the income of parents (the Malthusian assumptions), or at least if it is not strongly negatively related, then this model also has stable steady-state levels of the capital-labor ratio and per capita income. But these steady states depend on variables that change the demand for children.

One example is the consequences of an extended but temporary decline in income and productivity—perhaps due to the disorganization induced by a lengthy depression. In the neoclassical model this has no long-run effect on either per capita or aggregate income. In our modified model an extended decline in productivity can permanently lower *aggregate* income because birthrates may fall when productivity, wages, and interest rates fall. Recall the sharp decline in birthrates during the Great Depression.

Just over a decade age, Barro (1974) showed that a dose of family economics radically alters traditional conclusions about the effects of budget deficits on private savings. For example, deficits to finance social security payments tax future generations to support the elderly. Altruistic parents who leave bequests to their children do not seek an intergeneration redistribution of incomes, so they would increase their bequests to offset the effect on children of future taxes. If these families are common, social security payments and other public expenditures financed by taxes on future generations would not have much effect on private savings. This is the so-called Ricardian equivalence theorem.

A larger dose of family economics gives more radical implications in some respects but also has more conventional implications for the relation between social security and savings. Various comments on Ricardian equivalence emphasize that some families do not leave bequests; I will discuss these families in Section IV. Development economists have long recognized that parents value children who provide support during old age. A social security system that replaces child support of parents with public support raises the net cost of children to parents (not to society) since they are no longer as useful to elderly parents. As a result, a social security system tends to reduce the demand for children. Social security also reduces the demand for children by parents who do not receive support but provide bequests. The net cost of children to these parents also increases when they raise bequests to offset the effect of social security taxes on children.

For reasons given earlier, a lower demand for children raises the capital bequeathed to each child. Therefore, social security and other public transfers between generations would *raise* private savings *per child*, and as a result, raise wage rates and the capital-labor ratio in the next generation. Yet total private savings of the present generations would fall, as in a conventional life-cycle analysis with no bequests, if the decline in fertility exceeds the greater saving for each child.

Consider next an example from tax incidence. A tax on income from capital initially lowers after-tax returns and discourages investment. In the neoclassical model, capital then falls over time until the after-tax rate of return again equals the given rate of time preference. In public finance jargon, a tax on capital would be fully shifted in the long run.

A difficulty with this conclusion is the neoclassical assumption that fertility is fixed, which is especially inappropriate for very long-term changes in incidence. Fertility would fall as capital fell in response to the tax if fertility is positively related to per capita income. A fall in fertility lowers preference for present consumption and raises the demand for investment in each child through the interaction between the quality and quantity of children. Then the equilibrium after-tax rate of return must also fall, and the tax on capital is only partially shifted even in the long run.

The conclusion is more radical if fertility is negatively related to per capita income (for reasons discussed next). Fertility then increases when the stock of capital falls. Since the increase in fertility lowers investment per child, the equilibrium after-tax rate of return would have to increase. That is, we have the paradox that a tax on capital is eventually shifted by more than 100 percent! Let me assure the theorists that this strange result does not violate the second-order conditions.

Does a negative relation between fertility and per capita income imply that children are an "inferior" good (to use the economist's infelicitous language)? The answer is no because the cost of rearing children increases when the capital-labor ratio and per capita income rise since wage rates and the value of parents' time spent on children rise along with the capital-labor ratio. Fertility would fall if the positive effect on fertility of an increase in income is weaker than the negative effect due to the rise in cost. The substitution effect often dominates the income effect in rich countries, for child care in these countries requires considerable time and energy of parents.

If fertility is negatively related to per capita income, an increase in the capital-labor ratio above its steady-state level would reduce fertility and thereby encourage more investment per child. The capital-labor ratio would continue to increase over time if this positive effect on investment dominates the negative effect of a lower rate of return. Consequently, a negative relation between fertility and per capita income can destabilize what is otherwise a stable steady state (see the formal analysis in Robert Tamura 1986).

Demographers have long been aware that fertility eventually declines as a country develops. Less well appreciated (although see the earlier literature by R. R. Nelson 1956; Robert M. Solow 1956, 90–91; S. C. Tsiang 1964; and others on low-level " traps") is that a negative relation between a country's fertility and its income can destabilize a steady-state equilibrium and cause a protracted period of rising per capita incomes. However, although a decline in fertility is an important stimulus in early stages of development, it alone cannot explain sustained growth over a century or longer. In the absence of other forces, a growing economy with neoclassical production functions but without continuing technological progress eventually moves to a stable steady state with low fertility and high per capita incomes.

A promising approach to sustained growth that complements the role of fertility builds on the special properties of education and other learning. The important property for this purpose is that investments in education and other human capital are more productive when past investments are larger. That is to say, accumulation of knowledge and skills in the past eases the acquisition of additional knowledge. The mastery learning concept in education pedagogy uses this property to organize the teaching of mathematics and other subjects to children (see Benjamin S. Bloom 1976). Such a production technology implies that rates of return on investments in human capital may not fall and may even rise as the stock of human capital grows.

Perhaps it was reasonable in Malthus's time to neglect investments in human capital, but there is little excuse for the neglect in neoclassical growth theory. Modern economies spend enormous amounts on education and other training of children, and parents' investments in children are a far more important source of an economy's capital stock than are bequests or the life-cycle accumulation of physical capital. Dale Jorgenson and Barbara Fraumeni (1987) estimate that human capital comprises over 70 percent of the total capital stock in the United States. This estimate may be too low because it does not include the contribution of human capital to output in the household sector (the authors do try to estimate household output). Seventy percent may be higher than the true fraction because it makes no allowance for the contribution of "raw labor" to output. I would guess that the true ratio of human capital to the total capital stock may be as high as 90 percent or as low as 50 percent. Of course, even this lower percentage signifies a large contribution. The neglect of human capital in wealth and income accounts greatly distorts comparisons of savings propensities and the accumulation of wealth.

Only recently have growth models begun to appreciate the potential of the learning-by-having property of human capital for generating sustained growth in per capita incomes (see Paul Romer 1986; Robert E. Lucas Jr. 1988; and Robert G. King and Sergio Rebelo 1986; pioneering earlier work includes Kenneth J. Arrow 1962; Yoram Ben-Porath 1967; Hirofumi Uzawa 1965; and Sherwin Rosen 1976). Kevin M. Murphy and I are developing an analysis that combines such a human capital technology with unskilled labor, physical capital, and endogenous fertility that results from altruism. (See Gary S. Becker 1971, 204, 207–8, for an earlier effort to combine human capital, unskilled labor, and physical capital.) Our model has a "Malthusian" equilibrium where per capita income is constant and low and fertility is high. However, if this equilibrium receives big enough technology and other shocks—good luck may be required—the economy takes off toward a perpetual growth equilibrium with a decline in fertility and increased investment per child. Knowledge continues to grow through its embodiment in additional human capital.

Family economics is critical to the analysis since choices about number of children and investments in each child's human capital help determine whether the economy ends up at a "good" (i.e., growth) equilibrium or at a " bad" (i.e., Malthusian) equilibrium. Obviously, we do not have the full answer to economic growth—public policies, conglomeration effects, and other considerations are surely important—but I do believe that our story contributes a sizable part of the answer.

III. Short and Long Cycles

Let me now turn briefly to the relation between family behavior and cycles in aggregate output and other variables. For centuries marriages, births, and other family behavior have been known to respond to fluctuations in aggregate output and prices. In an early use of regression analysis in the social sciences, G. Udny Yule (1906) demonstrated that English marriages and births in the nineteenth century moved together with the business cycle. Subsequent studies showed that higher-order as well as first births, divorce rates, and possibly the labor force participation of secondary workers all fluctuated procyclically in many countries (see, for example, Becker 1960 and Morris Silver 1965). Birthrates in the United States apparently became countercyclical after many married women entered the labor force. Children are cheaper during recessions because the value of time spent on children by working mothers is low then (see William P. Butz and Michael P. Ward 1979). Investments in education and other human capital are much less procyclical than investments in physical capital also because the forgone value of time spent in school is cheaper during bad times (Linda N. Edwards 1975).

Of course, none of the competing macromodels of business cycles—be they Keynesian, monetarist, neoclassical, or real—rely on family behavior to cause business cycles. However, declining population growth was a major cause of the secular stagnation feared by Alvin H. Hansen (1939) in his presidential address to our association almost fifty years ago. Family behavior may play more than a negligible role even in generating ordinary business cycles. For example, an increase in the labor supply of married women or young people when household work or school becomes less attractive can induce cyclical responses in aggregate output and other variables. Cycles started by shifts in labor supply induce a negative relation between wage rates and aggregate output over business cycles. This would help explain why cyclical fluctuations in real wages appear to be less positively related to cyclical fluctuations in aggregate output than is implied by business cycles models that emphasize the demand side.

Although family behavior presumably has only a small part in the generation of ordinary business cycles, it is likely to be crucial to long cycles in economic activity. Malthus claimed that family choices cause long-term fluctuations in the economy through the lagged effects first of marriages on births and then of births on the size of the labor force (see Maw Lin Lee and David Loschky 1987). Modern demographic analysis generates long cycles in population growth rates through the relation between aggregate fertility and the age distribution, and perhaps also between fertility and the size of a cohort (see, for example, James C. Frauenthal and Kenneth E. Swick 1983 and Ronald Lee 1987a). In our modified Malthus-neoclassical model, family choices cause long cycles not only in population growth, but also in capital, output, and other variables if the elasticity of the degree of altruism per child with respect to the number of children declines as families get larger, a reasonable assumption. Fertility and per capita income then fluctuate in generation-long cycles whenever the economy is disturbed away from the steady state (for a proof, see Jess Benhabib and Kazuo Nishimura 1986).

In the 1920s, the Russian economist Nicholas D. Kondratieff claimed that capitalist economies exhibit long-term fluctuations of about fifty years' duration in output and prices (see Kondratieff 1935). Simon Kuznets (1958) later argued that long-term fluctuations only last about twenty years. If long cycles of the Kondratieff or Kuznets type exist—we will need another 200 years of data to determine whether they do exist or are just a statistical figment of an overactive imagination—they almost certainly will depend on fertility and other family decisions that biologically require a long time to implement.

IV. OVERLAPPING GENERATIONS

The intrinsic risks faced by the elderly, sick, and unemployed are surely no greater in rich countries like Germany and the United States than in poor countries like China and India, nor do these risks rise as a country develops. Yet the first large-scale social security program was introduced by Germany a mere 100 years ago. China, India, and numerous other countries still have only modest programs that exclude many of their old people. We take publicly financed schools for granted, but they were unimportant until the latter half of the nineteenth century. Public and private programs that protect against the consequences of illness and unemployment are even newer and less common than social security and public schools.

Throughout history the risks faced by the elderly, young, sick, and unemployed have been met primarily by the family, not by state transfers, private charity, or private insurance. Children usually cared for elderly or infirm parents, the unemployed looked to their families for temporary support, and parents have spent much time, money, and energy to rear and train their children. Despite the rapid growth of social security payments in the past few decades, almost 20 percent of women aged 65 and over in the United States still live with their children.

The altruism and love of parents, children, spouses, and other relatives have helped protect family members against the hazards of childhood, old age, and other risks. When altruism is insufficient—unfortunately, it often is—what sociologists call social norms frequently emerge that pressure children, parents, spouses, and other relatives into helping out family members in need. In addition, family members use their frequent interaction with one another to raise the level of guilt experienced by a member when he or she does not help out.

The formal analysis of the interaction among overlapping generations began with Paul A. Samuelson's brilliant paper in 1958. This spawned an enormous literature that continues up to the present. Although Samuelson had relevant obiter dicta about social compacts, altruism, and family obligations, his model and that of most of the subsequent literature assumes that each person enters the analysis as a young adult without personal connections to older cohorts. A long review of overlapping generation models in the recent *New Palgrave Dictionary* (see John Geanakopolos 1987) has no discussion whatsoever of familial relations between members of overlapping generations. I claim that the neglect of childhood and of the intimate relations among parents, children, husbands-wives, and other family members misled these studies sometimes into focusing on minor problems and diverted attention away from some important consequences of the overlapping of generations (the discussion in the next few paragraphs draws partly on Becker and Murphy 1988).

One example of the emphasis on unimportant problems is the concern with the plight of older people when there are few durable assets that can finance consumption at old age. In an influential literature on the demand for money, the social role of money is even attributed to a durability that enables older people to finance consumption by selling to the next generation money accumulated when young (see, for example, Thomas Sargent 1987, ch. 7, and Neil Wallace 1980). Yet when anthropologists study simple societies that do not have money or other durable assets, they find that old people finance their consumption mainly by relying for support on children and other kin. Indeed, children have been an important resource and money balances an unimportant resource of the elderly in practically all societies, whether simple or complicated.

General equilibrium theorists are concerned about the continuum of equilibria, inefficiency, and other problems that arise in models where overlapping generations persist indefinitely into the future (see, for example, Geanakopolos 1987 or Timothy J. Kehoe 1987). Although these problems would not completely disappear, I conjecture that they would be much less important if overlapping-generations models incorporated the informal trades and assistance available to parents, children, and other members of the same family.

Ever since Plato's *Republic*, philosophers have worried about whether parents invest sufficiently in the health, skills, and morals of their children. Overlapping-generations models usually neglect childhood and concentrate on savings by young adults and their trades with old adults. The treatment of children by parents not only is so important in its own right, but it also greatly influences the relations between older and younger adults. (Allan Drazen 1978 is one of the few earlier studies that recognizes the importance of investments in children for overlapping-generations models.)

I cannot do more on this occasion than present the bare bones of an analysis of how families respond to the demands of both old age and childhood. The analysis is straightforward when altruistic parents leave bequests to their children. The combination of altruism and bequests eliminates any difficulties in financing the wealth-maximizing investment in children's health, training, and other human capital. For if the marginal rate of return on additional human capital exceeds the rate on assets, both parents and children would be better off with additional capital. Parents can save less to offset the negative effect on their consumption of greater spending on their children's human capital, and they can reduce bequests to offset the effect of lower savings on consumption at old age.

Bequests also partly insulate parents from many risks of old age. The opportunity to draw on bequests provides an annuity-like protection against an usually long life and other risks of old age. For example, parents who live longer than expected reduce bequests to help finance consumption in the additional years. If bequests are not a large part of children's assets, bequests can give elderly parents excellent protection against various hazards, and yet changes in bequests do not have much influence on children's welfare. In effect, children help support their parents in old age, although their support is not fully voluntary.

The analysis is less simple when parents do not leave bequests, perhaps because they are not very altruistic or because they expect their children to be better off than they are. These families tend to underinvest in children and underprotect parents against the hazards of old age because bequests are not available to finance investments and old-age support.

Social norms, feelings of guilt, and similar mechanisms may greatly moderate the degree of underinvestments and underprotection. They can induce even selfish parents to invest in children and selfish children to care for sick or poor parents. Economists neglect concepts like norms and guilt because no one really knows how they evolve. Moreover, sociologists (perhaps I should say "we" sociologists since I am now officially also a sociologist) are too prone to use norms as a deus ex machina to explain behavior that is difficult to explain in other ways. Nevertheless, there can be little doubt that norms and other intangible mechanisms do greatly affect the relations between family members in many societies, although presumably, they do not work as well as bequests in linking generations together.

Parents in richer countries have more resources to spend on children and to protect against the hazards of old age. Why then have public expenditures on both the young and old grown rapidly during the 100 years as Western countries have become richer? One reason is that social norms are weaker in the anonymous urban communities of industrial countries where elderly parents often live far from adult children. A more analytically tractable reason is the high rates of return in modern industrial societies on investments in the health and training of children. Recall my discussion of the role of human capital in economic development. Parents are eager to finance profitable investments in children called for by economic development, as long as they can draw on gifts and bequests that they would give to children. But gifts and bequests would become nil in many families that invest a lot in their children. These families would underinvest in children, particularly when pressure from norms is weak! The growth in public support of schooling and other investments in children as countries develop would then appear to be mainly a response to the positive effect of economic development on the benefits from human capital.

Since families that do not leave bequests are vulnerable to the hazards of old age, it is not difficult to understand why public expenditures on social security and medical care for the elderly have also grown rapidly in industrial countries. However, you may be surprised to find out that public expenditures on the old have not been at the expense of the young. Since 1940 in the United States, the ratio of expenditures per child under age 22 to expenditures per adult age 65 or over has hardly changed. Our analysis that combines investments in human capital with old-age support does explain why expenditures on the old and young grew in tandem. By contrast, the popular view of generation fighting—that public expenditures on the elderly grew rapidly because the old became politically powerful as they became more numerous—cannot explain why expenditures on children grew just as rapidly.

The overlapping-generations framework is also a natural one to consider inequality and the transmission of wealth and poverty across generations. Families help perpetuate inequality because children inherit abilities and other "endowments" from parents. Moreover, parents are the major source of the assets and human capital of children. This enormous influence of the family led my esteemed teacher, Frank H. Knight, to claim that "where the family is the social unit, the inheritance of wealth, culture, educational advantages, and economic opportunities tend toward the progressive increase of inequality" (1935, p. 50).

Abilities and other endowments regress downward from parents to children in successful families where parents earn a lot, and they regress upward in unsuccessful families where parents earn little. The poor underinvest in each child also because they have larger families and less stable marriages. Therefore, children from poorer families tend to earn more than their parents but below the average of their generation, and children from richer families tend to earn less than their parents but above their generation's average.

Earnings depend not only on endowments but also on investments in human capital. Our earlier analysis implies that richer families do not tend to underinvest in their children's human capital because these families leave gifts and bequests. Poorer families do tend to underinvest in children because they are not likely to leave gifts and bequests. The poor underinvest in each child also because they have large families and less stable marriages. Therefore, the relation between the earning of fathers and sons in richer families would depend mainly on the relation between endowments, while the relation between earnings of fathers and sons in poorer families would depend also on the degree of underinvestment in children. Put differently, without offsetting government subsidies to investments in the human capital of poorer children, low earnings would be more persistent across generations than high earnings—the so-called culture of poverty across generations would exceed the culture of privilege.

In every country with data that I have seen—this includes the United States and several European countries (see table 1 in Becker and Nigel Tomes 1986), a few Asian countries, and some Latin American countries (James J. Heckman and Joseph V. Hotz 1986 consider the evidence for Panama)— earnings strongly regress to the mean between fathers and sons. Probably much less than 40 percent of the earnings advantages or disadvantages of fathers pass to sons, and few earnings advantages or disadvantages survive three generations. Evidently, abilities and other endowments that generate earnings are only weakly transmitted from parents to children. This tendency to go from "shirtsleeves to shirtsleeves" in three generations began long before industrialization and government support of education and other human capital. The fourteenth-century Arab historian and philosopher, Ibn Khaldûn, said (I owe this reference to my wife, Guity Nashat), "Prestige is an accident that affects human beings. It comes into being and decays inevitably. . . . It reaches its end in a single family within four successive generations" (1958, p. 279). "As a rule, no dynasty lasts beyond the [span] of three generations" (p. 343).

In all these countries, low earnings as well as high earnings are not strongly transmitted from fathers to sons, and Knight's claim about family life causing growing inequality is inconsistent with the evidence. Still, data for both the United States and England do appear to confirm the implication of our theory that low earnings persist more than high earnings across generations (see W. Stanley Siebert 1987). Of course, *incomes* of the rich regress down more slowly between generations than do their *earnings* because rich children receive gifts and bequests from parents (see Becker and Tomes 1986, table 2).

V. CONCLUDING REMARKS

I was attracted to the family by its obvious importance in all countries, no matter what the economic system or stage of development. People spend much of their time in a dependency relation—toward parents when children and toward grown children in old age—marriage is a crucial step for most people, children absorb time, energy, and money from their parents, divorce often causes economic hardship and mental depression, and so forth. Economic studies of the family are growing at a steady pace and they are influencing the way other social scientists look at this fundamental institution. The economic analysis of family behavior stimulated the development of techniques and prospectives that already has affected many parts of microeconomics, especially agricultural and labor economics, but also the study of industrial organization and preference theory. For example, the treatment of marriage as a sorting of men and women into small "partnerships" through a reasonably efficient marriage market influenced the analysis of how workers and managers are allocated to different firms. Viewing divorce as a joint decision by husbands and wives based largely on information gathered from living together encouraged some studies of employment separations to blur the analytical distinction between quits and layoffs and to emphasize the information about working conditions and productivity gathered from on-the-job experience.

The message of this address, however, is not the importance of the family per se, even though family welfare is the principal goal of a well-run economic system. Nor that analytical techniques developed to understand family choices are valuable in other parts of economics. The message is that family behavior is active, not passive, and endogenous, not exogenous. Families have large effects on the economy, and evolution of the economy greatly changes the structure and decisions of families. I illustrated how families and the economy interact through a discussion of economic growth and other issues in macroeconomics. A heightened awareness of the interaction between economic change and family choices will hasten the incorporation of family life into the mainstream of economics.

NOTES

Presidential address delivered at the one hundredth meeting of the American Economic Association, December 29,1987, Chicago, Illinois.

I received valuable comments from Robert Barro, Edward Prescott, Sherwin Rosen, George Stigler, and Robert Townsend. I was supported by the National Science Foundation under grant no. SES-8520258 and by the National Institute for Child Health and Development, grant no. SSP 1 R37 HD22054. I received useful research assistance from Michael Gibbs.

REFERENCES

Arrow, Kenneth. "The Economic Implications of Learning by Doing." *Review of Economic Studies* 29 (June 1962): 155–73.

Barro, Robert J. "Are Government Bonds Net Wealth?" *Journal of Political Economy* 82 (November/December 1974): 1095–1117.

———, and Gary S. Becker. "Fertility Choice in a Model of Economic Growth." Unpublished paper, Harvard University, 1987.

Becker, Gary S. "An Economic Analysis of Fertility." In *Demographic and Economic Change in Developed Countries*. Princeton: Princeton University Press for the National Bureau of Economic Research, 1960.

———. *Economic Theory*. New York: A. Knopf, 1971.

———. *A Treatise on the Family*. Cambridge, Mass.: Harvard University Press, 1981.

———, and Robert J. Barro. "A Reformulation of the Economic Theory of Fertility." *Quarterly Journal of Economics*. February 1988.

———, and Kevin M. Murphy. "The Family and the State." *Journal of Law and Economics* 31 (April 1988).

———, and Nigel Tomes. "Human Capital and the Rise and Fall of Families." *Journal of Labor Economics* 4 (July 1986): S1–S39.

Ben-Porath, Yoram. "The Production of Human Capital and the Life Cycle of Earnings." *Journal of Political Economy* 4 (August 1967): 352–65.

Benhabib, Jess, and Kazuo Nishimura. "Endogenous Fluctuations in the Barro-Becker Theory of Fertility." New York University, 1986.

Bloom, Benjamin S. *Human Characteristics and School Learning*. New York: McGraw-Hill, 1976.

Butz, William P., and Michael P. Ward. "The Emergency of Countercyclical U.S. Fertility." *American Economic Review* 69 (June 1979): 318–28.

Cass, David. "Optimal Growth in an Aggregative Model of Capital Accumulation." *Review of Economic Studies* 32 (July 1965): 233–40.

Drazen, Allan. "Government Debt, Human Capital, and Bequests in a Life-Cycle Model." *Journal of Political Economy* 86 (June 1978): 505–16.

Edwards, Linda N. "The Economics of Schooling Decisions: Teenage Enrollment Rates." *Journal of Human Resources* 10 (Spring 1975) 155–73.

Frauenthal, James C. and Kenneth E. Swick. "Unit Cycle Oscillations of the Human Population." *Demography* 20 (August 1983): 385–98.

Geanakopolos, John. "Overlapping Generations Model of General Equilibrium." *The New Palgrave Dictionary of Economics*. Vol. 3. London: Macmillan, 1987.

Hansen, Alvin H. "Economic Progress and Declining Population Growth." *American Economic Review* 29 (March 1939): 1–15.

Heckman, James J., and Joseph V. Hotz. "The Sources of Inequality for Males in Panama's Labor Market." *Journal of Human Resources* 21 (fall 1986): 507–42.

Jorgensen, Dale W., and Barbara M. Fraumeni. "The Accumulation of Human and Non-Human Capital, 1948–84." Cambridge, Mass.: Harvard University, 1987.

Kehoe, Timothy J. "Intertemporal General Equilibrium Models." Economic Theory Workshop, University of Chicago, January 1987.

Khaldn, Ibn. *The Muqaddimah.* Vol. 1. Franz Rosenthal, trans. New York: Basic Books, 1958.

King, Robert G., and Sergio Rebelo. "Business Cycles with Endogeneous Growth." Unpublished paper, University of Rochester, 1986.

Knight, Frank H. "The Ethics of Competition." In *The Ethics of Competition and Other Essays.* Chicago: Allen and Unwin, 1935.

Kondratieff, Nicholas D. "The Long Wages in Economic Life." *Review of Economics and Statistics* 17 (May 1935): 105–15.

Kuznets, Simon. "Long Swings in the Growth of Population and in Related Economic Variables." *Proceedings of the American Philosophical Society* 102 (1958) 25–52.

Lee, Maw Lin, and David Loschky. "Malthusian Population Oscillations." *Economic Journal* 97 (September 1987): 737–39.

Lee, Ronald D. (1987a). "Population Cycles." In *The New Palgrave Dictionary of Economics* Vol. 3. London: Macmillan, 1987.

——— (1987b). "Population Dynamics of Humans and Other Animals." *Demography* 24 (November 1987): 443–67.

Lucas, Robert E. Jr. "On the Mechanics of Economic Development." *Journal of Monetary Economics* 19 (1988).

Malthus, Thomas Robert. *An Essay on Population.* London: J. M. Deut, 1933.

Michael, Robert T., Victor Fuchs, and Sharon R. Scott. "Changes in the Propensity to Live Alone: 1950–1976." *Demography* 17 (February 1980): 39–56.

Mill, John Stuart. *Principles of Economics.* London, 1848.

Nelson, Richard R. "A Theory of the Low-Level Equilibrium Trap." *American Economic Review* 46 (December 1956): 894–908.

Romer, Paul. "Increasing Returns and Long-Run Growth." *Journal of Political Economy* 94 (February 1986): 1000–1037.

Rosen, Sherwin. "A Theory of Life Earnings." *Journal of Political Economy* 84 (August 1976): 545–568.

Samuelson, Paul A. "An Exact Consumption-Loan Model of Interest with or without the Social Contrivance of Money." *Journal of Political Economy* 66 (December 1958): 467–82.

Sargent, Thomas. *Dynamic Macroeconomic Theory.* Cambridge, Mass.: Harvard University Press, 1987.

Siebert, W. Stanley. "Inequality of Opportunity: An Analysis Based on the Microeconomics of the Family." In R. Drago and R. Perlman, eds., *Microeconomic Issues in Labor Economics: New Approaches.* Brighton, U. K.: Wheatsheaf Books, 1987.

Silver, Morris. "Births, Marriages, and Business Cycles in the United States." *Journal of Political Economy* 73 (June 1965): 237–55.

Solow, Robert M. "A Contribution to the Theory of Economic Growth." *Quarterly Journal of Economics* 70 (February 1956): 65–94.

Stigler, George J., and Gary S. Becker. "De Gustibus Non Est Disputandum." *American Economic Review* 67 (March 1977): 76–90.

Tamura, Robert. "The Existence of Multiple Steady States in One Sector Growth Models with Intergenerational Altruism." Unpublished paper, University of Chicago, 1986.

Tsiang, S. C. "A Model of Economic Growth in Rostovian Stages." *Econometrica* 32 (October 1964): 619–48.

Uzawa, Hirofumi. "Optimal Technical Change in an Aggregative Model of Economic Growth." *International Economic Review* 6 (January 1965): 18–31.

Wallace, Neil. "The Overlapping-Generations Model of Fiat Money." In J. H. Kareken and N. Wallace, eds., *Models of Monetary Economics*. Minneapolis: Federal Reserve Bank of Minneapolis, 1980.

Yule, G. Udny. "On the Changes in the Marriage- and Birth-Rates in England and Wales During the Past Half Century: With an Inquiry as to Their Probable Causes." *Journal of the Royal Statistical Society* 69 (March 1906): 88–132.

THE DIVISION OF LABOR, COORDINATION COSTS, AND KNOWLEDGE

Gary S. Becker
Kevin M. Murphy

· 25 ·

This paper considers specialization and the division of labor. A more extensive division of labor raises productivity because returns to the time spent on tasks are usually greater to workers who concentrate on a narrower range of skills. The traditional discussion of the division of labor emphasizes the limitations to specialization imposed by the extent of the market. We claim that the degree of specialization is more often determined by other considerations. Especially emphasized are various costs of "coordinating" specialized workers who perform complementary tasks, and the amount of general knowledge available.

I. INTRODUCTION

Adam Smith begins his study of the wealth of nations (1965) with three chapters on the causes and consequences of the division of labor among workers. His very first sentence claims that, "The greatest improvement in the productive powers of labor, and the greater part of the skill, dexterity, and judgement with which it is anywhere directed or applied, seem to have been the effects of the division of labor." A little later he adds that, "It is the

First published in the *Quarterly Journal of Economics* 107, no. 4 (November 1992): 1137–60. Reprinted by permission.

great multiplication of the productions of all the different arts, in consequence of the division of labor, which occasions, in a well-governed society, that universal opulence which extends itself to the lowest ranks of the people" (p. 11).

We believe that the priority Smith gives to the division of labor among workers is an enormous insight. But we differ with his claim, followed by many later economists, that the degree of specialization is limited mainly by the extent of the market. Specialization and the division of labor are also influenced by several other factors that often are far more significant than the extent of the market.

A variable of great importance is the cost of combining specialized workers. Modern work on principal-agent conflicts, free riding, and the difficulties of communication implies that the cost of coordinating a group of complementary specialized workers grows as the number of specialists increases.

The productivity of specialists at particular tasks depends on how much knowledge they have. The dependence of specialization on the knowledge available ties the division of labor to economic progress since progress depends on the growth in human capital and technologies.

The contribution of this paper is to show how specialization and the division of labor depend on coordination costs, and also on the amount and extent of knowledge. We explore implications of these relations for economic progress, industrial organization, and the activities of workers.

Section II develops a simple model of specialization among complementary tasks that links the division of labor to coordination costs, knowledge, and the extent of the market. Sections III, IV, and V then separately consider in greater detail coordination costs, human capital, and market size. Section VI models economic growth through endogenous increases over time in both human capital and the division of labor.

Section VII shifts the focus from the division of labor among tasks needed to produce one good to that between workers who contribute to current consumption, and teachers who engage in roundabout production by raising the human capital of others. In an efficient allocation, teachers have more human capital than workers, and teachers who contribute to the production of consumer goods in the more distant future have greater human capital than teachers engaged in less roundabout production.

A recent paper by Yang and Borland (1991) also relates the division of labor to "transactions" costs and learning through specialization. However, since they do not consider how general knowledge affects the division of labor, they have a very different interpretation of the relation between specialization and economic progress.

II. Division of Labor among Tasks

We follow Smith in recognizing that a very large number of tasks and processes are combined to produce even the most commonplace goods, such as pins or nails. All workers perform many tasks that could be refined into numerous distinct subtasks. For example, labor economics is a specialized field, but some economists concentrate on labor supply, others only consider the labor supply of married women, and others are narrower still, as they analyze the labor supply of young black mothers on welfare. Even finer labor specialties would emerge under appropriate conditions and incentives.

To model the unlimited divisibility of tasks, we assume that a continuum of tasks along a unit interval must be performed to produce the only good (Y) in the economy. "Must be performed" is modeled by the Leontief production function,

$$Y = \min_{0 \leq s \leq 1} Y(s), \qquad (1)$$

although much weaker assumptions about the complementarity among tasks would yield similar results about the division of labor. The rate of production from the sth task $(Y(s))$ equals the product of the working time devoted to s $(T_w(s))$ and the productivity of each hour $(E(s))$:

$$Y(s) = E(s)T_w(s). \qquad (2)$$

A worker who does not specialize and performs all the tasks himself allocates his working time and investments in specific human capital among tasks to maximize the common output on each one. However, it is possible for workers to do better by specializing in subsets of the tasks, and then combining their outputs with that of other workers who specialize in other tasks. The increasing returns from concentrating on a narrower set of tasks raises the productivity of a specialist above that of a jack-of-all-trades. For example, a doctor who specializes in surgery is more productive than one who performs an occasional operation because surgical skills are honed by operating, and because the specialist has greater incentive to invest in surgical knowledge.

We call a "team" a group of workers who cooperate to produce Y by performing different tasks and functions. They can be either part of the same firm, or they can engage in transactions across different firms. "Cooperation" and "team" should not be taken to signify that team members have the same goals or do not have conflicting interests, for conflicts among members are an important consideration in our analysis.

Instead of assuming that workers have intrinsic comparative advantages at different tasks (as in the Roy model [1951]), we follow Murphy (1986), Becker (1991, Chapter 2), and Smith too (1965) in assuming that workers are intrinsically identical. Specialization is what produces most comparative advantages; they do not arise at birth or in childhood. Although intrinsic differences are not negligible, we have no doubt—nor did Smith—that produced differences among workers are far more important.

Since the distribution of s does not have a natural metric, it is innocuous for our purposes to assume that all tasks are equally difficult and have the same degree of interdependence with other tasks. Therefore, each of the intrinsically identical members of an efficient team concentrates on an equal set of tasks, $w = 1/n$, where n is the team size. Output on each task depends on the size of the set and also on the general knowledge (H) available:

$$Y = Y(H,w), Y_h > 0, Y_w < 0. \qquad (3)$$

Increasing returns to specialization is captured by the assumption that $Y_w < 0$, for otherwise there is no gain from specialization.

To illustrate the process with a specific example, assume that

$$E(s) = dH^\gamma T_h^\theta(s), \qquad (4)$$

where $\theta > 0$ determines the marginal productivity of T_h, the time devoted to acquiring task-specific skills. General knowledge (H) is assumed to raise the productivity of the time spent investing in skills ($\gamma > 0$). The total time devoted to the sth skill is $T(s)$, so

$$T_h(s) + T_w(s) = T(s). \qquad (5)$$

Time is allocated between "investing" (T_h) and "working" (T_w) to maximize output, which implies that

$$Y(s) = A(\theta)H^\gamma T(s)^{1+\theta}, \qquad (6)$$

where $A = d\theta^\theta (1 + \theta)^{-(1+\theta)}$.

If each person allocates one unit of working time uniformly among a set $w = 1/n$ of tasks, then $T(s)w = T(s)(1/n) = 1$. Substitution into equation (6) then gives output on each task as a function of team size:

$$Y = AH^\gamma n^{1+\theta}. \qquad (7)$$

Output per team member equals

$$y = \frac{Y}{n} = B(H,n) = AH^\gamma n^\theta. \qquad (8)$$

Clearly, B rises with the size of the team as long as $\theta > 0$; that is as long as investments in task-specific skills have a positive marginal productivity.

This example can be generalized to include learning by doing and other considerations. But it would still retain the implication that per capita output grows with team size, so the gains from specialization are limited only by the extent of the market. If N people in a market could work with each other, equation (8) implies that output per person is maximized when $n = N$: when everyone in the market becomes part of the same team. Since each member specializes in tasks of width $w = 1/N$, the division of labor is then limited only by N, market size.

Sometimes the division of labor is limited by the extent of the market, but more frequently in the modern world it is limited by other forces. Our analysis will place the extent of the market in proper perspective by considering it along with other forces that affect the degree of specialization.

Conflict among members generally grows with the size of a team because members have greater incentives to shirk when they get a smaller share of the output (see, e.g., Holmstrom [1982]). Moreover, efforts to extract rents by "holding up" other members also grows as the number of members performing complementary tasks increases (see Chari and Jones [1991]). Further, the chances of a breakdown in production due to poor coordination of the tasks and functions performed by different members, or to communication of misleading information among members, also tends to expand as the number of separate specialists grows. In addition, coordination costs depend on whether workers trust each other, whether contracts are enforced, and whether governments maintain stable and effective laws.

Principal-agent conflicts, hold-up problems, and breakdowns in supply and communication all tend to grow as the degree of specialization increases. We call these problems part of the cost of "coordinating" specialists, and assume that the total coordination cost per member (C) depends on n (or w):

$$C = C(n), \qquad C_n > 0. \qquad (9)$$

Net output per team member (y) is the difference between benefits and costs:

$$y = B - C = B(H,n) - C(n), \qquad B_n > 0, C_n > 0. \qquad (10)$$

If B were independent of n, autarky or one-member "teams" are efficient as long as C rises with n. If C were independent of n, the division of labor is limited only by N, the extent of the market, as long as B rises with n. With both $B_n > 0$ and $C_n > 0$, an efficient team generally has more than one member and less than all workers in the market. The efficient amount of specialization is obtained by differentiating equation (10) with respect to n to get the first-order condition:

$$B_n \geq C_n, \tag{11}$$

where $B_{nn} - C_{nn} < 0$ is the second-order condition, and we assume that $B_n > C_n$ for small n. If $B_n > C_n$ for all $n \leq N$, the division of labor would be limited only by the extent of the market; otherwise, the optimal $n^* < N$ is found where $B_n = C_n$. The efficient division of labor is then limited by coordination costs, not by market size.

The rest of the paper assumes that actual teams are efficient and maximize income per member. We believe that this is a good approximation in competitive product and labor markets, although competition may not be sufficient to achieve efficient teams when members are in different firms. Still, contractual arrangements and buyouts can offset locational and other "externalities" across firms, and would limit the discrepancies between actual and efficient teams.

III. Coordination Costs

A few examples might help clarify the relation between specialization and coordination costs. Most pediatricians in a city, or even in a single HMO, do not specialize in particular childhood diseases. No doubt they would learn more about a disease through specialization, but the additional knowledge would require greater expenses in coordinating their care with that of other pediatricians. For parents often do not know what is wrong with their children, and would need to see several pediatricians to get adequate care if each were highly specialized. Yet we would expect to find, and do observe, more specialization in childhood diseases that require extensive knowledge to detect and treat, such as liver diseases and cancers.

If each historian specialized in the events of only a few years, they would become more expert on developments during these shorter time periods. But since events over a few years are not isolated from those in prior and subsequent years, each one would then have to coordinate his research with that of several other specialists. Such coordination costs can be greatly reduced by specialization in larger and more self-contained periods.

Economists and lawyers working on the relation between law and economics can coordinate their research, but coordination costs are reduced when economists also become lawyers or lawyers also become economists, as with the increasing number of persons who take advanced degrees in both law and economics. Yet it is not surprising that joint degrees are more common in law and economics than in health economics, since the investment required for a medical degree is much greater than for a law degree.

The family in most traditional societies has an extensive division of labor between husbands, wives, children, and sometimes other kin. Extensive specialization was made easier by the altruism and caring among family members. These lowered coordination costs by reducing the tendency for members to shirk and try to extract greater shares of their family's production (see the discussion in Becker [1991, Chapter 2]).

A rather enormous literature has studied the comprehensive division of labor found in insect colonies. Although genetically based, the degree of specialization does respond to changes in the environment. For example, the division of labor by age among honeybees is less extensive in smaller colonies—a measure of the extent of the market. The division of labor among bees also responds to the spatial organization of colonies, the demands of brood rearing, difficulties of communicating food sources, and other determinants that often can reasonably be considered to be "coordination" costs (see Winston [1987, pp. 101–7]).

An analysis of the cost of coordinating specialized tasks and functions provides insights into many aspects of the organization of firms and industries. Specialized members of a team who are employed by the same firm get coordinated by the rules of the firm, whereas specialists who are employed by different firms have their activities coordinated by contracts and other agreements that govern transactions across firms. Companies that cut the material for a dress manufacturer or supply car doors to General Motors are part of the "teams" producing particular dresses or General Motors cars. In market economies of the modern era, even firms involved in producing the simplest goods, such as pencils, use many downstream and upstream firms to produce these goods, so that modern teams are very large.

Companies are less "vertically" integrated when it is cheaper to coordinate specialized team members through market transactions. This is why companies are more specialized when they can economize on transactions costs by locating near each other—as the computer industry locates in Silicon Valley, the United States clothing industry was once concentrated on the West Side of Manhattan, and much of the small arms industry during the mid–nineteenth century squeezed into a small area of Birmingham (see Allen [1929]).

An important function of entrepreneurs is to coordinate different types of labor and capital: economists like John Bates Clark (1899) believed that this is their main function. Economic systems that encourage entrepreneurship would have lower costs of coordination, and presumably a more widespread division of labor among workers and firms. Since centrally planned economies throttle entrepreneurship as well as weaken the capacity of markets to coordinate transactions, workers and firms should be less specialized in these economies than in market economies. Unfortunately, there is no systematic evidence on the degree of specialization among workers in the formerly communist economies of Eastern Europe, although there is abundant evidence that firms were large and carried vertical integration to ridiculous extremes, or so it appears in comparisons with market economies.

In a stimulating article many years ago, Hayek (1945) stressed the importance to an economy of coordinating efficiently the specialized knowledge of different participants: "the problem of a rational economic order is . . . the utilization of knowledge which is not given to anyone in its totality," and "Through [the price system] not only a division of labor but also a coordinated utilization of resources based on an equally divided knowledge has become possible." Hayek's insight is that the cost of coordinating specialized workers is smaller, and hence the division of labor is greater, in economies that make effective use of prices and markets to coordinate tasks and skills across firms.

Hayek did not emphasize an even more significant implication of his analysis, although he must have been aware of it. The specialized knowledge at the command of workers is not simply given, for the knowledge acquired depends on incentives. Centrally planned and other economies that do not make effective use of markets and prices raise coordination costs, and thereby reduce incentives for investments in specialized knowledge.

IV. Knowledge and Specialization

The division of labor and specialization both within and between countries increased enormously during the past several centuries as much of the world became vastly richer. Sixteenth-century European cities had perhaps a few hundred occupations, whereas a telephone directory for even a small American city now lists thousands of specialized services. Probably no more than 15 percent of physicians in the nineteenth century were specialists—neither general practitioners nor pediatricians—while in recent years over 75 percent of United States physicians specialize.[1] The first three economic journals started in the United States were general-purpose journals—the Quarterly Journal of Economics in 1886, the Journal of Political Economy in 1892, and the American Economic Review in 1911—whereas most of the many journals established in recent years are highly specialized: the Journal of Applied Econometrics, the Journal of Legal Studies, and the Journal of Economic Demography are a few examples.

Engineers of the early nineteenth century were not highly specialized. But the growth of industries based on new technologies and greater knowledge of science during the nineteenth and twentieth centuries led to many engineering specialties. The British Institute of Civil Engineering started in

1818; the mechanical engineers started their own society in 1847; the electrical engineers in 1871; the automobile engineers in 1906; and so on until chemical and other specialized societies emerged during the past 70 years (see Buchanan [1989]).

The engineering, medical, and economics examples illustrate that much of the growth in specialization over time has been due to an extraordinary growth in knowledge. We assume as in equation (8) that an increase in the knowledge embodied in the human capital of workers not only raises the average product per team member, but also raises the marginal product of a larger team:

$$\frac{\partial}{\partial H}\left(\frac{\partial B}{\partial n}\right) = B_{nh} > 0. \tag{12}$$

The presumption built into equation (4) is that general knowledge is usually complementary with investments in task-specific knowledge.

By differentiating the first-order condition (11) that maximizes income per worker with respect to H, one gets

$$\frac{dn^*}{dH} = \frac{B_{nh}}{C_{nn} - B_{nn}} > 0, \tag{13}$$

where $B_{nn} - C_{nn} < 0$ is the second-order condition. The inequality in (12) signs these derivatives, and it is necessary if our model is to explain why economic development and the growth in knowledge raise specialization and the division of labor.

Equation (13) indicates that teams get larger and workers become more specialized and expert over a smaller range of skills as human capital and technological knowledge grow. Adam Smith recognizes the relation between specialization and knowledge when he states that the division of labor "is generally carried further in those countries which enjoy the highest degree of industry and improvement." (1965, p. 5). However, in his discussion the causation went from the division of labor to greater knowledge, while in ours it also goes from greater general knowledge to a more extensive division of labor and greater task-specific knowledge.

The "jack-of-all-trades'" is less useful than the specialist in economies with advanced technologies and an extensive human capital base. Although workers in modern economies have considerable knowledge of principles and have access to complicated technologies, a typical worker also commands a very much smaller share of the total knowledge used by the economy than do workers in simpler and more backward economies.

It is the extensive cooperation among highly specialized workers that enables advanced economies to utilize a vast amount of knowledge. This is why Hayek's emphasis on the role of prices and markets in combining efficiently the specialized knowledge of different workers is so important in appreciating the performance of rich and complex economies.

An "expert" has been facetiously defined as "someone who knows more and more about less and less." Highly specialized workers are surely experts in what they do, and yet know very little about the many other skills found in a complex economy. Modern expertise comes partly at the expense of narrowness, and of ignorance about what other people do.

Equation (12) also helps determine how workers with different knowledge get allocated to different sectors. The costs involved in "coordinating" specialists surely differ greatly among sectors; for example, costs are relatively low in dense urban communities, and in industries where suppliers and downstream firms locate near each other and communicate easily. The effects of higher coordination costs on specialization and the division of labor are exacerbated by the optimal allocation of workers among sectors.

An efficient allocation "assigns" workers whose productivity is least affected by coordination costs to the high-cost sectors. This implies that workers with lower human capital would be assigned to the high-cost sectors if greater coordination costs lower the marginal product of human capital (see Becker [1991, Appendix]). The first-order condition for n and the envelope theorem show that this is the case since

$$\frac{\partial^2 y}{\partial H \partial \lambda} = \frac{\partial(B_h)}{\partial \lambda} = B_{hn} \frac{\partial n^*}{d\lambda} < 0, \tag{14}$$

where λ is a coordination-cost-raising parameter, with $c_{n\lambda} > 0$, $B_{hn} > 0$ by equation (13), and $\partial n^*/\partial \lambda$ is clearly < 0. This analysis explains, among other things, why earnings are usually higher in large cities even after adjusting for observable measures of human capital—such as years of schooling and experience (see, e.g., Fuchs [1967])—because unobserved human capital is also attracted to cities by the lower coordination costs.

V. Extent of the Market

Adam Smith recognized that specialization had costs as well as benefits since it made workers "stupid" and "ignorant."[2] But Smith forcefully stated his belief that the division of labor is limited mainly by the extent of the market. The modern literature on specialization within a profession (Baumgardner 1988), increasing returns and specialization in international trade (Krugman 1987), the degree of brand proliferation (Lancaster 1975), and on the economic gains from population growth (e.g., Simon [1977] and Locay [1990]) has followed this emphasis on the limitations to the division of labor imposed by the extent of the market.

In our formulation also, the division of labor is limited by market size when n^*, the optimal number of team members, is greater than or equal to N, the number of workers in the market. In that case, each worker specializes in different skills, so that each has some monopoly power ex post (see Gros [1987]) and Baumgardner [1988]). This may well describe the position of many specialists in small towns and rural areas.

However, every reasonably large metropolitan area has several, often many, persons who have essentially the same specialized skills and compete in the same market. Pediatricians in the same HMO or psychiatrists who work out of a Psychoanalytic Institute have closely related skills and seek patients in the same geographic market. Any publisher in a major city has access to many copy editors and translators with very similar skills.

The division of labor cannot be limited mainly by the extent of the market when many specialists provide essentially the same skills. Our claim is that instead it is usually limited by the costs of coordinating workers with different specialties, as in the examples discussed in Section III.

We recognize that it is possible to reinterpret our examples by emphasizing quality differences among specialists who only appear to have the same skills, or by claiming they are in separate local markets. By the same token, however, the illustrations provided by Smith and others to support the emphasis on the extent of the market can often be reinterpreted in terms of coordination costs. For example, the division of labor may be greater in cities than in small towns not because markets are larger in cities, but because it is easier to coordinate specialists in more densely populated areas.

There even seems to be a problem with Smith's justly famous example of a pin factory, where workers specialize in various functions, including drawing out, straightening, and cutting the wire. Why didn't the several factories that made pins in Smith's England combine their activities, get a larger scale and market, and specialize more within each factory? If the answer is that the cost of combining these factories exceeded the gain from a greater division of labor, then specialization was limited by these costs of "coordination," not by the extent of the market.[3] Again, the answer may be that the pins were of very different qualities, or that each factory catered to a separate local market, although pins were cheap to ship and Smith does not mention the quality of pins.

Perhaps the most significant difference between our approach and that based on market size lies in the divergent interpretations of the enormous growth in specialization as countries develop. We claim that the huge increase in scientific and other knowledge and decline in coordination costs raised the benefits from greater specialization. The alternative view suggested by Smith's approach is that declines in transportation costs raised the effective size of markets. Surely both sets of forces were operating, although the expansion in knowledge and decline in coordination costs seem by far to be the more fundamental forces. Indeed, some of the growth in markets was not even exogenous, but rather the search for larger markets was induced by the increase in knowledge and decline in coordination costs that raised the gain from larger teams with more specialized members.

VI. THE GROWTH IN SPECIALIZATION AND KNOWLEDGE

However, the growth in knowledge also is not exogenous, for it depends on investments in new technologies, basic research, and human capital. The incentive to invest in knowledge depends partly on the degree of specialization and the level of task-specific skills. In other words, there is not a one-way correlation between knowledge and the division of labor, but mutual determination.

To show in a simple way the interaction between the division of labor, the accumulation of knowledge, and economic growth, we consider the functional form given by equation (8) after netting out a constant elasticity coordination cost function:

$$y_t = A_t H_t^\gamma n_t^\theta - \lambda_t n_t^\beta. \tag{15}$$

The first-order condition for optimal n implies that

$$n_t^* = \left(\frac{\theta}{\beta\lambda_t}\right)^{1/(\beta-\theta)} A_t^{1/(\beta-\theta)} H_t^{\gamma/(\beta-\theta)}, \tag{16}$$

where $\beta > \theta > 0$ is the second-order condition. Replacing n in equation (15) by the right-hand side of equation (16) gives optimal output as a function of general knowledge and various parameters:

$$y_t^* = k_t A_t^{\beta/(\beta-\theta)} H_t^{\gamma\beta/(\beta-\theta)}, \tag{17}$$

with

$$k_t = \lambda_t^{-\theta/(\beta-\theta)} \left[\left(\frac{\theta}{\beta}\right)^{\theta/(\beta-\theta)} - \left(\frac{\theta}{\beta}\right)^{\beta/(\beta-\theta)}\right] > 0. \tag{18}$$

Equation (17) divides the change in per capita income into the growth in human capital (H), the growth in technology (A), and the decline in coordination costs (λ):

$$\frac{d\log y}{dt} = \frac{\gamma\beta}{\beta - \theta}\frac{d\log H}{dt} + \frac{\beta}{\beta - \theta}\frac{d\log A}{dt} - \frac{\theta}{\beta - \theta}\frac{d\log \lambda}{dt}. \quad (19)$$

There is not a separate entry for coordination costs in the usual growth accounting calculus, so $-(\theta/\beta - \theta)$ ($d \log \lambda/dt$) would be considered part of the "residual" along with the effects of the growth in A, and some of the effects of changes in H.

To endogenize the accumulation of human capital, we consider a simple one-sector model where the human capital of period $t + 1$ is just the unconsumed output of period t (the next section considers a separate human capital sector):

$$\left.\begin{aligned} H_{t+1} &= y_t - c_t \\ &= A_t H_t^\gamma n_t^\theta - \lambda_t n_t^\beta - c_t \end{aligned}\right\}, \quad (20)$$

where c_t is consumption in t.

If $y < 1$, diminishing returns to the accumulation of knowledge discourage further investment as this stock of knowledge grows. Admittedly, knowledge is not subject to diminishing returns in the same obvious way as is physical capital because greater knowledge raises the productivity of further investment in knowledge. However, as knowledge continues to grow, limited human capacities tend to make it harder to pack more knowledge into a person without running into diminishing returns. This is why $y < 1$ seems to be a plausible assumption.

Autonomous technological progress in the neoclassical model offsets the diminishing returns to a higher capital-labor ratio. In our model the induced expansion in the division of labor as human capital grows raises the marginal product of additional knowledge. Equation (17) shows that the total elasticity of output with respect to human capital exceeds γ since $\beta > \beta - \theta$. The reason is that an increase in H has an indirect effect on y through the induced increase in n. This indirect effect is stronger the larger θ is relative to β: the bigger is n's effect on the productivity of specialized production compared with its effect on coordination costs. As it were, greater specialization enables workers to absorb knowledge more easily, which offsets to some extent the tendency toward diminishing returns from the accumulation of knowledge.

The model is completed with a conventional separable utility function defined over consumption into the indefinite future:

$$U = \frac{1}{\sigma}\sum_{t=0}^{\infty}\alpha^t c_t^\sigma, \quad \text{with } \sigma < 1. \quad (21)$$

Present consumption is transformed into future consumption through the production of human capital. If the rate of return on investment in human capital is denoted by r, the first-order conditions for optimal consumption over time are

$$\alpha(c_{t+1}/c_t)^{1-\sigma} = R_t = 1 + r_t, \qquad t = 0, 1, \ldots. \qquad (22)$$

With the given inherited knowledge stock, H_0, the first-order conditions in equations (16) and (22), and the production function in equation (15) determine the optimal path over time of c, H, and y. These variables converge to constant values at a steady state if the rate of return continues to fall without limit as capital grows, they converge to a steady-state growth path if the rate of return becomes independent of the capital stock, and they grow at increasing rates if the rate of return rises as capital grows.

Since a higher H_{t+1} means equally lower c_t (given y_t), the transformation between c_{t-1} and c_t gives the rate of return on changes in H_t. By the envelope theorem this equals the derivative of y^* in equation (17) with respect to H:

$$R_t = -\frac{dy_{t+1}}{dc_t} = \frac{dy_{t+1}}{dH_{t+1}} = \frac{\beta\gamma}{\beta-\theta} k_t A_t^{\beta/(\beta-\theta)} H_t^{[\beta\gamma/(\beta-\theta)]-1}, \qquad (23)$$

where k is defined in equation (20).

The rate of return falls, is constant, or rises with higher H, as $\beta\gamma \lessgtr \beta - \theta$. If $\beta\gamma = \beta - \theta$, and A and λ are constant over time, steady-state growth in y, H, and c starts from any initial H_0 at a rate equal to

$$1 + g = \frac{c_{t+1}}{c_t} = \frac{y_{t+1}}{y_t} = \frac{H_{t+1}}{H_t} = (R\alpha^{-1})^{1/1-\sigma}\delta. \qquad (24)$$

If $\beta\gamma < \beta - \theta$, and A is constant, the economy converges to a stationary state ($g = 0$). If $\beta\gamma < \beta - \theta$, and A is constant, rates of growth in Y, H, and c all increase over time. In Yang and Borland's model (1991) the growth rate must eventually decline because gains from a greater division of labor are eventually exhausted.

Equations (16) and (24) show that output per capita, knowledge, and the division of labor all grow together over time. Growth in these variables is interdependent, as causation runs from knowledge to the division of labor and output, as well as from the division of labor to knowledge and output. The equilibrium rate of growth at all moments is Pareto optimal since there are no externalities in the model.

Rates of growth in output and human capital are higher when the level of technology (A) is greater. These growth rates may be quite responsive to better technology because the induced expansion in specialization raises the exponent of A to $\beta/\beta - \theta > 1$.

Equations (18) and (23) show that rates of return on investments in knowledge depend on the cost of coordinating specialized workers (λ). Countries with lower coordination costs due to stabler and more efficient laws, or other reasons, not only have larger outputs, but they also tend to grow faster because lower costs stimulate investments in knowledge by raising the advantages of a more extensive division of labor.

VII. THE DIVISION OF LABOR BETWEEN SECTORS: TEACHERS AND WORKERS

Workers specialize in the production of different goods as well as in different tasks required to produce a single good. For example, an experienced steel-worker who has accumulated considerable skill at firing blast furnaces would be much less productive in the computer software industry. The discussion in previous sections of the advantages from specialization at tasks implies that workers become specialized to particular sectors partly because they become skilled at the tasks specific to a sector.

In discussing specialization across sectors, we continue to assume that all workers are identical to start, but they become different by investing in different skills at particular tasks. Each good is produced by teams that perform a very large number of specialized complementary tasks, where the productivity of each team depends on parameters of the relevant production function and the human capital of team members.

To analyze specialization across sectors, we consider the production function in each sector that has optimized out the endogenous team size. Output depends explicitly only on the human capital of team members, but implicitly it also depends on coordination costs and other parameters that determine specialization and the division of labor. The marginal products of human capital partly depend on the benefit and cost parameters that determine the optimal division of labor in each sector. Differences across sectors in these marginal products lead to sectoral differences in the human capital per worker. There is abundant evidence that years of schooling per worker differ greatly among industries (see Gill [1989] and Mincer and Higuchi [1988]).

Given our emphasis on the relation between the division of labor, the accumulation of knowledge, and economic progress, the discussion of specialization across sectors concentrates on differences between the consumption and investment sectors. We drop the assumption of Section VI that human capital is simply unspent consumer goods, and introduce more-realistic assumptions about the way human capital is produced.

To simplify the presentation, we consider only a special case of the production function for consumer goods in equation (17): $\beta\gamma = \beta - \theta$, and A and k are both normalized to unity. Therefore,

$$C_t = N_{ct}H_{ct}. \tag{25}$$

The term H_{ct} refers to the human capital of each person in the consumption sector in period t, N_{ct} is the number of these persons—we call this the number of "workers" in period t—and C_t is the aggregate output of consumer goods.

All persons who help produce human capital are called "teachers." We assume that human capital lasts for only one period, and that teachers in period t produce the human capital of both workers and teachers in period, or "cohort," $t + 1$. All persons in each cohort spend their "youthful" time as students acquiring the human capital that prepares them to become workers or teachers when they become adults. The human capital acquired by a student depends on the human capital of her teachers, and the number of teachers per student.

The human capital acquired by students is assumed to be proportional to the human capital of teachers (H_T), where the factor of proportionality depends on the number of teachers per student (τ):

$$H_{t+1} = F(\tau_t)H_{Tt}, \qquad F' > 0, F'' < 0, \tag{26}$$

where we shall show that ϵ, the elasticity of F with respect to τ, must fall as τ increases. Since this is a reduced form, H_T is the human capital of each teacher in a human capital production "team," and τ is the number of students per member of each team.

The assumption $F' > 0$ means that an increase in "class size"—a decrease in τ—reduces the human capital acquired by each student. This relation may not hold for all values of τ, but obviously it pays to economize on teachers when fewer teachers do not lower the human capital produced per student. Although many empirical studies do not find that larger classes reduce the learning of students (see the review in Hanushek [1989]), a good recent study by Card and Krueger (1990) finds that workers earn more if they went to schools with smaller classes. Moreover, an experiment conducted by Tennessee that randomly assigned students to classes of different sizes also found that smaller classes improved performance (see Finn and Achilles [1990]).

It is somewhat surprising that the concavity of F and the assumption that output in both the consumption and human capital sectors are proportional to the human capital of persons employed in each sector do not imply that students who prepare for different sectors acquire the same amount of human capital. Instead, the production functions in equations (25) and (26) imply a finely calibrated inequality between the human capital of workers and teachers in *efficient* allocations of persons and investments.

The teachers of workers in period j were students in period $j - 1$, their teachers were students in $j - 2$, and so on, continuing backward until one comes to the persons in the initial period who indirectly taught the workers in j. In essence, C_j is not simply produced by the workers in that period and their teachers, but also by the whole sequence over time of teachers who helped train these workers.

We define the jth "lineage" as this sequence of teachers and students in successive periods that ends in period j because the students in j become workers then. A lineage is a "team" of teachers, students, and workers in different periods who combine to produce consumer goods. The human capital of workers in later periods is produced with more "roundabout" methods, and hence has longer lineages, than the human capital of workers in earlier periods.

The roundabout methods used to produce human capital can be seen by substituting repeatedly into equation (26) to express the human capital of persons in period t who belong to the jth lineage as

$$H_{jt} = H_{j0}F\left(\frac{N_{j0}}{N_{j1}}\right) \ldots F\left(\frac{N_{jt-1}}{N_{jt}}\right), \qquad j = 0, \ldots, \infty, t \leq j, \quad (27)$$

where N'_{jt} is the number of teachers in lineage j in period $t'(< t)$, and H_{j0} is the human capital of the N_{j0} initial teachers in this lineage. By substituting equation (27) into (25), we get

$$C_j = H_{jj}N_{jj} = H_{j0}F\left(\frac{N_{j0}}{N_{j1}}\right) \ldots F\left(\frac{N_{jj-1}}{N_{jj}}\right)N_{jj}. \qquad (28)$$

We only consider accumulations of human capital that are efficient, that maximize consumption in any period, given consumptions in all other periods. It is obvious that the teacher-student ratios within a lineage then cannot be constant over time because marginal products in the lineage would be zero for all members. The negative effect on the production of human capital from having an additional student in a lineage would exactly cancel the positive effect of subsequently having an additional teacher. The appendix shows that efficient teacher-student ratios would fall over time within each lineage, so that teaching in a lineage would become less intensive as the lineage becomes closer to training workers who produce consumer goods.

Another important implication is due both to the concavity of the human capital production function with respect to the teacher-student ratio and the constant returns to scale in the consumption sector with respect to the number of workers. As a result of these assumptions, it is efficient to provide students who are further removed from becoming workers with more extensive training, so that teacher-student ratios would be higher in the more roundabout lineages (see the appendix). Consequently, the human capital of members of more roundabout lineages grows over time relative to those of less roundabout ones.

Even though the economy only has one consumption good and homogeneous human capital, the efficient accumulation of human capital creates an infinite number of sectors or lineages. Members of a particular sector would be specialized to that one partly because their human capital would be too little for the more roundabout sectors and too much for the less roundabout ones.

In addition, workers and teachers specialize in particular tasks within their sectors. Since more roundabout lineages have greater human capital, the analysis in Section II of the effects of human capital on the degree of specialization implies that members of the more roundabout sectors tend to specialize in a narrower range of tasks.

The distribution of human capital evolves over time. The human capital within each lineage grows at decreasing rates, but the slower-growing lineages are culled out over time when their members produce consumer goods, and the faster-growing lineages expand in size. Since lower-order lineages disappear over time, all human capital in later periods is "descended" from the teachers of persons in a small number of highly roundabout lineages in the initial period.

Inequality in the distribution of human capital at any moment expands over time because the human capital of sectors with greater human capital (the higher-order lineages) grows faster. However, the inequality would fall over time because the sectors with the least human capital (the lower-order lineages) are culled out and eliminated. We have not been able to reach any general conclusions about the net effect of these opposing forces on changes over time in the distribution of human capital.

What is rather remarkable about these rich implications concerning teacher-student ratios and the growth of human capital in different lineages is that they apply to any efficient path over time. Several additional properties hold if the economy is in a steady-state equilibrium, with consumption and human capital in each lineage growing at the same constant rate. For example, the inequality in this distribution of human capital across lineages tends to be greater when the steady-state growth rate is higher. However, we do not want to emphasize steady-state properties, for it is not clear that a steady state exists, given the restrictions on the teacher-student function implied by an efficient equilibrium.

VIII. Summary

This paper considers specialization and division of labor both within and between sectors. Workers concentrate on different tasks and combine their activities in "teams" to produce each sector's output. A more extensive division of labor raises productivity because returns to the time spent on tasks are usually greater to workers who concentrate on a narrower range of skills.

The traditional discussion of the division of labor inaugurated by Adam Smith emphasizes the limitations to specialization imposed by the extent of the market. Limited markets sometimes curtail the division of labor, but we claim that the degree of specialization is more often determined by other considerations. Especially emphasized are various costs of "coordinating" specialized workers who perform complementary tasks, and the amount of general knowledge available.

On this view, specialization increases until the higher productivity from a greater division of labor is just balanced by the greater costs of coordinating a larger number of more specialized workers. Consequently, principal-agent conflicts, holdup problems, communication difficulties, and other costs of combining specialized workers into productive teams play a major part in our approach. Since teams may include workers in different firms, costs of coordination also depend on the efficiency of markets and how well contracts are enforced.

Greater knowledge tends to raise the benefits from specialization, and thus tends to raise the optimal division of labor. This helps explain why workers become more expert on narrower ranges of tasks as knowledge grows and countries progress. Increased specialization in turn raises the benefits from investments in knowledge, so that the growth in tandem of specialization and investments in knowledge may allow an economy to continue to develop.

The paper considers the division of labor between workers who produce consumer goods and teachers who produce human capital. The analysis distinguishes among teachers of workers in the initial period, teachers of the teachers of workers in the following period, and so on for teachers engaged in more and more roundabout production of workers. We show that an efficient economy has a finely etched division of labor, where teachers have more human capital than workers, and teachers in higher-order lineages—in more roundabout production—have greater human capital than teachers in lower-order ranges.

Adam Smith's emphasis on the importance of specialization and the division of labor to economic progress is not simply an influential landmark in the development of economics. An analysis of the forces determining the division of labor provides crucial insights not only into the growth of nations, but also into the organization of product and labor markets, industries, and firms.

APPENDIX

Equation (28) implies that the marginal products of workers in any lineage are

$$\frac{dC_j}{dN_{jk}} = \frac{C_j}{N_{jk}}\left\{ \epsilon\left(\frac{N_{jk}}{N_{jk+1}}\right) - \epsilon\left(\frac{N_{jk-1}}{N_{jk}}\right)\right\}, \quad k < j \quad (29)$$

$$\frac{dC_j}{dN_{jj}} = \frac{C_j}{N_{jj}}\left\{ 1 - \epsilon\left(\frac{N_{jj-1}}{N_{jj}}\right)\right\}, \quad k = j > 0, \quad (30)$$

where $\epsilon(\tau) = F'(\tau) \times \tau/F(\tau)$ is the elasticity of the human capital production function with respect to the teacher-student ratio. Marginal products in the final period of a lineage are positive only if this elasticity is less than one in the period before the end of the lineage. Moreover, equation (29) shows that marginal products will not be positive in periods prior to the end unless in each lineage the elasticities with respect to the teacher-student ratio are increasing over time.

In addition, the marginal products in equation (29) would rise with a reduction in the number of members in a lineage only if the elasticity of human capital with respect to the teacher-student ratio falls as the ratio increases. Then a reduced number of members in the kth period raises the elasticity when they are teachers (since the teacher-student ratio falls) and lowers the elasticity when they are students (since the teacher-student ratio rises). Both effects imply that marginal products are positive only when the teacher-student ratio is falling over time within each lineage.

These results also have strong implications for differences across lineages. An optimal allocation of the labor force between lineages requires that the marginal rates of substitution between persons in any periods i and k be the same for members of all lineages (say j and m). By equations (29) and (30) this implies that

$$\left(\frac{N_{ji}}{N_{jk}}\right)\frac{\epsilon_{jk} - \epsilon_{jk-1}}{\epsilon_{ji} - \epsilon_{ji-1}} = \frac{N_{mi}}{N_{mk}}\frac{\epsilon_{mk} - \epsilon_{mk-1}}{\epsilon_{mi} - \epsilon_{mi-1}}, \quad (31)$$

where ϵ_{jk} is $\epsilon(N_{ji}/N_{jl+1})$, and $\epsilon_{jj} = 1$ for all j and k. When $i = j = 1$, $k = 0$, and $m = 2$, equation (31) becomes

$$\left(\frac{N_{11}}{N_{10}}\right)\frac{\epsilon_{10}}{1 - \epsilon_{10}} = \left(\frac{N_{21}}{N_{20}}\right)\frac{\epsilon_{20}}{\epsilon_{21} - \epsilon_{20}}. \quad (32)$$

Since ϵ_{21} must be less than one for the marginal product of workers in this lineage to be positive in period 2, then $\epsilon_{20} < \epsilon_{10}$ to satisfy equation (32). Given that elasticities decline with the teacher-student ratio, this ratio must be higher in period 0 for the second than for the first lineage.

Similar conditions hold over longer horizons. Not only must the teacher-student ratio decline over time within a lineage, but it also increases as a lineage becomes more roundabout. This implies that human capital grows faster over time in more-roundabout lineages.

Notes

We had valuable comments from Ronald Findlay, Sergio Rebello, Andrei Shleifer, Robert Tamura, Robert Vishny, two referees, and from participants in seminars at the University of Chicago, Duke University, the University of Iowa, Queens University, Pennsylvania State University, the Stockholm School of Economics, and the Conference on Human Capital and Economic Growth, Institute for the Study of Free Enterprise Systems, University of Buffalo, May 26 and 27, 1989. Support from the Lynde and Harry Bradley Foundation, NICHD grant #1 Rol HD22054, and NSF grant #SES85–20258 is gratefully acknowledged. David Meltzer and Rebecca Kilborn provided very useful research assistance.

1. See Peterson and Pennell (1962) and Shapiro (1989). Note, however, that U. S. physicians are much more specialized than those in Canada and Western Europe (see Fuchs and Hahn [1990]).

2. "The man whose life is spent performing a few simple operations has no occasion to exert his understanding or to exercise his invention . . . and generally becomes as stupid and ignorant as it is possible for a human creature to become" (Smith 1965, 734).

Due to this and similar statements, some scholars have seen a serious contradiction in Smith's approach to the division of labor: Book I extols its advantages, while Book IV points out its corrupting influence (e.g., see the discussions in Marx [1961] and West [1964], but see Rosenberg [1965]). But surely there is no necessary contradiction between Smith's recognition that the division of labor entails major costs, and his belief that the division of labor is crucial in promoting the wealth of nations. The contradiction is with Smith's belief that the division of labor is limited mainly by the extent of the market.

3. Stigler's important elaboration of the connection between the division of labor and the extent of the market (1951) recognizes that the Smithian view appears to lead to specialized producers and monopolistic suppliers. He asks, "Why does the firm not abandon the functions subject to increasing returns, allowing another firm (and industry) to specialize in them to take full advantage of increasing returns?" (p. 188). His answer that "these functions may be too small to support a specialized firm or firms" (p. 188) is inadequate because a firm need not specialize *only* in these

functions. Each firm could be the sole provider of some functions subject to increasing returns and one of several providers of functions subject to decreasing returns.

REFERENCES

Allen, George D. *The Industrial Development of Birmingham and the Black Country, 1860–1827.* London: George Allen & Unwin Ltd., 1929.

Baumgardner, James R. "The Division of Labor, Local Markets, and Worker Organization." *Journal of Political Economy* 96 (June 1988): 509–27.

Becker, Gary S. *A Treatise on the Family,* enlarged edition. Cambridge, Mass.: Harvard University Press, 1991.

Buchanan, R. A. *The Engineers: A History of the Engineering Profession in Britain, 1750–1914.* London: Jessica Kingsley Publishers, 1989.

Card, David, and Alan B. Krueger. "Does School Quality Matter? Returns to Education and the Characteristics of Public Schools in the United States." NBER Working Paper, May 1990.

Chari, V. V., and Larry E. Jones. "A Reconsideration of the Problem of Social Cost: Free Riders and Monopolists." Federal Reserve Bank of Minnesota, June 1991.

Clark, John B. *The Distribution of Wealth: A Theory of Wages, Interest and Profits.* New York: Macmillan, 1899.

Finn, Jeremy D., and Charles M. Achilles. " Answers and Questions about Class Size: A Statewide Experiment." *American Educational Research Journal,* 27 (fall 1990): 557–77.

Fuchs, Victor R. "Differentials in Hourly Earnings by Region and City Size, 1959." Occasional paper #101, NBER, 1967. An excerpt was published in *Monthly Labor Review* 90 (January 1967): 22–26.

Fuchs, Victor R., and James H. Hahn. "How Does Canada Do It? A Comparison of Expenditures for Physicians' Services in the United States and Canada." *New England Journal of Medicine* 323 (September 27, 1990): 884–90.

Gill, Indermit. "Technological Change, Education and Obsolescence of Human Capital: Some Evidence for the U.S." Ph.D. diss., University of Chicago, 1989.

Gros, Daniel. "Protectionism in a Framework with Intra-industry Trade: Tariffs, Quotas, Retaliation, and Welfare Losses." *International Monetary Fund Staff Papers* 34 (March 1987): 439–76.

Hanushek, Eric A. "The Impact of Differential Expenditures on School Performance." *Educational Researcher,* 18 (May 1989): 45–51, 62.

Hayek, F. A. "The Use of Knowledge in Society." *American Economic Review* 35 (September 1945): 519–30.

Holmstrom, Bengt. "Moral Hazard in Teams." *Bell Journal of Economics* 13 (fall 1982): 324–40.

Krugman, Paul R. "The Narrow Moving Band, the Dutch Disease, and the Consequences of Mrs. Thatcher: Notes on Trade in the Presence of Dynamic Scale Economics." *Journal of Development Economics* 27 (1987): 41–55.

Lancaster, Kelvin. "Socially Optimal Product Differentiation." *American Economic Review* 65 (September 1975): 580–85.

Locay, Luis. "Economic Development and the Division of Production between Households and Markets." *Journal of Political Economy* 98 (October 1990): 965–82.

Marx, Karl. *Capital.* Moscow: Foreign Languages Publishing House, 1961.

Mincer, Jacob, and Yoshio Higuchi. "Wage Structures and Labor Turnover in the United States and Japan." *Journal of the Japanese and International Economics* 2 (1988): 97–113.

Murphy, Kevin M. "Specialization and Human Capital." Ph.D. diss., University of Chicago, 1986.

Peterson, P. Q., and M. Y. Pennell. *Health Manpower Source Book.* Section 14: "Medical Specialists" Washington, D.C.: United States Public Health Service, 1962.

Rosenberg, Nathan. "Adam Smith on the Division of Labour: Two Views or One?" *Economica* 32 (May 1965): 127–39.

Roy, Andrew D. "Some Thoughts on the Distribution of Earnings." *Oxford Economic Papers* N.S. 3 (June 1951): 135–46.

Shapiro, David B. *Reference Data on Physician Manpower.* Chicago: American Medical Association, 1989.

Simon, Julian. *The Economics of Population Growth.* Princeton, N.J.: Princeton University Press, 1977.

Smith, Adam. *The Wealth of Nations.* New York: Modern Library, 1965.

Stigler, George J. "The Division of Labor Is Limited by the Extent of the Market." *Journal of Political Economy* 59 (June 1951): 185–93.

Winston, Mark L. *The Biology of the Honeybee.* Cambridge Mass.: Harvard University Press, 1987.

West, E. G. "Adam Smith's Two Views on the Division of Labour." *Economica* 31 (February 1964): 23–32.

Yang, Xiaokai, and Jeff Borland. "A Microeconomic Mechanism for Economic Growth." *Journal of Political Economy* 99 (June 1991): 460–82.

BECKER'S
PERSONAL OVERVIEW

◆ ◆ ◆ ◆ ◆ ◆ ◆

◆ *PART* ◆ *SEVEN* ◆

Nobel Lecture:
The Economic Way of
Looking at Behavior

· 26 ·

An important step in extending the traditional theory of individual rational choice to analyze social issues beyond those usually considered by economists is to incorporate into the theory a much richer class of attitudes, preferences, and calculations. While this approach to behavior builds on an expanded theory of individual choice, it is not mainly concerned with individuals. It uses theory at the microlevel as a powerful tool to derive implications at the group or macrolevel. The lecture describes the approach and illustrates it with examples drawn from my past and current work.

I. The Economic Approach

My research uses the economic approach to analyze social issues that range beyond those usually considered by economists. This lecture will describe the approach and illustrate it with examples drawn from past and current work.

Unlike Marxian analysis, the economic approach I refer to does not assume that individuals are motivated solely by selfishness or material gain. It is a *method* of analysis, not an assumption about particular motivations. Along with others, I have tried to pry economists away from narrow assump-

First published in the *Journal of Political Economy* 101, no. 3 (July 1993): 385–409. Reprinted by permission. © 1993 by The University of Chicago. All rights reserved.

tions about self-interest. Behavior is driven by a much richer set of values and preferences.

The analysis assumes that individuals maximize welfare *as they conceive it*, whether they be selfish, altruistic, loyal, spiteful, or masochistic. Their behavior is forward-looking, and it is also assumed to be consistent over time. In particular, they try as best they can to anticipate the uncertain consequences of their actions. Forward-looking behavior, however, may still be rooted in the past, for the past can exert a long shadow on attitudes and values.

Actions are constrained by income, time, imperfect memory and calculating capacities, and other limited resources, and also by the opportunities available in the economy and elsewhere. These opportunities are largely determined by the private and collective actions of other individuals and organizations.

Different constraints are decisive for different situations, but the most fundamental constraint is limited time. Economic and medical progress have greatly increased length of life, but not the physical flow of time itself, which always restricts everyone to 24 hours per day. So while goods and services have expanded enormously in rich countries, the total time available to consume has not.

Thus wants remain unsatisfied in rich countries as well as in poor ones. For while the growing abundance of goods may reduce the value of additional goods, time becomes more valuable as goods become more abundant. The welfare of people cannot be improved in a utopia in which everyone's needs are fully satisfied, but the constant flow of time makes such a utopia impossible. These are some of the issues analyzed in the literature on time allocation (for two early studies, see Becker [1965] and Linder [1970]).

The following sections illustrate the economic approach with four very different subjects. To understand discrimination against minorities, it is necessary to widen preferences to accommodate prejudice and hatred of particular groups. The economic analysis of crime incorporates into rational behavior illegal and other antisocial actions. The human capital perspective considers how the productivity of people in market and nonmarket situations is changed by investments in education, skills, and knowledge. The economic approach to the family interprets marriage, divorce, fertility, and relations among family members through the lens of utility-maximizing, forward-looking behavior.

II. DISCRIMINATION AGAINST MINORITIES

Discrimination against outsiders has always existed, but with the exception of a few discussions of the employment of women (see Fawcett [1918];

Edgeworth [1922]), economists wrote little on this subject before the 1950s. I began to worry about racial, religious, and gender discrimination while a graduate student, and I used the concept of discrimination coefficients to organize an approach to prejudice and hostility to members of particular groups.

Instead of making the common assumptions that employers consider only the productivity of employees, that workers ignore the characteristics of those with whom they work, and that customers care only about the qualities of the goods and services provided, discrimination coefficients incorporate the influence of race, gender, and other personal characteristics on tastes and attitudes. Employees may refuse to work under a woman or a black even when they are well paid to do so, or a customer may prefer not to deal with a black car salesman. It is only through *widening* of the usual assumptions that it is possible to begin to understand the obstacles to advancement encountered by minorities.

Presumably, the amount of observable discrimination against minorities in wages and employment depends not only on tastes for discrimination but also on other variables, such as the degree of competition and civil rights legislation. In the 1950s, a systematic analysis of how prejudice and other variables interact could begin with the important theory of compensating differentials originated by Adam Smith, and Gunnar Myrdal's pioneering *American Dilemma* (1944), but much remained to be done. I spent several years working out a theory of how actual discrimination in earnings and employment is determined by tastes for discrimination, along with the degree of competition in labor and product markets, the distribution of discrimination coefficients among members of the majority group, the access of minorities to education and training, the outcome of median voter and other voting mechanisms that determine whether legislation favors or is hostile to minorities, and other considerations. My advisers encouraged me to convert my doctoral dissertation into a book (Becker [1957]). I have continued over my career to write books rather than only articles, a practice that has become uncommon in economics.

Actual discrimination in the marketplace against a minority group depends on the combined discrimination of employers, workers, consumers, schools, and governments. The analysis shows that sometimes the environment greatly softens, while at other times it magnifies, the impact of a given amount of prejudice. For example, the discrepancy in wages between equally productive blacks and whites, or women and men, would be much smaller than the degree of prejudice against blacks and women when many companies can efficiently specialize in employing mainly blacks or women.

Indeed, in a world with constant returns to scale in production, two segregated economies with the same distribution of skills would completely bypass discrimination, and they would have equal wages and equal returns to other resources, regardless of the desire to discriminate against the segregated minorities. Therefore, discrimination by the majority in the marketplace is effective because minority members cannot provide various skills in sufficient quantities to companies that would specialize in using these workers.

When the majority is very large compared to the minority—in the United States whites are nine times as numerous as and have much more human and physical capital per capita than blacks—market discrimination by the majority hardly lowers its incomes, but may greatly reduce the incomes of the minority. However, when minority members are a sizable fraction of the total, discrimination by members of the majority injures them as well.

This proposition can be illustrated with an analysis of discrimination in South Africa, where blacks are some five times as numerous as whites. Discrimination against blacks has also significantly hurt whites, although some white groups have benefited (see Becker [1957 1971, 30–31]; Hutt [1964]; Lundahl [1992]). Its sizable cost to whites helps explain why apartheid and other blatant forms of Afrikaner discrimination were never fully effective and eventually broke down.

Many economists have the impression that my analysis of prejudice implies that market discrimination disappears in the "long run" (Arrow [1972] seems to be the first to make this claim). This impression is erroneous because I had shown that whether employers who do not want to discriminate compete away all discriminating employers depends not only on the distribution of tastes for discrimination among potential employers, but critically also on the nature of firm production functions (see Becker [1957 1971, 43–45]).

Of greater significance empirically is the long-run discrimination by employees and customers, who are far more important sources of market discrimination than employers. There is no reason to expect discrimination by these groups to be competed away unless it is possible to have enough efficient segregated firms and effectively segregated markets for goods (see Cain's [1986] good review of this and other issues regarding discrimination).

A novel theoretical development in recent years is the analysis of the consequences of stereotyped reasoning or statistical discrimination (see Phelps [1972]; Arrow [1973]). This analysis suggests that the *beliefs* of employers, teachers, and other influential groups that minority members are less productive *can* be self-fulfilling, for these beliefs may cause minorities to underinvest in education, training, and work skills, such as punctuality. The underinvestment does make them less productive (see a good recent analysis by Loury [1992]).

Evidence from many countries on the earnings, unemployment, and occupations of blacks, women, religious groups, immigrants, and others has expanded enormously during the past 25 years. This evidence more fully documents the economic position of minorities and how that changes in different environments.

The economic theory of discrimination based on prejudice implies that actual discrimination by firms or workers is measured by how much profits or wages they forfeit to avoid hiring or working with members of a group that is disliked. Discrimination by consumers is measured by the higher prices they pay to avoid products or services produced by those members. Evidence on forgone profits, wages, or prices is typically not available, so discrimination against a group is usually measured by comparing the earnings of members of the group with earnings of the "majority" who have the same years of schooling, job experience, and other measurable characteristics. Since this indirect approach has obvious defects, these studies have not dispelled some of the controversies over the source of lower incomes of minorities.

Recent studies on whether banks discriminate in their mortgage lending against blacks and other minorities compare the likelihood of getting a loan for minority and white applicants who are similar in incomes, credit backgrounds, and other available characteristics. The conclusion typically has been that blacks but not Asian-Americans are rejected excessively compared to whites of similar characteristics.

Unfortunately, these studies do not use the correct procedure for assessing whether banks discriminate, which is to determine whether loans are more profitable to blacks (and other minorities) than to whites. This requires examining the default and other payback experiences of loans, the interest rates charged, and so forth. If banks discriminate against minority applicants, they should earn *greater* profits on the loans actually made to them than on those to whites. The reason is that discriminating banks would be willing to accept marginally profitable white applicants who would be turned down if they were black.

III. Crime and Punishment

I began to think about crime in the 1960s after driving to Columbia University for an oral examination of a student in economic theory. I was late and had to decide quickly whether to put the car in a parking lot or risk getting a ticket for parking illegally on the street. I calculated the likelihood of getting a ticket, the size of the penalty, and the cost of putting the car in a lot. I decided it paid to take the risk and park on the street. (I did not get a ticket.)

As I walked the few blocks to the examination room, it occurred to me that the city authorities had probably gone through a similar analysis. The frequency of their inspection of parked vehicles and the size of the penalty imposed on violators should depend on their estimates of the type of calculations potential violators like me would make. Of course, the first question I put to the hapless student was to work out the optimal behavior of both the offenders and the police, something I had not yet done.

In the 1950s and 1960s, intellectual discussions of crime were dominated by the opinion that criminal behavior was caused by mental illness and social oppression, and that criminals were helpless "victims." A book by a well-known psychiatrist was entitled *The Crime of Punishment* (see Menninger 1966). Such attitudes began to exert a major influence on social policy, as laws changed to expand criminals' rights. These changes reduced the apprehension and conviction of criminals and provided less protection to the law-abiding population.

I was not sympathetic to the assumption that criminals had radically different motivations from everyone else. I explored instead the theoretical and empirical implications of the assumption that criminal behavior is rational (see the early pioneering work by Bentham [1931] and Beccaria [1797, 1986]), but again "rationality" did not imply narrow materialism. It recognized that many people were constrained by moral and ethical considerations, and they did not commit crimes even when these were profitable and there was no danger of detection. However, police and jails would be unnecessary if such attitudes always prevailed. Rationality implied that some individuals become criminals because of the financial and other rewards from crime compared to legal work, taking account of the likelihood of apprehension and conviction, and the severity of punishment.

The amount of crime is determined not only by the rationality and preferences of would-be criminals but also by the economic and social environment created by public policies, including expenditures on police, punishments for different crimes, and opportunities for employment, schooling, and training programs. Clearly, the types of legal jobs available as well as law, order, and punishment are an integral part of the economic approach to crime.

Total public spending on fighting crime can be reduced, while keeping the mathematically expected punishment unchanged, by offsetting a cut in expenditures on catching criminals with a sufficient increase in the punishment to those convicted. However, risk-preferring individuals are more deterred from crime by a higher probability of conviction than by severe punishments. Therefore, optimal behavior by the state would balance the reduced spending on police and courts from lowering the probability of conviction against the preference of risk-preferring criminals for a lesser certainty of punishment. The state should also consider the likelihood of punishing innocent persons.

In the early stages of my work on crime, I was puzzled by why theft is socially harmful since it appears merely to redistribute resources, usually from wealthier to poorer individuals. I resolved the puzzle (Becker [1968, 171n. 3]) by pointing out that criminals spend on weapons and on the value of the time in planning and carrying out their crimes, and that such spending is socially unproductive—it is what is now called "rent seeking"—because it does not create wealth, only forcibly redistributes it. I approximated the social cost of theft by the dollars stolen since rational criminals would be willing to spend up to that amount on their crimes. I should have added the resources spent by potential victims protecting themselves against crime.

One reason why the economic approach to crime became so influential is that the same analytic apparatus can be used to study enforcement of all laws, including minimum wage legislation, clean air acts, insider trader and other violations of security laws, and income tax evasions. Since few laws are self-enforcing, they require expenditures on conviction and punishment to deter violators. The U.S. Sentencing Commission (1992) has explicitly used the economic analysis of crime to develop rules to be followed by judges in punishing violators of federal statutes.

Studies of crime that use the economic approach have become common during the past quarter century. These include analysis of the optimal marginal punishments to deter increases in the severity of crimes—for example, to deter a kidnapper from killing his victim (the modern literature starts with Stigler [1970])—and the relation between private and public enforcement of laws (see Becker and Stigler [1974]; Landes and Posner [1975]).

Fines are preferable to imprisonment and other types of punishment because they can deter crimes effectively if criminals have sufficient financial resources—if they are not "judgment proof," to use legal jargon. Moreover, fines are more efficient than other methods because the cost to offenders is also revenue to the state. My discussion of the relations between fines and other punishments has been clarified and considerably improved (see, e.g., Polinsky and Shavell [1984]; Posner [1986]).

Empirical assessments of the effects on crime rates of prison terms, conviction rates, unemployment levels, income inequality, and other variables have become more numerous and more accurate (the pioneering work is by Ehrlich [1973], and the subsequent literature is extensive). The greatest controversies surround the question of whether capital punishment deters murders, a controversy that arouses much emotion but is far from being resolved (see, e.g., Ehrlich [1975]; National Research Council [1978]).

IV. Human Capital

Until the 1950s economists generally assumed that labor power was given and not augmentable. The sophisticated analyses of investments in education and other training by Adam Smith, Alfred Marshall, and Milton Friedman were not integrated into discussions of productivity. Then Theodore W. Schultz and others began to pioneer the exploration of the implications of human capital investments for economic growth and related economic questions.

Human capital analysis starts with the assumption that individuals decide on their education, training, medical care, and other additions to knowledge and health by weighing the benefits and costs. Benefits include cultural and other nonmonetary gains along with improvement in earnings and occupations, whereas costs usually depend mainly on the forgone value of the time spent on these investments. The concept of human capital also covers accumulated work and other habits, even including harmful addictions such as smoking and drug use. Human capital in the form of good work habits or addictions to heavy drinking has major positive or negative effects on productivity in both market and nonmarket sectors.

The various kinds of behavior included under the rubric of human capital help explain why the concept is so powerful and useful. It also means that the process of investing or disinvesting in human capital often alters the very nature of a person: training may change a lifestyle from one with perennial unemployment to one with stable and good earnings, or accumulated drinking may destroy a career, health, and even the capacity to think straight.

Human capital is so uncontroversial nowadays that it may be difficult to appreciate the hostility in the 1950s and 1960s toward the approach that went with the term. The very concept of *human* capital was alleged to be demeaning because it treated people as machines. To approach schooling as an investment rather than a cultural experience was considered unfeeling and extremely narrow. As a result, I hesitated a long time before deciding to call my book *Human Capital* (1964) and hedged the risk by using a long subtitle that I no longer remember. Only gradually did economists, let alone others, accept the concept of human capital as a valuable tool in the analysis of various economic and social issues.

My work on human capital began with an effort to calculate both private and social rates of return to men, women, blacks, and other groups from investments in different levels of education. After a while it became clear that the analysis of human capital can help explain many regularities in labor markets and the economy at large. It seemed possible to develop a more general theory of human capital that includes firms as well as individuals and that could consider its macroeconomic implications.

The empirical analysis tried to correct data on the higher earnings of more educated persons for the fact that they are abler: they have higher IQs and score better on other aptitude tests. It also considered the effects on rates of return to education of mortality, income taxes, forgone earnings, and economic growth. Ability corrections did not seem very important, but large changes in adult mortality and sizable rates of economic growth did have big effects. Meltzer (1992) recently has argued that the high death rates, especially from AIDS, of young males in many parts of Africa greatly discourage investments in human capital there.

The empirical study of investments in human capital received a major boost from Mincer's (1974) classic work. He extended a simple regression analysis that related earnings to years of schooling (Becker and Chiswick [1966]) to include a crude but very useful measure of on-the-job training and experience: years after finishing school, he used numerous individual observations rather than grouped data, and he carefully analyzed the properties of residuals from earnings-generating equations. There are now numerous estimated rates of return to education and training for many countries (for a summary of some of this literature, see Psacharopoulos [1985]); indeed, the earnings equation is probably the most common empirical regression in microeconomics.

The accumulating evidence on the economic benefits of schooling and training also promoted the importance of human capital in policy discussions. This new faith in human capital has reshaped the way governments approach the problem of stimulating growth and productivity, as was shown by the emphasis on human capital in the recent presidential election in the United States.

One of the most influential theoretical concepts in human capital analysis is the distinction between general and specific training or knowledge (see Becker [1962]; Oi [1962]). By definition, firm-specific knowledge is useful only in the firms providing it, whereas general knowledge is useful also in other firms. Teaching someone to operate an IBM-compatible personal computer is general training, whereas learning the authority structure and the talents of employees in a particular company is specific knowledge. This distinction helps explain why workers with highly specific skills are less likely to quit their jobs and are the last to be laid off during business downturns. It also explains why most promotions are made from within a firm rather than through hiring—workers need time to learn about a firm's structure and "culture"—and why better accounting methods would include the specific human capital of employees among the principal assets of most companies.

Firm-specific investments produce rents that must be shared between employers and employees, a sharing process that is vulnerable to "opportunistic" behavior because each side may try to extract most of the rent after investments are in place. Rents and opportunism due to specific investments play a crucial role in the modern economic theory of how organizations function (see Williamson [1985]) and in many discussions of principal-agent problems (see, e.g., Grossman and Hart [1983]). The implications of specific capital for sharing and turnover have also been used in analyzing marriage "markets" to explain divorce rates and bargaining within a marriage (see Becker, Landes, and Michael [1977]; McElroy and Horney [1981]) and in analyzing political "markets" to explain the low turnover of politicians (see Cain, Ferejohn, and Fiorina [1987]).

The theory of human capital investment relates inequality in earnings to differences in talents, family background, and bequests and other assets (see Becker and Tomes [1986]). Many empirical studies of inequality also rely on human capital concepts, especially differences in schooling and training (see Mincer [1974]). The sizable growth in earnings inequality in the United States during the 1980s that has excited so much political discussion is largely explained by higher returns to the more educated and better trained (see, e.g., Murphy and Welch [1992]).

Human capital theory gives a provocative interpretation of the so-called gender gap in earnings. Traditionally, women have been far more likely than men to work part-time and intermittently partly because they usually withdrew from the labor force for a while after having children. As a result, they had fewer incentives to invest in education and training that improved earnings and job skills.

During the past 25 years all this changed. The decline in family size, the growth in divorce rates, the rapid expansion of the service sector (where most women are employed), the continuing economic development that raised the earnings of women along with those of men, and civil rights legislation encouraged greater labor force participation by women and, hence, greater investment in market-oriented skills. In practically all rich countries, these forces significantly improved both the occupations and relative earnings of women.

The United States' experience is especially well documented. The gender gap in earnings among full-time men and women remained at about 35 percent from the midfifties to the midseventies. Then women began a steady economic advance, which is still continuing; it narrowed the gap to under 25 percent (see, e.g., O'Neill [1985]; Goldin [1990]). Women are flocking to business, law, and medical schools, and they are working at skilled jobs that they formerly shunned or were excluded from.

Schultz and others (see, e.g., Schultz [1963]; Denison [1962]) early on emphasized that investments in human capital are a major contributor to economic growth. But after a while the relation of human capital to growth was neglected, as economists became discouraged about whether the available growth theory gave many insights into the progress of different countries. The revival of more formal models of endogenous growth has brought human capital once again to the forefront of the discussions (see, e.g., Romer [1986]; Lucas [1988]; Becker, Murphy, and Tamura [1990]; Barro and Sala-i-Martin [1992]).

V. Formation, Dissolution, and Structure of Families

The rational choice analysis of family behavior builds on maximizing behavior, investments in human capital, the allocation of time, and discrimination against women and other groups. The rest of the lecture focuses on this analysis since it is still quite controversial, and I can discuss some of my current research.

Writing *A Treatise on the Family* (1981) is the most difficult sustained intellectual effort I have undertaken. The family is arguably the most fundamental and oldest of institutions: some authors trace its origin to more than 40,000 years ago (Soffer [1990]). The *Treatise* tries to analyze not only modern Western families but those in other cultures and changes in family structure during the past several centuries.

Trying to cover this broad subject required a degree of mental commitment over more than 6 years, during many nighttime as well as daytime hours, that left me intellectually and emotionally exhausted. In his autobiography, Bertrand Russell says that writing the *Principia Mathematica* used up so much of his mental powers that he was never again fit for really hard intellectual work. It took about 2 years after finishing the *Treatise* to regain my intellectual zest.

The analysis of fertility has a long and honorable history in economics, but until recent years marriage and divorce, and the relations between husbands, wives, parents, and children, had been largely neglected by economists (although see the important study by Mincer [1962]). The point of departure of my work on the family is the assumption that when men and women decide to marry, or have children, or divorce, they attempt to raise their welfare by comparing benefits and costs. So they marry when they expect to be better off than if they remained single, and they divorce if that is expected to increase their welfare.

People who are not intellectuals are often surprised when told that this approach is controversial since it seems obvious to them that individuals try to improve their welfare by marriage and divorce. The rational choice approach to marriage and other behavior is in fact often consistent with the instinctive economics "of the common person" (Farrell and Mandel [1992]).

Still, intuitive assumptions about behavior are only the *starting point* of systematic analysis, for alone they do not yield many interesting implications. The Marquis of Deffand said, when commenting on the story that St. Denis walked two leagues while carrying his head in his hands, that "the distance is nothing; it is only the first step that is difficult." The first one in new research is also important, but it is of little value without second, third, and several additional steps. (I owe this reference to the marquis and the comparison with research to Richard Posner.) The rational choice approach takes further steps by using a framework that combines maximizing behavior with the analysis of marriage and divorce markets, specialization and the division of labor, old-age support, investments in children, and legislation that affects families. The implications of the full model are often not so obvious and sometimes run sharply counter to received opinion.

For example, contrary to a common belief about divorce among the rich, the economic analysis of family decisions shows that wealthier couples are *less* likely to divorce than poorer couples. According to this theory, richer couples tend to gain a lot from remaining married, whereas many poorer couples do not. A poor woman may well doubt whether it is worth staying married to someone who is chronically unemployed. Empirical studies for many countries do indicate that marriages of richer couples are much more stable (see, e.g., Becker, Landes, and Michael [1977]; Hernandez [1992]).

Efficient bargaining between husbands and wives implies that the trend in Europe and the United States toward no-fault divorce during the past two decades did not raise divorce rates and, therefore, contrary to many claims, that it could not be responsible for the rapid rise in these rates. However, the theory does indicate that no-fault divorce hurts women with children whose marriages are broken up by their husbands. Feminists initially supported no-fault divorce, but some now have second thoughts about whether it has favorable effects on divorced women.

Economic models of behavior have been used to study fertility ever since Thomas Malthus's classic essay; the great Swedish economist, Knut Wicksell, was attracted to economics by his belief in the Malthusian predictions of overpopulation. But Malthus's conclusion that fertility would rise and fall as incomes increased and decreased was contradicted by the large decline in birthrates after some countries became industrialized during the latter part of the nineteenth century and the early part of this century.

The failure of Malthus's simple model of fertility persuaded economists that family size decisions lay beyond economic calculus. The neoclassical growth model reflects this belief, for in most versions it takes population growth as exogenous and given (see, e.g., Cass 1965; Arrow and Kurz 1970). However, the trouble with the Malthusian approach is not its use of economics per se, but an economics inappropriate for modern life. It neglects that the time spent on child care becomes more expensive when countries are more productive. The higher value of time raises the cost of children and thereby reduces the demand for large families. It also fails to consider that the greater importance of education and training in industrialized economies encourages parents to invest more in the skills of their children, which also raises the cost of large families. The growing value of time and the increased emphasis on schooling and other human capital explain the decline in fertility as countries develop, and many other features of birthrates in modern economies.

In almost all societies, married women have specialized in bearing and rearing children and in certain agricultural activities, whereas married men have done most of the fighting and market work. It should not be controversial to recognize that the explanation is a combination of biological differences between men and women—especially differences in their innate capacities to bear and rear children—and legal and other discrimination against women in market activities, partly through cultural conditioning. However, large and highly emotional differences of opinion exist over the relative importance of biology and discrimination in generating the traditional division of labor in marriages.

Contrary to allegations in many attacks on the economic approach to the gender division of labor (see, e.g., Boserup [1987]), this analysis does not try to weight the relative importance of biology and discrimination. Its main contribution is to show how sensitive the division of labor is to *small* differences in either. Since the return from investing in a skill is greater when more time is spent utilizing the skill, a married couple could gain much from a sharp division of labor because the husband would specialize in some types of human capital and the wife in others. Given such a large gain from specialization within a marriage, only a *little* discrimination against women or *small* biological differences in child-rearing skills would cause the division of labor between household and market tasks to be strongly and systematically related to gender. The sensitivity to small differences explains why the empirical evidence cannot readily choose between biological and "cultural" interpretations. This theory also explains why many women entered the labor force as families became smaller, divorce became more common, and earning opportunities for women improved.

Relations among family members differ radically from those among employees of firms and members of other organizations. The interactions among husbands, wives, parents, and children are more likely to be motivated by love, obligation, guilt, and a sense of duty than by self-interest narrowly interpreted.

It was demonstrated about 20 years ago that altruism within families enormously alters how they respond to shocks and public policies that redistribute resources among members. It was shown that exogenous redistributions of resources from an altruist to her beneficiaries (or vice versa) may not affect the welfare of anyone because the altruist would try to reduce her gifts by the amount redistributed (Becker [1974]). Barro (1974) derived this result in an intergenerational context, which cast doubt on the common assumption that government deficits and related fiscal policies have real effects on the economy.

The "rotten kid theorem"—the name is very popular even when critics disagree with the analysis—carries the discussion of altruism further, for it shows how the behavior of selfish individuals is affected by altruism. Under some conditions, even selfish persons (of course, most parents believe that the best example of selfish beneficiaries and altruistic benefactors is selfish children with altruistic parents) are induced to act *as though* they are altruistic toward their benefactors because that raises their own selfish welfare. They act this way because otherwise gifts from their benefactors would be reduced enough to make them worse off (see Becker [1974] and the elaboration and qualifications to the analysis in Lindbeck and Weibull [1988]; Bergstrom [1989]; and Becker [1991], 9–13).

The Bible, Plato's *Republic*, and other early writings discussed the treatment of young children by their parents and of elderly parents by adult children. Both the elderly and children need care: in one case because of declining health and energy, and in the other because of biological growth and dependency. A powerful implication of the economic analysis of relations within families is that these two issues are closely related.

Parents who leave sizable bequests do not need old-age support because instead they help out their children. I mentioned earlier one well-known implication of this: under certain conditions, budget deficits and social security payments to the elderly have no real effects because parents simply offset the bigger taxes in the future on their children through larger bequests.

It is much less appreciated that altruistic parents who leave bequests also tend to invest more in their children's skills, habits, and values. For they gain from financing all investments in the education and skills of children that yield a higher rate of return than the return on savings. They can indirectly save for old age by investing in children, and then reducing bequests when elderly. Both parents and children would be better off when parents make all investments in children that yield a higher return than that on savings, and then adjust bequests to the efficient level of investment (see sec. A of the appendix for a formal demonstration).

However, even in rich countries, many parents do not plan on leaving bequests. These parents want old-age support, and they "underinvest" in their children's education and other care. They underinvest because they cannot compensate themselves for greater spending on children by reducing bequests since they do not plan on leaving any.

Both the children and parents would be better off if the parents agreed to invest more in the children in return for a commitment by the children to care for them when they need help. But how can such a commitment be enforced? Economists and lawyers usually recommend a written contract to ensure commitment, but can you imagine a society that will enforce contracts between adults and 10-year-olds or teenagers?

Part of my current research considers an indirect way to generate commitments when promises and written agreements are not binding. I shall describe briefly some of this new work because it carries the economic approach to the family onto uncharted ground related to the rational formation of preferences within families.

Parental attitudes and behavior have an enormous influence on their children. Parents who are alcoholic or are addicted to crack create a bizarre atmosphere for impressionable youngsters, whereas parents with stable values who transmit knowledge and inspire their children favorably influence both what their children are capable of and what they want to do. The economic approach can contribute insights into the formation of preferences through childhood experiences without necessarily adopting the Freudian emphasis on the primacy of what happened during the first few months of life.

Again, I am trying to model a commonsense idea, namely, that the attitudes and values of adults are enormously influenced by their childhood experiences. An Indian doctor living in the United States may love curry because he acquired a strong taste for it while growing up in India, or a woman may forever fear men because she was sexually abused as a child.

Through its assumption of forward-looking behavior, the economic point of view implies that parents try to anticipate the effect of what happens to children on their attitudes and behavior when adults. These effects help determine the kind of care parents provide. For example, parents worried about old-age support may try to instill in their children feelings of guilt, obligation, duty, and filial love that indirectly, but still very effectively, can "commit" children to helping them out.

Economists have too narrow a perspective on commitments. "Manipulating" the experiences of others to influence their preferences may appear to be inefficient and fraught with uncertainty, but it can be the most effective way available to obtain commitment. Economic theory, especially game theory, needs to incorporate guilt, affection, and related attitudes into preferences in order to have a deeper understanding of when commitments are "credible" (see sec. B of the appendix for a formal discussion).

Parents who do not leave bequests may be willing to make their children feel guiltier precisely because they gain more utility from greater old-age consumption than they lose from an equal reduction in children's consumption. This type of behavior may be considerably more common than suggested by the number of families that actually do leave bequests, for parents with young children often do not know whether they will be financially secure when they are old. They may try to protect themselves against ill health, unemployment, and other hazards of old age by instilling in their children a willingness to help out if that becomes necessary.

This analysis of the link between childhood experiences and adult preferences is closely related to work on rational habit formation (see Becker and Murphy [1988]; also see the discussion by Kandel and Lazear [1992] of the creation of guilt among employees). The formation of preferences is rational in the sense that parental spending on children partly depends on the anticipated effects of childhood experiences on adult attitudes and behavior. I do not have time to consider the behavior of children—such as crying and acting "cute"—that tries in turn to influence the attitudes of parents.

Many economists, including me, have excessively relied on altruism to tie together the interests of family members. Recognition of the connection between childhood experiences and future behavior reduces the need to rely on altruism in families. But it does not return the analysis to a narrow focus on self-interest, for it partially replaces altruism by feelings of obligation, anger, and other attitudes usually neglected by models of rational behavior.

If children are expected to help out in old age—perhaps because of guilt or related motivations—even parents who are not very loving would invest more in the children's human capital and save less to provide for their old age. (For a proof, see sec. C of the appendix.) But equation (A12) of the appendix shows that altruistic parents always prefer small increases in their own consumption when old to equal increases in their children's *if* they have made their children feel guilty. This means that such parents always underinvest in the children's human capital. This shows directly why creating guilt has costs and is not fully efficient.

Altruistic family heads who do not plan to leave bequests try to create a "warm" atmosphere in their families, so that members are willing to come to the assistance of those experiencing financial and other difficulties. This conclusion is relevant to discussions of so-called family values, a subject that received attention during the recent presidential campaign in the United States. Parents help determine the values of children—including their feelings of obligation, duty, and love—but what parents try to do can be greatly affected by public policies and changes in economic and social conditions.

Consider, for example, a program that transfers resources to the elderly, perhaps especially to poorer families who do not leave bequests, that reduces the elderly's dependence on children. According to the earlier analysis I gave, parents who do not need support when they become old do not try as hard to make children more loyal or guiltier or otherwise feel as well disposed toward their parents. This means that programs such as social security that significantly help the elderly would encourage family members to drift apart emotionally, not by accident but as maximizing responses to those policies.

Other changes in the modern world that have altered family values include increased geographical mobility, the greater wealth that comes with economic growth, better capital and insurance markets, higher divorce rates, smaller families, and publicly funded health care. These developments have generally made people better off, but they have also weakened the personal relations within families between husbands and wives, parents and children, and among more distant relatives, partly by reducing the incentives to invest in *creating* closer relations.

VI. Concluding Comments

An important step in extending the traditional analysis of individual rational choice is to incorporate into the theory a much richer class of attitudes, preferences, and calculations. This step is prominent in all the examples I consider. The analysis of discrimination includes in preferences a dislike of— prejudice against—members of particular groups, such as blacks or women. In deciding whether to engage in illegal activities, potential criminals are assumed to act as though they consider both the gains and the risks, including the likelihood they will be caught and severity of punishments. In human capital theory, people rationally evaluate the benefits and costs of activities, such as education, training, expenditures on health, migration, and formation of habits that radically alter the way they are. The economic approach to the family assumes that even intimate decisions such as marriage, divorce, and family size are reached through weighing the advantages and disadvantages of alternative actions. The weights are determined by preferences that critically depend on the altruism and feelings of duty and obligation toward family members.

Since the economic, or rational choice, approach to behavior builds on a theory of individual decisions, criticisms of this theory usually concentrate on particular assumptions about how these decisions are made. Among other things, critics deny that individuals act consistently over time, and question whether behavior is forward-looking, particularly in situations that differ significantly from those usually considered by economists—such as those involving criminal, addictive, family, or political behavior. This is not the place to go into a detailed response to the criticisms, so I simply assert that no approach of comparable generality has yet been developed that offers serious competition to rational choice theory.

I have intentionally chosen certain topics for my research—such as addiction—to probe the boundaries of rational choice theory. William Blake said that you never know what is enough until you see what is more than enough (Jon Elster brought this proverb to my attention). My work may have sometimes assumed too much rationality, but I believe it has been an antidote to the extensive research that does not credit people with enough rationality.

While the economic approach to behavior builds on a theory of individual choice, it is not mainly concerned with individuals. It uses theory at the microlevel as a powerful tool to derive implications at the group or macrolevel. Rational individual choice is combined with assumptions about technologies and other determinants of opportunities, equilibrium in market and nonmarket situations, and laws, norms, and traditions to obtain results concerning the behavior of groups. It is mainly because the theory derives implications at the macrolevel that it is of interest to policy makers and those studying differences among countries and cultures.

None of the theories considered in this lecture aims for the greatest generality; instead, each tries to derive concrete implications about behavior that can be tested with survey and other data. Disputes over whether punishments deter crime, whether the lower earnings of women compared to those of men are mainly due to discrimination or lesser human capital, or whether no-fault divorce laws increase divorce rates—all raise questions about the empirical relevance of predictions derived from a theory based on individual rationality.

A close relation between theory and empirical testing helps prevent both the theoretical analysis and the empirical research from becoming sterile. Empirically oriented theories encourage the development of new sources and types of data, the way human capital theory stimulated the use of survey data, especially panels. At the same time, puzzling empirical results force changes in theory, as models of altruism and family preferences have been enriched to cope with the finding that parents in Western countries tend to bequeath equal amounts to different children.

I have been impressed by how many economists want to work on social issues rather than those forming the traditional core of economics. At the same time, specialists from fields that do consider social questions are often attracted to the economic way of modeling behavior because of the analytical power provided by the assumption of individual rationality. Thriving schools of rational choice theorists and empirical researchers are active in sociology, law, political science, and history and, to a lesser extent, in anthropology and psychology. The rational choice model provides the most promising basis presently available for a unified approach to the analysis of the social world by scholars from different social sciences.

APPENDIX

A

To develop a formal analysis, suppose that each person lives for three periods—young (y), middle age (m), and old age (o)—and has one child at the beginning of period (m). A child's youth overlaps his parent's middle age, and a child's middle age overlaps his parent's old age. The utility parents get from altruism is assumed to be separable from the utilities produced by their own consumption.

A simple utility function of parents (V_p) incorporating these assumptions is

$$V_p = u_{mp} + \beta u_{op} + \beta \alpha V_c, \qquad (A1)$$

where β is the discount rate, and the degree of altruism rises with α. For selfish parents, $\alpha = 0$. I do not permit parents to be sadistic toward children ($\alpha < 0$), although the analysis is easily generalized to include sadists.

Each person works and earns income only during middle age. It is possible to save then to provide consumption for old age (Z_{op}) by accumulating assets with a yield of R_k. Parents influence children's earnings by investing in their human capital. The marginal yield on these investments (R_h) is defined as

$$R_h = \frac{dE_c}{dh}, \qquad (A2)$$

where E_c is the earnings of children at middle age, and h is the amount invested. This yield is assumed to decline as more is invested in children: $dR_h/dh \leq 0$.

Parents must also decide whether to leave bequests, denoted by k_c. If parents can consume at different ages, leave bequests, or invest in the child's human capital, their budget constraint is

$$Z_{mp} + h + \frac{Z_{op}}{R_k} + \frac{k_c}{R_k} = A_p, \qquad (A3)$$

where A is the present value of resources.

One first-order condition to maximize parental utility determines their optimal consumption at middle and old age:

$$u'_{mp} = \beta R_k u'_{op} = \lambda_p, \tag{A4}$$

where λ_p is the parents' marginal utility of wealth. Another condition determines whether they give bequests:

$$\beta \alpha V'_c \leq \frac{\lambda_p}{R_k} = \beta u'_{op}, \tag{A5}$$

and the last determines investments in the human capital of children:

$$R_h \beta \alpha V'_c = \lambda_p. \tag{A6}$$

Equation (A6) assumes that the first-order condition for investment in human capital is strict equality, that some human capital is always invested in children. This can be justified with an Inada-type condition that small investments in human capital yield very high rates of return. In rich economies such as Sweden or the United States, investments in basic knowledge and nutrition of children presumably do yield a very good return. As long as parents are not completely selfish—as long as $\alpha > 0$—then such a condition does always imply positive investment in human capital. For completely selfish parents, equation (A6) would become an inequality.

Equation (A4) determines the accumulation of assets to finance old-age consumption. Whether parents leave bequests or want old-age support from their children is determined by the inequality in (A5). If this is a strict inequality, parents want support and would not leave bequests.

That inequality can be written in a more revealing way. If children also maximize their utility, then the envelope theorem implies that

$$\alpha u'_m < u'_{op} \quad \text{whenever} \quad \alpha V'_c < u'_{op} \quad \text{since } V'_c = u'_{mc}. \tag{A7}$$

Equation (A7) has the intuitive interpretation that parents do not give bequests when the utility the parents get from their children consuming a dollar more at middle age is less than the utility they get from a dollar more of their own consumption at old age. Obviously, such an inequality holds for completely selfish parents since the left-hand sides of equations (A5) and (A7) are zero when α is zero. The weaker the altruism (the smaller α), the more parents want from children.

Combining equations (A5) and (A6) gives

$$\frac{\lambda_p}{R_h} \leq \frac{\lambda_p}{R_k}, \quad \text{or} \quad R_h \geq R_k. \tag{A8}$$

Equation (A8) implies that the marginal rate of return on human capital equals the return on assets when parents do give bequests, and it is greater than the asset return when parents do not give bequests. Parents can help children either by investing in their human capital or by leaving them assets. Since they want to maximize the advantage to children, given the cost to themselves—parents are not sadistic—they help in the most efficient form.

Consequently, if strict inequality holds in equation (A8), they would not give bequests, for the best way to help children when the marginal return on human capital exceeds that on assets is to invest only in human capital. They leave bequests only when they get the same marginal return on both (some of these results have been derived in Becker and Tomes [1986]).

B

To analyze in a simple way the influence of parents over the formation of children's preferences, suppose parents can take actions x and y when children are young that affect their preferences when adults. I use the assumption of separability to write the utility function of middle-aged children as

$$V_c = u_{mc} + H(y) - G(x,g) + \beta u_{oc} + \dots \quad (A9)$$

I assume that $H' > 0$ and $G_x > 0$, which means that an increase in y raises the utility of children, but an increase in x lowers their utility. Interpret H for concreteness as "happiness" and G as the "guilt" children feel toward their parents, so that greater x makes children feel guiltier. The question is, Why would nonsadistic parents want to make their children feel guilty?

The variable g is the key to understanding why. This measures the contribution of children to the old-age support of parents; let us assume that children feel less guilty when they contribute more ($G_g < 0$). If $G_{gx} > 0$, then greater x both raises children's guilt and stimulates more giving by them.

The budget constraint of parents becomes

$$Z_{mp} + h + x + y + \frac{Z_{op}}{R_k} + \frac{k_c}{R_k} = A_p + \frac{g}{R_k}. \quad (A10)$$

The first-order condition for the optimal y is

$$\beta\alpha H' \leq \lambda_p. \quad (A11)$$

Since $H' > 0$, it is easy to understand why an altruistic parent may try to affect children's preferences through y since an increase in y makes children happier.

The first-order condition for x is more interesting, for even altruistic parents may want to make their children feel guilty if that sufficiently raises old-age support. This first-order condition can be written as

$$\frac{dV_p}{dx} = \frac{dg}{dx}\beta(u'_{op} - \alpha u'_{mc}) - \beta\alpha\frac{dG}{dx} \le \lambda_p, \qquad (A12)$$

were dG/dx incorporates the induced change in g. The second term in the middle expression is negative to altruistic parents because greater x does raise children's guilt, which lowers the utility of these parents ($\alpha > 0$). However, guilt also induces children to increase old-age support, as given by dg/dx. The magnitude of this response determines whether it is worthwhile for parents to make children feel guiltier.

Increased old-age support from children has two partially offsetting effects on the welfare of altruistic parents. On the one hand, it raises their old-age consumption and utility, as given by u'_{op}. On the other hand, it lowers children's consumption and, hence, the utility of altruistic parents, as given by $-\alpha u'_{mc}$. This means that altruistic parents who leave bequests never try to make children feel guiltier, for $u'_{op} = \alpha u'_{mc}$ for these parents. Since $dG/dx > 0$, they must be worse off when their children feel guiltier.

Equations (A5) and (A12) imply that

$$\frac{dg}{dx} - \frac{\alpha G_x}{u'_{op}} = R_x \le R_k. \qquad (A13)$$

The marginal rate of return to altruistic parents from making children feel guiltier (given by R_x) nets out the parents' evaluation of the loss in children's utility from their guilt. Selfish parents ($\alpha = 0$) ignore this loss and simply compare the effects of x and k on their consumption at old age.

C

Combine the first-order conditions in equations (A5) and (A6) to get

$$\frac{u'_{op}}{\alpha u'_{mc}} = \frac{R_h}{R_k}. \qquad (A14)$$

Both sides of this equation exceed unity when parents do not give bequests. Since greater old-age support from children lowers the left-hand side by lowering the numerator and raising the denominator, the right-hand side must also fall to be in a utility-maximizing equilibrium. But since R_k is given by market conditions, the right-hand side can fall only if R_h falls, which implies greater investment in children when parents expect greater old-age support from children. Even completely selfish parents ($\alpha = 0$) might invest in children if that would sufficiently increase the expected old-age support from guilty children.

REFERENCES

Arrow, Kenneth J. "Models of Job Discrimination." In *Racial Discrimination in Economic Life*, edited by Anthony H. Pascal. Lexington, Mass.: Lexington Books, 1972.

———. "The Theory of Discrimination." In *Discrimination in Labor Markets*, edited by Orley Ashenfelter and Albert Rees. Princeton, N.J.: Princeton University Press, 1973.

Arrow, Kenneth J., and Mordecai Kurz. *Public Investment, the Rate of Return, and Optimal Fiscal Policy*. Baltimore, Md.: John Hopkins University Press (for Resources for the Future), 1970.

Barro, Robert J. "Are Government Bonds Net Wealth?" *Journal of Political Economy* 82 (November/December 1974): 1095–1117.

Barro, Robert J., and Xavier Sala-i-Martin. "Convergence." *Journal of Political Economy* 100 (April 1992): 223–51.

Beccaria, Cesare, marchese di. *On Crimes and Punishment*. Indianapolis, Ind.: Hackett, 1986. Translation of *Dei delitti e delle pene* (1797).

Becker, Gary S. *The Economics of Discrimination*. Chicago: University Chicago Press, 1957. 2d ed. 1971.

———. "Investment in Human Capital: A Theoretical Analysis." *Journal of Political Economy* 70, no. 5, pt. 2 (October 1962): 9–49.

———. *Human Capital*. New York: Columbia University Press (for NBER), 1964. 2d ed. 1975.

———. "A Theory of the Allocation of Time." *Economic Journal* 75 (September 1965): 493–517.

———. "Crime and Punishment: An Economic Approach." *Journal of Political Economy* 76 (March/April 1968): 169–217.

———. "A Theory of Social Interactions." *Journal of Political Economy* 82 (November/December 1974): 1063–93.

———. *A Treatise on the Family*. Cambridge, Mass.: Harvard University Press, 1981. Enl. ed. 1991.

Becker, Gary S., and Barry R. Chiswick. "Education and the Distribution of Earnings." *American Economic Review Papers and Proceedings* 56 (May 1966): 358–69.

Becker, Gary S., Elisabeth M. Landes, and Robert T. Michael. "An Economic Analysis of Marital Instability." *Journal of Political Economy* 85 (December 1977): 1141–87.

Becker, Gary S., and Kevin M. Murphy. "A Theory of Rational Addiction." *Journal of Political Economy* 96 (August 1988): 675–700.

656 ◆ BECKER'S PERSONAL OVERVIEW

Becker, Gary S., Kevin M. Murphy, and Robert Tamura. "Human Capital, Fertility, and Economic Growth." *Journal of Political Economy* 98, no. 5, pt. 2 (October 1990): S12–S37.

Becker, Gary S., and George J. Stigler. "Law Enforcement, Malfeasance, and Compensation of Enforcers." *Journal of Legal Studies* 3 (January 1974): 1–18. Reprinted in *Chicago Studies in Political Economy*, by George J. Stigler. Chicago: University of Chicago Press, 1988.

Becker, Gary S., and Nigel Tomes. "Human Capital and the Rise and Fall of Families." *Journal of Labor Economics* 4, no. 3, pt. 2 (July 1986): S1–S39.

Bentham, Jeremy. *Theory of Legislation*. New York: Harcourt, Brace, 1931.

Bergstrom, Theodore C. "A Fresh Look at the Rotten Kid Theorem—and Other Household Mysteries." *Journal of Political Economy* 97 (October 1989): 1138–59.

Boserup, Ester. "Inequality between the Sexes." In *The New Palgrave: A Dictionary of Economics*, edited by John Eatwell, Murray Milgate, and Peter Newman. New York: Stockton, 1987.

Cain, Bruce E., John Ferejohn, and Morris Fiorina. *The Personal Vote: Constituency Service and Electoral Independence*. Cambridge, Mass.: Harvard University Press, 1987.

Cain, Glen G. "The Economic Analysis of Labor Market Discrimination: A Survey." In *Handbook of Labor Economics*, vol. I, edited by Orley Ashenfelter and Richard Layard. Handbooks in Economic Series, no. 5. New York: Elsevier Sci., 1986.

Cass, David. "Optimum Growth in an Aggregative Model of Capital Accumulation." *Review of Economic Studies* 32 (July 1965): 233–40.

Denison, Edward F. *Sources of Economic Growth in the United States*. Washington, D.C.: Commission on Economic Development, 1962.

Edgeworth, Francis Y. "Equal Pay to Men and Women for Equal Work." *Economic Journal* 32 (December 1922): 431–57.

Ehrlich, Isaac. "Participation in Illegitimate Activities: A Theoretical and Empirical Investigation." *Journal of Political Economy* 81 (May/June 1973): 521–65.

———. "The Deterrent Effect of Capital Punishment: A Question of Life and Death." *American Economic Review* 65 (June 1975): 397–417.

Farrell, C., and M. Mandel. "Uncommon Sense." *BusinessWeek*, October 26, 1992, pp. 36–37.

Fawcett, Millicent G. "Equal Pay for Equal Work." *Economic Journal* 28 (March 1918): 1–6.

Goldin, Claudia. *Understanding the Gender Gap: An Economic History of American Women*. Series on Long-Term Factors in Economic Development. New York: Oxford University Press (for NBER), 1990.

Grossman, Sanford J., and Oliver D. Hart. "An Analysis of the Principal-Agent Problem." *Econometrica* 51 (January 1983): 7–45.

Hernandez, Donald. *When Households Continue, Discontinue, and Form*. Washington, D.C.: U.S. Bureau of the Census, 1992.

Hutt, William H. *The Economics of the Colour Bar: A Study of the Economic Origins and Consequences of Racial Segregation in South Africa*. London: Deutsch (for the Institute of Economic Affairs), 1964.

Kandel, Eugene, and Edward P. Lazear. "Peer Pressure and Partnerships." *Journal of Political Economy* 100 (August 1992): 801–17.

Landes, William M., and Richard A. Posner. "The Private Enforcement of Law." *Journal of Legal Studies* 4 (January 1975): 1–46.

Lindbeck, Assar, and Jörgen W. Weibull. "Altruism and Time Consistency: The Economics of Fait Accompli." *Journal of Political Economy* 96 (December 1988): 1165–82.

Linder, Staffan Burenstam. *The Harried Leisure Class*. New York: Columbia University Press, 1970.

Loury, Glenn C. "Incentive Effects of Affirmative Action." *Annals of American Academic Political and Social Science* 523 (September 1992): 19–29.

Lucas, Robert E., Jr. "On the Mechanics of Economic Development." *Journal of Monetary Economics* 22 (July 1988): 3–42.

Lundahl, Mats. *Apartheid in Theory and Practice: An Economic Analysis*. Boulder, Colo.: Westview, 1992.

McElroy, Marjorie B., and Mary Jean Horney. "Nash-bargained Household Decisions: Toward a Generalization of the Theory of Demand." *International Economic Review* 22 (June 1981): 333–49.

Meltzer, David. "Mortality Decline, the Demographic Transition and Economic Growth." Ph.D. dissertation, University of Chicago, 1992.

Menninger, Karl. *The Crime of Punishment*. New York: Viking, 1966.

Mincer, Jacob. "Labor Force Participation of Married Women." In *Aspects of Labor Economics*. Universities–National Bureau Committee for Economic Research, no. 14. Princeton, N.J.: Princeton University Press (for NBER), 1962.

——. *Schooling, Experience, and Earnings*. New York: Columbia University Press (for NBER), 1974.

Murphy, Kevin M., and Finis Welch. "The Structure of Wages." *Quarterly Journal of Economics* 107 (February 1992): 285–326.

Myrdal, Gunnar. *An American Dilemma: The Negro Problem and Modern Democracy*. 2 vols. New York: Random House, 1944.

National Research Council. Panel of Research on Deterrent and Incapacitative Effects. *Deterrence and Incapacitation: Estimating the Effects of Criminal Sanctions on Crime Rates*, edited by Alfred Blumstein, Jacqueline Cohen, and Daniel Nagin. Washington, D.C.: National Academy of Sciences, 1978.

Oi, Walter Y. "Labor as a Quasi-fixed Factor." *Journal of Political Economy* 70 (December 1962): 538–55.

O'Neill, June. "The Trend in the Male-Female Wage Gap in the United States." *Journal of Labor Economics* 3, no. 1, pt. 2 (January 1985): S91–S116.

Phelps, Edmund S. "The Statistical Theory of Racism and Sexism." *American Economic Review* 62 (September 1972): 659–61.

Polinsky, A. Mitchell, and Steven Shavell. "The Optimal Use of Fines and Imprisonment." *Journal of Public Economics* 24 (June 1984): 89–99.

Posner, Richard A. *Economic Analysis of Law*. 3d ed. Boston: Little, Brown. 1986.

Psacharopoulos, George. "Returns to Education: A Further International Update and Implications." *Journal of Human Resources* 20 (fall 1985): 583–604.

Romer, Paul M. "Increasing Returns and Long-Run Growth." *Journal of Political Economy* 94 (October 1986): 1002–37.

Schultz, Theodore W. *The Economic Value of Education*. New York: Columbia University Press, 1963.

Soffer, O. "Before Beringia: Late Pleistocene Bio-social Transformations and the Colonization of Northern Eurasia." In *Chronostratigraphy of the Paleolithic in North Central, East Asia and America*. Novosibirsk: Academy of Sciences of the USSR, 1990.

Stigler, George J. "The Optimum Enforcement of Laws." *Journal of Political Economy* 78 (May–June 1970): 526–36.

U.S. Sentencing Commission. *Federal Sentencing Guidelines Manual*. Washington, D.C.: U.S. Government Printing Office, 1992.

Williamson, Oliver E. *The Economic Institutions of Capitalism: Firms, Markets, Relational Contracting*. New York: Free Press, 1985).

INDEX

patterns and, 290–92; motivation and, 59; of specific-type training, 45–54; of time, 102–4; wage increases and, 57–59
public expenditures: on education, 358, 389; for elderly parents, 388–92; family consumption and, 374–75; generation competition for, 396–97; human capital investment by, 357–58; impact on adoption by, 394; impact on children of, 358; model of taxation and, 546–51; social impact of, 649
public policy: compensation principle and, 551–53; for crime/punishment, 473–77, 493–94, 496–98; criminal fines as, 482–89; elderly support through, 388–92; for human capital investment, 386–88; justice for children through, 383; regulation/deregulation, 554–56; for support of elderly, 388–92. See also public expenditures
punishment, 463–64; behavioral relation shifts and, 477–82; costs of criminal, 472–73; developing optimal, 496–506; economic approach to, 637–39; fines vs., 484–88, 511n40, 639; of malfeasance, 523–28. See also crime

quality of children: costs vs. expenditures on, 264–68; described, 245–46, 260; marriage patterns and, 292; quantity vs., 261–63
quantity-quality interaction hypothesis, xxviii–xxix
Quarterly Journal of Economics (1886), 615

rates of return: earnings/costs and, 60–67; income gain and internal, 83nn41–51
rational behavior: assumption of, xl–xli; criminal behavior as, 638; habit formation as, 220–22; input prices changes and, 27–28; of voters, 557–58. See also human behavior; irrational behavior
rational firms, 50
rational habit model, 224–26
rationing theory, 114n10
Razin, Assaf, 383
"reciprocal altruism," 334, 341n10
regulation policies, 554–56
Reid, Margaret, 108, 110
"rent seeking," 639
Republic (Plato), 384, 600, 646
resources: common law regulation of, 383; discrimination and distribution of, 425;

"rotten-kid" theorem and, 165, 334, 339, 385, 388; scarce, xxvii–xlii, 6; transferred between family, 161–67, 173–74; transferred between spouses, 313, 324n9. See also endowments
restaurant pricing, 209–10, 214–16
Ricardo, David, 574, 577
risks: "life-cycle" explanation of, 71; liquidity and investment, 70–71
Roberts, Russell, 553
Robinson, Chris, 553
Rosen, Sherwin A., xxvi, 437
"rotten-kid" theorem, 165, 334, 339, 385, 388; altruism within, xxivii, 646; divorce and, 393
Ruhter, Wayne, 395
Russell, Bertrand, 643
Ryder, Harl E., 219, 220

Sadka, Efraim, 383
sale of children, 394
Samuelson, Paul A., 599
Sargent, Thomas, xliv
savings, Social Security and, 594–95
Say, J. B., 574, 579
Say's Equality, 571
Say's Identity, 568–71, 573, 579–81
Say's Law, 568, 573, 579–81
scarce resources, xxvii–xlii, 6
Schmoller, Gustav, xliii
Schultz, Theodore W., 640, 642
Schumpeter, Joseph A., 344
search theory, xxxiii
segregation: discrimination and economic, 418–19; market discrimination and, 409–12
self-insurance: as market insurance alternative, 129–33; market insurance and, 138–40
selfish behavior, xli
self-protection: market insurance and, 140–43; probabilities/moral hazard of, 133–38
Senior, Nassau, 151, 153, 154
service industries, 104
sex ratio, 296, 298
sexual division of labor, xxxii, 108, 441–42, 613–14, 645
sexual wage gap, xxxi–xxxiv, 281, 290–91
shadow prices, xxi–xxii
Smigel, Arlene, 494
Smith, Adam: on division of labor, 608–9, 611, 616, 618, 626; on education as

Gary S. Becker is a professor of economics and sociology at the University of Chicago, where he is currently studying formation of preferences, including addiction, as well as population growth and economic development.

♦   ♦   ♦   ♦   ♦

Ramón Febrero is a professor of economics at the Universidad Complutense de Madrid and director of the Economics and Business Administration Division of the Centro de Estudios Superiores "Ramón Carande."

Pedro S. Schwartz is a professor of the history of economic thought at the Autonomous University of Madrid and a special consultant at National Economic Research Associates.